"This excellent book compares the movements to reform women's legal status over half a century in seven South American countries. Its broad comparative approach challenges many facile generalizations about Latin American legal and women's history. A truly impressive achievement."

Silvia Arrom, *Jane's Professor of Latin American Studies Emerita, Brandeis University, United States*

"Carmen Diana Deere's work represents an excellent and necessary input for research and teaching from a gender and feminist perspective in the field of social sciences, especially for feminist economists in Latin America. Until now, we did not have material that informed us about this topic in historical and comparative terms for a large part of the region. Likewise, the work is essential to understanding the relationship between feminist demands, maternalism, and social, political and economic contexts."

Alma Espino, *President of the Interdisciplinary Center for Development Studies of Uruguay (CIEDUR)*

FIRST-WAVE FEMINISM AND WOMEN'S CIVIL AND POLITICAL RIGHTS IN SOUTH AMERICA

This book analyzes the context, process and content of the reform of married women's property rights in seven Spanish-speaking South American countries – Argentina, Chile, Colombia, Ecuador, Peru, Uruguay and Venezuela – between 1900 and the early 1950s.

It investigates how the reforms enacted earlier in the United States, England and continental Europe and national antecedents and conditions informed the ideas of feminists, jurists and politicians and shows how their interaction influenced the content of the reforms attained. It highlights the role of feminists and their organizations in achieving stronger property rights, emphasizing their proposals to reform the civil code. The book argues that while most feminists framed their arguments in maternalist terms – that they needed stronger rights to be better wives and mothers – their proposals to reform the marital regime fell along a continuum that ranged from accepting the husband as sole household head to gender equality in marriage. Since the long-run goal was to attain equal civil and political rights, the book also demonstrates how these two demands for stronger property rights and suffrage influenced their strategies and what feminists were able to achieve.

This book contributes to a long-standing discussion on the relationship between socioeconomic and legal change and brings the findings of recent scholarship and a vast array of primary materials only available in Spanish to an English-speaking audience, interpreting legal concepts and debates in a manner accessible to social scientists. Written from an interdisciplinary perspective, it supports the construction of a feminist legal history of marital regimes. It will be of interest to historians, legal scholars and feminists across a range of disciplines.

Carmen Diana Deere is Distinguished Professor Emerita of Latin American Studies and Food and Resource Economics at the University of Florida, Gainesville, FL, United States.

Routledge IAFFE Advances in Feminist Economics

IAFFE aims to increase the visibility and range of economic research on gender; facilitate communication among scholars, policymakers, and activists concerned with women's wellbeing and empowerment; promote discussions among policy makers about interventions which serve women's needs; educate economists, policymakers, and the general public about feminist perspectives on economic issues; foster feminist evaluations of economics as a discipline; expose the gender blindness characteristic of much social science and the ways in which this impoverishes all research – even research that does not explicitly concern women's issues; help expand opportunities for women, especially women from underrepresented groups, within economics; and, encourage the inclusion of feminist perspectives in the teaching of economics. The IAFFE book series pursues the aims of the organization by providing a forum in which scholars have space to develop their ideas at length and in detail. The series exemplifies the value of feminist research and the high standard of IAFFE sponsored scholarship.

21 Women's Economic Thought in the Romantic Age
Towards a Transdisciplinary Herstory of Economic Thought
Joanna Rostek

22 First-Wave Feminism and Women's Civil and Political Rights in South America
Carmen Diana Deere

For more information about this series, please visit www.routledge.com/Routledge-IAFFE-Advances-in-Feminist-Economics/book-series/IAFFE

FIRST-WAVE FEMINISM AND WOMEN'S CIVIL AND POLITICAL RIGHTS IN SOUTH AMERICA

Carmen Diana Deere

Routledge
Taylor & Francis Group
LONDON AND NEW YORK

Designed cover image: *Schlesinger Library, Harvard Radcliffe Institute*

First published 2026
by Routledge
4 Park Square, Milton Park, Abingdon, Oxon OX14 4RN

and by Routledge
605 Third Avenue, New York, NY 10158

Routledge is an imprint of the Taylor & Francis Group, an informa business

British Library Cataloguing-in-Publication Data
A catalogue record for this book is available from the British Library

ISBN: 978-1-041-11131-3 (hbk)
ISBN: 978-1-041-11130-6 (pbk)
ISBN: 978-1-003-65843-6 (ebk)

DOI: 10.4324/9781003658436

Typeset in Times New Roman
by KnowledgeWorks Global Ltd.

For those whose legacy we have built upon in hopes of inspiring the generations that follow us.

CONTENTS

FIGURES AND TABLES

Figures

Tables

PREFACE

The idea behind this monograph dates from the research Colombian sociologist Magdalena León and I conducted for our 2001 book, *Empowering Women: Land and Property Rights in Latin America*. That project focused on the agrarian reforms and counter-reforms of the second half of the twentieth century, on how rural and indigenous women began to organize around the demand for access to land and, more generally, on the demands and accomplishments of second-wave feminism. Early on, we realized that the marital and inheritance regimes embodied in the civil codes of the 12 countries studied shaped their respective reforms and influenced their outcomes for women.

I still have a vivid memory of the first time we encountered a civil code. In June 1997, Magdalena and I began our field research in Lima and requested our hosts, the Centro de la Mujer Peruana Flora Tristán, to arrange an interview with a feminist legal scholar. Ivonne Macassi León walked into the reception area carrying several tomes of the Peruvian civil code and proceeded to give us a two-hour tutorial. Given our lack of legal training, she might as well have been speaking Quechua. We dutifully photocopied the relevant sections on the marital and inheritance regimes for further study and repeated this process of interviews with experts in family law and the collection of materials in each country. We then spent the next several years trying to understand how and why these contemporary legal regimes differed by country and why such mattered.

At no time during our field research did anyone suggest that one of the reasons these differed by country could have been related to the demands and lobbying of first-wave feminists, those who organized in support of women's civil and political rights during the first half of the twentieth century. While historians of Latin America had begun to research the women's organizations of that period, most scholarship focused on their struggle for women's suffrage rather than on their demands for property and other civil rights. It was only as we were finalizing our manuscript that we came across Asunción Lavrin's (1995) pioneering comparative analysis of first-wave feminism in Argentina, Chile and Uruguay, which gave attention to reforms of the marital regime. This book, *First-Wave Feminism and Women's Civil and Political Rights in South America*, a comparative study of the Andes and Southern Cone, builds on Lavrin's work. In many ways, it constitutes what Magdalena and I wished we had in hand when we authored *Empowering Women*.

Our next collaborative project focused on the initial nineteenth-century civil codes of 14 of the new Republics. This was because one of the main findings of *Empowering Women* was how the default marital and inheritance regimes of Mexico and Central America were markedly different from those of South America. By then we were relatively proficient at reading civil codes and discovered that this divergence took place in the late nineteenth and early turn-of-the-century. Whereas most Central American countries reformed their initial civil codes during their respective Liberal Revolutions, those of South America entered the twentieth century with their regimes intact. Hence, the emphasis in *First-Wave Feminism* on the reforms of women's property and other civil rights in South America up through the 1950s, the gap in this story.

I began research for this monograph while affiliated with the Facultad Latinoamericana de Ciencias Sociales (FLACSO) in Quito, where I taught and conducted research for part of each year between 2009 and 2019. Up through 2015, I was part of an international team of feminist economists that undertook a comparative mixed-methods study of men's and women's accumulation of wealth in contemporary Ecuador, Ghana and India, co-directing the Ecuador study. As that project concluded, I began to explore the historical archives in Quito to see what they might reveal regarding factors that shaped women's ability to accumulate wealth, specifically, the impact of Ecuador's early reforms of married women's property rights and its adoption of civil divorce. My research in the national judicial archives was cut short by the indigenous uprising of November 2019. Then the eruption of the global COVID-19 pandemic in 2020 postponed my return to Quito until June 2022, when another indigenous uprising also cut short that research stay.

In the intervening years, while isolating at home in Gainesville, Florida, I discovered the wealth of historical materials now available on the internet. Whereas for our earlier project on the nineteenth century, Magdalena and I had to personally visit nearly every congressional and national library to locate and photocopy the civil codes, many of these, along with commentaries by jurists and subsequent editions of the code, are now available in digital depositories, particularly the HathiTrust and LLMC Digital collections. Moreover, many Latin American governments had begun to digitize their historical congressional records; feminists throughout the region were doing the same for the early feminist periodicals and writings of many of the pioneering feminists. Thus, what had begun as a modest project on Ecuador evolved into a seven-country comparative study of civil code reform and its interaction with the struggle for women's suffrage during the period of first-wave feminism.

My greatest debt in this process is to all those unnamed librarians, IT experts, feminists and their institutions whose digitization efforts have facilitated historical research on Latin America. In addition, librarians at many of the South American congressional libraries kindly answered my emails and facilitated copies of specific entries in congressional records when these were unavailable elsewhere. While the University of Florida has an outstanding Latin American and Caribbean Collection of which I made intense use, this project also relied heavily on UF's Inter-Library Loan services, which fulfilled my many requests for access to materials held at other universities. Two visits to the US Library of Congress in Washington, DC, and the support of staff at the Hispanic Division filled other gaps. Special thanks are also due to Elizabeth "Hiromi" Toguchi, librarian at Centro de la Mujer Peruana Flora Tristán, who shared copies of materials by and on early Peruvian feminists as well as images for this book. In addition, this project benefited from the capable research assistance of Abril Gómez in Bogota, Angela Quispe in Lima and María Gabriela Bourne in Guayaquil at various points.

When I returned to Quito in 2022, I discovered that the Property Registry contained the complete records of all married women in Quito who registered their property in order to manage it themselves under Ecuador's 1911 reform of its marital regime. I am grateful to the director and staff of the archives of the Registro de la Propiedad del Cantón Quito for facilitating access to these materials, as well as to the staff of the Archivo General de la Función Judicial for welcoming me back to complete some of my earlier research. I initially planned to pursue archival research in several other countries in order to document quantitatively women's use of these reforms. Due to their different scope and mechanics, I discovered that this was an almost impossible undertaking; in most cases it would have required the study of rarely indexed notarial records. Moreover, since I am officially retired, this study was self-financed, which limited extensive travel. Through the good offices of the Subdirección de Estudios y Desarrollo, Servicio de Registro Civil of Chile, I was able to at least gain access to administrative data for that country.

In writing this monograph, I was fortunate to be able to draw on the expertise of a number of good friends and colleagues across a range of disciplines. Among those who read the country and/or comparative chapters at various stages and provided valuable feedback or who provided guidance on specific matters were Ida Altman, Gina Alvarado, Florence Babb, Carollee Bengelsdorf, María Cuvi, Vanessa D'Alessandre, Carlos de la Torre, Alma Espina, Cristina Espinoza, Ana María Goetschel, Elsa Gómez, Terry Karl, Magdalena León, Nora Lustig, Susan Paulson, Mercedes Prieto, Marianne Schmink, Lars Schoultz, Ofelia Shutte, Danaya Wright and Reuben Zahler. I also benefited from the comments of participants in the Online Colloquium on Gender, History and Memory in Ecuador organized by Ana María Goestschel of FLACSO-Quito, during 2022–2023 where I presented an early version of the Ecuador chapter. I presented other chapters at the Latin American Studies Association congresses in Vancouver in 2023 and in Bogota in 2024 and at the International Association for Feminist Economics congresses in Rome in 2024 and Amherst, Massachusetts, in 2025. Silvia Arrom graciously read the full manuscript as an external reviewer for Routledge; her insightful comments improved the coherence of this work.

I am also grateful to Smriti Rao, the series editor of Routledge IAFFE Advances in Feminist Economics, for encouraging me to submit the manuscript to this series, and to Kristina Abbotts, Christiana Mandizha, and Riya Bhattacharya at Routledge for their advice, expertise and patience, which brought this project to completion.

ACRONYMS

AASF	Asociación Argentina del Sufragio Femenino (Argentine Association for Women's Suffrage)
ACF	Agrupación Cultural Femenina (Women's Cultural Association), Venezuela
AD	Acción Democrática (Democratic Action Party), Venezuela
AFE	Alianza Femenina Ecuatoriana (Ecuadorian Women's Alliance)
AN	Acción Nacional (National Action Party), Venezuela
ANMCH	Acción Nacional de Mujeres de Chile (National Action of Chilean Women)
APRA	Alianza Popular Revolucionaria Americana del Peru (American Popular Revolutionary Alliance of Peru)
AVM	Asociación Venezolana de Mujeres (Venezuelan Association of Women)
CIM	Comisión Interamericana de Mujeres (Inter-American Commission of Women)
CNM-A	Consejo Nacional de Mujeres Argentinas (National Council of Argentine Women)
CNM-C	Consejo Nacional de Mujeres de Chile (National Council of Chilean Women)
CNM-P	Consejo Nacional de Mujeres del Peru (National Council of Peruvian Women)
CNM-U	Consejo Nacional de Mujeres del Uruguay (National Council of Uruguayan Women)
FDN	Frente Democrático Nacional (National Democratic Front), Peru
FECHIF	Federación Chilena de Instituciones Femeninas (Chilean Federation of Women's Institutions)

IAWSEC	International Alliance of Women for Suffrage and Equal Citizenship
ICW	International Council of Women
IWSA	International Woman Suffrage Alliance
JV	Junta de la Victoria (Victory Board), Argentina
LIMIH	Liga Internacional de Mujeres Ibéricas e Hispanoamericanas (International League of Iberian and Hispanic Women)
MEMCH	Movimiento Pro-Emancipación de Mujeres de Chile (Movement for the Emancipation of Chilean Women)
NAWSA	National American Woman Suffrage Association
OFN	Organización Femenina Nacional (National Women's Organization), Colombia
ORVE	Movimiento de Organización Venezolana (Movement for Venezuelan Organization)
PAAAW	Pan American Association for the Advancement of Women
PAU	Pan American Union
PCF	Partido Cívico Femenino (Women's Civic Party), Chile
PDV	Partido Democrático Venezolano (Venezuelan Democratic Party)
PFN	Partido Feminista Nacional (National Feminist Party), Argentina
PFPN	Partido Femenino Progresista Nacional (Women's National Progressive Party), Chile
PIDF	Partido Independiente Democrático Femenino (Independent Democratic Women's Party), Uruguay
PRP	Partido Republicano Progresista (Progressive Republican Party), Venezuela
PSD	Partido Socialista Democrático (Socialist Democratic Party), Colombia
UAM	Unión Argentina de Mujeres (Argentine Union of Women)
UBA	Universidad de Buenos Aires (University of Buenos Aires)
UCE	Universidad Central del Ecuador (Central University of Ecuador)
UCR	Unión Cívica Radical (Radical Civic Union party), Argentina
UCV	Universidad Central de Venezuela (Central University of Venezuela)
UFC	Unión Femenina de Chile (Women's Union of Chile)
UFC	Unión Femenina de Colombia (Women's Union of Colombia)
UFN	Unión Feminista Nacional (National Feminist Union), Argentina
UMA	Unión de Mujeres Americanas (Union of American Women)
UNMSM	Universidad Nacional Mayor de San Marcos (National University of San Marcos), Peru
URP	Partido Unión Revolucionaria (Revolutionary Union Party), Peru
WILPF	Women's International League for Peace and Freedom

1

PATHWAYS TO REFORM OF THE MARITAL REGIME AND WOMEN'S SUFFRAGE

In late October 1911, shortly after Ecuador enacted its Economic Emancipation of Married Women Law, Alejandrina Gómez de la Torre de Guillén and her husband, Federico Belisario Guillén, visited the Property Registry in Quito so that Alejandrina could inscribe a notarized document.[1] This registration allowed her, a married woman, to manage independently the dwelling she had recently inherited from her mother. She thus became the first woman in Quito to exercise her rights under Ecuador's new law, the first in South America to strengthen married women's property rights in the early twentieth century.

With this registration, Alejandrina could execute contracts regarding the property, manage its earnings and represent herself in lawsuits. In its absence, the husband was the administrator of any assets that a wife brought to marriage or later inherited and any income generated by these as well as her wages or salary. While a wife did not require her husband's consent to exercise her rights under the 1911 law, Federico may have accompanied Alejandrina to the registry because he feared that the clerks might challenge her action if she was unaccompanied since it broke so deeply with tradition. He was undoubtedly a strong supporter of the reforms promoted by Ecuador's 1895 liberal revolution. He had been a delegate to the constitutional congress that produced the country's 1906 Constitution, one that did not explicitly exclude women from citizenship.[2]

1 Registro de la Propiedad del Cantón Quito (RPCQ), Subseries "Exclusión de Bienes," 1911, Class 4, entry #1, October 27, 1911.

2 A Federico Guillén signed the August 26, 1895, petition recognizing Eloy Alfaro as the Supreme Head of the Republic (reproduced in Aristizábal 1896, 54–5) and this constitution (Ecuador 1906). While his signature did not include a middle name or initial or a second last name, Guillén is not a common Ecuadorian surname; thus it is highly likely it is the same person.

DOI: 10.4324/9781003658436-1

During this period of liberal hegemony in Ecuador, women's rights organizations had not yet emerged. The government, however, was beginning to give attention to women's education, expanding public primary schools and teacher-training programs for girls and authorizing the first woman to enroll in university. In contrast, in Argentina women were completing secondary school and attending university in sufficient numbers that an association of university women had formed, which in 1910 hosted the First International Congress of Women in Buenos Aires.

At that congress physician Elvira Rawson (1911) presented a detailed proposal to reform Argentina's civil code, aiming to modify the marital regime to give wives the same property rights they held as single women and cede mothers the same rights over their children that fathers held. The congress attendees, primarily Argentine but also including Uruguayan, Chilean and Peruvian women, unanimously endorsed the proposal. Argentina's legislature had already entertained the first bill to strengthen married women's property rights; Uruguay and Chile's legislatures would also consider such proposals by the end of this decade.

This book examines the context, process and content of the reforms of women's civil and political rights in seven Spanish-speaking South American countries – Argentina, Chile, Colombia, Ecuador, Peru, Uruguay and Venezuela – during the first half of the twentieth century and the role played by feminists, jurists and politicians. These countries are those that reformed their marital regimes prior to the 1948 Inter-American conventions on women's equal civil and political rights.[3]

While the seven countries differed in the sequencing and substance of their reforms, they shared notable features, among them was their inherited legal tradition – colonial Hispanic law. As new Republics, they adopted their own initial civil codes between 1852 and 1873. Uniformly, single adult women (those who never married or were widows) held the same property rights and most of the other civil rights as men. The few restrictions on women because of their sex included serving as a legal witness and occupying certain occupations or positions. The main restrictions had to do with when they married.

All seven countries maintained the same marital regime of the colonial period, the *sociedad conyugal* (conjugal society), based on partial community property subject to *potestad marital*. It recognized three distinct types of property in marriage – the wife's, the husband's and the community property – but all were under the administration of the husband.[4] Under potestad marital the husband

3 "Inter-American Convention on the Granting of Civil Rights to Women" and "Inter-American Convention on the Granting of Political Rights to Women," signed at the Ninth International Conference of American States in Bogota, May 1948; https://www.oas.org/juridico/english/treaties/a-44.html. This study excludes Bolivia and Paraguay because they did not strengthen married women's property rights until 1972 and 1985, respectively. Prior to the convention on political rights, only three of the seven countries studied had granted women suffrage; by 1955 all had done so.

4 Brazil, a colony of Portugal, inherited a similar but distinct legal marital regime, full community property, where at marriage ownership of all assets was pooled. Its trajectory was also different because rather than in the nineteenth century, it did not enact its own civil code until 1916.

controlled both his wife's property and her person. She owed him obedience and as head of household he represented her and determined their domicile. Similarly, under *patria potestad* the father controlled both the person and property of the couple's legitimate children until the age of majority.

Another shared feature was the accelerated circulation of ideas, facilitated by developments in transportation, communication and growing integration into world markets.[5] By the beginning of the twentieth century, most jurists, politicians and nascent feminists were aware of the reforms of married women's property rights in the United States, England and parts of continental Europe and that women were beginning to attain political rights. In addition, South American countries were beginning to enjoy rising standards of living, albeit at markedly different rates, reflected in varying levels of industrialization, urbanization, literacy and women's labor force participation.[6]

One of the main questions motivating this study was whether the reform of married women's property rights in South America preceded or followed the emergence of women's movements demanding rights, a long-standing issue in feminist legal history (Basch 1986). Francesca Miller's (1991) and Asunción Lavrin's (1995) pioneering studies of these movements in Latin America establish that the emergence of organized women's groups demanding rights was strongly associated with the expansion of public secondary and higher education for women and their entry into the professions. Nonetheless, there were substantial differences in the region on when such occurred and when women achieved stronger civil rights and suffrage.

Another question regards the sequencing of feminist demands for civil and political rights. At the beginning of the century many reformist jurists, politicians and feminists in South America expected the region to follow a pattern similar to their progression in the United States and much of Europe. According to inherited wisdom, as summed up by Carrie Chapman Catt (1923b), one of the main leaders in the struggle for US women's suffrage, in the countries where by then women had the vote, they first began organizing around the demand for equal educational opportunities up through university; this was followed by demands for equal property rights and equal guardianship over children; and finally, by the demand for equal

5 On the influence of Western liberal ideals in the struggle for independence and in the subsequent Republican constitutions and new civil codes see Gargarella (2004), Guzmán Brito (2000), and Mirow (2004).

6 In 1913 the per capita GDP of Argentina, Uruguay and Chile was each more than twice that of Colombia or Venezuela (Bertola 2011, Table 2.2). In 1910–1914, the most urbanized were Argentina and Uruguay (with 31% and 29% of the population living in major cities, respectively), followed by Chile (14.5%), Ecuador (9%), Colombia (7%), Peru (5%) and Venezuela (4%) (Bulmer-Thomas 1994, Table 4.1). Literacy levels by 1925 were 73% in Argentina, 70% in Uruguay, 66% in Chile, but only 48% in Colombia, 38% in Peru and 34% in Venezuela (Newland 1994, Table 3). Historical estimates of women's labor force participation are not very reliable, largely because of the underestimation of rural women's work (Benería 1981; Deere and León 1982). The degree of urbanization, nonetheless, can serve as a proxy for women's wage employment opportunities.

political rights, the latter initially at the local level. And, indeed, South American women voiced the demand for access to more and a better education prior to demanding equal civil rights. When they initially organized around reform of the marital regime, they saw political rights as a long-run aspiration. Yet by the mid-1920s many feminists were simultaneously demanding stronger civil and political rights.

A third question regards what South American feminists wanted when they demanded equal property and other civil rights. Was it to retain the same rights when they married that they held as single women, or equal rights in marriage? A fourth is whether their ideas and demands influenced the content of the reforms attained.

This book aims to deepen our understanding of the role feminists and their organizations played in securing women's rights. It focuses on their objectives and proposals for civil code reform, the influence of reforms in the United States, England and continental Europe and how these ideas, along with national contexts and interactions with jurists and politicians, shaped these early twentieth-century reforms. The extensive historical material presented shows how the development of South American feminism was not simply derivative of US and European feminism but evolved in specific circumstances. It illustrates the interplay between South American feminist critiques of their own societies' restrictions, the circulation of ideas that informed their debates and how they came to formulate their own aspirations and demands.

While mindful of the critique of Katherine Marino and Susan Ware (2022) regarding the use of terminology that emerged in a different historical context, such as first-wave and second-wave feminism whose origins are in the chronology of US feminism, these terms are employed here following the Latin American feminist convention of distinguishing two periods with distinct aims. The first wave ran from the beginning of the twentieth century to the 1950s and focused on expanding women's access to education, civil rights and suffrage, initially in that order. During the second wave, from the late 1960s to the end of the century, feminists pursued equal rights in marriage, the property rights of those in consensual unions, reproductive rights, ending violence against women and effective political representation, among other issues. Notwithstanding, this study shows areas of overlap, for example, some first-wave feminists had their sights set on equal rights in marriage although it was a minority view.

Heterogenous Paths

This comparative study shows that feminist groups demanding rights first emerged in the Southern Cone countries of Argentina, Chile and Uruguay, and in Peru, and later in the Northern Andean countries of Ecuador, Colombia and Venezuela. This was largely because the expansion of women's access to public secondary and higher education took place later in the latter. Nonetheless, it reveals that the first successful reform of married women's property rights and the enactment of women's suffrage took place in a lesser developed Andean country, Ecuador, rather than in the more economically developed Southern Cone, and prior to the development of women's rights organizations.

A long-standing discussion in legal history has centered on the relationship between socioeconomic and legal change. Most analytical studies of the timing of the adoption of married women's property legislation are based on the experience of the United States, which adopted these reforms on a state-by-state basis during the second half of the nineteenth and early twentieth centuries. These studies assess whether socioeconomic change drives legal change, in this case, due either to the increased opportunity cost of women in the labor market or because the rise in the importance of human capital changed the economic calculus of fathers with respect to daughters (Doepke and Tertilt 2009). Among the findings is that US states with a higher level of per capita wealth, urbanization and women's school enrollment (Geddes and Lueck 2002) or that initiated a drop in fertility rates (Fernández 2014) adopted such reforms earlier.

The cases presented here reveal two distinct patterns with respect to the adoption of married women's property legislation in South America. In the Northern Andean countries of Ecuador and Venezuela, the initial reforms took place in a period of liberal ideological hegemony and were part of a package of reforms that included separation of church and state and the institution of civil marriage and divorce. The motive behind legal change in these cases was to spur socioeconomic change. In contrast, in the Southern cone, changing social norms, driven by industrialization, urbanization and women's rising education and labor force participation, created conditions favorable to legal reform. However, reform proposals met with concerted opposition from traditionalists, generally the Catholic Church and associated political parties. Feminist ideas and women's organizing, assisted by the press, served to move public opinion in support of reform adoption although the process was often piecemeal and drawn out.

Through its detailed attention to the reform proposals debated and adopted in South America, this study also contributes toward the construction of a legal history of marital regimes, an undertaking not systematically attempted until now. It contributes to a feminist legal history of these through its analysis of what organized women wanted to achieve. Among some of the common themes in their demands that stopped short of equal rights were that women not be in the same category as minors, criminals and the mentally deranged when it came to their civil capacities; that they should have some degree of autonomy over their own earnings and property; and that they should have a say in the raising of their own children. Not all challenged outright the husband's position as household head. This is why their proposals merit detailed study alongside analysis of what the reforms achieved.

Related to the point on what feminists wanted, this study offers insights into the context and meaning of "maternalist feminism" or what Karen Offen (1988, 135–6) terms "relational feminism." This approach highlights the centrality of the couple rather than the individual as the basic unit of society and emphasizes women's unique attributes and contributions as mothers and wives. Most first-wave feminists accepted the traditional gender division of labor whereby women's primary responsibility was to home and children and, as Miller (1991, 74) states, they even "cherished" or "celebrated" this role. They mobilized to be better able to fulfill this role, not to abandon it, arguing that stronger civil and political rights would make them better wives and mothers. But embracing these roles did not mean that they wanted to maintain separate spheres, the public and private. Rather, beginning with the demand for access to more and a better education, their objective was to expand the scope of women's activities beyond the domestic realm.

The metaphor of wives as "angels" or "queens" of the home was widely employed in South America from at least the last quarter of the nineteenth century and captured the Victorian idealization of the gender division of labor and glorification of motherhood.[7] In its Latin American variant, deeply fused with Catholicism, it both elevated the status of women because of their supposed moral superiority and justified their relegation to the domestic sphere, excluding them from the public. When at the beginning of the century feminists began demanding rights they were taking issue with the contradiction presented by women having responsibilities they deemed important, such as caring for children and the home, but not having the proper rights to be able to address or defend their interests.

The most glaring of these contradictions was patria potestad, the father's sole authority over his children. Legally, mothers carried equal responsibility for their care but did not have a voice in such fundamental matters as their education. Feminists also chaffed at how the law forced women into becoming the economic dependents of their husbands. They asked if they had no control over income except for what a husband might give them, how could a wife assure her household's well-being? While it was the husband's legal duty to provide for dependents, and it was frequent practice for wives to manage an allowance for daily expenses, what if their husbands were stingy, poor providers or spendthrifts? Moreover, since most women did not receive the preparation to provide for themselves they were quite vulnerable if they never married or if they did so, if abandoned by their husband or widowed. Hence women's need to access education and employment opportunities and some economic autonomy over their earnings and property to be better able to meet their responsibilities and maintain themselves under unforeseen circumstances. The argument that greater or equal civil rights would allow them to become better wives and mothers was not only strategic, in the sense that it made their demands more politically acceptable but also based on their lived experience.

7 LaGreca (2009) discusses the origins of this phrase simultaneously in England and Spain in the 1850s, and on its diffusion in Latin America through literature and manuals on proper behavior. See Alcibíades (2004) on the factors contributing to the diffusion of this ideal in Venezuela, and Szuchman (1988) and Shumway (2005) on the association between the rise in the perceived status of wives (valued for their domesticity and maternalism), acceptance of the idea that marriage should be based on romantic love, and the growing centrality of the conjugal unit in Argentina. These trends were similar to those in Europe (Giddens 1992; Coontz 2006).

South American feminists often had to defend themselves against the charge that in demanding rights they wanted to become like men. Often expressed in derogatory terms, that they were becoming *marimachos* (a third sex), feminists emphasized their feminity. They also laid out a vision whereby women could be true companions to men only if recognized as autonomous beings – persons with rights – and where marriage was based on mutual respect and consideration, not obedience and subordination. At the same time, they tended to distance themselves from individualistic arguments, such as those of Anglo-Saxon feminists who focused on personal independence, by emphasizing how women's rights would strengthen the family.

Feminists, nonetheless, differed in how far they were willing to go in the demand to end potestad marital; that is, around points on a continuum toward equal rights in marriage. For example, many Catholic feminists, following church teachings, had little interest in destabilizing male household headship, often referring to this view as properly understood feminism (*feminismo bien entendido*).[8] They considered those who challenged gender hierarchies more forthrightly as representing a poorly understood feminism (*feminismo mal entendido*). Nonetheless, they too wanted to improve women's education and employment opportunities and reduce their vulnerabilities. As a minimum this required wives to retain the rights they had when single, that is, control over their own earnings if not also the property they brought to marriage or later inherited.

Argentine historian Marcela Nari (2000) writes that what distinguished the maternalism of feminists in the early decades of the century from earlier Victorian versions was that it was a "political maternalism," one that emerged from the struggle to define what women had in common as women that transcended differences of class, religion and other divisions. "Feminists tried to reformulate traditional femininity and maternity within an ideology of complementarity and equivalence (if not superiority) of the feminine and of women with respect to masculinity and men" (Nari, 2004, 231). Moreover, over the course of the first half of the century the content of political maternalism changed as feminists interacted with the ideas of the medical establishment, organized labor and the state over the implications of socio-demographic changes and maternalist policies.

Partly as a result, maternalist arguments became even more pronounced in the struggle for women's suffrage. Feminists argued that because of sexual differences and their unique domestic roles and responsibilities, women would bring special and needed qualities to politics.[9] They incorporated the imaginary of "mothering the nation" – women's natural concern and expertise with all questions having to

8 See Uribe-Uran's (2023, 458–61) discussion of the Hispanic colonial heritage and how under Canon law, which was as important as civil law, patriarchal authority went together with the indissolubility of marriage.

9 Most analyses of South American maternalist feminism have been with respect to suffrage, not feminists' demands for civil rights; see Palermo (1998), Luna (2001b) and Osta (2023).

do with children, the family and social welfare. Given this predisposition, and their femininity and greater morality, they argued that women's participation in politics would result in more civilized discourse, national progress and even international peace.

Since the long-run goal of most feminists was to attain both equal civil and political rights, another contribution of this study is its analysis of how these two objectives interacted in their discourse, in the strategies of their organizations and in what they were able to achieve. Early on there was consensus among feminists and reformist politicians that women's civil rights must come prior to their attaining political rights. This was because to exercise citizenship women must be autonomous persons capable of exercising property and other civil rights. Nonetheless, the legislatures sometimes entertained bills in support of women's suffrage and reform of the marital regime simultaneously or prior to civil code reform. In some cases, feminist demands for both civil and political rights made the demand for stronger property rights appear less threatening to gender norms, fostering the conditions for the necessary political consensus to achieve civil code reform. In other instances, feminists became convinced that without political rights they would never achieve the equal civil status that they envisioned, especially after women secured the vote in England and the United States.

The chapters ahead show that among the reasons that demands for civil code reform often stopped short of equal rights in marriage is that, after achieving even modest strengthening of their property and other civil rights, most women's organizations turned their energies to the pursuit of suffrage, and in some countries, this struggle was particularly prolonged. Only in one country, Uruguay, did women attain suffrage prior to civil code reform. It was the last among the seven to strengthen married women's property rights but also came closest to attaining equal rights in marriage. This was partly because of its timing, taking place near mid-century and because female legislators participated in drafting the bill that became law.

Another key finding is that the reforms of married women's property rights in South America during the first half of the twentieth century enhanced the economic autonomy of wives while preserving the concept of community property. This required the pooling of the gains (*gananciales*) of the marriage at its end and their equal division between the spouses and/or their estates. Feminists and reform-oriented jurists and legislators debated the wisdom of adopting the separation of property regime as the default, as in the Anglo-Saxon reforms, and largely rejected its adoption. All three groups tended to view the more modest civil code reforms undertaken in France and Germany as more compatible with the region's legal and cultural legacy, particularly the adoption of the concept of "reserved property," which gave working wives the right to exclude from the conjugal society their wages and salaries to manage these themselves, while maintaining most of the other rules of the prevailing marital regime. Some countries innovated in important ways by producing their own unique combinations of regimes, variants of the "deferred community property" regime, a hybrid combining separation of property during the marriage with community property at its end (Glendon 1989, 118).

Another important finding is that irrespective of the advances in strengthening married women's property rights, limitations on the civil rights of wives and mothers continued through the 1950s. The early reforms diluted the concept of potestad marital as regards women's property, but a husband's control over the person of his wife endured. Most kept the requirement that wives obey their husbands and/or stipulated that the husband was the household head. In addition, while mothers gained greater rights over their children, fathers continued to play the dominant role in the exercise of patria potestad during the marriage; only Uruguay went as far as giving both parents equal rights over their children.

Sources, Concepts and Parameters

This comparative analysis of the goals and achievements of organized women during first-wave feminism is only possible because of the substantial growth of scholarship in women's history over the past 50 years. There is at least one major monograph on the emergence of feminism and the women's movements for most of these countries. Nonetheless, most tend to place greater emphasis on their struggles for suffrage rather than for civil rights and few examine their demands for reform of the marital regime in any detail. Similar tendencies characterize the far lengthier list of specialized contributions in journals and anthologies. Moreover, there are few comparative studies of these issues and these focus on either the Southern Cone or the larger Latin American countries.[10] Even recent handbooks on Latin American legal history give little or no attention to the reforms of marital and inheritance regimes in the first half of the twentieth century.[11] Yet these regimes play crucial roles in shaping the accumulation and distribution of wealth, particularly, gender income and wealth gaps (Deere and Doss 2006). For these reasons, this study gives greater attention to the debates over reform of the marital regime than to those on women's suffrage, which are better known.

In addition to the civil codes, constitutions and legislation for each country, the primary materials on which this study is based include the congressional records relevant to these reforms. Legislators often provided detailed rationale for the bills they presented, and these illustrate well the influence of the circulation of ideas and other motivations for reform, as do the congressional debates over these bills. In several cases, governments appointed civil code review commissions to update

10 Asunción Lavrin's (1995) study of Argentina, Chile and Uruguay was my starting point since she provided the first detailed, comparative study of the development of feminism and the pursuit of suffrage and civil code reform, among other topics. Also useful were Miller (1991), Giordano (2012) and Marino (2019).

11 The essays in Duve and Herzog (2024), for example, do not mention this topic at all and it gets short-shrift in Wisnoski (2023) and Uribe-Urán (2023).

their codes and their deliberations also provide insight into the influence of legal reforms elsewhere on their proposals. In addition, the study draws on the writings of contemporaries, especially legal scholars (including doctoral theses), as well as politicians and journalists on these issues.

Since an aim of this book is to discern the extent to which feminists developed their own autonomous proposals for reform and influenced legislation, this required a re-reading of the periodicals and other materials published by women's organizations and feminists in various venues with a different lens than utilized in previous studies. It revealed that women developed at least nine different detailed proposals for reform of the marital regime. This study also initially intended to investigate the extent to which women took advantage of these reforms and employed their new property rights. Due to the design of the reforms and accessibility of archival data, it was possible to pursue this important aspect only in two cases, for Ecuador and Chile.

This study uses the term "feminism" in its most ample sense, to include all those demanding civil and political rights for women, but for clarity of exposition, the term "feminist" is employed more narrowly to identify women who demanded these rights.[12] Sometimes it uses "feminist groups" and "women's organizations" interchangeably; the country chapters use the terms with which these associations self-identified. Since the largest constraint on women attaining equal civil rights were the restrictions on married women and their property rights, the study also often employs the terms civil and property rights interchangeably.[13] Note that in the Latin American context, the civil code delineates civil rights relevant to individuals, the family and property while electoral law defines political or voting rights, with both under the framework of the broader legal rights guaranteed under a country's constitution.

Technically, married women's property rights consist of the combination of a country's marital and inheritance regimes. While the marital regime defines the relationship between a person's ownership and administration of their property, the inheritance regime refers to the scope of an individual's right to bequeath their own property as well as rights to the property of others through kinship or marriage. The rules governing separation and divorce as well as custody and guardianship over children also define important aspects of women's property rights. For example, a critical component of parental rights over children, particularly over minors after the death of one parent, was control over their assets since legally, children inherited most of the assets of the deceased parent. Thus the welfare of widowed mothers often depended critically on whether the gains from the administration of children's property corresponded to them or an appointed guardian.

12 See Offen (1988) on the evolution of the term feminism globally, and Cuadro (2018) in the Southern Cone.

13 I do not use the concept of economic rights, as many economists do, since it is broader, encompassing labor and other related social rights, such as social security systems.

This book does not aim to provide a complete synthesis of what we now know about feminism and women's organizations in South America in this period. Since the focus is on the women's groups that demanded equal rights, this study centers on those inspired by liberal and socialist feminist ideas. Also, the platforms and activities of many of the women's organizations were much broader than the issues of concern here, often incorporating demands around labor and social rights as well as on moral issues; the book does not treat these topics in any depth.

The study focuses on the thinking and actions of white and mestizo middle- and upper-class women – those who had access to some education – who were the most likely to feel constrained by the restrictions on women's property and other civil rights. The reforms of married women's property rights that they demanded, nonetheless, were relevant to wives across social classes, not just those who owned property and were wealthy, for a key component of these reforms was control over their wages, salaries and other independent earnings. At the same time, feminists struggled to define what constituted the ideal marital regime, being aware that wives who worked or who inherited property were in a different position from those who did not and dedicated themselves full-time to the home and children.

Feminists were also cognizant that many working-class women lived in consensual unions and never married. Such women were legally single and had the same property rights as men. While they had greater economic autonomy than wives, they did not have any of the potential benefits that came from marriage, such as a claim to community property or inheritance rights, nor did their children have an automatic right to their father's patrimony. Feminists assumed the demand to strengthen the property rights of women in such unions only in Venezuela, although in most countries they gave attention to improving the inheritance rights of children born outside marriage and demanded that the civil code allow or expand the investigation of paternity.

Most feminists were genuinely concerned with the situation of working-class women and the often exploitative conditions under which they labored. Their organizations usually assumed the demand for equal pay for equal work, an issue relevant to both working-class and professional women. In addition, these organizations frequently sponsored education and training programs and other activities aimed at bettering the situation of poor women. Socialist feminists, in particular, fostered and supported the organization of working-class women around their own specific, class-based demands. But until the Popular Front coalitions of the 1930s and the focus on women's suffrage, with the exception of socialist women's groups, it was uncommon for working-class women to be members of women's rights organizations, especially to form part of their leadership.

To provide background for this comparative analysis, the next sections summarize the major features of family law in the nineteenth-century South American civil codes, trends in the reforms of marital regimes elsewhere and the process that gave rise to institutionalized global feminism, all factors that informed the deliberations of South American feminists, jurists and legislators.

Nineteenth-Century Civil Codes

The initial civil codes of the Hispanic American republics with respect to family law drew heavily on their colonial legal tradition while incorporating many of the legal innovations of the Napoleonic code of 1804 on other matters. All maintained the inherited marital regime that gave married women relatively strong ownership rights over their property but little economic autonomy as well as the inheritance regime that treated sons and daughters equally;[14] these mainly improved spousal inheritance rights.

Of the early nineteenth-century civil codes, the most influential on other countries in the region was the Chilean code of 1855 (effective in 1857), written by Venezuelan-born jurist Andrés Bello (Guzmán Brito 2000; Mirow 2004). Of the seven countries included in this study, the 1860 Ecuadorian and 1873 Colombian codes largely copied the Chilean while it also influenced the 1862 Venezuelan, 1868 Uruguayan and 1869 Argentine codes (Deere and León 2005; Deere 2023). Although the 1852 Peruvian Civil Code preceded the Chilean, they shared many features, both being rooted in the same colonial legal tradition and Napoleonic influence. Thus a summary of the key features of family law can be based on the Chilean code noting differences where appropriate.[15]

The civil codes offered one legal marital regime, the conjugal society, which recognized three types of property in marriage, the individual property of each spouse and the community property of the couple. Individual property consisted of what each spouse owned prior to marriage and later acquired as an inheritance or donation. Community property included the gains from such individual assets (rents, interest and profit), other earnings of each (wages and salaries) and any assets purchased during the marriage; together these constituted the gananciales. Particularly advantageous for wives was that irrespective of their relative contribution, when the conjugal society dissolved (due to death or judicial separation) each spouse retained their own individual property and they pooled and divided the community property into equal halves. The marital regime thus implicitly recognized the contribution of wives, through their domestic and caring labor, to the generation of the gananciales from the marriage. This gave wives a relatively strong fallback position in case of widowhood or separation (Deere and León 2001).

Not as favorable to married women was that partial community property was subject to potestad marital, which Andrés Bello formally defined as "the sum of rights that the law gives to the husband over the person and property of his wife" (Chile 1856, art. 132).[16] To emphasize its implications, he added the infamous Napoleonic phrase: "The husband owes protection to his wife, and she owes him

14 For Hispanic colonial America, the main treatise defining the marital regime and what wives could or could not do was the sixteenth-century *Leyes de Toro,* later reproduced in the *Novísima Recopilación* (Galván 1831). See Ots y Capdequi (1969) and Arrom (1985) on how married women had a legal personality and were only relatively incapable.

15 See the country chapters for references.

16 All translations from Spanish unless otherwise noted are the author's.

obedience" (Chile 1856, art. 131), which conformed to the colonial legal tradition.[17] Women's need for protection was the rationalization behind restrictions on the activities of wives combined with the perceived need for the household to have only one source of authority, that being of the stronger member, the husband.

During the marriage, the husband was the administrator of his wife's property as well as the community property. While he could not alienate her immovable property (land, dwellings and buildings) without her consent and the approval of a judge, he could do whatever he pleased with the community property. A married woman could not contract without her husband's permission – whether to purchase, sell, rent or mortgage property, make a loan or acquire debt, or be employed – nor receive a donation or inheritance, or be party to a lawsuit. A husband could grant his wife a general or specific license to engage in such acts. If she exercised a profession or engaged in remunerated work, the code assumed she had his permission although he could revoke this authorization at any time.

The only flexibility provided with respect to the management of assets was that a couple could make a prenuptial agreement known as *capitulaciones,* which specified that the wife could administer some (but not all) of her assets or a given sum of money.[18] In this case, the same rules applied to her management of these assets as under the "simple" separation of property. The latter took place either due to a permanent judicial or legal separation (called "divorce," but without the right to remarry) or by petition of the wife due to a husband's insolvency or fraudulent administration of the conjugal society. Under such a separation of property, the wife managed her own assets and her half of the gananciales although she still required her husband's permission or that of a judge to alienate immovable property or participate in a lawsuit (Chile 1856, 158–9).

Bello's code, and those modeled on his, eliminated the colonial concept of dowry, the requirement that fathers of means provide their daughters at marriage with a contribution toward the new couple's expenses, likely because of the steady decline in its practice.[19] The dowry legally belonged to the wife although it was under her husband's administration; at the dissolution of the union it held a privileged

17 Only Ecuador's 1860 and Colombia's 1887 codes copied both articles, the latter's 1873 code had not included the Napoleonic one on obedience. The 1852 Peruvian, 1862 Venezuelan and 1868 Uruguayan codes reproduced only the French article but delineated the ways that the wife was under the potestad of her husband or made her relatively incapable, with the husband her representative; Argentina's 1868 code did the latter.

18 Bello's concept was more restrictive than the capitulaciones of the *Novísima Recopilación* (Galván 1831, Bk. 10, tit. 4, law 5). Uruguay's 1868 code retained the most flexibility, allowing couples to specify what they found convenient as long as it conformed to good manners and did not abrogate potestad marital, patria potestad or succession law. Only the 1852 Peruvian code did not include the possibility of prenuptial agreements.

19 On its decline see Zeberio (2005) on Argentina and Hünefeldt (2000) on Peru although in the latter its nineteenth-century code maintained dowry as a parental requirement. Under colonial law, dowry was as an advance on a daughter's inheritance. Among the reasons for its demise was that it reduced the capital of the parental household during the parents' lifetime, becoming a constraint on economic expansion.

position versus third-party creditors.[20] In the 1855 Chilean code any parental contribution to the marriage was treated similarly to any other donation.[21] Those codes that did not eliminate the dowry dropped it as a parental requirement.

All the nineteenth-century codes incorporated the colonial legal concept of patria potestad – the rights of the father over the person and property of his legitimate children while they were minors. Only Argentina's civil code vested it in both parents, although the father administered the children's assets. The Chilean code and those of Ecuador and Colombia explicitly excluded mothers from exercising it. The codes of the other four were more generous, automatically conferring it upon the mother in the father's absence or death if he did not designate someone else in his will. The codes differed on the rules governing its exercise if a widow remarried, and on whether female relatives could serve as guardians over children. If a code did not prohibit women from being guardians, the explicit preference was for male over female relatives.

The colonial inheritance regime contained aspects favorable to women's ownership of property that the nineteenth-century codes maintained (Deere and León 2005). Most importantly, sons and daughters inherited equally from their parents whether in intestate or in a will. In principle, as forced heirs in the latter they received equal shares of the *legítima*, four-fifths of an estate.[22] Moreover, a wife did not require her husband's permission to accept an inventoried inheritance or write a will. She could designate one-fifth of her estate (which consisted of her individual property plus her half of the gananciales) to whomever she chose, just as he could. As a nod toward testamentary freedom, the 1855 Chilean code increased the share an individual was free to will to one-fourth of the estate. It also formalized the principle of gender equality in succession law, treating men and women equally in each order of succession and as surviving spouse (Chile 1856, art. 982).

The nineteenth-century civil codes improved the position of the surviving spouse when there was no will (intestate) (Deere 2023). Under colonial norms, husbands and wives did not inherit their spouse's estate unless the deceased had no living kin up through the 10th degree of kinship. The Republican codes reduced this to the 6th or 4th degree, and equally important, made the surviving spouse eligible for a share of the estate in the absence of legitimate descendants. These codes differed in whether in the 1st order of intestate, when there were descendants, the spouse received a conditional or unconditional share. In the Chilean and those

20 Other property, termed *bienes parafernales* (paraphernalia), not formally included in a dowry (such as her clothing, jewelry and household goods) that a bride brought to marriage remained under her control.

21 Also treated similarly to any other donation in Bello's code was the *arras*, a groom's gift to his wife, sometimes in recognition of her virginity.

22 The main source of potential inequality in the inheritance of legitimate children was through the *mejora*, a fixed share of the legítima that a testator could designate to only one child or grandchild. Chile's 1855 code reduced this share from the colonial one-third to one-fourth of the legítima; some codes eliminated it entirely (Deere and León 2005, 655–8).

codes that followed it most closely, the spouse received a conditional share, one depending on their relative poverty, termed the *porción conyugal*.[23] The Venezuelan and Argentine codes were more generous since the spouse had an unconditional right to a share equal to that of one child.

Under the initial Republican codes, children born outside of marriage ("illegitimate") did not fare very well in inheritance. As in the colonial period only "natural" children, those born to parents who did not have an impediment to marriage, held potential inheritance rights to a parent's estate. Previously, in addition to a parent, a court could grant such recognition; now only a parent could do so. Following the logic of the 1804 Napoleonic Code, the 1855 Chilean code (arts. 270–278) prohibited the investigation of paternity. A parent's recognition was strictly a voluntary act recorded in a public instrument or a will; a child or others could not contest a father's lack of recognition.[24] Moreover, in intestate, recognized natural children only inherited a share of the estate if the deceased parent left no legitimate children (Chile 1856, arts. 988–989), making it less likely that they would inherit.

The initial constitutions and civil codes maintained the Catholic Church as the one official church. The conditions for marriage, its nullification and permanent separation ("divorce" *a mensa et thoro*, of bed and board, without the possibility for remarriage) followed those of Canon law. In South America, the separation of church and state was a point of contention that dragged on well into the twentieth century. Struggles over the enactment of civil marriage and absolute divorce (*a vinculo matrimonii*) were at the heart of this conflict. The country chapters show that this process, the positions taken by feminists, and the outcomes were quite heterogenous.

Under the Hispanic colonial legal tradition, widows and single women above the age of majority had almost the same civil rights as men. The Chilean civil code reduced the age of majority for women, formerly 30 years, and made it the same for both sexes at 25; most others reduced it to 21 for both (Deere and León 2005, Table 3). Among the restrictions on women's civil rights irrespective of marital status was that they could not serve as witnesses of a public instrument (although in a few countries they could serve as witnesses to a marriage or a will), or a guardian

23 This was similar to the colonial *cuarta viudal*, although not limited to poor widows since poor widowers could also request it from a judge. Under the 1855 Chilean rules, if the surviving spouse owned no assets, this share could be equal to that of one child. However, deducted from that share was the value of any assets (whether a dowry or other assets acquired prior to marriage or a subsequent inheritance) of the wife as well as any gananciales that she received (Chile 1856, art. 1172). Although a spouse could renounce the gananciales and receive the porción conyugal if it were in their interest, this conditionality made it unlikely that a widow inherit anything at all.

24 As Milanich (2009, chpt. 1) explains, in colonial Chile lawsuits over recognition brought by such children or their mothers were fairly common and settled by judges who relied on proof provided by witnesses. Recognized natural children could inherit up to one-fifth of an estate. Under the 1855 code, if not recognized they could still sue for subsistence needs under new procedures.

unless they were the mother or grandmother of the child. Either the codes or other legislation excluded women from certain professions, such as being lawyers and notaries, and from government posts that required citizenship, for instance, being a judge.

The constitutions of the new republics differed on whether they explicitly denied women citizenship because some defined it in gender-neutral language.[25] Citizenship included only persons who were free and autonomous, and that usually required owning property and/or having a profession or trade as well as being a household head.[26] Electoral laws spelt out these conditions and usually explicitly restricted political rights to men.

In sum, among the reasons that discussions of the reform of married women's property rights in South America did not commence until the twentieth century was that under the governing marital and inheritance regimes, wives of means had relatively strong ownership rights although not over management of their property. Their lack of economic autonomy in marriage became a constraint principally when middle- and upper-class women gained sufficient education to enter the professions and non-elite women began to join the urban wage labor force in sufficient numbers.

Reforms of Married Women's Property Rights Elsewhere

During the period that Spanish American countries were developing their initial civil codes, the United States and England, countries following Common law, were taking first steps toward reform of married women's property rights. Reforms in continental Europe followed, some in countries with a community property tradition. In the late nineteenth century Mexico and Central American countries reformed their initial marital and inheritance regimes, differentiating them from those of South America where family law remained largely unchanged. While in their subsequent debates South American jurists and politicians referred to reforms of marital regimes in other countries (such as in Scandinavia and Switzerland), those of England, the United States, France and Germany proved most influential in their thinking.

Common Law and the Separation of Property Marital Regime

The marital regime of separation of property in England and the United States grew out of the Common law tradition of *couverture* or marital unity.[27] The law considered husband and wife as one, with the wife's legal personality subsumed under her

25 In Spanish the use of the male plural term such as "chilenos" includes women unless explicitly excluded; see Chile (1856, art. 25).

26 Portillo (2024) explains that the Latin American concept of citizen evolved from that of *vecino* in Hispanic colonial law who was an autonomous head of household.

27 It was also the default regime under Islamic law in the Ottoman Empire; see Deere and Doss (2006). This section draws primarily on Holcombe (1983) and Staves (1990).

husband. The wife's movable property (termed personalty) became her husband's property and he administered all her immovable property (realty – land, dwellings and buildings). While the husband could not sell his wife's immovable property without her consent, any earnings generated by her property (or by her, such as wages) belonged to him. Moreover, married women could not inherit property in their own names; any inheritance became property of the husband.

If widowed, a wife's immovable property returned to her control, as did her paraphernalia (clothing and jewelry). Her only claim on the gains accrued during the marriage was through the inheritance regime, the dower, a life-time interest in one-third of his property.[28] If she preceded him in death, and if there were children from the marriage, the husband retained a life-time interest (curtesy) in her immovable property; otherwise, it passed to her parents. Although from the eighteenth century on, men and single women were free to will their estates to whomever they chose, under coverture wives could not make out a will.[29] Under the tradition of primogeniture, the eldest son tended to inherit the entire estate, particularly all land, subject to the provisions for dower.

During the seventeenth and eighteenth centuries in England a parallel legal system of equity courts developed, which began to recognize women's separate property through prenuptial agreements. These could place under a trustee a separate estate for a wife's use that would not be under a husband's control or within the reach of his creditors. The agreement could give wives a range of rights, such as to contract or write a will and access to an independent income. But using these courts was expensive, thus as Lee Holcombe (1983) explains, the anomaly created by Common law for the poor versus equity for the wealthy was among the factors that created pressure for legal reform.

Marriage and divorce were under the purview of the Church of England that considered marriage a sacrament. Ecclesiastic courts only granted couples a permanent separation under certain grounds, including adultery, sodomy and excessive cruelty. In case of separation, the husband continued to control his wife's property, including any income from her real property as well as her wages. Divorce allowing remarriage was only possible through an act of Parliament and it was expensive as well as infrequent.

The first English reform of consequence for married women was the Matrimonial Causes Act of 1857, which transferred authority for separation and divorce from the Ecclesiastic courts and Parliament to the court system.[30] It strengthened the property rights of separated and divorced women by giving them the same rights as single women over their earnings and property; they could contract and

28 Jointure replaced dower during the eighteenth century, whereby a wife received a guaranteed income from her husband's estate (Staves 1990, 29).

29 With her husband's authorization, a wife could bequeath paraphernalia (Holcombe 1983, 22–3).

30 "Provisions Relating to Women's Property in the Divorce Act of 1857," in Holcombe (1983, Appendix 2 and 99–103); Shanley (1989, 36–46).

write a will. This law also instituted civil divorce although only on the grounds for adultery, with a double standard. A husband could divorce his wife based on adultery alone, while a wife had to prove adultery plus one of the aggravating conditions for a judicial separation (incest, rape, sodomy, bigamy, cruelty and intentional abandonment of at least two years). These courts also determined alimony and the custody and support of children, abrogating Common law whereby fathers held absolute rights over them.

The Married Women's Property Act of 1870 then allowed married women to own and dispose of their own wages and earnings and any assets acquired with such as their separate property.[31] They could own bank accounts, annuities and stocks in their own name; any inheritances via intestate below a certain value; and any rents and profits generated by their inheritance of freehold property. It also allowed wives to contract and participate in suits regarding this separate property and made them responsible for their own debts. The Married Women's Property Act of 1882 went further by granting married women the same property rights as single women.[32] Any property that they owned prior to or acquired during the marriage became a separate estate under their own management and full control. It authorized married women to conduct any trade or business with their separate property, and to contract, join suits, write a will and be responsible for their own debts.

By the time the United States became independent, there were already variations in the application of Common law in the different states, and only a few had equity courts (Salmon 1986). Moreover, the eight Western states that had once been part of colonial Spanish America entered the Union with a different marital regime, that of community property.[33] The strengthening of women's property rights was particularly drawn-out since it took place state by state over the course of the nineteenth and twentieth centuries, and in many cases through multiple pieces of legislation combined with judicial interpretation.[34]

The earliest reforms took place in the southern United States in the 1830s during a period of economic crisis to protect property (particularly slaves) from creditors. These recognized the assets that women brought to marriage as separate property so that creditors not hold such liable for the husbands' debts although husbands continued to manage their wives' assets. More effective strengthening of women's

31 "The Married Women's Property Act of 1870," in Holcombe (1983, Appendix 4).

32 "Married Women's Property Act, 1882," in Holcombe (1983, Appendix 5). Shanley (1989, 125–30), nonetheless argues that by retaining the language of equity and creating a separate estate, this law stopped short of placing married and unmarried women on the same legal footing. She and Holcombe agree that it did not go as far as some feminists wanted, which was equal property rights for husband and wife.

33 These were Louisiana (with origins in the Napoleonic code), Texas, California, Arizona, New Mexico, Idaho, Nevada and Washington (Sebree 1928; Warbasse 1987).

34 This summary draws on Speth (1982), Warbasse (1987) and Chatfield (2018); for Canada, where the reforms were at the provincial level and generally later than in the United States, see Backhouse (1988).

property rights began in the 1840s with legislation that recognized the property wives brought to marriage as a separate estate that they could manage independently of their husbands and/or that recognized their right to control their own independent earnings. In 1848, New York was the first to institute an effective Married Women's Property Act (MWPA), followed by an earnings law in 1860. Massachusetts passed the nation's first earnings law in 1846, followed by an MWPA in 1855.

By 1910, 45 of the 48 states had enacted either women's property and/or earnings legislation;[35] by 1920, 41 states had reformed both, so that married women had an independent legal personality and could own, manage, contract, inherit and bequeath their own earnings and assets and enter into suits (Geddes and Tennyson 2013, Table 1.1). Thus through a process focused on equalizing the rights of married and single women, the default marital regime became that of separation of property, one that does not recognize community property.[36] At the end of the marriage, any claim by a spouse on the property of the other depends on the rules of inheritance or of separation and divorce, and these also varied by state.[37]

Reforms in Community Property Regimes: France and Germany

The Napoleonic code of 1804 set the standard for modern civil codes with respect to technique and substance, the latter, by clarifying the rules governing property and contracts in capitalist economies. Although grounded in the principle of individual freedom, the French code famously included the phrase whereby the husband owed protection to his wife, and she obedience to him (Barrister of the Inner Temple [1904] 1999, art. 213), which was the basis for a wife's relative incapacity in marriage. A wife required her husband's authorization for any public act except to write a will or in limited cases, bring a suit against him.

The default marital regime was a variation of the partial community property regime described earlier, known as the "community of movables and acquests" (Glendon 1989, 119), where there were the same three forms of property in marriage (the wife's, the husband's and the community property of the couple). Where it differed from the Hispanic variant was that any movable property brought to marriage by either spouse became part of the couple's joint property, in addition

35 Community property states enacted these later than Common law states mainly because women's property rights were initially stronger (Geddes and Lueck 2002; Fernández 2014).

36 According to Siegel (1994), many of the early feminists favored joint property in marriage or a hybrid system depending on a wife's economic activities, with separate property for those who earned income but community property for those who did not. By the 1870s, as more women entered the professions, feminists came to place greater emphasis on attaining wives' control over their separate earnings as well as the assets they brought to marriage or inherited.

37 The legal trend in intestate was to favor spouses over more distant kin; to abolish dower for a fixed share of the husband's assets, usually one-third, but in a few, one-half; and to treat realty and personalty the same (Shammas, Salmon and Dahlin 1987, 69, 84–5). In divorce, it was toward codification based on fault (Friedman 1984).

to the gains from the immovable property of either spouse or any assets acquired with any income source during the marriage. Similarly, the husband managed a wife's individual property and the community property; at the dissolution of the marriage, each received half of the community property (Barrister … [1904] 1999, arts. 1401–1404; 1421, 1428).

Following the principle of individual freedom, the French code allowed couples in a prenuptial agreement to choose other regimes, such as separation of property, the dowry regime or full community property (where all assets, movable and immovable, constituted joint property irrespective of whom, how or when acquired) (Barrister … [1904] 1999, arts. 1387–1389). Under separation of property, a wife retained the right to manage her movables and immovables as well as the gains, but she could not alienate her immovable assets or participate in a suit without her husband's authorization. In this regime, the wife was to contribute up to one-third of her income for household expenses (Barrister … [1904] 1999, arts. 1536–1538).

The 1804 civil code also established that marriage was a contract, instituting obligatory civil marriage that allowed divorce with remarriage. Rescinded in 1816 because it was so controversial in this Catholic country, absolute divorce was not reinstituted until 1884 (Stetson 1987, 84–5). The grounds for divorce included adultery (under a double standard), excessive cruelty or injury and mutual consent after two years of marriage (Barrister … [1904] 1999, arts. 229–233).

During the late nineteenth and early twentieth centuries, wives acquired stronger property rights step by step. Legislation enacted in 1881 and 1886 allowed them to own individual post office savings accounts and to hold their own accounts in the old age pension fund. In the Napoleonic code, the inheritance rights of the surviving spouse had been particularly stingy. In intestate the spouse did not inherit if the deceased had living kin up to the 12th degree. An 1891 law improved these by assigning the spouse an automatic one-quarter share of the deceased's property although only in usufruct. In 1893, the country recognized the full civil legal capacity of women who obtained a judicial separation or a civil divorce and in 1897, all women above the age of majority became eligible to be legal witnesses.[38]

France's 1907 earnings law was a major step forward for working women since it gave wives the right to manage their own wages and independent earnings irrespective of marital regime, including the right to purchase and dispose of assets acquired with this income. The only restriction was that they could not donate these "reserved assets" (*biens réservés*) without their husbands' consent because at the end of the marriage these constituted community property. The legal thinking was that a donation would reduce their total value whereas a sale would not. Husbands had the right of redress if wives misused their right to manage their earnings (Herchenroder 1938, 198).[39]

38 Compiled from Herchenroder (1938, 197–8), Boring (2014) and Offen (2018, 509).

39 Both this reserved property law and the one recognizing women as witnesses were feminist initiatives under the leadership of Jeanne-E. Schmahl and the L'Avant Courrière group and (Metz 2007; Offen 2018).

Turning to Germany, prior to unification in 1871 the various regions of the German Empire followed different legal traditions, including the Napoleonic in the western region. After a lengthy drafting process, the country adopted a unified code in 1896, effective in 1900. Because of the different legal traditions, the civil code offered couples several marital regimes among which they could choose in a marriage contract, either before or after marriage.[40] The default was the "community of administration" whereby the husband assumed the administration of his wife's movable and immovable property. She, however, retained ownership of these assets, and he could not dispose of these without her authorization. At the dissolution of the union these returned to her management; there was no community property to pool and distribute since the code assumed that any gains from the wife's assets went toward household expenses (García Moreno 1897, arts. 1363, 1373–1376).[41]

The 1896 code also introduced the provision for married women's "reserved property" (*Vorbehaltsgut*), irrespective of marital regime. It included her earnings in a separate occupation or profession; objects destined for her exclusive use (personal items such as clothing and means of work); any assets stipulated as such in a marriage contract; and any gifts or inheritances given to her under the condition that she was to manage them. Notwithstanding, the wife required her husband's permission to be employed. If granted authorization, she could contract and pursue suits related to her separate economic activity (García Moreno 1897, arts. 1365–1371, 1405; Rheinstein and Glendon 2004, 4.43–44).

A salient feature of the German code was that it stipulated that the husband was the head of household while the wife had the right and responsibility to oversee domestic matters, thus enshrining the prevailing gender division of labor (García Moreno 1897, arts. 1354, 1356). It also required women to take their husbands' last names when they married (art. 1355). While this practice became common throughout Europe during the nineteenth century, rarely did codes include it as both a right and an obligation.

With respect to inheritance, the position of the surviving spouse in intestate was relatively favorable. Spouses received one-quarter of the deceased's estate if they had children or one-half if they did not and there were ascendants or in their absence, siblings of the deceased. If a husband or wife excluded the spouse in a will, the widow or widower automatically received half of the share due to them under intestate (García Moreno 1897, arts. 1931–1932, 2303–2305). Prior to approval of the civil code, the Law of Matrimony and Civil Registry of 1875 instituted

40 These alternative regimes differed according to the degree of sharing: full community property; the community of income and profits (the traditional Hispanic regime); and the community of movables and acquests (the French default regime). All three were under a husband's management (García Moreno 1897, arts. 1432, 1436).

41 The General German's Women's Association and August Bebel and his Socialist Democratic Party lobbied unsuccessfully to adopt separation of property as either the default or as an alternative regime (Evans 1976, 25–6).

civil marriage and divorce in certain non-Catholic regions; the 1896 code extended both nationally (García Moreno 1897, 304). Absolute divorce was only due to fault by one spouse, but in contrast to earlier divorce laws in England and France, in the case of adultery husbands and wives received equal treatment (García Moreno 1897, arts. 1564–1569).

Nineteenth-Century Reforms in Mexico and Central America

Since Mexico and Central American countries adopted some of the features of the European and US reforms in their civil code reforms of the late nineteenth and early twentieth centuries, it is also relevant to consider these antecedents. In its 1870 code, Mexico departed from the Hispanic colonial tradition of offering only one marital regime by following the French precedent of giving couples a choice.[42] In a prenuptial agreement a couple could opt for the conjugal society or the separation of property regime; if no regime was specified, the default was partial community property, with the husband its administrator.[43] This code also gave couples flexibility, for they could opt for separation of property at any point during the marriage whereby each spouse administered their own property and its gains as well as their own earnings; as in the French code, under this regime the wife still required her husband's authorization to alienate immovable assets.

Guatemala's 1877 code also introduced greater freedom of choice while maintaining the conjugal society as the default regime. Couples could opt for the separation of property before or during the marriage by mutual consent.[44] Unlike Mexico, under this option the wife had full legal capacity since she did not require her husband's authorization to sell her assets or appear in suits.

During the period of their Liberal revolutions, Costa Rica, El Salvador, Nicaragua and Honduras took the liberalization process a step further by adopting separation of property as the default and under this regime giving wives full legal capacity to contract and participate in suits.[45] But Costa Rica's 1887 Civil Code added an important new twist: when the marriage dissolved, any assets not documented as the individual property of either spouse were community property and divided equally.

42 During the period of French rule, Emperor Maximilian in 1866 promulgated the first two books of jurist Justo Sierra's draft as Mexico's first civil code. After the defeat of the French, another codification commission revised these drafts and produced the 1870 Civil Code for the Federal District and Territories (Méndez [1873] 1897). It served as the model for many other Mexican states.

43 Mexico (1870, arts. 198–213; 2099–2211). Its 1884 code maintained these provisions; in Mateos Alarcón (1904, arts. 189–202; 1965–2079). After its 1910 revolution, Mexico briefly adopted separation of property as the default in its 1917 Law of Family Relations (Deere and León 2005).

44 Guatemala (1877, arts. 149–160; 1090–1110; 1164–1175; 1185–1187).

45 Couples could also stipulate either prior to or during the marriage any arrangement they wished with respect to ownership and administration of their property. See Costa Rica (1887, arts. 73–79); for El Salvador, "Reformas al Código Civil" (*Diario Oficial*, August 4, 1902, 1569–74) and Suárez (1911); for Nicaragua, 1903 code in Santos Zelaya and Abaunza (1903, arts. 151–159); and Honduras (1906, arts. 167–175).

The 1902 Salvadorian, 1903 Nicaraguan and 1906 Honduran reformed codes also adopted this feature. Legal scholar Mary Ann Glendon (1989, 118) recognizes Costa Rica as among the innovators of this hybrid regime, deferred community property, which combines separation of property and community property (known as the *sociedad de gananciales* or *regimen de participación en las ganánciales*).

Although these Mexican and Central American reforms modified the doctrine of potestad marital regarding a woman's property, they maintained a husband's control over the person of his wife. Costa Rica and El Salvador kept the Napoleonic article that required wives to obey their husbands, as did Mexico and Guatemala, while Nicaragua and Honduras made explicit that husbands were the household heads. The husband still determined the household's domicile and held ultimate patria potestad over the children, although mothers sometimes had an enhanced role and automatically assumed it in the father's absence. Mexico and all five Central American countries adopted testamentary freedom – the freedom to bequest one's estate to whomever one chose – with only a few constraints. All also instituted civil marriage and absolute divorce with the possibility of remarriage (Deere and León 2005, Table 4).

Deere and León highlight how during their Liberal revolutions most Central American countries departed from the Hispanic tradition – and the countries of South America – by adopting separation of property as the default along with testamentary freedom.[46] They suggest that the Married Women's Property Acts in the United States and England and the Anglo-Saxon inheritance regime inspired these reforms. Central America was under the geopolitical sphere of influence of the United States and its revolutionary leaders considered it the model of the progress to which they aspired.[47] These countries, nonetheless, adopted separation of property as the default under quite different circumstances. Women's education and labor force participation were barely incipient and there is no evidence that women's groups demanding rights had yet formed, in contrast to the history of these reforms in the United States and England.

Multiple and ultimately unsuccessful attempts to promote political unification also fostered convergence among Central American leaders around liberal

46 They missed, however, the innovative nature of Costa Rica's reform, since they assumed that at the end of the marriage there was no community property to distribute. This is largely because in their interviews with lawyers in the late 1990s these considered separation of property to be the default, never mentioning the sharing requirement at the dissolution of the marriage. How this regime played out in practice requires further research. See Mateos Alarcón (1904) and Arrom (1985) on the discussions that led Mexico to reject separation of property as the default but to institute testamentary freedom in its 1884 code.

47 See the discussion in Deere and León (2005) on whether these reforms were actually gender-progressive since they had different implications for women depending on their class and kinship position. As Arrom (1985) highlights, the possibility of testamentary freedom could affect daughters and wives differently since daughters lost the guarantee of receiving an inheritance share equal to a brother; at the same time, husbands, if they wished, were now free to will to their wives a much larger share of their estate.

principles in family law. In addition to separation of church and state, among the principles adopted in the 1897 Treaty of Central American Unity was a commitment to "the absolute equality in the civil capacity of men and women" and the enactment of testamentary freedom (in Herrarte 1956, 128). The Central American reforms of married women's property rights thus constitute a case of reforms undertaken by liberal jurists and politicians in advance of socioeconomic change, motivated by the promise of progress embodied in the ideology of liberalism.

Emergence of Global Feminism

Another factor relevant to the development of feminism and demands for civil code reform and women's suffrage in South America in the early twentieth century was the development and diffusion of the ideas of a global feminist movement centered in the United States, England and continental Europe.[48] The formation of the International Council of Women (ICW) in 1888 in Washington, DC led to its institutionalization.

The ICW was born at an international conference organized by Susan B. Anthony and Elizabeth Cady Stanton of the National Woman Suffrage Association to celebrate the 40th anniversary of the 1848 Seneca Falls Declaration. Some 53 organizations from nine countries participated although most attendees were from the United States.[49] They established the ICW for the purpose of sharing information on women's progress internationally. It was to consist of representatives of national councils from each country, which were autonomous umbrella organizations of local women's associations. The first such national council was the National Committee of the United States formed at this conference. By 1901 there were national councils in Canada, Germany, Great Britain, Sweden, Australia, Italy, the Netherlands, Denmark, Switzerland, Argentina and France. ICW's president for many years was Lady Aberdeen of Scotland who promoted a genteel form of feminism that appealed to the women's philanthropic and social organizations that formed the bulk of the membership of the national councils in most countries (Evans 1977, 250; Rupp 2010).

Women's political rights were a contentious issue within the ICW. At its 1904 Berlin congress those demanding that the organization prioritize suffrage split off to form the International Woman Suffrage Alliance (IWSA). Carrie Chapman Catt, who was concluding her first term as president of the National

48 See Evans (1977) on the development of feminist organizations in these countries.
49 Drawn from www.icw-cif.com/history.

American Woman Suffrage Association (NAWSA),[50] served as IWSA president until 1923. By 1914 its membership was composed of women's suffrage organizations in 25 countries. Tensions at its 1915 congress over divided loyalties during World War I resulted in the formation of another influential organization in 1919, the Women's International League for Peace and Freedom (WILPF) (Rupp 2010, 140–1).

Prior to World War I, women attained suffrage in 1893 in New Zealand, followed by Australia, Finland and Norway (Towns 2019, Table 1.1; IAW 2005, 44). Between 1915 and 1919 an additional 20 European countries plus Canada recognized women's political rights, although in some it was conditional, such as in Great Britain where initially only women who were at least 30 years of age and property owners could vote. In the United States, where women began to vote and/or stand for office at the local level from the 1850s on, the process culminated in the passage of the Nineteenth Amendment to the US Constitution in 1920, which gave women nationally equal political rights to men. In 1928, women achieved the same in Great Britain, although not until 1944 in France.

The press amply diffused internationally the resolutions of the congresses of the women's organizations and their affiliates, and the process whereby women gained the vote. Earlier it had also brought to a South American audience the ideas of such canons of feminist thought as Olympe de Gouges' *Declaration on the Rights of Women and the Female Citizen* of 1792, and the *Declaration of Rights and Sentiments,* penned by Elizabeth Cady Stanton, Loretta Cott and others for the 1848 Seneca Falls Convention. The writings of Mary Wollstonecraft, John Stuart Mill and August Bebel were particularly influential in the thinking of South American intellectuals, going by the frequency of citations to them in the materials analyzed for this study.

Wollstonecraft's pamphlet, *A Vindication of the Rights of Women*, published in England in 1792, was immediately translated into French and then Spanish and serialized in the *Diario de Madrid* that same year, from which it made its way to Latin America (Lorenzo Modía 2003). Her argument that women were as mentally capable as men and deserved an education of similar quality resonated with Latin American women writers who from the last quarter of the nineteenth century began to question the position of women in society (LaGreca 2009).

Three years after its publication in England, Chilean Martina Barros de Orrego translated John Stuart Mill's 1869 *The Subjection of Women* into Spanish and published it in Santiago from where it circulated throughout the region (Barros with

50 NAWSA formed in 1890 from the fusion of the National Woman Suffrage Association led by Elizabeth Cady Stanton and Susan B. Anthony and the American Woman Suffrage Association formed by Lucy Stone, Henry Blackhead and others, each founded in 1869 (McCammon et al. 2001; Moehling and Thomasson 2020).

Castillo 2009). In the early 1890s writer Emilia Pardo Bazán also published in Spain a translation of Mill's text as well as of Bebel's 1879 *Woman and Socialism* (Freire and Ana 2021). Mill's call for the civil and political equality of men and women was particularly influential in the thinking of Liberal parties throughout Latin America and in the development of liberal feminism. Bebel's text played a similar role with respect to the Socialist parties formed in South America from 1895 on and in the development of socialist feminism. As the chapters ahead demonstrate, these writings, along with the commentaries of legal scholars on the reforms undertaken in Europe and North America, provided building-blocks for the debate that developed among feminists, jurists and politicians over the ideal marital regime and the reforms most compatible with South American needs and customs.

What follows are seven country studies, a comparative chapter and conclusion. Since the analysis of civil code reform drives the narrative, the order of the country chapters is roughly chronological according to when each enacted their major legislation reforming the marital regime. These thus begin with Ecuador followed by studies on Argentina, Chile, Peru, Colombia, Venezuela and Uruguay in Chapters 2–8. Table 1.1 provides a roadmap to their content. The timeline shows the year legislatures entertained the first bills to strengthen married women property rights as well as grant women suffrage; when they enacted their major pieces of legislation; and the decades during which women's organizations demanding rights emerged and were active. Since this process was sometimes piecemeal or phased, this table also indicates where an earnings law or municipal-level suffrage preceded a more profound reform. Chapter 9 compares the detailed feminist proposals for reform of the marital regime, summarizes the achievements of these reforms up to the early 1950s, and analyzes the extent to which women's proposals influenced legislation. The conclusion considers the relative role played by feminists, jurists and politicians in the different paths to these reforms, how discussions of civil and political reforms interacted and the potential impact of the civil code reforms on women.

TABLE 1.1 Timeline from First Bill to Major Law: Married Women's Property Rights, Women's Suffrage and Feminist Organizing

	1900s	*1910s*	*1920s*	*1930s*	*1940s*	*1950s*
Ecuador						
MWPR	B-	-L				
	(1909)	(1911)				
Suffrage		B-------------	-------------L			
		(1910)	(1929)			
Argentina						
MWPR	B-----------	---------------	----------L			
	(1902)		(1926)			
Suffrage		B	---------------	---------------	------------L	
		(1919)			(1947)	
Chile						
MWPR		B------	-------Le-----	-----Le		
		(1915)	(1925)	(1934)		
Suffrage		B---	---------------	-----Lm------	--------------L	
		(1917)		(1934)	(1949)	
Peru						
MWPR			CCRC/B----	----------L		
			(1922, 1925)	(1936)		
Suffrage		B--	---------------	----Lm-------	-------------	----L
		(1918)		(1933)		(1955)
Colombia						
MWPR			B------------	---L		
			(1921)	(1932)		
Suffrage				B---------	-------------	----L
				(1933)		(1954)
Venezuela						
MWPR		CCRC-Le	---------------	CCRC-------	---L	
		(1915, 1916)		(1930, 1936)	(1942)	
Suffrage					B-Lm---L	
					(1943, 1944, 1947)	
Uruguay						
MWPR		B---------	---------------	---------------	----------L	
		(1914)			(1946)	
Suffrage		B---------	---------------	---L		
		(1914)		(1932)		

Source: Author's compilation based on references cited in the country chapters.

Notes: Shaded rows indicate the decade that women's organizations demanding rights emerged and were then active. MWPR, married women's property rights; B, first bill introduced; L, law approved; CCRC, civil code review commission began work; Le, earnings law only; Lm, municipal suffrage law only.

2

ECUADOR IN THE VANGUARD ON WOMEN'S RIGHTS

In 1905, writer and journalist Zoila Ugarte de Landívar founded Ecuador's first feminist magazine, *La Mujer: Revista Mensual de Literatura y Variedades*, where she explained that feminism was "the voice of the oppressed woman who demands that which belongs to her …" (Ugarte 1905b, 100).[1] She stressed the need for women's economic independence and argued that the state must expand women's access to education and training so that they are able to earn an independent living when required, choose to remain single rather than be forced into marriage and are better prepared for widowhood. She also recognized that if women contributed economically to the household, husbands and wives would be in a more equal position in marriage.

Ugarte was careful to point out that she was not advocating for women to abandon their traditional roles: "We do not want to imply that women stop being the 'angel of the home' as mother and wife." Rather, "since they are gifted with intelligence and an exquisite sensibility, they are well suited to contribute to the social betterment and their attention should not be limited to the narrow circle of the family" (Ugarte 1905a, 31).

Few women at the time shared Ugarte's identification with feminism, although there were a good number of men who did. Inspired by reforms in Europe, the United States and Central America, Ecuador's legislature was the first in South America, in 1911, to enact a married women's property law. This reform was

1 Raised in a cacao plantation-owning family on the Coast, Ugarte never studied formally. An accomplished writer, she was one of Ecuador's first female journalists (Rodas 2011, 18–23). Note that if a woman was married when first mentioned, I provide her full married name; it was social convention to add the "de" plus a husband's last name. Subsequently, I refer to married women by their paternal surname.

DOI: 10.4324/9781003658436-2

unusual in that its provisions were particularly favorable to wives, giving their property privileged treatment compared to that of their husbands, a feature not repeated elsewhere. This resulted from it being a compromise – not between liberals and conservatives as in most countries – but rather between factions of liberals during the heyday of its Liberal Revolution.

Liberal policies fostered many of the conditions that subsequently facilitated approval of women's suffrage in 1929, Ecuador being the first Latin American country to enact it. While women's voices figured prominently in this debate, their acquisition of political rights also preceded the development of an organized women's rights movement. It was not until the mid-1930s that such emerged in the context of the need to defend the civil and political rights that women had already attained as well as the struggle to extend these and make them more effective.

The Liberal Opening

Liberalism became a political force in Ecuador relatively late compared to neighboring countries although its Liberal Revolution of 1895 accomplished much with respect to secularization and modernization. Liberal policies expanded individual freedoms while reducing the power of the Catholic Church.[2] These included many of the preconditions for women's greater participation in the public sphere, among them, the commitment to free and compulsory primary education to create an educated citizenry and the expansion of freedom of the press (Sinardet 1998; O'Connor 2007; Goetschel 2010).

Eloy Alfaro, president between 1895 to 1901 and 1906 to 1911, championed women's education and their incorporation into the labor force.[3] In his 1897 address to the legislature, for example, he stated that

> there is nothing more painful than the condition of women in our nation, where, relegated to domestic work, her sphere of her intellectual activity is limited and the possibilities for her to earn an independent and honorable living are even more restricted.
>
> *(Alfaro [1897] 1907, 334)*

2 Among the anti-clerical measures were dismantling church influence over education, undertaken between 1895 and 1906; secularizing cemeteries in 1900; and enacting the 1899 Ley de Patronato (Patronage Law) and 1904 Ley de Cultos (Law of Religious Cults) that restricted many Catholic Church activities and those of religious orders. The 1906 Constitution established total separation of church and state and the 1908 Ley de Beneficiencia resulted in the expropriation of properties owned by religious orders (Ayala Mora 1994).

3 RomoLeroux (1975) and Londoño (2011) attribute Alfaro's interest in improving women's position to the vital role they played both directly and indirectly in the civil wars that led to his successful revolution.

Noting how the expansion of women's rights and participation in the public sphere had contributed to social progress in the United States, he argued that women in Ecuador should have access to the university,[4] appropriate technical training and suitable public employment. He had already opened new occupations to women in the post and telegraph offices; he now asked the congress for legislation that would "emancipate the Ecuadorian woman from that very narrow circle in which she lives" (Alfaro [1897] 1907, 336).

The incorporation of women was into those sectors that required their labor and deemed appropriate for their gender (Goetschel 2010). The effort to expand public education and increase women's labor force participation were related, since these initiatives focused primarily on women's access to primary education and their entry into the teaching profession, with the first women's normal school established in 1901. The expansion of women's education along with public debate led to new magazines aimed at women that provided outlets for their creative work and spurred the circulation of ideas. Some of these exalted women's traditional roles, while others questioned them.[5]

With respect to family law, Alfaro's successor, President Leonidas Plaza (1901–1905; 1912–1916) established the civil registry in 1901, which took control away from the Church with regard to the record-keeping of births, marriages and deaths. The 1902 Law of Civil Matrimony instituted civil divorce with possibility of remarriage under a limited condition, only a wife's adultery; 1904 legislation added the husband's for "public and scandalous concubinage" and the sentencing of a spouse for an attempt on the other spouse's life.[6] In his 1905 message to the Congress, President Plaza ([1905] 1908, 320–1)) outlined his remaining legislative priorities – instituting testamentary freedom and divorce by mutual consent, and strengthening the property rights of married women:

> Let us defend women! In these days when feminism is the rallying call and an important point in the program of reformist parties...let us begin by giving the wife what is hers, that is, the free administration of her assets. Currently, these are in the hands of her husband who can pilfer them without accountability... Why is it assumed that a woman is less intelligent than a man in the management of her own affairs when we see daily proof of just the opposite? Why do we consider her as if she were an incapable minor when she is the heart of the home and the one who shapes the family?

4 In 1895, Aurelia Palmieri became the first woman to attend university by petitioning President Alfaro for permission to take the examinations to enter the Faculty of Medicine at the University of Guayaquil. Due to the lack of women's secondary schools, she did not hold the necessary diploma, the *bachillerato* (Estrada 1980, 48).

5 Goetschel (2006) and Handelsman (1976, 42–4) discuss the other new women's magazines.

6 "Reformatoria, Ley de Matrimonio Civil," *Registro Oficial* 929, November 5, 1904. See Moscoso (1996a, 1996b), O'Connor (2007) and Rodas (2009) on the debates over these bills.

The liberal agenda on family law reform in Ecuador was like the set of policies adopted in Central America after their earlier liberal revolutions. Both Alfaro and Plaza spent years in Central America, usually in political exile, and were in communication with liberal leaders throughout the hemisphere (Ayala Mora 1988, 121–2; 1994, 78–82, 134). Hence, it is not surprising that they had similar ideas regarding how to improve the position of women, focusing not only on their education and employment but also on enhancing their property rights so that wives maintain those that they had as single women; gender equality within the family was not the aim.

Ecuadorian legal scholars were aware of the reforms of married women's property rights in other countries. In his treatise on civil law, Francisco José Urrutia (1902, 51) explained how feminist demands had led to these reforms in the United States, England and Germany and that they sought to deepen individual liberty. He observed that the "seduction of feminist reforms had not yet found echo in the young republics of Latin America," although some of these ideas might be worth pursuing. Among those he found attractive was giving couples the freedom to make whatever arrangements they wished with respect to their property in prenuptial agreements, such as opting for the separation of property marital regime. He warned, nonetheless, against making it the default regime as Anglo-Saxon countries had done, considering it too drastic a change. Irrespective of regime, Urrutia stressed the importance of maintaining potestad marital for the unity of the family.[7]

A decade later, in his 1911 thesis for a doctorate of law at the Universidad Central del Ecuador (UCE), José María Suárez (1913) concurred with Urrutia that the code should maintain the conjugal society as the default regime but that it should offer separation of property as an option at the time of marriage. He argued that if single women were perfectly capable of managing their own property, they should have the option of continuing to do so after marriage. This would require only a minimal reform of the code, which currently allowed women to specify in a prenuptial agreement (capitulaciones) that they would continue to manage some but not all of their property.

Suárez also recommended specific changes to the rules governing the conjugal society. He thought it imperative that women have the right of redress if they disagreed with their husband's management of the community property. Currently, the only way that a wife could safeguard her interests was to sue her husband for separation of property if he blatantly mismanaged such property or committed fraud (Ecuador 1889, arts. 234, 258–260). This was difficult to prove, and women rarely used this mechanism. He suggested simplifying this procedure by adopting the rules employed when disagreements occurred among business partners. In addition, he recommended the adoption of an innovation of the 1896 German code,

7 The main features of the marital regime are in Ecuador (1860, arts. 124–144, 1708–1742), only slightly modified in Ecuador (1889).

married women's reserved property, so that wives be able to manage their own independent earnings and the assets acquired with this income.

While Suárez did not propose eliminating potestad marital, his thinking was bolder than Francisco Urrutia's. He proposed that in marriage, each spouse hold the same obligations, for example, rather than requiring the wife to live where the husband determined, the code need only specify their mutual obligation to live together. Moreover, he proposed that the grounds for separation or divorce due to adultery be the same for both spouses. With respect to patria potestad, while Ecuador's 1889 code (arts. 234, 258–260) did not exclude mothers explicitly from exercising it, as had its initial 1860 code (art. 234), they could only exercise it in the absence of fathers, that is, when they widowed or the father was legally incapacitated. Suárez thought a mother should at least have the right to appeal if she disagreed with her husband's decisions regarding the education of their children. He believed such reforms would emancipate women, legally and socially, while reducing marital conflict and strengthening the family (Suárez 1913, 101).

Deepening the Liberal Reform: Married Women's Economic Emancipation

During President Alfaro's second term, there was considerable discussion over what should come first, legislation in support of married women's property rights, civil divorce by mutual consent, or women's suffrage, all items on the agenda of the radical wing of the Liberal Party.[8] As it turned out the legislature considered all three, approving civil divorce by mutual consent and reforming the marital regime while failing to recognize women's political rights.

In an editorial in *El Tiempo*, Francisco de Paula Soria ([1909] 1912) argued that the logical order of reforms to emancipate women was instituting civil divorce by mutual consent first, followed by strengthening their property rights, and finally, recognizing their political rights. He reasoned that for marriage to be successful, it must be based on individual choice; like any other contract, spouses should have the option of ending it. Moreover, divorce by mutual consent was the most dignified manner of dissolving unhappy marriages. The forced nature of the conjugal society also went against individual choice and was a source of conflict in marriage. It led men to marry for the wrong reason, for economic motives rather than for love. He favored the separation of property regime since it recognized that wives were competent to manage their own economic affairs and did not subject them to their husbands' tutelage. He recommended the gradual introduction of these three

8 The Liberal Party that ruled until the mid-1920s emerged in the late 1890s from a coalition of supporters of Eloy Alfaro who considered themselves "radicals" and the more elite "liberals" of the coastal oligarchy around their common anti-clericalism. Many of the former would refer to themselves as "liberal-radicals" or also "Alfaristas," as opposed to "civilistas" who supported his successor, Leonides Plaza (Coronel 2022, 130–211).

reforms with political rights coming last because women were not yet prepared for suffrage, noting that "the reasons should be obvious to any liberal …," implying that they were too much under the influence of the Catholic Church (de Paula Soria [1909] 1912, 6).

The Chamber of Deputies addressed all three issues, first considering a bill entitled "the Economic Liberty of Women" that a group of liberal-radical deputies introduced in September 1909.[9] It sought to replace Ecuador's legal marital regime of the conjugal society with separation of property and end the relative incapacity of married women in civil and commercial acts. According to its sponsors, "the economic liberty of married women is the logical extension of the general principle of liberty."[10] In other words, women should have the ability to manage their own economic affairs and thus have the same legal capacity as men to contract and participate in lawsuits. In their view, this required abolishing the conjugal society that gave husbands control over their wives' property as well as the community property. Among other rationales mentioned was the declining rate of marriage, which they attributed to the forced imposition of community property that made marriage unattractive to men. In addition, current arrangements whereby wives needed their husbands' permission for every transaction or act was a source of marital discord.

In his introductory comments, co-sponsor Julio E. Fernández recognized that he was proposing "a radical law," since it changed the traditional marital regime. Nonetheless, "the time has now arrived to lift women out of the slavery under which they have lived, because, unfortunately, we must recognize that is how we have considered them … Why not make their civil rights equal to those of men?"[11] During the initial discussion, Deputy Miguel Angel Montalvo proposed inclusion of an additional measure, to institute complete testamentary freedom in place of the traditional restricted freedom of what an individual could do in a will.[12] The co-sponsors agreed to include this classic liberal policy, and the bill passed to the commission on legislation for further consideration.

The deputies addressed women's political rights the next year. Four deputies introduced a bill to reform the electoral law so that it specified that electors include "all Ecuadorians (men or women) who are qualified according to the Constitution and this law."[13] They assumed that women were citizens with political rights since the constitutions of 1897 and 1906 did not specifically exclude them as citizens, as had the earlier 1884 Constitution, with citizenship defined in gender-neutral

9 *Actas de la Cámara de Diputados* (ACD) (1909, session 19, September 10, 419–25); unpublished, handwritten version in the Archivo-Biblioteca de la Función Legislativa, Quito.

10 ACD, 419.

11 ACD, 425.

12 ACD, 419. These had followed the 1855 Chilean code's rules described in Chapter 1; Ecuador (1889, arts. 1171–1174).

13 Article 1, "Reformas a la Ley de Elecciones," ACD (1910, September 7, 432).

language.[14] The purpose of the bill was simply to implement this constitutional right. An amendment was immediately proposed by its opponents to delete the phrase "men or women" in the definition of electors.

The arguments raised for and against women's suffrage in this debate preview those made in other South American countries over the next several decades. Those against women's political rights argued that such was contrary to natural law given the gender division of labor. As Deputy Cesar Borja Cordero put it, "women have been raised for a higher purpose, to be queen of the home; by their nature they must dedicate themselves to the domestic tasks of their sex." For them to take on masculine roles, such as direction of public affairs, "would be moral prostitution."[15] Moreover, it was argued that women were not prepared to vote given their lack of education; they lacked the necessary independence since they were economic dependents of their husbands or fathers; and politics were far too corrupt for women to get involved.[16] Borja Cordero also emphasized that if in countries that held free elections "female suffrage has led to long debates, so that even today it has not been achieved, how are we going to do so here …?"[17] This latter factor would, of course, change during the next decade.

The bill's co-sponsors summarized the arguments in favor of women's suffrage. Col. Nicolás López attacked Borja Cordero's position as being based on outdated "colonial ideals" that considered women inferior to men and pointed to a contradiction: how could it be "affirmed that women were the queen of the home when we negate her the management of her own assets, and what is even worse, as widows, patria potestad over her children?"[18] Luciano Coral emphasized how women were already exercising citizenship since they occupied positions of authority in public administration and nothing prevented them from doing so.[19] Angel Barrera argued that it was time to move beyond the "theoretical liberalism" of the constitution and put liberalism into practice. While he favored universal suffrage (extending the vote to those who were illiterate), he considered that approval of this bill, which extended the vote to women under the same conditions as men, as the necessary next step in expanding democracy.[20] Regarding international trends, he noted how just in 1907 women had gained the vote in four additional countries as well as four more US states.[21]

14 See Prieto and Goetschel (2007) and Rodas (2009) on the discussion of citizenship. The main difference between the two constitutions was the minimum age, which the 1906 Constitution raised from 18 to 21; both required literacy (Ecuador 1897, art. 8; 1906, art. 13).

15 ACD (1910, September 9, 460).

16 ACD, summary of comments during the two-day discussion.

17 ACD, September 7, 439–40.

18 ACD, 436. Under the 1889 Civil Code (arts. 258–260), a widow held patria potestad over her children, although the father in his will could appoint an advisor to manage the children's patrimony with her. If she remarried she lost the right to administer such assets.

19 ACD (1910, 448–9).

20 ACD, 433–5.

21 ACD, 459.

A vote on the amendment to exclude the clause "men and women" in the definition of electors passed 21 to 13, bringing this debate to a close.[22] The divide was one primarily among liberals, between those who considered women's political rights as essential to deepening democracy and those who feared any change in gender roles.

Since the Senate had just approved a bill on divorce by mutual consent, the Chamber turned to this reform next, which was also controversial. The main issues were whether marriage was just like any other contract that its parties could dissolve at will, and whether divorce would be liberating or prejudicial to women.[23] The Chamber approved divorce by mutual consent by a small margin and President Alfaro promulgated this 1910 reform of the Law on Civil Matrimony.[24]

The commission reviewing the Economic Liberty of Women bill recommended it favorably.[25] There was little substantive debate over the bill in the Chamber, particularly in comparison to the recent heated discussion over women's political rights and divorce by mutual consent. This was largely because there was consensus that strengthening women's civil rights was a precondition to their eventually exercising political rights, and if women were not yet prepared for the latter, it was important to take the next logical step. The deputies approved only one amendment so that married couples who wished to maintain the conjugal society under its previous terms (with the husband as the administrator of his wife's property) could do so via a notarized document; those who subsequently married could opt for the conjugal society in a marital contract.[26]

The Debate over Alternative Regimes

The Senate took up the Women's Economic Liberty bill in mid-1911 and held a much more substantive discussion over what it meant to change the default marital regime before approving a much revised version.[27] The Senate's commission on legislation, chaired by jurist Victor Peñaherrera, was in favor of strengthening women's property rights but it took issue with the Chamber's approach and

22 ACD, 471.

23 ACD, September 22, 214–75. See Rodas (2009, 117–9) for greater detail on this debate.

24 "Ley Reformatoria a la de Matrimonio Civil." *Registro Oficial* 1359, October 4, 1910, 1864.

25 ACD (1910, October 7, 387). The commission on legislation's report deleted the proposed article regarding freedom of testimony, either because this topic pertained to a different section of the civil code than this bill or for lack of support. The Congress did not consider this idea again; it was the only liberal reform of those enacted in Central America not adopted in Ecuador in this period.

26 ACD, Extraordinary Session, October 10, 241–3. The Deputies' approved bill is in *Diario de Debates de la Cámara del Senado* (DDCS) (1911, August 1, 42–3).

27 DDCS, September 9, 11 and 15, 89–152. O'Connor (2007, 93–7), who analyzes this same source, provides a good analysis of legislators' views of proper gender roles but does not consider the legal substance of this debate, which was over alternative marital regimes.

proposed amending the bill, herein referred to as the commission's alternative.[28] Nonetheless, debate proceeded on the Deputies' bill, focusing on its article 1, which abolished the conjugal society in favor of the total separation of property regime.

Although the Senate was entirely composed of liberals, there were both ideological and regional divisions over the bill. Among the main defenders of the Deputies' bill were three liberal-radicals from the Coast, Federico Intriago and Angel Hidalgo, of the province of Manabí, and Manuel de Calisto, of Los Ríos. In his opening comments, Intriago argued that "women's emancipation should be total, that is, the default by law should be that she administers her own assets, without need for lawsuits or administrative procedures that do not accomplish anything other than dissuade the interested party."[29] Under the current code, couples had no choice in the matter since it imposed the conjugal society on all marriages, which abrogated individual freedom. An appealing feature of this bill, according to Intriago, was that while separation of property became the default, couples could choose to make other arrangements at any time, such as opting for community property and deciding on its manager. He also noted the precedent set by those countries "of the Saxon race," which had successfully adopted separation of property, referring to the United States and England.[30]

Several senators commented on how difficult it was for women to obtain a separation of property due to their husband's mismanagement or bankruptcy, the only reasons the code allowed. Hidalgo viewed this reform as protecting women, "that disgraced being who until now has been subject to potestad marital, which is an iron ring from which she cannot easily escape."[31] De Calisto argued that wives were currently "slaves" of their husbands; the separation of property regime would give them full civil capacity. He drew an analogy to how legal business partnerships were based on the principle of equality between its members, saying that, similarly, the proposed regime was based on the principle of equality between the spouses.[32]

Senator Peñaherrera, who represented the highland province of Imbabura, strongly opposed making separation of property the default regime on the grounds that partial community property protected women's interests, primarily by entitling

28 The commission proposed replacing the first five articles of the bill (establishing separation of property as the default) with three of its own. These allowed wives to request a judge to declare the separation of property of all or some of her assets and for her to administer these and appear in suits without need for her husband's or a judge's permission. If a wife made use of this provision, the husband could then request a total separation of property, i.e., the liquidation of the conjugal society (DDCS 1911, 89).

29 DDCS, 91.

30 DDCS, 94.

31 DDCS, 96.

32 DDCS, 98.

wives to half the gananciales generated during the marriage, a share they deserved because of the gender division of labor:

> The man dedicates himself to the heavy labors of the street, manages the capital and makes it produce, in sum, he is the one who generates the wealth… The woman dedicates herself to the home, she is in charge of caring for the family, raising children and their rudimentary education, and saving and economizing; that is, she also helps to augment the capital of the marriage indirectly… Without the conyugal society, what would happen? The husband would be the only wealthy one, since the wife would not have the right to participate in the gananciales even if she had spent ten years dedicated to the care of the family, contributing indirectly to the formation of its fortune.[33]

Hence, the pooling of resources and division of the gananciales at the end was a form of compensation to wives:

> Her contribution to the formation of capital is so effective, that although her labor does not appear to be pecuniary labor, in fact, it is because it makes the labor of her husband more productive since he need not be concerned with domestic affairs. The conjugal society thus corresponds perfectly to the interests of a married woman and the very fundamentals of marriage, because if the fortunes of the spouses are the same, it is natural that they share the benefits of this society."[34]

Peñaherrera recognized that the Deputies' bill would allow couples to voluntarily opt for the conjugal society regime in a marital contract but argued that no one used capitulaciones: "When couples are about to marry they do not pay attention to such formalities or safeguards, because women do not know yet what dangers they might incur or because recognizing them could affect the potential marriage."[35] Since women marry for love, "they would not want to offend" their partner. Thus, he concluded that it was preferable for women to marry under the conjugal society regime and be able to ask for a separation of property if required. He also recognized that it was currently difficult for women to request a separation of property. This was why in the Commission's alternative proposal wives would have the right to request the separation of their property at any point during the marriage without having to justify doing so.

Senator Juan B. Vela of Tungurahua, another highland province, supported Peñaherrera's arguments. He stressed that he was a good liberal-radical and for

33 DDCS, 92.
34 DDCS, 93.
35 DDCS, 93.

reasons of "justice and humanity" he wanted to end a husband's control over a wife's assets.[36] In his 40 years of practicing law, he had seen many cases of husbands abusing this right. Nonetheless, he would not support any reform that might weaken family ties, since the family "was the basis of society and of the nation."[37] Senator Roberto Andrade of Carchi, who also identified as a liberal-radical, was concerned that "given the state of civilization" of Ecuador, "women were not prepared to independently manage their assets, as they were in other countries."[38] If separation of property were the default, priests, who liberals viewed as exerting too much sway over women, would end up influencing women's economic decisions.

In the preliminary vote on article 1 of the Deputies' proposal, to change the default regime to separation of property, senators failed to approve it, with all but one of those from the Sierra voting against it and those from the Coast uniformly favoring it. The next day, Peñaherrera agreed to continue the discussion of this article since "all of us want to improve existing institutions to better favor women but differ on the means to accomplish it" and called for deliberate consideration, as had happened with the French and German reforms since it was a matter of civil law, not a political or religious issue.[39]

Senator Adolfo Páez of Imbabura considered that the main argument of those who favored making separation of property the default was that they considered wives to be the slaves of their husbands. According to him, "without the conjugal society, wives would be deprived of the gananciales that are more commonly generated by husbands than wives, and thus they would fall into the worst kind of slavery, which is poverty."[40] While women's labor force participation was increasing in this period, particularly in the education and health sectors, it was still quite low (Goetschel 2007; Clark 2012). Thus, unless women inherited property, they were unlikely to have any assets or income to manage. Páez also stressed that laws should reflect the situation of the majority of couples, which was that most marriages were happy. They should not be legislating for the minority, those cases where husbands abandoned their wives or pilfered their assets. Moreover, if there was choice in the matter, men would never opt for community property; hence, making the separation of property the default regime would harm women. Another concern he raised was that if they adopted this as the default regime, this would result in "two authorities in the home," which would surely threaten the ties of love between husband and wife.[41]

36 DDCS, 95.
37 DDCS, 95.
38 DDCS, 98.
39 DDCS, 102.
40 DDCS, 109.
41 DDCS, 109–10.

After more discussion, Peñaherrera proposed the following compromise as an amendment to article 1:

> Married women at any time will have the right to exclude from the marital society all or a portion of their own assets to manage independently without need to rely on or give proof of the civil code motives for the separation of property. Regarding this administration, they have full legal capacity to engage in any act or contract, including the sale or mortgage of real estate and to appear in suits.[42]

It was a compromise because it differed from what the commission initially had in mind. It made women's exclusion of assets from the conjugal society an automatic right rather than an option they could request from a judge.

Since it maintained partial community property as the marital regime and the wife's rights to the gananciales, Peñaherrera argued that his amendment was "more feminist than the bill proposed by the Chamber of Deputies," for theirs imposed separation of property on all wives. His compromise, in contrast, would make "the conjugal society a requirement for men, but voluntary for women."[43] By preserving married women's rights to the gananciales, Peñaherrera considered that it recognized that the wife's savings and sacrifices were of equal value to a husband's efforts. Also, enabling a woman to exclude her own assets at any time to manage these herself was not unlike the marital contract allowed in the civil code, except that currently, couples could only choose this option prior to marriage and in regard to some, not all her assets. Hence, his amendment gave wives more flexibility since they could exclude their assets at any point if they felt the need to do so. After more discussion, Peñaherrera's motion passed 13 to 11.

Intriago introduced a new idea during the final debate, one that would preserve the concept of community property but allow each spouse to freely administer their own assets during the marriage, with equal rights and legal capacity.[44] Once the marriage dissolved, the spouses would share and divide the gananciales equally. This alternative is what would come to be known as deferred community property, combining aspects of separation of property with community property in a manner like what most Central American countries had instituted earlier, although Intriago did not mention these antecedents.[45]

Peñaherrera summarized the three alternatives before the Senate as follows. The Deputies' bill abolished the conjugal society while both his compromise and Intriago's new proposal preserved it. The latter two differed in the degree of choice exercised by women and as to whom would head this society. In his proposal, the

42 DDCS, 113.
43 DDCS, 114.
44 DDCS, 139.
45 It may have been an idea original to him since he was not a lawyer and thus would not have formally studied comparative civil law.

default was partial community property under the administration of the husband. It was the wife's prerogative to opt to exclude her properties when she deemed it appropriate. In contrast, in Intriago's proposal, the default was separation of property even if the gananciales would eventually be equally divided. According to Peñaherrera, "what seems absurd is that the society of husband and wife would not have a head, and to a certain extent, the marriage would have two husbands."[46] His proposal assumed that the husband would "continue to be, as he should be, the head of the family and the supreme authority of the home."[47] Moreover, he warned that too abrupt a change from traditional practice, as would be the case with both the Deputies' bill and Intriago's proposal, might give women "the idea that they are totally emancipated from their husbands to the point of their no longer respecting or obeying them, which would be very prejudicial for domestic order and family well-being."[48]

The question of headship and the need to maintain potestad marital generated much discussion. Most senators agreed that women were incapable of heading the conjugal society and some doubted that they could even manage her own assets. Páez asserted that women in Ecuador "are ill-prepared to manage the business of life … they cannot be compared with the American woman, who some take as a model."[49] Senator Belisario Torres of Guayas challenged this assertion, noting how in Ecuador "many single women easily administer their own assets, and since they have full civil capacity, some do so more successfully than men."[50] Moreover, he reminded the senators that most wives managed domestic finances without difficulty, and "if they have shown aptitude at a small scale, why not at a larger scale?"[51] Intriago's amendment was then defeated.

In the final discussion, the winning argument was that women should have the option of choosing what they considered to be in their best interest. Whereas the original bill and Intriago's proposal applied to all marriages, Peñaherrera's would only apply in the case that a wife wanted to manage her own assets. Whereas under current law, she could file suit for simple separation of property only if the husband mismanaged the assets or committed fraud, in his proposal, a wife could exclude her property without having to provide a reason and do so relatively easily through a notary public (and if immovable property, inscribing such in the property registry) rather than going to court. The Senate approved Peñaherrera's amendment by a vote of 13 to 6.

During this debate, it was clear that the senators were primarily thinking of what was in the best interest of women of their own social class who were housewives.

46 DDCS, 140.
47 DDCS, 140.
48 DDCS, 141.
49 DDCS, 146.
50 DDCS, 147.
51 DDCS, 147.

Almost as an afterthought, Peñaherrera proposed an additional article to benefit those who worked outside the home: "The assets that a woman acquires with her own capital or through her own work or industry will be administered by her and will be considered with respect to third parties as her exclusive property."[52] While there was some opposition, senators approved this amendment. Without this last-minute addition regarding women's earnings, Ecuador's reform would have potentially benefited only those wives who brought or inherited assets during marriage, giving the law a potential class bias. What became article 8 of the law, covering women's earnings, broadened its beneficiaries to include working-class and professional middle-class women who did not own property.[53]

Approved by the Senate in September, President Emilio Estrada Carmona, who briefly followed Eloy Alfaro in the presidency, promulgated the Economic Emancipation of Married Women Act in early October 1911.[54] It strengthened the property rights of married women but only if they explicitly chose to exclude their assets or earnings from the conjugal society to manage these themselves. In this case, they could enter into contracts and dispose of their assets freely and participate in lawsuits related to these.[55] It was also a law particularly favorable to wives since it gave them a privilege that their husbands did not have – of excluding the gananciales generated by such assets from the sharing principle of community property. Nonetheless, this reform did not modify the civil code provisions that enshrined male household headship and required a wife's obedience to her husband, including on whether she worked for an income. These restrictions continued to apply to all married women, even if they had excluded their property from the conjugal society. Moreover, wives who did not own assets nor earn an income, who may have been in the majority, continued to be subject to the traditional rules of the conjugal society.

Inputs and Reaction to the 1911 Law

Little is known about what women themselves were thinking about their property rights at the beginning of the twentieth century. Although Zoila Ugarte recognized the importance of women's economic autonomy, she did not raise property rights explicitly in 1905, the year that she edited the short-lived publication *La Mujer*. During the 1910 congressional debates on women's property rights, suffrage and

52 DDCS, 150.

53 O'Connor (2007, 94–5) and Clark (2012, 16) miss this point as well as what happened to the gains from excluded property or earnings. These became the wife's property, not forming part of the community property managed by the husband.

54 *Registro Oficial* 29, October 6, 1911, in Ecuador (1912, 25–6).

55 The next year, the Congress made it explicit that wives who excluded their property or earnings did not require their husband's authorization to engage in any contract, including the sale of their assets (Ecuador 1913, 153). The full text of the 1911 bill and its 1912 amendment are in a footnote in Ecuador (1930, 37–8) and incorporated into the text in Ecuador (1950, art. 195).

FIGURE 2.1 Ecuadorian Writer and Journalist Zoila Ugarte de Landívar (1864–1969), ca. 1915.

Source: In *Zoila Ugarte de Landívar, La escritora, pensamiento y obra. Semblanzas y necrologías, 1892–1948*, Vol. I, edited by Myriam Landívar de Arteaga (Casa de la Cultura Ecuatoriana Benjamin Carrión, 2015). Landívar Family Archive, courtesy of Myriam Landívar Silvers.

divorce by mutual consent, Ugarte was a journalist at *La Prensa* and she became the main female public advocate for women's civil and political rights (Goetschel 2010, 227) (Figure 2.1). In a series of seven articles under the title "Women's Emancipation," she made the case for why women needed "complete and absolute civil equality" with men (Ugarte 1910a, Sept. 15).[56]

Ugarte reviewed legal advances in England, France, Germany and the United States; the progress made with respect to women's entry into the professions and industry worldwide; and took on the arguments of "anti-feminists" regarding women's innate inferiority to men. Noting that "all oppression is based on economic dependence," she argued that the type of education women received had to change

56 From personal archive of Myriam Landívar, Quito; facilitated by Ana María Goetschel.

since what they received currently did not allow them to support themselves, but rather trained them to become total dependents (Ugarte 1910a, Sept. 15). For this reason, she supported giving women stronger civil rights prior to their exercising political rights. Ugarte, nonetheless, like many liberal-radical legislators, did not believe that the constitution barred women from voting or standing for office. She also found it absurd that the electoral rules allowed barely literate men to vote while denying well-educated women the opportunity.[57]

She directed her strongest ire to the limitations that the civil code placed on married women. Drawing on John Stuart Mill, she argued that "marriage is the only servitude recognized by the law" (Ugarte 1910a, Sept. 22). Specifically, the code dispossessed the wife of her property; deprived her of a legal personality, reducing her to "the ignominious state of a minor or an incompetent"; and denied her the right to demand a full accounting of the assets managed by her husband.[58] What made marriage akin to slavery, was that a wife "was forced to love and to follow, for all of her life, someone who perhaps she may hate and who subjects her to insults and moral indignities" (Ugarte 1910a, Sept. 22). Hence, besides advocating for women's equal civil rights, she supported making divorce easier by allowing it by mutual consent, a proposal that the legislature was considering at the time.

Prior to the Chamber taking up discussion of the "Economic Liberty of Women" bill, in a separate article "On the Conjugal Society," Ugarte (1910b) went into greater detail on the economic aspects of marriage.[59] Highlighting the differences between the conjugal society and a normal society of business partners, she explained how in the latter, partners had the right to supervise the administration of a business and to hold the manager accountable. Moreover, each partner received the profits from their joint endeavor. The conjugal society could not differ more from this model:

> While the woman contributes her capital and her labor, particularly, her ability to economize and save through her good management of the household, as well as her good advice, what does she get? Absolutely nothing. If the husband is good, honest and just, the wife will enjoy with him all the benefits... But she does not have a right to any of the capital or earnings of this society except what he voluntarily gives her...The husband, meanwhile, can do anything he wants with the gananciales and most of the capital, without restriction, except for selling the physical assets that the wife brought to marriage or inherited.
>
> *(Ugarte 1910b, 2)*

57 For more detail on Ugarte's writings on political rights, see Rodas (2011, 131–2) and Landívar (2015).

58 Married women could perform some civil acts without their husbands' permission, such as writing a will and serving as a witness to a marriage or a will (Ecuador 1889, art. 1002), thus Ugarte was not entirely correct regarding married women lacking a legal personality; it was a relative incapacity.

59 Personal archive of Myriam Landívar; Rodas (2011, 122–3) also includes excerpts.

Ugarte denounced the "monstrous difference" the conjugal society created in the position of husbands and wives and urged abolishing it in favor of giving couples the freedom to determine their own arrangements regarding the ownership and management of property. While she did not state that she backed the 1910 Deputies' bill, one can infer that she supported its main features. What she thought of the 1911 Senate compromise that maintained the conjugal society while giving wives the option of excluding their property is unknown. She may have seen the wisdom behind it since it expanded their options while surely disappointed that it did not automatically give wives full civil capacity. In subsequent articles, she only mentioned that it was encouraging that women elsewhere in South America had recently formed a Pan American Women's Federation with the aim of obtaining women's equal rights, which gave her "great hope for the future."[60]

One of the main themes that appears repeatedly, both in the legislative debate and in writings on women in Ecuador in this period, is the excessive sway that the Catholic Church held over many women, an influence that continued well into the second half of the twentieth century. For example, the church mobilized women against civil marriage and divorce and in defense of the religious orders and religious education (Moscoso 1996a and 1996b; Goetschel 2010).

According to Gioconda Herrera (2010), the Catholic Church, nonetheless, developed a more nuanced position with respect to women's economic situation. In 1909, as part of the celebrations around the Centennial of Independence, it sponsored the First Congress of Catholic Ladies in Quito. Among the objectives of this meeting, which led to the founding of the Liga Nacional de Damas Católicas (National League of Catholic Ladies), was "the moral, intellectual and economic betterment of women" (Herrera 2010, 248). Analyzing the resolutions of this congress, Herrera argues that these representatives of Catholic women's organizations were positioning themselves for a role in public affairs, one that went beyond the domestic realm. Besides being concerned with women's employment, they also discussed how a religious education should prepare women to manage their household's economic affairs should their husbands turn out to be incompetent managers. Their discourse on pilfering husbands, according to Herrera, was not that much different from that of legislators debating the Economic Emancipation of Married Women bill; she implies that in principle, Catholic women did not oppose this reform.

Other authors, however, such as historian Raquel Rodas (2011, 124), suggest that many Catholic women considered any reform a threat that might destabilize the family, a view encouraged by some in the Catholic Church as well as the conservative press. Rodas (2009, 117) cites an article published in the conservative

60 "Plumadas," August 24, 1911, in Landívar (2015, 333–4). This short-lived Federation was the outcome of the First International Women's Congress held in Buenos Aires in 1910; see Chapters 3 and 8.

newspaper *El Comercio* in 1910 that came out against married women managing their own assets and appearing in lawsuits, considering these activities improper. In addition, the growth and direction of European feminism was causing alarm.

As Adelaida Velasco Galdós ([1914] 2006, 81–2), writing in the religious women's periodical *El Hogar Cristiano*, warned:

> Many minds, unfortunately, have been invaded by utopic and deceiving theories of a poorly understood feminism, which will hardly ennoble or honor it... One has only to look at England where a significantly large number of women, wanting to usurp rights that are incompatible with their sex and condition, have undertaken a very violent campaign, drawing the attention of the world...under shouts of "Votes for Women, Yes."

Velasco went on to stress how women's place was in the home, not to be involved in elections. This echoed a theme recurrent in the literature of the period that "well-understood feminism" favored women's progress through education with the purpose of better preparing them for their traditional roles as wives and mothers. This position followed Pope Pious X's discourse on the topic, which kept their political participation off the table (Goetschel 2006, 22–3).

Among the few academic critiques of the 1911 law was that of jurist Francisco Pérez Borja (1913). While sympathetic to strengthening married women's property rights, he took issue with the way that law mixed what he considered to be two incompatible marital regimes, separation of property and the conjugal society. It would have been preferable in his view to have strengthened their property rights by requiring a wife's consent to alienate the immovable property of the conjugal society or by offering the separation of property regime as an option at the time of marriage. Moreover, he was concerned that the law did not make any provisions requiring women who excluded their property to contribute to the expenses of the household, something he considered damaging to its economic well-being and a potential source of marital discord. His journal article, however, did not spark a debate.[61]

To disseminate what Ecuador had accomplished, Victor Peñaherrera (1922), its intellectual author and now dean of the UCE law faculty, published a booklet that included excerpts of the Senate debate on this historic piece of legislation. Nonetheless, few jurists in other South American countries cited this pioneering reform of married women's property rights as an antecedent or model, perhaps because this law was so favorable to wives.

61 There were no further articles on this topic during this or the next decade in the *Revista de la Sociedad Jurídico-Literaria* nor in the newly founded journal of the Academia de Abogados (Academy of Legal Scholars), the *Revista Forense*.

Women's Use of the Law

A feature of Ecuador's 1911 law was that women had to take the initiative in order to benefit from it. To manage her own assets and earnings, a wife had to declare her intention to do so before a notary public and in the case of immovable property, inscribe this document in the municipal property registry. Archival records of the Quito property registry allowed investigation of the extent to which women took advantage of this law.

By 1920, 425 women had excluded their property from the conjugal society to manage it themselves, representing 2.1% of Quito's married women.[62] This seems like a reasonable uptake rate since relatively few individuals owned immovable property in this period, particularly urban property, meaning relative few women had the possibility of inheriting such, and women's labor market participation rate was still quite low. These factors have led researchers, such as Raquel Rodas (2009, 105) to assert that it was only women who "held a fortune" who benefited from the 1911 law.

It is true that some very wealthy women registered their properties, such as Eufemia Chiriboga de Muñoz who in 1912 inscribed the hacienda San Isidro in Sangolquí and its annex plus its livestock and equipment and the debts of workers residing there and some lots in Santa Prisca, all inherited from her mother. Including cash from various sources, the value of the assets she wanted to manage amounted to S/. 24,700 (Ecuadorian sucres).[63] The assets of some of the other women who inscribed their properties, however, were quite modest, such as Rosa Tobar de Paredes who inscribed a lot in Santa Prisca inherited from her father valued at only S/. 200.[64]

For tax purposes, the property registry classified these inscriptions into eight "classes," with those categorized as "1," paying the lowest fee (for property valued at S/. 200 or less) and those categorized as "8," the highest (for property worth over S/. 30,000). Of those registering in 1920, 15% of the transactions were in class 1, 46% in class 3, 30% in class 4, 3% in class 5 and 6% in class 7.[65] This shows that women in what were likely varied socioeconomic positions took advantage of this law although those of the middle and upper classes were the main initial beneficiaries.

62 This estimate is based on extrapolating the average rate of growth of marriages from the 1906 Quito census and the first national population census of 1950 to arrive at the figure of 20,521 married women in Quito in 1920 (Terán 1906, Table Ñ; Ecuador 1952, Table 6).

63 *Registro de la Propiedad del Cantón Quito* (RPCQ), 1912, Class 8, entry #2 of November 8 and Class 6, entry #1 of December 5. Hers was a complicated estate and it took the couple two attempts to sort out what constituted Eufemia's individual assets versus community property. She paid a total of S/. 57 in taxes.

64 RPCQ, 1912, Class 1, entry #2 of December 24; she paid S/. 0.40 in taxes.

65 Author's database, RPCQ subseries "Exclusión de Bienes," which includes information on all the entries for 1911–1912, 1920, 1930 and 1940, and a random sample of 66% for 1950 and 50% for 1960.

There was some confusion initially on whether wives could exclude not only their own assets but also their half of the community property for them to manage themselves, which the law did not allow.[66] Also, it was often difficult to distinguish the assets that belonged to the wife from those that constituted community property, such as when a property had been acquired with a combination of funds, for example, from the sale of an asset she brought to marriage plus joint funds, leading to some lawsuits (Avellán 1940). Attention, nonetheless, soon turned to the pending issue of women's political rights.

The Incipient Women's Movement of the 1920s and Suffrage

After World War I, liberal policies, such as the expansion of women's access to education and employment, began to bear fruit. As Kim Clark (2012) observes, the discourse on women's rights expanded in tandem with their public roles. These policies also led to the growth of a middle class, with its two pillars being government workers and the national army. The period of liberal rule ended with the 1925 Juliana Revolution led by young military officers (Coronel 2022, 395–7). Among its consequences was that women gained the vote.

The example of European women during the war raised Ecuadorian women's aspirations and led to the formation of new women's groups and periodicals. As the editors of *Flora*, Rosaura Emelia Galarza and her sister Celina María Galarza expressed it, their objective in founding this magazine in 1918 was "broader than to cultivate the flowers of literature." They admonished women "to not live like parasites, to stop considering themselves incapable of earning their own living and being a perpetual dependent. Women should be men's partners … while realizing that marriage or the convent do not define their destiny."[67]

The new women's groups included the Centro Feminista La Aurora de Instrucción y Beneficiencia (The Dawn Feminist Center for Training and Welfare), formed in Guayaquil in 1918, and the Centro Feminista Luz del Pichincha (Light of Pichincha Feminist Center) in Quito in 1921.[68] Both were formed by middle-class women in order to expand opportunities for working-class women through their education and training, with the dual objective of drawing middle-class women out of the

66 There were three such cases in 1912 suggesting that there was some demand for the full separation of property regime.

67 "Proemio," *Flora* 1918, 156, in Handelsman (1976, 63).

68 Agustín R. Freire, the editor of the labor journal *La Aurora,* initiated the Guayaquil group. Heracial de Lombeida served as its first president with Freire's wife, Clara Aurora Potes de Freire, as treasurer and editor of its periodical. It aimed to eventually establish a women's industrial, commercial and arts school. With over 50 members, by 1921, it was offering courses in English, Spanish and first aid, a sewing workshop, and childcare to working women. The "intellectual director" of the Quito group was Zoila C. Rendón, which initially had 60 members; Zoila Paredes was its first president (*La Mujer Ecuatoriana* 1918, 10–1, 53–4; 1919, 125–6, 173–7; 1921, 401). In 1922, it opened a night school for women (Vásconez 1922a).

home and into the public realm. According to Clara Aurora de Freire, the editor of *La Mujer Ecuatoriana* (1918, 5), the Guayaquil group's periodical, "it was time for the feminine sex to unite." She admonished her peers to "leave aside vanity and selfishness" in order to work for women's social and economic betterment across social classes (*La Mujer Ecuatoriana* 1918, 9).

The women writers who considered themselves feminists tended to agree on certain core principles, for example, that women's primary calling was to be a wife and mother; they required greater education to be able to better fulfill those roles as well as to prepare themselves for the labor force should the need arise; they had the same intellectual capacity as men; and they needed strong civil rights (Rendón 1923; Vásconez 1922a, 1922b).[69] They differed in their views on gender equality in marriage and on whether women needed political rights.

Zoila Rendón was the epitome of maternalist feminism, not only accepting the traditional gender division of labor but also glorifying women's femininity and role as queen of the home (Goetschel 2006, 14–5, 23–4). The latter, nonetheless, included wives having strong property rights. She described the 1911 Economic Emancipation of Married Women law as "a giant step towards progress and civilization" (Rendón 1923, 161). In her view, it addressed two social ills: it gave wives whose husbands might squander their capital an alternative, and it diminished the incentives for marriages of convenience, where rather than for love, men married only to access their wives' wealth. Rendón fully expected most wives to prefer their husbands to manage their assets, while recognizing that the law increased their bargaining power: "For his own dignity, he will manage those assets well, for he would not want to find himself in the embarrassing position where his spouse would ask for their management to revert to her" (Rendón 1923, 161).

Notwithstanding, Rendón fully accepted the husband's role as household head. She considered "a society without subordination a fanciful dream, and similarly, women's subordination to her husband in the home." She expected wives to use their feminine charms "to get whatever they wanted from him" (Rendón 1923, 26). She extended this argument to political rights, saying that women "do not need to vote to elect candidates sympathetic to their views, it is sufficient to influence their husbands, brothers and sons to obtain their votes," through their subtle powers of persuasion, i.e., drawing on their femininity (Rendón 1923, 20).

Educator Victoria Vásconez Cuvi (1922b, 3) held a different view of marriage, that it must be based on companionship and equal rights, for feminists "did not want to be subordinate or superior to men, but their equal." Although in her writings, she did not go into the specifics of needed reforms to the civil code, she clearly chaffed at how it treated women the same "as minors, the deaf-mute and the mentally impaired" (Vásconez Cuvi 1925, 23). Moreover, she considered that the

69 In the issues published between 1918 and 1921 *La Mujer Ecuatoriana* did not mention women's property rights; its focus was primarily on women's access to employment and their labor rights.

"acquisition of civil and political rights was not an exaggerated ambition of crazy women, nor an effort by women to become like men, but rather, a question of absolute justice and profound necessity" (Vásconez Cuvi 1925, 46).[70]

Ecuadorian feminists also began to develop ties with their regional counterparts. *La Mujer* Ecuatoriana, for example, published news of the founding and activities of women's organizations in other countries. Zoila Ugarte became involved in Pan American women's activities while she was director of the National Library (Rodas 2011, 165–7). The Second Pan American Scientific Congress held in Washington, D.C. in late 1915 hosted a concurrent Women's Auxiliary Conference that resulted in the formation of the International Pan American Women's Committee with representatives from each country. Ugarte and two ladies of the liberal elite served as Ecuador's representatives, tasked with organizing a local committee in support of Pan American initiatives.[71] They recruited leading women intellectuals to participate in Pan American conferences, such as Victoria Vásconez who sent a paper to the women's auxiliary conference of the Third Pan American Scientific Congress in Lima in 1924.

Ugarte was also the Ecuadorian representative of the Liga Internacional de Mujeres Ibéricas e Hispanoamericanas (LIMIH).[72] Founded in New York City in 1923, the LIMIH offered an alternative to Pan American Union (PAU)-related initiatives that some considered too dominated by the interests of the United States. These were just a few of various efforts to create a regional women's movement, which gained greater momentum by the end of that decade with the founding of the Comisión Interamericana de Mujeres (CIM, Inter-American Commission of Women) in 1928 at the Sixth International Conference of American States in Havana.

How Women Obtained the Vote

Ecuador experienced a sharp economic crisis in the early 1920s as the price of its principal export, cacao, fell sharply in international markets, precipitating labor unrest, its repression, and then further political turmoil. Charges that liberals won the 1924 election by fraud led to a coup by young military officers in what is known as the Juliana Revolution. New labor organizations and political parties then formed, such as the Socialist Party that included disaffected liberals from the radical wing of the Liberal Party (Reyes [1938] n.d., 260). Among its founders was María Luisa Gómez de la Torre, an educator and feminist activist.[73]

70 Up through 1921, there was only one article in *La Mujer* Ecuatoriana (1919, 244–5) on women's political rights, which was supportive; several articles mentioned in passing how women were acquiring suffrage elsewhere.

71 These were the First Lady, Avelina Lasso de Plaza, and her half-sister, Clemencia Lasso de Alfaro who was married to a son of former president Eloy Alfaro (Women's Auxiliary 1921, 2).

72 See Chapter 6 on Colombia where this organization was more active.

73 She later joined the Communist Party when in 1931 it split from the Socialist Party. On her career trajectory, see Clark (2005).

These developments coincided with the precipitating action toward woman's suffrage by Matilde Hidalgo de Procel, the country's first female physician.[74] While studying in Quito, she met Zoila Ugarte and María Luisa Gómez de la Torre and became involved in the local Pan American women's committee (Estrada 1980, 71; Rodas 2011, 166, 227). After moving to the coastal province of El Oro to join her husband, a lawyer, Hidalgo had the audacity to present herself before the local election board in 1924 to register to vote, taking advantage of the fact that the 1906 Constitution did not explicitly prohibit women from voting.

The election board sought advice from the Council of State, which informed it that there was nothing constitutionally that prevented women from voting nor any social nor moral reason to deny them suffrage (Prieto and Goetschel 2007; Rodas 2009).[75] The timing of Hidalgo's precipitating action and the deliberations of the Council of State coincided with discussions around a questionnaire on the legal status of women distributed by the PAU. José María Pérez Echanique, a member of the Legal Scholar's Academy, and Homero Viteri Lafronte, a UCE law professor, authored Ecuador's reply. Drawing on the fact that recent Ecuadorian constitutions did not specify that only men could be citizens, they reported to PAU that "... we can say that women have full right of suffrage and can vote and be elected under the same terms as men" (Pérez and Viteri 1924, 213).[76]

The military-civilian junta was planning to step down after a new constitution was drafted and elections held and thus appointed a Constitutional Review Commission.[77] Made up of prominent liberals, socialists and conservatives, this commission in its 1925 draft defined citizens as including "all Ecuadorians of 21 years of age who could read and write, without distinction of sex."[78] The Council of State ruling and the commission's draft led to a vigorous debate in civil society over the pros and cons of women having the vote. According to Mercedes Prieto and Ana María Goetschel's (2007, 306–9) study of press reports, the legal argument that women were citizens and should be able to vote and stand for office was uncontroversial. The points of contention were whether women were sufficiently prepared and interested in doing so and how their political participation might impact the

74 Hidalgo completed her medical degree at UCE in 1921; Estrada (1980) and Clark (2005) provide her biography. The first woman doctorate in law, Obdulia Romelia Luna completed her degree in 1927 at the University of Guayaquil (Estrada 1980, 118).

75 Estrada (1980, 98–102) reproduces this July 1924 report.

76 Rodas (2009, 121) reports that during 1924, the Senate received two telegrams from women's groups in southern Ecuador demanding suffrage. Its commission on legislation replied that a law was unnecessary since the constitution did not exclude women from citizenship nor the exercise of political rights. Among those who signed the reply were senators Agustín Cueva and J. M. Pérez, the latter who was likely the same co-author of Ecuador's reply to PAU.

77 *Actas de la Asamblea Nacional Constituyente 1928–1929 (AANC)* (1928, October 9, 11 and 15). Members of this commission included Alfredo Baquerizo Moreno, a former liberal president (1916–1920); Federico Intriago, the liberal-radical senator who in 1911 had advocated in favor of the separation of property regime; and Homero Viteri, co-author of the 1924 reply to PAU.

78 See Title IV, article 16 of the 1925 draft in AANC (October 15, 1928).

family and the quality of Ecuador's political system, a debate in which women participated and took distinct positions.

Zoila Rendón came out against women having the vote because she thought they best exercised a political role by exercising their influence on men. Moreover, if they entered the tumultuous world of politics they would lose their femininity.[79] Victoria Vásconez (1925, 48) strongly supported suffrage, arguing that

> women need the vote as a strict matter of justice, because they obey the law while also suffering more from its insufficiencies and they have the same legal responsibilities as men and pay the same taxes; in sum, because they have accepted all the same obligations but lack the same rights.

She was, nonetheless, concerned with whether women were prepared to vote given their inadequate education and was ready to accept a conditional form of suffrage, whereby initially only educated women voted or participated first only at the municipal level.[80]

According to María Angélica Idrobo ([1928] 2006, 112–3), who considered women to be citizens, the problem was that few women had tried to exercise their right to suffrage because they feared facing ridicule if they did not adhere to "a well-understood feminism," one that preserved their femininity. She did not accept the argument that women were not yet prepared to vote, pointing to the progress made in women's education under the liberal revolution. While she agreed that its quality needed to improve, among the reasons so that mothers could instill democratic values in their children, she made no mention of instituting a conditional or phased vote for women. Both she and Victoria Vásconez emphasized how women's political participation, given their unique sensibilities, would result in better institutions and more just legislation, such as equal wages for equal work and equal rights for children irrespective of the conditions of their birth.

During the 1928 Constitutional Assembly, the commission charged with reviewing the 1925 draft constitution maintained the critical clause that the right to vote should be "without distinction of sex" in the version it recommended for debate. Several delegates then tried to undermine this explicit recognition of women's political rights by excluding this clause, leaving it ambiguous; by making this option only available sometime in the future; or through amendments regarding the qualifications to vote.[81] In the end, the Assembly reached consensus that it was preferable to make women's participation explicit.

79 Prieto and Goetschel (2007, 316) cite her 1924 article in the Guayaquil daily *El Universal*, which apparently summarized the argument she made earlier in Rendón (1923) and repeated in Rendón ([1928] 2006).

80 Following the Council of State's report, the city of Guayaquil elected the first woman to a municipal council (Prieto and Goetschel 2007, 319).

81 AANC (1928, December 14).

Ecuador's 1929 Constitution thus defined citizens as men and women who were 21 or older and literate and specified that suffrage was the right of all citizens (Ecuador 1929, arts. 13 and 18). It became the first Latin American country to give women the vote and the right to stand for national office on the same terms as men. It also instituted a form of affirmative action, saying that "the State is under obligation to give special attention to women …" to prepare them for positions in public administration (Ecuador 1929, art. 168). A 1930 law followed that gave women with the appropriate qualifications equal access to public posts.[82]

Authors such as Quintero (1980, 241) and Clark (2012, 22) who conclude that women gained the vote in the absence of a female suffrage movement are technically correct, in the sense that a strong and effective feminist organization or broad-based women's movement had not developed by the late 1920s. Isabel Castillo (2023, 88) in her comparative study goes further, arguing that the Ecuadorian case shows that "the lack of a movement might actually promote women's suffrage by decreasing opposition;" that is, neither liberals nor conservatives felt it was a threat to the existing gender order. She concludes that because of this, the issue did not become politicized and neither political party paid much attention to whether expanding suffrage would work to their electoral advantage;[83] in this case, the normative argument – the principle of equality – proved decisive.

But the reason that women's suffrage did not become politicized was that there was broad acceptance of the notion that women were citizens and theoretically had the right to vote and participate in elections, as demonstrated by the positive reply to the 1924 PAU questionnaire that confirmed that women in Ecuador had political rights. Moreover, among the reasons that women's suffrage might not have been threatening was because women had been exercising stronger property rights – widely held as a precondition to political rights – since 1911 without this having any notable negative effects. At the same time, as Prieto and Goetschel (2007), Rodas (2009) and O'Connor (2024) argue, it is unlikely that women would have obtained the vote in 1929 if prominent feminists had not demanded it.

Backlash, the Building of the Women's Movement and Reforms of the 1930s

During the 1930s, women's political and property rights came under challenge. Women defended these in their writings and in new periodicals that also laid the groundwork for the subsequent development of a mass-based women's organization. This decade was particularly tumultuous because of the effects of the Great Depression. Ecuador's main export, cacao, had already been in decline, thus the

82 "Ley de Régimen Político Administrativo," December 11, 1930; *Registro Oficial,* January 3, 1931.

83 Quintero (1980) emphasizes that at this time conservatives potentially stood to gain more than liberals from ceding women the vote, given their religiosity and the church's support of Conservative Party candidates.

fall in all export prices provoked a general economic crisis, with high unemployment, inflation, social unrest and political instability. Indicative is that between 1931 and 1940, the country had 17 short-lived presidents (Cueva 1988, 96).

The most successful of the new women's periodicals was *Nuevos Horizontes*, edited by acclaimed writer Rosa Borja de Ycaza and published in Guayaquil between 1933 and 1937.[84] It was the voice of the Legión Femenina de Educación Popular (Women's Legion for Popular Education), a social welfare organization that Borja founded in 1932 that grew to have branches in several cities and affiliates in several countries.[85] During the thirties, she and members of her organization played an important role in defending women's suffrage.

Women first voted in the 1931 and 1933 elections and the backlash began when conservatives won the presidency. Although they represented only a fraction of the electorate, liberals and progressives blamed women for the political instability and their own defeat (Reyes [1938] n.d., 274; Quintero 1980, 245). They accused women of being under the influence of the clergy, too subject to manipulation and not autonomous actors (Prieto and Goetschel 2007, 319).[86]

Among those defending women's suffrage was María Esther Martínez Macias (1934) of the *Nuevos Horizontes* editorial team who took on the arguments of those who romanticized women's domesticity, wanting to limit them to traditional roles, or who viewed them as pawns of those upon whom they depended. In her view, women were excelling in the search for solutions to a range of social problems, from defending children to world peace, and their political participation was absolutely necessary to improve the situation of families and the nation.

After the military deposed the short-lived elected president in 1935, Federico Páez became Supreme Commander and among his initial acts was to appoint a commission to draft a new constitution. The rumor began to circulate that his intention was to replace the 1929 Constitution with that of 1906 in which women's right to vote was not explicit. In response, Rosa Borja wrote a letter to Páez advising him that backtracking on women's suffrage would be totally against all "modern tendencies of evolution and social justice."[87] Explaining that the Women's Legion that she headed was committed to "promoting and defending by whatever means

84 Veteran feminists Zoila Ugarte, Victoria Vásconez, María Angélica Idrobo and Rosaura Emelia Galarza also launched the short-lived periodical, *Alas,* in Quito in 1934 while they were all teachers at the Liceo Fernández Madrid (Lodoño L. 2011), a periodical I was unable to locate.

85 Its annual reports show that in the mid-1930s, its main activities were adult education classes, training workshops and mobile libraries aimed at poor women and initiatives on behalf of orphans and street children (*Nuevos Horizontes* 1935, 2 (12), 23–5; 1937, 4 (19), 14–23). When Mary M. Cannon (1943, 601) of the Women's Bureau of the US Department of Labor visited the Guayaquil group in 1943, it had around 100 members.

86 O'Connor (2024, 261–6) provides a nuanced political analysis of the 1930s and how this backlash was also related to fears around the growth of leftist and indigenous movements.

87 Borja de Ycaza to Federico Páez of November 20, 1935, in Doris Stevens Papers, Series V. Inter-American Commission on Women, sub-series A. Correspondence: Ecuador, 1937–1942.

the gains in women's rights and prerogatives," she warned that rescinding women's suffrage would lead to protests, including internationally, which would negatively affect the country's prestige. She reminded him that Ecuador had been one of the few countries to sign the Equal Rights Treaty proposed by the CIM but not formally approved at the 1933 Seventh International Conference of American States in Montevideo, a draft treaty that recognized women's equal civil and political rights.[88]

The issue of women's suffrage surfaced again in early 1937 and drew international attention due to a memo written by Rosa Huerta de Viteri Lafronte, the country's CIM representative between 1931 and 1938. She alerted CIM chair Doris Stevens that the government had issued a decree that took away women's right to vote in the upcoming elections for deputies to a new constitutional assembly.[89] Although she thought this might just be a temporary suspension of women's political rights, with the outcome to be determined by the new assembly, she urged Stevens to act.

Stevens wrote President Páez on behalf of the CIM and launched a major international letter-writing campaign (Álvarez Giménez 2019, 120). She drew attention to how Ecuador had signed the Equal Rights Treaty and how it was "morally bound" to guarantee men and women equal rights."[90] She asked him "to use his influence and power to safeguard women's right to vote" in the new constitution and, moreover, that his government ratify the Equal Rights Treaty. As it turned out, the government had issued the new electoral law a few days before Steven wrote her letter and it maintained the same qualifications for voting as in the 1929 Constitution.[91] Journalist Hipatia Cárdenas de Bustamante sent Stevens a copy and explained that the problem was that the new procedures to register and vote were so complicated that only government workers and soldiers would likely do so; moreover, a free election was not assured.

Meanwhile, women's organizations wrote dozens of letters to President Páez.[92] Among those protesting this alleged assault on women's political rights from the United States were the National Council of Women, the National Women's Party, and various chapters of the Federation of Women's Clubs and the International

88 See Chapter 8 and Marino (2019) on the origin of the draft Equal Rights Treaty and the 1928 Sixth International Conference of American States in Havana that established CIM.

89 Memorandum by Rosa Huerta de Viteri Lafronte, n.d., in Doris Stevens Papers, Series V, sub-series A. Correspondence: Ecuador, Campaign to abolish vote, file 1.

90 Doris Stevens, Chairman, to President Federico Páez, May 1, 1937, in Doris Stevens Papers, Series V, sub-series A. Correspondence: Ecuador, Campaign to abolish vote, file 1.

91 "Ley para la elección de Representantes a la Asamblea Nacional," *Registro Oficial* 480, May 4, 1937; included as an attachment in Hipatia Cárdenas to Doris Stevens, May 22, 1937, in Doris Stevens Papers, Series V, sub-series A. Correspondence: Ecuador, Campaign to abolish vote, file 2.

92 Doris Stevens Papers, Series V, sub-series A. Correspondence: Ecuador, Campaign to abolish vote, file 4, includes a list of 30 organizations that wrote letters and sent a copy to CIM; copies of many more individual letters are in these files or referenced.

Federation of Business and Professional Women's Clubs. The International Alliance of Women for Suffrage and Equal Citizenship (IAWSEC, the renamed IWSA) also mobilized its international network, and Páez received protest letters from women's organizations in France, Ireland and the Philippines as well as Argentina, Chile, Mexico and Costa Rica. Páez's office responded to at least one, writing the president of the New York-based Unión de Mujeres Americanas (UMA, Union of American Women) to confirm that women in Ecuador still had the vote and that many were registering to participate in the upcoming elections for a constitutional assembly.[93] This assembly did not end up reforming the constitution; rather, it only formally elected Páez as interim president.[94] It is difficult to judge the extent to which plans to eliminate women's right to vote were shelved due to the international outcry this raised, but it was likely among the factors that contributed to it.

A few months later General Alberto Enríquez Gallo deposed Páez and by early 1938 rumors were again circulating that he also planned a constitutional reform that would take away women's right to vote. In an article in *El Día*, Hipatia Cárdenas noted how every time elections came up men wanted to reverse women's right to vote: "Infelicitous men do not seem able to solve the political problem of Ecuador … thus they fall back on the argument of needing to put women aside to see if they can then move forward." [95]

The draft electoral law that circulated in March did not exclude women, but in Cárdenas' analysis, it presented so many obstacles as to whom could vote that it implicitly diminished their potential participation; for example, it required proof of having completed primary school and being economically solvent.[96] Cárdenas reported that she had spoken to General Enríquez about the injustices in this proposal. He must have had second thoughts because the final electoral law issued in April 1938 maintained women's suffrage without the proposed restrictions; the main change was that it dropped the age at which either men and women could vote to 18.[97]

During the 1930s, feminists strengthened their regional and international networks around women's rights and international peace issues. Rosa Borja's

93 Teodoro Alvarado Garsicos to Evangelina A. de Vaughan y Antonia de Castro López, July 5, 1937. Copy attached in Vaughan to Steven, August 31, 1937, along with a press clipping describing UMA activities on behalf of women's suffrage in Ecuador; in Doris Stevens Papers, Series V, sub-series A. Correspondence: Ecuador, Campaign to abolish vote, file 2. See Chapter 5 on UMA's 1934 founding.

94 In his memoir, Páez (1939, 72) explained the difficulties in drafting a new constitution but he does not mention the issue of women's political rights.

95 Published under her pseudonym "Aspasig," this article, "El voto femenino y la suficiencia de los hombres," appeared in *El Día*, February 1, 1938, and is in Cárdenas (1943, 33–5) and Goestschel (2006b, 169–70).

96 "El proyecto de Ley Electoral, *El Día*, March 14, 1938, in Cárdenas (1943, 103–5).

97 "Ley de Elecciones de la República del Ecuador expedida el 25 de abril de 1938," Delegación del Ecuador, Washington; in Doris Stevens Papers, Ecuador Campaign, file 4.

Women's Legion developed branches in Colombia, Chile, Bolivia, Panama and Venezuela (Álvarez Giménez 2019, 125–7). It was one of the founding members of UMA; Borja chaired its Ecuadorian section.[98] Another feminist and writer associated with Borja's Guayaquil group, María Piedad Castillo de Levi, became Ecuador's delegate to the CIM, serving from 1940 to 1952 (CECIM 2006, 7; Goetschel 2006, 31, 33).

The most notable organizing effort of this decade was the formation of the Alianza Femenina Ecuatoriana (AFE, Ecuadorian Women's Alliance), a broad-based organization of women from across the political and class spectrum founded in 1938 by socialist leaders Nela Martínez, María Luisa Gómez de la Torre and others. It aimed to defend the civil and political rights women had already obtained and to further the struggle for equal economic, social and political rights (Goetschel 2006, 181–3). Its initial advisory board included veteran feminists Zoila Ugarte and María Angélica Idrovo. Others who played leadership roles in the organization in the 1940s were Hipatia Cárdenas, Matilde Hidalgo and noted indigenous leader Dolores Cacuango. Through a decentralized structure, with base units in factories, universities and communities, by the mid-1940s, some 124 women were active in leadership positions (Salazar 2018, 169). When Nela Martínez, its secretary-general,[99] visited feminist activists in Colombia in 1945, she claimed that the organization had some 5,000 members.[100]

Among the AFE's initial activities was lobbying for women's concerns in the discussions around the 1938 Labor Code, specifically for equal wages for equal work, paid maternity leave and childcare centers. It also sought legislation protecting unorganized women in different sectors, ranging from street vendors to domestic servants. Drawing on the expertise of some of its members, it organized workshops on maternal and child health and delivered health services in poor neighborhoods, conducted literacy programs and operated food kitchens. Through these social welfare activities, it formed alliances with women across the class divide (Salazar 2018, 173–5; Troya et al. 2022, 23–4).

Further Civil Code Reform

Feminists in the 1930s were not only defending women's right to vote and their rights as workers but also seeking to enhance women's civil rights and those of

98 The letterhead of UMA (in Doris Stevens Papers) shows that Ana Gallegos de Torre served as the Women's Legion representative in New York and secretary of its international executive committee.

99 Nela Martínez wore multiple hats, serving on the central committee of the Communist Party and in the leadership of the Popular Movement against Totalitarianism (Troya et al. 2022, 21–2).

100 Report on the visit by Martínez to the Unión Femenina Colombiana, in *Agitación Femenina* (1945, 4, 4). Mercedes Prieto, in a personal communication, considers this number exaggerated; it may represent the estimated number of women participating in AFE-led marches around the 1944 Revolution.

children. Decrees issued by the civilian-military government that ruled between 1935 and 1938 fortified women's labor rights and the inheritance rights of illegitimate children, while both strengthening and weakening married women's property rights.

Several feminists raised how it was time to eradicate potestad marital from the civil code. María Esther Martínez (1933) considered wives to have gained some degree of independence under the 1911 Married Women's Economic Emancipation law but that the spirit of that law was to protect women's assets, not necessarily their freedom of action, since potestad marital still governed marriage. For example, since a husband still represented his wife, he could undermine her conducting any public function. She called for a review of all of Ecuador's codes to make sure these were consistent with women's constitutional rights as citizens. Poet Aurora Estrada Ayala de Ramírez Pérez ([1934] 2006) also addressed the need to end the subjugation of wives to their husbands so that all married women be able to act without their husband's permission. She advocated eliminating specific civil code articles, such as the one requiring a wife's obedience.

Although unknown whether he was responding to the demands of feminists, President Páez's Minister of Government, liberal Aurelio Armando Bayas, sought the advice of the Academy of Legal Scholars (of which he was a member) to propose reforms to the civil code (Balarezo 1937).[101] These jurists recommended further strengthening married women's property rights through what became known as the "double signature" law. Páez issued Supreme Decree No. 279 in 1936 that instituted the requirement that a husband obtain his wife's consent to sell or mortgage any immovable property acquired during the marriage as well as to take out a loan backed by community property.[102] Thus, wives acquired a voice and the right of redress regarding management of community property.

This decree addressed a grievance first raised by Zoila Ugarte in her 1910 *La Prensa* articles and one recommended by legal scholars Suárez (1913) and Pérez (1913). It responded to the general demand of feminists of the 1930s to end potestad marital, weakening although not fully eliminating it.[103] Nonetheless, it was a particularly important measure for housewives who did not own individual property nor worked for income and who could not benefit from the 1911 law.

The reform that recognized the rights of children born outside marriage also indirectly strengthened women's property rights. Supreme Decree No. 94 of November 1935 allowed the investigation of paternity and, if recognized by a parent, gave illegitimate children stronger inheritance rights.[104] These were now in

101 On how Páez started out with a reformist agenda and had several socialists and reformist liberals in his cabinet but ended up as a repressive dictator, see Cueva (1988, 102–3) and Vega (1987, 28–9).

102 "Reforma al Código Civil," *Registro Oficial* 228, July 1, 1936, 526.

103 Zoila Rendón ([1948] 2006) mentioned this 1936 decree favorably as an example of how much ideas had progressed since the 1911 law.

104 *Registro Oficial* 46, November 22, 1935; in Torres (1942, 15).

the first order of intestate succession, alongside legitimate children, although they received only half their share. This reform directly strengthened the property rights of wives by increasing the share that the surviving spouse received when there were no legitimate descendants.[105] The ascendants, spouse and illegitimate children each (by category) inherited one-third; previously, the ascendants received one-half, and the other categories, one-fourth of the estate each.[106] The position of the surviving spouse also improved if there were no descendants or ascendants. While previously the spouse then shared the estate with the siblings of the deceased, the decree now allocated the full estate to them. This improvement in the position of widows and widowers in intestate seems like an incidental by-product of the move to strengthen the inheritance rights of illegitimate children but it conformed to the growing consensus among Latin American jurists that the surviving spouse should receive favored treatment over collateral relatives.

The reform of the rules governing civil divorce issued by the Páez government, Supreme Decree No. 112 of December 1935,[107] responded to a long-standing demand of feminists to end the double standard with regard to adultery, making the grounds the same for husbands and wives. It also made divorce by mutual consent easier by distinguishing between "express consent," when both spouses agreed to it, and "tacit consent," when one spouse had been abandoned for at least three years.[108] Moreover, if the husband was the guilty party to a divorce, and the wife lacked assets to maintain her customary living standard and there was no community property to divide, she became automatically entitled to one-third of her husband's assets, which improved her position.[109]

Provisions in Ecuador's first labor code and in the national social security system enacted in these years strengthened the economic autonomy of wage-earning women. The 1938 labor code specified that wives had the legal capacity to sign work contracts and to exercise its rights and obligations, including to file lawsuits related to their wage employment.[110] In the savings bank established by the social security system, working wives were considered "the free administrators of their

105 Ecuador's 1860 code copied the 1855 Chilean code on succession that was less generous to spouses than other nineteenth-century codes (Deere 2023).

106 Based on the comparison of Ecuador (1930, arts. 978 to 982) and the decree, incorporated into Ecuador (1950).

107 "Reforma de la Ley de Matrimonio Civil en lo concerniente al divorcio," *Registro Oficial* 56, December 4, 1935; see Torres (1942, 105) for other subsequent modifications.

108 It is unknown how feminists reacted to this specific feature. In the 1920s, Vásconez (1925, 22–3) had been concerned that divorce was too easy for men and that women and children ended up worse off.

109 This one-third share followed the inheritance rules governing the porcion conyugal (spousal share), which the surviving spouse could request depending on relative need. Deducted from the maximum share was the value of any assets they owned or gananciales received.

110 Código de Trabajo of 1938, art. 32, in Torres (1942, 526), which includes the articles modifying the civil code. Although drafted by the Páez government, the next Junta promulgated it.

assets with respect to deposits, benefits and related acts and contracts."[111] Taken together, these provisions led lawyer Mercedes Herrera García (1956, 104) to conclude that married women workers "freely dispose of the product of their work"; i.e., their wages and salaries.

An unfavorable development followed under the junta led by General Enríquez Gallo regarding the implementation of the 1911 Economic Emancipation law. The 1938 reform of the Code of Civil Procedures strengthened the hand of men whose wives excluded their property from the conjugal society by allowing them to petition a judge for a complete separation of property (Ecuador 1938, art. 883). In other words, if a woman exerted her right to exclude her assets or earnings from her husband's management, she stood to lose access to any future gananciales based on her husband's capital and effort. While this redress to men placed husbands and wives in a parallel position – under separation of property, each managed their own property and captured their own gains – it was unfavorable to women given men's much higher labor force participation rate and the gender wage gap. It meant that for the rest of the marriage a wife would not receive compensation for her contribution to enhancing her husband's gains through her domestic and caring labor.

This change in procedures was an initiative of the Academy of Legal Scholars, instigated by a query put to them regarding apparent inconsistencies relating to the 1911 law between the civil code and the code of civil procedures.[112] During their lengthy discussion, some Academy members voiced concern that this law was unfair to men since it gave wives privileges not available to husbands: their earnings formed part of the conjugal society whereas those of their wives, if they chose to exclude their own assets or earnings, did not.[113] A consensus was reached to recommend men's right of redress on the grounds that it honored Senator Peñaherrera's initial intentions.[114] The Academy then submitted their recommendations to the Minister of Government and the Enríquez Gallo government promulgated these reforms of the code of civil procedures the next year.[115]

The elected government of Carlos Alberto Arroyo del Río enacted one other reform favorable to women that had been under discussion for some time. The 1940 Law of Family Patrimony allowed the owner of a household's principal residence to designate it as *patrimonio familiar* if children under the age of majority resided

111 Ley del Instituto Nacional de Previsión y de las Cajas de Previsión, art. 90, of 1935, in Torres (1942, 554).

112 Avellán Férres (1940) and "Actas," Academia de Abogados, nos. 15–22, 1937, in *Revista Forense* (1938, 127, 240–303).

113 "Actas," Academia de Abogados, no. 30, 1937, in *Revista Forense* (1938, 128, 3–6).

114 Aware that some might view the special privileges to wives as unfair to husbands, Peñaherrera (1922, 40) had included such a clause in the legislative commission's amended draft bill but in the heat of the Senate's debate did not bring it up for discussion.

115 Another reform enacted at that same time made it unnecessary for a husband to obtain the approval of a judge to alienate the property of his wife that he managed directly; only her consent was now necessary (Ecuador 1938, art. 837).

there. In this case, to rent, mortgage or sell the dwelling required special permission, essentially excluding it from any action by creditors.[116] Inspired by the hardship caused by the Great Depression and adopted throughout Latin America, this mechanism intended to protect families in the case of unemployment or bankruptcy.

Men Seeking Redress and Women Autonomy

Not all men accepted the enhanced economy autonomy of their wives that the 1911 Economic Emancipation law facilitated. There are several cases in the Quito property records of women who had inscribed their assets but later rescinded the action because of their husbands' discontent. For example, in December 1929, Manuela Shimtasi registered a house and lot that she had inherited from her parents in the parish of Sangolquí. A few weeks later, she returned to the Property Registry to rescind her inscription saying that she "had not known the effects that this would have in my home" and that she "had no reason to doubt the honesty of my husband."[117]

The law did not require a husband's consent for a wife to exclude her property from the conjugal society. However, if he was not present when the wife requested such an exclusion, the notary public had to notify the husband. In the initial decades of its application, husbands were present during the execution of these documents in only around one-quarter of the cases. The tendency was for a greater share of husbands to be present and declare their agreement with their wives' action: 43% in 1930 and 60% in both 1940 and 1950.[118] This suggests that one impact of the 1938 change in the rules was to encourage couples to agree on this option before a wife pursued it.

The 1938 decree that gave husbands greater redress did not discourage women from availing themselves of the benefits of the 1911 law. As Figure 2.2 illustrates, during the 1940s, there was a significant increase in the number of women inscribing their assets at the property registry annually. By 1950, a cumulative 4.3% of the married women in Quito had taken advantage of this law,[119] compared to only 2.1% in 1920. Its increased use during the 1940s coincides with the growth in women's labor force participation as well as of the women's movement, which emphasized the importance of women's economic autonomy.

Women continued to take advantage of this law irrespective of social class.[120] Information on the composition and form of acquisition of the registered assets illustrate some of the important changes. As Table 2.1 shows, up through the 1930s, most of the registrations were of immovable properties – dwellings and/or land.

116 "Patrimonio Familiar," *Registro Oficial* 56, November 8, 1940, in Torres (1942, 321–52).
117 RPCQ, Subserie Exclusión de Bienes, entries 1929 #39 and 1930 #1.
118 Author's database, RPCQ, Subserie Exclusión de Bienes.
119 Estimate is based on the number of married women in the district of Quito reported in the 1950 Population Census (Ecuador 1952, Table 6).
120 See Deere (2025, Table 3).

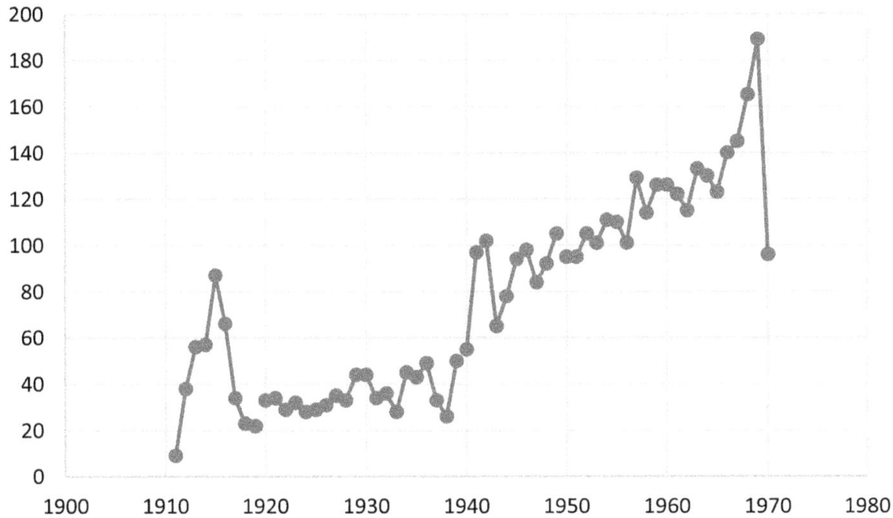

FIGURE 2.2 Number of Women Inscribing Their Exclusion of Property, Quito, 1911–1970.

Source: Compiled by the author from Registro de la Propiedad del Cantón Quito, Subserie Exclusión de Bienes.

TABLE 2.1 Type of Assets Registered by Married Women in Quito

Year	*Dwelling*	*Land*[a]	*Consumer goods*	*Financial assets*[b]	*Business*	*Unspecified*
1911–12 n = 46	70%	48%	9%	11%	–	9%
1920 n = 33	64%	39%	27%	21%	–	12%
1930 n = 44	57%	41%	16%	–	5%	16%
1940 n = 55	31%	20%	31%	42%	15%	4%
1950 n = 62[c]	19%	23%	29%	40%	20%	10%
1960 n = 63[c]	16%	13%	41%	46%	24%	5%

Source: Author's database compiled from Registro de la Propiedad del Cantón Quito, Subserie Exclusión de Bienes.

Notes:

[a] Includes urban lots, haciendas and farms.

[b] Includes cash, bank accounts and loans to third parties.

[c] The "n" represents a random sample of entries.

TABLE 2.2 Form of Acquisition of the Registered Assets

Year	*Inheritance*	*Gananciales from a previous marriage*	*From own work or business*
1911–12	54%	9%	2%
1920	76%	3%	3%
1930	45%	2%	5%
1940	35%	2%	20%
1950	32%	8%	27%
1960	25%	–	44%

Source: Author's database compiled from Registro de la Propiedad del Cantón Quito, Subserie Exclusión de Bienes.

Thereafter, consumer goods (furniture, jewelry and consumer durables), financial assets and businesses appear more frequently, even though the law did not require women to inscribe movables in the registry.[121] In the initial decades, consumer goods only appear when included with immovable property, as in "a house and its furnishings." From 1940 on, a larger share of entries (between 8 and 11%) were of women who only reported such items. The composition of the consumer items also changed over time. Whereas in 1940, the most frequent were Singer sewing machines and Phillips radios; in 1950, consumer durables such as refrigerators and washing machines appear more often; by 1960, some women were registering automobiles.

From 1940 on, it also became quite common for a woman to register a given sum of money that could represent the value of an inheritance (given to her as cash or property subsequently sold), or her savings from prior or current work. More women began to inscribe financial assets such as loans they had made to third parties from their own resources. Moreover, prior to 1930, there was no mention of women owning non-agricultural businesses; thereafter, these inscriptions grew steadily, and included fruit stands as well as restaurants and hotels, and textile workshops and factories. Whereas in 1940, 15% of the women registered a business, this figure increased to 20% in 1950 and 24% in 1960.

The information on the form of acquisition also provides evidence of women's increased labor force participation (Table 2.2). Up until 1930, most women acquired their assets through inheritance from a parent or other relative; few mentioned their own work or a business as being its source. In 1950, over a quarter of the women reported that they acquired these through their own labor efforts either prior to or during the marriage, reaching 44% in 1960.

The judicial archives for Quito provide further information on the impact of the 1938 reform in the code of civil procedures. In two (of the four) Quito civil courts, there were only 28 cases between 1938 and 1954 of men suing their wives for the

121 This increase may have resulted from the reform of the 1938 code of civil procedures mentioned earlier that also explicitly allowed women to exclude movable property from the conjugal society.

separation of property due to a woman's exclusion of assets from the conjugal society.[122] Assuming the incidence of such cases was similar in all the Quito courts, fewer than 4% of wives' inscriptions in the property registry resulted in husbands demanding the separation of property. Men's lawsuits were of two types: opposition because their wives had excluded community property rather than their own individual property (and this was against the law), or for the separation of property, following the new 1938 rules. There were only two cases filed because of the former reason, one of which was successful.[123]

In most cases, the husband concurred with his wife's exclusion of her property but as was his right, demanded the separation of property. The reasons that some men sought redress were often similar to the sentiment expressed by Wilfredo Gallegos Páez in the demand that he placed against his wife Aida María Fierro de Gallegos in 1943: "It is not possible to continue in a conjugal society where I am the only partner sustaining gains and losses, with my wife only reaping the gains without having made any contribution."[124] Wilfredo, of course, was not taking into account his wife's non-monetary contributions, such as her domestic labor and child-rearing contributions. In other cases, it is apparent that the couple preferred the separation of property of regime, and since this regime was not an option when they married, they were going through the process of women's exclusion of assets, followed by the husband's demand for separation of property as a means of attaining this outcome. In most of these cases, the wife owned her own business.[125]

Constitutional and Civil Code Reform at Mid-Century

In 1944, a broad-based political coalition, the Alianza Democrática Ecuatoriana (Ecuadorian Democratic Alliance), ended the presidency of Arroyo del Río prematurely in a revolution known as "La Gloriosa" in which members of the AFE were active participants. Nela Martínez herself led the group that occupied the national palace and served as Minister of Government for three days. The constitutional assembly that followed included provincial-level representatives as well as "functional" delegates representing various social sectors, and the AFE lobbied, apparently unsuccessfully, to be included as the representative of women (Troya

122 Author's database compiled from the archives for the First and Second Civil Courts of Quito, *Archivo General de la Función Judicial* (AGFJ). See Deere (2025) for a fuller discussion of these cases.

123 AGFJ, Second Court, 1942, case #9, and First Court, 1950, case #82, which was incomplete.

124 AGFJ, First Court, 1943, case #502.

125 See Deere (2025, Table 4) for a comparison of these lawsuits with those pursued by women to obtain a separation of property due their husband's poor administration of or fraud regarding community. There were fewer such suits, only 22 in this same period, in part because the 1936 "double signature" decree reduced the need; these cases had never been common (Suárez 1913).

et al. 2020, 29–30).[126] Martínez, nonetheless, was selected as the alternate delegate of the labor movement and was able to address the assembly, raising such issues as women's ability to administer their own assets, the structure of authority of the conjugal society and the legal status of illegitimate children (Salazar 2018, 176–80). This assembly drafted the socially oriented 1945 Constitution that included the principle of equality of spousal rights in marriage (Ecuador 1945, art. 142).[127]

While this principle had been adopted without much commentary in the short-lived 1938 Constitution (Ecuador 1938b, art. 159 (19)), its interpretation now sparked a heated debate. If interpreted narrowly, it only meant that spouses had equal rights before the law, for example, to contract marriage; if interpreted more broadly, it abolished potestad marital. Alfredo Pérez Guerrero ([1946] 1954), a well-known progressive and UCE law professor, took the latter position arguing that this clause meant that marriage no longer rendered women relatively incapable and that they had the same legal right as husbands to act on their own behalf, whether in administering their own assets or determining the household's domicile. Jurist Juan María Pérez Echanique ([1946] 1954), rebutted Pérez Guerrero, arguing that this article had not changed anything at all: by agreeing to marry, the "subjection of a woman to potestad marital was an obligation to which she enters freely" and thus conformed to the principle of equality. In his view, "it was inconceivable that there would be a society without a figure of authority, much less a society of two people with equal authority" (Pérez Echanique [1946] 1954, 190).

The Legal Scholar's Academy spent several months studying the issue. The main defender of the position that this clause gave husbands and wives equivalent rights in marriage was lawyer Mercedes Herrera García who represented the Colegio de Abogados (Bar Association) on this prestigious body, likely the first woman to do so. The Academy ended up concluding that the clause did not establish complete equality between the spouses and that their rights and responsibilities as laid out in the civil code remained unaffected.[128] The consensus was that any change required implementing legislation.

President José María Velasco Ibarra's voiding of the 1945 Constitution cut short this discussion and the new one he promulgated in late 1946 made no mention of gender equality in marriage.[129] The 1946 Constitution also made women's vote

126 Ecuador (1945, 125–28) includes the list of delegates signing the 1945 Constitution, and Martínez does not appear among them.

127 Unfortunately, I was unable to locate the proceedings of the session where Martínez made her presentation or where this constitutional article was discussed. It may be that only the first six volumes of the *Diario de Debates de la Asamblea Constituyente de 1944* were ever published.

128 Actas, March 19, 1946, in *Revista Forense*, Época II (1954, 1, 157–95). Posso and Cortés (1946) discuss the court cases around this clause.

129 Appointed president in 1944 following the La Gloriosa uprising, he won the presidency through elections in 1934, 1952, 1960 and 1968. He mobilized large numbers of women in his support by promoting a maternalist discourse that was silent regarding furthering women's civil rights. Sosa (2020) considers his female supporters as relatively indifferent to these.

optional while maintaining men's as compulsory (Ecuador 1946, art. 22).[130] Although removed from office shortly afterward, Velasco Ibarra's 1946 Constitution remained in effect.

The 1945 debates on gender equality in marriage did spur further reform likely at the instigation of the Comisión Legislativa.[131] The 1950 Civil Code included a new article that recognized the full legal capacity of married women who exercised a liberal profession (Ecuador 1950, art. 175); that is, they could conduct any economic or legal transaction without permission of their husbands or a judge. This was probably in recognition of the growing number of women lawyers, physicians and teachers and their political visibility in the 1944 Revolution. The 1938 Labor Code had given married women wage workers explicit rights that those in the professions did not have, such as the capacity to sign a labor contract and receive their own wage, thus, this measure established equivalence in their legal status. Nonetheless, for women in other forms of employment, such as self-employment, the code still presumed that if they worked, they had the permission of their husbands to do so unless they objected (Ecuador 1950, art. 176).[132]

As lawyer Mercedes Herrera García (1956), now vice-president of the International Federation of Women Lawyers reported at its ninth congress, Ecuador had made noteworthy progress in elevating the legal status of women over the past 50 years although restrictions remained on their civil capacity. Most wives could not manage the property they brought to marriage or inherited unless they declared their intent to do so via a notarized document inscribed in the Property Registry. Most women still could not be guardians of a minor nor a witness to public documents, other than to wills and the act of marriage. Moreover, while mothers shared some of the responsibilities over children with fathers, legally fathers had the last word. A widow exercised patria potestad over her children and if she remarried, she retained some rights, such as to represent them, but she could not administer their assets. It was not until the second wave of feminism before all elements of potestad marital were fully rescinded.[133]

130 Sosa (2020, 110–1) discusses the differences in these constitutions but does not explain why Velasco Ibarra wanted to make women's vote optional.

131 It was an extra-parliamentary group created by the 1946 Constitution charged with reviewing the nation's codes and laws to draft revisions to submit to the Congress. It was composed of a senator, a deputy, a representative of the president and one of the judiciary as well as the dean of the UCE Faculty of Law (Ecuador 1946). Such a body first appeared in the short-lived 1945 Constitution as the Comisión Legislativa Permanente, but with a broader composition (Ecuador 1945).

132 In a 1956 reform, the Comisión Legislativa also initiated a few changes in the rules regarding married women's right to exclude their property. If a wife took this action either spouse could demand the separation of property, thus establishing gender parity. Also, if a wife excluded all her assets, this included all her future earnings and assets without need for further action. *Registro Oficial* 53, November 6, 1956, and in Ecuador (1960).

133 Prior to the ending of potestad marital in the 1989 Civil Code, the reform of 1970 abrogated the provisions of the 1911 law regarding women's right to exclude their property from the conjugal society (RomoLeroux 1975).

Conclusion

In 1911, Ecuador became the first South American country to strengthen married women's property rights primarily because of the strength of convictions of the leaders of its 1895 Liberal Revolution and the influence of legal reforms in Europe and the United States on the thinking of liberal jurists and legislators. While presidents Eloy Alfaro and Leonidas Plaza were no doubt influenced by the accomplishments of the liberal revolutions in Central America, it is noteworthy that its intelligentsia looked elsewhere – to the legal reforms in more advanced countries – for inspiration in developing their own unique reform.

Except for journalist Zoila Ugarte, Ecuadorian women's voices were absent during this debate among liberal legislators, all who were committed to strengthening married women's property rights. The issue dividing them was how much economic autonomy to cede wives. For many, the adoption of separation of property as the default was going too far as well as disadvantageous to wives since they would lose access to the gananciales from the marriage. The challenge was how to conciliate the need for wives' greater autonomy with the least disruption to potestad marital and male household headship.

The compromise that emerged was particularly beneficial to wives. They could opt to manage their own earnings and assets with the right to keep the gananciales they generated, while benefiting from the right to share in their husbands' gananciales at the end of the marriage. The law was radical for its time by giving wives a special privilege not available to husbands. At the same time, it was of limited scope since only those who owned assets or worked for income could opt for strong property rights. Wives also had to take action to receive its benefits, notarizing their intention to manage their assets themselves and, in the case of immovables, registering the document in the Property Registry and paying a tax.

The finding that by 1950, 4.3% of married women in Quito registered their assets demonstrates the keen interest of many women in managing their wealth. It is likely that an even larger share benefited from the law, since to manage movables (such as earnings and savings) a wife required only a notarial document.[134] Nonetheless, housewives who did not own property or earn income had little choice but to accept the terms of the conjugal society, with the husband as its sole manager who could do whatever he pleased with the community property. The 1911 law also did not touch other aspects of potestad marital, such as the husband's control over the person of his wife. Legally, she still had to obey him and he decided if she could work independently and where they would live, and held sole patria potestad over the children during the marriage.

Ecuador's extension of suffrage to women in 1929 was also unique in that it preceded the development of a large-scale woman's movement although many feminist intellectuals were demanding it. Liberal policies that expanded women's

134 An analysis of its full uptake would require a systematic examination of notarial records, which would be challenging since the National Archive has not yet catalogued these by type of record.

access to education and employment facilitated it, along with the fact the 1906 Liberal Constitution did not explicitly exclude women from citizenship and that their political rights had been under discussion since 1910. This helped normalize the idea that women were citizens, particularly after women obtained the vote in a growing number of countries, especially the United States. It did not become a partisan issue because from 1911 on many wives were exercising stronger property rights without significantly destabilizing the patriarchal family. The unique political moment that followed the Juliana revolution also facilitated it since political alignments were in a process of reconstitution.

Nonetheless, fears that women's votes favored conservatives induced a backlash that led the military-civilian juntas of the mid-1930s to consider reversing women's suffrage. That women were able to maintain their right to vote is partly attributable to the mobilization of the global women's movement against this attack. This backlash, in concert with the upheaval of the Great Depression, also fostered the conditions for the emergence of a large cross-class women's organization demanding rights, the AFE.

The AFE's mobilization of women around labor rights was no doubt influential in the military-civilian juntas' reform of the labor code that resulted in women wage workers gaining control over their own earnings and other benefits such as maternity leave. Feminists also demanded the eradication of potestad marital from the civil code, resulting in its amelioration, not its elimination. The 1936 double signature law required husbands to obtain their wives' consent to alienate joint immovable property or take out a loan backed by such. Since this law automatically applied to all married women, its scope was broader than the 1911 law.

Excluded from all these improvements in women's property rights were women in consensual unions. According to the 1950 census, they made up 11.9% of women 12 years or older and were a much higher share on the Coast (27.1%) than in the Sierra (2.4%) (Ecuador 1952, Table 6). Nonetheless, children born outside marriage, if formally recognized, gained stronger inheritance rights; it also became easier to pursue the recognition of paternity. The share of women excluded from political rights due to the literacy requirement was notable. In 1950, 48.9% of women (age 10 or above) were illiterate compared to 38.4% of men, with the greatest disparity being between rural and urban areas (Ecuador 1952, Table 10), meaning that rural indigenous women were the largest group excluded from the vote.

The first wave of feminism flourished during the period of the country's greatest political instability, from 1925 to 1948, when Ecuador had 23 different administrations in as many years (Cueva 1983). In the period of political stability that followed, from 1948 to 1960 when three democratically elected presidents finished their terms, women's demands became muted as they joined political parties or women's associations in support of Velasco Ibarra, the populist leader who occupied the presidency on five separate occasions. Not until the second wave of feminism was the elimination of potestad marital, the extension of property rights to couples in consensual unions or universal suffrage discussed seriously.

3

ARGENTINA'S PIONEERING FEMINISTS

Limited Early Gains in Property Rights and Delayed Suffrage

The first scholarly effort in the region to explain the demands and achievements of global feminism was likely Elvira López's 1901 doctoral dissertation. She was one of the first women to finish a PhD in the recently formed Faculty of Philosophy and Arts at the University of Buenos Aires.[1] Her published thesis on the feminist movement served as a primer for her contemporaries on the rights women were attaining elsewhere,[2] examples that encouraged organizing efforts in Argentina. As feminist leader Elvira Rawson de Dellepiane (1921, 73) later observed, "inspired by the example of English and North American women more than anything since they were the most advanced and energetic, Argentine women began the struggle for their redemption."

López (1901, 259) considered the feminist movement a "historical necessity," and supported its long-term goals. Nonetheless, she thought that the urgent task in Argentina was to enhance women's education to better prepare them to exercise greater civil and political rights. While she supported enacting some reforms to achieve a better balance between women's rights and their familial duties, such as mothers exercising patria potestad on the same terms as fathers, she made no specific recommendations regarding reform of the marital regime.

1 Her sister, Ernestina López, who authored a dissertation on Latin American literature, graduated at the same time. They were the daughters of a well-known Argentine painter (Gago 2009).

2 López (1901) summarized what the United States, England, Northern Europe and Argentina had accomplished in terms of women's education, employment and legal status. She likely introduced many of the pioneering feminists – from Olympe de Gouges, María Deraismes and Leon Richer in France, to Millicent Garrett Fawcett and Lady Aberdeen in England, and Susan B. Anthony, Elizabeth Cady Stanton and Lucretia Mott in the United States, among others – to an Argentine audience.

DOI: 10.4324/9781003658436-3

In the subsequent decade, feminists in Argentina developed the first proposals by South American women to reform the marital regime so that wives could manage their own earnings and assets. By then women had formed a national umbrella association of women's organizations, some explicitly feminist groups had emerged, and the legislature had entertained the first two bills to strengthen married women's property rights. Argentina's feminist movement developed earlier than in other South American countries largely because it led the region in women's literacy, access to secondary and higher education and labor force participation (Miller 1991; Lavrin 1995).[3] With a vibrant movement that mobilized effectively and strong allies in the legislature, women attained stronger property and other civil rights in 1926 although due to conservative opposition, the reform fell short of their demands.

By that decade, many feminist groups were seeking both equal civil and political rights simultaneously. They came close to gaining suffrage in the early 1930s when conservative women joined the cause. At the same time, the country's reform of married women's property rights up through mid-century was not as deep as those approved later in other South American countries because in the mid-1930s, feminists had to organize to defend what they had already achieved, and the struggle for suffrage was so lengthy. Women did not attain political rights until after World War II, which delayed further efforts to reform the marital regime and enact civil divorce.

Feminist Thinking and Organizing in the Early Decades

By the beginning of the century, middle- and upper-class women in Argentina were already active in the public sphere in those activities deemed appropriate for them, primarily social welfare organizations. During the decade of the 1900s, they began to form professional associations and women's rights groups. As a result of their divergencies, women's organizations held two competing conferences during the 1910 centennial celebrations of Argentina's independence. At one, women glorified their contributions to the nation, while at the other they shared their aspirations for emancipation and discussed proposals to reform the country's 1867 Civil Code.

Indicative of the density of women's social welfare organizations at the turn of the century is that when Cecilia Grierson, the country's first female physician,[4] and

3 See Barrancos (2007, 107–13) and Carlson (1988, 62–86) on the commitment of mid-century liberal governments to women's education, the expansion of normal schools in the 1870s and 1880s, and how teaching became a female occupation. By 1895 women's literacy rate, although lower than men's, was already 41.5% (Hammond 2011, 24). In greater Buenos Aires in that same year women's economic activity rate was almost 22% and they constituted 20% of the industrial workforce (Rocchi 2000, 226).

4 The founder of Argentina's first nursing school, Grierson completed her medical degree at the University of Buenos Aires (UBA) in 1889 (Vasallo 2000; Vignoli 2021).

aristocratic Alvina van Praet de Sala[5] sent out invitations to the inaugural meeting of the Consejo Nacional de Mujeres Argentinas (CNM-A, National Council of Argentine Women) in 1900, they contacted some 250 organizations nationally. It formed at the urging of the International Council of Women (ICW) with the CNM-A becoming its first Latin American affiliate.[6] Representatives from 28 women's organizations and six periodicals attended the first meeting; by mid-1905, the CNM-A had 68 institutional members, which included social welfare, professional and immigrant women's organizations, and 141 individual members (*Revista del Consejo Nacional de Mujeres,* RCNM, 1901, 1, 7; 1905, 19, 38–41).

Much of the intellectual energy behind the CNM-A came from the professional women organized in the Asociación de Universitarias Argentinas (Universitarias, Association of Argentine University Women) formed in 1902 (Vignoli 2018). Among its founding members were educators Elvira López and Ernestina López, dentist Sara Justo, medical student Julieta Lanteri and physicians Cecilia Grierson, Elvira Rawson,[7] and Petrona Eyle.[8] The Universitarias were particularly active in its outreach commission, with the two López sisters editing its periodical.

The thinking of the CNM-A during its initial decade reflected the evolutionary view of women's progress developed by Elvira López in her thesis (Vasallo 2000). If women were to eventually attain equal civil and political rights to men's, they must first receive an equivalent education. In López's (1901, 15) words: "Some say that feminism pretends to make the sexes equal, which is absurd if equality is taken to refer to identity; but if it refers to equivalence, it is quite just." Equivalence required recognizing the differences between the sexes, while at the same time aiming for "… absolute equality, to the extent possible, with respect to civil rights in private and personal life, family life, in society and in the State." Once women had a solid education, they could aspire to be "in the same condition as men, whether single or married, with respect to property, contractual and commercial relations, and with respect to patria potestad and guardianship" (López's 1901, 20). And once they attained these rights, she envisioned women gaining political rights and participating in government.

5 Van Praet de Sala was the former president of the prestigious Sociedad de Beneficencia (Beneficence Society) of Buenos Aires, founded in 1823, which gave women an important public role (Carlson 1988, 47–57; Guy 2009).

6 The ICW president, May W. Sewall, invited an American educator, Isabel King, who had been teaching at an Argentine normal school to represent Argentina at its first conference in 1893 in Chicago. King asked Grierson's assistance in preparing her report on the status of Argentine women and Grierson subsequently attended the 1899 ICW congress in London (Vasallo 2000; Vignoli 2021).

7 Elvira Rawson also authored a thesis on a topic related to feminism for her medical degree in 1892, on the role of hygiene in modern motherhood, contrasting women's crucial reproductive role with their lack of civil rights (Guy 2009, 66).

8 All were single at the time. Both Elvira Rawson and Julieta Lanteri married during 1910 and thereafter went by Rawson de Dellepiane and Lanteri Renshaw (Giordano 2012, 83; Bellotta 2001, 86). Rawson married Luis Dellepiane, a leader of the Unión Cívica Nacional (UCR, National Civic Union or Radicals), a secular, liberal democratic party founded in 1890 made up primarily of the expanding middle class. She had been active in this party since its founding.

While López considered a woman's primary mission as being a wife and mother, she stressed that marriage should not be her only aspiration. Women needed an appropriate education to better fulfill these roles and to contribute to social progress through their paid employment. She thus supported women being able to enter any profession that "was not contrary to her dignity or her sex," while emphasizing the importance that they maintain their femininity, that "women should always be women" (López 1901, 20). In her discussion of the limitations on women in Argentina, she referred to some of the legal restrictions, such as not being able to be a witness to a public instrument or a will, but she considered most of the constraints on their employment to be the result of social convention.

López (1901, 126) recognized that Argentina's marital regime placed wives in an inferior position to their husbands but believed that men's authority was necessary to "safeguard the interests of the family." In her words,

> in the current state, giving married women certain rights would be bad for the family and for the woman herself. It is indispensable that she first be capable of exercising such rights through her greater education, independence of spirit and understanding of what is in her interests.
>
> *(López 1901, 142)*

In contrast, she was adamant about widowed mothers who remarried being able to maintain patria potestad over their children, since mothers should always have the same rights as fathers, both during the marriage and after its dissolution (López 1901, 131–3).

López (1901, 146–50) also favored instituting absolute divorce, given the many situations where continuation of a marriage became impossible, such as when abandonment, domestic violence or alcoholism were involved, among other reasons. A permanent legal separation in such cases was insufficient because in her view, it led to either women's social isolation or endangered their morality (i.e., if they formed a second union outside of marriage). For her, any discussion of women's political rights in Argentina was premature: "Suffrage is the end goal of feminist evolution and here it is only beginning." Other reasons why it would be inconvenient that she mentioned were "the deficiencies in women's education, in their less than liberal spirit, and in the influence that the Church has over them" (López 1901, 240).

Under van Praet's presidency, the CNM-A was committed to women's advancement through education, primarily to make them better mothers that would strengthen the family and Argentine society. As Cecilia Grierson reported in a 1901 questionnaire distributed by the National American Woman's Suffrage Association, while women now had access to all levels of education, relatively few women pursued secondary or higher education and that needed to change (RCNM 1902, 6, 27–9). The CNM-A supported enhancing women's civil rights but distanced itself from the more radical demand of *equal* rights for men and women or women's suffrage. According to Grierson, public opinion was against women's participation in politics and "women do not have the right of suffrage nor do they wish to have it" (RCNM 1902, 29).

María Abella Ramirez

FIGURE 3.1 Uruguayan-Argentine Educator María Abella de Ramírez (1863–1926), ca. 1900.

Source: In *Álbum biográfico de los Librepensadores de la República Argentina en el primer Centenario de su independencia* (El Progreso, 1910). Courtesy of the Centro de Documentación e Investigación de la Cultura de Izquierdas Argentina, Buenos Aires.

The first groups with an explicit equal rights agenda grew out of the socialist and freethinking movements.[9] From its founding in 1896, the Socialist Party's platform included women's equal civil and political rights. In 1902 it supported the formation of the Centro Socialista Femenino (Socialist Women's Center) by the Chertkoff sisters (Fenia, Adela and Mariana), Carolina Muzzilli, Sara Justo and others. Its objectives were to promote women's equal rights, civil divorce and the protection of women and child wage workers (Carlson 1988, 129–33; Lavrin 1995, 261).[10]

Another current of early Argentine feminism grew out of the Freethinkers movement. Among its adherents was Uruguayan-born educator María Abella de Ramírez (Figure 3.1) who in 1902 founded one of the first feminist periodicals, *Nosotras*, with socialist Justa Burgos Meyer as co-editor.[11] In this short-lived

9 See Molyneux (2001) and Gallo (2004, 10–1) on how in the 1890s the earliest feminists were primarily anarchist immigrants. They defined their struggle as being against the state, capital and religion, and did not have a reform agenda around women's civil and political rights.

10 Also see "Tres Luchadoras," *Vida Femenina* (1935, 21, 17–9).

11 Abella trained as a teacher in Uruguay and moved to La Plata (the capital of the province of Buenos Aires) after she widowed and remarried. Justa Burgos, also an educator, was the secretary of the Socialist party in La Plata (Rey 2021).

magazine, they advocated for women's civil and political rights and discussed the differences among socialist, freethinking, anarchist and liberal feminists (Lavrin 1995, 21; Rey 2021).[12]

Abella and Spanish feminist and freethinker Belén de Sárraga de Ferrero were two of the main speakers at the 1906 International Congress of Freethinkers held in Buenos Aires. In "Towards a Minimum Program of Feminist Demands," Abella ([1908] 1965, 13–5) laid out a 17-point platform that called for men and women's equal education and the opening of all professions and government employment to women at similar salaries. With respect to the civil code, she demanded eliminating potestad marital,[13] whereby a woman needed the authorization of her husband for just about every transaction, including whether to be employed, study or travel internationally, and he determined the household's residence.

Abella had two specific ideas about needed reforms to the marital regime: that in a prenuptial agreement, women have the option of reserving for themselves the management of all of their current and future property; and that if married under the regime of the conjugal society, the wife have access to half of the gananciales for her to manage independently with the expectation she cover half the expenses. Her main concerns were that the law not force wives into becoming dependents of their husbands – that is, made dependent on their generosity to meet their needs – and that they have a choice on how to manage their economic affairs.

Abella also wanted mothers to exercise patria potestad on the same terms as fathers, and if they widowed and then remarried for them to maintain the same rights, just as widowers did. Argentina's 1869 Civil Code was unusual in that it was the only South American code were both parents held the same rights and responsibilities except that the father alone was responsible for managing the children's assets. At his death, the widow automatically assumed full rights but lost them if she remarried.[14] Also included in the minimum program was the need for absolute divorce by demand of either spouse; ending the double moral standard regarding the treatment of adultery; equalizing the rights of children irrespective of the conditions of their birth; and women's full political rights, among other points. The congress endorsed her platform by consensus.

12 See Nari (2000, 247–50) for a discussion of their substantive differences.

13 The 1869 Argentine code (Argentina 1874) did not incorporate the concept of potestad marital explicitly or the offensive Napoleonic article on a wife's obedience. It did require wives to have their husband's authorization for just about every transaction and established him as the conjugal society's sole head, capturing its essence (Segovia 1881, arts. 184–197, 1218–1291). I cite Segovia's annotated edition since he numbers the code's articles consecutively and Argentina (1874) did not.

14 If she remarried, the widow was to notify a judge who could appoint her as guardian or someone else. If she did not provide notice, she and her new husband were jointly responsible for her children's assets, with the gains accruing to the new conjugal society. If the widower remarried, he continued to exercise the same rights, with the gains from children's assets accruing to him (Segovia 1881, arts. 239, 264, 287, 293, 305 and 309).

Among those attending the Freethinkers' congress were writer and educator Alicia Moreau and Julieta Lanteri, Elvira Rawson and Sara Justo of the Universitarias. During this 1906 congress, they decided to establish an autonomous organization committed to advancing women's rights, the Centro Feminista (Feminist Center), with Moreau serving as its first president.[15] Rawson followed in the presidency, subsequently renaming the association the Centro Manuela Gorriti after the acclaimed nineteenth-century Argentine writer.[16]

Julieta Lanteri and María Abella co-founded the Liga Nacional de Mujeres Librepensadoras (National League of Women Freethinkers) in 1909 and launched the periodical, *La Nueva Mujer*, the next year (Lavrin 1995, 260). The Liga's platform included six points: attaining women's political rights, equal civil rights, the rights of children, absolute divorce, mixed-sex secular education and the dignification of work (Barrancos 2002, 50).[17]

Abella also founded a different organization, the Liga Feminista Nacional (National Feminist League), in La Plata with the aim of creating feminist centers dedicated to "women's emancipation" throughout the country (Rey 2021, 156–7). Its program included women at marriage not losing the property rights they had when single, attaining women's political rights and absolute divorce and protecting childhood.[18] The more detailed platform explained that in a prenuptial agreement, a woman should be able to declare her intention to manage her current and future assets, and if she did not do so or bring assets to the marriage, that the husband be obliged to declare how much he would provide her as a monthly allowance. Abella had apparently rethought her earlier demand that the husband automatically turn over half of the gananciales to the wife for her to manage, perhaps because it was too impractical or controversial. Other specific demands were that the couple jointly determine the household's residence, that both parents exercise patria potestad on the same terms and legal equality between legitimate and illegitimate children.

Historian Marcela Vignoli (2018) suggests that the 1906 Freethinkers conference and the organizing activity that followed served as the incubator of

15 On the founding of the Centro Feminista, see Moreau ([1919b] 2004) and *La Prensa*, October 5 and 8, 1906. Moreau left the leadership to begin medical school and was then involved with the *Revista Socialista Internacional,* edited by Enrique del Valle Iberlucea. In 1910, she co-founded Ateneo Popular, a popular education initiative, becoming editor of its magazine, *Humanidad Nueva* (Henault 2002; Valobra 2012).

16 The women of the Centro Manuela Gorriti and the Centro Socialista Femenino later collaborated in publishing *Unión y Labor* in which Sara Justo played a leading role (Bellotta 2001, 62–3; Gallo 2004, 11; Hammond 2011, 57–8).

17 In 1911, Lanteri formed another organization, the Liga para los Derechos de la Mujer y el Niño (League for Women and Children's Rights), which gave rise to Argentina's child welfare movement and spearheaded two foundational conferences, the 1913 First Argentine Congress on the Child and the 1916 First Pan American Congress on the Child (Carlson 1988, 108–13; Guy 2009, 33–4, 68–9).

18 Rey (2021) reproduces the program and platform that appeared in *La Nueva Mujer* in June 1910.

both feminism as well as anti-feminism in Argentina because it was after 1906 that the society ladies of the CNM-A became increasingly uncomfortable with the concept of feminism. She reports that after the International Woman's Suffrage Alliance (IWSA) broke off from the ICW in 1904 to focus on women's political rights, it distributed a questionnaire to ICW affiliates worldwide. The Argentine Council refused to fill it out because it considered women's suffrage unthinkable.

While initially the professional women in the CNM-A and those of the charity and welfare organizations found common cause in elevating the status of women, the tensions around their differing visions of feminism broke out in the open around discussions of organizing a national women's congress. The Universitarias withdrew from the CNM-A in 1908 and founder Cecilia Grierson broke with it in 1910, which left its leadership firmly in the hands of the society ladies (Vignoli 2021). The commemoration of Argentina's Independence Centennial in 1910 thus featured two separate women's congresses. The CNM-A organized the official one, the First Patriotic Congress of Women, with the aim of raising awareness of women's contributions to the nation, largely in those arenas where it was socially acceptable for women to participate.[19] In contrast, the congress organized by the Universitarias focused on women's social, economic and legal inequality and the need for reform (Carlson 1988, 87–106; Vasallo 2000; Barrancos 2007, 132).

Demands at the 1910 International Women's Congress

The Universitarias co-organized the 1910 International Women's Congress with the Centro Socialista Femenino and the Liga Nacional de Mujeres Librepensadoras. Julieta Lanteri served as secretary-general and Cecilia Griersen as the congress chair. The participants included 158 women from Uruguay, Chile, Peru, Paraguay, Italy, Spain and France, with almost two-thirds being Argentine; some 20 organizations also sent representatives (Asociación de Universitarias Argentinas 1911, 25–9). The papers presented covered a broad range of topics with the largest number focusing on some aspect of women's education.[20]

Elvira Rawson (1911) presented her detailed proposal for reform of the marital regime whose objective was for wives to maintain the same rights they had as single women. She proposed that without need for permission from their husbands, wives be free to exercise any profession or industry; manage their own earnings and any assets they brought to marriage; acquire, sell, mortgage and donate the assets that belong to them; and hold bank accounts and join cooperatives and mutual

19 See Cuadro (2018, 169) on the CNM-A conference where many presentations reflected a Christian feminist perspective. Several speakers condemned absolute divorce and women's suffrage.

20 See Lavrin (1995, 29–32) for a fuller discussion of the conference papers. I focus on those presented in the congress' law section relevant to women's civil and political rights.

aid societies. Moreover, she demanded that for a husband to dispose of any community property, he require his wife's consent.[21]

Rawson also considered the situation of formally separated women, demanding that they be able to manage and dispose of all their assets without need for authorization from their estranged husband or a judge, and that mothers have preference in the custody of children. In addition, during the marriage, mothers should exercise patria potestad on the same terms as fathers; unmarried parents should be able to administer their children's property on the same terms as those who were married; and the civil code should allow the investigation of paternity. Finally, she proposed that all women, irrespective of marital status, be eligible to serve as guardians and as witnesses (Rawson 1911, 428–9). At the time, other than the mother, only widowed grandmothers could serve as guardians. The congress approved a resolution in support of all these proposed changes to the 1869 Argentine Civil Code.

Carolina Muzzilli of the Centro Socialist Femenino addressed the importance of instituting absolute divorce, with the possibility of remarriage. The legislature was currently considering such a bill and she urged participants to endorse its approval.[22] After a lengthy discussion, those attending approved a motion to support divorce "as long as it is regulated so that it not be subject to abuse," reflecting a concern that in some countries, it was proving to be to women's disadvantage. Another successful motion justified divorce as a measure that would contribute to the "moral purification of matrimony," because the inability to remarry currently led permanently separated women to live in concubinage with their new partner (Asociación de Universitarias Argentinas 1911, 425).

Four of the conference papers argued in support of women attaining full political rights (Asociación de Universitarias Argentinas 1911, 400–14, 368–78). Among the arguments was that women must have the vote to achieve a fully functioning democracy. Several raised how many women now worked and paid taxes but did not have a voice on state expenditures; moreover, public policies impacted all women. These also referred to the experience of the many US states as well as Australia where women now voted, arguing that such had not caused political disturbances nor resulted in women neglecting their domestic and maternal duties.

The paper by Ana A. de Montalvo on civil and political rights addressed other common arguments against women's suffrage. To those who argued that women did not understand or were not interested in politics, she replied that if currently they were not involved, it was because politics was of no use to them since they did not benefit from being engaged. To those who questioned the use that women

21 The only restriction on a husband's management of gananciales in the 1869 code was that he could not donate immovable assets without his wife's consent or that of a judge; he could sell or mortgage these assets freely. The husband's sale of his wife's assets, however, required her consent or that of a judge (Segovia 1881, arts. 1809, 1254).

22 Argentina instituted obligatory civil marriage in 1888 but civil divorce was contentious. Between 1901 and 1954, the Congress considered multiple bills to institute it (Rébora 1926, vol. 1, 103; Lavrin 1995, 236–41).

would make of the vote, she emphasized that it could not be worse than men's use, acknowledging that only a small minority of men and women were sufficiently prepared to vote wisely. She asked whether "it was just that thousands of intellectual women enjoy fewer rights than the most ignorant and gross man?" (Asociación de Universitarias Argentinas 1911, 411). De Montalvo's proposal that those attending draft a women's suffrage bill to present to the legislature, however, failed to gain support. Her other proposals resulted in the following successful resolution: "The International Women's Congress supports all the different countries of the world dictating laws that would equalize the civil and legal rights of men and women" (Asociación de Universitarias Argentinas 1911, 414).

The Liga Nacional de Mujeres Librepensadoras and the Centro Socialista Femenino presented their respective platforms.[23] Of the Liga's two motions, the congress approved the following: "The International Women's Congress, considering that women are capable of exercising political and civil rights, supports recognition of their right to suffrage" (Asociación de Universitarias Argentinas 1911, 415). The second, more specific motion to name a commission to petition the Argentine legislature to recognize women's political rights failed, demonstrating how many women still considered suffrage to be premature.

Asunción Lavrin (1995, 31) argues that the women at the congress were "prepared to adopt principles but not ready to take practical steps to obtain such goals." She suggests that this was because of the diversity of the women attending and because many of them did not consider suffrage as the most critical issue. This pattern of supporting general principles over recommending specific legislative action also characterized the discussion of divorce. But it did not characterize the discussion of reform of the civil code, where those gathered recommended that the Argentine legislature adopt Rawson's list of proposed reforms, confirming the unanimity that existed around the need to first strengthen women's property and other civil rights. The main conclusion of the congress was that the urgent task was to prepare women for their eventual citizenship through education (Asociación de Universitarias Argentinas1911, 469–79).

The Thinking of Legal Scholars and Legislative Proposals on the Marital Regime

The major treatises on Argentine's civil code show that while legal scholars were well aware of the reforms taking place in Europe, most refrained from making specific recommendations to reform the marital regime. It was often their students who

23 The Centro Socialista Femenina presented an eight-point platform, which besides women's political rights and civil divorce, included four points related to the rights of women workers and two on education. By the time of their intervention, the congress had already approved proposals on suffrage and divorce thus it did not again discuss these topics (Asociación de Universitarias Argentinas 2011, 426–7).

later as legislators developed such proposals. The Congress discussed nine different proposals to strengthen married women's property rights before the approval of the successful 1926 bill. These differed on whether wives should be able to control only their own earnings, or their earnings *and* the assets they brought to marriage or subsequently inherited; how much say they should have over the gananciales, from zero to total control over those generated by them; and the degree of choice offered to couples with respect to the marital regime. They also differed on whether they addressed women's lack of other civil rights, such as patria potestad or their inability to serve as guardians or witnesses.

Of the jurists writing treatises on the civil code, only José Olegario Machado ([1898] 1922, 360) directly addressed the concerns of feminists. He observed that

> it is time that our legislation take into account the intellectual progress of women and liberate them from the perpetual tutelage to which they are subject and reduce potestad marital to that absolutely necessary for the direction of the business of the conjugal society.

He commented favorably on the 1896 German Civil Code that allowed wives to change a prenuptial agreement (termed *convenciones nupciales* by him) at any time, suggesting this reform was worthy of further study. Moreover, he noted that the civil incapacity of married women in Argentina was based on the notion that a household should have only one head to direct and govern the family. Given the progress made in women's education and changing social norms, he envisioned that the day was not far off when women might have equal civil rights (Machado [1898] 1922, 374, 563). Jurist Raymundo M. Salvat (1922) criticized the existing code for offering only one marital regime but did not offer alternatives. His main recommendation was to allow women to be witnesses in civil matters.[24]

When in 1902, Deputy Luis María Drago of the Partido Autonomista Nacional (National Autonomist Party) presented the first relevant bill to Congress, women were just beginning to organize around their rights. He had a long-standing interest in women's economic status in the family, having earlier authored his thesis on this topic for his UBA law degree (Barrancos 2007, 138). Drago was critical of Argentine codifier Dalmacio Vélez Sarsfield's interpretation of Roman law in his 1869 Civil Code that had resulted in the total subordination of women in marriage.[25] He noted how the publication of Mary Wollstonecraft's 1791 book, *A Vindication of the Rights of Woman*, had provoked a fierce debate internationally between advocates of legal equality in marriage and those who believed that the stability of the family required wives' subordination to their husbands. In his view, the result was

24 Some treatises discussed recent legal reforms in Europe but did not even mention those on women's property rights, such as the didactic text by Rodolfo Rivarola (1901).

25 *Diario de Sesiones de la Cámara de Diputados* (DSCD) (1902, vol. 1, 287–91).

that married women in England now had the same property rights as single women, and that most US states had adopted similar legislation. Drago urged Argentine legislators to join this march "toward progress" by reforming its marital regime.

Drago proposed allowing couples prior to marriage to make any arrangement they wished regarding the administration of their property. In the absence of a prenuptial agreement, he maintained the default regime of partial community property with new management rules. Husband and wife were to have almost parallel rights over their own individual property: each would administer the movable and immovable property each brought to marriage; any inheritances subsequently received; the fruits and gains of such property; and the earnings from the administration of children's assets from a prior marriage. Wives were free to manage and dispose of this property without need for anyone's permission and to participate in lawsuits regarding it. The only exception to this parallel treatment favored women: whatever wives earned from their independent activities was their own to keep and excluded from the community property; in contrast, whatever husbands earned formed part of it. The husband remained the administrator of the community property, shared equally at the marriage's end.[26] Diego did not explain why wives should receive this favored treatment although it was likely because he wanted to give special protection to working women.

Among those commenting favorably on the Drago bill was socialist Justa Burgos (Lavrin 1995, 204). In an article in *Nosotras*, she emphasized how it addressed the vulnerability of the growing number of working wives whose husbands appropriated their hard-earned wages because legally they could do so. Drago's innovative proposal, however, never made it out of committee.[27]

Five years later, Alfredo Palacios, the first Socialist Party deputy, presented a bill that he said originated with the Centro Feminista.[28] It was more modest than Drago's bill with respect to property rights since it only focused on the needs of working women. This 1907 bill gave wives the right to work in any profession or industry and full control over their earnings and any assets acquired with such earnings. At the dissolution of the conjugal society, the assets that were under a wife's management formed part of the gananciales, which the spouses and/or their estates divided equally. In effect, Palacios was proposing adopting the concept of reserved property for married women established in the civil code reforms of Germany, Sweden, Norway and Geneva, and awaiting approval in France, among the antecedents he mentioned. The terms were not as favorable to working wives as the

26 Moreau (1919a, 15) and Lavrin (1995, 201) refer to Drago's bill as establishing the separation of property regime; however, he was proposing a mixed regime, one that maintained the concept of community property and its sharing principle while giving wives a special privilege. It was not unlike what Ecuador adopted in 1911.

27 Drago left the congress to become Minister of Foreign Affairs and after he was re-elected in 1914, he re-introduced the same bill. It also did not prosper (DSCD 1914, vol. 4, 840–5).

28 DSCD (1907, vol. 1, 1066–8).

Drago bill although becoming the international standard in community property countries.

Palacios' bill was also broader than Drago's since it addressed several other feminist demands. It proposed allowing wives to join mutual aid societies and cooperatives and to manage savings accounts without need for their husband's authorization. It gave legally separated women the right to fully manage and dispose of their own assets without requiring the permission of a husband or judge, a current limitation. Unmarried parents gained the right to exercise patria potestad over their children on the same terms as those who were married. Further, the bill strengthened the civil rights of all women by allowing them to be witnesses in civil matters and expanding the list of those who could serve as guardians to include aunts or sisters of minors who were single or widowed. This bill also died in the Chamber's commission on codes.[29]

In Elvira Rawson's (1921,75) retelling, after the 1910 International Women's Congress, the Centro Feminista asked Deputy Palacios to present her civil code reform proposal to the Congress. She explained that her group

> gave it to a committee of lawyers for review to then give to Dr. A. Palacios for submission to the Congress. While recognizing the proposal as just, this committee mutilated it, considering it to be too broad, and they suppressed those articles that challenged masculine interests.

This account does not conform to the sequencing of events because after the Women's Congress, Palacios in 1913 and 1915 unsuccessfully reintroduced his same 1907 bill without modification.[30] Since he credits the Centro Feminista for having originated his 1907 bill, it is likely that Rawson confused the dates in the passage above, and that she was referring to the process that resulted in his 1907 bill, for it does resemble a heavily redacted version of Rawson's proposal. Two critical components of her proposal were missing: giving married women full control over the assets they brought to marriage or later inherited (not just those acquired with their earnings) and requiring mutual consent for the disposition of community property.

Following this reasoning, Rawson probably drafted her proposal in late 1906 or early 1907, although she did not present it publicly until the 1910 women's conference. She likely wrote it in dialogue with María Abella's proposal as well as Luis María Drago's 1902 bill, both of which allowed wives to administer the assets they brought to marriage or later inherited although through different mechanisms. That

29 In 1909, deputy Juan Antonio Argerich presented a bill that incorporated Palacios' concerns regarding the property rights of formally separated women and patria potestad and guardianship, in addition to some changes to succession law, which was also unsuccessful (DSCD 1909, vol. 2, 798–9). Argerich had previously presented unsuccessful proposals to make succession law more favorable to surviving spouses (DSCD 1905, vol. 2, 467–8; 1909, vol. 1, 442–3).

30 DSCD (1913, vol. 3, 41; 1915, vol. 1, 657–8).

the lawyers advising Palacios dropped this demand conforms to Rawson's analysis that they "mutilated" her proposal because it "challenged masculine interests," likely viewing it as a more radical demand than working wives managing their own wages and salaries.

The first strengthening of the property rights of wives came about indirectly, through the passage of the 1914 law creating the Caja Nacional de Ahorro Postal (National Post Office Savings Bank), aimed at encouraging the habit of saving among Argentina's working class.[31] Its regulations allowed wives to establish savings accounts in their own names and to make deposits and withdrawals without need for their husbands' authorization.[32] The rationale was that in working-class families, wives were more likely than their husbands to save and to use these savings wisely; thus why should they have to ask permission of someone who was potentially irresponsible (who might drink away their savings) or from whom they were possibly estranged.

Subsequently in 1918, Enrique del Valle Iberlucea, the first Socialist Party senator, presented a comprehensive "Civil Emancipation of Women Bill."[33] In its lengthy justification, he argued that Argentina's civil code did not conform to the country's constitution, which promised equality before the law, nor did it address the needs of a modernizing Argentina. The 1914 national census revealed that women constituted 22% of the labor force, a share almost equal to that in Germany. Argentina, nonetheless, was falling behind "most civilized nations" regarding the legal status of married women as well as in its lack of civil divorce legislation. Drawing on John Stuart Mills and August Bebel, he argued that the so-called "mental inferiority of women is not a product of nature, but of man, who has wished to make her submit to his authority."[34] He linked the development of the feminist movement to the development of industry and the progress of democracy, and noted "the parallel march of free institutions and the civil and political emancipation of women."[35] He also provided a detailed review of the reforms undertaken to date in the United States, Europe and Latin America.[36]

Del Valle proposed giving all women full civil rights, including the right to engage in any occupation and to hold any position or conduct any civil function. Moreover, his bill explicitly abolished the legal incapacity of wives, arguing that if

31 Law 9.527, September 29, 1914. http://mepriv.mecon.gov.ar/Normas/9327.htm.

32 Successful models of postal savings banks in Europe inspired this bill. Socialist deputies played a key role in removing restrictions on married women from the original bill (DSCD, 1914, vol. 1, 828–9 and vol. 4, 783–822).

33 *Diario de Sesiones de la Cámara del Senado* (DSCS) (1918, vol. 1, 38–78). Giordano (2012, 109) reports that del Valle wrote his 1902 doctoral law thesis on the need for women's economic emancipation and absolute divorce.

34 DSCS (1918, vol. 1, 49).

35 DSCS (1918, vol. 1, 53).

36 Specifically, he mentioned the new 1916 Brazilian civil code and the reforms in Costa Rica, El Salvador and Nicaragua, the earliest mention I have found to these Central American antecedents. He did not mention Ecuador's 1911 reform.

women did not have any natural incapacities, there was no reason to subject them to potestad marital or other restrictions. He gave couples complete flexibility to stipulate anything they wished regarding the ownership and management of their property in a prenuptial agreement. Since marriage was a contract, he believed that individuals should be free to determine its content.

With regard to the default regime, Del Valle proposed adopting separation of property during the marriage combined with the shared division of gananciales at its end, similar to the provisions in Costa Rica's 1887 code. Each spouse maintained and managed what they owned prior to marriage as well as whatever else they subsequently acquired, irrespective of source, with the right to freely dispose of their property. Except for those assets brought to marriage or later inherited or so stipulated in a marital contract, when the marriage ended, all other assets of both spouses (the gananciales) constituted community property, pooled and divided between them. This regime is what is now known as deferred community property. For those couples who had already married under the regime of the conjugal society (or who initially opted for it in a prenuptial), wives had the right to opt for separation of property under these new rules at any time simply by declaring this intention in the civil registry.

In his justification, del Valle argued that separation of property was not only the simplest regime and the most just, but it "was the only one that really safeguards women's interests" and "guarantees women's full civil capacity and autonomy."[37] In his view, this was the reason that feminists at the 1900 Paris Congress on Women's Rights favored it. Aware that critics might contend that such a regime would destroy the family, he reviewed studies of the implementation of separation of property in the states of New York and Pennsylvania to show that to the contrary, "women are treated with more consideration by their husbands."[38] In good marriages, he also observed, wives often turned over their assets to their husbands to manage, but this was a voluntary act and one that they could rescind at any time. Del Valle did not mention the shortcoming of this regime as it developed in the United States and England that at the end of the marriage, there was no community property to divide. However, it was implicit in his explanation as to why he adopted the Costa Rican variant – to protect housewives who were not employed nor owned assets – so that when the marriage dissolved, they receive half of the gananciales.

Del Valle also proposed that, irrespective of the marital regime, certain property automatically constitute the "reserved patrimony" of married women. Besides not requiring their husband's permission to work, wives had the free administration and disposition of the earnings and assets acquired through their own effort and

37 DSCS (1918, vol. 1, 62, 68). In addition, Del Valle considered the regime of full community property as an alternative regime likely to favor women but only in the case that it provide for joint administration of the community property by husband and wife.

38 DSCS (1918, vol. 1, 68).

could participate in lawsuits related to these activities. He also considered the case of family enterprises where the wife and husband worked together and proposed that the wife was entitled to half of the profits as her reserved patrimony. Drawing on the German Civil Code, he also included as part of this reserved patrimony a woman's personal effects and work instruments; any asset she might have reserved in a prenuptial agreement; an inheritance that stipulated her sole management; and any compensations resulting from lawsuits or insurance related to her economic activities. Neither spouse was responsible for any debts the other might incur through their separate management.

For those who chose (or maintained) the partial community property regime, del Valle proposed a change in its rules that had been part of Elvira Rawson's 1910 proposal: a husband would be unable to mortgage or sell the community property without his wife's consent. Moreover, under this or the mixed default regime, he incorporated the idea from Drago's 1902 proposal that included the assets acquired via the husband's earnings in the community property but not those generated through women's reserved property, thus giving favored treatment to a wife's wages and salaries. In the case of judicial separation, the rules of the separation of property regime were automatically to apply, with a woman being able to exercise all civil acts without need for authorization from her husband or a judge. Other measures in the del Valle bill equalized the position of mothers and fathers with respect to patria potestad, whether the children were legitimate or natural. In contrast to previous bills, del Valle included a list of the specific changes required to the relevant articles of the civil code.

The Debate over the 1918 del Valle Bill

For the first time, a married women's property rights bill generated broad public discussion and vigorous lobbying efforts by women. The day prior to presenting his bill to the Senate, del Valle gave a major address at the Museo Social Argentino where he laid out the rationale for his reform.[39] This institution then sponsored two public forums where distinguished legal scholars commented on the bill, including five UBA civil law professors, and later published this discussion.[40] Their comments foreshadowed the content of the eventually successful 1926 bill that strengthened married women's property rights.

These scholars recognized the need for some reform of the marital regime to meet current social trends, principally, women's growing labor force participation. But apart from professor Enrique Jorge, most considered the del Valle bill to be too

39 This speech (del Valle 1918) was identical to the justification that he subsequently presented on the Senate floor.

40 See Boletín Mensual (1918, 530–73). The *Revista Argentina de Ciencias Políticas* also reproduced del Valle's lengthy justification over four issues during 1918, and published articles both in support and against the bill.

extreme, that it went too far, too fast and preferred a more partial and gradual approach. The most controversial points were granting women equivalent civil rights to those of men and establishing separation of property as the norm during marriage even though it maintained community property at its end.

Professors Esteban Lamadrid and Hector Lafaille opposed giving women equivalent civil rights, not because they were inferior but because of their physical and psychological differences with men. Lafaille argued that women were ideally suited to managing the home because of their maternal role. It was due to this "natural" sexual division of labor and the level and type of education they received that women were incompetent to act in the public sphere. In his view, prior to even thinking about equal rights required improving their education. Also, the civil code needed to include safeguards to ensure the stability of the family. He observed that the German code had maintained such safeguards when it strengthened married women's property rights. For example, while wives could manage their own earnings, they needed their husbands' consent to work outside the home, for such independent activities could not come at the cost of the well-being of the children or a well-maintained home. The collective interests of the family, in his opinion, were more important to society than individual interests.

Both Lamadrid and Lafaille supported maintaining the traditional conjugal society as the default, arguing that it promoted the aims of marriage better than other regimes since it assured a coincidence of interests and affections between spouses. For Lamadrid, marriage was not a contract, but rather an institution designed to promote the collective interests of the family. He opposed even offering the separation of property as an option in a prenuptial agreement. Jorge and jurist Raymundo Salvat, on the other hand, favored offering this option in the name of individual freedom. While Lafaille was open to offering separation of property as an option, he opposed allowing couples to change regimes during the marriage, as in del Valle's proposal. Salvat considered such flexibility an eventual possibility but currently premature since it was not clear that many couples would opt for separation of property. Only professor Alfredo Colmo voiced support for the idea of requiring mutual consent for husbands to dispose of community property, the demand in Elvira Rawson's earlier proposal.

There was consensus on the need to establish something like the German or French mechanism of reserved property for married women, so that wives who worked outside the home be able to manage their own income and the assets so acquired. They rejected Del Valle's idea that these gananciales should receive special treatment at the end of the marriage (remaining as the wife's individual property) in favor of these forming part of the community property. Several referred to how the 1907 Palacios bill had been premature in proposing reserved property, but that the substantial number of working women in Argentina now justified it. Colmo and Juan A. Figueroa also favored del Valle's proposal to recognize the full legal capacity of single women and of those legally separated from their husbands.

These legal scholars also debated the wisdom of undertaking partial reforms of the civil code at this time. Figueroa argued that the code required a complete updating and that any reform needed to maintain its internal cohesion. He hoped that the government would soon appoint a commission of legal scholars to undertake this work, a recommendation seconded by Lamadrid. Only Jorge recommended approval of the del Valle bill with modest modifications.

Alicia Moreau wrote an enthusiastic review of the del Valle bill in *Humanidad Nueva*, the periodical she edited, which she later published as a booklet.[41] She considered del Valle's justification for the bill "a brilliant defense of the rights of women and a complete and profound study of the question" (Moreau 1919a, 16). She reported that he was aware that his proposed default regime (deferred community property) departed drastically from customary practice and he fully expected most couples to choose the traditional conjugal society. This is why he built important safeguards so that under its new rules, marriage was as equitable as possible, with wives having greater economic independence: they no longer required their husband's permission to engage in a trade or profession; they were automatically entitled to manage and dispose of reserved property from such work and as partners in joint family enterprises; the consent of both spouses was required to pawn, mortgage or sell community property; and a wife could revoke the mandate she gave her husband for him to manage her property at any time, instituting the separation of property under its new, more favorable rules. Moreau also foresaw that it was unlikely that the Congress would approve such an ambitious bill and planned to initiate a movement in its support in the hopes that it would lead to at least some progress.

The Senate commission on codes subsequently recommended the del Valle bill for debate, albeit with important modifications.[42] It deleted the phrase that abolished married women's legal incapacity across the board; instead, their legal capacity was to be determined by the marital regime. It rejected the separation of property regime as the default but maintained it as an option couples could specify in a prenuptial agreement; under this option, wives would have full legal capacity. The provision regarding the reserved property of married women remained intact except that these assets were to form part of the gananciales pooled at the end of the marriage, eliminating del Valle's special treatment. The Senate, nonetheless, never scheduled the bill for discussion.

The Push for Civil *and* Political Rights

Up through World War I, most Argentine feminists assumed that attaining women's civil rights should come prior to efforts to obtain political rights. When the del Valle bill stalled in Congress, many began to think that without the vote, they

41 Dreier (1920, 241–56), a North American feminist who spent six months in Argentina, included a translation of parts of Moreau's 1918 *Humanidad Nueva* article.

42 DSCS (1920, vol. 1, 561–3); Font (1921, 227–31).

might never attain women's civil equality with men. Thus several new feminist organizations formed with the dual objective of attaining both women's civil and political rights, encouraged by how women were attaining suffrage in a growing number of countries (Moreau [1919b] 2004).[43] Irrespective of their goal of equal rights, feminists did not refrain from using maternalist arguments in making their case, how enhanced civil and political rights would make them better wives and mothers.

The same pioneering feminists of the previous decade led most of the new post-World War I organizations that formed to lobby for women's rights: Alicia Moreau founded the Unión Feminista Nacional (UFN, National Feminist Union); Elvira Rawson, the Asociación Pro-Derechos de la Mujer (Women's Rights Association); and Julieta Lanteri, the Partido Feminista Nacional (PFN, National Feminist Party) (Carlson 1988; Lavrin 1995, 269–70). The growing number of women entering universities assisted this organizational effort. While in 1915, women represented less than 3% of all graduates, their share increased steadily after a 1918 university reform (Suárez 2012, 161, 164).

One of the founding principles of the UFN was support for all efforts to change laws "that place women in an inferior position to men" (Moreau 1919a, 25).[44] Its immediate aim in 1918 was to lobby for the del Valle bill (Rawson 1921). To disseminate its content more broadly, the first issue of its periodical, *Nuestra Causa, revista mensual feminista*, reproduced this hefty bill in its entirety.[45] It organized a petition drive in its support that gathered some 7,000 signatures (Lavrin 1995, 272).

Up until then, Moreau and those affiliated with the Socialist Women's Center had held the view that women should attain the vote in phases, beginning at the municipal level (Valobra 2012). She decided to pursue full suffrage after visiting the United States to attend two conferences in 1919, a trip that took place shortly after the US Congress approved women's suffrage. While there, she had the opportunity to meet Carrie Chapman Catt, the president of NAWSA who led that struggle (Nari 2000, 193). Catt was also president of the IWSA and she invited UFN to join, and

43 Indicative of the change was that in the 1911 and 1912 debates around reform of the electoral law to institute universal male suffrage the issue of whether women should be citizens and exercise suffrage never even came up. The electoral registry was to be based on enrolment for military service and only men were subject to compulsory military service; see Giordano (2013, 47–9).

44 The UFN brought together women from the Centro Socialista Femenino, the Agrupación Femenina Socialista (Socialist Women's Association) and a few independent CNM-A members (Henault 2002, 69). In late 1918, it had 120 members (Dreier 1920, 232). Although she ran in socialist circles, Moreau did not join the Socialist Party until the early 1920s, around the time she married its founder, Juan B. Justo, who had widowed.

45 Shown in Gallo (2004, 119), who provides a complete index of the articles published in this journal during its two-year run. The index and articles reproduced in her book also demonstrate how almost all the prominent Argentine women intellectuals of this period contributed to it, as did leading feminists from other countries.

FIGURE 3.2 Argentine Physician Elvira Rawson de Dellepiane (1867–1954, Front Row, Fourth from Left) and Other Founders of the Asociación Pro-Derechos de la Mujer, 1919. By Baldisserotto.

Source: Courtesy of Special Collections, Hesburgh Libraries, University of Notre Dame.

in 1920, the UFN became IWSA's second Latin American affiliate.[46] As discussed subsequently, the pages of *Nuestra Causa* increasingly focused on the need for women to attain political rights.

Elvira Rawson's Women's Rights Association (Figure 3.2), founded in early 1919, was a non-partisan organization of men and women formed to lobby for women's civil, economic and political rights (Rawson 1921, 76). Among its notable members were deputies Alfredo Palacios (a socialist) and Rogelio Araya (a radical) and writer Alfonsina Storni.[47] Its top priority was attaining women's full civil rights:

> ...removing from the codes and laws any articles that establish differences between men and women that are prejudicial to them, such as those that consider

46 *Nuestra Causa*, 1920, in Gallo (2004, 37). In 1922, Moreau was the official Argentine delegate to the First Pan American Women's Congress hosted by the National League of Women Voters in Baltimore. Moreau and her collaborators initiated the idea of holding a regional women's conference and in Catt's correspondence with Moreau, she apologized for the League preempting their efforts. Catt to Moreau letters of September 13, 1920, and September 8, 1921, Carrie Chapman Catt Papers, Box 4, Correspondence: Alicia Moreau; also see Marino (2019, 22–5).

47 Among the founding members depicted in Figure 3.2 are, front row, far left, Emma Day and far right, Adelia di Carlo, and top row center, Rogelio Araya. Its membership included many Universitarias and some members of the CNM-A and of the Radical Party (Nari 2000, 193).

> women to be relatively incapable, so that they be able to exercise all the rights corresponding to conscientious and responsible beings.
>
> *(Rawson 1921, 78)*

Moreover, it lobbied for specific reforms, such as the addition of mutual consent for a husband to alienate community property because the exclusion of wives from its management led to their total dependence and was prejudicial to the well-being of the family. In Rawson's view, it was all too easy for a husband to dissipate a family's fortunes, be it through drinking, gambling or other vices, without the wife even learning of this until it was too late to ask for the only redress the civil code provided – to ask for the separation of property due to his poor mismanagement – since there was no property left to protect. Hence, the reiteration of the demand she had made in her 1910 proposal to the Women's Congress.

The Association's platform also included women's full political rights; appointment of women as school administrators and justices; equal pay for equal work; protection of maternity and illegitimate children and the right to investigate paternity; and abolition of regulated brothels (Rawson 1921, 78–9). To garner support, Rawson sent the platform to all the political parties and numerous civic organizations and newspapers, asking for endorsements. In her cover letter, she stressed how it called for nothing less than the civil, economic and political rights that women had attained in "the most culturally advanced countries of Europe and North America" (Rawson 1921, 83).[48]

Julieta Lanteri founded the National Feminist Party in 1919 to support her candidacy for the Chamber of Deputies. She was able to run for office through a rather unusual process. Born in Italy, as a child she immigrated to Argentina with her family, completed a medical degree and applied for citizenship after she learned it was necessary to obtain the university lectureship that she sought. While a judge approved her application for naturalization, a federal prosecutor took issue with her case, arguing that women could not become citizens because they did not have political rights (Bellotta 2001, 86–90; Barrancos 2002, 52–3). Lanteri appealed, aided by María Angélica Barrera, Argentina's first woman lawyer.[49] A federal panel of judges finally ruled in her favor, declaring her a citizen with the corresponding rights and duties.

48 Representatives of five political parties answered her letter, with only two endorsing it, the Socialist Party and the Partido Unitario (Unitary Party). The others, including Rawson's UCR, replied that while they were sympathetic to its ideals, the platform required further study (in Font 1921, 84–7).

49 Barrera completed her law degree at the National University of La Plata in 1909 and participated in the 1910 International Women's Congress (Corva and Gómez 2021).

Lanteri thus became the first woman to vote in Argentina, participating in the 1911 Buenos Aires municipal elections. She also attempted to register to vote in national elections but was unsuccessful because being on the voters' list required having registered for military service. Studying the 1911–1912 electoral laws, she observed that while registering to vote required military service, being a candidate for office did not. Thus, Lanteri founded the PFN to launch her candidacy in the 1919 national elections (Bellotta 2001, 90–4, 114–9; Barrancos 2002, 52–3).

The top item on the PFN's platform was attaining women's political and civil rights on the same terms as men.[50] Other demands included instituting absolute divorce, legal equality between legitimate and illegitimate children, protective legislation for women, equal wages for equal work and a host of other educational and public health reforms. The UFN and the Women's Rights Association supported her campaign. Lanteri received only a small number of votes, 1,730, although she was pleased the results demonstrated that a woman could attract the votes of more than a handful of men (Bellotta 2001, 134–42).[51]

For the 1920 elections, the UFN decided to stage a mock election where women could vote and it formed a broad-based Comité Pro-Sufragio Femenino (Committee for Women's Suffrage) for this purpose. Inspired by similar events in France, the idea was to generate enthusiasm among women in attaining the vote since many were indifferent; some 4,000 women participated.[52] This committee then replicated this event for the Buenos Aires municipal council elections that followed and even more women participated, almost 6,000. The press gave much attention, both favorable and unfavorable, to these mock elections. Lanteri continued to run unsuccessfully as the PFN's candidate for deputy in every federal election until 1930 as well as in several more municipal elections before her inopportune death (Bellotta 2001, 157–60, 179–205; Barrancos 2002).

Feminists honed their arguments for political rights and what women might do with the vote in the pages of *Nuestra Causa*. Elvira Rawson ([1919] 2004), for example, carefully explained that by demanding equal civil and political rights, women were not seeking to rival men nor where they planning to forget their duties as wives and mothers. As María Abella ([1919] 2004, 99) put it, they were not seeking

> the absurdity of becoming like men, nor to abandon the home, but to be a worthy companion of today's man, intelligent and free, a mother capable of educating her children well, in sum, women at the level of progress that the nation merits.

50 Dreier (1920, 230–1) reproduced the PFN platform and described in detail Lanteri' s first campaign.

51 Lanteri then tried to register for military service unsuccessfully and filed a lawsuit; it took the Supreme Court ten years to rule against her (Bellotta 2001, 142–9).

52 There are different interpretations of this mock event, primarily on whether Moreau, Rawson and Lanteri were candidates as suggested by Carlson (1988, 158–62) and Nari (2000). The articles in *Nuestra Causa*, reproduced in Gallo (2004, 36–7; 112–4), show that women voted separately and unofficially for the same candidates as male voters.

Julieta Lanteri ([1919] 2004, 28–9), after noting that women were obtaining the vote in a growing number of countries and that Argentina "was on the path to realizing that aspiration," expected that once women could vote, they would prioritize both their own and their children's needs; that they would undo the "inhumane laws" that women were subject to, including the double moral standard; and that they would work for a more just distribution of wealth as well as world peace.[53]

As these quotes illustrate, even the most ardent feminists, such as Lanteri and Abello, did not hesitate to appeal to women based on sexual differences, their biologically and socially defined role as mothers. As Marcela Nari (2000, 199) argues, feminists accepted maternity as key to their femininity and the basis for what united them as women. But they politicized maternity as a public issue, reformulating it as a social function that required both recognition and protection by the State, "… to construct a more just society where men and women would continue to be different but under equal conditions," that is, with equal civil, social and political rights (Nari 2000, 200).[54]

In the pages of *Nuestra Causa*, feminists now argued that women needed suffrage if they were ever to secure equal civil rights:

> How can we tolerate any longer a civil code that maintains the incapacity of women, containing dispositions that are repugnant to our culture and customs, which subordinates a wife under her husband's tutelage, even for her to exercise a profession or administer her own assets?

They highlighted how "daily life imposes the same obligations on women as men," with an increasing share of women in the labor force, and since they were not exempt from taxes nor responsibilities, "it is just that they achieve their complete civil and political emancipation."[55]

In elite circles, nonetheless, there was greater consensus around the need to strengthen women's civil rights than to cede them political rights. This is evident in the responses to a questionnaire distributed in 1916 by journalist Miguel Font to over 60 public figures, both men and women. Among those who responded, there was nearly unanimous support for strengthening women's civil rights. Only 22 respondents favored granting women suffrage, while 36 opposed it, showing that the idea was gaining traction but not generally accepted (Font 1921). In this context, the push to enhance women's civil rights was successful decades before the attainment of women's political rights.

53 Also see the 1921 editorial in *Nuestra Causa*, in Gallo (2004, 42–3).

54 Nari (2004) provides a detailed analysis of the interactions between feminists and the medical establishment, the eugenics movement, organized labor and state concerns, which resulted in greater state involvement in what were previously viewed as family issues and in the adoption of some maternalist policies favoring wage-working women. She and Valobra (2024, 129) both provide a thorough discussion of the nuances in the maternalist argument.

55 "A las mujeres de la República Argentina," editorial in *Nuestra Causa*, 1920, in Gallo (2004, 38–9).

Converging on the 1926 Law on Women's Civil Rights

Feminists' demands for both civil and political rights may have been the factor that turned the tide in favor of strengthening married women's property rights in the legislature because expanding women's civil rights was less threatening than suffrage. McCammon, Arch and Bergner (2014) term this a "radical demand effect," which they observed at play in the debates in the United States decades earlier. When faced with both demands, legislators coalesced around enacting the less radical feminist demand. Between 1919 and 1924, deputies of the ruling Radical Party, the UCR, filed four separate bills to strengthen women's property rights and the first two bills on women's suffrage; socialist senators introduced a more modest proposal to reform the marital regime than the earlier del Valle bill.[56] The latter served as the model for the 1926 Law on Women's Civil Rights that ended up being a compromise between those who favored women's equal rights and those determined to preserve the male-headed household.

Elvira Rawson's Women's Rights Association endorsed two of the bills introduced by UCR deputies, those of Rogelio Araya and Herminio Quirós. The 1919 Araya bill was like the earlier Palacios bill, focusing primarily on giving wives control over their own earnings while augmenting a few other civil rights, such as allowing women to be witnesses.[57] The bill also allowed wives to join mutual societies and cooperatives and to manage their own savings accounts without authorization of their husbands, features also included in other UCR-sponsored bills. While Rawson ([1919] 2004) praised this bill, she noted that it fell short since it did not allow wives to manage their own assets or have a say in the management of the community property.[58]

Rawson's association was more enthusiastic about Quirós' 1922 bill, leading a petition campaign on its behalf.[59] This bill recognized men and women's equal

56 Bravo (1927) reproduced all the married women's property rights bills presented up through enactment of the 1926 law. He also discussed the reforms undertaken already in 16 countries worldwide, including Ecuador.

57 DSCD (1919, vol. 2, 841–2).

58 Her association did not endorse the bill submitted by Deputy Carlos F. Melo in 1919 that gave couples complete flexibility in marital contracts before or after marriage to determine the management of their own property. This was probably because it maintained the conjugal society as the default and required the husband's permission for a wife to manage her assets; it did incorporate mutual consent for either spouse to alienate gananciales (DSCD 1919, vol. 4, 676–82). There is also no record of her association supporting UCR Deputy Leopoldo Bard's 1924 bill, which established the full legal capacity of married women, made it a requirement when couples married to choose either separation of property or the conjugal society, and provided for women's reserved property under either option. However, if married under the conjugal society wives had to declare their intention to manage their own assets, which is why Rawson probably found it objectionable (DSCD 1924, vol. 5, 494–596).

59 DSCD (1922, vol. 4, 458).

civil rights and explicitly established the full legal capacity of married women.[60] Under the default regime of partial community property, husbands or wives could each manage and dispose of their own assets without need for permission while requiring mutual consent to sell or mortgage the gananciales. It thus encompassed much of Rawson's 1910 proposal. In addition, the Quirós bill allowed couples to make marital contracts either before or after marriage, thus they could adopt the separation of property regime at any time. Notably, this bill also received the support of the CNM-A, demonstrating that even more conservative, upper-class women thought it was time for women to attain equal civil rights.[61]

Hoping to achieve consensus, in 1924, socialist senators Mario Bravo and Juan Justo submitted a less ambitious bill than those of the Radical deputies.[62] It did not give wives full legal capacity nor offer the option of the separation of property regime or flexibility with respect to marital contracts. Rather, it focused on giving wives the right to manage and dispose of their own assets and earnings; that is, to give them equivalent property rights to single women. Given the consensus in favor of strengthening the property rights of wives, the Congress appointed a bicameral, multiparty commission to reconcile the various bills, with Senator Bravo serving as chair and conservative Deputy Angel Sánchez Elías as secretary. The commission focused its deliberations on the 1924 Bravo-Justo bill since it presented the simplest formulation of what they wanted to achieve. The commission presented its consensus bill to the Senate in August 1925, which approved it the same day.[63]

During 1925 and 1926, organized women conducted an intensive campaign to press the Chamber to approve the Senate's bill (Sieben 2012). The CNM-A and the Socialist Women's Center sponsored separate lecture series on the reform, demonstrating its broad support across class, religious and ideological divides, events that garnered much press attention. In addition, the influential Colegio de Abogados (Bar Association) of Buenos Aires endorsed the Senate's bill and it had the support of the UCR government of President Marcelo Torcuato de Alvear. When the Chamber finally began its discussion in August 1926, Minister of Justice Antonio Sagarna urged its passing, arguing that such a reform was long overdue and that "the legal situation of Argentine women was much inferior to her economic, educational and social condition."[64]

Over the four days of general discussion, with women packing the gallery, supporters of the bill reiterated the arguments for expanding the property rights of married women. Deputies stressed how women in the most advanced countries

60 DSCD (1922, vol. 2, 8–9). At this same time, Quirós submitted another bill establishing the legal equality among all children irrespective of the conditions of their birth and making the state responsible for the investigation of paternity (DSCD 1922, vol. 2, 10–14). He resubmitted his property rights bill in 1924 (vol. 3, 460).

61 DSCD (1924 vol. 2, 590).

62 DSCS (1924, vol. 1, 750–7).

63 DSCS (1925, vol. 2, 457–66 and appendix, 473–80).

64 DSCD (1926, 848–9).

had full civil and political rights, and that such were necessary for Argentina's development. Also emphasized was that this bill had been 20 years in the making; that it drew on previous proposals by conservatives, socialists and radicals; and that representatives of all three major parties had participated in the commission that drafted the Senate-approved bill. They made repeated references to the petition circulated by the Women's Rights Association and the lecture series hosted by the CNM-A and the Socialist Women's Center.

Various legislators brought up how they considered strengthening women's property rights a precondition for their attaining political rights. Socialist Deputy Enrique Dickmann remarked, for example, regarding women's suffrage, "we know that we are not ready for this last and great reform, but the law of women's civil rights prepares them. It is the crucial link for Argentine women to gain political rights."[65]

The strongest opposition to the bill came from some of the UCR's more conservative members.[66] Deputies Jorge Ferri and Hector Bergalli argued that the bill did not speak to a real need and was too broad, too advanced and would change the civil code too much. They mentioned how President Alvear had just appointed a special commission of jurists to revise the code and urged the Chamber to reject the bill or at least send it back to committee and await its recommendations. Other Radicals were ready to support the bill but proposed a variety of amendments, some that strengthened women's rights or improved technical aspects of the bill, while others diluted its intent, reducing wives' potential autonomy.

The Senate-approved bill gave single, separated and widowed adult women the same civil capacity as men. Since it was not clear if this included such functions as being a guardian or a witness, to leave no doubt, the deputies amended this article to include "civil functions" but without specifying them. They then approved another amendment that spelt out that wives could be guardians, executors and witnesses, and could accept donations without need for their husbands' authorization. These amendments thus strengthened the civil rights of all women.

The main point of contention regarding married women's property rights was whether wives should be able to both manage and dispose of their individual property without their husband's authorization. The Senate-approved bill allowed women to sell or mortgage this property (*a título oneroso*) but not donate it. Radical Deputy Guillermo R. Fonrouge proposed an amendment deleting this restriction, so that women would be able to "freely dispose" of their assets, giving them the greatest economic autonomy. Deputy Francisco E. Correa, of the Partido Demócrata Progresista (Democratic Progressive Party), on the other hand, wanted to delete a wife's ability to dispose of her own property altogether, although maintain her right to manage it. He argued that if a wife could sell her property without her husband's consent this would reduce the capital of the conjugal society and

65 DSCD (1926, 58).

66 See Sieben (2012) on the divisions among Radicals at this time and the political alignments in the legislature.

undermine potestad marital. Voting on the amendment word-by-word, the deputies approved maintaining the wife's right "to dispose" of her own assets but the addition of "freely" failed. This discussion revealed the schism over how far members were willing to go in granting married women greater economicautonomy.[67]

Deputy Correa then introduced a change that inverted the logic of the Senate's bill. Implicit in that bill was that if a wife did not want to manage her own assets, she could always give her husband a special mandate to do so. Correa's amendment proposed doing the inverse, for the law to assume that the husband had a mandate to administer his wife's assets unless she declared her intention to manage and dispose of her own assets in a special registry. In other words, the default was similar to the original 1869 code: husbands were the administrators of their wives' assets and of the community property although a wife could choose to manage her individual's assets herself. Socialist Deputy Antonio de Tomaso argued against this measure since it would reduce the scope of the reform, in practice maintaining the status quo. In Correa's view, this was exactly the point: the amendment would facilitate the transition to new rules and avoid complications, precisely because most couples would continue with traditional practice.

Even the staunchest supporters of the reform, such as Hector González Iramain, a socialist deputy on the bicameral commission, did not expect many women to want to manage their own assets. Hoping to allay the fears of those opposed to the bill, he had earlier stressed that even in the United States and England, most wives (he claimed 90%) turned over their assets to their husband's management. According to him, the point of the original wording was to give women a choice; if they wanted their husbands to manage their assets, this would happen by consent and not "by the hateful imposition of a law."[68] Nonetheless, the Chamber approved the unfortunate Correa amendment without much further discussion.

The amended bill then returned to the Senate where Senator Bravo urged its approval, arguing that the Chamber had not modified its substance unduly; the Senate approved the bill that same day.[69] The Law on Women's Civil Rights was thus a compromise between those who wanted to give married women equal civil rights and those who wanted to guarantee the stability of patriarchal, male-headed households. While Law 11.357 greatly reduced a wife's relative incapacity, it did not eliminate it. Article 3(2) laid out explicitly what she could do without permission of her husband or a judge: be a guardian, executor of an estate and a witness; participate in suits regarding her own person or property; accept a donation or an assessed inheritance; join civil or commercial associations and cooperatives; and participate in any profession, employment or trade.

67 DSCD (1926, 425–38).
68 DSCD (1926, 839–46).
69 DSCS (1926, September 14, 639–49); "Ley sobre los Derechos Civiles de la Mujer," Law 11.357, *Boletín Oficial*, September 23, 1926, 978–9.

The law maintained partial community property as the only marital regime. The main advance with respect to the economic autonomy of wives was that in this regime, they could now exercise a profession or occupation without need for their husband's permission and administer and dispose of their own earnings and any assets acquired with these earnings.[70] They could also manage and sell the assets that they brought to marriage or later inherited although only if they previously registered their intention to do so.[71] At the end of the marriage, the gananciales under a woman's control were pooled with those of the husband and divided equally between them and/or their estates.

Other notable components of this law included wives gaining the right to manage their husbands' assets as well as the gananciales in certain circumstances, such as his being incarcerated. In the husband's absence, mothers continued to automatically assume patria potestad over their children. What changed was that if a widow remarried, she now continued to manage her minor children's patrimony independently, with the gains on such assets accruing to her alone, as was the case for widowers. Parents of natural children also obtained it under the same conditions as those of legitimate children.

As Alicia Moreau (1919a) had anticipated, the final law did not go as far as organized women would have liked, requiring a compromise on important issues. It maintained potestad marital over the person of the wife as well as over the property she brought to marriage or subsequently inherited if she did not go out her way to register these assets to manage them directly. Husbands continued to be free to do almost anything they wanted with the community property, although wives who earned an independent income now managed some of the gananciales – those resulting from their reserved property. As Senator Bravo (1927, 179) explained, compromise was necessary since he was afraid of "losing the good by wanting the best."

Carlson (1988) and Lavrin (1995) concur that one of the reasons that the Congress finally passed the 1926 law was that its more conservative members considered this bill the lesser evil compared to the idea of granting women suffrage. In other words, a radical demand effect resulted from organized women pursuing both civil and political rights in favor of the less radical demand. Conservatives were willing to accommodate piecemeal reforms to meet the changing role of women in Argentina's modernizing economy, particularly the needs of working-class women; hence, the greatest consensus was around granting those who were income-earners full control over their own earnings. The assets of middle- and upper-class women in traditional families were another matter. In subsequent decades, rather than pressing to deepen this reform, the energy of the feminist movement focused on the defense of their newly won rights and attaining suffrage.

70 The sales receipt was to note if a woman purchased the asset with her own earnings.

71 If a wife managed these assets separately, the husband was not responsible for the wife's debts, and vice versa.

Backlash: Total Reform of the Civil Code?

Feminists were unable to savor their newly won civil rights for long before some of these came under attack. Legal scholars had been calling for a complete revision of the 1869 Civil Code and in July 1926, President Alvear had appointed a commission to undertake its thorough revision. While the Congress never approved the proposed new code, partly because of the opposition of feminists, the commission's draft of the volume on family law (Argentina 1936) is worth examining for what it reveals about the thinking of eminent legal scholars on married women's rights.

The members of the Civil Code Revisory Commission consisted of 12 lawyers, with the president of the Supreme Court, Roberto Repetto, serving as chair (Argentina 1936, xii). Among its members were four civil law professors from each of the main faculties of law, and some of their opinions on women's civil rights were already well known. UBA professor Hector Lafaille had been among those opposed to the 1918 del Valle bill. Juan Carlos Rébora (1927, 1929) of the University of La Plata also favored incremental reform but was more progressive; as dean of its law faculty, he had admitted its first woman (Corva and Gómez 2021). Juan Antonio Bibiloni, the representative of the prestigious Academia de Abogados (Academy of Legal Scholars), assumed the drafting of the initial text. Between 1927 and 1933, as he finished writing each volume, commission members reviewed them and he revised them.[72] Before his death in 1933, he concluded revising only two volumes, including the one on family law, published posthumously (Bibiloni 1939). Jurist Lafaille and Gastón Federico Tobal completed the revisions and in October 1936, submitted the final draft to the government (Argentina 1936, xvi–xxii).

When feminists learned that the proposed civil code would reverse some of their newly won rights, they formed the Unión Argentina de Mujeres (UAM, Argentine Union of Women) in March 1936 to defend these (Giordano 2012, 157–9). Well-known writer Victoria Ocampo served as its first president with philanthropist Ana Rosa Schleiper de Martínez Guerrero and writers Susana Larguía and María Rosa Oliver playing important roles. Its membership included veteran feminists Elvira Rawson and Alicia Moreau as well as Carmela Horne de Burmeister, a suffragist leader of the 1930s. The UAM brought together communist, socialist and radical women as well as independents in what was a typical Popular Front feminist organization of the mid-1930s, one that worked in support of women's rights as well as anti-fascism and the defense of democracy and world peace (Marino 2019, 145–7).

Overall, the proposed new code represented an attempt to modernize potestad marital by emphasizing the mutual rights and responsibilities of husbands and wives, while maintaining its essence – the supremacy of the husband as household head – and anchoring it in the gender division of labor. The proposal emphasized the reciprocal obligations of spouses: they owed each other fidelity, protection and

72 The initial scheme included seven volumes, with all aspects relevant to family law brought together in volume 5. Bibiloni (1939) contains both his first draft and the second, revised draft of this volume and the General Section. By the Bibiloni draft, I am referring to this second draft.

assistance and a commitment to live together. The husband retained his traditional right to decide on the couple's residency and responsibility to maintain the household. An innovation was its recognition of the wife's right to advise her husband and "to attend the home"; that is, the code made women explicitly responsible for domestic and caring labor (Argentina 1936, art. 361). Thus, each spouse had reciprocal responsibilities built around the gender division of labor.

The most controversial change proposed by the Commission was the abrogation of article 3(2) of the 1926 Law on Women's Civil Rights, which allowed wives to conduct numerous activities without need for a husband's permission. Instead, the proposed code required mutual consent for wives to seek employment, to join a civil or commercial association, to receive or reject a donation or inheritance, or to donate any of the assets that she administered (Argentina 1936, art. 365). The UAM viewed mutual consent for such activities as an unjustified regression in women's rights since it amounted to once again requiring a husband's permission.[73] It would only create unnecessary obstacles and disincentives and, moreover, generate discord in the family. Instead, they argued for improvements in the 1926 so that wives attain fully equal rights.

In its final report, the commission explained that it had striven to establish reciprocal rights and obligations, but that "the cohesion of the family" required it to give husbands primacy in determining household residence and in deciding whether wives could work for remuneration (Argentina 1936, 45). They drew on Bibiloni's (1939) reasoning, who justified the need for a husband's permission for a wife to work as one derived from the marital contract, not women's civil capacity. Given women's responsibility for domestic work and childcare, he found it incomprehensible that women abandon these tasks for paid work unless the husband concurred it was in the family's best interest. In his words, "her civil capacity is not at play; she freely accepted being a wife, becoming a mother" (Bibiloni 1939, 230).

The commission returned to the language of the country's 1869 code, which assumed that if a woman worked, she had her husband's approval. However, rather than allowing the husband to revoke this implicit permission at any time without cause, if a husband opposed his wife's employment, he could ask a judge to settle the dispute (Argentina 1936, art. 366). Besides unjustly reversing the 1926 law, the UAM thought this procedure would be time consuming and costly.

The draft code maintained partial community property as the only marital regime but it expanded what couples could do in a prenuptial agreement by allowing wives to retain *all* their assets, not just some, to manage themselves, with the gananciales accruing to the conjugal society (Argentina 1936, art. 399). It also maintained two central features of the 1926 law, a wife's management of her earnings from separate

73 "Merecemos las mujeres argentinas este agravio? Proyecto absurdo de Reforma del Código Civil," a pamphlet published by UAM in 1937. In an undated flyer, "Los derechos civiles de la mujer," it compared the wording of the 1926 law to the articles it found objectionable in the proposed new code. In Doris Stevens Papers, Series V. IACW, sub-series Correspondence: Argentina: Ana Rosa Schlieper de Martínez Guerrero.

employment, and the option for her to manage the assets she brought to marriage or later inherited by registering her intent to do so. However, it added such conditions and consequences to these actions that the UAM drew the conclusion that it ended the ability of wives to freely dispose of their own earnings or manage their assets.[74] With respect to a wife's reserved property, the proposed code required a wife to inform her husband of her transactions, and if he found them imprudent, he could appeal to a judge to remove her as the administrator, with management of her earnings reverting to him (Argentina 1936, arts. 425 and 430). And while a wife could still declare her intention to manage the assets she brought to marriage by declaring such in the Property Registry, the husband could appeal this action by asking for an immediate separation of property (Argentina 1936, art. 432).

Bibiloni (1939, 313–4) initially had been skeptical that women could wisely manage their own assets and feared that a wife's separate management would be harmful to family unity. To assess whether women were taking advantage of the option provided by the 1926 law and its potential impact, he requested the relevant data from the city of Buenos Aires Property Registry. Between 1926 and 1930, there were only 852 cases of wives separating their property through various mechanisms, not only as a result of the 1926 law but also including judicial separations or after a wife's successful lawsuit over her husband's mismanagement. Since women did not appear to be using the 1926 option frequently, Bibiloni concluded that it was not a threat to the well-being of the family and maintained this right in his draft code.

Bibiloni (1939, 314) also recognized that this right protected women whose "husband failed in his responsibility," since it made it much easier for a wife to gain control of her assets than under the traditional mechanism of having to file a lawsuit and publicly charge her husband with poor administration or fraud. However, he gave husbands the right of redress given the potential harm that could result from the decentralization of asset management (Bibiloni 1939, arts. 659–662). As he put it, "this decision of the wife could have grave personal consequences for the man, affecting his wealth … and it is unjust that he continues to work for the common benefit when the woman is spending her income unproductively"; hence the right he gave husbands to demand the separation of property (Bibiloni 1939, 314).

Since in the final draft the commission maintained Bibiloni's proposed redress for husbands if wives excluded their assets from the conjugal society (Argentina 1936, art. 432), this made the option of women declaring that they wanted to manage their own assets potentially less favorable to them.[75] It also maintained the traditional demand for separation of property as the redress for wives whose husbands mismanaged their property. Thus, under limited circumstances, either spouse could now petition a judge for the full separation of property. In either case, it led to the dissolution

74 "Merecemos las mujeres…," pamphlet cited earlier.

75 The UAM did not comment explicitly on this feature. It was like what Ecuador adopted in 1938 that diluted the benefits for women of its 1911 law.

of the conjugal society, with each spouse receiving half the gananciales; thereafter, neither would benefit from access to the gananciales generated by the other.

In addition, Bibiloni (1939, arts. 626–630) had proposed giving wives greater say in the husbands' management of the conjugal society by requiring a wife's consent for the husband to sell immovable community property, like what Elvira Rawson had demanded in her 1910 proposal but that was not included in the 1926 law. Following the logic of mutual obligations, he also would have required husbands to keep their wives informed of matters regarding their administration. As it turned out, the Commission did not include these potentially beneficial features in its final 1936 draft. The only constraint maintained on the husband's management of the community property was the traditional one, which required mutual consent for donations to third parties (Argentina 1936, art. 419); otherwise, the husband could do whatever he wanted with this property. It also maintained the few traditional limitations on what he could do regarding his wife's property if under his administration. The UAM was particularly displeased that the husband remained the sole administrator of the conjugal society.

Another aspect of the proposed code that the UAM considered a setback was that the 1926 law had allowed widowed mothers who remarried to manage the assets of their minor children and for the gananciales generated by these to accrue to them. The draft 1936 code allowed mothers to continue to manage these assets but their gananciales were now to form part of those of the new conjugal society rather than be owned by the mother. The same rules, nonetheless, applied to both widows and widowers (Argentina 1936, art. 423).

The draft 1936 code potentially improved the inheritance position of wives, an aspect on which the UAM did not comment. In intestate, if the only heirs were the surviving spouse and natural children, the spouse inherited half of both the deceased's individual property and his/her share of gananciales, a point on which the 1869 code had been unclear.[76] An innovative provision was that childless widows gained the right to a share in the estate of her in-laws equal to one-fourth the share that her husband would have received if he were living (Argentina 1936, arts. 1998–2001). With respect to wills, the proposed code increased the share that a testator was free to will to whomever from the previous one-fourth to one-third of an estate; in the absence of descendants and ascendants, this free share increased to one-half, with the reserved half going to the surviving spouse as a forced heir (Argentina 1936, art. 2010).

The issue of civil divorce divided the commission to the point that in the final draft, it presented the Executive with two options (Argentina 1936, arts. 371–384). The majority position held that marriage was indissolvable and only provided for judicial separation, arguing that the stability of the family was more important to society than individual choice. The minority followed the recommendation of Bibiloni,

76 The draft code maintained the 1869 code's restriction that if the spouse inherited along with descendants or ascendants, they only receive a share of the deceased's individual property, not of his/her share of the gananciales.

which allowed separating spouses to choose between a judicial separation or an absolute divorce; even if the guilty party, a spouse who married under the rules of the Catholic Church could insist on a judicial separation rather than divorce. The UAM did not take a position on this issue, likely because they did not have a unified stand.

After the Revisory Commission delivered its draft civil code, President Agustín Pedro Justo, who assumed office in 1932 as the Concordancia candidate (an alliance among conservatives forces), recommended to Congress that it approve the draft civil code in its entirety without discussing it article by article, as had taken place with the 1869 code. The Congress then set up a bicameral commission of seven representatives from each chamber to study the code and act on its behalf.

Even before publication of the final draft, the proposed reforms drew numerous commentaries and generated a relatively large scholarly literature. The volume on the family drew less attention, perhaps because there were still relatively few women lawyers at the time.[77] It was primarily the UAM who called attention to its nefarious aspects, writing and distributing flyers and pamphlets explaining how its provisions represented a setback for women. It also organized numerous events to discuss the problems presented by the proposed code and lobbied members of the Revisory Commission to change their stance (Oliver 1969, 353–4; Giordano 2012, 161–2).

That the bicameral commission never issued a report recommending adoption of the proposed new civil code was likely due to a confluence of factors, among them, that the influential newspaper *La Nación* came out against approval of the new code without its detailed discussion in the legislature (Giordano 2012, 163–4). Argentine feminists were also able to draw attention to and build support for maintaining the civil rights that women had already attained through discussions and resolutions approved at major international peace conferences held in Buenos Aires in late 1936. These included the civil society-organized Conferencia Pro-Paz de América (Popular Peace Conference) in November and the official Inter-American Conference for the Maintenance of Peace convened by the Roosevelt administration in December. While women's rights had not initially been on the agenda of either, largely at the instigation of CIM and Argentine women's rights organizations, the former passed a resolution in support of women's equal rights and the latter, a weaker one to this same effect in recognition of women's role in the maintenance of peace.[78]

77 Risolia (1940) published a 20-page bibliography of journal and newspaper articles on the proposed reform up to 1940 and no women authors were among them. Only 11 entries addressed the volume on the family.

78 See Deutsch (2023, 26–33) for a full discussion of these conferences, including the earlier Argentine Conference of Women for Peace, and Marino (2019, 134–40) on the role of CIM, UAM and AASF in the two international conferences and the close links between feminism, pacifism and anti-fascism. *Vida Femenina*, the socialist feminist journal edited by María Luisa Berrondo, amply covered Alicia Moreau de Justo's leadership in organizing the Popular Peace Conference. Several issues of this periodical between 1934 and 1938 mention the on-going threat to women's civil rights although overall it gave much more attention to women's suffrage (*Vida Femenina*, 43, 16; 44, 18–9; 56, 3).

The Tortuous Path to Women's Political Rights

Between 1919 and 1947, legislators considered at least 21 unique bills relating to women's suffrage, with several submitted multiple times.[79] The bills differed in scope and whether the qualifications for women were different from those of men.[80] Women came close to attaining political rights during the Great Depression when the Chamber of Deputies approved such a bill, which then stalled in the Senate. During this "infamous decade," electoral fraud was rampant and anti-democratic forces were in the ascendancy. It was not until the end of World War II, when women's political rights became an international concern that momentum resumed, with women's suffrage enacted in 1947 under the populist government of Col. Juan Domingo Perón. The Congress did not again discuss women's civil rights until then, although the courts began to interpret the 1926 law broadly, strengthening married women's property rights.

A new women's organization, the Asociación Argentina del Sufragio Femenino (AASF, Argentine Association for Women's Suffrage), founded by Carmela Horne, led efforts to secure the vote in the early 1930s (Lavrin 1995, 177–9; Hammond 2011, 122). It joined the IAWSEC and broadened the appeal of suffrage to conservative women by accepting the restrictions favored by conservative parties (limiting the vote to literate and native-born women who were at least 22 years of age). It also linked the need for women to have the vote to stopping the enactment of a bill allowing absolute divorce that the Chamber was also considering (AASF 1932).[81] The Women's Rights Association and the Socialist Women's Center lobbied for equal political rights and it was their legislative allies, primarily radicals and socialists, who were responsible for the Chamber's approval of the 1932 bill that recognized women's suffrage on the same terms as men's. The Senate, however, did not discuss the Chamber's bill during the Infamous Decade.

Indicative of the political climate was that its right-wing government abstained from supporting the Lima Declaration in support of women's equal civil and political rights at the 1938 Eighth International Conference of American States, irrespective of the efforts of Ana Rosa Schleiper, UAM president then and Argentina's representative to the CIM (Hammond 2011, 133).

79 This count is based on those reproduced in Cocca (1948) and my review of DSCD and DSCS.

80 The controversial issues included whether women should only be eligible to vote or both vote and stand for office; whether to qualify they should be older than men and/or literate; if they should have to perform some type of alternative military service; and whether their registration and vote should be optional rather than compulsory. Cocca (1948), Palermo (1998), and Hammond (2011) consider the multiple bills in detail. See Valobra (2024) for an overview and critique of the historiography.

81 The AASF initially favored women's unconditional political rights but changed its position to broaden its appeal. It collected 80,000 petitions in support of suffrage with such restrictions, and the Asociación Nacional de Damas Patricias Argentinas (National Association of Argentine Patrician Ladies), which was strongly against divorce, collected an additional 56,000. Carmela Horne de Burmeister to Chamber of Deputies president Juan F. Cafferata, August 8 and 9, 1932, in DSCD (1932, vol. 5, 62–4). The CNM-A also came out in favor of women's restricted suffrage (Nari 2000).

During the late 1930s and early 1940s, the war in Europe became the focus of feminist organizing activities, women's suffrage became further politicized around ideological lines, and the issue of furthering women's civil rights receded (Hammond 2011, 136–7; Palermo 1998). In 1941, the UAM morphed into the Junta de la Victoria (JV, Victory Board), a war relief organization led by Schleiper, María Rosa Oliver and Cora Ratto de Sadosky. By 1943, JV brought together some 45,000 communist, socialist, liberal and Catholic women around an anti-fascist, pro-peace and pro-democracy agenda. It trained women in the practice of democracy for their eventual political participation and linked the anti-fascist struggle at home and abroad. It gave little specific attention to advancing women's civil or social rights (Valobra 2005; Deutsch 2012).[82]

That women's civil rights receded in importance may also have been because the courts began interpreting the 1926 Law on Women's Civil Rights broadly. While that law abrogated civil code provisions that were contrary to it, it left it up to the courts to determine the articles that still applied. This led to a multitude of lawsuits as well as conflicting court interpretations in Argentina's federal system.[83] Settled early on to women's benefit was that this law opened all occupations and professions to women, whether public or private (Spota 1953, 199), a long-standing feminist demand.

Another issue the courts settled in favor of wives was related to the clause that required them to inscribe in a special registry their intention to manage their own individual property for them to be able to sell, rent or mortgage such property.[84] Beginning with a 1930 suit, the courts began to recognize a wife's right to alienate her property even though she had not registered her intention to manage it (Díaz de Guíjarro 1942, 5–7). According to Spota (1953, 201), by the early 1950s, "the doctrine that prevails today is that married women above the age of majority exercise their capacity to act when they demonstrate that they administer their own property whether or not they have registered their intent as foreseen in the law."

The Congress did not again consider women's civil rights until 1946 when Senator Lorenzo Soler, a member of the Radical splinter party UCR-JR (Junta Renovadora or Renovation Board) that formed part of President Juan Perón's political coalition, submitted a bill giving women full and equivalent rights to men and abrogating any articles in the civil code or other legislation opposed to this principle.[85] According to Soler, "my bill not only establishes equal political rights, but also equal civil, economic, social and human rights. And I have done this deliberately so that the situation of women in the Republic of Argentina finally changes."[86]

82 See Deutsch (2023) for a comprehensive treatment of the origins of JV in the pacifist and anti-fascist organizations of the 1930s and how it successfully managed to create a multi-class organization across religious and political lines while blending maternalism and women's empowerment.

83 Rébora (1929) provides an exhaustive analysis of the early lawsuits that resulted.

84 I was unable to confirm whether these special registries were ever set up or whether many women ever formally registered their properties.

85 DSCS (1946, 303).

86 DSCS (1946, 304).

The Senate's commission on constitutional affairs subsequently reduced the bill's scope to only women's political rights and responsibilities, endorsing women's suffrage under the same conditions as men's except for military service, like the 1932 Chamber-approved bill.[87] During the discussion, Soler did not again bring up furthering women's civil and other rights. Rather, in his long speech in support of the revised bill, he gave credit to the decades-long struggle for women's suffrage by Argentine feminists and legislators from across the political spectrum.[88] Since Perón had promised to give women the vote, and all the senators elected in 1946 were Peronistas (being either members of the UCR-JR or the Laborista party), there was no real dissent on granting women equal political rights. The Senate approved the bill in August 1946 with only minor changes in wording.

Discussions in the Chamber dragged on another year as deputies introduced new bills and debated whether women's registration and vote should be optional or obligatory, whether they should be subject to auxiliary military service and over issues of implementation.[89] Eva Duarte de Perón (Evita), who had been organizing women into Peronist Civil Centers, led the final lobbying effort, to the discomfort of feminists who saw Peronism as a form of neofascism. Finally, under pressure to act, the Chamber voted almost unanimously to approve the Senate bill and Perón signed Law 13.010 on women's equal political rights into law in September 1947.[90] Perón and Evita took full credit for the attainment of women's suffrage, ignoring the previous legislative initiatives of radicals, socialists and conservatives and, particularly, the long struggle of feminists for political rights (Palermo 1998; Barry 2011).

Many former JV members joined a new organization launched in 1946 under Communist Party leadership, the Unión de Mujeres de la Argentina (Union of Argentine Women) (Valobra 2005). With women's suffrage attained, its 1948 platform focused on the long-pending issues of women's equal civil rights and absolute divorce (Bordagaray 2014, 26). While the Perón government enacted civil divorce in 1954, the military junta that deposed him overturned the measure two years later. Married women did not attain full legal capacity until the reform of 1968 (Deere and León 2001, Table 2.1).

Conclusion

Given its relatively high level of female literacy and labor force participation, Argentina provided an auspicious context for the reform of women's civil and political rights at the beginning of the century. These conditions, particularly its relatively large contingent of normal school and university graduates, produced the earliest organized women's movement in Spanish-speaking South America. Nonetheless, the Congress considered some nine proposals, beginning in 1902, before approving the 1926

87 DSCS (1946, August 21, 29).
88 DSCS (1946, 33–39).
89 See DSCD (1947, September 9, 203–58) for a summary of the new bills and the final discussion.
90 *Boletín Oficial* 15.877, September 27, 1947, 1.

Law on Women's Civil Rights. Achieving women's equal political rights required an even greater number of legislative attempts over an even longer period, 1919 to 1947.

There were three main reasons why women's civil rights came prior to consideration of women's political rights. First, most feminists and reformist politicians agreed that women must first be recognized as capable legal beings and wives, given some degree of economic autonomy. Second, the relatively large presence of women in the labor force made the issue of the need for their control of their own earnings one that was difficult to ignore. And third, women from across the political spectrum reached a relatively early consensus around the need to strengthen married women's property rights.

Rawson's proposal at the 1910 International Women's Conference for reform of the marital regime code encompassed three main demands: women's control over their own earnings; their control over the assets they brought to marriage or later inherited; and their right to a say in the management of the community property. The greatest consensus among jurists and politicians across party lines was on working wives being able to manage their earnings, explaining why most feminists supported the minimalist Palacios and Araya bills and why most bills and the final law included this point.

Regarding women's control over the property they brought to marriage or later inherited, the consensus position among the early feminists, reflected in Rawson's proposal, was that wives should be able to maintain the same property rights and capacities they had as single women. The various bills differed on how best to assure wives greater autonomy. The menu included offering couples' flexibility in what they could do in prenuptial agreements; the option of declaring the separation of property at any time; instituting the latter as the default regime; or del Valle's mixed regime of separation of property during the marriage with the pooling of the gananciales at the end (deferred community property). Organized women mounted their first large-scale lobbying effort around Enrique del Valle's 1918 proposal. They never voiced much support for instituting the separation of property regime as the default or having it as an option. Rawson's Women's Rights Association found the 1922 Quirós bill the most attractive since it maintained partial community property while allowing each spouse to manage and dispose of their own assets without need for each other's permission and mutual consent to dispose of community property.

The 1926 law partly met Rawson's second core demand, allowing women to manage the property that they brought to marriage or later inherited. That the Chamber of Deputies diluted this right by making it an option rather than the default by requiring wives to register their intent to manage such property did not elicit comment from them, although it surely reduced the potential impact of the law.

Regarding the third demand, Rawson's proposal did not challenge male headship or specifically the husband's control over the community property. This was perhaps because of the emphasis feminists placed on linking greater civil rights to becoming better mothers and companions to their husbands. Rather than undermining the traditional patriarchal family, they sought to make marital relations more equitable. Thus, they only asked that wives have a say over the disposition of the gananciales, the minimum on a continuum toward equal rights in marriage. Instituting parallel or joint management of the gananciales was never among organized women's explicit demands.[91] The demand for mutual consent to dispose of community property was sufficiently controversial that the Bravo-Justo bill that served as the model for the 1926 law excluded it. Mutual consent challenged the privileges and status of husbands as household heads too directly to be palatable to most legislators. Regardless of its shortcomings – principally, diluting rather than eliminating potestad marital – the 1926 law was unquestionably an advance, and feminists and their organizations took and deserve credit.

The deliberations over the reform of the code in the mid-1930s illustrate how firmly implanted the concept of potestad marital was in the thinking of many jurists. The most controversial proposal in the 1936 draft code – the one that rallied the UAM to successfully oppose it – was the undoing of a feature of the 1926 law that allowed married women to conduct most economic activities, including the decision on whether to work without the authorization of their husbands and replacing it by that of mutual consent. Feminists paid little attention to how the reform proposal would have even more firmly cemented the traditional gender division of labor, giving women the right and responsibility of overseeing the home, likely because they did not see this as objectionable. And likewise, with respect to how the reform proposed parallel rights and means of redress for both husbands and wives in many matters.

In retrospect, there was an interactive process between the different waves of feminist organizing and their priorities, and developments in the legislature. The failure of the Senate in 1918 to consider a revised version of the del Valle bill provided the incentive for feminists to form new organizations to lobby for both women's civil and political rights, what had been a minority position before this, advocated primarily by freethinking women. That women gained stronger civil rights in 1926 was because there was greater consensus among legislators and conservative women that stronger property rights for wives was more acceptable than political rights for all women. Legislators' resistance to granting women suffrage resulted in bills that granted women the vote under more restrictive conditions than men. Feminist organizations continued to press for full political rights, reaching a pinnacle in 1932, when the Chamber of Deputies approved a bill to grant women equal political rights that then stalled in the Senate.

The rise of fascism and World War II, combined with the rightward shift in Argentine politics, focused the attention of the next generation of feminist leaders on issues of peace and preserving democracy. The pending issue of political rights, combined with the fact that the courts interpreted the 1926 law to include the right of wives to manage their own property, likely dissuaded organized women from pressing further on attaining greater equality in marriage for another generation.

91 While feminists groups supported the del Valle bill that included parallel management of gananciales, they did not highlight this aspect.

4

CHILE'S PIECEMEAL PROCESS TOWARD WOMEN'S CIVIL AND POLITICAL RIGHTS

Chile led South America in the opening of higher education to women. From 1877 on women could sit for university entrance exams, which encouraged the expansion of public and private secondary schools for girls and women's entrance into the professions.[1] In 1898 Lawyer Matilde Brandau authored the first doctoral thesis in law on women's civil status by a South American woman.

Brandau (1898) analyzed the property rights of wives and mothers' rights over children in antiquity and in England, France, Germany, Spain, Argentina and Chile. She argued that if in the ancient past women lacked civil rights because of their sex, with the development of civilization their exclusion was primarily because of marriage. Most countries recognized women's civil capacity when they were single or widowed, with the remaining limitations largely derived from custom. In her view, married women's civil incapacity existed for no other reason than to make wives dependent on their husbands.

According to Brandau (1898, 109),

> married women's civil incapacity was not meant to protect them because of their inexperience or weakness nor to favor their interests. Rather, it was established only and exclusively because a husband's authority—the bundle of rights that he has over the person and assets of his wife—requires it.

The Napoleonic code article that the 1855 Chilean code copied, which established that a man owed his wife protection while she owed him obedience,

1 The first two women received medical degrees in the 1880s, followed by the first two with law degrees in the 1890s, all from the University of Chile (Pereira 1978, 111–30).

DOI: 10.4324/9781003658436-4

summed up the essence of this relationship. She argued that women's subordination was unnecessary to the objectives of marriage, pointing to the "splendid results" of England's 1882 reform of married women's property rights (Brandau, 1898, 109). Since wives administered their own property, it required household decisions to be based on mutual accord, strengthening rather than weakening marriage.

With respect to patria potestad, Brandau found the 1855 Chilean Civil Code to be more restrictive than other codes since it excluded mothers from exercising it under most conditions. This was unjust because mothers shared the same responsibilities with fathers but did not have similar rights and it was contrary to natural law because women were more apt to care for infants and young children than fathers.[2] While she favored both spouses holding patria potestad jointly, with decisions over children to be based on mutual consent, Brandau recommended that as a minimum, mothers exercise it in the father's absence, as in Argentina. She supported giving married women full civil rights by ending potestad marital although she did not specify a preferred marital regime, that is, whether Chile should adopt the separation of property regime as in England or offer various options as Germany did. It was over the next two decades that women began to discuss the alternatives and advocate for specific changes to the marital regime.

These promising antecedents, nonetheless, did not lead to either a very rapid or deep reform of married women's property rights. Reflecting Chile's social conservatism, the process was gradual and piecemeal. Secular women's groups demanding rights emerged later than in Argentina, not until the late teens, coinciding with the first legislative initiatives to enhance women's civil and political rights. Organized women participated in these debates and in 1922 made their first proposal to strengthen married women's property rights, which served as an input into the country's initial, 1925 reform of women's civil rights. More modest reforms in 1934 and 1943 followed, with a more significant one in 1952 that gave wives a voice in the disposition of community property. Overall, by mid-century married women in Chile gained less economic autonomy than in many other South American countries.

Conservatives initiated the push for women's political rights, which they acquired in phases, at the municipal level in 1934 and nationally in 1949. Among the reasons why Chile made comparatively less progress in strengthening married women's property rights was because the struggle for political rights was so prolonged. This was largely due to the recalcitrant role of the anticleric parties even as the country became more ideologically and politically pluralistic.

2 Brandau noted that in case of spousal separation Chilean law recognized this point since mothers automatically held guardianship of children under five years of age.

The First Phase of Women's Organizing

Women began to organize around their rights during the late 1910s and 1920s. The emergence of secular women's organizations coincided with the expansion of the country's middle class as well as growing numbers of women completing secondary education and graduating from university. Enhanced international ties among professional women spurred and supported organizational efforts.

Some 75 Chilean women participated in the First Pan American Scientific Conference held in Santiago in late 1908.[3] Among them were Eloisa Díaz and Matilde Throup (the country's first female physician and lawyer, respectively), and educators Amanda Labarca and María Espíndola de Muñoz. A few of the pioneering feminists from neighboring countries were also in attendance, such as physicians Cecilia Grierson and Petrona Eyle, who had recently founded Argentina's University Women's Association, and Uruguayan physician Paulina Luisi. Likely because of the ties developed at this conference, some 20 Chilean women (the largest contingent from outside of Argentina) participated in the congress this association organized in Buenos Aires in 1910, the First International Congress of Women (Asociación de Universitarias Argentinas 1911, 24–9).

Among the Chileans who presented papers at the Buenos Aires congress was lawyer Matilde Throup (1911), on the topic of why the Latin American civil codes needed reforming. She compared the unfavorable civil status of women in Argentina and Chile with recent advances in the 1896 German code and found the latter's concept of women's reserved property particularly attractive since it gave wives control over their own earnings, personal items and means of work. Throup urged congress participants to adopt a resolution to petition governments to establish equal civil rights between men and women.

María Espíndola, who served as the congress' honorary president, called for the organization of a Latin American federation of women to work for the common purpose of elevating women's position (Asociación de Universitarias Argentinas 1911, 51).[4] One of the outcomes of this congress was the attempt to organize such a regional network, the Federación Femenina Panamericana.[5] In the closing session, the participants agreed to hold a second international women's congress in 1913 in Chile to launch the federation, although it appears that such was never held (Pernet 2000, 666).

Another participant at the Buenos Aires congress, Spanish freethinker Belén de Sárraga, subsequently influenced discussions in Chile.[6] At the invitation of

3 Swiggett (1916, Appendix A) contains a list of attendees. Prior to its sponsorship by the Pan American Union, Southern Cone scholars held three scientific conferences between 1898 and 1902 in which some women participated (Miller 1991, 51–2).

4 The conference program shows that Espíndola was the official delegate of the Asociación Educacional de Chile (Chilean Educational Association) and also represented two women's groups in Chillán.

5 See Chapter 8 for a discussion of its platform.

6 Sárraga was residing in Uruguay at this time; see Chapter 8. Her paternal last name was "de Sárraga" but while she was married (until around 1911) she went by Belén Sárraga de Ferrero. In Chilean publications, her surname often appears as "de Zárraga."

the Radical party daily, *La Razón*, de Sárraga gave a series of nine lectures in Santiago where she laid out the views of the international freethinking movement on women, the family and the Catholic Church (de Sárraga 1913). According to cultural historian Bernardo Subercaseaux (2011, 99) her lectures and ideas, while quite controversial, served to legitimize discussion of women's issues both among anti-clericals and those defending the church.

At the behest of the recently organized Socialist Labor Party, de Sárraga traveled to the northern mining regions where many of the country's wage workers were located. There she helped found several women's group that were subsequently named Centros Femeninos "Belén de Zárraga." These focused more on labor and social issues than on women's civil or political rights, nonetheless, the party's newspaper, *El Despertar de los Trabajadores*, gave ample attention to the struggle for women's rights in the United States and Europe (Kirkwood 1986, 96–103; Gaviola et al. 1986, 31–3).

Most elite women participating in the public sphere at this time engaged in philanthropic and church-related social welfare activities.[7] With the support of the Archbishop, aristocrats Amalia Errázuriz de Subercaseaux and María Luisa McClure de Edwards founded the Liga de Damas Chilenas (Chilean Ladies League) in 1912. Its purpose was to expand the church's social outreach activities and to "combat evil" and immorality in public and private life.[8] Much of this group's initial energy focused on censoring theatre performances as well as the lectures of Belén de Sárraga. It also condemned the series of lectures that educator Amanda Labarca gave at the University of Chile upon her return from pursuing graduate studies at Columbia University (Subercaseaux 2011, 96).[9]

Labarca's lectures focused on the high level of participation of women in American civil society, which she attributed to the expansion of public secondary and higher education, a topic anathema to Catholic women defending church control over education. She published a book on the topic (Labarca Hubertson 1914) and convinced the editors of the women's magazine, *Familia*, where she authored a book review column, to sponsor a women's literary discussion group like those found in the United States and Great Britain. The aim of the Círculo de Lectura de Señoras (Ladies Reading Circle) was to elevate the level of culture of its members and by sponsoring literary contests for women, to do so more broadly;

7 See Maza Valenzuela (1995, 165–7) for more detail.

8 "El Espíritu de la Liga," *El Eco de la Liga de Damas Chilenas* 1 (2), 1912. This Catholic movement originated in France and led to the organization of an international federation of such groups in 1910.

9 Labarca was a graduate of the Instituto Pedagógico (Pedagogical Institute) of the University of Chile and worked as a teacher and educator prior to receiving government fellowships to study at Columbia University and later, the Sorbonne. She was appointed to a temporary faculty position in 1922 and the next year became the first woman to receive a regular faculty appointment at the University of Chile, in the Faculty of Philosophy and Education (Chaney 1979, 57). By convention Labarca's full married name would have been Amanda Pinto Sepulveda de Labarca Hubertson, but according to her biographer (Paul 1968, 20), her father opposed her marriage and in rebellion, Amanda dropped his surname and adopted her husband's although without the "de."

by 1916 it reportedly had some 300 members (Lavrin 1995, 286; Verba 1995; Maza Valenzuela 1998).

Soon after the founding of Ladies Reading Circle, the more aristocratic ladies in the group, led by Delia Matte de Izquierdo and writer Inés Echeverría de Larraín, split off to form the Club de Señoras (Ladies Club), whose objectives were more social and philanthropic and like those of the elite men's club, the Club de la Unión (Union Club). Historian Asunción Lavrin (1995, 287) considers that both institutions "embodied a form of genteel feminism that promoted new roles for women but adhered to traditional female activities and pursued only limited changes." Nonetheless, both groups sponsored lectures and discussions on the need for civil and political reforms and developed links to international feminism.[10]

Two members of the Ladies Club, Delia Matte and Elena Edwards de López, were among the philanthropists who funded *La Voz Femenina*, a newspaper that circulated in 1916 and 1917 under the direction of Teresa Valderrama Larraín.[11] In its first issue the editors explained that they had deliberately chosen the word "femenina" (women or feminine) rather than "feminista" (feminist) for the periodical's name because the former captured women's "just and legitimate aspirations" whereas the latter was associated with the violent actions of the British suffragettes and brought only ridicule (*La Voz Femenina* 1, 1). The most important Santiago newspaper, *El Mercurio*, had described their militancy during 1913 in the most disparaging terms, calling the suffragettes "fanatics," "audacious assailants" and "vandals," tarnishing the term "feminism" in public opinion (Caffarena de Jiles 1952, 104). The pages of *La Voz Femenina* demonstrate that while progressive elite women considered women's primary mission to be that of wife and mother, they supported a process of evolutionary change, beginning with raising women's level of education so that it led to their greater economic independence and eventual political rights.

The first women's organization founded to pursue women's rights was the Consejo Nacional de Mujeres de Chile (CNM-C, National Council of Chilean Women), established in 1918 by journalist Celinda Arregui de Rodicio (a participant at the 1910 Women's Congress), Eloisa Díaz, Amanda Labarca, Juana Aguirre de Aguirre and others, with physician Díaz serving as its first president.[12] Its purpose was "to better women's civil, economic and juridical rights" while remaining

10 Amanda Labarca, Delia Matte and Inés Echeverría became the Chilean representatives to the Pan American International Women's Committee that emerged from the Women's Auxiliary conference at the Second Pan American Scientific Conference in Washington, DC in late 1915 (Women's Auxiliary Committee 1921, 2).

11 Only five issues of this newspaper are available; also see Lavrin (1995, 289).

12 On whom served as its inaugural president, I follow Sánchez Manriquez (2006, 311), whose rendering conforms to a 1918 letter from Uruguayan Paulina Luisi to Eloisa Díaz congratulating her on her presidency (Ehrick 2005, 47).

independent of partisan politics or any religion.[13] Its membership overlapped with that of the Ladies Reading Circle and Ladies Club and included a number of social welfare organizations. Labarca was CNM-C's president from 1919 to 1925, and under her leadership the Council first focused on women's full civil rights. She considered these a precondition to political rights since women's secular education and stronger property rights were likely to promote their independent thinking (Labarca 1934, 125–6; Lavrin 1995, 287).[14]

Amid labor unrest and growing calls for social reform, the early 1920s were propitious for women's organizing. Among the new groups that formed were two that called themselves political parties. The Partido Femenino Progresista Nacional (PFPN, Women's National Progressive Party), founded by Sofia de Ferrari Rojas in 1921, grew out of the women's magazine, *Evolución*. Its platform called for reform of the country's constitution and civil and penal codes in support of women's rights (Lavrin 1995, 291–2). Ester La Rivera de Sangüeza in 1922 formed the other non-partisan, autonomous organization, the Partido Cívico Femenino (PCF, Women's Civic Party), with the objective of promoting legislation in support of women's civil and political rights (*Acción Femenina* 1922, 1, 10). While disavowing "anarchic" feminism (associated with the British suffragettes), it used the term feminism to characterize the type of moderate change it advocated. Its incidence was primarily through its magazine, *Acción Femenina*, which aimed to raise women's consciousness and re-signify motherhood and domesticity in pursuit of rights (Kirkwood 1986, 109).

The PCF actively championed women's suffrage and took on the arguments of critics who asserted that women would lose their femininity or neglect the home if they had the vote:

> There are those who deny women their political rights based on their being "the angel of the home," an angel of innocence and sincerity...Why would women lose their innocence and charm if they expressed their thinking about the governing of the country? Why would they stop being "the queen of the home" if they could influence with their generous sentiments the destiny of their homeland?[15]

Women from several of these organizations attended the 1922 First Pan American Congress of Women in Baltimore, with Graciela Mandujano representing the CNM-C and Sofia de Ferrari Rojas, the PFPN (Lavrin 1995, 288, 292). An outcome

13 "Consejo Nacional de Mujeres," in Guérin (1928, 630–2). The CNM-C also aimed to create departmental- level councils and by 1927 had established two, in Chañaral and Copiapó.

14 This was also the thinking of the Radical Party of which Labarca was an adherent; her husband was a prominent figure in this party (Paul 1968; Maza Valenzuela 1998).

15 1923 editorial in *Acción Femenina* cited in Errázariz (2005, 274). Various articles in this periodical also stress the importance of bettering women's education as a precondition to suffrage.

of the Baltimore congress was the formation of the Pan American Association for the Advancement of Women (PAAAW), with Carrie Chapman Catt (the president of the IWSA) as honorary president. Subsequently, Catt undertook a five-country trip to South America to recruit women's organizations to join PAAAW. Mandujano arranged her February 1923 visit to Chile, which included a public session hosted by the CNM-C and an interview with President Arturo Alessandri Palma.

Catt encouraged the CNM-C to join the ICW and the IWSA (Pernet 2000, 674–5). The CNM-C's membership in the ICW was already in process; it officially became its third Latin American affiliate later in 1923, following those in Argentina and Uruguay (ICW 1996, Appendix 11). Labarca did not pursue CNM-C membership in the IWSA since political rights, while on its agenda, were a long-term objective.

Chile hosted the Fifth International Conference of American States in Santiago during March-April 1923, which provided another boost to feminist organizing efforts. Writer Elvira Santa Cruz Ossa (pen name, "Roxane"), one of the founders of the Ladies Reading Circle and a CNM-C member, was a journalist with *El Mercurio* and in her column drew attention to how issues of concern to women, such as their lack of civil rights, were absent from the conference's agenda. She wrote how Chile's civil code was unjust to women, resulting in their "economic and political servitude," and highlighted the situation of "the heroic mother whose salary is spent by her husband in the taverns or brothels, wives who suffer humiliation and torment, widows who see their children's patrimony pilfered by unscrupulous guardians."[16]

Roxane called for elimination of all the civil code articles that placed women in a position of civil inferiority and argued in favor of the right of married women to manage their own salary; for mothers to exercise patria potestad over their children; and for the opening of positions in public administration to women. She mentioned that a bill including some of these points was before the legislature and hoped it would be discussed seriously and, moreover, that the Pan American conference consider placing women's rights on its agenda.

In her next column, Roxane reported that one of the delegates at the conference, Guatemalan writer Máximo Soto Hall, responded to her call and the lobbying of other women and presented a resolution asking member countries to study how to expand and improve women's education and their civil and political rights, so that these could be discussed at the next Pan American conference.[17] Since some of the delegates had asked her for more specifics on women's demands, she reproduced the CNM-C's reform proposal in her column, discussed in the next section.

The secretary general of the conference, Chilean diplomat Manuel Rivas Vicuña, endorsed Soto Hall's motion and formalized a proposal that asked those attending to recommend to PAU that "in the program of future conferences it include a study of ways to abolish constitutional and legal incapacities based on sex with the aim

16 Roxane, "La mujer y la V Conferencia Panamericana," *El Mercurio* (1923, March 29, 3).

17 Roxane, "Los derechos de la mujer en la V Conferencia Panamericana," *El Mercurio* (1923, April 22, 3).

of ...[women] attaining the same civil and political rights as men."[18] Moreover, women were to be included in the preparation of this study and in the delegations to future conferences. Approved unanimously, this proposal placed women's rights on the official hemispheric agenda for the first time (Marino 2019, 36).[19]

The momentum provided by this conference led to the 1926 International Women's Congress in Santiago and the formation of the Bando Femenino de Acción Social y Cultural (Women's Group for Social and Cultural Action) to implement its accords. Celinda Arregui, a CNM-C founder, led this initiative and served as president; Martina Barros, the translator of John Stuart Mill, was honorary president (Bando Femenino 1928).[20] Its platform called for women's equal civil and political rights, as well as a social code like the one Uruguay had recently adopted to protect mothers, children, the infirm and elderly. It set up seven commissions, one of which focused on attaining women's equal rights. It was among the Chilean organizations that signed a letter urging the upcoming Sixth International Conference of American States in Havana to support women's equal civil and political rights.

In the port city of Valparaíso, educator Aurora Argomedo (another attendee of the 1910 Women's Congress), Graciela Lacoste and others founded the Unión Femenina de Chile (UFC, Women's Union of Chile) in 1927 as a non-partisan, multi-class organization.[21] Among its objectives was to raise "the moral, intellectual and economic position of women" and "to improve women's civil, political and economic rights."[22] It sponsored the magazine *Nosotras*, edited by Delia Ducoing de Arrate (pen name, "Isabel Morel"), who also served as UFC president between 1929 and 1933. Consider now the role played by these feminists and their organizations in the first round of reform of married women's property rights.

Legislative Initiatives and the First Reforms

Between 1915 and 1925 the Congress considered three bills on married women's property rights and one on civil divorce. The property rights bills proposed contrasting approaches to reforming the marital regime – incorporating the mechanism

18 "Los derechos de la Mujer, discurso de Manuel Rivas Vicuña," *El Mercurio* (1923, April 26, 23).

19 "En la sesión plenaria se rinde un homenaje a la mujer a aprobarse una ponencia sobre sus derechos." *El Mercurio* (1923, April 27, 20). See Miller (2010) for a brief summary of how this led to the establishment of the CIM in 1928 and its role at subsequent PAU conferences, and Marino (2019) for more detailed treatment. PAU took this mandate seriously because after the 1923 conference it sent out a questionnaire to member governments requesting information on women's civil and political rights; see Chapter 2 on Ecuador's response.

20 Bando Femenino's (1928) founding document, signed by 24 women, mentions that it succeeded the Partido Demócrata Femenino (Women's Democratic Party), a short-lived group formed around discussion of the 1925 Constitution, and received its assets, which included a free clinic for poor workers.

21 See Guérin (1928, 639) and "Síntesis de la acción desarrollada por la U.F. Ch.," *Unión Femenina de Chile* (1934, 1, 2). It reportedly had around 1,000 members by 1929.

22 Its statutes are in Morel (n.d.).

of married women's reserved property into the existing regime versus adopting separation of property as the default. The CNM-C developed its own proposal focusing on women's earnings although it ended up supporting a bill to adopt the separation of property regime. A military junta enacted the 1925 decree that recognized married women's reserved property along with the option of full separation of property in a prenuptial agreement. A 1934 law then clarified some of the provisions of this decree while modifying a few other civil code restrictions on women. The divorce bill, in contrast, died in committee.

Prior to 1915 the only modest step strengthening married women's property rights was a by-product of an initiative regarding state-financed, low-income housing. A 1907 law allowed working wives to open accounts in their own name in the Cajas Nacionales de Ahorro (National Savings Banks) and to freely manage these for the purpose of purchasing housing.[23] Then in 1915 liberal Senator Luis Claro Solar, a well-regarded jurist,[24] introduced legislation to reform numerous articles of the civil code dealing with marriage and the family.[25]

In the preface to his bill, Claro Solar (1915a, 1–6) explained that the regime of the conjugal society (partial community property) worked well for women in well-to-do families who did not work outside the home since they received half the gananciales at the dissolution of the marriage irrespective of whether they had contributed assets. In contrast, in poor or working-class households where wives needed to earn income, the rules of the civil code were unfavorable to them, since husbands could claim their wives' wages or earnings and use these as they wished. He was concerned that men sometimes spent women's earnings on their own vices, to the detriment of the family. Observing how in Chile, as in more developed countries, women's labor force participation was increasing, he reviewed how other countries had dealt with this situation. Several had adopted the mechanism of reserved property for wives who conducted independent economic activities, which he thought met Chilean needs.

Chile' 1855 civil code (Chile 1856, art. 150) presumed that a wife who exercised a profession or occupation had her husband's authorization to contract regarding her own economic activities but was silent regarding the management of these earnings. Claro Solar (1915a) proposed amending this article so that working wives have the explicit right to manage their own earnings, including the purchase or sale of assets acquired with their own income. While in his bill husbands

23 Law 1969 of July 18, 1907, www.leychile.cl. Claro Solar (1915b) mentions this law as an antecedent, as does Giordano (2012, 142–3).

24 Claro Solar, professor of civil law at the University of Chile, was the author of a detailed commentary on the 1855 Civil Code (Claro Solar 1902). His treatise did not contain recommendations regarding the legal position of women, although he noted some of the code's inconsistencies and praised the recent German code for moving furthest toward equal rights and responsibilities in marriage.

25 *Diario de Sesiones de la Cámara del Senado* (DSCS) (1915, 651)and Claro Solar (1915a).

retained the right to oppose their wives' employment, if a husband denied permission a wife could appeal to a judge. Husbands gained the right of redress if a wife mismanaged her earnings; he could appeal to a judge to gain control of her income. At the dissolution of the marriage this reserved property formed part of the gananciales divided between the two spouses and/or their estates.

Other relevant aspects of Claro Solar's bill included giving legally separated women the right to manage, alienate and join suits regarding their movable and immovable property without need for the authorization of their husband or a judge.[26] Also, in the fathers' absence (due to death or legal incapacity), mothers automatically assumed patria potestad although if a widow remarried she lost this right.[27] In addition, he proposed reducing the age of majority for both men and women from 25 to 21.

Claro Solar's 1915 bill spurred debate in women's organizations and academic circles, the latter evident in the growing number of university theses on the topic of married women's property rights (Arteaga Infante 1922, 84). Among those arguing that working wives should have control over their earnings was the thesis by Guillermo Búrgos (1917) presented to the law faculty at the University of Concepción, which reviewed the precedents for this measure in the reforms in Great Britain, Scandinavia, Belgium and France. He also noted how countries that had adopted the 1855 Chilean code, such as Ecuador and Colombia, gave more rights to mothers than did Chile, since in those countries they exercised patria potestad in the fathers' absence. Búrgos also considered Chile to be behind other countries in maintaining restrictions on women being witnesses or guardians of children who were minors.[28]

Among the groups that Claro Solar (1915b) addressed to promote his bill was the Ladies Reading Circle. He explained how the 1870 English reform was the precedent for his proposal to give wives control over their own earnings and that other European countries were adopting similar provisions. He emphasized how the 1907 Chilean law that allowed married women to own and manage savings accounts was a first step toward this end, but it was important to go further, as did his proposed bill, to give wives greater economic independence.

26 Under the existing rules, the wife could demand the simple separation of property due to the mismanagement of her property or the community property. If granted by a judge, the wife then administered her own assets (irrespective of source) along with half of the gananciales; she required, nonetheless, the permission of the husband or a judge to sell or mortgage immovable assets (Chile 1856, arts. 158 and 159).

27 In 1877 Liberal Deputy Julio Zegers had proposed both these measures and while recommended favorably by a legislative commission a decade later, the bill was never taken up by the full Chamber of Deputiest (Zeger 1918). The Zeger bill received the support of the women's group that formed in 1877 around the literary and cultural magazine, *La Mujer*, with the aim of supporting women's "social advancement," particularly their access to education (Pereira 1978, 132, 166).

28 See Chile (1856, arts. 367 and 1012).

His bill also gained the support of Catholic women attending the 1918 Congreso Mariano Femenino (Marian Women's Congress) sponsored by the Chilean Ladies League and the Archbishop. Isabel Irarrázaval de Pereira (1918, 276-80), the vice-chair of the congress, presented the only paper focusing on women's rights. After summarizing how Christianity had improved the position of women, she focused on how many aspects of the civil code were, in fact, "uncivil" as well as unjust to women. She found two aspects particularly prejudicial to wives: that they did not have equal rights to fathers over their children, and that in the working-class husbands controlled the wages of working wives, often resulting in a family's immiseration. Some 126 women at the congress signed a petition urging the Senate to pass the Claro Solar bill since it "contained their legitimate aspirations as to needed civil reforms" (Congreso Mariano Femenino 1918, 398–9). The emergence of a Catholic feminism that supported an improvement in women's civil rights may have been among the factors that spurred secular women to organize the CNM-C to pursue that aim that same year.

Another paper at the Congreso Mariano Femenino (1918, 205) raised how the enemies of the Church were threatening the stability of the family by introducing a bill to institute civil divorce. In October 1917 Radical party Deputy Ramón Briones Luco and ten others had introduced a bill that allowed absolute divorce under limited conditions: adultery, willful abandonment for at least three years, and the long-term imprisonment of one of the spouses.[29] Briones Luco emphasized how these grounds were among those required for a permanent judicial separation. It maintained the dual standard in the grounds for adultery, whereby any form of infidelity by a wife constituted grounds, while for a husband it required a public scandal, that he introduced a concubine into the home, or his infidelity plus by any of the other conditions required for separation. The bill also kept the provision that punished the guilty party to a divorce with the loss of their share of the gananciales. Nonetheless, it added an important new cause for a judicial separation, mutual consent after five years of marriage.

As a presidential candidate for the Alianza Liberal – a coalition of radicals, democrats and reformist liberals[30] – Arturo Alessandri Palma assumed the banner of women's rights. In his 1920 nomination acceptance speech, he denounced a woman's legal status in Chile as one that "humiliates and depresses her and does not conform to the needs and aspirations of modern civilization" and lamented how Chile was falling behind other countries in elevating women's position (cited in Giordano 2012, 106). His reformist agenda received staunch support from

29 *Diario de Sesiones de la Cámara de Diputados* (DSCD) (1917, 103–7).

30 The Radical party, founded in 1888, and the Partido Demócrata, founded in 1889, tended to represent the expanding middle-class that grew concurrently with the expansion of the state. Both parties admitted women members (Gallo Chinchilla 1945, 64–6). Alessandri Palma was a liberal of the reformist tendency.

the middle- and upper-class women in the CNM-C and later the PCF (Giordano 2012, 139).

Once president, in his 1921 message to the opening of Congress, Alessandri specifically indicated his support for the Claro Solar bill that was pending in the Senate.[31] A year later, he reaffirmed how bettering the legal condition of women was a priority of his administration and that a special commission of the Congress was now studying such a reform. He hoped that the "rights of Chilean women as mothers and as owners of assets that they brought to marriage and of those they acquire through their personal effort would soon be achieved, becoming law."[32] In this passage he advocated going beyond the Claro Solar bill, since he addressed the property women brought to marriage. He also indicated his support for absolute divorce because by allowing legally separated women to marry their new partner it would be a moralizing influence on society.

In 1922 liberal Senator Eliodoro Yañez introduced a more radical bill on married women's property rights than Claro Solar's, since it proposed replacing the partial community property regime with separation of property as the default.[33] Under the latter, wives would automatically have the free administration of the assets that they brought to marriage and any assets they acquired while married including from their earnings; each spouse managed and kept their own gananciales, thus no community property was formed. He, nonetheless, maintained an important restriction on a wife's economic activity: while she could make contracts regarding her own separate property, she could not sell or mortgage her immovable property without her husband's permission. The Yañez bill furthered women's other civil rights by ending all limitations on their serving as witnesses or guardians except that to serve in the latter capacity, wives required the consent of their husbands or a judge. Like Claro Solar's bill, it gave mothers patria potestad in the fathers' absence; it did not address the situation of widows who remarried.

Yañez's proposal to change the default regime to separation of property provoked much discussion. Among those supporting this change was *El Mercurio* journalist Claudio Arteaga Infante (1922, 15–23), who argued that potestad marital placed wives under a form of legal slavery. Under the guise that they required their husbands' protection, the law forced women when they married to turn their property over to them. Rather than imposing the husband's management, Arteaga considered it preferable to adopt separation of property as the default; if a woman wanted her husband's protection in the management of her property, it would be

31 "Mensaje leído por S.E. el Presidente de la República en la apertura de las sesiones ordinarias del Congreso Nacional," June 1, 1921, 40. In Mensajes Presidenciales, www.bcn.cl/historiapolitica.

32 Congreso Nacional, Sesión de las Cámaras Reunidas el 1 de junio de 1922, 20. In Mensajes Presidenciales.

33 The Yañez bill is in Vásquez Rencoret (1922, 7–8). I was unable to locate it in the *Diario de Sesiones* since some January and February 1922 sessions are missing in the BCN electronic archive; the microfilm copy at the US Library of Congress is illegible.

her choice. He also thought this regime was the most effective way of giving wives equivalent rights to those of husbands over their own assets and earnings.

Inés Echeverría, a well-regarded writer under the pen name "Iris" (and member of both the Ladies Reading Circle and the Ladies Club), wrote the preface to Arteaga's book where she commended the Yañez bill for fostering women's economic independence. While the civil code allowed couples to make capitulaciones that specified that the wife might manage some (but not all) of her assets, couples rarely made these because for a young woman to mention such a possibility to her betrothed was "offensive" and "signaled distrust" (Arteaga Infante 1922, x). Thus changing the default regime to total separation of property would be a better way to ensure that women managed their own property if they wished. Iris expected most upper-class women to voluntarily turn over management of their assets to their husbands, which would be more dignified than all her assets being taken away without her consent. Moreover, if problems developed with his management, she could always revoke her consent without having to file suit against him. Echeverría's analysis implicitly acknowledged that this regime would increase the wife's bargaining power, since husbands would behave better, "being more considerate of her" (Arteaga Infante 1922, xiii).

The thesis written by Humberto Vásquez Rencoret (1922) for his law degree at the University of Chile is representative of those that favored strengthening married women's property rights but who considered Yañez's proposal inappropriate. His strongest argument in favor of maintaining the existing marital regime was that under the conjugal society the wife got half of the gananciales at the end "even if she did not contribute to it"; in his view, this more than compensated for a wife's loss of autonomy (Vásquez Rencoret 1922, 34). He also thought the adoption of separation of property as the default would impose a financial penalty on women for it was doubtful that they would be able to compensate for the loss of the gananciales through their own endeavors, given their lack of preparation and "natural weakness." At the same time, Vásquez recognized that wives who worked were in a special situation and their earnings needed protection from irresponsible husbands who might squander them. He thus favored Claro Solar's 1915 bill, considering it like the earnings legislation enacted in many US states and England. He also raised the possibility of allowing couples to choose between the two marital regimes, as a growing number of countries were doing.

Legal scholar Alejandro Valdés Riesco (1922), analyzing the wide variety of marital regimes that had emerged internationally, voiced a third opinion. He considered the separation of property regime to be the simplest and most equitable since it allowed wives to administer their own assets and whatever they acquired after marriage, including from their employment. While he supported the Yañez bill, he suggested that it was important to maintain community property with respect to what husbands earned during the marriage, implicitly suggesting a mixed system, such as deferred community property. He did not, however, further develop this idea.

FIGURE 4.1 Chilean educator Amanda Labarca Hubertson (1886–1975), ca. 1920.

Source: In *Chileans of To-day*, edited by William Belmont Parker (G.P. Putnam's Sons, 1920). Courtesy of Harvard University.

The CNM-C Proposal, the Maza-Sánchez Bill and the 1925 Decree

While the Women's Civic Party lobbied for adoption of the Yañez bill (Lavrin 1995, 293), the CNM-C was unsatisfied with it and in early 1922 drafted its own bill. According to Amanda Labarca (1952, 120) (Figure 4.1), two lawyers, Pedro Aguirre Cerda (the husband of CNM-C co-founder Juana Aguirre and a future president) and Arturo Alessandri Rodríguez (the son of president Alessandri Palma) assisted her in drafting the CNM-C proposal. In some of its demands it coincided with the Claro Solar bill, while in others with the Yañez bill; at the same time, it contained aspects that were further-reaching than what those bills contained.

The CNM-C proposal assumed the conjugal society continued as the default regime and expanded the property rights of wives primarily by giving them control over their earnings.[34] While it resembled the Claro Solar bill that established

34 This analysis is based on the CNM-C proposal reproduced by Roxanne in her article in *El Mercurio* (1923, April 22, 3).

women's reserved property, it differed in that it assumed that a wife could freely engage in any employment or profession so that a husband would have to petition a judge to prohibit her from doing so. It also went further than his bill in two other ways: (i) by establishing that wives had the same rights as single adult women regarding their own earnings and the assets acquired with such – they could freely contract and dispose of these earnings and assets and enter into suits without need for a husband's authorization; and (ii) by specifying that the gains from such independent activities belonged exclusively to the wife – such did not enter into the gananciales to be pooled at the end of the marriage. To differentiate it from Claro Solar's "reserved property," the proposal termed this arrangement "married women's exclusive property." It also considered the situation of wives who collaborated with their husbands in family businesses. It recognized the wife as an equal partner in such enterprises and proposed that when the business dissolved half of the net profits were the wife's exclusive property.

The CNM-C's proposal on wives' independent earnings was actually closer to the married women's earnings legislation adopted by many US states than Claro Solar's, the key difference being that women's earnings and any assets generated by them belonged to them alone. Although Amanda Labarca Hubertson (1914) does not mention property rights in her book on US women and their organizations, she was likely familiar with the US Married Women's Property Acts. It is also possible that Senator Enrique del Valle's 1918 bill that was under discussion in the Argentine legislature inspired this proposal, since it gave wives' earnings this privileged treatment as well as control of half the net profits of family enterprises. Labarca was in regular correspondence with Argentine and Uruguayan feminists and may have received the first issue of *Nuestra Causa*, which reproduced del Valle's bill. Nonetheless, the CNM-C proposal made no mention of the assets that women brought to marriage or later inherited, as del Valle's bill did, assuming these would remain under the husband's control and contribute to the generation of the gananciales.

The CNC-C proposal did demand the elimination of all the incapacities the civil code placed on women because of their sex. It proposed that women be eligible to be guardians under the same conditions as men although it concurred with the Yañez bill that wives should have their husbands' authorization or that of a judge to assume this responsibility. It did not explicitly mention women being able to be witnesses, as did the Yañez bill, although such would fall under the general demand of removing all incapacities based on sex. The CNM-C also proposed that in the father's absence, for whatever reason, the mother automatically assume patria potestad; it accepted Claro Solar's indication that a widow would lose this right if she remarried. This proposal also mentioned women's political rights, envisioning a phased process whereby women attained municipal suffrage prior to national suffrage. Recognition of women's citizenship was necessary if women were to have access to positions in public administration, another CNM-C demand.

In 1923 liberal deputies José Maza Fernández and Roberto Sánchez García submitted a revised version of the CNM-C bill to the Chamber of Deputies.[35] It was co-signed by another 12 deputies representing six political parties, including three from the Conservative Party, suggesting that the idea of improving women's civil rights had broad consensus. Somewhat surprisingly, the Maza-Sánchez bill proposed changing the default marital regime to that of full separation of property, moving away from the CNM-C's focus on women's exclusive property from employment. It was thus like the Yañez bill but went further by specifying that under this regime, married women were free to engage in any form of employment or economic activity. Husbands, nonetheless, had the right of redress; if they objected to their wives' employment, they could file suit with a judge to prohibit it. As in the Yañez bill, while wives were free to manage their own assets, they required the permission of their husbands to sell or mortgage their own immovable assets.[36]

The Maza-Sánchez bill retained the CNM-C's concern with the situation of wives who collaborated with their husbands in a family enterprise. However, it made these subject to the general rules of a business society regarding the distribution of expenses and profits and assumed that the husband was the administrator of the joint enterprise. Since the proposed default regime was separation of property, the Maza-Sánchez bill allowed couples to opt for the conjugal society in a prenuptial agreement. Regarding other civil rights, it allowed women to be witnesses or guardians and like the Yañez bill it required wives to have their husbands' authorization for the latter. Mothers gained the right to exercise patria potestad in the absence of the father; if a widow remarried, however, she automatically lost this right.

In an essay in the journal *Ateneo,* Labarca (1924) explained why the CNM-C backed away from its initial proposal and now embraced the separation of property marital regime: maintaining the conjugal society under the husband's administration had too many defects. It gave young husbands with little preparation too much power since no one held them accountable for what they did with the community property. Also, it led to marriages of convenience and was "too tempting for lazy husbands who were married to industrious women," to live off their earnings or assets and dissipate these through their vices (Labarca 1924, 384). Her main argument in support of adopting separation of property was that if adult single women could manage their own earnings and assets, why should married women be unable to do the same. Also, making it the default regime did not preclude wives in harmonious marriages, where husbands were good managers, from giving them a mandate to administer their earnings and assets, echoing the argument made earlier by Inés Echeverría.

35 DSCD (1923, 1362–7).

36 This is because the bill made the separation of property regime subject to the same rules governing the simple separation of property in the existing code.

With regard to the concern that adopting separation of property would deny women access to the gananciales, Labarca (1924, 386) thought that the Maza-Sánchez bill protected widows, since they gained full patria potestad over their children, which meant that they managed their patrimony, which could be the bulk of the deceased father's estate. If they were good administrators, widows earned income from this activity since the gananciales on such assets would accrue to them rather than to an external guardian. She also expected that in good marriages husbands provided for their wives by designating them as the beneficiary of the one-quarter share of their estate that the code's inheritance rules allowed a parent to will to whomever they chose. But Labarca also acknowledged that adopting separation of property as the default would require further changes in the rules of intestate inheritance to ensure that widows receive a fair share of their husband's estate.[37]

Labarca had visited the United States twice by then and was likely familiar with how the separation of property regime worked in practice. What is curious, nonetheless, is that, as Corrine Pernet (2000, 669–70) emphasizes, in her writings she was often critical of what she considered the excessive individualism of North Americans, this being among the factors that led to the adoption of the separation of property regime in Anglo-Saxon countries and that this regime further encouraged. Nonetheless, deputies Maza and Sánchez likely convinced her that this regime facilitated attaining the objective of wives holding the same property rights as single women and that, strategically, presenting a bill that was like the Yañez bill in the Senate stood a better chance of approval than a bill asking for special privileges for wives if only over their earnings. Also, feminists such as Inés Echeverría, Elvira Santa Cruz and PCF members supported Senator Yañez's bill.

In her essay, Labarca (1924) also explained that the Maza-Sánchez bill contained a minimum program of reforms since it included only the points on which there was the greatest consensus. A full "feminist program" required the additional demands of absolute divorce and women's suffrage. The bill did not address suffrage because women's civil rights were a precondition to their political rights.[38] Even though Labarca herself supported absolute divorce, the bill did not include this demand since the CNM-C did not want women's civil rights to become embroiled in religious divisions.[39]

The Senate, meanwhile, had appointed a special commission to consider the Claro Solar and Yañez bills and in August 1923 received its two reports.[40] Senator Yañez

37 As discussed in Chapter 1, the rules of intestate succession were not very favorable to widows, entitling them only to the *porción conyugal* if there were legitimate children (Chile 1856, art. 1172).

38 In Labarca (1952, 120) she cites a CNM-C accord of 1923 ("Memoria del Consejo Nacional") as containing women's political rights. I am assuming that the CNM-C proposal reported in Roxanne's *El Mercurio* article, analyzed earlier, is based on this document, which I was unable to locate.

39 On her support for divorce, see Labarca (1934, 203–15). *Acción Femenina* (1923) also published articles in favor of divorce. Stuven and Araya (2004) provide a detailed study of the Catholic Church's opposition to divorce.

40 DSCS (1923, 943–8).

and three others (a liberal, a radical and a conservative) wrote the majority report while Senator Claro Solar authored the minority one. They had reached consensus on the most important point, maintaining the conjugal society as the default marital regime. The compromise was that couples would be able to opt for the total separation of property in a marital contract at any point, before or during the marriage. The two reports differed, however, on how much economic autonomy wives gained if they chose this regime. Whereas in the Yañez report the wife was fully capable with respect to the property that she separately administered, in Claro Solar's she could not sell or mortgage immovable property without her husband's permission.[41]

Both reports also recommended adopting the mechanism of reserved property for wives and agreed on its rules: a wife could manage her earnings from independent labor autonomously, acquire assets and enjoy its fruits; when the marriage ended these assets formed part of the community property. While married women could freely decide whether they wanted to work, the husband could file suit if he objected, with a judge determining the outcome. The majority report recommended that all women be able to serve as witnesses to public acts as well as guardians over children although wives required the consent of their husbands to exercise this latter function; the minority report did not address these points. Both reports gave mothers in the absence of fathers the same right of patria potestad. They differed in what happened when a widow remarried, mothers losing this right in Claro Solar's but maintaining it in Yañez's report.[42]

In a public lecture held at the CNM-C in 1923, President Alessandri Palma reiterated his continuing support for enhancing women's civil and political rights (Lavrin 1995, 290) and at the opening session of Congress in 1924, he once again urged it to address women's civil rights noting that these constituted "an unpaid debt" to Chilean women. Moreover, attaining civil rights would "put them on the path to attaining administrative and political rights…" and place Chile in the vanguard of the sentiments expressed at the Fifth Pan American conference held in Santiago the previous year.[43] Alessandri also urged approval of the Briones Luco bill allowing absolute divorce.

Neither the Chamber's Maza-Sánchez bill nor the Senate Commission's reports had come to the floor for debate when in September 1924 a military coup disbanded the Congress. But shortly before its dissolution and under pressure from the military the Congress approved two important pieces of labor legislation. These

41 The Claro Solar report lifted this restriction in the case of a permanent judicial separation so that a woman could also alienate her immovable property.

42 Senator Ramon Briones Lucas, who signed the majority report, was disappointed that the commission had not had time to address divorce and re-introduced the same bill that he had submitted in 1917 as a deputy; DSCS (1923, 948–9). The Union Patriótica de las Mujeres de Chile (Patriotic Union of Chilean Women), in its publication of the same name, took credit for preventing the Congress discussing his divorce bill due to its mobilization of women against it; *Union Patriótica de las Mujeres de Chile* (1926, 20, 1).

43 Congreso Nacional, Sesión de las dos Cámaras reunidas en 1 de junio de 1924, 26, in Mensajes Presidenciales, www.bcn.cl/historiapolitica.

included provisions for working wives to receive their own pay without the intervention of their husbands and to administer their earnings freely.[44]

The reform-oriented junta subsequently promulgated some aspects of the Maza-Sánchez bill and Senate reports at the instigation of José Maza who served as its Minister of Justice (Labarca 1934). Decree Law 328 of March 1925 (known as the "Maza Decree"),[45] differed from the Maza-Sánchez bill principally in terms of the default marital regime. Rather than instituting the separation of property regime as the default, this decree offered it as an *option* that couples could choose in a prenuptial agreement, following the consensus position of the Senate commission.[46] This option was to follow the rules governing the simple separation of property: wives could manage their own property but they could not dispose of immovable property without their husbands' permission. Thus it followed the more restrictive proposal in Claro Solar's rather than Yañez's report that would have given wives greater autonomy.

The decree maintained the provisions of the Maza-Sánchez bill and the two Senate reports whereby wives could freely choose to dedicate themselves to any economic activity and regarding married women's reserved property.[47] Women's right to employment was subject, nonetheless, to the same important caveat, that husbands could petition a judge to prohibit them from doing so. Irrespective of marital regime, wives who earned independent income were "considered to be separated in goods for purposes of administration of those assets that were the result of their professional work or industry," and could participate in lawsuits relative to such activities (Chile 1925, arts. 9 and 10).[48]

It also strengthened all women's civil rights by allowing them to serve as witnesses and guardians although wives required their husbands' authorization for the latter. In the father's absence, a mother gained the same rights of patria potestad but if widowed and she remarried she lost this right. Hence, the Maza Decree of 1925 was a compromise that drew on the different ideas of how to strengthen married women's property rights that had been under discussion in the legislature and civil society for the previous decade.

Felícitas Klimpel (1962, 52) credits the CNM-C's "intense campaign" for the country finally having improved married women's property rights. Labarca (1934, 174) herself claimed the victory while making clear that the Maza

44 Art. 18, Ley de Contrato de Trabajo, Law 4053, September 1924, and art. 14, Ley sobre Contratos de Trabajo entre patrones y particulares, Law 4059, September 1924, https://www.bcn.cl/leychile. Also mentioned in Klimpel (1962, 56) and Giordano (2012, 143).

45 Available at https://www.bcn.cl/leychile.

46 The decree did not go as far as the Yañez majority report would have liked, making this option also available at any point during the marriage.

47 The decree itself does not use this term, but legal scholars such as Alessandri Rodríguez (1935, 619) commonly employed it to refer to this provision.

48 Under the rules of simple separation of property a wife required her husband's permission to engage in lawsuits, so this was an important concession.

Decree did not contain everything that the CNM-C would have wanted. While it conformed to their initial 1922 demand that women be able to manage their own earnings, it was not under conditions as favorable as she had hoped. Nonetheless, it gave couples greater flexibility when they married and was an important step toward recognizing the legal capacity of married women.

The 1934 Civil Code Reform

Not long after the promulgation of the 1925 decree, Elena Caffarena, who was just finishing her law degree and in subsequent decades would become a prominent feminist leader, published a critique. She considered the Maza Decree to contain "a minimum program" of women's demands, for while it got rid of the most "unjust and irritating constraints" on women, it fell short of reforms in other countries (Caffarena Morice 1928, 77). While single women and widows now had the same civil rights as men, potestad marital continued to constrain married women's property rights.

Caffarena argued that the provisions for the separation of property regime, the new option in the decree, were inadequate since it tied what women could do with their assets to the existing rules for the simple separation of property, such as wives needing permission to sell their immovable assets. This undermined the economic autonomy that this regime was meant to further. Moreover, since it was not customary for couples to make prenuptial agreements, it was unlikely that many would opt for this regime. She criticized the decree for not allowing couples to change a prenuptial agreement or to opt for separation of property during the marriage since it was only once they were married that spouses got to know each other well and that a wife could assess whether her husband was a good manager.

In addition, Caffarena (1928, 80) was critical of the way the decree defined women's reserved property, considering that it did little "beyond prohibiting husbands from directly receiving the fruits of women's labor," being simply an extension of the previous 1924 labor laws to women's general income earning activities. The wording was also confusing and the decree did not specify what happened at the marriage's dissolution to the assets that women acquired as separate property. She thought Claro Solar had provided a better formulation of this concept in his 1915 bill.

A few years later, Caffarena and lawyer Flora Heredia were among those participating in the committee led by Aída Parada, Chile's representative to CIM, which drafted the report on women's civil and political rights in Chile in preparation for the 1933 Seventh International Conference of American States in Montevideo (CIM 1933). It is curious that this report only mentioned one provision of Decree Law 328, the article allowing women to be witnesses under the same conditions as men. This might be because they felt that this decree lacked clarity and had not been fully implemented.[49]

49 Creditors, for example, continued to require the authorization of the husband for any transaction that a wife conducted with her own salary (Klimpel 1962, 57).

Moreover, efforts were underway to supplant the Maza Decree. In 1924, prior to its promulgation, the dean of the law faculty of the University of Chile had appointed a faculty committee to study potential reforms to the civil code that would strengthen women's civil rights. But before this committee finished its report, the military junta approved the 1925 statute. After Arturo Alessandri Rodríguez became dean and chair of this committee, he submitted the commission's completed report to the Congress in 1926 but it did not act upon it (Alessandri Rodríguez 1935).

After Arturo Alessandri Palma returned to the presidency in 1932, his son, jurist Alessandri Rodríguez urged him to consider the draft bill on women's civil rights contained in the University of Chile report since it improved upon the 1925 statute by providing greater clarity and amended specific articles of the civil code, something that the decree had not done (Alessandri Rodríguez 1935, 624–6). The government assumed this bill as its own and the Congress approved it with minor modifications.[50]

Law 5521 of December 1934, Equalizing Women before the Law,[51] rescinded the 1925 statute while incorporating most of its content into existing articles of the 1855 civil code. For example, the 1934 law maintained the provision allowing couples to stipulate the full separation of property regime in a prenuptial agreement. The main change was that rather than following the previous rules for the simple separation of property, it now followed new rules for judicial separations, whereby such separated women could freely dispose of their own property (movable and immovable) and appear in lawsuits.

Law 5521 maintained the earlier decree's clause whereby, irrespective of marital regime, wives could freely engage in an economic activity unless a judge, at the husband's petition, prohibited such. With regard to the income or earnings of such independent activity, for this sole purpose women were under a separation of property regime (meaning that it constituted reserved property although not using this term). It was incumbent upon working wives to prove what assets they acquired through their own independent activities. The law clarified that at the dissolution of the union, women's reserved assets and its fruits constituted community property. A woman maintained her right to renounce the gananciales if she found it in her interest to do so, and in this case she kept her reserved assets.

This law also maintained the previous provision automatically giving mothers patria potestad in the absence of the father. An improvement on the decree was that if a widow remarried, she no longer lost this right. She was to notify a judge of her impending marriage who could then appoint her or someone else; if she did not provide notification, she and her new spouse shared the responsibility and gains

50 DSCD (1934, 1116–8), contains the version of the bill edited by the Senate that it returned to the Chamber for final approval, and a summary of the process.

51 In https://www.leychile.cl.

from managing her children's assets. Overall, the 1934 law addressed many of the points raised by Caffarena (1928) although it did not allow couples to opt for the separation of property regime during the marriage.

Alessandri Rodríguez (1935, 630) acknowledged that although the reform reduced the incapacity of wives, it did not eliminate potestad marital; moreover, the assets that women brought to marriage or acquired through inheritance continued to be under a husband's management. He considered this approach appropriate since a more radical reform – such as a change in the default regime to separation of property or deferred community property – would have required a more complete revision of the civil code and particularly, of the inheritance regime. He considered the existing intestate rules unfavorable to widows and, unless changed to favor them, separation of property could leave wives unprotected if they widowed because there were no gananciales from the marriage to divide.

Although all the various feminist organizations included women attaining equal civil rights in their platforms, most did not pay much attention to this 1934 reform of married women's property rights. For example, in her 1934 inaugural speech on becoming UFC president Graciela Lacoste did not even mention this reform although she highlighted the male bias embodied in the civil code, which restricted the civil rights of wives. She emphasized how women needed the vote to reform the code so that it favor the interests of women and children.[52]

A 1936 editorial in *La Mujer Nueva,* the newspaper of the recently formed Movimiento Pro-Emancipación de las Mujeres de Chile (MEMCH, Movement for the Emancipation of Chilean Women), mentioned approval of this reform, lamented that its content was not well known and wished that women's organizations had given as much attention to this reform as they were giving to suffrage, for the reforms to date fell short of women attaining legal equality.[53]

Founded in 1935 by lawyer Elena Caffarena (Figure 4.2), journalist Marta Vergara, educator Aída Parada and others, MEMCH aimed to bring together all women's organizations and women of different political parties as well as independents around a comprehensive program that included their "legal, economic, and biological emancipation" (MEMCH 1936). Besides middle-class women, its membership included a fairly large contingent from the working-class, many of whom were affiliated with the Communist Party.[54] Under Caffarena, its secretary general until 1941, its activities and campaigns were broad ranging, from promoting women's political

52 This speech is embedded in "Recepción del nuevo Directorio," *Unión Femenina de Chile* (1934, 4, 4–5).

53 "Un balance," *La Mujer Nueva* (1936, 8, 3).

54 Elena Caffarena was not a member of any political party although in 1929 she married lawyer Jorge Jiles Pizarro who was a member of the Communist Party (Poblete 1993, 19). Marta Vergara, who edited its periodical, was a member of the Communist Party from 1936 until 1939 when the party expelled her (Marino 2014).

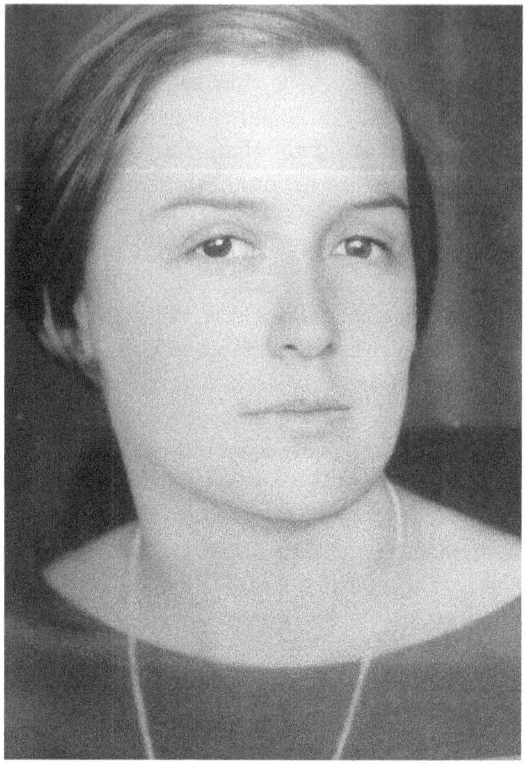

FIGURE 4.2 Chilean lawyer Elena Caffarena Morice de Jiles (1903–2003), ca. 1935.
Source: Courtesy of Jiles Caffarena family and granddaughter, historian Ximena Jiles.

rights and civic education to labor rights and peace in the face of fascism,[55] and lobbying for women's rights in regional forums.[56]

MEMCH's (1936) program of action included reforms to the marital regime. Reflecting Caffarena's (1928) earlier thinking, it proposed making the separation of property option more flexible so that couples by mutual consent could choose this regime at any point in the marriage. It also proposed broadening the conditions under which wives alone could demand a separation of property. It was critical of how women's reserved property, the main gain for wives in the 1925 and 1934 reforms, worked in practice. Due to the proof required, it was difficult for working

55 See Pernet (1996) and Rojas and Jiles (2020) for detailed analyses of its activities and the problems of maintaining multi-class unity.

56 As a result of MEMCH's lobbying, President Alessandri Palma appointed Graciela Mandujano as Chile's CIM delegate to the 1938 Conference of American States in Lima; it also lobbied him unsuccessfully to sign the CIM's Equal Rights Treaty presented at the 1933 Montevideo conference. See Pernet (2000, 678) and Marino (2014).

women to establish their right to manage the assets they acquired with their own earnings. Thus if wives were to gain economic autonomy, a complete separation of property might be preferable. MEMCH also championed the enactment of absolute divorce and the adoption of a comprehensive code of the child that would allow investigation of paternity and establish the legal equality of children irrespective of the conditions of their birth.[57]

MEMCH was likely the first South American women's organization to advocate in favor of women's reproductive rights.[58] Its 1936 program advocated emancipating women from "forced maternity" by making birth control widely available and bringing abortion out of the shadows through state regulation. Its advocacy of women's biological emancipation immediately earned it the wrath of Catholic women recently organized in Acción Nacional de Mujeres de Chile (ANMCH, National Action of Chilean Women) who in an advertisement in *El Mercurio* denounced MEMCH for going against nature and morality and being anti-family as well as communists.[59] It was also a factor that made it difficult for some progressive women's organizations, such as the UFC, to align with MEMCH under a common program.[60]

Regarding divorce, Radical legislators once again introduced bills in its support in 1933 and 1935, but these were unsuccessful (Lavrin 1995, 235–6). Besides MEMCH, two of the feminist periodicals, *Nosotras* and *Acción Femenina,* voiced their support for these bills. The Catholic Church and various Catholic women's organizations continued their campaign against the Congress even discussing divorce legislation. While the issue of divorce continued to divide organized women on religious grounds, the struggle for political rights during this decade would unite them.

A Gradual Path toward Women's Political Rights

In contrast to most other South American countries, in Chile the Conservative Party presented the first bill to enact women's suffrage. Moreover, the anti-clerical parties resisted enfranchising women for close to three decades precisely because they

57 Between 1900 and 1929 slightly over one-third of children born in Chile were legally illegitimate (Milanich 2009, Table 1.1). Milanich considers few Chilean feminists to have advocated on behalf of illegitimate children perhaps unaware that MEMCH incorporated this issue into its platform. She shows that discrimination against illegitimate children was a frequent topic of law theses. Radical legislators introduced bills to remedy this situation in 1916 and 1928 (Milanich 2009, 222, 229–30).

58 In Uruguay in this period, Sara Rey Álvarez, editor of *Ideas y Acción*, also advocated in favor of voluntary maternity and abortion for therapeutic reasons although it was not part of her party's program. See Lavrin (1995, 173–92) for a detailed discussion of the debate over decriminalizing abortion in the Southern Cone and how feminists only timidly engaged in it. While they rarely discussed women's sexuality, most condemned the double sexual moral standard and its consequences – a relatively high rate of illegitimacy as well as of infant mortality.

59 Clipping of September 7, 1935 from *El Mercurio* and Elena Caffarena's response in Archivos Mujeres y Géneros, https://www.archivonacional.gob.cl/archivos-mujeres-y-generos/galerias/memch-movimiento-pro-emancipacion-de-las-mujeres-de-chile.

60 See the MEMCH correspondence, Letters no. 69 and 76, in Rojas and Jiles (2017, 81, 85–6) and the comments by the editors.

feared that women would favor the party of the Church. This, and the fact that most organized women favored a gradual approach, were among the reasons this country followed a two-phased process toward women's political rights, first recognizing them at the local, then national level.

When a group of Conservative Party deputies, led by Luis A. Undurraga, introduced the first bill to grant women suffrage in 1917 few women were demanding suffrage.[61] That began to change as women obtained the vote in more countries and consensus built around women's participation in municipal governance. Both men and women viewed their participation at this level as more appropriate than at the national, since municipalities primarily dealt with local-level services, issues related to women's domestic roles.

In its 1922 program the CNM-C proposed that women be enfranchised on the same terms as men, but that for the first eight years after its enactment women's participation be limited to the municipal level, to facilitate their gradual political incorporation.[62] During discussions around the 1925 Constitution some secular women organized the short-lived Partido Demócrata Femenino with this objective and Catholic women also began to ask for the municipal vote although they favored restricted suffrage, limiting it to women who were taxpayers.[63] This constitution left it to future legislation on municipal governance to determine if women and resident foreigners could exercise suffrage at the local level.[64]

Under the authoritarian presidency of General Carlos Ibáñez a limited group of women gained the right to vote in local elections although not the right to stand for office under a short-lived 1931 municipal elections law.[65] It enfranchised women who were literate, at least 25 years of age and were asset owners, independent professionals or tradeswomen and inscribed in the appropriate registry (for property or a business) and paid taxes. Men could vote at age 21 if they were literate irrespective of whether they owned property, worked or paid taxes. A military coup toppled Ibañez before implementation of this law. By then more women from across the political spectrum were calling for women's equal suffrage at the local level.

Among the new women's organizations formed with this objective were Acción Nacional de Mujeres de Chile, founded by Adela Edwards de Sala (a founding

61 DSCD (1917, 56); Errázariz (2005, 271) and Gaviola et al. (1986, 35).

62 In Roxanne, *El Mercurio* (1923). An editorial in *Las Ultimas Noticias*, reproduced in *Acción Femenina* (1923, no. 7), also mentions both Labarca and Elvira Santa Cruz endorsing women's municipal-level suffrage.

63 "Presentación que hicieron las damas a la Excelentísima Junta de Gobierno cuando iniciaron públicamente la campaña pro-municipio," signed by María Luisa MacClure de Edwards and 11 others; undated petition in *La Union Patriótica de las Mujeres de Chile* (1926, 22, 2).

64 Although article 104 (Chile 1925) did not mention women, it referred to future voter registries; the sub-committee on constitutional reform that proposed the wording said its intent was for the legislature to determine when it was appropriate to extend suffrage to women. See Gallo Chinchilla (1945, 25) on the discussion around this and the 1926 debate in the Congress.

65 Decree 320, in https://bcn.cl/2hzso; mentioned in Rojas M. (2011, 410).

member of the Chilean Ladies League and president of the welfare organization Cruz Blanca), and the Partido Femenino Nacional (National Women's Party) under the leadership of Celinda Arregui of the Bando Femenino (Maza Valenzuela 1995, 171–3; Lavrin 1995, 300). The UFC, which favored full suffrage, took the lead in uniting the various groups in 1933 in the Comité Nacional Pro Derechos de la Mujer (National Committee for Women's Rights) to pressure Congress to give women at least municipal-level suffrage, organizing a national petition campaign with this objective.[66]

After his reelection to the presidency in late 1932, Arturo Alessandri Palma wanted to hold municipal elections quickly and asked Congress to pass a short bill to allow this although it meant using the same electoral registry as in the recent presidential election. According to the editors of *La Mujer Nueva* (1936, 8), it was only because of the tenacity of the women's groups that the Chamber took issue with his approach, incorporating women's participation into the bill. Led by Radical Deputy Pedro Opitz Velázquez, its commission on internal affairs proposed that in municipal elections women could vote and stand for office on the same terms as men. The discussion in both chambers was contentious, with some wanting to go further and give women full political rights and others not wanting women to participate in any elections at all (Errázuriz 2005). The Congress approved the Opitz bill as a compromise. Women thus attained partial political rights in January 1934 when President Alessandri Palma promulgated Law 5357.[67]

During the debate over women's participation in municipal governance the issue of women's civil rights came up tangentially. For example, Senator Aurelio Nuñez, a radical socialist who supported the bill as a short-term measure, considered it contradictory to enable women to participate in local elections when they did not even have the right to manage their own assets and the civil code treated them "like minors."[68] He went on to propose a set of reforms that included changing the default marital regime to that of separation of property; deleting the stipulation that women obey their husbands; and specifying that wives have the right and obligation to be in charge of the household's domestic affairs. It is not clear whether he was speaking sarcastically when he said these measures, particularly the latter, would "legally make women 'the queen of the home'."[69]

Once women had achieved municipal-level suffrage, a major issue facing them became whether they should become active in male political parties, establish their own separate parties to support women candidates for local office, and/or

66 Felisa Vergara González of the UFC served as secretary general, which included ANMCH member Elena Doll de Díaz and Amanda Labarca as honorary president; see *Nosotras* (1933, 38, 1) and Antezana-Pernet (1996, 55).

67 Art. 19, "Fija las normas relativa a las elecciones…de las municipalidades," Law 5357, January 15, 1934; in www.bcn.cl.

68 DSCS (1933, 336).

69 DSCS (1933, 336).

form coalitions of women's organizations to push a feminist agenda. Both the Socialist and Radical parties organized women's sections. The National Committee for Women's Rights evolved into the Agrupación Nacional de Mujeres de Chile (National Association of Chilean Women) in May 1934, under the leadership of UFC member Romelia de Badilla. It aimed to unify the various women's groups around an equal rights agenda, with its top objective being attaining full suffrage so that they could enact a rather long list of specific reforms, including reform of the civil and penal codes.[70] It also fielded candidates for municipal office and mobilized women to register to vote.

Elcira Rojas de Vergara revived the PCF with a broad-range program that included women attaining full civil and political rights; its immediate objective was to make sure women registered to vote.[71] Catholic women of the right also formed new organizations and got involved in municipal politics. Besides the ANMCH, an off-shoot with similar objectives, Acción Patriótica de Mujeres de Chile (APMCH, Patriotic Action of Chilean Women), formed that published the magazine *Voz Femenina* from 1935 on (Gaviola et al. 1986, 60–2; Lavrin 1995, 305–6, 313). As candidates for municipal office, women of both left and right stressed how as women and mothers they would bring special qualities to politics, such as a moral voice and greater concern for daily bread-and-butter issues that affected family and social welfare (Rosemblatt 2000, 243).[72]

In the late 1930s, MEMCH was the largest and most influential organization demanding women's suffrage (Kirkwood 1986; Gaviola et al. 1986; Lavrin 1995).[73] In the 1938 presidential elections, MEMCH and the PCF supported the Popular Front candidate, Radical Pedro Aguirre Cerda, whose coalition included the Socialist, Communist, and Democratic parties as well as the Chilean Labor Federation (Poblete 1993, 48). While Aguirre Cerda voiced his support for women's equal

70 Among the specific civil code reforms mentioned was allowing recognition of paternity of children born outside of marriage. "Agrupación Nacional. Declaración de Principios," *Unión Femenina de Chile* (1934, 5, 4–6); Graciela Lacoste letter to Doris Stevens of May 10, 1934, Doris Stevens Papers, Series V. IACW, sub-series A. Correspondence: Chile, 1935–1938. Also see Lavrin (1995, 309–10).

71 Rojas edited its magazine, once again named *Acción Femenina,* from 1937 on; Amanda Labarca was coordinator of its editorial council (Lavrin 1995, 307–9, 312).

72 See Maza Valenzuela (1995) on women's participation in the 1935 elections. Some 65 women ran for municipal council positions with 35% of these elected. Most of the latter were members of the ANMCH, APMCH and/or the Conservative party, including Adela Edwards and Elena Doll (Maza Valenzuela 1995, Table 3). Of the candidates of the Agrupación Nacional, only Romelia de Badilla, its president, was successful. After the 1935 elections, the Agrupación Nacional became the Partido Nacional de Mujeres de Chile (National Party of Chilean Women) (*Unión Femenina de Chile* 1935, 10, 6).

73 While its membership fluctuated, its local committees spanned Chile geographically; in 1944 38 were active (Rojas and Jiles 2017, 551). In 1945 MEMCH fused with the Unión de Mujeres de Chile, led by María Marchant de González (Rojas and Jiles 2017, 529, 559).

civil and political rights, not much happened during his first few years in office.[74] Thus in January 1941 MENCH leaders publicly asked him to adopt their draft bill to grant women full political rights.[75] A few days later, Aguirre Cerda submitted his own bill to Congress to establish women's equal political rights.[76] He died later that year and the suffrage bill never made it out of committee.[77]

Some 200 women's organizations participated in the First National Congress of Women in October 1944 which resulted in the founding of the Federación Chilena de Instituciones Femeninas (FECHIF, Chilean Federation of Women's Institutions), with Amanda Labarca as its president.[78] It immediately turned to drafting a bill in support of women's political rights and lobbying senators to support it (Gaviola et al. 1986, 68; Antezana-Pernet 1996, 347). Due to their efforts, a group of nine senators, representing all the major political parties– Radical, Liberal, Socialist, Communist, Democratic and Conservative—co-signed the June 1945 bill that drew upon their proposal and eventually was successful.[79] The preamble stressed many of the same points contained in Aguirre Cerda's 1941 bill, for example, that justice and the expansion of democracy demanded women's equal political rights, and that they had more than proved themselves as competent and contributing citizens. What was new was the stress on the need for Chile to act on its international commitments regarding women's suffrage and the emphasis on how it was falling behind other Latin American countries.

MEMCH and FECHIF launched full-scale lobbying efforts, holding rallies outside the congressional palace and weekly lectures on suffrage that engaged the interest of the press. They also successfully lobbied individual senators; the Senate approved the bill in December 1946.[80] Even though the bill had the support of all the major political parties and the backing of President Gabriel González Videla (a Radical elected by the Popular Front), it got stuck in the Deputies' commission. Feminists such as Amanda Labarca blamed this delay on the lingering fear of politicians over whom women would support at the polls. The two-year delay was also

74 "Mensaje de S.E. Don Pedro Aguirre Cerda en la apertura de las Sesiones Ordinarias del Congreso Nacional," May 21, 1939, Cámara de Senadores, *Boletín de Sesiones Ordinarias* (1939, 8). In the late 1930s, Democracia Unificada (Unified Democracy Party) and the Conservative Party both presented bills in favor of women's suffrage that died in committee (DSCD 1937, 650, 716; 1939, 1084–9).

75 Reproduced in "Voto Político Femenino," *La Mujer Nueva* (1941, 27, 7); Gaviola et al. (1986, 68).

76 DSCD (1941, 1745).

77 See Antezana-Pernet (1996, 322–41) and Gallo Chinchilla (1945, 59) on the disarray within MEMCH at this time and the ineffective lobbying effort of the new Women's Rights Committee formed for this purpose.

78 Many of the veterans of the women's movement were on the congress coordinating committee, among them Amanda Labarca, Felisa Vergara, Flora Heredia, and Aída Parada. The FECHIF executive committee included María Aguirre, Graciela Mandujano (now president of MEMCH), and María Correa (Gallo Chinchilla 1945, 61).

79 DSCS (1945, 460, 473–9).

80 DSCS (1946, Extraordinary Session 8, 370); Antezana-Pernet (1996, 348).

because of their wrangling over the finer points of the election law and what advantage or disadvantage such changes might offer them. Also, the discussion was taking place in an overall context of increased repression, related to the broader Cold War politics of the period.[81]

To push the bill over the finish line, women formed another coordinating committee, the Comité Unido Pro Voto Femenino, but their unity soon come under strain. FECHIF held a second National Women's Congress in Valparaíso in 1947 under the theme "Women want to vote in the next elections." Labarca, apparently without consulting other members, invited President González Videla to attend and his aggressive anti-communist speech led Elena Caffarena and other MENCH members to walk out. Shortly after, Congress approved his government's "Permanent Defense of Democracy Act," Law 8987, known as the "Ley Maldita" (Accursed Law) since it proscribed the political participation of the Communist Party and made other changes to the electoral law. MEMCH members were among those harassed, persecuted and jailed under the Ley Maldita. When the FECHIF leadership failed to demand the protection of human rights, MENCH withdrew its membership (Gaviola et al. 1986, 75–6; Rojas and Jiles 2020).

By 1948 all the major newspapers were calling on congress to act since it had become a national embarrassment that Chile was among the Latin American countries where women did not hold full political rights (Klimpel 1962, 94–6). One final coordinating committee, the Comando Unido Nacional Pro-Voto Femenino (United Command for Women's Vote), organized a "Pro Women's Suffrage Week" of intense activities in September of that year (Gaviola et al. 1986, 76). In response to this pressure, the Chamber held a preliminary discussion of the suffrage bill to a packed gallery of women.[82] Each of the major political groupings (conservative, liberal, radical and independent) expressed their support for the bill, emphasizing how their party platforms included women's suffrage.

González Videla needed to shore up his democratic credentials given the condemnation he received over the Ley Maldita, thus he finally agreed to designate the bill as urgent. The commission reviewing it subsequently issued its second report.[83] Among the changes it made to the bill was removing the phrase "men and women" from those required to register to vote so that it specified only "Chileans," leaving it understood that the term included men and women. Gender neutral language was employed throughout, with any explicit reference to men removed (except for the

81 González Videla initially included three Communist party members in his cabinet as part of the Popular Front coalition. After the communists obtained 17% of the national vote in the 1947 municipal elections and they continued to support labor strikes, González Videla expelled these cabinet members and began to suppress the labor movement (Gaviola et al. 1986, 74–5; Antezana-Pernet 1996, 355).

82 DSCD (1948, 2415–22).

83 DSCD (1948, 2415–22). Extraordinary Sessions 14 and 18, 542–5 and 727–40; Klimpel (1962, 100–4) and Errázuriz (2005, 283) summarize the discussion.

separate registries for men and women). The provisions dealing with women's registration were only to become effective 120 days after enactment of the law, which assured that women would not be able to vote in the upcoming 1949 elections.

Both chambers approved the bill without modification and González Videla signed Law 9.292 granting women full political rights in early 1949.[84] He did not invite feminists such as Elena Caffarena who had struggled for women's suffrage for over a decade to the official ceremony and soon after his administration revoked Caffarena's electoral registration along with that of several thousand women for being communists or communist sympathizers under the Ley Maldita (MEMCH 1983, 5, 73).[85]

Further Reforms of the Civil Code

During the 1940s and early 1950s Chile continued with its piecemeal approach to the reform of married women's property rights. Reforms made the option of the separation of property regime more flexible by allowing its adoption at any time during the marriage; improved the position of the spouse in intestate inheritance; and gave wives a say in the disposition of gananciales. The reforms did not include civil divorce. Those enacted were largely the initiative of legal scholars, although they responded to demands of women's organizations.

During the 1945–1948 discussion of women's political rights in the Congress, several legislators brought up how wives still did not have full legal capacity. Former president Arturo Alessandri Palma, now president of the Senate, refuted the need for further civil code reform on the grounds that the code did not discriminate against women. Rather, the restrictions that remained on married women's legal capacity were related to the need to maintain a sole household head who was properly the husband.[86] Nonetheless, gender inequality in marriage combined with the inability to obtain a civil divorce were generating contradictions. For instance, couples who wanted to divorce were seeking annulments on technical grounds, known as "divorcio a la chilena." In 1945–1947 these represented an average 2.2% of new marriages, a share that would continue to increase (Rojas 1997, 353).

In an essay entitled "Home, Sweet Home," Amanda Labarca (1947, 200–7) focused on the growing disconnect between the aspirations of educated, middle-class housewives to be their husbands' companions and the unchanging attitudes of men. In her story of why a young wife recently separated from her husband,

84 "Modifica la ley general sobre inscripciones electorales," Law 9292, January 8, 1949, in www.LeyChile.ch.

85 According to Caffarena, her removal from the electoral lists was due to her having defended the women and children held at a detention camp for their political activities (Eltit 1994, 105, 119). MEMCH by then was affiliated with the WILPF and it took her case to the UN Commission on Human Rights (Poblete 1993, 50).

86 DSCS (1946, 201–2).

Labarca cited him as saying that he would welcome his wife home only "on the condition that she accept once for all that I am the one who rules the home, her obligation is to obey me." Moreover, he accused her "of being intrusive, she wants to know how I spend my time, my money and even tries to immerse herself in my business" (Labarca 1947, 203–4). In the wife's view, they were simply incompatible, "the woman he wants for a wife is not me" (Labarca 1947, 200). In another essay, Labarca (1947, 227–30) emphasized how attaining democracy in the home was a precondition for the construction of Chilean democracy.

In the early 1940s the Instituto Chileno de Estudios Legislativos (Chilean Institute of Legislative Studies), a nonpartisan institute of the University of Chile under the leadership of Arturo Alessandri Rodríguez undertook a general analysis of the civil code with the aim of updating it and making it more internally consistent. Among its relevant proposals was lowering the age of majority from 25 to 21 and allowing couples to opt for the separation of property regime at any point during the marriage. Recall that under the 1934 law it was only an option in a prenuptial agreement, thus the only way for those married under the conjugal society to obtain it (other than by a judicial separation) was for the wife to file suit against her husband due to his fraud or impending bankruptcy, an onerous and time-consuming process that was also embarrassing. This is among the reasons that MEMCH's 1936 program included allowing couples to choose this regime at any point among its demands.

According to Alessandri Rodríguez (1943), couples were seeking a separation of property under false pretenses and many in the legal profession favored making its conditions more flexible. The government of Juan Antonio Ríos embraced this reform and in 1943 the Congress approved it without much discussion.[87] The legal scholars of the Institute were aware that separation of property might prove detrimental to wives if they opted for this regime without considering its consequences because if widowed they could find themselves in a vulnerable position. The Institute even placed newspaper ads explaining how under this regime wives lost any claim to future gananciales from the marriage and if widowed they might not inherit anything from their husbands (Klimpel 1962, 61–2).

The inheritance regime had not been a real issue of concern to feminists up to now since most women who married did so under the conjugal society that gave them a certain degree of protection when they widowed since they automatically received half of the gananciales as a property right. But recall that when Amanda Labarca (1924) supported instituting separation of property as the default in the 1920s she assumed it would require changes to the inheritance rules to protect widows.

The Institute for Legislative Studies focused next on reforming the inheritance regime. Its primary aim was to improve the inheritance provisions for children

87 "Modificaciones al Código Civil," Law 7612 of October 11, 1943, in www.leychile.cl.

born outside of marriage and facilitate their recognition, issues that had been under discussion for some time (Klimpel 1962, 58), and as shown earlier were also on the MEMCH list of demands.[88] Nonetheless, the Institute's proposal also increased the likelihood that a widow or widower might inherit from their spouse's estate by eliminating the requirement that a spouse plead relative poverty to claim the porción conyugal. If there were legitimate children, the surviving spouse automatically inherited alongside them and their share was twice the share of a child; if there was only one child they received up to half the estate. While the porción conyugal became a spousal right, the actual amount the spouse received still depended on whether they owned individual assets or received gananciales, with these values deducted from the final share. Hence the position of the spouse in intestate improved although it was still stingy compared to countries that did not require such deductions.

According to Klimpel (1962, 58), the reform related to the management of the community property enacted at this same time originated with the Partido Femenino de Chile (Women's Party of Chile), a party founded by María de la Cruz in 1946.[89] It had studied the consequences of when husbands sold all or some of the community property without informing their wives; families were oftentimes reduced to poverty. The party raised the issue with the Women's Office (established in 1947 under the González Videla government to comply with a CIM mandate) to see if there was a way to require husbands to seek their wives' consent to alienate such property, which then turned to Alessandri Rodríguez's Institute for assistance.[90]

The Institute agreed to incorporate this change on the management of the conjugal society to the package of civil code reforms that it had submitted since the Congress had not yet considered them. The new clause required the husband to obtain the wife's consent to sell, mortgage or lease any immovable property acquired during the marriage. If a wife denied her consent, a husband could appeal to the courts. Its rationale for including mutual consent was that "it does not disturb the husband's management of the community property in marriages that are harmonious,

88 The Institute proposed that if the deceased left both legitimate and recognized natural children, that in intestate the latter be eligible for a share of their parent's estate, although this share could only be equal to half that of a legitimate child and the maximum share that could be claimed by all such children was one-quarter of the estate. In the absence of legitimate children, the parents of the deceased, the spouse and the natural children each received a one-third share by group. Previously in the second order of inheritance the parents received three-fifths of the estate and the spouse and the natural children only one-fifth each (Chile 1856, art. 989), hence the share of both improved. The proposal also simplified the conditions for recognition and legitimation of natural children and allowed for the investigation of paternity. See Rioseco (1948) for a detailed discussion of the proposal and final law.

89 In 1953 de la Cruz became Chile's first female senator (Gaviola et al. 1986, 78–9).

90 Antezana-Pernet (1996, 375) suggests that one of the first initiatives of the Women's Office under its first director, Ana Figueroa, was to compile all the previous MEMCH and FECHIF proposals for civil code reform and to present these as her own. I was unable to confirm whether these earlier proposals included the demand for mutual consent to alienate community property.

but it should be a measure protective of women who are in the weakest position in cases of the husband's abuse or spousal discord" (cited in Klimpel 1962, 58). Without much discussion, the Congress approved Law 10.271 in February 1952 that incorporated this measure plus the changes to intestate inheritance and recognition of natural children described earlier.[91]

This reform in the management of the community property was an important step toward greater equality in marriage. The labor force participation rate of married women was still relatively low thus most would not have benefited directly from the 1925 and 1934 reforms that recognized women's reserved property over their labor earnings.[92] As housewives, their security largely depended on the gananciales generated during the marriage. The new requirement that made their consent necessary for husbands to dispose of community property thus likely enhanced their bargaining power in marriage.

Feminist Ideas on Alternative Marital Regimes

Prior to the initiative by the Women's Party discussed above, MENCH leader Elena Caffarena observed that compared to the energy that they dedicated to suffrage, feminist organizations and the women's sections of political parties appeared almost apathetic when it came to demanding changes in women's property rights. She lamented that not one organization had undertaken "a serious and sustained campaign to change the default marital regime and thus end the incapacity of married women" (Caffarena de Jiles 1944, 9). This did not mean that women were satisfied with their legal status or that the marital regime met their needs. Rather, according to Caffarena, the problem had to do with legal literacy – women's lack of knowledge of the law – and the very complexity of the civil code.[93] This made it difficult for those not trained as lawyers to begin to think about alternatives. Thus the purpose of her 1944 book, to educate women on their property rights and its shortcomings, and to develop a proposal for an alternative marital regime.

Caffarena (1944, 17) argued that the name of the 1934 law, Equalizing Women before the Law, was a misnomer for it did not make men and women equal; rather, married women continued to have limited legal capacity. First, very few couples opted to marry under the separation of property regime, less than 1%. This meant that relatively few wives managed the property that they brought to marriage or

91 "Diversas modificaciones en el código civil," Law 10.271, February 29, 1952; www.leychile.cl.

92 While direct estimates of women's labor force participation rates by marital status are unavailable, the 1952 Census revealed that the rate was highest in the age group 20 to 24, where 35.1% were economically active but only 37.3% of the total were married. Thereafter, the labor force participation rate fell as the share who were married rose. Derived from Chile (1952, tables 20 and 5).

93 To its credit, during 1937 MENCH's newspaper, *La Mujer Nueva*, published articles aiming to educate women on their rights, for example, on parental rights and potestad marital and on women's legal capacity under different marital regimes. It also offered a required training workshop on this topic at its 1940 Second National Congress (*La Mujer Nueva* 1941, 27, 1–2).

later inherited. Second, while the adoption of reserved property for wives who worked was an important advance, it was only of "mediocre value" (Caffarena de Jiles 1944, 49). While wives could manage the assets they acquired with funds earned while married, they could not manage any assets they had purchased from their earnings prior to marriage. Since it was more common for women to work while they were single than once they married, this limited its benefit. Moreover, many women worked in family enterprises with their husbands, income that did not qualify for reserved property status, since it was not from an independent activity.

Another problem was that each time wives purchased an asset they had to prove that the funds came from such independent economic activities and many women, particularly those who worked only occasionally, did not engage in such bookkeeping. Caffarena (1944) asked rhetorically if this situation was any different from what prevailed in the past, with a wife having to ask her husband for permission to undertake any economic transaction. In sum, the mechanism of reserved property did not facilitate married women's economic autonomy.

Caffarena carefully reviewed the benefits and limitations of each of Chile's two marital regimes, separation of property and the conjugal society. While the former offered a woman the greatest economic autonomy since she was legally capable, the latter provided the greatest security because at the dissolution of the marriage, the wife received half the gananciales irrespective of her contribution. She stressed how the benefits and limitations of each regime depended on a woman's class position. A woman who married with a personal fortune or who was in a lucrative profession would be better off under separation of property since this gave her the greatest economic freedom. For those who married without assets and were homemakers, however, the conjugal society was preferable, since their right to half of the gananciales represented "compensation for the work, sacrifice and assistance encompassed in managing a household and raising children" (Caffarena de Jiles 1944, 75).

For Caffarena (1944, 75–80) the ideal marital regime was one that combined the strengths of each, the "regime of participation in the gananciales." Under this regime each spouse managed their own assets and earnings independently during the marriage but at its dissolution the gananciales of each constituted community property and subject to its equal division. She noted that Costa Rica, Honduras and Colombia had already adopted such a hybrid regime as the default. She said Chilean legal scholars were aware of this innovation, citing jurist Alessandri Rodríguez (1935)'s tome, but no one had championed it previously. She considered it the ideal default marital regime because it would dignify women, meeting their aspirations for full legal capacity, while assuring equity since it combined economic autonomy with the community of interests in marriage. She did not mention the potential benefits of requiring the alienation of gananciales to be subject to mutual consent (the reform that was subsequently enacted) likely because she thought it was time to change the default marital regime.

Caffarena (1944, 69, 82) viewed positively the 1943 reform that allowed couples to choose the separation of property regime at any time because it was only

TABLE 4.1 Number of Couples Opting for a Separation of Property, by Time Period and Mechanism, Chile, 1920–1960

Period	*Prenuptial*	*Average per year*	*After marriage*	*Average per year*		*Average per year*	*Total*	*Average per year*
Via:	*Notary*		*Notary*		*Judicial*			
1920–1924	5	1	83	16.6	17	3.4	105	21
1925–1934	45	4.5	482	48.2	35	3.5	562	56.2
1935–1944	148	14.8	1,814	181.4	24	2.4	1,986	198.6
1945–1954	776	77.6	4,946	494.6	29	2.9	5,751	575.1
1955–1960	1,991	331.8	1,112	185.3	0	1.5	3,112	518.7
Total	2,965 26%	72.3	8,437 73%	205.8	114 1%	2.8	11,516 100%	280.9

Source: Compiled by the author from the database provided by Chile, Servicio de Registro Civil, Subdirección de Estudios y Desarrollo, February 2024.

Note: Judicial includes separation of property due to a permanent separation or because of a woman's lawsuit against her husband for mismanagement.

after marriage that couples could determine the regime that best served their interests. Nonetheless, she thought the new law did not go far enough in providing couples with the flexibility required. For example, it did not allow couples who had chosen separation of property in a prenuptial agreement to later change their mind and opt for partial community property.[94]

Administrative data from the Civil Registry confirms Caffarena's conclusion that few couples opted for the separation of property regime before marriage and moreover, that even after the rules became more flexible relatively few did so. As Table 4.1 (last column) shows, considering all the different means that led to a separation of property, the average number of couples per year opting for it nationally was miniscule until the late 1940s–early 1950s when it reached an average 575 cases annually; this was primarily because of an increase after the 1943 law allowed this option at any time.[95]

94 The other reform that Caffarena (1944, 82) proposed had to do with adultery as a cause for a judicial separation. Not only were women held to a higher moral standard than men, but if a husband successfully sued his wife for a permanent separation based on her adultery she lost access to the gananciales from the marriage. Moreover, he continued as the administrator of her individual property, a point Caffarena considered particularly unjust since it relegated her to poverty.

95 Prior to this law those executing this action via a notary public were likely cases of marriage annulment, which produced a separation of property in the combined process of dissolution of the conjugal society and the marriage bond.

Between 1920 and 1960 very few couples obtained the separation of property via the traditional mechanisms of it resulting from either a judicial separation or a wife's lawsuit against her husband for his mismanagement of the community property. The number opting for it in a prenuptial agreement was also quite small until the late 1950s. The subsequent increase may have been in reaction to the change in the management of the gananciales; that is, a backlash among grooms who found the separation of property regime preferable to the conjugal society due to the 1952 reform that gave wives a say over the disposition of community property. This increase may have also been related to changing social norms that resulted after the option of separation of property at any time during the marriage became possible; this may have made the discussion of financial matters prior to marriage more acceptable. In any case, through the 1950s the share of marriages under separation of property irrespective of mechanism remained less than 1% of total marriages.[96] Thus the reform that potentially was the most beneficial to the largest share of wives was the 1952 reform that gave them a voice over the disposition of the gananciales. The country did not undertake further reforms until well into the second wave of feminism.[97]

Conclusion

Chile opened public secondary and university education to women earlier than other countries in the region, positioning it to be in the vanguard of the struggle for women's rights. Women's organizations demanding equal civil rights emerged concurrently with the first legislative proposals and thus engaged in the debates over reform right from their initiation. Yet what women attained by the mid-1930s was less than in neighboring countries, only control over their own earnings and the option of choosing the separation of property regime in a prenuptial agreement, an option not frequently used.

In comparative perspective there was greater attention in Chile than in other countries to the potential adoption of the separation of property regime as the default. This regime was the centerpiece of two of the three mains bills considered prior to the adoption of the 1925 decree and backed by prominent feminists. While the CNM-C's initial proposal had been different, focusing on working women

96 The 1952 census revealed that a total of 1.1 million women were "ever-married" (including those currently married, widows, in annulled marriages or permanently separated) (Chile 1952, Table 5). Of these, between 1920 and 1952 a total of 7,032 attained separation of property through some mechanism, representing 0.6%. In the 1955–1960 period when the number opting for separation of property at marriage reached an all-time high, these represented only 0.6% of the total 332,216 new marriages (derived from Chile-INE 1958, 102 and Chile-INE 1963, 94).

97 The need for a wife to obey her husband remained in the code until the reform of 1989. The deferred community property regime favored by Caffarena became an optional marital regime in 1994, while the enaction of civil divorce was not until 2004. Laws 18.802, May 23, 1989; 19.335, September 12, 1994; and 19.947, May 17, 2004, respectively, www.leychile.cl.

controlling their earnings with exceptional privileges, it subsequently supported adopting separation of property as the default primarily because it allowed wives to maintain the same property rights that they held as single women.

The Maza decree of 1925 met several of the demands put forth by women's organizations regarding women's civil capacity: women could now be witnesses as well as guardians and in the absence of the father, a mother could exercise patria potestad. But these and the property rights they gained came with important restrictions. In the compromise that led to it, the country adopted the separation of property regime as an option in a prenuptial agreement rather than as the default regime and instituted married women's reserved property under conditions that limited their economic autonomy.

Jurist Arturo Alessandri Rodríguez of the University of Chile played an outsized role in Chile's incremental process toward strengthening women's rights. He led the effort that resulted in Law 5.521 of 1934, which cleared up some of the deficiencies of the 1925 decree, such as giving women full control over their earnings and allowing a widowed mother who remarried to maintain patria potestad over her children. Later, as president of the Instituto Chileno de Estudios Legislativos, he drafted the legislation that allowed couples to choose the separation of property regime at any time; that improved the position of the surviving spouse in intestate inheritance; and that, under the conjugal society, curtailed the absolute control that husbands had over a couple's community property by requiring the consent of wives to alienate it.

All of these reforms responded to feminist demands. Elena Caffarena's (1928) critique of the Maza decree highlighted some of the specific problems that the subsequent 1934 law sought to address. MEMCH's 1936 program included the demand for greater flexibility in the choice of regime, so that couples could choose the separation of property after marriage; it also raised the demand to improve the position of children born outside of marriage. Amanda Labarca (1924) had a long-standing concern regarding the need to improve the position of widows in inheritance, particularly in conjunction with adoption of the separation of property regime. And the reform that gave wives a voice in the disposition of the community property was the result of the combined initiative of the Women's Party of Chile and the Women's Office that brought it to the attention of the Instituto Chileno.

The 1952 reform requiring the wife's consent for a husband to alienate community property was the most consequential because, as shown, relatively few couples opted for the separation of property either before or after marriage. The great majority married under the regime of the conjugal society, with husbands managing the assets women brought to marriage and any subsequent inheritances they received, and married women's labor force participation was still quite low, thus a minority could take advantage of the benefits of women's reserved property.

Worth noting is that while most feminist groups, including Catholic feminists, voiced the demand for equal civil rights, few ever called outright for the ending of potestad marital or voiced the goal of equal rights in marriage. The idea that united secular women was that when women marry they retain the property rights they had as single women. It is not clear if all Catholic feminists were willing to go that far. They principally advocated in favor of poor working-class women being able to control their own wages, alongside an improvement in the rights of mothers over their children, a long-standing demand that united women across religious and political divides. Elena Caffarena first voiced the demand for equal rights in marriage in her 1944 book, a considered analysis of the pros and cons of the two marital regimes (separation of property and the conjugal society). Neither jurists nor politicians in this period considered the adoption of the deferred community property regime, one that in her analysis combined the best features of each.

Among the reasons why progress on strengthening married women's property rights was slow and piecemeal was because the struggle for women's political rights was so prolonged. Nonetheless, women's political rights went from being a feminist aspiration in the 1910s and early 1920s to a demand in the 1930s primarily because of the growing consensus among organized women of both left and right that they needed political rights to achieve further reforms to benefit women and children. Many of the organized women's groups supported attaining suffrage in phases, beginning at the local level, in a pattern not unlike that of the United States, England and several European countries. That it took place in phases is also related to features of the country's political legacy. Unlike most other South American countries, it was the Conservative Party in Chile that had historically supported women's political rights, having introduced the first bill to this effect in 1917. While liberals and radicals embraced women's suffrage in principle, in practice, strategic considerations took precedence. They feared that women were too much under the sway of the Catholic Church, which would electorally favor conservatives. Hence the political consensus to grant women suffrage in phases to observe their voting behavior.

That it subsequently took another 15 years after women achieved municipal suffrage for them to attain full political rights was not for lack of effort. The women's organizations that emerged in the mid-1930s, especially the MEMCH with its large working-class base, expanded the composition and numbers of those demanding suffrage. Full political rights appeared in reach under the Popular Front government of Aguirre Cerda but his premature death combined with the uncertainty provoked by World War II reduced this momentum.

Other factors subsequently accelerated it, such as the growing international consensus around women's political rights in the immediate post-World War II period and the fear of Chile falling behind; that FECHIF united all the major women's organizations across the political, religious and class spectrum around this demand; and that the maintenance of democracy required women's political participation. The latter argument was pivotal as Chile veered to the right under Cold War politics and the regime of González Videla, after issuing the Ley Maldita, required internal and external legitimacy. The enactment of women's suffrage served as reaffirmation of the country's commitment to democracy.

5

PERU'S LENGTHY PATH TO CIVIL CODE REFORM AND WOMEN'S SUFFRAGE

Sometime prior to 1922 Zoila Marca de Ruedas and her sister inherited the family land that they farmed in the province of Lima.[1] When they decided to formally divide up this inheritance between them Zoila faced an obstacle. As a married woman, she could not represent herself in court to request this division without her husband's permission. She and her husband had separated informally some years before and he was now refusing to authorize this transaction, according to Zoila, out of spite. Her main recourse was to hire a lawyer and seek permission from a judge to represent herself to then execute this division of the property.

This petition appeared in a handbook written by lawyer Pedro Delgado (1922) on women's civil rights. To facilitate the work of other lawyers, he provided samples of 86 petitions that he had filed in court on behalf of women on a variety of issues, for example, on the right to marry without parental consent, guardianship, inheritance and wives' economic transactions (Delgado 1922, 276–343). In several, wives requested a judge to approve an action that their husbands had unjustly denied, such as to negotiate a contract or represent themselves in court. They also reveal how cumbersome it was for wives to act if their husband had abandoned them, was absent for a prolonged period or the couple had separated informally. Moreover, these petitions demonstrate that husbands effectively exercised potestad marital – their rights over the property and person of their wives – and that wives used the main recourse available to them, appealing to a judge when their interests required it. But this came at a cost in both time and money. By the 1920s many women were beginning to feel that such constraints on their activities were not only degrading, but also unproductive, given women's new economic roles.

1 Petition no. 52, in Delgado (1922, 318–9).

DOI: 10.4324/9781003658436-5

Peruvian feminists began organizing and speaking out for women's rights in the decade of the teens, although it was not until the 1920s that they began lobbying the legislature systematically, first to strengthen their civil rights and then to gain political rights. During this latter decade they developed their own proposals for civil code reform that sought to change the marital regime and eliminate most vestiges of potestad marital. These efforts coincided with the appointment of a commission charged with updating the country's code and with legislative initiatives to strengthen the property rights of wives. Their debates reveal the influence on Peruvian legal thinking of particular reforms in other countries as well as the extent to which feminist ideas and lobbying efforts influenced the content of its 1936 Civil Code.

By the time the Congress approved the new code, some of the reforms of married women's property rights that had seemed progressive in the 1920s appeared less so. Wives gained the right to manage and dispose of their own earnings and individual property but husbands continued as the sole managers of the community property. This meant that women such as Zoila Marca could now freely manage their inheritances; nonetheless, as long as they remained married, husbands managed the gains such property generated, half of which was theirs when the marriage dissolved. However, the new civil code allowed absolute divorce and made a legal separation easier, so women could more easily end a toxic relationship and any future claims on their property and labor.

Women's lobbying efforts led to a political compromise in the writing of the country's 1933 Constitution whereby literate adult women could vote and stand for office at the municipal level. It was not until 1955, in the context of post-World War II international consensus around women's political rights, that they attained suffrage. Given the lengthy struggle to achieve full political rights, feminists gave little attention to further strengthening married women's property rights beyond the reforms attained in the 1936 code.

Emergence of the Women's Movement

Some 18 Peruvian women, mostly educators or philanthropists, participated in the First International Women's Congress held in Buenos Aires in 1910 (Asociación de Universitarias Argentinas 1911, 25–9). Some had been the first to attend university in a period where their admittance required a special presidential or congressional decree.[2] Esther Festini in 1904 was the first woman to complete a Ph.D. in the Faculty of Philosophy and Letters at the Universidad Nacional Mayor de San Marcos

2 Universities formally opened to women under Law 801 of November 7, 1908. Prior to that only 14 women had been able to either enroll or take university classes. The first accepted by petition was Trinidad María Enríquez who in 1875 enrolled in the Faculty of Law at the University of San Antonio de Abad in Cuzco. Although she completed the course of study, the faculty never allowed her to take the exams needed to become a lawyer (Valladares 2012, 114–5 and Table 1).

(UNMSM). She and María Elvira Rodríguez Lorente as well as participants Teresa González Fanning and Elvira García y García established and/or directed schools for women. Among the philanthropists was Juana Alarco de Dammert who in 1902 founded the first maternity hospital in Lima (Salazar 2001, 83–92).

Other elite women of this generation established magazines aimed at women or centers to train working-class women for employment.[3] Among the latter was the Centro Social de Señoras (Ladies Social Center), co-founded in 1905 by Festini, writer Zoila Aurora Cáceres, physician Laura Rodríguez Dulanto[4] and others (Pachas 2019, 31, 34). With around 200 mostly society women as members, it ran a school that provided women with technical training for a range of new careers, from nursing to commerce, following a model common in Europe (Araujo 2009, 174).

Zoila Aurora Cáceres, who would become one of Peru's foremost feminists, was the daughter of General Andrés Avelino Cáceres, a hero of the War of the Pacific who served two terms as president of Peru.[5] She received a privileged education, studying in England, Germany and France, and graduating in 1906 from the School for Advanced Studies at the Sorbonne where she authored a thesis on "Feminism in Berlin," based on interviews with notable German feminists (Pachas 2019, 29; Valdivia 2019, 425). In 1909 she published *Mujeres de ayer y de hoy* (Women of Yesterday and Today), likely the first account of the accomplishments of feminism in Europe by a Latin American woman who had the opportunity to experience and report on these first-hand.

While much of Cáceres' (1909) book focused on famous women in antiquity and in literature, it included her reporting on the militant suffragists in England (of whom she was critical), the diverse views of feminists in France and Germany and the 1908 Feminist Congress in Paris that she covered for the International Press Association. In addition, she reported favorably on the 1907 legal advance in France that gave wives who worked outside the home the right to control their own earnings as reserved property. Her book likely contributed to subsequent discussions in Peru on the need to enact a similar reform.

Most of the papers presented by Peruvians at the 1910 Buenos Aires Congress advocated prioritizing women's education and employment as a precondition to

3 Salazar (2001, 77–83) distinguishes those of the Generation of 1890 who took on public roles from the Generation of 1870, the precursors of feminism, who as writers questioned women's intellectual inferiority and their unequal access to education. The best known writers were Clorinda Matto de Turner, Mercedes Cabello de Carbonera and Argentine-born Juana Manuela Gorriti. Also see Cáceres (1909, 187–203) and Villavicencio (1992: chpts. 3 and 4).

4 In 1900 Rodríguez Dulanto was the first woman to earn a medical degree from UNMSM and founded Peru's first school of nursing (Pachas 2019, 34).

5 Cáceres lived in Buenos Aires during her father's exile and it was there that she began her literary career under the mentorship of Clorinda Matto who, also in exile, edited the periodical *El Búcaro Americano.* She published her first article under the pseudonym "Eva Angelina" (later "Evangelina") (Valdivia 2019, 421; Pachas 2019, 27–8).

FIGURE 5.1 Peruvian educator María Jesús Alvarado Rivera (1878–1971), ca. 1911.

Source: Courtesy of Centro de la Mujer Peruana Flora Tristán.

equal civil rights, including the paper presented (in absentia) by educator María Jesús Alvarado Rivera (Figure 5.1), another of the country's pioneering feminists.[6] Alvarado (1911, 271–2) thought "it was premature to demand women's absolute legal equality," referring to citizenship and political rights, since social prejudices that held women to be inferior must be changed first, along with the "unequal and humiliating civil condition of women." A few of these conference papers raised specific reforms required to the nation's 1852 civil code, discussed subsequently.

In 1911 the Geographic Society of Lima invited Alvarado to address its members, an event subsequent feminist scholars consider the debut of Peruvian feminism (Chaney 1979; Villavicencio 1992; Zegarra 2006). In "El Feminismo" Alvarado ([1912] 2012) argued that a basic principle of feminism was its recognition of the equal intellect and capacity of men and women, hence, they should be equal before the law. Her list of needed reforms included elevating the level of women's

6 An autodidact, Alvarado was a journalist, novelist and teacher who acquired her credential by exam without having attended a normal school (Zegarra 2006; Ysla 2022, 22–6).

education to that of men; opening government positions and all liberal professions to women; enhancing women's property rights so that when they married, they retain those they had when single; and eventually attaining women's equal political rights (Alvarado Rivera [1912] 2012, 9).

Noting the advances of feminism elsewhere, Alvarado ([1912] 2012, 15–6) lamented the situation of Peruvian women where "erroneous concepts and medieval prejudices" still predominated, such that a woman's destiny was to become a wife or a nun, which then supposedly justified the lack of attention to their education. While a small but growing number of women were accessing secondary education and entering new occupations, this had not yet led to sufficient numbers demanding civil or political rights. She expected this to change once more women received a better quality education and joined the labor force.

The name and program of the organization that Alvarado founded in 1914, Evolución Femenina (Women's Evolution), the country's first explicitly feminist organization, reflected this evolutionary perspective. Among its 77 founding members were several of the women who had attended the 1910 Buenos Aires conference, including Dora Mayer, Teresa González Fanning, Juana Alarco, and Elvira Rodríguez Lorente, with Alvarado serving as its president and law student Miguelina Acosta Cárdenas as secretary.[7] In her inaugural address, Alvarado (1914, 3) stressed that "we are not going to do a revolution, an initiative that would fail in this unfavorable context. We are only going to advocate for an evolution of the feminine mentality…." She committed the organization to defending "women's real interests and rights," which included their right to an education and to enter the liberal professions and government posts. She also defended motherhood, "women's first and most noble mission," and planned to assist women becoming better mothers through education and training in home economics, hygiene and childrearing (Alvarado Rivera 1914, 6). She stressed how motherhood was perfectly compatible with work in the professions and the exercise of civil and political rights.

Alvarado (1914, 5) also promised a thorough study of the 1852 Civil Code and of laws that impacted women, "seeking to modify those that are prejudicial…and that deny married women the right to administer and dispose of their own assets," among other norms. Noting the recent legal advances of women in Germany and Italy, she highlighted how these strengthened rather than weakened marriage and the family, since "when both [spouses] have the same rights and responsibilities, they hold each other in mutual esteem and respect" (Alvarado Rivera 1914,6). Thus, the founding principles of Evolución Femenina included men's and women's

7 Alvarado, Mayer and Acosta were also involved in the Asociación Pro-Indigena (Indigenous Rights Association), the organization founded by Pedro Zulen in 1909 where Dora Mayer, a German-Peruvian writer-journalist, played a leading role and edited its periodical, *El Deber Pro-Indígena* (Ysla 2022, 60–2). After the founding of the Geneva-based WILPF in 1915, Mayer was its Peruvian correspondent. Miguelina Acosta was from a well-to-do family in the rubber trade in department of Loreto and studied in Europe prior to attending university in Peru (Rojas 2020, 11).

equal civil capacity and equality in marriage.[8] One of Alvarado's first acts as president was to send a memo to the Chamber of Deputies in October 1914 demanding reform of the civil code because of all the ways that it discriminated against women (Castorino 1969, 71–2).

Evolución Femenina's first major campaign, nonetheless, aimed to enhance women's roles in the public sphere in an activity in which they were already engaged – for them to become official members of the semi-public institutions that organized welfare activities at the departmental level, the Sociedades de Beneficencia Pública (Public Beneficent Societies). While women were the main volunteers, they could not hold office or vote on policy, in contrast to countries such as Argentina where women had long run such organizations. A bill to allow women to become official members of the Beneficencias had languished in the Congress since 1913, thus Alvarado launched a successful two-year campaign in its support (Guardia 1985, 71).[9]

Alvarado also focused on improving the situation of poor women, establishing the Escuela-Taller Moral y Trabajo (School-Workshop for Work and Morality) in 1915 that trained them for participation in the labor market (Ysla 2022, 52–3). It was one of several new centers founded to address the situation of women workers, some organized by anarchist women who were in the vanguard of labor organizing between 1911 and 1924.[10] Miguelina Acosta and Dora Mayer participated in other initiatives, such as the Sociedad de Labor Feminista (Society for Feminist Work)[11] and in 1919 organized housewives in the Committee to Lower the Cost of Living. In addition, Acosta was among the organizers of the Women's Committee of the Labor Movement that participated in the national strike of May 1919; its repression resulted in over 400 deaths (Salazar 2001, 102).

More conservative feminists, such as María Wiesse, the editor of *Familias*, condemned the actions of these activist feminists. In a June 1919 editorial, she wrote that

> the real and only feminism that should receive support is that which does not deprive women of their aura. It is not the conquest of the rights of men, such as to speak in the plazas – as done recently by a group of hapless and irresponsible women who have caused a ruckus, exposing themselves to ridicule.[12]

8 "Estatutos de la Institución Evolución Femenina," art. 2e, in Alvarado Rivera (1914, 7).

9 Law 4526, September 23, 1922. Conforming to Peru's civil code, this law required women who were married to obtain their husband's permission to serve as members (Salazar 2001).

10 On women's participation in labor unions and other initiatives to benefit working-class women, see García Naranjo (2009, 62–89) and Salazar (2001, 97–102).

11 This Society's activities included education and training, legal aid and an employment agency. In 1918 Corina Prado was president with Acosta serving as auditor and Mayer as editor of its periodical, *Revista Labor Feminista*; press report in *La Verdad*, reproduced in *La Mujer Ecuatoriana* (1918, 34–5). Mayer and Acosta were also co-editors of the weekly *La Crítica*, a periodical of political commentary.

12 Reproduced as "El verdadero Femenismo," in *La Crítica* (1919, 97, 7).

She praised the work of philanthropist Juana Alarco for exemplifying "true feminism," and having "broadened women's horizons" by leaving "the narrow confines of the home to collaborate with men." However, if women departed from those activities considered proper for their sex they risked losing "the charm of their femininity."[13] The fact that women's charity work was socially acceptable was likely the reason Evolución Femenina's first campaign challenging gender inequality focused on the Beneficencias. But María Jesús Alvarado soon turned her organization's focus to reforming the civil code, since it constrained women's activities as wives, mothers and workers.

Critiques of the Civil Code and Women's Organizing

As women's labor force participation became more widespread and visible, the constraints on their activities began to draw attention. Law students began to write doctoral theses on women's lack of rights while educated women began to demand specific civil code reforms and to lobby for them.

Among the law theses presented at UNMSM that argued in support of women's civil emancipation was Lorenzo Mori y Chávez's (1906) thesis.[14] He considered the unequal treatment of men and women in the 1852 Civil Code to be unjust, especially the marital regime. While wives could manage some individual property (the *bienes parafernales* – those that were not part of a dowry), they could not sell, mortgage or acquire such property or appear in suits without their husbands' permission; moreover, the husband was the sole manager of the community property and if she had one, her dowry.[15] Also, a mother could exercise patria potestad over her minor children only in the absence of the father; if a widow remarried she lost these rights (Fuentes and de la Lama 1870, arts. 285, 293).

Mori y Chávez (1906) argued that the rationale for this unequal treatment was based on two inter-related arguments: men's natural superiority over women, and the idea that the husband must be the head of the conjugal society to maintain order in the family. The code's articles that limited the civil capacity of both single and married women, such as not allowing them to be a witness to a will, serve as a guarantor of a loan or be guardians of minors, all reflected the assumption that men were naturally superior to women.[16] Women's presumed inferiority then justified the limitations placed on the activities of wives, allegedly to protect the weaker

13 *La Crítica* (1919, 97, 7).

14 Zegarra (2006, 494–5) found 11 UNMSM theses on the status of women between 1884 and 1922, including two on women's civil rights. I was unable to locate these but found an additional four, some from other universities.

15 The restrictions on wives and the marital regime are in Peru (1852, arts. 173–190, 955–1076); hereafter, I use the 1870 official edition of Fuentes and de la Lama (1870).

16 See Fuentes and de la Lama (1870, arts. 683, 314 and 331). If a parent did not name a guardian in a will, guardianship fell to the grandparents, with preference to the father's line over the mother's, and men always preferred over women.

sex.[17] He considered this argument to be a pretext to ensure their dependence on husbands and bolster men's position as household heads. Cognizant of the reforms undertaken in Europe and the United States, he recommended "a radical reform" of the Peruvian code so that it treat men and women equally. Nonetheless, he did not provide specific suggestions regarding the changes required in the marital regime.

A thesis for a law doctorate at the University of Cuzco by Julio Jiménez Pacheco (1913) covered similar terrain, challenging the argument that women were naturally inferior to men and arguing in favor of equal civil rights. He viewed the process of women's emancipation much as María Jesús Alvarado did, that it should evolve in phases, beginning with improving their education followed by stronger civil rights and finally, political rights. Nonetheless, he also did not make any specific recommendations regarding needed reforms. Only one of these law theses recommended a specific reform, a UNMSM doctoral thesis by Enrique Barriga Alarcón (1907). He proposed requiring a wife's consent for the husband to dispose of community property, viewing such a requirement as both just and consistent with the logic of the code. Since the husband was only the administrator, not the sole owner of the community property, he should not be able to do anything he pleased with property in which a wife had a shared interest.

Several of the papers presented by Peruvians at the 1910 Buenos Aires Women's Conference criticized specific aspects of the civil code. Dora Mayer (1911, 247–8) argued that it "was flagrantly biased against women," and considered "that any law that makes a woman depend upon a man for her personal transactions is an abuse. Any person who does not administer directly their own assets exposes themselves to potential deceit." Similarly, Teresa González Fanning (1911, 280) demanded that the code allow wives to manage the assets that they brought to marriage. She also thought widows should have the right to manage "the couple's total fortune"; that is, that the gananciales remain under a widow's control rather than their division between her and her deceased husband's estate. Both papers stressed how men and women should be subject to the same moral standard and, specifically that in the case of a legal separation due to adultery, the same standard apply to the guilty party, whether husband or wife. Another paper presented under the pseudonym "Rignas" argued that given the substantial number of illegitimate children, the civil code needed to allow the investigation of paternity (Asociación de Universitarias Argentinas 1911, 387).

Miguelina Acosta Cárdenas (Figure 5.2), one of the first two female lawyers, undertook the first comprehensive analysis of needed reforms for her 1920 doctoral thesis at UNMSM. Among her recommendations was changing the language in the 1852 Civil Code so that the gender-neutral concept of "persons" replace references to "man" or "men," as in article 2 that stated, "man from birth has all the rights

17 What wives could and could not do without permission of their husbands is in arts. 176–188 (Fuentes and de la Lama (1870).

FIGURE 5.2 Peruvian lawyer Miguelina Acosta Cárdenas (1887–1933), 1920.

Source: In *Miguelina Acosta Cárdenas. Pensamiento y acción*, edited by Joel Rojas (Lima: Heraldo Eds., 2020). Courtesy of Joel Rojas and the Archivo Familia Acosta.

that the law declares." Such a change would give women equal civil capacity to conduct all acts, such as being a witness or a guardian (Acosta Cárdenas 1920, 35). With respect to marriage, she proposed abolishing all elements of potestad marital, including the infamous phrase copied from the Napoleonic Code that the husband owed the wife protection and the wife obedience to him, and replacing it with a dual-headed household, "household governance by both spouses" (Acosta Cárdenas 1920, 51).

Acosta recommended maintaining the existing marital regime of partial community property (termed the *sociedad legal*) that recognized the individual property of each spouse as well as the community property generated during the marriage, the gananciales. Her innovation was to propose a change in its management. Wives were to fully manage their own individual property, including the right to mortgage or sell such without need for a husband's permission, while the couple was to jointly manage the gananciales. In addition, she proposed the adoption of reserved property (*bienes reservados*) for married women who did not own assets, so that they be able to manage their own wages, salaries and other earnings generated through their own independent labor, similar to the 1907 French reform except that its gains, as men's, were to be jointly managed. She also recommended abolishing the dowry and arras, since these were legal relics.[18] Finally, Acosta advocated giving mothers equal and joint rights with fathers in the exercise of patria potestad.

Since Acosta was on the board of Evolución Femenina, she likely worked with María Jesús Alvarado on the petition drafted on its behalf in November 1922 that Alvarado presented to the Chamber of Deputies and the newly appointed Civil Code Review Commission. Alvarado ([1923] 2019) found it objectionable that the civil code often lumped women together with minors, idiots, and those who were physically or morally impaired to deny them civil rights. She demanded that the code allow all women to serve as guardians over children as well as witnesses to a will. She deplored the subjugation of the wife to the husband's authority, especially that she owed him obedience, and demanded recognition of a wife's full civil capacity, including her right to contract and to represent herself in lawsuits, rights that she held as a single woman.

With respect to the marital regime, Alvarado highlighted the disparity in the code's treatment of the contributions and rights of each spouse:

> If the gananciales are acquired with the labor of both spouses or the use of the assets of each, and these represent not only the work of the man but also the energies and savings of the wife, and if she, because of her maternal love and her own convenience is just as interested in the welfare of the family, why is only the husband able to alienate such joint assets, while the woman cannot dispose of even those assets that she brought to the marriage or acquired by inheritance or donation…?
>
> *(Alvarado Rivera [1923] 2019, 45)*

Since husbands and wives had parallel obligations in marriage – to provide fidelity and assistance to each other – Alvarado thought that it was only fair that the treatment of their assets be the same. Moreover, note her emphasis on the wife's equal contribution to the generation of the gananciales through her domestic labor. Her petition implied that each spouse should manage their own assets, subject to the same constraint: each would need the consent of the other to dispose of these assets as well as the gananciales they generated. This parallelism suggests that her goal was equal spousal rights in marriage. While she does not clearly define the marital regime she had in mind, its outline suggests something like what is known as deferred community property, that is, a combination of separation of property during the marriage with the gananciales shared equally at the end.

18 See Hünefeldt (2000) on the decline of the practice of dowry over the nineteenth century.

Alvarado's petition also demanded that the code allow the investigation of paternity of children born outside marriage since it was unjust to punish illegitimate children by not recognizing their right to support from their parents. It did not mention mother's equal exercise of patria potestad, as did Acosta's proposal, perhaps because she thought that demand might face more objections than those around women's property rights. Although the Chamber's legislation commission shelved the petition upon its receipt, Alvarado publicized its contents in the press and began a campaign around its endorsement.

Women's organizing efforts grew in the 1920s in tandem with their improved educational attainment and increased labor force participation.[19] Social norms among the middle- and upper-class regarding women's employment were changing, at least for single women. As Elvira García y García (1925, 855) explained:

> Traditional prejudices that criticized women who worked have in large measure disappeared…, the events surrounding the European War and the good example offered by North American women have led a good number of women to the conviction that if one has energy and intelligence it is better to work than to be an eternal parasite of the family. It is no longer rare to see ladies from "good society" personally directing their own businesses, and many *señoritas* seek positions in commercial establishments or in schools for girls.

The new women's organizations of the 1920s included women's professional organizations of teachers, nurses and employees in commerce. Elisa Rodríguez Porras de García Rosell founded the Legión Feminista Pro-Cultura (Feminist Legion for Culture) in 1922 to prepare young women for work, which also focused on women's rights and peace issues.[20] Others had a more social welfare focus, such and the Sociedad del Bien del Hogar (Society for Household Welfare) in which educator Esther Festini was involved that trained working-class women in the domestic sciences (Salazar 2001, 112–3).

Given the growing number of women completing university, an alumni association formed, the Federación de Universitarias Graduadas, that advocated for women's rights, with Miguelina Acosta serving as president, as well as an International Committee of University Graduates, chaired by Esther Festini who was in contact

19 Census data for the province of Lima for 1920 and 1931 show that the largest number of women reporting an occupation were in the manufacturing sector or domestic servants. Between these censuses, among the occupations where women's participation grew relatively rapidly were those in commerce and the liberal professions broadly defined (Peru 1927, Tables 65 and 66; Peru 1932, Table 78).

20 It was affiliated with the WILPF (García y García 1925, 373–5, 682–92, 854). Rodríguez was on the governing board of the Consejo Superior del Trabajo y Prevision Social (Superior Council of Work and Social Welfare), a semi-official organization, and inspected factories and establishments that employed women. She later founded the women's magazine *Universal. Revista Femenina Ilustrada*.

with its counterpart in the United States (García y García 1925, 695–7). Other activist women, such as writers Angela Ramos and Magda Portal, became associated with the periodicals founded by José Carlos Mariátegui in 1926, *Amauta* and *Labor*, and joined his Socialist Party (later Communist Party), which advocated for women's emancipation alongside the class struggle (Guardia 1985, 74).

Women from several of these new groups along with traditional women's welfare organizations came together to form the Consejo Nacional de Mujeres del Peru (CNM-P, National Council of Peruvian Women) in 1923. The catalyst behind its formation was a February 1923 visit to Peru by Carrie Chapman Catt, the IWSA president and honorary president of the PAAAW. María Jesús Alvarado took advantage of the lecture series that she arranged for Catt to present Evolución Femenina's petition for women's civil rights and gather signatures, including that of Catt (Castorino 1969, 38–43).

Among those who failed to endorse the petition was the CNM-P's first president, philanthropist Mercedes Gallaguer de Parks.[21] Earlier, she had shared the petition with her cousin, a judge, who thought that its demands might require a fundamental rewriting of the civil code, one that would challenge "the existing social basis of society." Thus Gallaguer concluded that "it would be better if things continue as they were if changing them in a society as immature and loosely consolidated as ours, would weaken the family."[22] Alvarado ended up presenting her petition to the Civil Code Review Commission in June 1923 with 135 signatures but without the Consejo's endorsement (CCRC 1923, 194).

Some 36 organizations joined the CNM-P and there was disagreement among them over priorities, with Evolución Femenina being the most explicitly feminist and some not being interested in enhancing women's rights at all. In reference to Alvarado's petition, the representative of the Unión Católica de Señoras (Catholic Ladies Union) was cited in the press as saying that women's civil rights were incompatible with the principles of its organization (Chaney 1979, 335).[23] Carrie Chapman Catt had foreseen that it might be particularly difficult to consolidate an effective women's umbrella organization in Peru, given the strong influence of the Catholic Church and that the country was marked by stark class and ethnic divisions, including between white Hispanic women and middle-class mestizo women; all the university graduates whom she met belonged to the latter group.[24]

21 Gallaguer was a member of the Pan American Women's Committee organized in each country after the Pan American Women's Auxiliary Conference in Washington, D.C. in late 1915. Other notable members of this committee were writer Lastenia Larriva de Llona, Luisa Dammert and Elvira García y García (García y García 1925, 925).

22 Letter of Gallaguer to Alvarado of December 1922 reproduced in Córdova (1969, 132).

23 Also see Ysla (2022, 50–1) on the opposition of many elite women to women's greater civil rights. The CNM-P's first activity under Gallaguer was a morality campaign directed at cinemas and the press (García y García 1925, 718–9). It officially joined the ICW in 1926.

24 Carrie Chapman Catt Papers: Diaries Europe and South America, 1922 to 1923, 2 of 4, "En route Peru to Panama," Roundabout letter of February 6, 1923.

The organization of the CNM-P coincided with preparations for the Pan American Union's Third Scientific Conference in Lima in late December 1924 and its parallel Women's Auxiliary Congress over which Mercedes Gallaguer eventually presided.[25] Alvarado was scheduled to present four papers at the women's congress, including one on women's rights, but the day it was to begin she was arrested and jailed for her work in support of workers opposed to the Leguía regime and subsequently went into exile in Buenos Aires (Castorino 1969, 44–50, 57).

Zoila Aurora Cáceres then picked up the banner of feminism. Although a decade earlier she had been a founding member of the Catholic Ladies Union, after another stay in France she returned to Peru in 1924 to found Feminismo Peruano, an explicitly secular and non-partisan organization whose primary objective was to promote women's equal civil and political rights (Pachas 2019, 42). It was the first Peruvian organization to embrace the demand for women's recognition as citizens with the ability vote and stand for office in both municipal and national elections. It did not join the CNM-P because of that organization's resistance to women's suffrage and the excessive religiosity of some its affiliated members (Cáceres [n.d. a] 2019).

Among the civil code reforms Feminismo Peruano demanded was recognition of the full civil capacity of married women so that they be able to administer their own assets including the gananciales they generated during the marriage, as well as allowing all women to be guardians, witnesses, guarantors of loans and legal representatives.[26] Its platform also called for the same minimum age (18) for men and women to marry; for mothers to exercise the same rights of patria potestad as fathers; and for the code to allow the investigation of the paternity of unrecognized children.

In her arguments in favor of equal civil and political rights, Cáceres highlighted the injustices that women suffered because of their lack of property rights, and why as mothers and patriots they deserved greater rights. Her ideas blended liberal and Catholic feminisms, except when it came to divorce, which she personally opposed.[27] She drew attention to the success of reforms in Europe and the activities of the IAWSEC (the renamed IWSA), which Feminismo Peruano joined (Cáceres [n.d. a] 2019). The press gave broad coverage to its program and Cáceres' speaking

25 Often called the Second Pan American Women's Congress, the International Pan American Women's Committee organized it and not the PAAAW, which emerged from the 1922 First Pan American Women's Congress in Baltimore; PAAAW's next meeting was the 1926 Inter-American Women's Congress in Panama. At the Lima meeting, Peruvian women presented some 96 papers, mostly focused on women's education, employment and philanthropic activities (García y García 1925, 925–36).

26 "Programa de Principios de Feminismo Peruano," *La Prensa*, October 2, 1924, in Pachas (2019, 42).

27 When freedom of religion was under discussion in the Congress in 1915, Cáceres defended the church's position, which wanted to maintain its standing as the official religion. Also, after she separated from her husband she did not pursue a civil divorce although she could have done so while residing in France since she had married there. She eventually got her marriage annulled but never remarried. See Araujo (2009), Valdivia (2019), and Pachas (2019) for more detail on her ideas and on Catholic feminism.

engagements since she was a well-known public figure (Aguilar 2006; Pachas 2019, 41–5). It was in this context of the growing visibility of women in the public realm and increasing agitation for women's civil and political rights by a vocal minority, that the Congress considered women's rights and the Civil Code Review Commission undertook its deliberations.

Congressional Initiatives on Women's Rights

In the late teens the legislature entertained bills to recognize women's political rights and institute absolute divorce prior to the first bills to strengthen married women's property rights. Feminists ignored the early suffrage bill, considering it unfeasible, and differed in their support for civil divorce. There was broader support for civil code reform, which the Congress finally addressed in the mid-twenties. None of these legislative initiatives were successful although the discussions they generated began to move public opinion in favor of strengthening women's civil rights.

During the presidency of José Pardo, a deputy in the anti-Pardo faction from Huancavelica, Celestino Manchego Muñoz, introduced the first bill to give women suffrage in 1918. It limited the vote to a small group of well-educated women, including those engaged in a liberal profession (that he defined as lawyers, physicians, engineers, pharmacists or dentists), university graduates and those holding a doctorate in any field, journalists who had edited a periodical for at least three years and published writers.[28] The next year Augusto B. Leguía led a successful coup against the elected president and dissolved the Congress. A National Constitutional Assembly then confirmed Leguía as president and drafted a new constitution. During its deliberations, Manchego, elected as a supporter of Leguía, re-introduced his bill to grant suffrage to educated women.[29] There is no record that the Assembly seriously considered it.

The published documents of Evolución Femenina do not mention these suffrage initiatives although María Jesús Alvarado was surely aware of them. At the time she was lobbying the Congress on behalf of the bill regarding women's participation in the Beneficencias. She likely did not take Deputy Manchego's efforts seriously because she considered it far-fetched that women attain suffrage prior to stronger civil rights.

Also in 1918, senators Angel Gustavo Cornejo and Mariano Lino Urquieta presented a bill to make civil marriage mandatory for all (rather than limiting it to non-Catholics as the 1897 law had) and allow for civil divorce with the possibility of remarriage.[30] The Senate approved the bill that year and in September 1920 the Chamber did so as well. President Leguía did not sign the bill since he did not want

28 *Diario de los Debates de la Cámara de Diputados* (DDCD) (1918, October 14, 915).

29 *Diario de los Debates de la Asamblea Nacional de 1919* (1919, vol. 1, 246).

30 In the 1852 Civil Code ecclesiastical law governed marriage. See Cornejo (1921, 203–4 and 270–84) on the debates over civil marriage during the nineteenth century, and absolute divorce in the early twentieth.

to destabilize his relations with the Catholic Church and returned it to the Congress with observations.[31]

Prior to 1920 the activists of Evolución Femenina had not taken a stand in the debate over civil marriage and divorce likely because the group included both secular and Catholic women and this issue could potentially divide them. But once the Senate approved the bill, two of the leaders of Agitación Femenina came out in favor of absolute divorce. Miguelina Acosta (1920, 36) addressed the issue in her doctoral thesis where she argued that marriage was a contract and just like any other contract couples should be able to dissolve it; civil divorce was the logical extension of civil marriage.

María Jesús Alvarado announced her support for divorce by publishing a short pamphlet where she argued that it would strengthen marriage and the family. In Alvarado's analysis, marriage must be based on love and mutual respect; if those elements were missing, marriage was akin to "legalized prostitution" (Alvarado Rivera 1922, 14). Achieving harmony in marriage also required ending the wife's legal subordination, for their civil incapacity made them "the slave of their husbands" (Alvarado Rivera 1922, 5, 12).[32] Since marriages were indissoluble, women had no bargaining power if their husbands turned out to be tyrants. Hence, to establish the basis for truly companionate marriage – founded on love and mutual respect – required both instituting divorce and men and women having equal civil rights. That is why civil code reform was such a priority.

The Debate on Married Women's Property Rights

Although President Leguía in 1922 appointed a Civil Code Reform Commission to update the country's 1852 civil code, by 1925 it had not yet addressed married women's property rights. Thus a group of Leguía deputies in the Chamber led by Juan Francisco Pazos Varela decided to act and presented a bill to give wives the right to freely dispose of their bienes parafernales without need for authorization by the husband or a judge.[33]

The 1852 Civil Code defined these as the individual assets that a woman brought to marriage that were not part of a dowry plus as any inheritances or donations that

31 After Luis M. Sánchez Cerro deposed Leguía, Decree Law 6890 of October 8, 1930, fully incorporated the 1920 bill approved by the Chamber; Decree Law 6889 of the same date nullified Leguía's observations. The allowed causes for absolute divorce were based on fault and the same as those specified by the 1852 code for a judicial separation (Fuentes y de la Lama 1870, art. 192).

32 Mannarelli (1999, 208–19) and Zegarra (2006, 499) highlight Alvarado's critique of marriages of convenience which she claimed led to extra-marital affairs and illegitimate children. But also embedded in this pamphlet was a strong critique of potestad marital.

33 DDCD (1925, April 17, 95). Pazos Varela was a former director of the daily *El Tiempo;* among the co-signers was Celestino Manchego who had earlier introduced the first suffrage bill. All were members or allies of Leguía's Partido Democrático Reformista (Democratic Reformist Party) (Reaño 1928).

a wife received after marriage. While the wife was the owner of these assets and she could opt to manage them, she could not sell or mortgage them without her husband's permission or that of a judge. If she did not bring a dowry, the code required a wife to turn over half these assets to her husband for him to manage. The gananciales derived from these individual assets formed part of the community property. Pazos Varela's bill proposed two important changes: allowing a wife to mortgage or sell the bienes parafernales without need for her husband's or a judge's approval; and designating the gains from these individual assets as the property of the wife alone rather than forming part of the community property.

It is unknown whether these deputies were responding to the demands of Evolución Femenina's 1922 petition. This bill went beyond their demand that married women be able to manage their own property, since it proposed giving wives the right to manage and *retain* the gananciales accruing from such individual property, an exceptional privilege.[34] Its petition asked for parallel treatment in the ownership and management of the property of each spouse, not special privileges.

The Chamber's commission on legislation subsequently forwarded the bill to the Supreme Court for its advisory opinion, and the court's majority report accepted the bill's first proposal but not the second. Since wives owned and managed the bienes parafernales, it reasoned this should include the right to freely dispose of these assets without need for the permission of anyone.[35] But it opposed anything that might weaken the conjugal society and thus rejected that the gananciales from such individual property accrue to the wife alone. It stressed how the civil code treated the individual property of husbands and wives similarly and that this proposal would introduce a fundamental inequality in favor of women that would undermine its basic principles. Two of the justices issued a minority report that adamantly condemned the whole bill since it weakened the concept of potestad marital and the position of the husband as head of the conjugal society, factors they considered detrimental to the well-being of the family. Moreover, they were against Congress undertaking any partial reform of the marital regime while the Civil Code Reform Commission was working on these same issues.

In its report, the Chamber's commission concurred that wives should have the right to dispose of their bienes parafernales without need for anyone's permission.[36] It also agreed that the other proposition – to give married women exclusive rights to the gains generated by these assets – would weaken the conjugal society. Instead, to protect women's interests, it recommended that husbands be unable to sell or mortgage immovable community property without their wives' consent. This

34 The bill's special treatment of the wife's parafernales was like what neighboring Ecuador had adopted as an option in its 1911 reform (see Chapter 2). It is unknown if the bill's authors were familiar with this reform.

35 Ruling of April 12, 1926, in Corte Suprema (1927, 187–96).

36 In *Diario de los Debates de la Cámara Nacional de Diputados* (DDCND) (1926, December 16, 1270–1).

proposal was like what Evolución Femenina had demanded in its 1922 petition. Nonetheless, while the commission considered the reform of the rules regarding wives' management of their own property as important, it did not view it as urgent. It thought that many more wives were employed and earning income than those who owned property; thus, it was more urgent to give working women the right to manage their own earnings. However, it was hesitant to recommend these partial reforms before the Civil Code Reform Commission concluded its work.

The commission ended up proposing a substitute bill to accomplish two things: it would abrogate articles 1038 and 1039 of the civil code, so that married women had full property rights over their bienes parafernales; and it would make the sale or mortgage of community property subject to the consent of both spouses, which in effect was giving the same treatment to community property as the code currently gave to the dowry. That is, the husband would be unable to alienate it without his wife's consent.

During the Chamber's discussion of this substitute bill, Pazos Varela, the author of the original bill, agreed to it although he considered his own initial proposal, to allow wives to retain the gananciales their own property generated, to be superior. [37] Plácido Jiménez, the chair of the legislation commission, was afraid that such a change might pave the way for the institution of the separation of property regime, one that he considered to be against the interests of most wives because of men's and women's different capacities to earn income and acquire assets. He also argued that the legislature should not make such a fundamental change to the marital regime, one that gave wives special treatment, while the Civil Code Reform Commission was working on a new code. Jiménez had discussed his substitute bill with its members and they concurred that his proposal only added consistency to the administration of bienes parafernales and the community property.

A deputy from Puno, Carlos A. Calle, voiced the main opposition to the substitute bill, arguing against requiring the wife's consent for a husband to sell community property because such a measure would undermine his position as household head. He urged the Chamber to postpone this debate in order to give the Civil Code Reform Commission time to complete its work. Pazos Varela and Jiménez wanted the legislature to act now although for different reasons. Pazos Varela thought it important that the Congress take a stand in support of women's property rights in principle, while Jiménez was worried about how long it might take the Reform Commission to finish its work. After the motion to delay consideration of the bill failed, the deputies approved the first part of the substitute bill, to abrogate the two inconsistent articles of the civil code.

There was more discussion on the second, with Deputy Calle continuing to object to requiring the wife's consent for the husband to alienate community property. Pazos Varela offered an eloquent defense of how women contributed to the

37 DDCND (1927, vol. 3, 5 and 15–27; 6, 12–26).

generation of gananciales and should have a say over their disposition: "The man works to sustain the family…but the woman also works in the home, since she needs to look after the children, to educate and care for them."[38] He stressed how marriage was a partnership, and even if the husband was the only one contributing income, the wife contributed through her savings and good domestic management, with both responsible for generating the gains from the marriage. Thus not only feminists such as María Jesús Alvarado recognized the value of women's domestic labor.

Deputy Calle then proposed substitute language as a compromise: "the sale or mortgage *of a woman's share* of the community property are subject to the same restrictions and formalities as the dowry" (author's highlighting).[39] To move the bill forward, Pazos Varela and Jiménez agreed to this change, which the deputies approved. The Senate's commission on legislation, however, never considered the bill. This congressional debate, nonetheless, influenced public opinion and led to growing consensus that it was time to strengthen married women's property rights.

Deliberations of the 1922 Civil Code Reform Commission

President Leguía's charge to the Civil Code Reform Commission was to update the 1852 Civil Code to reflect the country's evolution in the intervening years as well as modern legal thinking.[40] Since the commission decided to write a completely new code rather than just revise the previous one, it ended up taking seven years, until 1929, to produce a full draft.[41] To ensure transparency and gather feedback, the commission published a daily record of its proceedings, the *Actas*, in eight volumes between 1923 and 1930. Among the main points of contention in its deliberations on family law were: (i) whether married women should have full legal capacity; (ii) the extent to which the marital regime should encompass parallel rights and responsibilities; (iii) the degree of flexibility allowed couples; and (iv) the role of mothers in the exercise of patria potestad.

Without much discussion, the commission agreed early on that "men and women enjoy the same civil rights with the exception of those restrictions explicitly established by law" (CRCC 1923, 36). Their first major debate was on whether married women should be among those defined as relatively incapable – those who could conduct only some but not all civil acts (CRCC 1923, 60–63). Chair Juan

38 DDCND (1927, vol. 3, 5 and 15–27, 6, 24).

39 DDCND (1927, vol. 3, 5 and 15–27, 6, 24).

40 According to legal scholar Carlos Ramos Nuñez (2011, vol. 1), Leguía took a neutral position with respect to the revisions and the members of the commission, four lawyers and a physician, represented different political tendencies and regions of the country. Four held academic appointments at UNMSM; the chair, Juan José Calle, was prosecutor of the Supreme Court.

41 One of the Commission's first decisions was to divide the revised code into five books, rather than the previous three, and to distribute the drafting among the four lawyers. The new Book II was to bring together the previously dispersed material on marriage and the family.

José Calle included wives in this group along with those between 18 and 21 years of age, those judicially declared as spendthrifts and indigenous persons who did not speak Spanish. Commission member Alfredo Solf y Mura disagreed with his inclusion of wives among the relatively incapable, arguing that it required rethinking since the recent legal trend was to broaden their rights. Drawing a parallel with business societies, he argued that the position of wives was equivalent to that of a business partner who did not manage the society.

Calle replied that their informal understanding was that the new code would maintain the existing legal marital regime (the conjugal society or partial community property with potestad marital) as the only regime. In this regime, "a married woman depends on the husband" because he managed the community property and her individual property and she could not sell or mortgage her own assets without her husband's consent (CRCC 1923, 61). In his view, if there were some actions that wives could not exercise, they did not have full capacity and hence, they were relatively incapable. This was due to "the necessity of recognizing the husband's role as head of the family" (CRCC 1923, 61). To do otherwise, specifically, to establish the complete equality of the spouses would require a different marital regime, that of separation of property, and the intention of the commission was to leave the legal marital regime unchanged.

Manuel A. Olaechea concurred, stressing that the relatively incapacity of married women was not because of their sex but rather because "it is necessary to recognize one head in the society formed by the union of two spouses"; that is, to maintain his authority (CRCC 1923, 62). Pedro M. Oliveira highlighted the inconsistency in Calle's position, while he had agreed to the principle of women's equal civil rights he wanted to consider wives as relatively incapable. Nonetheless, he agreed that the commission should not adopt separation of property as the default regime since it was "entirely alien to our customs" (CRCC 1923, 62).

It was at this point in their deliberations, in June 1923, that the commission received two petitions from women's groups, one from Evolución Femenina and the other from the Liga Peruana de Laboradoras Pacifistas (Peruvian League of Pacifist Women Workers), demanding recognition of the full civil capacity of married women and changes to the marital regime (CRCC 1923, 194). The commission also received comments from five departmental Superior Court judges on the issue of married women's relative incapacity, all who favored strengthening married women's civil rights but for different reasons.[42] Some did not consider the restrictions on married women exercising certain rights as incapacities, the point raised by commission member Solf y Mura. Others thought wives should have at least the capacity to manage and dispose of their own assets without their husbands' authorization. This latter point was precisely what Evolución Femenina's petition demanded, showing that this idea had some support in legal circles.

42 CRCC (1924, 473); see Ramos Nuñez (2011, vol. 2, 91) for a more detailed discussion.

The commission maintained the relative incapacity of wives in its second draft of Book I, "On Persons," (CRCC 1926b, 11) but then dropped it during its 1929 revision; the draft presented to the government did not include it (CRCC 1936). This shows how the commission's thinking evolved over the 1920s in response to the congressional debates and broader public discussion of the need to strengthen women's civil rights.

Before the commission turned to the discussion of the draft of Book II, "On the Family," commission chair Calle, the most traditionalist of its members, introduced a proposal on married women's reserved property (CRCC 1926a, 23–7). This was likely because deputy Pazos Varela's 1925 Bienes Parafernales bill was before the Chamber, and he feared that its provisions would undermine the conjugal society, a regime he considered perfectly suited to Peruvian needs. In Calle's view, when a woman marries "she gives her heart and everything else she has, it is the most natural thing in the world that he who is the owner of her will and her body, also be the owner of her patrimony" (CRCC 1926a, 22). He also argued that it was not women who owned assets who were demanding reform but rather those who worked for a living and it was important to protect their wages from husbands who might pilfer them. Influenced by the writings of Spanish legal scholar Carlos Posada y Díaz (1915) and drawing on the recent innovations in the German and Swiss codes, he proposed that the reserved property of wives encompass a woman's personal goods, such as clothes and jewelry; those assets that she used in her profession or industry; the product of her work outside of domestic chores; and those assets she acquired via donation or inheritance. Wives could buy and sell these reserved assets without authorization by a husband although at the end of the marriage these constituted gananciales.

Pedro Oliveira, who was responsible for drafting Book II, finally presented his draft to the commission in August 1926 (CRCC 1926a, 246–59). It represented a substantial reformulation of the 1852 code, and overall, took it in a more gender-equitable direction. He reformulated Calle's proposal regarding the reserved property of wives, allowing those who engaged in independent activities to freely manage their earnings and dispose of the assets purchased with these earnings. In this case, the husband had the right to require the wife to contribute to household expenses from her earnings in an equitable manner. When the conjugal society dissolved, this reserved property formed part of the community property.

Citing the recently approved 1926 Argentine law as precedent, Oliveira proposed that each spouse have the right to freely administer their own assets, including the ability to sell or mortgage these.[43] With respect to the community property, he maintained the husband as the sole administrator, with the right to alienate such property. The wife, nonetheless, had redress if the husband committed fraud with

43 In referring to the Argentine law, Oliveira failed to note that it required women to formally declare their intention to manage their own assets; if not, the husband automatically managed these. His proposal made the wife's management of these the default position.

such property since she could appeal to a judge. His proposal thus did not go as far as the Chamber's approved bill that required mutual consent for the husband to alienate his wife's half of the gananciales. On other points, however, he favored mutual consent, such as for the wife or husband to renounce an inheritance, which they might want to do if encumbered with debt.[44]

Oliveira also spelled out married women's rights in a more positive manner and placed greater stress on the mutual and parallel obligations of each spouse, although with caveats. He deleted the offensive article that Peru's code had copied from the Napoleonic code that the wife owed the husband obedience. While a wife had the right to engage in a profession or industry it was only with the express or tacit consent of her husband; if he denied it, however, she could appeal to a judge. Similarly, wives could appear in lawsuits and contract and dispose of assets "with the only limitations being those derived from the legal regime," which assumed his consent (CRCC 1926a, 248). His proposal required a couple to live together, but this obligation ceased if it threatened the health, honor, or the prosperity of the businesses of either, like similar provisions in the Swiss and Brazilian codes. Another new article, also inspired by the Swiss code, gave greater recognition to the potential agency of wives, stipulating that "for the ordinary needs of the household, it can be represented by either" (CRCC 1926a, 247). Another laid out the conditions under which a wife might assume the direction and representation of the conjugal society, such as a husband's disappearance or his imprisonment for more than a year.

At the same time, Oliveira's draft maintained the core elements of male household headship: the husband was responsible for the direction of the conjugal society and the family's financial support and determined the household's domicile. Moreover, he added a new article (surely inspired by Germany's 1896 code) that stipulated that upon marriage a wife must add her husband's last name to her paternal name, a customary practice but one not previously codified, which served to reinforce male household headship.

The draft section on the separation of property during marriage was quite innovative (CRCC (1926a, 260–62). In the 1852 code, except for death, only a permanent judicial separation dissolved the conjugal society, giving each spouse the ownership and full administration of their own patrimony (Fuentes and de la Lama 1870, art. 208). In Oliveira's proposal wives gained an important right of redress over their husbands' actions because they could petition a judge to declare the separation of property if the husband was not meeting his obligations to provide for the family; if he could not provide the required guarantees for any of her property over

44 Oliveira's draft also maintained the dowry although it made it optional. While some commission members favored its elimination, making this practice subject to the same rules as other donations as in the 1855 Chilean code, Oliveira and Calle defended maintaining it notwithstanding its lack of use in Peru. Its discussion came up during multiple sessions; see CRCC (1929b, Section 2, Title III) for the proposed new rules.

which he had control; if he committed abuses in the administration of the community property; and if the administration of the community property had passed to her and she did not want to assume it. Also, if either spouse declared bankruptcy a separation of property took place automatically.

Peru's 1852 Civil Code was unusual because unlike most others it did not allow couples to make prenuptial agreements regarding the management of any of their property. Early in the discussions Oliveira introduced the idea of allowing couples to make marital contracts regarding the ownership and management of their property either prior to or during the marriage (CRCC 1925, 159–65), and in his 1926 draft he maintained this flexibility. Calles had objected since these were not part of Peruvian legal tradition and would weaken the marriage bond. Olaechea, who had previously been against including the possibility of such contracts, now surprised the other members by proposing that the code offer the regime of separation of property as an option (CRCC, 1929a, 152–4). While he endorsed Oliveira's draft and concurred that the conjugal society was the best regime, he thought it would be useful to offer this alternative regime because it was becoming more generalized internationally and the French, Swiss, Spanish and Brazilian civil codes all offered multiple regimes.

In Olaechea's analysis, the separation of property regime strengthened the legal personality of women since each spouse owned and administered their own property and had full capacity to conduct all acts related to such administration (CRCC 1929a, 252, 259–64). Moreover, it responded to feminist aspirations by enhancing married women's civil capacity and economic autonomy. Nonetheless, he thought that couples in Peru would use this option infrequently, being potentially of most interest to those who had complicated estates and where the spouses had different economic interests. If the commission rejected the possibility of spouses being able to contract with each other, he proposed that they should at least allow them to choose between regimes. He pointed out that in accepting the mechanism of reserved property for wives, they were in fact approximating the regime of separation of property, and should take the next step, adding this regime as a formal alternative.

There was little support among commission members for offering this alternative regime. Solf argued that while he understood Olaechea's reasoning, it would break custom and was inappropriate for Peru. Moreover, he thought that the introduction of women's reserved property introduced sufficient flexibility, as did Calle. The commission thus dropped the idea of offering the separation of property regime as an option and maintained the article that stated that neither spouse could renounce the legal marital regime (the conjugal society). Also dropped was Oliveira's proposal to allow spouses to make marital contracts regarding the ownership and management of their property. Hence the main changes to the existing marital regime were the recognition of the wife's earnings as reserved property; her right to manage the assets she brought to marriage or inherited; and the expanded conditions under which a separation of property could take place due to fault (CRCC 1929b).

The discussion of enhancing the role of mothers in the exercise of patria potestad over children was particularly contentious and took place in a piecemeal fashion over these years. Chair Calle consistently objected to any change in the traditional right of fathers to exercise sole patria potestad, for "giving mothers the right to intervene would violate the unity of the father's direction of the family" (CRCC 1923, 68). Besides going against Peruvian tradition, he thought it would only enhance marital conflict.

In Oliveira's original draft, both parents were to exercise patria potestad although in the case of disagreement, the father had the last word. In the final revision of Book I during 1929, its exercise resulted less equitable to mothers (CRCC 1930, 41). The commission added a phrase that made the father alone the legal representative and administrator of the children's assets, diluting the concept of its joint exercise. The commission completed its work in October 1929 but before it could submit a final draft of the new code to the government, a military coup overthrew the Leguía regime. This partly explains why it took some seven more years to promulgate it since the top priority became drafting a new constitution.

Municipal Suffrage as a Consolation Prize

Lt. Col. Luis M. Sánchez Cerro's 1930 coup against President Leguía coincided with the beginning of the Great Depression and the subsequent economic contraction led to social unrest and political instability. The Junta called a Constitutional Convention, which provided the opening for feminists to intensify efforts in support of women's suffrage. In the 1933 Constitution women ended up with the right to participate in municipal elections as a consolation prize.

Zoila Aurora Cáceres, who had been out of the country for several years, returned in November 1930 to reconstitute Feminismo Peruano (now carrying her initials, "Z.A.C." behind its name)[45] and lead an intense campaign to women's suffrage. She began by organizing women's groups around the country and publishing articles on suffrage in all the major newspapers. The campaign initially focused on influencing the electoral commission to include women among those who could vote to elect delegates to the Constitutional Congress.[46] When that failed, Cáceres then focused on lobbying candidates to support the cause and convincing notable political figures to declare their support for women's political rights (Aguilar 2002, 2006).

45 See Pachas (2019, 47–9, 59) on its change in name and the expansion of its social base. Among those collaborating with Feminismo Peruano Z.A.C. in the early 1930s were Miguelina Acosta and Dora Mayer.

46 Since Leguía's 1920 Constitution had not explicitly excluded women from citizenship, nothing prevented the inclusion of women as electors. In April 1931 Cáceres sent a letter to the president of the Junta with over one thousand signatures supporting this demand (Pachas 2019, 64, 160–1).

The main contenders in the concurrent presidential election were Sánchez Cerro, who founded the Partido Unión Revolucionaria (URP, Revolutionary Union Party) for this purpose, and Victor Haya de la Torre, the founder of the newly constituted Alianza Popular Revolucionaria Americana del Peru (APRA, American Popular Revolutionary Alliance). Largely because of the role of Magda Portal, a co-founder of APRA who led its new women's secretariat, this party's 1931 platform included a commitment to women's civil and political rights (Burns 1983). While the URP's 1931 platform did not mention women's rights, after Sánchez Cerro became president he began to support women's suffrage in recognition of the positive role they played in his campaign.

At the beginning of this Congress, things looked quite favorable. An ally of Cáceres who favored women's equal rights presided over it and the commission that issued the majority report on voting rights recommended extending the vote to women. The debate on women's suffrage took place over seven days, with women always present in the galleys.[47] Roisida Aguilar (2002) stresses how there was greater consensus around the need to give women equal civil rights than on their political rights. This may have reflected what McCammon, Arch and Bergner (2014) call a "radical demand effect," where feminist demands for both civil and political rights made the demand for stronger property rights appear less threatening to gender norms.

Nonetheless, the issue of women's civil rights played into the arguments regarding suffrage in different ways. Some opposed women's suffrage because they believed that without civil rights they were not qualified to exercise political rights. Others thought that the most urgent task was to reduce a wife's total dependence on her husband, thus civil code reform must precede women's suffrage. Several opposed strengthening either women's civil and political rights arguing that the role of the state was to protect women and that it did this best by preserving the sanctity of the male-headed household. Still others, seeing latent opposition to women's civil rights, argued that women needed the vote if they were ever to attain their full emancipation (Aguilar 2002; Poulsen 2016).

Once the motion to institute women's suffrage failed, granting them the vote and ability to stand for office at the municipal level emerged as a compromise. Proposed by URP Delegate Victor Arévalo, he argued that partial suffrage would at least show some progress on the issue and demonstrate that Peru was not falling behind the times (Poulsen 2016, 157). It became the consensus position based on the reasoning that local elections were less political than national ones, and that the issues under the purview of local government, such as health and welfare, were more suited to women's interests and experience. By slowing down the process toward full suffrage, it also assuaged those who were worried over the influence of the Church on women or the instability that their vote might introduce, as well

47 See Aguilar (2002) and Miloslavich (2015) for a detailed summary of the arguments pro and con.

as the threat that it represented to male privilege (Aguilar 2002). Thus the 1933 Constitution's article 86 excluded women from citizenship, but if they were at least 21 (or younger, if married or household heads) and literate, they could participate in municipal elections.

Since APRA's voting bloc could have produced a different outcome, the failure of women to achieve full citizenship and suffrage at this time could be blamed on them, although the UR was also divided on the issue.[48] In an interview years later, Portal told Sara Guardia (1985, 81–4) that Haya de la Torre had not been present at APRAs 1931 congress, only returning from exile later, and that he considered the 1931 platform to be excessively progressive. Moreover, he feared that if Catholic housewives obtained the vote they would favor conservatives. Thus the Aprista delegates initially derailed the discussion of giving women full political rights by proposing that only educated women or those who worked should vote, although they finally backed giving women suffrage gradually, first at the municipal level. This would give the party time to organize and prepare women to vote. At the time, Portal backed APRA's position and was disdainful of efforts of elite feminists such as Zoila Aurora Cáceres who she viewed as pursuing a foreign model rather than being concerned with promoting the profound social change that Peru required (Burns 1983; Poulsen 2016).[49]

Zoila Aurora Cáceres ([n.d. b] 2019, 385–6) was clearly disappointed with the outcome of the Constitutional Congress since early in the deliberations it seemed that the goal of full political rights was within reach. Allowing women's participation in municipal elections at least constituted progress toward this goal. Another advance was that this constitution recognized a wife's right to choose her nationality if she married a foreigner (Peru 1933, art. 6), a reform that allowed Peru to ratify the Treaty on the Nationality of Women approved at the Seventh International Conference of American States in Montevideo, a treaty for which feminists had fought.[50]

Approval of the 1936 Civil Code

The assassination of President Sánchez Cerro in 1933 led to greater political instability and thus it was not until 1936 that the three remaining living members of the 1922 Civil Code Reform Commission delivered the draft of their new code to the government. A comparison of this final draft (CRCC 1936) with the second draft of Book II (CRCC 1929b) suggests that in the intervening years the commission made only a few relevant changes. Approved without much discussion in either the

48 See Castillo (2023, 85) for an analysis of this vote.

49 Portal (1978, 215–7) later explained that she never considered herself a feminist since initially feminists seemed anti-men and she believed that women had to join men in the class struggle. Nonetheless, she criticized APRA for its repeated failure to support women's suffrage.

50 See Chapter 8 for details on this Treaty.

Congress or civil society, it represented another step forward while falling short of feminists' demands.

One notable change in the final 1936 draft was that it included obligatory civil marriage and divorce with the right to remarry (CRCC 1936, arts. 242, 248). This was because in 1930 the Military Junta promulgated obligatory civil marriage and absolute divorce, which the Constitutional Congress ratified in 1934.[51] The commission thus revised its final draft to conform to this legislation and also incorporated a long-standing feminist demand: it treated both spouses similarly if the divorce was due to adultery.[52]

The Reform Commission made one notable change in the obligations and rights born of matrimony. While it maintained the husband as the household head, it added that the wife: "owes the husband assistance and counsel for their common prosperity and has the right and duty to personally supervise the home" (CRCC 1936, art. 153). Husbands continued to determine the household's residency but wives gained greater latitude in that "a woman was not obliged to accept her husband's decision when this constitutes an abuse of her rights" (CRCC 1936, art 155). Thus while the proposed code reaffirmed the traditional gender of division of labor, it recognized a greater role for wives in decision-making and placed greater limits on that of husbands.

It expanded the concept of women's reserved property to include whatever a woman might earn resulting from her legal usufruct of her children's assets from a previous marriage, since a widow who remarried could now potentially retain full rights of patria potestad over her children (CRCC 1936, art. 200).[53] Another change that responded to feminist demands was that all women became eligible to be guardians of underage children. For a married woman to fulfill this role, however, she required her husband's authorization (CRCC 1936, arts. 475–490).

The Reform Commission also made some substantive changes to the rules of intestate succession. It improved the inheritance rights of natural children by including them in the first order of succession although if there were also legitimate children they were each entitled to only half the share of a legitimate child. Regarding spouses, in its 1926 draft it had given widows and widowers parallel inheritance rights, whereby they automatically inherited a share of their spouse's estate in usufruct in all orders of succession. The final draft improved on this by giving the spouse full property rights over this share (CRCC 1936, arts. 760–765). If there

51 Law 7893, which incorporated divorce by mutual consent, and Law 7894, which made this option available after three years of marriage, of May 22, 1934 (Toledo 1938).

52 Some of the putative aspects of divorce remained in the code, however, such as the guilty party losing their right to gananciales from the marriage (CRCC 1936, art. 260).

53 Another change worth noting was that the commission deleted from the community property assets acquired via transfer from the state (CRCC 1929b, art. 110). In future years this would have detrimental implications for women in Peru's agrarian reform, since the State could title the lands it distributed in the name of just the husband, with this becoming his individual property (Deere and León 2001, 99–106).

were legitimate children from the marriage, the spouse inherited a share equal to a child; in the absence of any children, ascendants and siblings of the deceased, they inherited the full estate. However, the draft maintained some limiting conditions from the 1852 code. If there were other legal heirs, deducted from the share the surviving spouse received were any gananciales accruing to them; and if there were children from the marriage but no gananciales to deduct, the spouse's share could not exceed one-quarter of the deceased's estate. Thus while the new code improved the inheritance rights of wives these were still not as generous as those in other South American countries (Deere 2023).

The remaining commission members also adopted a measure that other countries were instituting in response to the effects of the Great Depression, the right of household heads to declare the household's main residency as family patrimony (*bienes de familia*). In this case the owner could not alienate the home while minor children resided there, protecting it from creditors. A farm or industry that provided the family's main sustenance could receive similar designation (CRCC 1936, arts. 453–473).

In anticipation of receiving the final draft, the Minister of Justice requested that the Congress authorize promulgation of the code by the Executive, subject to its review by a commission appointed by its members. The Congress did so, subject to the caveat that the approved code incorporate any civil legislation it had enacted, including the laws on mandatory civil marriage and absolute divorce.[54] This review commission made only minor changes to the Reform Commission's final draft,[55] and President Gen. Oscar R. Benavides promulgated the code in August 1936.

In sum, Peru's 1936 code was 14 years in the making and over these years the country reached greater consensus around the need for women to hold stronger civil rights, if not gender equality in marriage. The 1922 Reform Commission took seriously its charge to produce a modern code for Peru, one that reflected the evolution of legal thinking in Europe and the Americas. There were frequent references to the reforms that expanded women's property rights in Germany, Switzerland and France as well as Brazil and Argentina. At the same time commission members were concerned about not breaking too radically from Peruvian customary practice and what they deemed as socially acceptable. In the analysis of its deliberations, it is interesting that no single member of this group was consistently a traditionalist – refusing to break with past legal norms – nor a proponent of women's full economic autonomy or gender equality. They often switched positions to reach consensus. Nonetheless, they never broke ranks on one point, the need to maintain the husband as household head. Hence, there was little debate over whether

54 *Diario de los Debates del Congreso Constituyente de 1931* (133, 3403–16).

55 Comparing CRCC (1936) and the approved civil code, Peru (1939), shows that the few small substantive changes made were related to divorce, for example, divorce by mutual consent became slightly easier. See Toledo (1938, 34–47) on the controversy that ensued.

the husband should retain the sole right to manage the community property and similarly, that he be able to alienate such property without his wife's consent.

In its discussions, the Commission never considered Miguelina Acosta's 1920 proposal that the marital society be jointly managed and represented by both spouses because the idea that the household have two heads was inconceivable. While there was support in the Chamber of Deputies for María Jesús Alvarado's proposal to at least institute mutual consent for the sale of community property, they diluted this proposal in the bill approved in 1927. The Commission ignored the compromise in that bill, to include the need for the wife's consent for the husband to sell assets that represented her share of the gananciales. And the Commission accepted only in part Alvarado's proposal that husbands and wives hold parallel rights in marriage. The 1936 reform treated what men and women each brought to marriage, inherited during it and acquired through their own labor in a parallel fashion; each could manage and alienate such individual property. The gains from such property (the community property), nonetheless, remained the preserve of the husband to administer.

The Commission did rid the civil code of the inherited notion of married women's relative incapacity, since this was incongruent with recognizing their greater economic autonomy with respect to their own individual earnings and property. Also, the 1936 code established the conditions under which wives were able to administer the conjugal society and assume patria potestad over their children, legal actions that required them to be legally capable. While both husband and wife were to hold patria potestad over minor children, in the case of any disagreement between them, the father had the final word. Moreover, only fathers could manage their children's assets and represent them,[56] thus recognition of joint patria potestad was only a moral victory in many ways. Nonetheless, the conditions for a widow or widower if they remarried to retain it, including management of the children's assets, were now the same, representing another step toward gender equality. Moreover, now all women could also be guardians and witnesses, a demand included in Alvarado's 1922 petition.

The 1936 code was also traditionalist in that it maintained the regime of the conjugal society as the only marital regime. While the 1922 commission considered offering separation of property as an option regime, it rejected this proposition as representing too much economic individualism that would be detrimental to the unity required of marriage. There was greater support among commission members for including greater flexibility in the code by allowing couples to make prenuptial agreements that might include the separation of property, but it discarded this option for similar reasons. Worth noting is that feminists never demanded a change in the default regime or greater flexibility to choose a regime, since they

56 Peru (1939, arts. 391 and 392).

implicitly recognized the benefits of community property. Rather, their focus was on enhancing women's autonomy by giving them parallel rights and responsibilities within the partial community property regime.

After approval of the new code, Zoila Aurora Cáceres credited the activities of Femenismo Peruano for its advances while noting its shortcomings. Among the deficiencies that she mentioned was that the code maintained the outdated notion that women needed protection, primarily because the husband remained as the sole household head (Cáceres [1938] 2019, 369). It was thus that she declared that women needed full political rights if they were ever to attain equal civil rights: "Only the right to citizenship, which constitutes the one and fundamental basis of individual liberty, will facilitate women's conquest of civil rights" (Cáceres [1938] 2019, 370).

With respect to the impact of the 1936 reform, its magnitude is difficult to estimate because data on the share of wives who worked or who owned property is unavailable. The 1931 census for Lima province did provide information on the sex of those who owned immovable property (a dwelling, lot, agricultural land, or building), although not on their marital status. Some 8.5% of men and 7.7% of women (over 15 years of age) reported owning such property (Peru 1932, Table 45). The small gender asset gap suggests that it is likely that married men and women each reported owning immovable property when they acquired it together as community property. But since husbands still solely managed the community property under the 1936 reform, only wives who brought property to marriage or inherited it benefited from being able to manage their assets, a share that was likely relatively small, certainly below 7.7%. The overall trend in this province, Peru's most urban, was toward an increase in the number of women employed in the non-agricultural sector. Surely many were working wives who gained greater autonomy through the possibility of managing their own wages, salaries and other labor earnings.

The Slow Process Toward Full Political and Greater Civil Rights

Peru ended up being among the last Latin American countries to recognize women's political rights, with suffrage not attained until 1955. Among the reasons that it took so long to achieve was that while new women's rights groups continued to emerge to lobby for suffrage, these never fused into a strong national, cross-class women's movement as in neighboring countries. The only progress toward deepening women's civil rights was a reform that made women eligible for all government positions.

The demand for women's suffrage gained new momentum around activities organized before and after Peru hosted the Eighth International Conference of American States in December 1938. Among the new groups that formed prior to this event to lobby for equal rights was the Comité Nacional Pro-Derechos Civiles y Políticos de la Mujer (National Committee for Women's Civil and Political

Rights), formed in 1934 by Elisa Rodríguez Porras of the Feminist Legion.[57] The next year Mary Doris Clark de Velasco founded UMA Peruana, and in 1936 Alicia del Prado organized Acción Femenina Peruana (Women's Action) to bring together women from APRA, the Communist Party and independents.[58]

UMA Peruana was a chapter of the regional Unión de Mujeres Americanas (UMA), established in New York City in 1934 by Mexican CIM delegate Margarita Robles de Mendoza. Its objective was to bring women of the Americas together to promote their civil, social, economic and political rights. It sought the "emancipation of women by cooperating with men, not by creating a battle between the sexes, but by showing the necessity of equality between men and women as members of one human family" (UMA 1936). While autonomous of CIM or of any political party, it aimed to promote CIM's goals and activities.[59] Its international council consisted of representatives from national councils in each country. Peruvian Evangelina Antay de Vaughan, who earlier had been a founding member of Evolución Femenina (Ysla 2022, 44), served as its first president from 1935 through 1938.[60]

Antay recruited Mary Doris Clark, an engineer who was president of the Unión Femenina de Ciencias, Letras y Artes (Women's Union for Science, Letters and the Arts) to form the Peruvian chapter (UMA Peruana 1936). It grew quickly to include 18 institutional members in Lima, among them Feminismo Peruano Z.A.C., the Women's Rights Committee and Acción Femenina, plus six affiliated women's organizations or chapters in other departments.[61] Clark served as secretary general and María Jesús Alvarado, who had returned from exile in Argentina, was a member of its executive board for the 1935–1937 term. In advance of the upcoming Pan

57 Rodríguez found CIM's activities on behalf of women's equal rights at the 1933 Pan American conference inspiring, which may have motivated her to form this new organization. See her letter to Doris Stevens of July 20, 1934, in Doris Stevens Papers, Correspondence: Peru: Elisa Rodríguez Parra. Peru sent a delegate to CIM's initial 1930 meeting in Havana and later appointed Belén de Osma as its official representative but as this correspondence shows, Peruvians had not been active CIM members.

58 Based on the popular front model of the mid-1930s, this group conducted political activities against fascism and in defense of democracy and advanced demands around women's equal economic, social and legal rights (Cannon 1943; Guardia 1985, 77, 90).

59 In her correspondence with CIM Chair Doris Stevens during 1934, Margarita Robles shared her plan to organize the UMA as an autonomous organization, sending her a draft of its objectives and by-laws, and said her intent was for it to mobilize broadly in support of the Equal Rights Treaty championed by CIM. In Doris Stevens Papers, Correspondence: Mexico, Margarita Robles de Mendoza, 1933–1936.

60 In a letter dated November 23, 1936, to CIM Chair Doris Stevens, Antay said that since the two organizations shared the same goals she hoped they would collaborate. UMA already had affiliated organizations in ten countries, in South America, in Peru, Chile, Venezuela and Uruguay. Doris Stevens Papers, Correspondence: UMA, 1935–1938.

61 Its members included some of the more traditional elite women's organizations such as the Ladies Social Center and the Catholic Ladies Union as well as new women's professional organizations and alumni associations of women's secondary schools.

American conference, UMA Peruana hosted the First National Women's Congress in Lima in November 1938.[62] The organizing committee, chaired by Clark, included Alvarado, Cáceres and lawyer Rosa Pérez Liendo of the Feminist League, among others. The conference focused on eight themes, with women's political rights figuring prominently alongside the need for further reform of the civil, commercial and penal codes.

Prior to the opening of the Pan American conference, Femenismo Peruano Z.A.C. circulated a petition that garnered some 890 signatures (Pachas 2019, 78). It asked the official delegates to make:

> ...a solemn declaration in support of women's vote in conditions of complete equality with men, given that women, just as men, work, are subject to the same laws, and pay taxes. The Peruvian woman, without any personal ambition, will exercise her right to vote to defend her interests as a mother, wife, and worker, and to protect her children and ensure the integrity of the family, and will collaborate with men in patriotic causes and state affairs.[63]

By this time, the CNM-P, now under the leadership of educator Ester Festini, also supported full political rights for women and it employed even more maternalistic arguments. It circulated a different petition that asked for the vote:

> not because we want to actively get involved in political life, but when necessary, [to] use it to support the institution that represents the pillar of political life [the family],...and also to attain or support existing laws that protect women and children.
>
> *(quoted in Aguilar 2019, 450)*

The main aim of CIM at this conference was to secure approval of a Convention on the Political Rights of Women that specified that "the right of women to vote and be elected shall not be denied or abridged on account of sex" (IACW 1938, 8).[64] CIM delegates participated in the conference's Fourth Committee,

62 Evangelina Antay letter to Doris Stevens of November 1, 1938, includes a copy of the program. Doris Stevens Papers, Correspondence: UMA, 1935–1938.

63 Pachas (2019, 403–22) includes copies of these petitions with the names of all those who signed.

64 See Chapter 8 on CIM's activities at the 1933 Seventh International Conference of American States in Montevideo where it presented proposals for an Equal Rights Treaty and a Convention on the Nationality of Women, with the conference only approving the latter. IACW (1933) included a detailed analysis of the discrimination against women in all the Latin American civil codes; IACW (1938) only updated that earlier report with the reforms enacted in the intervening period, including Peru's 1936 code, which it called "an immense forward step" (IACW 1938, 130). This report also provided a detailed analysis of women's political rights and of legislation related to women's work and maternity.

on Political and Civil Rights of Women.[65] Numerous women gathered in a non-official capacity to accompany the proceedings and support CIM delegates in their efforts.[66] Once it was clear that the passage of such a convention was unlikely, CIM delegates focused on securing at least a strong declaration on women's rights. Peruvian delegate Victor A. Belaunde (who had supported women's suffrage during the 1931–1933 debate) played a critical role in mediating the compromise that emerged (Aguilar 2019).

The Lima Declaration on Women's Rights approved in December 1938 declared "that women have the right to political treatment on the basis of equality with men; to the enjoyment of equality as to civil status; to full protection and opportunity for work; to the amplest protection as mothers" (IAC 1940, 250). Another resolution gave CIM permanent status within the PAU and gave PAU the authority to name CIM's chair among the country delegates appointed by their respective governments (IAC 1940, 252).[67]

In the aftermath of the Pan American conference, some of the Lima women's groups, such as Acción Femenina expanded nationally and worked to support the Allies in the war effort, while others continued to press for women's suffrage. In 1941 Elisa Rodríguez's Women's Rights Committee organized another petition drive for women's suffrage. The Congress entertained a bill to amend the constitution to this effect but it failed to garner support (González del Riego 2005, 36; Miloslavich 2015, 124).

In the mid-1940s a new women's organization emerged from the mobilizations around the high cost of living, the Frente Nacional de Mujeres (Women's National Front) under the leadership of Nina Flores.[68] It assumed the banner of women's suffrage, published its own newspaper, *Nuestra Voz*, established affiliates in several departments and ran a female employment agency. It was part of the Frente Democrático Nacional (FDN, National Democratic Front) coalition (one that

65 The official delegations from the United States, Brazil and Mexico each included a woman (Marino 2019, 149–55). The photograph on the book cover, of those at a reception hosted by Feminismo Peruano Z.A.C. for CIM members, includes front row center, CIM Chair Doris Stevens, with Zoila Aurora Cáceres and the Dominican Republic CIM representative, Minerva Bernadino, to the viewer's right. In the second row, behind Stevens, is the Argentine CIM representative Ana Rosa Schleiper de Martínez Guerra with Susana Larguía, the Argentine alternate representative, to the left. Doris Stevens Papers, Series V. Inter-American Commission, sub-series: Photographs, Lima Album.

66 The campaign to collect signatures continued, with Feminismo Peruano's petition finally gathering 5,000 and the CNM-P's, 4,000 signatures (Aguilar 2019, 450–4).

67 See Marino (2019, 149–64) on the politics of this conference, especially the efforts of the Roosevelt administration to oust Doris Stevens as CIM chair and establish greater control over CIM so that it would align better with US foreign policy interests. Some of the CIM delegates affiliated with feminist popular front organizations in Latin America were also active in the effort to remove her because they resented her domineering and sometimes condescending leadership.

68 Ramos (1990, 491) interview with Nina Flores.

included the recently legalized APRA)[69] that in 1945 elected José Luis Bustamante y Rivero as president.

Since the promised municipal elections of the 1933 Constitution never took place, among the first acts of the FDN-dominated Congress was to adopt a transitional two-step, indirect process that included women.[70] María Jesús Alvarado, who had revitalized Evolución Femenina with the objective of attaining women's political rights, was among those backing this initiative. She argued that while this 1945 law did not provide for direct elections, it was, nonetheless, important for women to participate since this would be the first occasion that they exercised the rights gained in the 1933 Constitution (Miloslavich 2015, 126). Four women were subsequently elected to the Lima municipal council, including Alvarado; at least 27 women served on these councils nationally (Bedoya 2020, 27).

In 1946 the Senate considered another bill to give women full political rights, with Evolución Femenina sending a petition to Congress in its support (Miloslavich 2015, 126). While unsuccessful, these discussions resulted in Congress approving a law that allowed women, irrespective of their lack of citizenship, to occupy all government administrative positions.[71] This was another long-standing feminist demand, one that Feminismo Peruano Z.A.C. had included in its 1938 platform.[72] It was a particularly important measure for women lawyers because until then they could not occupy government-appointed positions such as judgeships (Poulsen 2016, 178–9).

In 1948 General Manuel A. Odría staged a coup against the Bustamante government and then stepped down in 1950 to run for president in an election where he was the only candidate (Poulsen 2016, 161). The final push for women's suffrage began in 1953 when several deputies submitted bills to amend the 1933 Constitution to make women eligible to vote in national elections. Various women's groups sent petitions in support of these bills[73] and several new ones formed to demand

69 Once legal, in 1946 APRA organized its first congress of Aprista women but this party tended to focus on women's domestic role in building the party, not women's rights issues. Magda Portal resigned from the party in 1948 when at its Second Congress it announced that since women were not citizens, they were no longer eligible to be official party members (Portal 1978, 217; Burns 1983, 124–5).

70 Law 10233, approved in September 1945, charged the departmental Superior Courts with forming municipal electoral assemblies (made up of representatives of a wide range of civil society organizations) to nominate and elect by secret ballot those who would serve on the municipal and provincial Juntas Transitorias (Transitional Boards). These would elect their own mayor and other officials (Bedoya 2020, 236–7).

71 Law 10.552, April 14, 1946. https://docs.peru.justia.com/federales/leyes/10552-apr-14-1946.pdf

72 Besides women's equal political rights, its 1938 platform included ending all existing barriers to women's access to high posts in the state, judiciary and diplomatic service (Guardia 1985, 72; Pachas 2019, 78, 385s).

73 Among those submitting petitions were the Women's Rights Committee, the Asociación Femenina Universitaria (Women's University Association), and the Asociación de Abogadas Trujillanas (Women Lawyers Association of Trujillo) (González del Riego 2005, 37). María Jesús Alvarado was again active in this campaign, writing in support of women's political rights in *La Crónica* (Miloslavich 2015, 127).

suffrage including the Unidad Nacional de Mujeres Peruanas (National Unity of Peruvian Women), a cross-class and multi-party coalition, and the Movimiento Cívico Femenino del Perú (Peruvian Women's Civic Union), a non-partisan organization formed to prepare women for the vote (Salazar 2001, 133; Aguilar 2024, 291–3). By then many felt that women's suffrage was imminent, given the passage of the 1948 Inter-American Convention on Women's Political Rights and the fact that women had already attained the vote in most South American countries.

The 1953 bills were not successful, but in an apparent bid to gain greater legitimacy, the Odría government submitted its own bill the next year (Miloslavich 2015, 127–9). Women were once again present in the galleys during this round of congressional debate. Both chambers approved the bill during 1954, which gave women the right to vote and stand for elections on the same terms as men (being literate and at least 21 or 18 if married, with obligatory registration), and then, as required for a constitutional amendment, again the next year, this time unanimously. President Odría promulgated Law 12391 in September 1955 and women voted for the first time in national elections the next year, with nine women elected to Congress (Aguilar 2024, 293).

Worth mentioning is that the literacy requirement continued to exclude a large share of the adult population from political rights, particularly indigenous rural women.[74] None of the political parties seriously demanded universal suffrage and, moreover, it never appeared as a demand of the women's movement. Married women would not gain full legal capacity until decades later, when it became a demand of second-wave feminism.[75]

Conclusion

The gender scholarship of the 1970s and 1980s viewed the attainment of women's political rights in Peru as General Odría's "gift" to women, reproducing his own, self-congratulatory view of its enactment. For example, according to Elsa Chaney (1979, 73), "...the conferring of the vote on women by General Odría in 1955 caught most women by surprise; it came as a gift for which they had not expended any large amounts of energy."[76] As Miloslavich (2015), Poulsen (2016), and Aguilar (2002, 2024) argue, and this chapter has shown, this was hardly the case.

Moreover, Chaney (1979, 73) considers that prior to the second wave of feminism, "women never succeeded in building a movement in Peru," a statement that requires qualification. What differentiates Peru and Chile, the two countries she compares, is that feminists in Peru were unable to build a *unified* women's

74 According to the 1961 census 51.7% of women and 25.6% of men were illiterate (UNESCO 1988, Table 8).

75 Their demands resulted in the civil code reform of 1984 (Deere and León 2001, Table 2.1).

76 Burns (1983, 119) follows this line of analysis, stating that "...General Odría practically gifted it to women, thinking that they would vote for him in the next elections." Klarén (2004, 374) gives the president's wife, María Delgado de Odría, the credit for women having attained the vote.

movement around either their civil or political rights. While Peruvian women continued to organize new rights organizations in the 1940s and 1950s, they never attained the cohesion of a national force, as was the case with FECHIF in Chile, partly explaining why women attained political rights much later. But as the more recent scholarship has demonstrated, Peruvian women and their political allies certainly expended energy to attain such.

Chaney's (1979) contribution is to show that, going back to the late nineteenth century, different policies with respect to public education and particularly, the late development of the expansion of women's secondary public education in Peru, made it more difficult to organize large groups of women in that country compared to Chile. Miller (1991, 81) further develops this comparison, highlighting the deeper class and ethnic divisions in Peru that made it difficult to mobilize women across social classes. A fuller explanation of these impediments, however, must also reckon with the detrimental role played by APRA – the most successful group in mobilizing working-class women over these decades (even if illegal for much of this time), one which provided little space for feminist concerns and used women most instrumentally.

Over the first half century, the number of organized women actively demanding rights was never large and principally centered in Lima. Nonetheless, a critical mass of feminist activists developed in the teens who, under the leadership of María Jesús Alvarado and Evolución Femenina, placed women's civil rights firmly on the national agenda. During the next decade, Zoila Aurora Cáceres and Femenismo Peruano did the same with respect to women's political rights and, moreover, extended the network of activist women nationally. The new generations of feminists they mentored kept the demand for women's rights in the public discussion over four decades.

Feminists and jurists developed their ideas for reforming the civil code at about the same time, and Peru is among the South American countries where feminist thinking and activism contributed to the substance of its 1936 reform. The reform included some of the demands of Evolución Femenina, such as women being able to be legal witnesses and guardians, and married women's control over their earnings and the assets they brought to marriage or inherited. International antecedents – the earlier reforms of married women's property rights in European countries with similar community property regimes – clearly influenced the thinking of the Civil Code Review Commission and facilitated reform adoption. This was particularly the case with respect to married women's reserved property plus the fact that the Brazilian, Chilean and Argentine codes had adopted this mechanism.

There was not much interest in either the Reform Commission, the legislature nor among organized women in even offering the separation of property regime as an option prior to marriage. Maria Jesús Alvarado was keenly aware of the benefit of maintaining partial community property as the legal regime due to the recognition that it provided to women's contribution to the gananciales from the marriage through their domestic labor, a rationale acknowledged by some politicians and jurists.[77] The issue for feminists was how to make this marital regime more equitable, either through the joint management of the community property (as in Miguelina Acosta's formulation) or by giving husbands and wives parallel rights over their own assets and the gananciales (as in Alvarado's proposal).

The 1936 reform did not meet feminists aspirations in this regard, for control of the gananciales remained with husbands who continued as the sole manager of the conjugal society. The reform thus reinforced male household headship, and while it ameliorated potestad marital, it did not eliminate it. Still, women attained greater civil rights and mothers gained greater recognition in the exercise of patria potestad, notably equal rights in widowhood if they remarried. Overall, Peru's 1936 reform ended up going beyond what Argentina or Chile had earlier attained with respect to married women's property rights since it included women's control over the assets they brought to marriage or later inherited, that is, upon marriage, they did not automatically lose the rights they held as single women nor formally have to opt to do so. But it did not go as far as Colombia's (1932) reform, which in addition included their control over the gananciales that they generated, considered in the next chapter.

Initially most feminists viewed suffrage as a long-term goal. By the mid-1920s a group of activist women were demanding the vote and they came close to achieving it in the political opening provided by the fall of the Leguía regime and the upheaval of the Great Depression, which led to the formation of new coalitions and the constitutional reform of 1933. The fact that by then feminists were demanding both civil and political rights led to consensus around the need to improve their civil rights and the compromise between political factions around ceding women municipal-level suffrage. While this also fell short of the demands of Feminismo Peruano, the attainment of partial suffrage in 1933 and then its implementation in 1945, contributed to eroding the resistance to women's political participation among both men and women. Maternalist arguments took on even greater weight in the struggle for women's suffrage than they had in the earlier debates over civil code reform, as feminists argued that women's unique attributes would contribute to better legislation and social welfare.

By the 1950s women were firmly in the public space and the arguments against their political participation were now outdated (Poulsen 2016, 180). The international consensus behind women's suffrage and the legitimacy that it conferred on countries aspiring to be democratic was difficult to ignore, even by authoritarians, particularly, since most Latin American countries had already ceded women the vote. In sum, Peru's two-step process toward women's suffrage was in this way like that of Chile, but it made the struggle for suffrage even more prolonged; it was parallel in time to its attainment in Colombia, a country where the women's movement developed much later.

77 According to Valverde (1942, 544–6), there was broad consensus among jurists that the gananciales were the product of the joint efforts of husband and wife, justifying their equal division. While this idea may have been implicit in the deliberations of the 1922 Civil Code Reform Commission, it did not come out very strongly in their discussions.

6

COLOMBIA AS AN INNOVATOR IN MARITAL REGIME REFORM YET A LAGGARD IN WOMEN ORGANIZING FOR RIGHTS

A 1930 lawsuit filed by Encarnación R. against her husband Jesús Antonio P. in Medellín[1] illustrates well why women needed stronger property rights in marriage. Under the regime of the conjugal society a husband was the administrator of his wife's individual property and earnings and the community property. While he could authorize his wife to manage her own assets, he could revoke this permission at any time. According to Encarnación, when she married she already owned several urban properties that Jesús Antonio allowed her to continue to manage and rent out. She purchased several additional properties with this rental income and built a sizable asset portfolio. Although illiterate, as many non-elite women were before the expansion of public education, she was aware that the assets accumulated during the marriage (the gananciales) legally belonged jointly to both her and her husband.

Conflict erupted when after 23 years of marriage, Encarnación became ill and could no longer work. Jesús Antonio rescinded his permission for her to manage the properties, threw her out of their home and refused to support her economically. She sued for a separation of property because, besides needing to secure her sustenance, she feared that her husband would mismanage the properties, reducing the patrimony that she would eventually leave her only son (born prior to her marriage) with whom she was then living.

A 1922 reform of the civil code is what allowed Encarnación to seek a separation of property. Previously, under Colombia's 1887 code a wife could obtain a separation of property only if she could prove that her husband was insolvent or committed fraud with her assets or the community property (Colombia 1895, art.

1 Drawn from López Oseira (2013, 287–9), whose research was in the Judicial Archives of Medellín.

DOI: 10.4324/9781003658436-6

200). The legislature, in the first successful bill to modestly strengthen women's property rights, had expanded the conditions under which wives could sue for such a separation to include situations where husbands were no longer meeting their sustenance obligations to their wives and children. But even if the lawsuit proved successful, she would still require her husband's authorization or that of a judge to sell or mortgage her immovable property. This case shows the vulnerability of wives under potestad marital, how they were dependent on their husbands' good will and why women began to demand stronger property rights.

An organized women's movement demanding rights – initially access to public secondary education and stronger civil rights – did not emerge in Colombia until around 1930. Its relatively late development was largely because of the extended period of hegemony of the Conservative Party (1886 to 1930) and its alliance with the Catholic Church, which had a near monopoly over education. The first legislative bills to strengthen women's civil rights preceded its emergence. Nonetheless, partly as a result of the concerted actions of the women participating in the Fourth International Congress of Women in Bogotá in 1930 – an event that coincided with the return to power of the Liberal Party – the country thoroughly reformed its marital regime in 1932. It instituted the mixed regime of deferred community property, which combined separation of property during marriage with community property at its dissolution. This legislation, nonetheless, left many aspects of potestad marital intact as well as a father's right of patria potestad over the children.

A stronger and broader based women's movement did not develop until the 1940s when women began to organize around attaining suffrage. A 1945 constitutional reform formally recognized women as citizens although only for the purpose of occupying government positions that required such; they still could not vote or stand for office. The political polarization that gave rise to civil war contributed to Colombia being among the laggards in enfranchising women. They did not attain full political rights until 1954, when women from all political tendencies joined together to demand both suffrage and an end to the internal conflict.

Antecedents to the Reform of Women's Civil Rights

While liberal legal scholars began writing about the need to improve married women's property rights at the turn of the century, it took several more decades before some of the political parties assumed this concern and women themselves began to demand rights. That women were doing so by 1930 is partly because of the ties they began to develop with the regional women's movement.

Among the liberal legal scholars who raised the issue of women's civil rights during the 50-year period of conservative hegemony was Eduardo Rodríguez Piñeres (1899, 151–5). Inspired by the writings of John Stuart Mill, in an 1898 address to the Law Society he argued that the practice of liberty and equality must begin with justice in the family. He favored removing most restrictions on women's civil rights and giving couples flexibility in determining the marital regime that best suited them.[2] Specifically, he proposed allowing couples to make or change marital contracts over their property at any time, including opting for the full separation of property. Such a reform would allow married women to manage their own earnings and property if they so wished.

Between 1898 and 1919 four jurists published major treatises on the civil code, conservative scholars Fernando Vélez, Antonio José Uribe and Nicasio Anzola, and liberal Rodríguez Piñeres. The teaching of civil law in law faculties was usually based on these treatises, thus they were influential in the training of law students, many of whom went into politics. Legal historian Isabel Jaramillo (2013) finds that these jurists agreed that women's relative civil incapacity in marriage was not based on the assumption of their natural inferiority to men. The three conservative scholars justified women's incapacity either because there were advantages to having only one administrator of the conjugal society and/or because it was necessary to have only one person in charge of protecting the moral interests of the family, and they considered men better equipped for this role. Only Rodríguez Piñeres found no justification at all for the maintenance of potestad marital (Jaramillo 2013, 266).

Ricardo Uribe Escobar (1914) wrote a scathing critique of the country's civil code as his doctoral law thesis at the University of Antioquia. Going beyond Rodríguez Piñeres' analysis, he argued that the code placed women in a subordinate position to men under the dubious rationale that it was for their protection. The mechanism was via the forced nature of the conjugal society whereby at marriage the husband became the administrator of his wife's assets as well as of the "social assets" (the gananciales or community property) generated during it. By making her civilly incapable, the marital regime "converted her into a dependent of her husband" (Uribe Escobar 1914, 38).

Uribe Escobar (1914, 43) likened the regime of the conjugal society to a business where one partner had all the rights and privileges, and the other, no rights, which he considered "inconceivably absurd" and "an unjust inequality." Husbands could do anything they wished with the assets acquired during the marriage, while wives could not conduct any transaction without their husbands' permission. The only potential autonomy granted wives was if in a prenuptial agreement (capitulaciones) the couple explicitly designated some of her assets for her to manage or a certain amount of money for her to spend. This flexibility was illusory since couples rarely concerned themselves with economic matters at the time of marriage. He was not aware of a single case of a couple having made a prenuptial agreement.

The wife's only say in her husband's management was that he could not sell her immovable assets without her permission and the authorization of a judge. According to Uribe Escobar (1914, 42), this protection was also illusory because

2 The restrictions on married women and the details of the marital regime are in Colombia (1895, arts. 176–195, 1771–1836).

a husband could easily circumvent it, using threats or deception to acquire her consent, "by having her sign a paper whose content and scope she does not understand." The main safeguard that the code gave wives regarding the community property was that if the husband declared bankruptcy or committed fraud she could ask for separation of property, whereby her assets and half of the gananciales came under her control. Nonetheless, by the time a wife followed this recourse there were usually no assets left to divide. Among working-class households where the only asset might be the dwelling, he did not consider it unusual for a husband to sell it without her knowledge, "pocketing the proceeds and leaving the poor woman on the street, deceived and miserable" (Uribe Escobar 1914, 42), not unlike the case of Encarnación, discussed earlier.

Thus Uribe Escobar (1914, 43) proposed the adoption of separation of property as the default regime "to protect women against husbands who defraud, are spendthrifts or incapable of good management of the social assets." He expected its adoption to not only end wives' dependence upon their husbands and their power over them, but also that it would transform them. Nonetheless, the type of education women received also had to change, since currently it only prepared them for marriage, not employment. His analysis closely followed the thinking of Frederick Engels and August Bebel, whom he cited favorably in terms of the expected liberating effect of women joining the labor force.

Uribe Escobar (1914, 51) also viewed positively the advances in women's political rights in the United States although in Colombia he thought such rights would be premature: "Before giving her the right to vote she needs civil and social rights; because only once she has a civil personality…will she have the capacity to exercise her political rights." That women's civil rights must come first was the consensus position among most liberal and some conservative politicians.

Several of the political parties began to champion women's civil rights prior to the emergence of the first women's groups demanding them. From its founding in 1919, the Socialist Party included women's civil and economic rights in its platform. By then women workers in the textile industry were participating in strikes and some women's labor centers had formed to advocate for their specific interests, such as working conditions and maternity leave.[3] That same year the directorate of the Liberal Party also recognized the need to address married women's civil rights and to improve the working conditions of women (Camacho et al. 1919, 26, 28), perhaps because socialists were addressing these issues. Its 1922 party platform included improving married women's civil rights (Velásquez Toro 1989, 23).

3 One of the noted labor activists of the 1920s was María Cano, a middle-class intellectual who rose to prominence in the labor struggles in Medellín, the center of Colombia's textile industry, who became a leader of that party. Its newspaper, *Humanidad*, regularly publicized the advances of women in other countries, called for men's and women's equal access to education and drew attention to women's double exploitation as workers and as women (Velásquez Toro 1989, 23, 42–4; Villarreal 1994, 73–4).

With deep ties to the Catholic Church, the Conservative Party established its hegemony after brutal civil wars under the so-called "Regeneration." The Constitution of 1886 reaffirmed Catholicism as the official religion and reasserted Church control over marriage and the content of private and public education.[4] The calls by nascent feminists to reform the content of women's education beyond its focus on women's domestic role, and particularly their demand for public secondary schools for women, faced powerful resistance. For example, after studying in the United States, educator María Rojas Tejada returned home to Medellín to start a private secondary school for girls based on progressive education principles. The Church forced her to close it down, which is why she ended up in the small town of Pereira to set up her school and start the periodical *Femeninas* in 1916 that focused on the importance of women's access to education (Londoño 1995; Wills 2007, 98–9). Women always presented their demands for better access to education in terms of how this would make them better wives and mothers and strengthen the family, that is, in the framework of maternalist feminism.[5]

The first public secondary schools that admitted women were normal schools for teacher training established after an 1870 decree authorized one in each department. But the number of these, a precondition to the expansion of public primary education, only increased after the passage of Law 8 of 1903 that established that there were to be separate normal schools for men and women in each departmental capital, since the Church was strongly against mixed-sex education (Velásquez Toro 1989, 26–8). The government, nonetheless, did not give serious attention to the quality of women's teacher training until 1927 when it established the National Pedagogical Institute. Even the private Catholic schools at that time did not offer a course study at the secondary level that could lead to university entrance.

Among the first secular women's organizations whose purpose went beyond philanthropic activities[6] were the Centro Femenino de Estudios (Women's Study Center) in Medellín and Centro Femenil de Acción Social (Center for Feminine Social Action) in Bogotá, both established in 1929 (Cocker 2000; Cohen 2001; Luna 2004). The Centro Femenino was a study group associated with the periodical

4 During the 1853–1880 liberal period under the Federation, most states instituted the separation of church and state and civil marriage; a few adopted absolute divorce. The conservative Regeneración enacted the centralized 1887 Civil Code and the 1888 Concordant with Rome whereby Catholics could only marry according to Catholic rituals (Miranda Salcedo 2011). Deere and León (2021) show how this code was less favorable to wives than the initial 1873 code.

5 According to Londoño (1995), most of the early women's periodicals were religiously oriented. The first edited by a woman focusing on "the modern woman" was *Colombia, La Revista de Damas,* published in 1907 in Bogotá. By the 1920s this latter category included *Athenea* in Medellín and *Revista Hogar* in Bogotá, both of which promoted women's access to a better education, including access to university (Cohen 2001, 6; Gomez de Monroy 2002, 104–5).

6 As elsewhere, upper-class women were active in charity organizations linked to the Catholic Church since this was among the few socially approved public activities for women of their class (Velásquez Toro 1989, 44).

Letras y Encajes, which focused on promoting women's artistic, literary and scientific development and accomplishments as well as Catholic values. Founded by philanthropist Alicia Merizalde de Echevarría and writers Sofía Ospina de Navarro and Angela Villa (later, de Toro), Teresa Santamaría (later, de González) edited it for most of the lengthy period, 1926 to 1959 it was in circulation (Londoño 1995; Cohen 2001, 6).

Educators Georgina Fletcher and Claudia Múnera founded the Centro Femenil with the objective of improving the situation of women. It promoted a Christian and rational feminism meant to prepare women to collaborate with men as equals (Cohen 2001, 50). While Fletcher identified with the Liberal Party, the Centro's initial leadership was composed of prominent middle- and upper-class women from across the political spectrum.[7]

Although no Colombian woman attended the First International Women's Congress in Buenos Aires in 1910 (Asociación de Universitarias Argentinas 1911), during the 1920s a few began to participate in such congresses. Múnera, for example, presented papers and those of others at the Women's Auxiliary Conference of the 1924 Second Pan American Scientific Congress in Lima, the 1926 Inter-American Congress of Women in Panama, and the 1928 Third International Congress of Women held in Buenos Aires (Cohen 2001, 38–42). Fletcher was also in regular correspondence with the founder and secretary general of the Liga Internacional de Mujeres Ibéricas y Hispanoamericanas (LIMIH), Mexican writer Elena Arizmendi, who lived in exile in New York City, and its president, Spanish writer Carmen de Burgos Seguí.

The origins of the LIMIH are related to the 1922 First Pan American Women's Congress in Baltimore, which caused Arizmendi to become concerned over US leadership of the nascent Latin American women's movement.[8] She founded LIMIH in 1923 to strengthen ties among Spanish-speaking women in the Americas and Spain. Its objectives were to elevate the position of women through their education, both for their own development and to make them better mothers, and the pursuit of civil rights; equal political rights were a distant goal (Ezama 2014). LIMIH soon had national committees in 15 countries, composed primarily of writers, journalists and other professional women (Cuadro 2018, 255). Poet Blanca Isaza de Jaramillo Meza was Colombia's first representative although shortly after its first congress in Mexico City in 1925, Fletcher replaced her, and it was she who invited the LIMIH to hold its 1930 congress in Bogotá (Cohen 2001, 38–48). One

7 Colombia's first lady, Leonor de Velasco de Abadía Méndez, wife of the conservative president, was its honorary president (Cohen 2001, 49).

8 Arizmendi felt offended by the attitude of superiority of US feminists toward Latin American women at the Baltimore congress, and even more so after Carrie Chapman Catt, who toured South America on behalf of the PAAAW published articles on the poor prospects for feminism in the region (Catt 1923a, 1923b; Cuadro 2018, 247, 254). Catt was co-founder of the National League of Women Voters who organized the 1922 conference and president of IWSA.

of the main topics of discussion at this congress was a legislative bill to reform the marital regime, thus it is relevant to first consider the civil code reform initiatives undertaken prior to 1930.

First Steps in the Legislature

During the 1920s the Congress considered three bills to improve married women's property rights and one regarding women's access to higher education. Even though the country was industrializing at a much faster pace that its neighbors, Ecuador and Venezuela, where working wives had gained the right to control their earnings, the conservative Senate nixed the two bills approved by the Chamber of Representatives that recognized women's reserved property. The bill the Congress approved in 1922 only minimally improved the property rights of wives while taking a modest step toward expanding women's other civil rights.

The first bill proposing to reform the marital regime was a 1921 bipartisan initiative by two congressmen from Cundinamarca, Conservative Party Deputy Nicasio Anzola (one of the jurists discussed previously) and Nemesio Camacho, leader of the Liberal Party.[9] It gave wives the right to administer and dispose of their own earnings from a profession or industry, like the reserved property of the 1907 French law and the earlier German reform. Women's personal items, such as clothing, jewels, furniture and instruments of work received similar treatment. The bill also declared married women as being legally capable of managing their own assets subject to two caveats: to sell immovable assets they required a judge's approval and during the marriage the husband had the usufruct right to their immovable property for the purpose of covering expenses of the marriage.

While the bill provided only illusory gains when it came to a wife's management of assets such as housing or land, as opposed to her own wage or salary, it likely represented a compromise between the two deputies. Only a few years before Anzola (1918) had published his treatise on the civil code where he had only proposed one small change, related to divorced women's property rights. The presentation of this bill coincided with marked labor unrest and the attention that Socialist and Liberal parties were placing on improving the situation of working women. In this context, Anzola was able to draw on sufficient conservative support for the Chamber to approve it.

The Senate's commission on legislation sent the Anzola-Camacho bill to the Supreme Court for its input and the discussions between them produced a vastly different bill that was subsequently approved. Notably, married women's control over their own earnings along with the idea that wives were legally capable as regards the administration of their own property disappeared. Law 8 of February 1922 only reiterated what the civil code already allowed: that with respect to their

9 *Anales de la Cámara de Representantes* (ACR) (1921, Series 3, 58, September 29, 239).

own property, wives had the use and management of those assets specified in a prenuptial agreement and personal items and work instruments related to their profession or occupation.[10] What was new was that neither wife nor husband could dispose of these assets (mortgage, sell or donate them) without the consent of the other. Thus it focused on giving married women added protection while diminishing their autonomy since previously they could dispose of their clothing and jewelry (Colombia 1895, art. 1795).

Law 8 was, nonetheless, much broader than the original Anzola-Camacho bill, including several other points that had been under discussion in legal circles. It made all adult women eligible to be witnesses on the same terms as men. Women's exclusion from such basic civil functions as witnessing a will or a marriage had been based on notions of women's inferiority–that their word was worth less than that of a man. Thus by recognizing women's civil capacity in this instance the 1922 reform laid the groundwork for future recognition of their equal civil rights.

Another aspect favorable to women and surely a concession to those who wanted a stronger reform was that it expanded the reasons under which wives could demand the simple separation of property. This redress had previously been available only if the husband mismanaged the wife's assets or committed fraud; now the conditions included any of the grounds for a permanent legal separation when the husband was the guilty party.[11] It did not, however, change the existing limitations on separated women's administration of their property. While they could manage their own assets and their half of the gananciales, they could not alienate any of their immovable property or appear in suits without permission of their husbands or a judge (Colombia 1895, art. 204).

The 1922 law also improved the situation of women who had caused a judicial separation due to their infidelity. While it left the double standard regarding adultery intact (with any form of adultery by women, but only men's concubinage being grounds), it ended the specific punishment of women whereby in this case only wives lost the right to the gananciales from the marriage. Both conservative and liberal legal scholars agreed that this penalty was unjust as well as unconstitutional (Jaramillo 2013, 260–1). It was unconstitutional because the constitution prohibited confiscation, and the loss of gananciales was a form of confiscation since during the marriage a wife contributed to generating these through her domestic labor and savings (if not her earnings and assets). Since in the case of adultery the code also deprived the wife of the right to any support from her husband, it left such women in indigency.[12] The code did not punish men who caused a divorce due to their notorious adultery in a similar fashion.

10 Law 8, "Por la cual se adiciona el Código Civil," *Diario Oficial* 18.130, February 23, 1922.

11 These included the husband's concubinage; habitual drunkenness; abandonment and unfulfillment of his obligations as a husband and father; and cruel mistreatment of his wife (Colombia 1895, art. 154).

12 See Anzola (1918, 65–6), for this specific reasoning.

In her research in the judicial archives in Medellín, López Oseira (2013, 286–7) found only 14 cases between 1915 and 1945 of women demanding a separation of property, confirming that wives did not use this recourse very frequently. Besides Encarnacion's case, two others (from 1926 and 1931) show that wives took advantage of the new 1922 clause that allowed them to sue for separation of property due to the grounds for legal separation in combination with concern that the husband was dissipating her assets or the community property.

The next year Liberal Party Deputy Absalón Fernández de Soto presented a comprehensive bill to expand women's civil rights.[13] He noted how Colombia was falling behind not only European but also Latin American countries such as neighboring Ecuador "whose culture is not more advanced than our own."[14] He was inspired by a bill authored by Uruguayan President Baltasar Brum that was under consideration by its legislature, which abolished the forced nature of the conjugal society by replacing it with one that was voluntarily entered into by the woman. Brum (1923) proposed combining the principle that a married woman was the owner and administrator of her own assets with the presumption that she gave her husband an implicit mandate to manage these, a mandate she could rescind at any time.

In Fernández de Soto's bill, prior to marriage couples would decide in a marital contract whether to form a conjugal society and if so, who would manage the community property. They could stipulate, for example, that the wife manage both her own assets as well as the community property with the same rights that the current code gave to husbands. In this voluntarily contracted conjugal society, the non-administrating spouse (whether wife or husband) had the right to ask a judge at any time to separately administer the assets that he or she brought to or acquired during the marriage. If a couple did not enter a prenuptial agreement (and he expected this to be the case, since they rarely did), the bill assumed that the wife gave her husband an implicit mandate to administer her assets and those that she might acquire during the marriage except for those assets related to her own independent profession or occupation. Irrespective of regime, a wife who exercised a profession or occupation automatically retained the right to administer and dispose of her earnings and the assets thereby acquired; that is, it recognized a working wife's reserved property similar to the original 1921 Anzola-Camacho bill.

Fernández de Soto's bill also eliminated the civil code article that required the husband to provide his wife protection and the wife obedience to him, replacing it with a provision for mutual support, respect and protection, and established that the couple was to jointly determine the household's domicile. Further, both father and mother were to exercise patria potestad over their minor children, including the administration of their assets. As in the case of the conjugal society, he assumed

13 "Proyecto de ley sobre Derechos de la Mujer y Exposición de motivos" (ACR, 1923, October 11, 381–4). Also discussed in Cohen (2001, 28–9) and Gómez Camargo (2019, 218).

14 ACR (1923, October 11, 382). He erroneously dated Ecuador's reform as being of 1918 rather than 1911.

that a wife would voluntarily defer to her husband so that these assets were under one sole administrator. His intent was to establish women's property rights in principle, not necessarily that they would exercise them in practice, surely to assuage the opposition to his bill.

The bill also expanded the reasons for a judicial separation and gave such separated women the right to manage and dispose of their assets without need for anyone's authorization. Also, irrespective of marital status, women who administered their own property could serve as guardians,[15] be a guarantor of a loan or hold power of attorney for another person and appear in suits regarding their own property. In addition, the bill specified that women had the right to be employed in any job, profession or honest occupation, including any form of public employment that did not involve supervision or authority, and to attend universities on the same terms as men. According to him, legal barriers did not prohibit women from attending university or being employed in the liberal professions or in government but it was socially inappropriate for women to be involved such activities. Thus legislation was necessary to establish that these opportunities were open to them.

The commission studying the bill recommended it favorably, observing that while unscrupulous husbands were the exception rather than the rule, women needed more protection.[16] It supported the idea of making the conjugal society voluntary but was concerned with whether couples would make prenuptial agreements, since such went against traditional practice. There was also hesitancy about granting wives so much freedom of action, and particularly, granting mothers equal patria potestad over children, since it considered wives to be ill-prepared for such a role. Notwithstanding the favorable report, the Chamber never discussed the bill.

A few years later, conservative Senator Luis Ignacio Andrade assumed the cause of women's higher education. His 1927 bill allowed women to attend universities and created the necessary secondary education track for them to qualify to take the entrance exams. Most conservatives opposed the measure since the Catholic Church was firmly against expanding public education and especially any type of mixed-sex education. Since they controlled the legislature, the bill did not prosper although it served to further public discussion around women's need for higher education to be able to enter the professions. Women were among those who sent memos to the Congress and published articles in the press in support of this bill (Cohen 2001, 12, 29–30).

Deputy Fernández de Soto resubmitted his Women's Civil Rights bill to the Congress in 1928, now co-sponsored by liberal Nemesio Camacho.[17] This time

15 Under the 1887 Civil Code, if the father did not specify a guardian for his children in his will, the only women who could serve as guardian of a minor were the mother or grandmother; specifically excluded were sisters and aunts (Colombia 1895, arts. 457, 587).

16 ACR (1923, October 11, 384).

17 "Proyecto de ley sobre derechos de la mujer" (ACR 1928, Series 2, 35, June 16, 224–8).

his bill was accompanied by the expressed support of women, such as well-known writer Isabel Pinzón Castilla, who sent a memo to the Congress.[18] Parts of the bill had the support of a few conservative deputies, and a special commission reduced its scope before it was discussed on the floor; during that discussion it was reduced still further because of the opposition of most conservatives.[19] The substitute bill, which the deputies approved in November 1928 contained only six articles rather than the original 29.[20]

The approved bill allowed the admission of women to universities and for them to exercise all professions, including those in public administration. It laid out explicitly that the wages and salaries earned by married women belonged to them exclusively. It extended the previous requirement of a wife's consent for a husband to sell any immovable property that she brought to marriage, to any that she might inherit. The bill strengthened the position of separated women by giving them the same status as widows or single women to manage and dispose of their own movable and immovable property. It also streamlined the process for a judicial separation of assets under the conditions allowed by the code.

Conservative senators then further diluted the bill by voting down the article that would have provided for women's control over their own earnings.[21] Rather than vote on this modest bill, to deny a quorum, many of them walked out and the bill died. Their behavior caused an uproar in the press, with the director of *El Tiempo*, for example, describing the debate as embarrassing and insulting to women. Several prominent intellectuals, including Georgina Fletcher, wrote letters deploring the Senate's actions (Cohen 2001, 35).

Besides the minimalist 1922 law, the only other relevant reform undertaken during this period of conservative rule was an indirect gain attained under Law 124 of 1928 regulating savings institutions. It provided for married women to be able to own and establish their own bank accounts.[22] Worth emphasizing is that although the Chamber approved two bills that provided for women's control over their own earnings, conservative senators consistently refused to accept this concept. Allowing wives to own bank accounts in their own name, nonetheless, was a step in this direction.

The 1930 Women's Congress and the 1932 Reform

After a long hiatus, the Liberal Party returned to power in 1930 with the election of Enrique Olaya Herrera to the presidency. He constituted a coalition government with conservatives around a program to extricate the country from the

18 "Proyecto de ley sobre derechos de la mujer" (ACR 1928, 228), also mentioned in Cohen (2001, 29).
19 ACR (1928, Series 7, 153, 1090–1; 154, 1098; 155, 1106–7; 156, 1114).
20 The Chamber's approved version is in *Anales del Senado* (AS) (1928, Series 7, 167, 1127).
21 *Anales del Senado* (AS) (1928, Series 7, 170, 1148). Cohen (2001, 32–4) draws on press reports to provide a detailed analysis of this debate; little of its substance appears in the Senate record.
22 *Diario Oficial* 20.959, December 1, 1928, art. 12, and noted in Amezquita de Almeyda (1977, 255).

economic, social and political crisis of the Great Depression. Enhancing women's civil rights was part of his campaign platform, a campaign actively supported by many women (Cohen 2001). Nonetheless, it took four attempts, with bills containing different mechanisms to strengthen married women's property rights, before the successful enactment of Law 28 of 1932. The approval of this law was very much due to the lobbying of women, a process initiated at the 1930 Women's Conference.

Olaya Herrera's support for women's rights preceded his presidency. Under the previous government he had served as Colombia's ambassador to Washington, DC and headed its delegation to the 1928 Sixth International Conference of American States in Havana (Rodríguez 1979, 131). At this conference he endorsed the demands of the Latin American and US feminists who had gathered in a parallel meeting for permission to present their proposal for an Equal Rights Treaty. While the delegates rejected the women's proposal, at Olaya Herrera's insistence, they endorsed the formation of the Inter-American Commission of Women (CIM, as it is known in the region) (Marino 2019, 57–65, 260, n.260).[23]

Shortly after Olaya Herrera's inauguration, a group of women met with him to lobby for implementation of his campaign promises and to ask his support of the upcoming Fourth International Congress of Women.[24] He reportedly replied that he was pleased that women were finally interested in their rights and that one of the first bills he would present to Congress would be to strengthen their property rights (Uribe 1963, 189). He also agreed to government sponsorship of the women's congress as part of the celebrations around the centennial commemoration of Bolivar's death and provided some modest funding.

As the first public forum of women, the congress was to include two delegates from each of the country's departments appointed by their respective governors as well as representatives of all interested organizations. Reflecting the level of interest in such a congress, over 100 women participated in the planning meeting that determined its five central themes.[25] Among them was the promotion of legislation favorable to women and children (Cohen 2001, 54).

23 María Elena de Ricardo Hinestrosa was Colombia's first representative although Alicia Rico de Herrera attended CIM's 1930 inaugural meeting (IACW 1935).

24 This was the fourth non-Pan American related women's conference, following the 1910 Buenos Aires conference hosted by the Universitarias, the 1926 conference held in Chile, and the 1928 Buenos Aires conference hosted by Club Argentina de Mujeres. After its initial 1925 conference in Mexico, LIMIH co-sponsored the 1928 Buenos Aires conference, making the Bogotá 1930 conference technically its third (Cuadro 2018, 263–9).

25 Uruguayan Paulina Luisi, who was second vice-president of LIMIH and unable to attend, later wrote how the agenda of the Bogotá congress was "timid" in its themes, which she thought reflected the very recent organization of Colombian women and their limited access to university (Cuadro 2018, 268).

The Olaya-Restrepo Capitulaciones Bill

In August 1930 Olaya Herrera's minister of government, Carlos E. Restrepo (a former conservative president), presented a bill to the Chamber to reform sections of the civil code on the marital regime, which became known as the Olaya-Restrepo or "capitulaciones" bill.[26] Drafted by legal scholar Eduardo Rodríguez Piñeres, it contained the proposal he had made three decades earlier (Rodríguez Fonnegra 1965, 9). It gave couples the option of making marital contracts at any point – not just prior to marriage – and that these could include all or some of their current or future assets. It went beyond this by specifying that if a couple had not made a prenuptial, a wife could ask for a partial or total separation of property at any time without need to justify such an action.

In their cover letter, Olaya Herrera and Restrepo said features of the German civil code, such as its flexibility, inspired their proposal. Prior to marriage women could rarely foresee the problems that might later develop, thus the importance of couples having the flexibility to make a marital contract at any point. Moreover, they considered it crucial for wives to be able to request a separation of property without having to prove cause, for currently a wife needed to prove her husband's incompetence, bankruptcy or alcoholism, all causes "dishonorable to the husband." In their view, a woman would rather lose all her assets than embarrass or shame her husband in such a manner; in addition, it was often difficult to obtain the required evidence to prove such behavior.

The editors of *Letras y Encajes* (1950, 811–2) enthusiastically endorsed the bill since if approved: "…married women will have gained a major victory and will move beyond the status of perpetual minors to which they have been relegated since time immemorial." This is the first indication that the very Catholic elite women of Medellín embraced the demand for enhancing women's property rights.

The Chamber's commission on civil legislation presented its report on the Olaya-Restrepo bill just as the women's congress was about to begin.[27] In their majority report, conservative deputies firmly rejected it, for "it would have grave consequences for marital assets that could disturb the union and peace of the family."[28] Since the bill drew on the German and Swiss civil codes, they also viewed these ideas as foreign and incompatible with local traditions and norms. Moreover, they justified the relatively legal incapacity of wives in the Colombian civil code as being based not on their intellectually incompetency but rather on the fact that the conjugal society required that there be only one head, "who could not be any other but the husband."[29] Allowing wives to fully manage their own assets via marital contracts was also inconsistent with other parts of the civil code that prohibited

26 "Proyecto de ley reformatorio del Código Civil" (ACR, 1930, Series 2, 27, August 25, 183).
27 ACR (1930, Series 6, 130, December 16, 1011–3).
28 ACR (1930, Series 6, 130, December 16, 1012).
29 ACR (1930, Series 6, 130, December 16, 1012).

women from acting without their husband's consent. Further, if a couple could change these during the marriage this would introduce confusion regarding the origin of the gananciales. In addition, they found it "inconvenient" to allow women to separate their property during the marriage without providing specific reasons, since besides undermining potestad marital, it would deprive husbands of needed capital to meet the debts of the conjugal society. They found it preferable to allow couples to choose between the separation of property regime and the conjugal society at the time of marriage, as the 1804 French civil code allowed.

The commission thus proposed a substitute bill to replace the Olaya-Restrepo bill consisting of two articles.[30] The first allowed couples in prenuptial agreements to opt for partial or total separation of property. The second expanded the conditions under which a wife could petition a judge for separation of property during the marriage to include his inept administration or dissipation of her assets due to his drunkenness or other vices; if her assets fell by 20% or more in value due to his mismanagement; and if he did not contribute to her and her children's appropriate support. The minority report, authored by two liberals, refuted the arguments of the majority report while suggesting a few minor modifications.[31]

The Women's Congress and Lobbying Efforts

At the 1930 Women's Congress, Ofelia Uribe de Acosta,[32] a teacher by training, presented a keynote entitled "A Contribution to the Study of the Olaya-Restrepo Reform of the Capitulaciones Regime." Georgina Fletcher, the chair of the women's congress, invited the entire Chamber of Representatives to this session and three deputies as well as Minister Restrepo attended (Cohen 2001).

Uribe (1931, 23) began by denouncing the injustice of the current marital regime, especially because "the first rule and basis of the [marriage] contract is obedience and absolute submission" by the wife. Moreover, "lack of recognition of a woman's judgement and ability to reason, a characteristic of all conscious beings, is ridiculous and deeply offensive." She then responded to some of the specific criticisms raised by the commission's majority report, for example, that the bill copied innovations developed under different customs than Colombia's. She stressed how the nation's civil code was outdated and did not correspond to contemporary needs. Its rigidities, such as couples not being able to opt for an alternative regime after marriage, left a wife defenseless if she later realized her husband had married only

30 ACR (1930, Series 6, 130, December 16, 1013).

31 ACR (1930, Series 6, 134, December 22, 1052–4). *Letras y Encajes* (1931, 873–5) published the entire minority report.

32 Uribe, the daughter of a liberal provincial family of educators, was a graduate of normal school and taught primary school prior to her marriage to a liberal lawyer. She attended the 1930 congress as a delegate appointed by the governor of Boyacá and later became a leading feminist journalist and editor (Torres 1986, 28–30).

for material gain. In her view, the reason some men opposed the Olaya-Restrepo reform was because they simply did not want to give up their privileges.

Uribe (1931) also laid out how the Olaya-Restrepo bill addressed only the minimum concerns of feminists, and that if anything, it did not go far enough in establishing married women's economic independence. For example, it did not establish civil equality between men and women, for it maintained the concept and content of potestad marital. At the same time, she recognized that women were not yet prepared for full equality. They needed access to more and better quality education before they could be men's full partners in marriage, which was the goal. Thus, to the criticism of those who opposed the bill because it only gave women the right to contract with their husband but maintained their civil incapacity in other matters, she answered that it was precisely this middle road that was currently appropriate. She urged congress participants to lobby the legislature to approve the bill, considering it a major step forward.

Fletcher subsequently appointed a delegation that included Uribe, Clotilde García de Ucros and others to observe the congressional debate over the Olaya-Restrepo bill. Many other women also attended these sessions, filling the gallery and cheering those who supported the bill (Cohen 2001; Gómez Molina 2015). By the time the Women's Congress concluded, however, the Chamber had not yet acted. In her closing remarks Claudina Múnera emphasized how passage of this bill was a top priority of the women in attendance, along with improving and expanding women's education.[33]

In January 1931 Clotilde García and others sent a memorandum to the Chamber's president asking him to prioritize the Olaya-Restrepo bill, given its strong support by Colombian women. The Chamber's leaders tended to place the bill far down on the daily agenda and although a liberal deputy attempted to mark off a given afternoon for its sole consideration, the Chamber voted down this motion. The bill thus died during this legislative session (Cohen 2011). Nonetheless, this experience with the Olaya-Restrepo bill served as both a civic and legal education for many of those who attended the Women's Congress, as well as those who followed its discussions in the press. Most of the congress participants were teachers or writers and while relatively well educated, they were not necessarily well informed of the details of the civil code nor of the different options available to strengthen married women's property rights.

Building Consensus in the Legislature

Concurrently with the capitulaciones bill, the Chamber's commission on civil legislation considered several other modest ones that partially reformed the civil code in ways favorable to women. Those approved by the Congress that were

33 "Del Congreso Femenino, discurso de la señorita Claudina Múnera," *Letras y Encajes* (1931, 871–2).

uncontroversial included a 1930 law that finally established that legally separated women had full legal capacity with respect to administration of their own assets.[34] It also specified that a husband could not alienate a married woman's inheritance without her consent and the approval of a judge, adding the latter to give wives greater protection.

To protect the family against some of the adverse consequences of the Great Depression, in 1931 the Congress approved legislation that allowed an owner to designate the household's principal residence as "family patrimony," making it immune from seizure in case of bankruptcy. If minors resided in the home, the owner could not mortgage or sell it without consent of his or her spouse.[35] Even if there were no minor children remaining at home, it protected widows from eviction by giving them preference in buying out any heirs. The labor legislation of this period also contained an important recognition of the property rights of wives, attesting to the growing visibility of women wage workers. Married women were to receive their wages directly and entitled to manage these themselves.[36] This was an important step forward since only a few years earlier the Senate had rejected the idea of wives managing their own earnings.

After the 1931 elections that renovated the Senate, the Olaya Herrera administration again attempted to reform the marital regime. This time a conservative senator who was an ally of the president, Mario Fernández de Soto, presented the government's bill on capitulaciones.[37] The main change in the 1931 version was that, because of the strong opposition it had generated, a wife would no longer be able to obtain a separation of property without providing reason. She now had to prove that her husband was squandering assets or that there was danger of these diminishing. Notwithstanding the many telegrams sent by women urging its passage even under these restricted conditions, this bill also died in committee (Gómez Molina 2015, 55–6).

Absalón Fernández de Soto was now a senator and in 1931 he submitted the same bill to this chamber that he had unsuccessfully introduced as deputy in 1923 and 1928.[38] His bill was much more ambitious than that of Olaya-Restrepo and it faced opposition from those opposed to enhancing women's civil rights as well as by those who championed them.[39] The latter group was concerned that its provisions might encourage women to choose the separation of property regime, one

34 Law 67, *Diario Oficial* 21.570, December 18, 1930.

35 Law 70, *Diario Oficial* 21.706, June 5, 1931. To qualify, there could not be a mortgage on the dwelling and its value had to be less than 10,000 pesos.

36 Law 83, art. 24, *Diario Oficial* 21.735, June 10, 1931. Peláez (1944, 60) and Velásquez Toro (1989, 34) cite this as an important precedent.

37 "Proyecto de Ley reformatoria del Código Civil" (AS, 1931, Series 1, 11, August 3, 73–4).

38 "Proyecto de ley sobre derechos de la mujer" (AS, 1931,Series 3, 53 and 54, September 24, 375–80).

39 See Gómez Molina (2015, 47) for more details of this debate.

they considered detrimental to women who married without any assets or who did not work for income, since it did not recognize the contribution of wives through their domestic labor and childcare to their husband's accumulation of assets. Recall that under this regime when the marriage dissolves, there is no community property to redistribute. This bill also died in committee.

President Olaya Herrera remained resolute in his determination to strengthen married women's property rights since he considered these crucial to his modernization project, among other reasons, to provide incentives for women to join the labor force.[40] He thus asked his presidential lawyer, Luis Felipe Latorre, to devise a new approach. Inspired by his study of recent reforms in Scandinavia and Hungary, Latorre (1934) proposed combining separation of property during the marriage – so that wives and husbands have full and parallel rights over their own property and the gananciales each generated – with the conjugal society at its end, requiring the pooling and equal division of the gananciales to benefit both spouses. The government presented the new bill to the Chamber in July 1932, which became the basis for the approved law.[41]

In his exposition, Latorre (1934, 28) argued that by mixing regimes his proposal gave wives economic independence during the marriage while assuring them equity at its end. He viewed it as particularly beneficial to housewives who married without assets, for it recognized their domestic labor and contribution to the formation of the gananciales from the marriage.[42] It thus improved upon the classic separation of property regime since in that regime at the marriage's end wives had no claim to community property. Summarizing how most advanced countries had by now strengthened married women's property rights, Latorre (1934, 32) argued that it was imperative for Colombia to join "this contemporary universal movement in favor of women's economic emancipation and recognition of their civil capacity…" In the more developed countries there had not been any negative consequences from these reforms and it was unlikely that there would be so in Colombia, "unless we erroneously suppose that Colombian women were intellectually and morally inferior to women in countries where they now have such rights" (Latorre 1934, 32).

In his minority report to the Chamber's legislation commission and in his later comments, conservative Deputy Joaquín Emilio Sierra summarized the thinking of

40 Comments to the Chamber when it was about to begin its second debate on the bill (Colombia 1939, 145–6). This source, *Historia de las Leyes*, contains the congressional debates behind each approved bill, and is my primary source in the subsequent discussion of the 1932 law.

41 Gómez Molina (2015) initially drew my attention to how three failed bills preceded the successful 1932 law. Villarreal (1994), Velásquez Ocampo (2015) and Dueñas (2024) wrongly imply that the 1930 capitulaciones bill eventually became law. The 1932 law was quite different since separation of property during the marriage became the default, not just an option as in that bill; moreover, the law combined it with community property at its end.

42 Latorre (1934, 28–9) cited Belgian lawyer Georgette Ciselet to this effect who had analyzed the Hungarian legislation in a 1930 book. He did not mention that Central American countries had adopted such a mixed regime several decades earlier.

those opposed to the bill.[43] While he favored protecting women from unscrupulous husbands, he considered such situations to be the exception rather than the rule. Moreover, he objected to the import of a legal institution that was meant to solve a problem of only a minority, for this could destabilize the family. Women in Colombia had not reached the same level of "civilization" as those in Europe, being neither educated sufficiently nor prepared to manage their own assets or businesses. He also found it absurd as well as contrary to legal theory to try to mix two marital regimes, separation of property and partial community property. In his words, how could one speak about "the dissolution and liquidation of something that did not exist" during the marriage? (Colombia 1939, 153). A better alternative in his view would be to maintain the conjugal society, with the husband as the administrator of the community property and household head, while allowing each spouse to manage their own assets during the marriage.[44]

Latorre and defenders of the bill, such as liberal deputies Eduardo Esguerra Serrano and Jorge Eliécer Gaitán, argued that it was precisely this mixing of regimes that offered the greatest benefits. Separation of property during the marriage gave wives needed economic autonomy while the equal division of the gananciales upon its dissolution recognized their economic contribution to the household, that is, their domestic labor and childcare responsibilities (Colombia 1939, 157–74). This formula took care of the concerns expressed by both liberals and conservatives in the earlier debates over proposals to institute the separation of property regime, either via prenuptial agreements or as an alternative regime. Conservative Deputy Eleuterio Serna, for example, who had opposed the capitulaciones bill, explained that he had considered that alternative too difficult to implement, given social norms. But he was not "anti-feminist" and considered the formula proposed in this bill a just alternative. While he supported women's civil rights, he made a point of noting that their political rights were another matter (Colombia 1939,165–6).

Clotilde García once again mobilized groups of women to observe the legislative debates during which several conservative deputies derided their presence in the balcony (Uribe 1963, 195–6). The press widely reported these incidents and the substance of the debate, which served to raise public consciousness of the need for reform and assisted in moving public opinion in favor of the bill (Velásquez Toro 1989; Gómez Molina 2015). After some re-writing for greater clarity and the addition of new articles on transitory measures, the Chamber approved the bill.

In the Senate, its commission on legislation voiced concern that Colombia was not yet ready for such a radical reform (Colombia 1939, 194–8). At the same time, the commission recognized that enhancing married women's property rights was just and overdue. It acknowledged that women's participation in the labor force was proving compatible with their traditional responsibilities in the home.

43 Colombia (1939, 146–7, 152–6); see Gómez Molina (2015) for greater detail.

44 Sierra's proposed solution was like what Peru adopted in its 1936 Civil Code; see Chapter 5.

Nonetheless, it would have preferred a more gradual approach, such as that of the original Olaya-Restrepo bill that gave couples flexibility in what they could do in marital contracts. Among the reasons the commission gave to move the bill forward were that public opinion favored it; the Colegio de Abogados (Bar Association) had approved it; the government considered it indispensable; the Chamber had adopted it almost unanimously; and that "the worthiest ladies of our society support it enthusiastically" (Colombia 1939, 197).

The Senate approved the bill by a vote of 31 to 10 without much discussion. Nine of those opposed, all members of the Conservative Party, requested that the congressional record include their reasons for dissent: the bill was conceptually contradictory, since it mixed two regimes; it did not protect women and could be prejudicial to their interests; it would destabilize the family; and went "directly against the unity of conjugal bond, which is the basis of Catholic marriage" (Colombia 1939, 205).

Women's mobilization in support of the 1932 bill was crucial to its passage. Among the petitions read on the floor of the legislature was one by Claudina Múnera and a group from Manizales who considered the current bill to be far superior to the earlier capitulaciones bill and urged the Congress to approve it (Cohen 2001, 106). The Feminine Social Action Center sent a petition signed by Georgina Fletcher and 60 other women also urging Congress to quickly approve it.[45] The next month they sent another with over 100 signatures stressing how the bill would enhance marital harmony since men would no longer marry for material considerations but rather for love (Velásquez Toro 1989, 25). Another petition by a group of women in Neiva asked the Congress to remove "all that dishonors the dignity of women" from the civil code (Colombia 1939, 156).

As Magdala Velásquez Toro (1989, 25) observes, Law 28 of 1932[46] abolished most elements of potestad marital related to the property of married women, but not those regarding their personhood. With marriage, women no longer automatically lost their right to manage their own property or what they acquired through inheritance or labor. Husbands ceased to be the legal representatives of their wives, who could now contract and appear in suits. At the same time, a wife still owed her husband obedience, and he determined the place of residence and could oblige her to live wherever he chose. Moreover, fathers continued to exert exclusive patria potestad. Gómez Molina (2015, 68) thus overstates the case when she says that with Law 28 women achieved their "complete civil capacity."[47]

In the new marital regime, each spouse held parallel rights to administer and dispose of the assets each brought to marriage and those acquired during it, irrespective of source. The novelty was that, at its dissolution, this regime assumed

45 ACR (1932, Series 2, 79, October 1, 470).

46 *Diario Oficial* 22.139, November 17, 1932.

47 Rodríguez Fonnegra (1965, 37) maintains that since the wife still owed the husband obedience, he could prevent her from working or establishing a business, a point that the courts never clearly settled.

that community property existed from the moment of its inception.[48] Hence, all the assets acquired during marriage by either spouse (except those acquired via inheritance) were community property, along with any gains from individually owned assets and divided equally between the two or their estates. In Colombia this regime is known as the regime of "participation in gananciales" or the "society of gananciales," and internationally, as differed community property. Legal scholars Arturo Valencia Zea and Álvaro Ortíz Monsalve (1995, 63) consider it essentially the same as what Costa Rica adopted in its 1887 civil code using different terms, separation of property as the default with the pooling and division of gananciales at the dissolution of the marriage. Nonetheless, it is worth highlighting how neither Latorre who proposed it, nor the legislators who debated its finer points ever referred to its Central American antecedents.

There was also a downside to the way Colombia formulated this mixed regime. Housewives who had no earnings or assets to manage did not gain any economic autonomy during the marriage and remained dependent on their husbands.[49] Although they received half of the gananciales at its end, during it they had no say over how their husbands managed these. As in the past, if he was a poor manager or dissipated these a wife's main recourse was to sue for separation of property. López Oseira (2013) shows that only a few wives continued to utilize this remedy. She considers one of the main effects of Law 28 to be that the courts began to rule more consistently in women's favor in the case of marital conflict over property.

Other Advances and Setbacks for Women in the 1930s

Under the presidency of Olaya Herrera and his liberal successor, Alfonso López Pumarejo, the Congress approved several other reforms favorable to women, including expanding women's access to education and public employment and improving mothers' rights over children and the inheritance rights of wives and of illegitimate children. Two issues were particularly contentious, civil divorce and women's political rights.

Shortly after the enactment of Law 28, the Congress approved legislation providing for women's equal access to secondary education and facilitating their enrollment in universities, meeting long-standing feminist demands (Velásquez Toro 1989, 27).[50] For some feminists, the possibility of women attaining the bachillerato

48 This interpretation was a source of dispute among jurists; see Gomez R. (1961) and Rodríguez Fonnegra (1965).

49 The labor force participation rate of married women remained quite low through the 1950s. The 1951 census revealed that the highest rate for wives was in the 35-44 age group when it reached only 7.3%. In comparison, in that same age group it was 11.4% for those in consensual unions, 34.8% for widows, and 37.5% for separated and 42.1% for single women (Iregui-Bohórquez et al. 2021, Table 5).

50 Decree 1874 of 1932 opened universities to women and Decree 227 of 1933 established that both public and private women's secondary schools could offer the bachillerato; they were subsequently modified by Decree 1972 of December 1, 1933; *Diario Oficial* 22.460, December 12, 1933, 13.

was as important an achievement as married women being able to manage their own property. As Idalia Vassalis (1934, 9) reported in a missive sent to *Nuevos Horizontes*, an Ecuadorian periodical, Law 28 "freed wives from the guardianship of husbands who dissipated their assets or were inept"; for girls to complete the same course of study as boys allowed them to cultivate their intellectual capacities and opened new careers to them. But while the number of women's secondary schools offering the bachillerato degree soon began to expand, women's university enrollment grew slowly.

One of the outcomes of the 1930 Women's Congress and the three year-long debate over the marital regime was that some of the women's publications, such as *Femeninas* and *Letras y Encajes*, that had previously focused on bettering women's traditional role through education became strong advocates of women's rights across the board, including their political rights (Villarreal 1994, 83; Cocker 2000, 697–8). New women's periodicals such as *El Heraldo Femenino* and Georgina Fletcher's *Hogar y Patria* honed the arguments on why women should have the vote (Villarreal 1994, 86–7; Velásquez Ocampo 2015, 23, 28). The latter's name reflected how its mission linked maternalist values such as women's domesticity and sensibility to service to the nation, which required women to have expanded rights to play a complementary role to men.[51]

Historian Lola Luna (2004) argues that two strands of what she terms "suffragette subjects" emerged in the 1930s. "Conservative suffragettes" favored women's education and civil and political rights primarily to make them better wives and mothers. "Feminist suffragettes," such as Ofelia Uribe, focused on women's emancipation from traditional roles while seeing no contradiction between women working and voting and being good wives and mothers. While these early feminists had heterogenous perspectives, political allegiances and relation to Catholicism, a factor that united them was a sense of injustice around their being denied citizenship (Mendoza 2018).

In her memoir, *Una voz insurgente* (An Insurgent Voice), Ofelia Uribe (1963, 199) acknowledged that in the 1930s the number of feminists and secular women's organizations was small. An article in the Bogotá daily *El Tiempo* mentioned only six women as forming the Colombian chapter of the Legión Femenina de Educación Popular, the Guayaquil organization founded by Ecuadorian writer Rosa Borja de Ycaza in 1932 with regional pretensions.[52] After the regional Unión de Mujeres Americanas formed in New York City in 1934, only one Colombian

51 Mendoza (2018) discusses how Fletcher's periodical, *Hogar y Patria*, founded in 1935, mirrored the Christian feminism of the LIMIH.

52 See Chapter 2 and "*Nuevos Horizontes* en el exterior," *Nuevos Horizontes* (1934, 1 (5): 23, 27). Among those mentioned were Teresa Santamaría de González in Medellín, Claudina Múnera in Manizales and members in Bucaramanga, Cúcuta, Tunja and Barranquilla.

organization joined, the Federación Nacional de Empleadas (National Federation of Female Employees).[53]

Many women did not want to be associated with feminism or ask for rights "not appropriate to their sex." Too many people viewed feminism and femininity to be incompatible, considering feminists to be *marimachos* (belonging to a third sex), a derogatory term. As Enriqueta Angelo (1931, 983–4) felt she had to explain in a lead article in *Letras y Encajes*, feminists were not "against men" nor did they wish "to start a war between the sexes." Neither were they "ridiculous marimachos who pretend to be superior to the stronger sex." She emphasized how access to education, the ability to manage one's own property and the vote would not lead women "to abandon their good taste, circumspection and delicate qualities."

A group of conservative deputies apparently agreed, because in 1933 they presented the first bill to extend citizenship to women so that they could exercise political rights (Chavarriaga 1940, 431–3; Velásquez Ocampo 2015, 30–1). The bill proposed deleting the word "men" (*varones*) in article 15 of the 1886 Constitution and lowering the age of citizenship from 21 to those at least 20 years of age while maintaining the requirement that citizens must exercise a profession or occupation and have a proven means of generating their subsistence. The deputies argued that women would bring moderation to politics through their morality and civility and that it was the logical next step after the passage of Law 28 of 1932, which they considered to have recognized women's full civil capacity and absolute equality with men.

While the full Chamber never discussed this bill, it fostered public debate. The conservative Medellín newspaper *El Colombiano* conducted a survey of women on whether they wanted the vote, assuming they would soundly reject it. Angela Villa and Teresa Santamaría of *Letras y Encajes* were among those who replied that they supported women's suffrage, arguing that the vote would not change women's primary domestic role nor go against Catholic doctrine (Velásquez Toro 1995, 201–2).

One of López Pumarejo's main objectives when he took office in 1934 was to reform the antiquated 1886 Constitution to enable greater state intervention, reduce the power of the Catholic Church, and broaden democracy through universal male suffrage. Liberals dominated this congress since the Conservative Party had abstained from running candidates in the 1935 parliamentary election as in the recent presidential one. While there was consensus that it was time to eliminate the property and income requirements on voting and standing for office, universal suffrage was contentious and particularly, the potential inclusion of women. While some liberals favored extending citizenship to women, others of the same party

53 On UMA, see Chapter 5. Several Colombian women who resided in New York City served on UMA's international board in the mid-1930s. Doris Stevens Papers, Series V, sub-series A. Correspondence: UMA, 1936–1938. On the Female Employees Federation, founded in 1932, and its publication, the *Heraldo Femenino*, see Gómez de Monroy (2002, 70, 74, 100–2).

were adamant that women's place was in the home, not in politics (Chavarriaga 1940, 433–7; Velásquez Toro 1989, 49).

In the constitutional reform of 1936, citizens ended up being defined as men who were 21 years of age or over (without a literacy requirement) and the vote, standing for office and public employment that involved authority or supervision of others limited to those who were citizens.[54] But the compromise that emerged was to allow qualified women to hold any form of public employment, including positions exercising supervision or authority over others, under the same conditions as male citizens. This concession was related to the opening of universities to women, since these graduates required employment opportunities. It meant, for example, that the new generation of women studying law could aspire to be public advocates and judges.

For feminists, the extension of the vote to illiterate men while denying all women the vote was contradictory and an injustice (*Letras y Encajes*, 1936, 2064–7). However, while they argued for suffrage in their magazines, they did not organize around attaining the vote at this time. This led María Currea de Aya, a feminist who was appointed as Colombia's next CIM representative to declare that "in Colombia there is not one women's organization worthy of its name."[55] Nonetheless, many feminists thought that they gained an important concession in the 1936 Constitution since being deemed eligible for government positions, together with the measures that strengthened women's property rights and opened universities to them, reinforced the argument that women were capable beings and, thus, eventually worthy of the vote (*Letras y Encajes,* 1937, 2283–4).

Overlapping the discussion of women's suffrage was the divisive issue of civil matrimony and divorce. At its 1935 convention, the Liberal Party reiterated its commitment in principle to absolute divorce since it was essential to furthering the civil rights of both men and women (Beltrán y Puga 2020, 89–101). But there was not unanimity on whether to pursue it at this time, since embracing it was politically risky given the adamant opposition of the Catholic Church. Nonetheless, liberal deputies continued to present bills, and the Chamber approved one in 1935 that allowed civil divorce under nine conditions, including mutual consent; the Senate never even discussed it. It was also an issue during discussions of the constitutional reform of 1936 and liberal deputies and senators presented bills in 1937 and 1939; all failed to gain traction.

Encouraged by the Church, women led much of the opposition to enacting civil divorce. Among those who vehemently opposed it were the wives of liberal presidents López Pumarejo and Olaya Herrera. The Centro Femenino de Estudios led a petition drive against it in Medellín, signed by the founders and editors of *Letras*

54 Acto Legislativo 1 de 1936, "Reformatorio de la constitución," *Diario Oficial* 23.263, August 22, 1936, 1–5.

55 Letter from María Currea to Doris Stevens, April 21, 1938, in Doris Stevens Papers, Correspondence: Colombia, María Currea Aya, 1937–1939.

y Encajes (1935, 1699–1700). According to Alma Beltrán y Puga (2020, 92), the issue of divorce divided feminists since many were Catholic and followed church teaching on such matters. Many also believed that divorce would be harmful for women, for example, by allowing men to abandon wives for younger women. Secular feminists were in a bind, since their primary objective at this time was to attain the vote and in their arguments they emphasized how it would not alter women's role as wives and mothers but rather serve to strengthen the family. In this context, it was difficult to mobilize women around the idea that marriage was a civil contract, which just like any other contract the parties could terminate, or that just the threat of divorce would increase women's bargaining power since they would leave the marriage with half the gananciales.[56]

In contrast to divorce, there was much broader support across religious and party lines for reform of patria potestad and the inheritance regime. Another advance for women under the López Pumarejo administration was Law 45 of 1936 that vested patria potestad over children in both parents although mothers could only exercise it in the fathers' absence, whether due to his death or judicial incapacity. [57] This reform did not go as far as those in other South American countries because if a widow remarried she lost this right; a judge then determined who was to serve as guardian and manage the children's assets. Moreover, the code continued to discriminate against women being guardians because any male relative could assume such but the only women who could were a child's mother or grandmother.

This 1936 law also established the right of unwed mothers' to patria potestad over their children and loosened the rules for investigation of paternity so that their recognition became easier. It also improved the inheritance rights of recognized natural children so that in the first order of succession such children receive a share of their parent's estate that was half that of a legitimate child. Previously, such children did not inherit at all if there were legitimate children; in their absence, in the second order, they received a one-fifth share of the estate as a group, irrespective of their number.[58] Now they were to share three-fourths of the estate with the deceased's parents by head.

Following the regional trend, this reform of intestate inheritance slightly improved the position of the surviving spouse. If there were no legitimate children, in the 2nd order of succession the spouse received one-fourth of the estate; previously,

56 I did not locate any writings by women in this period in favor of divorce.

57 *Diario Oficial* 23.147, March 30, 1936. Colombia's civil code had initially copied the 1855 Chilean code where mothers were explicitly excluded from exercising patria potestad. Law 153 of 1887 gave mothers the automatic right to replace fathers in the exercise of patria potestad if they widowed, although in that law only fathers were officially vested with patria potestad, thus the latter was the main change. See Rodríguez Piñera (1923, art. 288).

58 Amézquita de Almeida (1977, 288–9) mentions the advance with respect to recognition of paternity, but not how this law improved the inheritance rights of recognized natural children and the surviving spouse.

the widow or widower received only a one-fifth share. Moreover, if there were no ascendents (or natural children), the spouse became entitled to half the estate, with the other half going to the remaining category of heirs. As in the previous code, in the 3rd order the spouse shared the estate with the deceased's siblings; only if there were none (including their issue) did they inherit the full estate.[59] Thus even with this reform, inheritance provisions were much less favorable to the surviving spouse than in other South American countries (Deere 2023).

An anomaly in this period of liberal rule were decrees passed during the Oyala Herrera and Eduardo Santos administrations that required married women to use their husbands' last name with the prefix "de" (of); in other words, signaling that they belonged to their husband (Deere and León 2023). While this was a long-standing practice, its formalization in the rules for identity cards reinforced the fact that the 1932 reform of women's property rights had not ended all aspects of potestad marital. There was no mention of this new requirement in the women's periodicals of the 1930s and 1940s, perhaps because a woman's addition of her husband's last name upon marriage was social convention.

Also, the reforms in education were slow to take root largely because of the opposition of the Catholic Church to mixed-sex education and the lack of government funding for additional public secondary schools. For example, in 1943, after their daughter completed normal school, Ofelia Uribe and her husband, Guillermo Acosta enrolled her at the public men's secondary school in Tunja so that she could acquire the bachillerato degree to apply to university (Torres 1986, 36). The director of the school, a Liberal, had enrolled several girls that year, which caused a scandal, with the bishop denouncing the director and the families involved and complaining to the governor and the church hierarchy. Even the liberal Minister of Education urged the Acosta couple to withdraw their daughter. The Acosta family resisted, pointing to the contradiction of a so-called liberal government making such a request. The government finally resolved the issue by opening a women's section at the Tunja men's school and appointing a female director to supervise the girls. Ofelia's daughter later passed the entrance exams and attended university. Few women or men had access to university during these years. In 1938 women represented only 2% of the 284 graduates from all Colombian universities, a share that rose to 15% of the 865 graduates in 1950 (Velásquez Toro 1989, 30).[60]

A 1940 editorial in *Letras y Encajes* was pessimistic that women would attain political rights anytime soon, primarily due to the misalignment between strategic political concerns and views on gender. It considered the country to be in a vicious cycle since prior to coming to power, the Liberal Party had included women's suffrage in its program. "Now that it is in the majority it is the greatest force opposed

59 The 1950 Civil Code incorporated these changes; in Ortega (1950, arts. 1045–1048).

60 It was not until 1925 that the first woman earned a medical degree, and 1942, a law degree (Velásquez Toro 1989, 30; Cohen 2001, 151).

to giving us the vote" because it considers "women by nature" to be conservative, too subject to the influence of the clergy, and that if they voted they would return the Conservative Party to power. On the other hand, "when conservatives oversaw the destinies of the country, they would not even allow discussion of female suffrage because it was against women's dignity" (*Letras y Encajes* 1940, 4739-40).

Organizing for Political Rights: A Mutilated Citizenship

Although the number of women university graduates and professionals grew slowly, by the mid-1940s there was a sufficient core to support the formation of stronger women's rights organizations. Thus when the opportunity opened again to discuss reform of the constitution, organized women lobbied for political rights more effectively. While the Congress seriously considered the issue, during the 1940s women only attained formal recognition of their citizenship, what feminist leader Lucila Rubio de Laverde (1965, 88–9) called "a mutilated citizenship" since they still could not vote nor stand for office.

The impetus for the formation of the Unión Femenina de Colombia (UFC, Women's Union) in 1944 was an uproar caused by the appointment of Rosa Rojas Castro, the first woman lawyer, to a judgeship in Bogotá. Conservatives challenged this appointment on the grounds that women were not citizens, this coming seven years after they had become constitutionally eligible to hold such positions (*Mireya* 1943, 1, 27–8; Villarreal 1994, 100; Velásquez Toro 1995, 208). Some of the women who came to Rojas' defense founded the UFC, among them Rosa María Moreno Aguilera, who served as its first president.[61] Initially consisting of some 70 professional women, it hoped to unite women from all social classes, political parties and religious beliefs in support of women's cultural and economic advancement, and to lobby for recognition of women's rights and other demands.[62]

Several new periodicals appeared that voiced support for women's rights. Josefina Canal de Reyes and Mercedes Triana de Castillo edited *Mireya, Revista Femenina*, published in Bogotá between 1943 and 1945, which was similar in style and content to *Letras y Encajes*, addressing women's traditional domestic concerns while aiming to elevate their cultural level.[63] Ofelia Uribe (Figure 6.1) published *Agitación Femenina* between 1944 and 1946 in Tunja, which was explicitly feminist and political, with women's suffrage as its main concern. According to Uribe (1963, 202–8), she founded this periodical to counter the negative commentary around women's potential political rights that erupted in the press after the López Pumarejo administration submitted its constitutional reform proposal to the Congress.

61 Among those often mentioned as UFC founders or regularly active were Ilda Carriazo, Alicia Ruiz de Amórtegui, Gabriela Peláez, Camila Uribe, Lucila Rubio, Aidé Anzola, Josefina Canal and Ofelia Uribe (Uribe 1963, 201; Villareal 1994, 82, 88, 100; Luna 2001a, 111, 2004, 72).

62 "Unión Femenina de Colombia. Objeto y Programa de Acción" (*Agitación Femenina* 1944, 1, 2).

63 See Luna (2004, 71–2) on how they represented conservative suffragettes.

FIGURE 6.1 Colombian journalist Ofelia Uribe de Acosta (1900–1988), ca. 1960.

Source: Archives of *El Tiempo*, Bogotá, by permission.

The reform proposed instituting direct elections for the presidency and the senate and dropping the term "men" in the definition of citizenship. While women could stand for election and hold government positions with authority over others, they could not vote; that was to depend on future action by the Congress.[64] Minister of Government Alberto Lleras Camargo explained that the government's objective was to open the door to women's eventual equal political rights, with the legislature to decide when it was convenient to do so. Granting women citizenship and allowing them to run for office would end the anomaly in the 1936 Constitution whereby women could be judges without being citizens. Moreover, he claimed that "women had not asked for full citizenship."[65] Among the UFC's initial acts was to send a petition to the Congress in support of women attaining full citizenship, including both the ability to vote and to stand for office.[66]

Minister Lleras called for public discussion of the issue, and the media followed up, asking women to write or call in with their views.[67] *Agitación Femenina* regularly published letters by women explaining why they needed full political rights. In its pages and those of *Mireya* feminists perfected their arguments on why

64 "Proyecto de Acto Reformatorio de la Constitución Nacional" (ACR 1944, Series 1, 12, November 13, 109–16). Also discussed by Gómez Camargo (2019, 288–9).

65 ACR (1944, November 13, 121).

66 Signed by 84 women with an attached letter of support signed by 74 from the city of Tunja (ACR 1944, Series 1, 22, November 24, 252–3).

67 See Velásquez Toro (1995, 219–22) on the mix of ideological positions contained in the writings of those opposed to women's suffrage.

women needed full citizenship, emphasizing how women wanted to participate in politics not for their own individual benefit but to propose and support legislation that would contribute to the wellbeing of the family and nation.[68]

The way the issue of women's political rights played out in the legislature was different than in other countries, since a consensus finally emerged around recognizing women as citizens but not on two of its critical components, standing for office and voting. The only party that enthusiastically favored recognizing women's full political rights was the Partido Socialista Democrático (PSD, Socialist Democratic Party), the successor to the Communist Party; most liberals and conservatives were either lukewarm or opposed the proposal. The Chamber, nonetheless, approved the government's proposal with one amendment; the legislature would not consider giving women the vote for at least three years.[69]

The opposition was stronger in the Senate than in the Chamber, with many not wanting to extend citizenship to women under any circumstances or if willing to grant it to them, that it be without the right to stand for office or vote.[70] During this debate several senators mentioned that married women had acquired strong property rights via Law 28 of 1932 but drew different lessons. Liberal Senator Arturo Santos Cabrera, who favored giving women political rights, recalled how in these debates legislators had used similar arguments to undermine approval of that law: that women were not yet prepared to manage their own property or that it went against tradition and would undermine the family. He considered that "there was no reason to regret having approved that law" and that it had solved certain social problems, such as husbands marrying for economic gain or their dissipating their wives' earnings and assets.[71] Another liberal senator, Eduardo Fernández Botero, considered Law 28 "an admirable concession to women," although it had not yielded the expected benefits since most had not showed much interest in managing their own assets.[72] He was thus in no hurry to grant them suffrage.

In the end, the Senate was not willing to compromise very much. The constitutional reform enacted in February 1945 granted citizenship to all Colombians 21 years of age or older while specifying that "the function of suffrage and the capacity to be elected by popular vote is reserved to men."[73] Ofelia Uribe (1963, 218–9) blamed the failure of women attaining full political rights at this time on the actions of nine Liberal senators.[74] Exasperated by the position of politicians

68 See *Agitación Femenina* (1944, 1, 3; 3, 1; 1945, 1, 23–5; 4, 16; 1946, 14, 4, 10) and *Mireya* (1944, 14, 2–3, 47).

69 ACR (1944, Series 1, No. 20, November 22, 217–55).

70 The Senate discussion of this bill on December 6 and 8, 1944 appears in AS (1945, Series 1, 56, May 28, 642–5).

71 AS (1945, Series 1, 56, May 28, 643).

72 AS (1945, Series 1, 56, May 28, 645).

73 "Acto Legislativo No. 1," February 16, 1945; *Diario Oficial* 25.769, February 17, 1945.

74 Velásquez Toro (1995, 222–7) provides a detailed analysis of why they opposed women having the vote.

who viewed women's political rights only in terms of strategic interests – by which party might gain the electoral advantage by women's vote – an editorial in *Agitación Femenina* (1945, 4, 1) reflected that "… the genesis of liberalism was the struggle to attain individual rights and public liberties" and during the first century after independence, "these principles were the essence and substance of liberal programs." Thus it was difficult to understand "why those who hold the majority in Congress, who consider themselves to embody the liberal tradition, dedicated all their energies into blocking Colombian women from attaining their individual and human dignity by recognizing their full rights of citizenship" (*Agitación Femenina* 1945, 4, 1).

UFC president Rosa María Moreno vowed to keep fighting for women's full political rights and the focus of this organization now turned to building a national, cross-class movement in support of suffrage (*Agitación Femenina*, 1945, 5, 4). It held its First National Congress of Women that spring, organized by two members of the PSD, Lucía Querales and labor leader Mercedes Abadía, who were successful in bringing women workers together with students and middle- and upper-class professional women. Participants at that meeting decided to create a new umbrella organization, the Alianza Femenina de Colombia (Colombian Women's Alliance), to be truly national in scope and composed of departmental or regional women's organizations, with the primary goal of attaining women's suffrage. Lucila Rubio, its first president, laid out why women's unity around suffrage was so important. It was the means to ensure that they gain access to more and better education and equal wages for comparable work, and for mothers to get the support they deserve as well as greater protection for their children (*Agitación Femenina*, 1945, 7, 5).

According to historian Norma Villarreal (1994, 102–3), among the ways that the UFC and the Alianza differed was that many Alianza leaders had ties to the various leftist parties and prioritized incorporating working class women into the struggle for suffrage.[75] Those active in the UFC were mostly professionals and linked to either the Liberal or Conservative parties. The UFC affiliate group in Tunja, led by collaborators of *Agitación Femenina*, was composed primarily of liberals; in Medellín conservative women active in Acción Católica led the local affiliate.[76] Catholic women emphasized how their participation would bring greater morality to politics and more attention to the plight of disadvantaged groups, a position emphasized in *Letras y Encajes* and subsequently endorsed by the Catholic Church (Villarreal 1994, 108; Cocker 2000, 705). A change in the position of the Vatican after World War II, who under Pope Pious XII began to endorse women's political rights as part of its strategy to combat fascism and communism, facilitated the support of growing numbers of Catholic women (Velásquez Toro 1986, 200).

75 Among the organizations they launched were the Alianza Femenina del Valle and the Alianza Departamental Femenina del Atlántico.

76 The UFC also had affiliate groups in Cali and Gámeza (*Mireya* 1945, 20, 4, 45).

The UFC and the Alianza employed multiple strategies to recruit more women to the cause and develop momentum toward suffrage. Particularly effective was the use of radio in reaching women from across the class and geographic spectrum. Both Ofelia Uribe and Lucila Rubio developed their own weekly radio programs, as did some of the UFC's and Alianza's affiliate groups. They also undertook lecture tours and held meetings at workplaces and in communities and effectively used the press to publicize their cause (Villarreal 1974, 118; Cocker 2000, 701–2). They kept up the pressure on congress with the UFC circulating another petition in support of women's political rights in May 1945 that gathered over 1,000 signatures, followed by one by the Alianza that garnered 4,000.[77] PSD Deputy Pedro Pérez Sotomayor submitted a new bill, backed by these petitions, but the Chamber shelved it (Gómez Camargo 2019, 292).

In its call for participation in the Second National Congress of Women in June 1946, the Alianza highlighted how Colombia had signed the UN Charter and thus an international commitment by the state backed their demand for suffrage (*Agitación Femenina* 1946, 16, 4). During 1946 deputies of the Conservative, Liberal and Social Democratic parties all submitted different bills on women's political rights. A Chamber committee then combined these into one that emphasized that it was time to recognize women's suffrage because the country's adherence to the UN Charter required it.[78] This bill never came to a vote largely because of the opposition of liberals who still held a majority in the congress. According to Uribe (1963, 221) this was the final blow; the Liberal Party "lost its last opportunity to be true to the principle of equality" for which it stood.

Even the most progressive wing of this party, led by Jorge Eliécer Gaitán, feared the Catholic Church's influence over women. At its convention, the party only agreed to give women suffrage in phases, beginning with municipal elections. Deeply divided, in the 1946 presidential elections liberals ran two separate candidates against each other; Gabriel Turbay represented the more traditional wing, and Gaitán, those wanting to deepen the social reform effort, a division that led to the presidency of conservative Mariano Ospina Pérez (Velásquez Toro 1989, 54–5; Villareal 1994, 114).

The Status of Women's Civil Rights in the 1940s

Given their focus on attaining political rights, feminists paid little attention to the fact that the 1932 reform had only been partial, giving married women economic autonomy but maintaining husbands' control other aspects of their lives, such as fathers' control over the children. While they lobbied in support of the regional conventions on women's rights approved at the Pan American conference held in Bogotá in 1948, they did not mobilize around subsequent legislative attempts

77 For the UFC petition, see *Letras y Encajes* (1945, 7375–6), and for Alianza's, *Mireya* (1945, 21, 13).
78 Gómez Camargo (2019, 295–9) provides a detailed discussion of this consensus bill.

to make Colombia's civil code consistent with the Convention of Women's Civil Rights.

Most of the references to the 1932 law in *Agitación Femenina*, for example, were laudatory, praising the Oyala Herrera regime for this achievement without emphasizing its limitations.[79] The main concern of Ofelia Uribe was that many women were still unaware of this law; she thought that perhaps because they did not understand its benefits, they were indifferent to pursuing their political rights. In 1946 she launched a regular column in this periodical, "What every woman should know," written by legal scholar Enrique Callero de la Cruz, to explain the property rights that women had achieved.[80] Nonetheless, there were also difficulties in its implementation (*Agitación Femenina* 1946, 19, 14). Some institutions were unwilling to accept a contract signed by a married woman alone, continuing to require the authorization of her husband, which denied her economic autonomy.

There were also disputes among jurists and in the courts regarding its impact on couples who had married prior to January 1, 1933, when the 1932 law became effective.[81] The law specified the process that couples should follow to dissolve their existing conjugal society and manage their property separately. Jurist José Gómez R. (1961, xii) observed that while in the preceding three decades "a not insignificant number" of couples married before 1933 had followed instructions and divided their community property, many had not. He thought this was because in harmonious marriages where the husband managed his wife's assets well, they did not see any reason to do so.

In 1937 the Supreme Court determined that irrespective of whether the assets had been divided, the principle of two administrators with equal civil capacity applied; thus the consent of both spouses was required to alienate assets previously acquired by the conjugal society.[82] Nonetheless, in 1946 Congress passed a law establishing that those couples who had married prior to 1933 and who had not already liquidated their conjugal society were understood to be governed by the previous marital regime; that is, the husband remained the default administrator of his wife's assets and all the community property.[83] Ofelia Uribe (1963, 344) considered this 1946 law to have established two marital regimes depending upon when a couple had married. Gómez R. (1961, xii) opined that the 1932 law still protected wives who had married under the previous regime because they could ask to manage their own assets at any time. Ambiguities thus remained in the interpretation of this law.[84]

79 See *Agitación Femenina* (1944, 1, 3; 1945, 8, 1).
80 *Agitación Femenina* (1946, issues 14, 15, 16 and 17).
81 Gómez R. (1961) and Rodríguez Fonnegra (1965) review the disputes and court rulings.
82 Supreme Court Sentence of October 20, 1937, reproduced in Gómez R. (1961, 166–8, n46).
83 "Ley 68 de 1946, Aclaratoria de la Ley 28 de 1932" (*Diario Oficial* 1946, 26.317, December 30, 4).
84 It led to lawsuits but the Supreme Court ruled in February 1948 that it was constitutional. See "Summary of Jurisprudence" on Law 68 in https://www.suin-juriscol.gov.co/viewDocument.asp?id=1619072#ver_16190753.

Due to the perseverance of CIM, women's civil and political rights were on the agenda at the 1948 Ninth International Conference of American States in Bogotá. To the consternation of organized women, the official Colombian delegation did not include the country's CIM delegate María Currea, a UFC and Alianza member. Both the UFC and the newly formed Liga de Acción Feminista Colombiana (Colombian League for Feminist Action) considered this an affront to women, particularly since this conference was to discuss issues vital to them. They lobbied the government to vote in favor of the two proposed conventions (on women's civil rights and on their political rights) that the conference was to discuss and stressed how Colombia was a retrograde in the region, being among the few where women did not have the vote (Reyes Cardenas and Velásquez Toro 1995, 234–5; Aguilera 1997, 69). The Colombian delegation voted in favor of the two conventions although the Congress did not ratify them until 1959 (Pinzón 2011, 245).

Following the conference, Liberal Deputy Andrés Augusto Fernández in 1948 and then Deputy Nestor Pineda again in 1949 introduced the same bill to make the civil code consistent with the principles established in Law 28 of 1932 and the equal rights envisioned in the UN Charter and the 1948 Inter-American Convention.[85] Notably, the bill eliminated civil code article 177 that defined potestad marital as the right of a husband over the property and person of his wife.[86] It established that both married men and women were legally capable at 18, not just husbands. It also rid the code of some of the remaining restrictions on wives' activities, such as the need for their husbands' authorization to be a guarantor for a loan or an executor of an estate or the approval of a judge for a widow who remarried to continue as the executor of her husband's estate. Also, widows who remarried would automatically continue to exercise patria potestad on the same terms as widowers. Further, it proposed ending the discrimination against women being guardians, so that in the case of ascendants or siblings, both sexes be equally eligible; moreover, if a woman guardian married, she would not require her husband's permission to continue exercising this function. This bill failed to gain traction, partly because the attention of both organized women and the political parties was on the growing political violence in the country (Gómez Camargo 2019, 323–4).

The Final Push for Suffrage

The assassination of liberal political candidate Jorge Eliécer Gaitán in April 1948 initiated the period of political violence known as *La Violencia*, a civil war between liberals and conservatives. Under deteriorating conditions, the Congress continued to consider bills to give women the vote. Consensus was illusive largely because

85 "Sobre reformas civiles (derechos de la mujer)," *Anales del Congreso* (1949, 82, October 15, 1434–8).

86 Reflecting the ambiguities raised by the 1932 law, the 1942 annotated edition of the civil code by jurist Jose Antonio Archila (1942, 74) already considered this article abrogated by that law.

the political parties continued to view the issue in terms of which would gain or lose electoral advantage.[87] It was the ability of organized women to organize across party lines in support of peace and women's suffrage that finally tipped the scales in 1954 in favor of their full political rights.

The Liberal party did not participate in the 1950 presidential elections, leading to the election of conservative Laureano Gómez, a sympathizer of the Spanish Falangists. He aggravated the internal conflict by closing Congress, convoking a National Constitutional Assembly and appointing a Comisión de Estudios Constitucionales (CEC, Constitutional Study Commission) made up entirely of conservatives to propose reforms along corporativist lines. The CEC's 1953 report recommended a gradual approach to women's suffrage, beginning with women voting and standing for office in municipal elections. It also included what it considered a pro-family measure, that in elections the votes of married men and women carry twice the weight of those who were single (Velásquez Toro 1997, 12).

Liberal lawyer Esmeralda Arboleda and conservative Josefina Valencia de Hubach, long-time friends from the department of Popayán, subsequently co-authored a memorandum that opposed the CEC's phased approach to women's suffrage as well as the weighted voting scheme according to marital status. They demanded full and equal political rights as provided for in the various international accords that Colombia had signed. They presented this petition to the CEC in June 1953 with 3,000 signatures (Velásquez Toro 1997, 12; Pinzón 2014, 127–8). The clamor for an end to the violence had grown sufficiently strong that liberal and conservative leaders came together that same month to back a military coup by Gen. Gustavo Rojas Pinilla to restore peace. The National Constitutional Assembly subsequently confirmed him as president, and he named a new CEC that included some liberals.

The new political conjuncture provided the opportunity for feminists to redouble efforts. Once the reconstituted CEC went into session, Arboleda and Valencia presented their memorandum in person; at this session many women spoke in its favor while others sent letters, garnering ample press coverage.[88] Moreover, President Rojas Pinilla declared his support for women's suffrage. Since CEC members divided on the issue, they did not issue a recommendation and opted for the Constitutional Assembly to decide the question (Velásquez Toro 1997, 13–5; Pinzón 2014, 128–31).

In April 1954 Esmeralda Arboleda and Josefina Valencia founded the Organización Femenina Nacional (OFN, National Women's Organization) to

87 Between 1947 and 1949 the Congress considered at least four bills to give women either full political rights or only at the municipal level, including one submitted by President Ospina so that Colombia meet its international obligations (Gómez Camargo 2019, 300–4).

88 Aguilera (1997, 72–91) reproduces many of these speeches. At least one woman spoke out against suffrage before the CEC, arguing that politics were already too inflamed, women's participation could only aggravate it, and that women were better off as a moral force (Velásquez Toro 1997, 14).

unite women of all political parties and social classes behind the demand for women's political rights (Pinzón 2014, 133–4). Bertha Hernández de Ospina, the wife of the former conservative president, served as president and feminist María Currea as vice president. The current first lady, Carola Correa de Rojas Pinilla, also endorsed its platform (Reyes Cárdenas and Velásquez Toro 1995, 250–1).

Women of all political persuasions were now behind attaining the vote although with different aims. Bertha Hernández, with close ties to Acción Católica and the Archbishop of Bogotá, represented those who sought the vote primarily on maternalist grounds while also arguing that women's political participation was necessary to bring peace to the country. Socialist women organized in the new Asociación Democrática de Mujeres Colombianas (Democratic Association of Colombian Women) and their periodical, *Nuestra Mujeres*, considered women's political participation a precondition for more profound social transformation. The UFC, now under the presidency of Ofelia Uribe, wanted women to represent a third force in politics, staying out of traditional bipartisan politics and pushing their own independent agenda (Velásquez Toro 1989, 54; Villareal 1994, 130–7; Luna 2001b).

Among OFN's specific demands was that women participate in the Constitutional Assembly, a demand that Bertha Hernández ably negotiated with Rojas Pinilla who then appointed Valencia and Arboleda to this legislative body (Villareal 1994, 135–6; Velásquez Toro 1997, 16–7). They co-authored and presented the bill to grant women full political rights. Heated discussions followed and its passage by the Assembly was in no way guaranteed. Rojas Pinilla played a pivotal role by dispatching one of his ministers to announce that he was absolutely committed to women attaining full suffrage now (Uribe 1963; 222; Rubio 1965, 89; Gómez Camargo 2019, 319–20).

During the final debate five conservatives walked out rather than vote on the bill; the Assembly then approved it unanimously (Velásquez Toro 1997, 17–8; Pinzón 2014, 137–45). Legislative Act No. 3 of August 1954, modified the constitution by granting women the vote and ability to stand for office under the same conditions as men, at age 21 or older, without a literacy requirement.[89] Women first exercised suffrage in the 1957 plebiscite that approved a new constitution, one which enshrined women's political rights along with a new governance structure; once in office women legislators continued to press for further civil code reform.[90]

89 "Reformatoria de la Constitución Nacional," *Diario Oficial* 28.576, September 14, 1954, 3. See Dueñas (2024) for a more detailed analysis of the politics of this period.

90 Esmeralda Arboleda became the country's first woman senator and in 1959 presented the next bill to strengthen women's civil rights (Pinzón 2014, 253–7). The civil code reform of 1974 rescinded potestad marital and again changed the default marital regime (Deere and León 2021). The country enacted civil divorce in 1976 for non-Catholics and in 1991 for all.

Conclusion

In 1932 Colombia adopted what many would come to regard as the ideal marital regime, deferred community property, which combined the advantages of the separation of property and community property regimes. It gave wives full control over their assets and earnings during the marriage while at its dissolution assuring them access to half the gananciales generated by the couple's combined assets and efforts. Several factors explain why legislators reached consensus on a reform with these features. First, during the decades of the 1920s and 1930s conservatives and liberals were not as polarized as they had been previously or would later become. Recall that several of the early married women's property bills were co-sponsored by liberals and conservatives, and that the 1930 Oyala-Restrepo bill that eventually led to the successful 1932 law was a bi-partisan initiative.

Second, the bills presented between 1921 and 1932 contained contrasting approaches to strengthening married women's property rights, separately or in combination: instituting women's reserved property over their earnings; allowing a couple to determine the management of their assets in a marital contract at any time; giving wives the prerogative to seek the separation of property during the marriage; and abolishing the forced nature of the conjugal society by assuming that women gave their husband a mandate to manage their property, one that they could revoke. The Chamber, although not the Senate, approved two of the bills that proposed instituting women's reserved property over their earnings. During this 11-year discussion the Congress strengthened aspects of women's civil rights in a piecemeal fashion, allowing all women to serve as witnesses and working wives to hold savings accounts and manage their own wages, and recognizing the full legal capacity of separated women.

Presidential advisor Luis Felipe Latorre's 1932 bill to institute deferred community property took the predisposition to grant wives more autonomy to the next level by combining separation of property during the marriage with community property at its end, an idea for which he cited European precedents, not those in Central America of which he may not have been aware. This combination of regimes overcame the objections of those who thought separation of property through the mechanism of marital contracts was insufficient since couples rarely made these and those who wanted to maintain community property to protect women's interests. Moreover, the fact that this bill focused only on the marital regime and did not touch other aspects of potestad marital made it more palatable to those committed to maintaining the husband as sole household head.

Women's voices were absent from the debate over civil code reform until around 1928, when their views began to appear in the press. Without doubt, the 1930 Women's Congress that brought together many of the country's educated women, those who had some secondary education, served as the catalyst for women to mobilize in support of their civil rights. Notably, women actively supported all the bills presented between 1930 and 1932, regardless of the mechanism employed to strengthen their property rights, although one of the women's petitions recognized that the final Latorre bill was superior to earlier ones. Women's lobbying and the broad attention garnered in the press galvanized public opinion in favor of strengthening women's property rights. As the group of conservative senators opposed to the reform noted, because of these factors and the staunch support behind the bill by the Olaya Herrera administration and the legal profession, it did not block the successful bill from moving forward.

Feminists had long demanded equal access to public secondary education and universities and once they secured these and women's property rights they began to demand political rights. But they did not launch any significant organizing effort around the first suffrage bill of 1933 nor around discussions of the 1936 constitutional reform. Moreover, they were not involved in the civil code reform of the late 1930s that focused on children born outside marriage, patria potestad and inheritance, a reform whose impetus came from liberal jurists and politicians. But many, especially Catholic feminists, mobilized against what they considered the threat of absolute divorce, a legislative initiative that proved unsuccessful.

In this seven-country study, Colombia stands out for how long it took to develop strong women's rights organizations, partly because it was only in the mid-1940s that women began to complete a secondary degree and attend university in sufficient numbers and because of the strong influence of the Catholic Church over women. While in 1932 women had gained exceptionally strong property rights – parallel rights to husbands over the management of their property and the gananciales – it was not until the 1940s feminists began to discuss gender equality in other aspects of marriage. Even after the passage of the 1948 Inter-American Convention on Women's Civil Rights organized women did not lobby actively in favor of a bill that attempted to ameliorate remaining aspects of potestad marital. But this was also because suffrage and the ending of the civil war were the most pressing issues.

Whereas in the early 1930s, at the initiative of liberals, collaboration between liberal and conservatives led to the expansion of women's property rights, during the 1940s partisan polarization and divisions among liberals delayed the attainment of their political rights. These factors contributed to Colombia's unique distinction of being the only South American country where a constitutional reform granted women citizenship without the right to vote or stand for office. As more conservatives came to favor women's suffrage for the electoral gains it might provide them, liberals became more recalcitrant to expand the size of the electorate, concerns that intensified during La Violencia. The rising clamor to end the civil war then created the conditions that brought conservative and liberal women together in an alliance around securing internal peace and women's suffrage. The change in the position of the Catholic Church in favor of women's political rights facilitated their collaboration in a unified organization, as did the international context, the fact that women had obtained the vote in so many other Latin American countries by then and that international accords supported women's suffrage.

Velásquez Toro (1997, 13) considers that the most important rights obtained by Colombian women to have been due to the determined actions of sympathetic presidents rather than a product of the democratic commitment of elected politicians of either the left or right. Feminists certainly acknowledged the positive role played by Oyala Herrera in leading the quest for civil rights and Rojas Pinilla in tipping the balance in favor of women's suffrage. Finally, in both 1932 and 1954 male legislators voted in favor of women's property rights and suffrage because of the efforts of feminists who successfully overcame their own political and religious divisions to mobilize public opinion in favor of expanding women's rights.

7

VENEZUELA'S STAGGERED ADVANCES FOR WOMEN UNDER LIBERALISM AND A DEMOCRATIC TRANSITION

In a 1937 radio address, Luisa Martínez, editor of Venezuela's first feminist periodical, *Nos-Otras*, explained to her audience why women needed stronger property rights. The main way that a wife could manage her own assets was if she specified so in a prenuptial agreement. However, rarely was this done: "What woman in love is going to insist on such a clause?" (Martínez 1937, 7). The marriage would start out badly since it signaled that the wife had little confidence in her husband. Thus almost all marriages took place under the default regime of the conjugal society where the husband was the administrator of the property a wife brought to marriage or later inherited as well as the community property. This made her dependent on his goodwill, and especially if she did not work for income or bring assets to the marriage. Hence, the importance of reforming the civil code so that wives be able to manage their own assets and have a say in the use of the gananciales of the marriage.

Women's rights organizations emerged relatively late in Venezuela compared to other South American countries, not until the country's political opening of the mid-1930s. But in less than two decades they accomplished much, strengthening married women's property rights and attaining full political rights. Among the reasons why organized women were successful in getting many of their demands met relatively quickly was because of the country's liberal legal tradition. In the late nineteenth century Venezuela began enacting some of the reforms that were on the agenda in other South American countries in the twentieth, such as being able to opt for the separation of property regime in prenuptial agreements and civil divorce. Moreover, liberal jurists were responsible for a 1916 reform that granted wives who worked independently control over their own earnings. Thus feminists of the 1930s could focus on other demands, such as ending the obligation of wives to obey their husbands, managing their own assets and sharing patria potestad.

DOI: 10.4324/9781003658436-7

Another reason they were relatively successful was that soon after their founding the women's organizations joined together to develop their own reform proposal and formed an umbrella association with relatively broad cross-class participation to lobby effectively for their demands. At the same time, these were not as radical as those of feminist in other countries in the 1930s, stopping short of equal rights in marriage. Among their main achievements was ridding the code of some of the aspects they considered most humiliating and attaining recognition of the property rights of women in consensual unions, the first South American country to recognize these. Women's organizations then formed an even broader coalition to lobby for suffrage. In 1945 they attained the ability to vote and stand for office at the municipal level and two years later, full suffrage.

The Liberal Legal Legacy

The historiography on Venezuela's civil codes (Machado 1940; Pérez Perdomo 1983) or on its women's movement (Friedman 2000; Rivas 2006; Huggins 2010) has not paid much attention to how women's civil rights gradually improved over the country's long period of liberal rule. During the second-half of the nineteenth and early twentieth century the country undertook reforms related to patria potestad and guardianship, spousal inheritance rights, the marital regime and instituted civil divorce, all at the initiative of liberal jurists and politicians who considered these perfectly compatible with women's role as the "queen of the home."[1]

Venezuela adopted these reforms earlier than other South American countries because it was one of the new American republics most influenced by liberalism. As an outlier in the Spanish empire, colonial institutions were less entrenched and there was greater receptivity to new ideas regarding liberty and individual freedom. The Wars of Independence began here and were more devastating than in neighboring countries, and since these decimated its colonial elite, it resulted in a less rigid class structure and institutional framework. Specifically, the Catholic Church was never able to establish the strong institutional and ideological control that it secured in Colombia (Karl 1997, 74–5; Zahler 2013).

Notwithstanding the recurrent civil wars among *caudillos* (political-military strongmen) and frequent periods of dictatorship, the unifying project between 1822 and 1935 was the attempt to create a modern liberal state. Its many constitutions and civil codes were heavily liberal in that they sought to build coherent norms to guarantee property rights and individual liberties. This took place irrespective of recurring struggles between liberals and conservatives over issues such as federalism and centralization and the fact that when in power these caudillos only paid lip-service to some liberal ideals, such as free elections or freedom of the press (Pérez

1 See Alcibíades (2004) on the development of the cult of domesticity from the 1850s on and Zahler (2013) on the construction of "Republican motherhood."

Perdomo 1983; Zahler 2013). Moreover, although civil codes and constitutions changed frequently,[2] these tended to maintain the key reforms regarding family law and women's civil rights enacted under previous administrations, becoming part of the country's unique liberal legal legacy.

As a result of freer trade and the circulation of ideas, by the time the country adopted its first civil code in 1862, authored by liberal jurist Julián Viso and enacted under President Gen. José Antonio Páez, social conventions regarding marriage and the family had undergone considerable change (Deere 2023). This code departed from colonial tradition in that in the father's absence a mother automatically exercised patria potestad over her children; notably, women maintained this right even if as a widow they remarried (Venezuela 1862, Book I, Title VII, art. 27). It also differed from the colonial norm with respect to the intestate inheritance rights of the surviving spouse. Viso's code provided for either the widow or widower to inherit an unconditional share of the estate equal to a child.[3] Although this code was short-lived, the 1873 and 1880 civil codes promulgated under liberal dictator Antonio Guzmán Blanco and subsequent codes retained these features.

Strongly anti-clerical, Guzmán Blanco instituted civil marriage and, in the interest of furthering individual freedom, the 1873 civil code expanded what couples could do in a prenuptial agreement. It allowed couples to establish "their own assets regime" as long as it "was not contrary to the law or common decency..." (Venezuela 1873, arts. 1318–1319). Legal scholar Anibal Dominici (1897, 261) later explained that in the capitulaciones a couple "could opt for the regime of separation of property that gives the wife the right to administer those that she owns or to reserve for herself the right to administer part of her own patrimony."[4] Hence, Venezuela entered the twentieth century as the only South American country where prior to marriage a couple could choose the separation of property regime,[5] an option maintained in subsequent codes.

The 1896 code promulgated under President Gen. Joaquin Crespo made more categories of women eligible to be guardians over children who were minors, adding sisters and aunts if they were single or widows (Venezuela 1896, art. 310). Previously, if the deceased parents had not specified a guardian in their wills, the only

2 Venezuela enacted five civil codes during the nineteenth century and four in the first half of the twentieth (Deere and León 2005). Pérez Perdomo (1983, 721) reports that between 1822 and 1935 the country had 18 constitutions although not all incorporated major changes.

3 Venezuela (1862, Book III, Title V, Law 1, arts. 3–13); see Deere (2023) on colonial intestate norms and how of the nineteenth-century codes, Venezuela's was the most favorable to spouses.

4 Earlier, jurist Luis Sanojo (1873, 223) had interpreted this flexibility more narrowly, suggesting that wives still needed their husbands' permission to contract or dispose of the assets they managed since potestad marital still applied. Dominici's and Sanojo's treatises on the civil codes formed part of the basic curriculum of the law faculty at the Universidad Central de Venezuela (UCV, Central University), influencing generations of legal scholars and politicians (Pérez Perdomo 2013, 100).

5 Recall from Chapter 1 that Mexico and Guatemala had already included this option either in a prenuptial agreement or at any point of the marriage.

women who could serve in this position were widowed grandmothers, with preference to the paternal side. After another civil war, President Gen. Cipriano Castro's "Liberal Restorative Revolution" concluded the process of secularization in 1904 by instituting civil divorce allowing remarriage (Venezuela 1904, arts. 151–155). The Catholic Church, which had never been extraordinarily strong, was in disarray and unable to mount an effective opposition to this measure (Acosta Prieto 1989).

The grounds for divorce in the 1904 Civil Code were relatively ample if unequitable, being the same as those for a permanent separation: any instance of adultery by a wife was cause but for a husband only if he had a concubine in the home or such circumstances that produced grievous insult to the wife.[6] After five years of separation either spouse could request a divorce.[7] The main point of contention in the subsequent decades was whether to allow divorce by mutual consent without first requiring a judicial separation, or if required, for a shorter time period.

The 1916 Reform: Women's Reserved Property

The 1916 reform that resulted in wives gaining control over their independent earnings was part of an overall reform of the civil code undertaken under the presidency of General Juan Vicente Gómez who governed the country directly or indirectly between 1908 and 1935.[8] The deliberations of the civil code review commission that he appointed shed light on the influence of reforms elsewhere on legal thinking in Venezuela. The adoption of reserved property for wives was an idea ahead of its time since the country was still heavily rural with a miniscule urban working class, which included relatively few women wage workers or professionals.

In 1912 President Gómez appointed seven distinguished jurists to serve on the civil code review commission.[9] He intended its deliberations to be relatively transparent and financed a monthly bulletin, the *Gaceta Jurídica*, to disseminate its

6 The other grounds were voluntary abandonment; brutality, grievous insults or excesses that made sharing daily life impossible; attempts to prostitute the wife or the children; and the imprisonment of either spouse (Venezuela 1904, arts. 151–155).

7 If the permanent separation were the fault of the husband, the wife could ask for a separation of property, which would return her property and half the gananciales to her administration; while the wife could freely manage her movable property, she still required the authorization of her husband or a judge to alienate immovable property. If the separation was the wife's fault, the husband maintained the administration of the community property but had to provide her with sustenance (Venezuela 1904, arts. 156–160).

8 Gómez took over in a military coup and became the elected president in 1909. While others served in the presidency between 1913 and 1922, he remained the power behind the presidency, serving an elected term between 1922 and 1929, and then taking over again directly between 1931 and 1935. Notwithstanding his authoritarianism, his accomplishments included ending the previous tendency toward recurrent civil wars, strengthening the state, and furthering a liberal legislative agenda (Ewell 1984; Pérez Perdomo 2013).

9 All were doctors in law and five were members of the prestigious Academia de Ciencias Políticas y Sociales (ACPS, Academy of Political and Social Sciences) (Pérez Perdomo 2013, 116).

discussions (Machado 1940; Clagett 1947). José Loreto Arismendi, a leading expert on civil law, made the first modest proposal to strengthen the property rights of wives (*Gaceta Jurídica* 1913, 2 (20), 50–3). Noting the growing interest among the legal profession in safeguarding the economic interests of married women, he observed that other countries had done so either by giving wives control over their own earnings and/or instituting the marital regime of separation of property as the default. He considered both these alternatives too extreme for Venezuela (*Gaceta Jurídica* 1915, (3), 218–21).

Arismendi viewed allowing wives who worked to manage and dispose of their earnings without need for their husbands' approval or that of a judge, as approved in the French 1907 civil code reform, as incompatible with the marital regime of the conjugal society. He thought it would be prejudicial to the stability of the family, for if wives were free to manage their own earnings, this implied that they would also be free to make contracts and to manage their own time. He objected to the other approach, replacing the conjugal society with the separation of property regime since it potentially benefited only wealthy women who owned assets. He thought it prejudicial to poor women because under this regime they did not have access to the gananciales from the marriage. He thought other less drastic measures could address the plight of wives married to spendthrifts or whose husbands mismanaged their assets.

Arismendi proposed allowing such a wife to seek a judge's authorization to manage her own earnings.[10] This measure would provide her relief without altering the situation of all married women. In addition, he proposed allowing an abandoned wife to request a judge to embargo a share of her husband's wage. He considered these measures sufficient to deal with any problems that might arise from a husband's irresponsibility and that his solutions were superior to the alternatives since they were perfectly compatible with the current marital regime.[11]

Commission members José Santiago Rodríguez and Cristobal L. Mendoza wanted to go further in strengthening women's economic autonomy (*Gaceta Jurídica* 1914, 2 (22), 112–4). They had a copy of Ecuador's 1911 Economic Emancipation of Married Women Law and asked the other members to study it to see if Venezuela might adopt something similar. Ecuador's law was more favorable to women than the French concept of reserved property since it allowed wives to exclude from the conjugal society both their earnings and the assets they brought to

10 In Venezuela's various codes, women had the right to ask a judge for a separation of property if a husband mismanaged or committed fraud with their assets. Arismendi's idea was to simplify this process by giving women control over their earnings without requiring a full separation of property.

11 Arismendi also opposed allowing women to become lawyers and join the judiciary. Among the reasons he gave for barring them from this profession was that besides their "feminine sensibilities, ….it is detestable to see women arguing" (Arismendi 1916, 144). The UCV law faculty did not admit women until the 1930s.

marriage or later acquired to manage these themselves, with the gananciales these generated becoming their own individual property.

Rodríguez must have had second thoughts about adopting a change as profound as Ecuador's 1911 reform, for the next year he formally proposed adopting the French formulation of reserved property for wives (*Gaceta Jurídica* 1915, 3 (33–34), 125). Married women would thus be free to manage and dispose of their independent earnings from a profession, industry or commerce subject to the restriction, as in France, that wives could not donate such earnings or the assets purchased with them. The thinking behind this restriction was that if a wife donated her assets such would diminish the mass of gananciales available to pool at the marriage's end; selling them would not necessarily do so, since the income generated was reincorporated into the pool. While Rodríguez acknowledged that reserved property did not go as far as the reforms undertaken in England and the United States, he thought it a better fit for Venezuela and an adequate means to strengthen the property rights of wives for now. The commission adopted his proposal over Arismendi's continued objections (*Gaceta Jurídica* 1915,155; 3 (35–36), 218–9).

In its final report, besides some simplification in marriage procedures, the commission recommended two other relevant reforms.[12] In the 1904 code, for a husband to sell an immovable asset of his wife required both her consent and that of a judge; it eliminated the latter in the interest of expediency. In the case of a judicial separation, a wife would no longer require her husband's or a judge's authorization to dispose of her immovable property, which considerably strengthened her property rights.

Minister of Interior Pedro M. Arcaya then reviewed the commission's recommendations and accepted its proposed changes on women's property rights while making additional changes to their proposals on the formalities of marriage and recognition of natural children.[13] He was concerned about Venezuela's high rate of illegitimacy because between 1908 and 1911 only 30% of recorded births were legitimate. He wanted to encourage marriage by further simplifying its formalities and allowing a broader range of government officials as well as priests to conduct civil marriages.[14]

12 "Resumen de los trabajos de la Comisión..." (*Gaceta Jurídica* 1915, 3 (37), 297–321). Earlier, Rodríguez and Mendoza had also proposed allowing all women to serve as guardians over minor children, including wives if they had their husband's approval, but they apparently dropped this idea.

13 "Exposición que dirige el ciudadano Ministro de Relaciones Interiores a la Cámara del Senado sobre el proyecto de código civil..." (*Revista de Derecho y Legislación* 1914–15, 4, 81–97).

14 Compared to other Latin American civil codes, the requirements, formalities and documents required for marriage seemed excessive (Venezuela 1904, arts. 63–114), which is why these were frequently discussed. Moreover, the average nuptiality rate in 1910–1912 was 6.5 per 1,000 inhabitants, which was low by regional standards. Civil divorce, however, had made marriage more attractive; in 1904–1909 the rate had averaged only 4.7 per year. Calculated from Venezuela (1915, Table 6).

In its discussion of the bill, the Senate focused on whether allowing priests to conduct civil marriages would be a set-back to the separation of church and state and the country's liberal tradition.[15] Several senators, nonetheless, wanted to go beyond what the review commission had proposed with regard to married women's property and other civil rights.[16] Senator José Gil Fortoul, a well-regarded liberal jurist,[17] proposed giving the wife the right to freely administer and dispose of her assets irrespective of how these were acquired and eliminating or amending other code articles relevant to potestad marital. [18] Those opposed to his amendment thought that the commission's proposal (for wives to control their own earnings) was already favorable enough to women. They viewed Venezuelan women as being less educated than those in Europe and unprepared to manage their own assets. A special committee was then set up to review the issue, which recommended against Gil Fortoul's proposal. The Senate then approved the original recommendations of the review commission.

The Chamber of Deputies entertained two relevant amendments to the bill although both failed.[19] Discarded was a proposal to end the double moral standard in the treatment of adultery as grounds for divorce. Also controversial was reducing the time required for a legal separation to become grounds for a divorce. Those opposed successfully argued that reducing the time from the current five to two or three years was a backdoor to the introduction of divorce by mutual consent. The civil code reform bill finally approved in July 1916 was essentially what the review commission had proposed plus additional measures simplifying the procedures for civil marriage and recognizing the inheritance rights of children born outside of marriage to the patrimony of their unwed mothers (but not their fathers) (Venezuela 1916).[20]

The lack of attention by feminist scholars to the 1916 reform of married women's property rights may be because contemporary legal scholars did not draw attention to this aspect. Jurists who commented on its salient features with respect to family law did not even mention that wives attained the right to manage and dispose of their earnings (Martínez Paz 1917; Machado 1940). Moreover, relatively few women were formally employed with their numbers limited to schoolteachers

15 The record of this debate is in "El proyecto de Código Civil en el Parlamento. Cámara del Senado" (*Revista de Derecho y Legislación* 1914–1915, 4, 127–99).

16 Also raised were divorce by mutual consent and broadening the conditions for investigation of paternity.

17 Gil Fortoul was a writer, historian and diplomat who briefly served as provisional president in 1913; notwithstanding his liberal and democratic ideals, he worked closely with the Gómez regime. https://www.venezuelatuya.com/biografias/jose_gil_fortul.htm.

18 Speech of April 26, 1916, in *Revista de Derecho y Legislación* (1923, 12, 74, 143–7).

19 The Chambers' 1916 discussion is in *Revista de Derecho y Legislación* (1924, 13, 38–82; 1925, 14, 112–270).

20 The Congress partially reformed the code again in 1922 although the changes to family law were minimal (Venezuela [1922] 1928).

and those working in tobacco factories and offices.[21] While women had become a growing share of the teaching profession, universal primary education grew quite slowly, hence also the demand for teachers.[22] In addition, most teachers were single and non-elite women who were wage workers tended to be in consensual unions rather than marriages (Friedman 2000, 74), hence they did not derive direct benefits from the 1916 expansion of married women's property rights. This reform is thus an example of legal change undertaken in advance of social change or to promote it, rather than its result.

The Gómez regime expanded women's public secondary educational opportunities in the early teens, establishing the first professional women's teaching college, a women's trade school and a school of nursing (Friedman 2000, 57). Although a few women attended the Central University in Caracas sporadically from the 1890s on, until mid-century there were relatively few women university graduates or in liberal professions other than teaching.[23]

Rise of the Women's Movement

Women's greater involvement in the public sphere dates from the late 1920s[24] and is related to the expansion of the urban working and middle classes associated with the development of the petroleum sector and the expansion of the state under the Gómez regime.[25] Moreover, the 1928 student uprising against dictatorial rule served as the catalyst for many women to become politically active and begin to engage with feminism. The death of Gómez in 1935 then created the political opening for the founding of the first women's rights organizations as well as the opportunity for them to press their own demands for civil code reform.

While few women were university students at the time of the 1928 student uprising, many participated in efforts to support those imprisoned by the Gómez regime (Huggins 2010). Among the groups formed around these support activities was the Sociedad Patriótica de Mujeres Venezolanas (Venezuelan Women's

21 Travieso (1961, Appendix) reports women being employed in factories and offices from 1908 on, with the first women's labor union, the Asociación Obrera de Mujeres, founded in 1909 (Vargas 2007, 158).

22 Compulsory primary education (for both boys and girls from age 7 to 14) dates from the presidency of Guzmán Blanco in the 1870s and the establishment of the first normal schools for women (Martínez V. 2008).

23 While the first woman dentist graduated in 1904, the first female physicians and lawyers did not graduate until 1936, all from UCV (Quintero 2000; Martínez V. 2008). In 1936 only 2.3% of university students were women, a figure that rose to 10% in 1946 (Friedman 2000, 47).

24 Prior to this elite women had founded and participated in religious charity organizations (Huggins 2010, 170) and some women writers founded and/or published in cultural periodicals for a female audience (Ramón 1985, 12).

25 See Karl (1997) on the expansion of the petroleum sector under Gómez and its impact, including the decline in agriculture. By 1929–1930 the petroleum sector was the main source of state revenues and in 1935 oil constituted 91% of Venezuela's exports (Karl 1997, 79).

Patriotic Society), one of the first secular middle-class women's organization (Travieso 1961, 12).[26] Equally important was the politicization of many young women, some of whom the regime detained or imprisoned for their activism, such as Ada Pérez Guevara and Carmen Travieso, both who subsequently emerged as feminist leaders (Dagnino 2019, 14–7, 28–32). Such women provided the readership for the first feminist periodical, *Nos-Otras*, founded in 1927 by journalist Luisa Martínez.

The number of women employed in white collar positions grew sufficiently that in 1929 Martínez also formed the Asociación Cristiana Venezolana de Mujeres Trabajadoras (Venezuelan Christian Organization of Working Women).[27] Dedicated to the moral, intellectual and material betterment of working women through such activities as mutual self-help and training and education, its membership included teachers, office workers and employees in the retail trades. Among this group's demands was for an eight-hour working day and the right to a two-week annual vacation.

A few middle- and upper-class women began participating in the new regional women's organizations, some while in exile due to the repression of the Gómez regime. While residing in Spain, poet María Edilia Valero became coordinator of LIMIH's Fifth International Congress, scheduled to be held in Madrid in 1933.[28] Among the Venezuelan women who signed the call for papers were writers Ada Pérez, Carmen Escobar Saluzzo, and Clotilde Crespo de Arévalo (Ezama 2014, 58; Dagnino 2019, 14–7).[29] While residing in exile in New York City, Ana Esther Gouverneur de Trujillo co-founded with Mexican writer Margarita Robles de Mendoza the Unión de Mujeres Americanas (UMA) in 1934.[30]

The Gómez administration appointed writer and historian Lucila Luciani de Pérez Díaz as the country's initial representative to the CIM in 1928, followed by

26 This organization may have been the same group or related to the Sociedad Pro-Patria that Friedman (2000, 56) says that Ana Esther Gouverneur formed in 1928 while in exile in New York City. The latter was a mutual aid society that also worked to raise awareness of Gómez's brutal dictatorship in the United States.

27 News item from *El Universal*, December 6, 1929, in *Bulletin of the Pan American Union* (1930, 64 (3), 322) and Álvarez (2010, 66).

28 See Chapter 6 on Colombia where the LIMIH was more active. Valero founded the cultural center Hogar Americano in Madrid in 1934 and was the impetus behind a similar cultural center in Caracas formed around the same time (Márquez Macías 2022).

29 Pérez and Escobar were among the founders of the cultural institution Ateneo in 1931 (Dagnino 2019, 14–7, 76–9). Dagnino also attributes the founding of the Asociación Cultural Interamericana to Pérez.

30 See Chapter 5 on UMA' s regional activities, as well as UMA (1936) and "Discurso pronunciado por la señora Evangelina Antay de Vaughan," March 5, 1937, Doris Stevens papers, Series V, sub-series A. Correspondence: UMA, 1935–1938. Gouverneur served on the UMA's international board of directors from 1935 to 1936, as did her sister, Dora H. Gouverneur, and another Venezuelan, Celia Delgado.

Clotilde Crespo who served in this capacity until 1937.[31] Both received repeated requests from the CIM to pressure the government to fill out its questionnaires on women's civil and political status, ones that it had apparently failed to submit.

The death of dictator Juan Vicente Gómez in 1935 provided the political opening for organizing around democratic rights, including women's rights. In December of that year a group of women under the leadership of Ada Pérez and poet and educator Luisa del Valle Silva sent a letter to interim President Gen. Eleazar López Contreras demanding the government's protection of mothers and children.[32] Initially signed by 38 women, they noted in this petition how "in this moment of awakening of national civic sentiment," it was incumbent upon them as current and future mothers to remind him that the future of the country depended on its children.[33] They included a long list of specific demands, ranging from the need for childcare centers and orphanages, to courses on childrearing, to maternity leave for women workers.[34]

Several of the new leftist political parties committed to strengthening democracy formed women's secretariats to encourage their participation.[35] Women from a broad array of political tendencies, nonetheless, felt the need to form their own organizations around their own gender-specific demands (Friedman 2000, 58). Among the most important was the Agrupación Cultural Femenina (ACF, Women's Cultural Association), founded in 1935. Its aim was to elevate the "cultural level of Venezuelan women" and, specifically, to fight for their civil and political rights, effective social security and maternity legislation, and the organization of women wage workers, employees and peasants.[36] Its members were primarily middle- and upper-class women, many of whom were also active in the new political parties. Among those affiliated with what would become the Communist Party who were founding or early ACF members were journalist Carmen Travieso, a veteran of the

31 Luciani's letterhead shows her as the director of the magazine *Iris*, the organ of the Centro de Damas Católicas (Catholic Ladies Center); Luciani to Doris Stevens, December 30, 1928, Doris Stevens Papers, Correspondence: Lucila Luciani de Pérez. Also see IACW (1936, 15).

32 "Mensaje de las mujeres venezolanas al General Eleazar López Contreras," December 30, 1935; in Travieso (1961, Appendix). Most scholarship on Venezuela dates the beginning of the women's movement to this initiative; see Friedman (2000, 59).

33 When *Nos-Otras* published this letter in February 1936 the petition had gained an additional 134 signatures; in Travieso (1961, Appendix).

34 These women must have had some influence because once named president López Contreras included the protection of mothers and children in his 1936 and 1938 National Plans. Moreover, the 1936 Labor Law included maternity leave, on-site nurseries and the stipulation of equal pay for equal work. The government, however, rarely enforced these measures (Friedman 2000, 59, 71). See Ewell (1984, 74–6) on this turbulent transition period.

35 These included the Partido Republicano Progresista (PRP, Progressive Republican Party) which later became the Communist Party and the Movimiento de Organización Venezolana (ORVE, Movement for Venezuelan Organization) that later meshed into Acción Democrática (AD, Democratic Action Party) under the leadership of Rómulo Betancourt. In late 1936 they briefly joined together as the Partido Demócrata Nacional (National Democratic Party) (Yarrington 2014).

36 The ACF program of action appeared in *Ahora*, December 30, 1938; in Álvarez (2010, 141).

1928 protests, labor leader Eumelia Hernández, and Ana Senior. Those of other political tendencies included Lola Morales Lara, Imelda Campos, Carmen Delgado de Quintero, Josefina Ernst, journalist Analuisa Llovera and educator Mercedes Fermín (Leonardi 1983, 391; Álvarez 2010, 74–84).[37]

To engage working-class women, the ACF established the Casa de la Obrera (Working Women's Center), which ran a night school to promote literacy and skills training and a clinic and hosted cultural events. The organization became well known nationally through its weekly page, "Cultura de la Mujer" in *Ahora*, a daily newspaper with a country-wide circulation of over 10,000 readers. Edited for many years by Travieso, it covered developments in union organizing, the struggle for equal wages for equal work, the gains in women's civil and political rights in other countries as well as news on ACF activities and those of other women's organizations.[38]

Ada Pérez and Luisa del Valle, the initiators of the 1935 women's petition, and Panchita Soublette Saluzzi and others founded the Asociación Venezolana de Mujeres (AVM, Venezuelan Association of Women) the next year. Its primary activities included organizing an orphans' home, a prenatal clinic, childcare centers and running hygiene campaigns. It also sponsored a weekly women's page in another daily newspaper, *El Universal* (Friedman 2000, 69–71; Rivas 2006, 180). It too was concerned with enhancing women's civil rights and during 1937 it sponsored a lecture series of legal scholars to educate women on the topic.[39] This gave rise to the formation of a working group around the need for civil code reform (AUPR 1942, 14).

Upon her return from exile, Ana Esther Gouverneur formed the Venezuelan branch of UMA, the regional organization she had co-founded. Other new organizations with a predominantly female membership were the Juntas Pro-Fomento de los Barrios (Community Development Boards) and the Federación Venezolana de Maestros (FVM, Venezuelan Federation of Teachers), the latter founded by ACF's Mercedes Fermín who served as its first president,[40] and UVM's Luisa del Valle.

With all this organizing activity among women, it may seem surprising that suffrage was not among their immediate demands since by then women had the vote

37 Among those signing the 1935 petition to interim President López Contreras as representing the ACF were, besides Imelda Campos and Lola Morales, Cecilia Nuñez Sucre, María Cristina Hernández and Lila Trujillo, they thus must also have been among the founding members; "Mensaje…" in Travieso (1961, Appendix).

38 Álvarez (2010, 123–60) reproduces many of these articles.

39 Friedman (2000, 69–71) considers the AVM to have been more apolitical and maternalist in orientation than the ACV. While the AVM gave primary attention to mothers and children, it is difficult to argue that they were less political, given the leadership role played by Pérez, del Valle and other AVM members in the struggle for women's civil and political rights. But perhaps AVM members were less likely than those of the ACF to also be activists in the various leftist parties.

40 Fermín was a public primary school teacher who later was among the first women graduates of the Instituto Pedagógico (Pedagogical Institute) of Caracas (Dagnino 2019, 80–3).

in Ecuador, Uruguay and Brazil, and at the municipal level in Peru and Chile.[41] The progressive parties that emerged in the mid-1930s all demanded universal suffrage at the age of 18 and direct elections for the presidency, conditions they considered necessary for a transition to an effective democracy. But only the PRP explicitly included women's equal political rights in its immediate demands (Yarrington 2014, 170). The 1937 program of ORVE's Women's Secretariat mentioned the need to enhance women's civil rights, specifically to attain equal rights in marriage, and increase women's participation in political organizations to prepare them for political rights, but it did not demand suffrage.[42]

When the Congress, still made up of many Gómez supporters, revised the constitution in 1936 it restricted suffrage to men who were at least 21 and literate (Venezuela 1936, art. 14). This reduced rather than expanded suffrage since the previous 1929 Constitution did not have a literacy requirement nor limit voting to one sex (Venezuela 1929, art. 12). There were apparently no protests at the time over the explicit exclusion of women (Quintero 2001, 60–2). Elizabeth Friedman (2000, 85) suggests that ACF members – many of whom were affiliated with the leftist parties – were hesitant to call themselves feminists or viewed as suffragists. Such carried negative connotations, given its identification with the militant feminist movement in England. They frequently had to explain that their intent was not to replace or rival men, but rather to be their companions in the building of a more just, democratic society. Moreover, just their organizing activities and being publicly visible was anathema to conservatives and the hierarchy of the Catholic Church who viewed women's place as in the home. The progressive parties also viewed women's greater religiosity as a risk, for they might vote conservatively and undermine the very transition to democracy (Quintero 2001, 60–2; Yarrington 2014, 175).

According to ACF leader Carmen Travieso, the reason feminists began their organizing around married women's property rights rather than suffrage was because women first needed to improve their rights in marriage. As she put it,

> when a woman in Venezuela does not have a voice or vote within the boundaries of her own home, it would be laughable to have the vote nationally…It is a question of logic, to begin to fight for that which our women most need.[43]

In a subsequent essay, Travieso ([1944] 1977, 136) explained how for women "the struggle for economic liberty is the basis for all other liberties." She greatly

41 The only mention of women demanding suffrage at this time was by Mercedes Carvajal de Arocha, who wrote under the pen name of Lucila Palacios (1985, 110). She said it was an aim of the Junta Patriótica Femenina (Women's Patriotic Board) that she founded in February 1936 to assist those injured in the government repression. But since women's groups were proliferating, she disbanded the group to prevent diluting efforts.

42 "Esbozo del programa," Secretaria del Movimiento Femenino, Movimiento de Organización Venezolana, in Travieso (1961, Appendix). Lucila Palacios and four other women signed this document.

43 "Cultura de la Mujer," *Ahora,* March 24, 1939, cited in Friedman (2000, 85).

admired what feminists in the United States had achieved and among the lessons she drew from their experience was the need to gain economic autonomy and property rights before political rights, a process facilitated by rapid industrialization and economic development. Cognizant that conditions were quite different in Latin America, Travieso took heart that in a few Latin American countries "women were beginning to liberate themselves," and saw glimmers of this process in Venezuela, "when women begin to work and liberate themselves economically, they become cognizant of the need to fight for the conquest of their other rights" (Travieso [1944] 1977, 136).

Civil Code Reform Commissions and Organized Women's Demands

In response to the student uprising, President Gómez appointed a new civil code review commission in 1930. Following his death, newly installed President Gen. Eleazar López Contreras appointed another such commission in 1936. The 1936 commission followed many of the recommendations of its predecessor on women's property rights, and these ideas also influenced the demands of organized women who developed their own proposal for civil code reform.

The long-time advocate of women's property rights, José Gil Fortoul, was among the group of liberal jurists who in the aftermath of the student uprising urged President Gómez to appoint a new commission to again review the civil code, a commission on which he served. His views on feminism were well known. In the first issue of *Nos-Otras*, he published an article that argued that "all men of culture should necessarily be feminists; that is, they should urge an end to the customary inequalities in rights and liberty that have resulted simply from women being less educated than men" (Álvarez 2010, 65).

Not surprisingly, the agenda of the 1930 Comisión Revisora de Códigos Nacionales (National Codes Review Commission) included enhancing married women's property rights.[44] Members Cristóbal Mendoza and Juan B. Bance made the first proposal, to give married women the automatic right to manage their own assets with the ability to contract and appear in lawsuits. While each spouse was to administer their own assets, the gains each generated constituted community property under the administration of the husband. Jurist Luis Bastides strongly opposed this proposal, arguing that it mixed two different marital regimes (that of the conjugal society and the separation of property regime), and doing so "mutilated both" (cited in García de Astorga 1983, 250).

Gil Fortoul wanted to go even further than the Mendoza-Bance proposal and rid the code of all vestiges of married women's relative incapacity. He also wanted to give couples flexibility in deciding how to manage their property, proposing that they be able to make marital contracts to this effect at any time (Rangel 1936, 83).

44 I could not locate this commission's deliberations, thus draw on Rangel (1936) and García de Astorga (1983).

Most commission members were not ready to end all aspects of potestad marital or introduce that much flexibility in marriage. In their 1931 report they approved the Mendoza-Bance proposal, a report the Congress never even discussed. The attention of the government at this time was on other matters, principally dealing with the effects of the Great Depression.[45]

The need to further strengthen married women's property rights began to gain greater public support after neighboring Colombia passed its 1932 reform because in comparison, Venezuela appeared as a laggard. Legal scholar Amenodoro Rangel (1936, 84–5) considered Colombia's reform that instituted the regime of deferred community property "truly revolutionary" but far too advanced for Venezuela. In contrast, the 1930 commission's proposal was ideally suited for the country. He would only have added the requirement of mutual consent for the husband to alienate community property, an idea the women's movement subsequently embraced. Articles on women's civil rights also began to appear sporadically in newspapers (Ramón 1985, 32–3) and in some of the magazines aimed at a female audience.[46]

After the death of Gómez, President López Contreras in 1936 appointed a new commission, the Comisión Codificadora Nacional (National Codification Commission), to review all the country's codes.[47] Two of its members, Juan B. Bance and Cristóbal Mendoza had served on the 1930 review commission; its recommendation were the point of departure for the new one (Clagett 1947, 19). The women's organizations demanding rights – the ACF, AVM and UMA – then joined together to develop their own proposal for civil code reform.

Among the demands the women's coalition presented in its 1937 petition to the commission was that rather than requiring the wife's obedience, the code should establish the need for mutual protection, respect and consideration between spouses.[48] It should automatically allow a married woman to have the free administration of the assets she brought to marriage and acquired thereafter. If the husband continued as the administrator of the community property, the code should require him to obtain a wife's consent to mortgage or sell such assets. In addition, a wife should

45 The depression devastated agricultural exports but oil exports compensated for this decline in export revenue and thus the country experienced less economic turmoil than others; moreover, its policies of repression prevented political and labor organizing (Yarrington 2014, 164).

46 According to Quintero (2000, 255–6) most of the articles in *Progreso y Cultura* and *Ecos de Gloria* related to women's status were on the need to increase their literacy and the quality of their education and/or to expand their employment, particularly in professions that were compatible with their traditional role as wives and mothers.

47 The judiciary, the ACPS, the Colegio de Abogados (Bar Association) of the Federal District, and the government nominated its 13 members.

48 "Petición de las mujeres venezolanas," *Boletín de la Comisión Codificadora Nacional* (1937, 9, 43–6), signed by five AVM members (Leticia M. de Nouel, Irma de Sola Ricardo, Luisa del Valle, Ada Pérez and Josefina Bello de Jiménez); two of ACF (Lola Morales and Praxedes Abraham); and Ana Esther Gouverner of UMA. Other groups of women also submitted letters in support. Rivas (2006, 181) reproduces an abbreviated version.

not need her husband's permission to purchase, mortgage or sell her assets nor to engage in any contracts or appear in suits, and in the case of reserved property resulting from her employment, she should be able to donate such assets also without need for approval. With respect to divorce, the petition demanded that the grounds include the incompatibility of the spouses (mutual consent), and if for adultery, it should be under the same conditions for either spouse; they also wanted a simplification in the procedures for divorce.[49] The petition also demanded full recognition of married women's legal capacity so that they could be guardians as well as civil judges in matters regarding children. In terms of patria potestad, its proposal was modest, that parents share decisions over education of their children.

The coalition's most innovative proposal was for the code to recognize the property rights of couples in consensual unions, a demand that reflected the large share of women with partners who had children together but never married.[50] Technically, these women were single and thus controlled their own earnings and whatever assets they acquired independently; however, irrespective of the length of their union, they had no rights to any property that might have resulted from their joint efforts nor to inherit from each other. Moreover, their children, unless explicitly recognized by their fathers, did not have inheritance rights to their father's patrimony. The petition also wanted the code to allow the investigation of paternity. The ACF and AVN initiated a national discussion around these reforms through their respective women's pages in the two major newspapers (AUPR 1942, 15).

In her 1937 radio address and in *Nos-Otras*, Luisa Martínez (1937, 9–10) also explained why reform of the civil code should be important to women, advocating not only in support of married women's property rights but also in favor of mothers attaining equal rights of patria potestad.[51] She thus went beyond the demand contained in the ACF-AVM-UMA petition, highlighting the need for parents to share these rights and responsibilities. She found it paradoxical that the Venezuelan code gave unwed mothers patria potestad over their illegitimate children (a result of the 1916 civil code reform) but denied mothers who were married the same rights over their legitimate children.

Martínez was also concerned that current divorce law made it too easy for husbands to divorce wives for abandonment and deprive them of raising their children. She cited a recent court case where a man had charged his wife with voluntary

49 Since divorce was only available for fault, it was difficult for women to access. The 1936 national census reported only 3,237 divorced women (0.3% of the share of women 15 years or older); calculated from Venezuela (1957, Table 20).

50 In the censuses, women in consensual unions appear as single along with those who are unpartnered. The share of women over 15 reported as single was always more than twice the share reported as married, 69.5%, 68.3%, and 63.2%, respectively in the 1936, 1941 and 1950 national censuses, attesting to the large number in consensual unions (Venezuela 1957, Table 20).

51 Martínez at the time was Venezuela's CIM representative and a member of its legal research committee that prepared CIM's report to the Eighth Pan American Conference in Lima (IACM 1938, 209–10).

abandonment even though she had not left the marital home because of her refusal to sleep with him (the *deber conyugal*). A judge ruled in his favor and since she was the guilty party to the divorce, denied her access to her children (Martínez 1937,11).

The women's organizations continued their coalition-building around plans for the First Venezuelan Congress of Women.[52] While they did not hold a national congress because of insufficient funding and organizational capacity for a truly national meeting, the preparatory conference held in June 1940 brought together several hundred women representing some 69 groups (C.V.M. 1941, 9–11). Among them were representatives from 16 unions, labor committees and factories, besides numerous community organizations, suggesting this conference was successful in incorporating working-class women.

The conference was organized around a five-point platform that included equal pay for equal work; reform of all laws and codes that placed women in an inferior position to men; reform of the constitution and electoral law so that women have the right to vote on the same terms as men; an end to the distinction between legitimate and illegitimate children; and the simplification of the procedures for matrimony and divorce (C.V.M. 1941, 20; Travieso [1944] 1977, 117).[53] Much of the emphasis in the 11 papers presented was on how women needed equal civil rights to be better mothers (Friedman 2000, 75–7).

AVM and UMA member Panchita Soublette (1941) (Figure 7.1), a law student at the time, presented the main paper on the needed reforms to the civil code. She summarized women's progress over previous decades, such as attaining higher levels of schooling and some attending university; broad representation in the labor force, including in the civil service; and ample participation in social programs of all types. She emphasized how women's responsibilities had increased while their rights had not, and how when they married they lost the property rights that they held as single women. She also took issue with how the code required a wife's obedience to her husband, arguing that marriage should be based on mutual comprehension, responsibilities and consideration rather than women's subordination.

Soublette also acknowledged the progress made in strengthening women's property rights – that since the late nineteenth century women could stipulate in a prenuptial agreement that they manage all their own assets. Social convention, nonetheless, dissuaded women from exercising this right, for if they raised the topic, men took this as an affront to their dignity since it signaled a lack of trust. As a result, few couples made these. She also recognized the importance of the 1916 reform that allowed married women workers to manage their own earnings and the

52 The ACF, AVM and Ateneo led the planning committee that included 23 women (C.V.M. 1941, 11).

53 As Milanich (2009, 122–4) points out in the case of Chile, demands around eradicating distinctions among children based on the conditions of their birth and simplifying marriage procedures were interrelated, since illegitimate children often found it difficult to marry, for example, due to not having birth certificates or identifiable kin.

FIGURE 7.1 Venezuelan lawyer Panchita Soublette Saluzzo (1912–1987), ca. 1950.

Source: Photographer unknown, in *Diccionario Biográfico de Venezuela*, Garrido Mezquita y Compañía editors (Madrid: Talleres Blass S.A., 1953). Courtesy of George A. Smathers Libraries, University of Florida.

assets purchased with such income. Nonetheless, she considered it unjust that they could not gift such assets, since husbands could make modest donations from the community property they controlled without wives having a say.

Soublette's recommendations for reform of women's property rights reiterated most of the points contained in the 1937 ACF-AVM-UMA petition to the Congress discussed earlier. Her recommendation regarding the management of community property was slightly different than the demand of the ACF-AVM-UMA; she proposed that only donations of community property be subject to mutual consent, not alienation. This is likely because it was already known that the codification commission had discussed and rejected the idea that each spouse manage the gananciales from the property that they administered individually, with these pooled at the end of the marriage (as in the 1932 Colombian law). But there was consensus on the commission around the idea that each spouse manage his or her own assets subject to the constraint that they could not donate these (or accept an inheritance) without the approval of the other spouse.[54] As tentatively approved, the husband remained the administrator of most of the gananciales; the exception were those generated from a wife's employment (the reserved property) that remained under her control. Thus Soublette focused on making sure that the community property under a

54 This proposal was like the one that the 1930 review commission approved (García de Astorga 1983, 244–7) and its reasoning regarding donations was similar. The main advance for women was that this limitation now applied to the individual assets of each spouse, not just those of wives.

husband's control be subject to the same condition as individual property – mutual consent for its donation.

She added a new demand to the ACF-AVM-UMA proposal, giving mothers equal rights to fathers in the exercise of patria potestad. Soublette argued that mothers were subject to the same obligations as fathers and that it was unfair that their rights and privileges were unequal. Overall, her proposal was based on the principle of wives maintaining the same property rights that they had as single women but went beyond it to include a few parallel rights during marriage. Of the demands in the ACF-AVM-UMA proposal that Soublette did not include in hers was the issue of the property rights of women in consensual unions.

During the discussion of Soublette's presentation, conference participants urged the inclusion of this demand so that after five years' duration consensual unions hold the same property rights as marriages (C.V.M. 1941, 109). Advocates argued that such unions were often as stable as marriages, and that their lack of legal recognition was particularly harmful to children. Moreover, recognizing their right to gananciales from the union might even promote marriage, since it would reduce the incentive for men not to marry. Those attending approved this recommendation along with all the other points contained in Soublette's paper. The conference organizers then submitted the list of demands to the codification commission and the Congress (C.V.M. 1941, 109; AUPR 1942, 16).

Soon after, the ACF, AVM, and other groups represented at the women's conference formed the Frente de Asociaciones Unidas Pro-Reforma del Código Civil (Frente, United Front of Organizations for Civil Code Reform) to advance their demands.[55] It launched a large-scale campaign that included convoking meetings and sponsoring lectures as well as effective use of their weekly women's pages in the newspapers to publicize these events as well as their demands. Lucila Palacios included a questionnaire in the magazine *Elite* seeking the opinion of women on the need for reform, which served to increase public awareness of the issues and generated much discussion (AUPR 1942, 16; Rivas 2006, 182–4).

The coalition also made its demands for women's civil rights an issue in the 1941 presidential elections, receiving the support of writer Rómulo Gallegos, the candidate of the recently formed Acción Democrática (Friedman 2000, 81–2). The winning candidate in these indirect elections (by the Congress) was Isaías Medina Angarita, of the Partido Democrático Venezolano (PDV, Venezuelan Democratic Party), who had served as López Contrera's Minister of Defense.

The 1942 Civil Code Reform

The reforms proposed by the 1936 commission in its final report (Comisión Codificadora [1942] 1968) met many of the demands of organized women. Its recommendations that weakened potestad marital, however, met opposition in the

55 The main organizers were Panchita Soublette for the AVN and Carmen Travieso for the ACF. https://venezuelaenretrospectiva.wordpress.com/2018/02/17/panchita-soublette-saluzzo/

Congress. Thus while considerably strengthening married women's property rights by giving them similar property rights to single women, the 1942 civil code reforms did not go as far as feminists had hoped in establishing the basis for equal rights in marriage.

Soon after the codification commission submitted its report, the Frente responded with a detailed analysis of its content. In the pamphlet *La Mujer ante la Ley* (Women Before the Law) it provided a side-by-side comparison of the wording of the existing code, the commission's proposed changes, and their demands.[56] Among the gains they highlighted was the commission's recommendation to rid the code of the article that required the wife's obedience to her husband as well as the need for his authorization for her to be employed, to contract or appear in suits. Also, married women gained the right to manage the assets they brought to marriage subject to the constraint that neither spouse could donate any individual property without the other's approval. While the husband remained the administrator of most of the community property (except for the gananciales from the wife's reserved property), he could not donate these assets without his wife's consent, a condition that the women's coalition had agreed was sufficient. As the Frente (AUPR 1942, 26) noted with respect to these specific articles, "the woman is rightfully considered as she should be in the conjugal society–not as a minor or an irresponsible person – and her assets are protected against her husband's potential dissipation."

Organized women were also pleased that the commission had adopted their recommendations to recognize the property rights of women in consensual unions as well as mutual consent as a grounds for a civil divorce. They were disappointed, nonetheless, that it ignored their demand to end the discriminatory treatment of women in the case of adultery. They were also concerned that the commission had not added safeguards to abandonment as a ground for divorce.[57] They concluded that "the reforms of the Code, even though weak, undoubtedly better the situation of women as well as that of illegitimate children in civil law, and we support them" (AUPR 1942, 17).

In his comments to the Chamber accompanying the commission's report, Minister of Interior Tulio Chiossone (1942, 125–35) observed that while their proposal updated the country's code according to modern legal thinking, it had gone too far with respect to the family. He considered Venezuelan society to be very conservative on family matters.[58] He was most worried about how the commission

56 The co-authors of this report were Panchita Soublette and Lucila Palacios, working with Ada Pérez, Luisa del Valle and Ateneo member Anna Julia Rojas. https://www.bibliofep.fundacionempresaspolar.org.

57 This pamphlet began with the story of a man who divorced his wife on the grounds of abandonment when after his verbal abuse she had left their home to stay with her mother. She was hoping that her absence would make him appreciate her more but instead, to her surprise, he filed for divorce on the grounds of willful abandonment. Since she was legally the guilty party he gained custody of their children (AUPR 1942, 3–5).

58 Quintero (2000, 248–54) provides a good description of how women's idealized role centered on being a wife and mother, at least for the middle and upper class.

had totally rewritten the code's chapter on the traditional rights and obligations in marriage, giving women what he considered "an exceptional degree of autonomy" (Chiossone 1942, 34). Chiossone opposed, for example, giving wives more flexibility with respect to the obligation that they reside where their husbands determined since it would create discord and destabilize the family. He also opposed divorce by mutual consent preferring that this only be a cause for legal separation, not divorce, and proposed that after two years (rather than the current five) such a separation become a no-fault divorce.

The Minister was also concerned that the commission's recommendation to legalize consensual unions might justify concubinage, undermining efforts to encourage marriage. Nonetheless, he supported efforts to strengthen the inheritance rights of natural children, making the recognition of paternity easier, and recognizing the contribution that women in consensual unions made to their partner's patrimony. He recommended, nonetheless, that a woman's right to a share of the gananciales generated in such a union depend on whether she directly contributed income or assets. This, of course, ignored the contribution women made to their generation through their domestic and caring labor.

Shortly after the Congress began discussion of the commission's recommendations, Frente leaders sent them their detailed analysis. In this message they commended the commission for "restoring to the Venezuelan woman those rights that correspond to her as a natural person…that the act of marriage has taken from her, placing her in a humiliating condition of inferiority…" and, overall, noted that the proposed reforms "merited the support of all responsible Venezuelan women" (AUPR 1942, 17). They highlighted again how the commission had adopted one of their demands, giving property rights to women in consensual unions. They thought this should mitigate the poverty in which such women found themselves upon the death of their partner. They also reiterated the points on which the reform fell short, for example, with the respect to the grounds for civil divorce. Nonetheless, they urged approval of the reform and lobbied heavily for it.[59]

According to María Teresa Rivas (2006, 189–203), the main opposition to the proposed reforms came from the members of Acción Nacional (AN), the conservative party with the strongest ties to the Catholic Church, along with some members of the ruling PDV who did not want to change the code's sections related to family law at all. As Minister Chiossone had foreseen, they viewed any weakening of potestad marital as destabilizing to marriage and the family, whose unity they considered to be based on the husband's authority.

The opposition first fought against changing the existing right of the husband to determine the household's residency.[60] The commission had loosened this authority, giving a woman the right to temporarily leave the home to meet professional

59 News items in "Cultura de la Mujer" in *Ahora* during May 1942 report groups of women going to meet with members of the Chamber to discuss the civil code reforms. Its pages also include letters in support of the reform from women in the interior of the country; in Álvarez (2010, 159–64).

60 Discussion in the Chamber, May 7, 1942, reproduced in Congreso (1987), tome 9, 21 (37), 315–34.

obligations, although the husband could appeal such an action in court. Deputy Rafael Caldera, a AN leader, took issue with the analysis of the women's groups that the obligation of the wife to obey and follow her husband was anti-democratic, asking if it was anti-democratic or humiliating to have to obey a law written to safeguard the state's superior interest in protecting the family. While he applauded women who pursued a profession, once they married motherhood must be their top priority, and he urged the deputies to reject the commission's proposed wording of this article. The opposition won this battle, with the original code wording maintained that "the woman should follow the man to wherever he resides." A wife gained the right to appeal if she considered her husband's decision to be against her best interests (Venezuela 1942, art. 138). Rivas (2006, 196) emphasizes how this shows that the dominant ideology, while becoming more tolerant of women working and being in the public sphere, still considered women's primary duty to be to the home and children.

AN Deputy Lara Peña took issue with the fact that nowhere in the commission's recommended articles on marital relations did it state that the husband owed the wife protection, as the 1922 code did. He thus proposed adding this phrase, and this amendment also passed. Lara Pena's main goal, however, was to preserve the old article that stated explicitly that the husband was the head of the household. The commission had maintained the principle of male household headship, but diluted it somewhat by proposing alternative wording, that "the decisions relating to marital life correspond to the husband." The opposition was adamant that the conjugal society should have only one head – the husband – and that he should have complete authority over the family. Supporters of the commission's wording, such as Deputy Blanco, argued that the new wording, while giving husbands the final word over any decision, presumed that couples discussed the issue first, which reflected how in practice households made most decisions. Most deputies favored the Commission's revised version of this concept and maintained it.[61]

There was little opposition to the articles that reformed the marital regime. The main change, allowing wives to manage their own assets, had been under discussion for some time and viewed as an extension of the concept of women's reserved property. The provision that maintained the husband as the sole manager of the gananciales assuaged any potential dissent. Recognizing the property rights of women in consensual unions was another matter. The opposition argued that giving them the same rights as marriages would reduce the incentive to marry. Just as Minister Chiossone had recommended, the deputies amended the proposed article so that for a woman to benefit from the gananciales she had to prove that she contributed to or enhanced her partner's patrimony.

The inclusion of mutual consent as grounds for civil divorce was also controversial since it might weaken the institution of marriage. The Catholic Church fought hard against this measure, launching a press campaign against it (Rivas 2006). The

61 Congreso (1987), tome 9, 21 (37), 325–7.

opposition won this battle and the approved version deleted mutual consent. The bill, however, retained it as grounds for a permanent separation that after two years could result in a no-fault divorce. The Congress approved the proposed reforms as amended and President Medina signed the new civil code into law in August 1942.[62]

The government lauded the 1942 reforms as having "liberated married women economically and judicially" (González 1942, 46). While not ending potestad marital, the reform improved married women's property rights by ending their relative civil incapacity. Whereas the 1916 code had only given women the ability to manage their own earnings from employment, these rights now included all her property, irrespective of its origins (whether brought to marriage, inherited or purchased with earnings) (Venezuela 1942, art. 152). The only restriction on the free administration of individual property by either the wife or husband was a parallel obligation – that each could not donate this property nor refuse an inheritance without the permission of the other spouse (Venezuela 1942, art. 154).

The husband remained the administrator of the community property, except for the gananciales acquired through a wife's employment and its fruits, which remained under her management during the marriage (Venezuela 1942, art. 168). While husband and wife were equally free to contract with the gananciales under their respective management, they required each other's consent to donate such assets (Venezuela 1942, art. 170). This met the demand of the women's movement in terms of parallel rights and responsibilities, although it still left the bulk of the gananciales from the marriage under the control of husbands; organized women had not asked for more, such as joint management over all the gananciales.

The civil code recognized the property rights of women living in consensual unions for the first time, assuming that such unions generated community property, like marriages, with the caveat noted earlier, that women had to prove that they had contributed directly to the generation of gananciales (Venezuela 1942, art. 767).[63] Children of these unions gained inheritance rights to the patrimony of both parents. The inheritance rights of children whose father was married to someone other than the mother also improved. For the first time, if recognized, such children were in the first order of inheritance of the father although they could only inherit half the share of his legitimate children (Venezuela 1942, art. 823).[64] Moreover, the position of all illegitimate children improved in that if they were minors and not legally recognized and hence not eligible to receive an inheritance, they were entitled to claim subsistence support (*alimentos*) from their father's estate

62 *Gaceta Oficial*, extraordinary issue, September 1, 1942.

63 Mexico in 1928 was the only other Latin American country to have given similar property rights to those in consensual unions (Deere and León 2021, Table 2).

64 The 1942 code maintained the same provision from the 1916 code whereby natural and legitimate children were equal heirs of their mothers.

(Venezuela 1942, art. 830). In addition, the code now supported the investigation of paternity, increasing the chances that fathers recognize children born outside of marriage.

With respect to patria potestad, the 1942 code retained it as the prerogative of fathers, but it bettered the position of mothers by stating that they shared it with fathers "with respect to domestic matters and the supervision of children" (Venezuela 1942, art. 261). In the case of natural children, if both parents recognized the child, it corresponded to the father; otherwise, to the mother or father alone depending on who had recognized them (Venezuela 1942, art. 262). Another advance was that if a widow or widower remarried, they maintained patria potestad with the same rights and duties.[65] The reform expanded all women's civil rights by allowing them to be guardians and witnesses to wills and other public instruments, irrespective of marital status. Finally, it simplified the formalities associated with matrimony to make it more accessible. The reform failed, however, to change the unequal treatment of spouses with respect to adultery in the grounds for civil divorce.

Overall, while not meeting all the demands of organized women, the 1942 reform of the civil code was quite responsive to them. Friedman's (2000, 83) conclusion that this code represented "a limited victory for women" is rather harsh, since this reform gave wives similar property rights to single women and was a significant step toward gender equality in marriage due to the parallel constraints that it imposed on both husband and wife. It was also a major step forward for women in consensual unions and their children, an achievement directly attributable to feminist demands. What they achieved, as Friedman notes, was in large measure due to the coalition-building that organized women's groups engaged in across civil society.[66] These groups then repeated this process of coalition-building to attain women's political rights.

Recognition of Women's Political Rights

While a resolution in support of women's political rights had been approved at the 1940 Women's Conference, suffrage was not actively pursued because organized women focused on what they considered most urgent, the recognition of their civil capacity and property rights.[67] Once these reforms were attained, in 1943 the leaders

65 This was an advance since beginning with the 1867 code a family tribunal decided whether a widow who remarried continued to manage a minor's assets; it could appoint an advisor to the mother, a stipulation not applicable to widowers (Venezuela 1867, arts. 168 and 172).

66 Friedman (2000) tends to give more credit to the ACF than the AVM in this coalition-building. Given the leadership role of lawyer Panchita Soublette and Ada Pérez of the AVM in the Frente, especially in the drafting of its various documents suggests members of both organizations played crucial roles.

67 Friedman (2000, 72, 83) also suggests that the AVM divided over the issue of women's suffrage although I did not find clear evidence of this.

of the ACF and AVM formed another coalition, the Comité Coordinadora Pro Sufragio de la Mujer (Women's Suffrage Coordinating Committee), to lobby for the vote.[68] During the next two years this committee conducted an intense press campaign, wrote letters and presented petitions to the congress, and organized support in the interior of the country and within political parties, attaining suffrage in a two-step process.[69]

In its first petition the Suffrage Committee only asked the Congress to set up a commission to study a constitutional reform to give women political rights on the same terms as men.[70] Each chamber dedicated at least one session to discussion of their petition. Deputy Andrés Eloy Blanco, a co-founder of AD, was the main advocate of women's suffrage in the Chamber. He gave an impassioned speech where he reviewed the long struggle of women in the United States to obtain the vote, among other points. To critics who saw women's fundamental mission as maternal, he posed the question of whether Venezuela would have had "fewer revolutions, war and human casualties, if women could defend their children against unjust wars."[71]

The recent approval of the 1942 civil code reform informed the debate in different ways. To some, this reform meant that men and women had equal civil rights and equal political rights were simply a logical extension of the same principle. For others, the reform had rightly maintained potestad marital, meaning that wives were not autonomous persons, a factor which they considered a precondition to their attaining equal political rights. For Deputy Blanco this showed why women needed the vote if they were ever to attain full equality with men. The Senate finally replied to the women's commission saying that it was inopportune to consider women's suffrage at this time although it recognized that universal suffrage was the aim of any true democracy and that in theory there was no reason to deny women the vote.[72]

To build momentum, during its first celebration of International Women's Day the Suffrage Committee launched a petition campaign and collected 11,436

68 The coordinating committee included Luisa del Valle, Ada Pérez and Panchita Soublette of the AVM, Mercedes Fermín of the ACF, and Graciela Rincón Calcano. https://venezuelaenretrospectiva.wordpress.com/2018/02/17/panchita-soublette-saluzzo/.

69 Among the new organizations active in this effort were the Comité de Mujeres Trabajadoras pro Voto Femenino (Working Women's Committee for Women's Vote) and the Unión de Amas de Casa (Housewives' Union), the latter resulting from mobilizations around the rising price of food. See the excerpts of "Cultura de la Mujer" in *Ahora,* in Álvarez (2010, 171–88), Friedman (2000, 86) and Quintero (2000, 259; 2001, 65–6) on their arguments for suffrage.

70 "Representación de damas ante la Cámara de Diputados" April 18, 1943, DDCD (1943, 5, May 17, 6–7), reproduced in Congreso (1987, 301–3); and Quintero (2001, 63–4).

71 Discussion of May 19, 1943 (DDCD, 1943, 7, May 21), in Congreso (1987, 346–74).

72 "Informe de la Comisión Permanente de Relaciones Interiores de la Cámara del Senado sobre el Voto Femenino," *Diario de Debates de la Cámara del Senado* (DDCS) (1943, June 23, 304) in Congreso (1987, 311–3) and Quintero (2001, 64).

signatures by April 1944.[73] PDV Senator Julio Medina Angarita responded to the delivery of these petitions to Congress by saying that his party was about to propose a constitutional reform bill and since the draft did not include women's suffrage, he would convoke a special session of his party to consider it. As a result of the intense lobbying by women, the PDV reached a compromise to support a gradual process toward women's suffrage.[74] The bill that PDV deputies subsequently presented amended article 32 of the constitution to give women the right to vote and be candidates for municipal councils. It also included another concession, allowing the appointment of women to all public offices, including judgeships, thus meeting another demand of organized women.[75]

Deputy Blanco argued that the PDV reform bill did not go far enough since it excluded universal suffrage and women's equal political rights as well as direct election of the president. He was disdainful of what it meant to give women suffrage at the local level, noting that this came just when municipalities were losing autonomy, making them nothing more than "family councils" with no real power. Nonetheless, he was willing to support the package of constitutional reforms since, overall, it represented some progress toward the goal of democratization of the country.[76]

Those who favored the government's bill argued that illiteracy in the country was still too high to institute universal suffrage and that given the many years of dictatorship, most people had no experience in politics. The 1941 national census revealed that while there had been some gains over the previous decade, 57.2% of the population above the age of 15 was still illiterate, with it being much higher among women (60.6%) than men (53.5%) (Venezuela 1957, Table 35). They also argued that women's full suffrage was premature since they were not prepared to participate in politics, that this demand came from only a small group of feminists, and that most Venezuelan women had no interest in participating in politics. A two-stage process offered the advantage of giving women time to prepare themselves for civic duties and the political parties time to see if and how women voted. Moreover, there was consensus that local level issues such as municipal services were perfectly compatible with women's interests and responsibilities in the home as compared to national issues (Quintero 2000; 2001).

To inform the congressional debates and influence public opinion, Ada Pérez (1944) published a pamphlet on behalf of the Suffrage Committee summarizing

73 "Representación de las mujeres al Senado sobre el voto femenino," April 18, 1944 (DDCS 1944, May 11) in Congreso (1987, 315–8). The petition had 50 signatures including those of Ada Pérez, Luisa del Valle, Panchita Sublette, Lucila Palacios and Mercedes Fermín and attached 11,386 others.

74 "Las mujeres venezolanas," *Diario Popular*, reprinted in *Agitación Femenina* (1945, 8, 6).

75 DDCS (1944, May 27), in Congreso (1987, 17–41).

76 DDCD (1944, July 6) in Congreso (1987, 144–5).

the status of women's suffrage internationally and efforts in Venezuela. She highlighted how most of the country's previous constitutions had not explicitly denied women political rights, since the language was either gender neutral or stated that only men could stand for office with the language on voting being gender neutral. Only the constitutions of 1901 and 1936 explicitly prohibited women from exercising political rights.

Reviewing the efforts of women's groups in favor of suffrage since 1940, Pérez (1944, 8–10), stressed how this demand now included women from all of Venezuela's states and across social classes, as was evident in their petition. She refuted those who objected to women's suffrage on the grounds that it would pull them away from their domestic duties, arguing that voting would not require more than a few hours every few years, and more important, that it was precisely because many women were mothers that they needed the vote, to socialize children as good citizens.

To the fears over how women would vote, Pérez responded with a detailed analysis of how diverse groups of women might vote, concluding that women would not vote as a block and would not sway elections in one direction or another. She also analyzed the role that women might play if elected or appointed to public offices, predicting that they would give more attention to issues focusing on the family and children, such as education and public health as well as moral issues. Perhaps anticipating that the compromise that might emerge would be to give women the right to participate in municipal-level elections, she stressed their potential contribution to local, practical matters. Pérez's most impassioned arguments were regarding the contribution that women's suffrage would make to the consolidation and stability of Venezuelan democracy. Drawing on a recent CIM report that called on women to promote democracy in the Americas,[77] she emphasized how women's participation was necessary for "genuine democracy," something that could not happen while "half of humanity was free, and the other half were slaves" (Pérez Guevara 1944, 14).

The Medina Angarita government signed the bill of constitutional reforms in late 1944, with these going into effect in 1945. The requirements for suffrage were the same as in the previous 1936 Constitution – 21 years of age and the ability to read and write – and similar for men and women, although it limited women's participation to the municipal level. In addition, the revised constitution specified that women could hold appointed public offices (Venezuela 1945a, arts. 14, 33). Shortly after, lawyer Panchita Soublette became the first woman named to a judgeship (Ramón 1985, 48–9).

The leaders of the Suffrage Committee then formed a new organization, Acción Femenina (Women's Action), with the dual objective of attaining women's

77 See Chapter 5 on how CIM's initiatives in the Pan American Union led to the 1938 Lima Declaration, and Chapter 6 on the 1948 conventions on women's civil and political rights.

full suffrage and furthering their civic education.[78] Panchita Soublette served as its first secretary general,[79] and Ada Pérez and Flor María Zambrano edited its newspaper, the *Correo Cívico Femenino*.[80] With chapters throughout the country, the organization reached a membership of around 1,500 women. It held mock elections for women to practice voting and organized the Second Preparatory Conference for a Venezuelan Women's Congress, held on International Women's Day in 1945 (Friedman 2000, 87–88).[81] In lobbying for full suffrage, organized women were now able to draw upon several international conventions besides the 1938 Lima accord that Venezuela had signed in support of their demands, Resolution 28 of Chapultepec and the United Nations Charter.[82]

A military coup in October 1945 deposed Medina and led to a civilian-military Junta presided over by AD's Rómulo Betancourt. This party had championed universal suffrage since its founding and supported women's full suffrage in the earlier debate. Thus the Junta's Decree 217 of March 1946 called for a constitutional convention with the election of delegates to be based on universal suffrage by those 18 or older irrespective of gender or literacy. Women were able to stand for election and vote for the first time for members of this assembly and among the 12 women elected were prominent feminists Panchita Soublette, Lucila Palacios, Mercedes Fermín, and Analuisa Llovera (Leonardi 1983, 408; Friedman 2000, 88–9).[83]

The women delegates demanded that the new constitution enshrine universal suffrage with equal political rights for men and women, a demand that met little opposition. They also championed the defense of the family, the protection of women workers, and equal wages for equal work, among other issues (Quintero 2000, 260–1). The 1947 Constitution incorporated these and many other

78 Friedman (2000, 87) dates it founding to mid-1944 and, drawing on Miller (1991, 115), says that the CIM began organizing groups by that name throughout the region after the 1938 Lima Conference of American States. I did not find evidence of such a regional initiative, although groups with that same name appeared in several countries.

79 Other founding officers included Josefina Coronil, Ada Pérez, Mercedes Gil Santana, Eumelia Hernández, Ana Esther Gouverneur and Luisa del Valle (Álvarez 2010, 94).

80 Álvarez (2010, 94–9) contains excerpts from several of the 18 issues published between 1945 and 1947.

81 Friedman (2000, 89) mentions that among its activities was successfully lobbying for reform of the 1919 Commercial Code. However, the September 1945 partial reform of this code did not modify any of the articles dealing with married women. Left intact were articles 14 and 18 of the previous code that assumed that married women had the tacit or explicit authorization of their husbands to exercise this activity, including the husband's right to revoke his permission (Venezuela 1945b). Married women did not attain the right to engage in commercial activity autonomously (without any kind of authorization) until the codes next reform in 1955 (Venezuela 1955).

82 Mentioned in the letter sent by Acción Femenina to the Colombian Congress of July 1, 1945, in support of women's suffrage in Colombia; in *Agitación Femenina* (1945, 10, 4). That feminists in Colombia and Venezuela were in close contact is also evident in the pages of "Cultura de la Mujer" in *Ahora,* in Álvarez (2010).

83 Huggins (2020) mentions 13 and Quintero (2001, 69) 15 women elected, with the difference perhaps due to whether the count includes alternate delegates.

social rights along with women's equal political rights and direct elections for the presidency and congress. It instituted universal suffrage at 18; standing for office required either men and women to be at least 21 (Venezuela 1947, arts. 63, 81 and 82).

In the last issue of *Correo Cívico Femenino*, published in January 1947, Ada Pérez reflected on how much the women's movement had accomplished in the dozen years or so of its existence (in Álvarez 2010, 99). But unjust differences remained in the treatment of men and women in the civil, commercial and penal codes. The military coup of 1948, however, brought further organizing efforts around women's demands to a halt. In subsequent years, as women became increasingly active in political parties their activism in support of gender issues through autonomous women's organizations declined until the second wave of feminism (Leonardi 1983; Espina 1994; Friedman 2000, 97–8).[84]

Conclusion

Women's attainment of broader civil rights in Venezuela took place in two phases with different protagonists. The first phase, from the mid-nineteenth to the early decades of the twentieth, was under liberal caudillo regimes without the participation of women. These piecemeal reforms of the civil code were the initiative of jurists inspired by liberal principles and the reforms of married women's property rights in Europe, the United States and perhaps Central America.[85] The second phase coincided with the transition toward democracy. Also led by liberal jurists, it now included participation by women's rights organizations that pressed their own set of demands.

As a result of the first phase, women entered the twentieth century with stronger rights than in other South American countries, particularly as mothers and widows; they held patria potestad over children in the father's absence and strong inheritance rights as a surviving spouse. There was also more flexibility in the marital regime since couples could opt for the regime of separation of property at the time of marriage, with Venezuela being the first South American country to institute this option. Moreover, when it instituted civil divorce in 1904 it was under more grounds than Ecuador (the first to do so) initially allowed. This phase culminated with married women gaining control over their own earnings in 1916, in a period in which women's labor force participation and educational opportunities were still quite limited and no women's organizations demanding reform had yet emerged.

84 The civil code reform of 1992 finally recognized equal rights in marriage (Deere and León 2001, Table 2.1).

85 While I did not find any direct references to the Central American liberal reforms in Venezuelan discussions, that these coincided in time suggests a circulation of ideas in the circum-Caribbean region.

As in Ecuador, these reforms took place in advance of social change and largely to spur modernization.

The second phase commenced in the tumultuous years following the 1935 death of strongman Juan Vicente Gómez when several women's organizations formed with the objective of securing equal civil rights and later, political rights. That such organizations emerged comparatively late in the regional context is related to the country's slow pace of urbanization, expansion of schooling and development of a middle class. These conditions began to develop during the Gómez dictatorship, driven by the expansion of the petroleum industry and the state, which coincided with the circulation of ideas regarding true democracy and feminism, particularly after 1928.

That organized women were able to attain greater civil as well as full political rights in a relatively short period – within 12 years of the founding of their organizations – is related to several factors, but foremost, their timing. It coincided with a period of transition to democracy in a regional context where women had already gained stronger property rights and the vote in several countries. Also, the women's groups proved particularly adept at constructing broad coalitions across class and religious divides in pursuit of their objectives. Moreover, the Frente and then the Suffrage Committee lobbied successfully across political lines, emphasizing how greater rights strengthened women's maternal role and contribution to social welfare.

The appointment of a new commission to reform the civil code shortly after the death of Gómez provided organized women the opportunity to directly impact its content. The proposal they approved at the 1940s Women's Conference was based on the idea that women when they married should maintain the same rights they held as single women combined with a vision of spouses holding parallel rights in marriage. Nonetheless, they did not demand fully equal rights and got close to what they demanded.

The 1942 civil code reform diluted potestad marital by getting rid of the requirement that wives provide obedience to their husbands but did not eliminate it. Although married women could now manage their own assets as well as their earnings, husbands still managed the couple's community property, the exemption being that working women managed the gananciales from their employment. The parallelism was that neither spouse could make donations from the gananciales they controlled without mutual consent. Venezuela's reform of the marital regime ended up being closer to Peru's 1936 reform rather than Colombia's 1932 legal advance with respect to management of the community property.

Feminist demands, nonetheless, were solely responsible for the 1942 reform recognizing the property rights of the large share of partnered women who never married. Although the terms were more restrictive than they had wished, Venezuela became the first country in South America to recognize such rights. Also, through the 1942 reform all women irrespective of marital status could be witnesses in civil matters and guardians over children. Probably most disappointing among the demands feminists did not achieve was with respect to patria potestad. Although mothers gained a voice in childrearing, during the marriage they did not attain equal rights to fathers over their children, although widows and widowers held similar rights and maintained these if they remarried.

With stronger civil rights, organized women immediately turned their attention to securing equal political rights in a context in which the progressive political parties were pushing for universal suffrage and direct election of the presidency. Again, due to their united efforts in a broad cross-class coalition and through effective lobbying, they attained partial suffrage as a compromise in 1945, the ability to vote and stand for office at the local level. The next year the military-civilian junta led by the progressive party, Acción Democrática, ceded women the vote and the right to be candidates for the Constitutional Assembly. Women thus participated directly in the process of constitutional reform that in 1947, in the context of universal suffrage, recognized their full political rights.

8

URUGUAY'S UNIQUE PATH

Women's Suffrage Prior to Property Rights

Uruguay's trajectory was unique in South America because women acquired the vote before they obtained stronger property and other civil rights. That they inverted the conventional order is partly because Paulina Luisi, the founder of the Consejo Nacional de Mujeres del Uruguay (CNM-U, National Council of Uruguayan Women), rejected the evolutionary view of women's emancipation. From its founding in the teens, the CNM-U pursued political and civil rights simultaneously since it considered that women's suffrage might be necessary for women to achieve equal civil rights.

The country's 1893 Civil Code certainly needed reforming. Consider the situation of this wife of a white-collar worker who wrote the editors of *Acción Femenina*, the CNM-U's periodical, in 1918 asking if there was a law that might protect her.[1] Her husband earned 95 pesos monthly but because of his vices, most of his salary disappeared within a week, leaving almost nothing for household expenses; moreover, store owners were no longer willing to extend the family credit. With six children to support, she earned income by occasionally working for a shoe repair shop. She wished to know whether it were possible for her to directly access half of her husband's salary. The editors replied that the civil code allowed a husband to do whatever he wished with his salary without her consent, while he had the legal right to manage any income that she earned independently. Her main alternatives were either to divorce him, which since 1913 she could easily do, or to resign herself to this unfortunate situation.

Feminists came close to achieving both stronger civil and full political rights in 1932; after they attained suffrage, the president's abrupt closing of Congress

1 "Una gestión importante. Los derechos civiles de la mujer" (*Acción Femenina* 1918, 5–6, 86–8).

DOI: 10.4324/9781003658436-8

interrupted this momentum. As a result of women having political rights, Uruguay is the only country of the Americas where female legislators led and co-authored the successful bill that reformed the marital regime, drawing on previous feminist proposals. The 1946 civil code reform instituted deferred community property as the default regime, eliminated potestad marital and recognized shared patria potestad over children, thereby coming closest legally to achieving equal rights in marriage.

Batllismo and Other Antecedents

In the early twentieth century, various strands of feminism circulated in Uruguay as in Argentina, from the liberalism of John Stuart Mill to freethinking, anarchist, socialist and Christian feminisms, which would later intersect with the rights-oriented global feminist movement (Ehrick 2005; Cuadro 2018). The birth of the first organization committed to attaining women's rights that endured coincided with the emergence of a core group of professional women. Historian Asunción Lavrin (1995, 321) considers that women's rights organizations emerged later in Uruguay than in Argentina precisely because women began entering university later.

The history of feminism in Uruguay intertwines with the presidency of José Batlle y Ordoñez (1903–1907, 1911–1915) who renewed the Colorado Party under a platform committed to a mix of liberal and social democratic principles, among these anti-clericalism, the expansion of public education and social assistance and a commitment to women's eventual civil and political rights (Ehrick 2005; Sapriza 2011; Cuadro 2018). As previous scholarship has shown, many of the women's organizations that formed prior to World War I were a product of Batllismo policies, formed either in support of or opposition to these policies.

The priorities of the Batlle administration with respect to secularization included reducing the influence of the Catholic Church over education, attaining the full separation of church and state, and instituting civil divorce. While the country established obligatory civil marriage in 1885, this did not include absolute divorce, and it became Batlle's priority for both political and personal reasons. He had experienced first-hand the injustice of women not being able to leave an unhappy marriage, since the husband of the love of his life, Matilde Pacheco de Michaelsson, had abandoned her with four children and left her penniless. Batlle and Matilde scandalized Uruguayan society by living together for ten years and having two children together before she widowed and they were able to marry (Rodríguez and Sapriza 1984, 74; Vigil 2003).

The Congress considered the first bill allowing absolute divorce in 1902 and in 1907 enacted a divorce law that included mutual consent as grounds after two years of marriage.[2] In 1912, some Colorado deputies wanted to go even further, allowing

2 Law 3.245, October 29, 1907; https//www.impo.com.uy/bases/beleyes/3245-1907. See Rodríguez and Sapriza (1984, 75–9) and Lavrin (1995, 228) on the debate around this first divorce law.

no-fault divorce by demand of either spouse after three years of marriage. Whereas the initial debate around instituting divorce was between anti-clericals and conservatives, this debate was one among liberals. The thinking of Uruguayan philosopher Carlos Vaz Ferreira, who developed what became known as the "feminism of compensation" as a critique of Mill's "feminism of equality," influenced the outcome (Lavrin 1995, 38–41, 232).

Vaz Ferreira ([1933] 1945) argued that women needed special protection from the state, not because they were intellectually inferior but because biological differences placed them at a disadvantage in their socioeconomic roles. Treating men and women equally under all circumstances could lead to unjust situations. Thus, if women were in a less favorable position for physiological or social reasons, they deserved compensatory action by the state. In the case of divorce, if husbands and wives had equal rights to demand it without cause, this could be prejudicial to women because divorce had different social and economic consequences for them. Moreover, mutual consent favored husbands since they were the dominant party in a marriage; a woman might agree to it not out of choice, but rather to avoid the scandal that would result if he sued her for divorce for cause, such as adultery or abandonment. Vaz Ferreira thus advocated giving *only* women the right to unilaterally demand divorce since they would pursue this avenue only if it were in their own best interests. Ceding women such a right was a form of compensation because it would increase their bargaining power in marriage. Thus the unique 1913 law that instituted divorce by demand of the woman alone, without cause, after 18 months of marriage. It maintained the previous grounds for divorce, including mutual consent.[3]

The discussion of instituting divorce provoked the first large-scale mobilization of women although of those opposed to it under any conditions. The Catholic Church began organizing women around a 1905 petition campaign to defend the sanctity of marriage, one that collected tens of thousands of signatures (Ehrick 2005, 46). The next year, the Archbishop of Montevideo promoted the organization of the Liga de Damas Católicas (Catholic Ladies League) around the concept of Christian feminism, the premise that true feminism was based on the teachings of Christianity. This organization opposed not only divorce but also Batlle's other anti-clerical actions, such as the expansion of public schools at the expense of a Catholic education. The League supported enhancing women's education and public role to the extent that it strengthened their moral development and the

3 Law 4.802 of September 15, 1913; https://www.impo.com.uy/bases/leyes/4802-1913. This law, nonetheless, did not change other discriminatory aspects of divorce on the grounds of adultery. A man was adulterous if he had a concubine, committed an infidelity in the family home or caused a public scandal, whereas any form of infidelity by the wife was sufficient. The consequences were also more severe for wives since they lost their share of the gananciales, while husbands did not (Uruguay 1914, arts. 148 and 182).

family.[4] Its elite women members also formed committees throughout the country to counter the influence of anarchists and socialists in working-class communities by providing social assistance programs and occupational training to women, and promoting marriage (Ehrick 2005, 52).

Soon after, freethinking women formed the Asociación de Damas Liberales (Liberal Ladies Association) to advance secular policies (Cuadro 2018, 86–108). Besides the complete separation of church and state, freethinkers considered religion one of the main obstacles to women's advancement. The catalyst to the formation of this group was the visit of Spanish freethinker Belén de Sárraga de Ferrero, who stopped to give lectures in Montevideo on her way to the 1906 International Congress of Freethinkers in Buenos Aires.[5] She later immigrated to Uruguay and became the editor of *El Liberal*, a daily published between 1908 and 1910 that advanced secular policies from a feminist perspective.

Among Batlle's policy goals were to expand women's access to education and employment. While Uruguay adopted free, compulsory mixed-sex primary education in the late 1870s and set up the first women's teacher training institute in 1882,[6] the only institutions that offered a secondary degree (the bachillerato) that prepared students for university examinations were all-male high schools. The first public secondary school for women, known as the "Women's University," opened in 1913 and Clotilde Luisi (Paulina Luisi's sister and the first woman lawyer) served as its first dean.[7] Also founded in this period were the first nursing and midwifery schools and the government expanded the industrial school for women (Rodríguez and Sapriza 1984, 89–93). Batlle also supported giving women preference in hiring for vacant government jobs.[8]

With respect to social policy, historian Christine Ehrick (2005, 72–3) highlights how Vaz Ferreira's ideas of compensation influenced Batlle's thinking on the role of the state, on how it should compensate for social and economic inequalities by protecting the weak. Among the accomplishments of this period was the institution of the eight-hour working day, old-age pensions and a national public assistance program. Legislation also strengthened the inheritance rights of natural children

4 The model was the French Ligue des Dames Françaises, established in 1901 to counter similar secularization policies (Ehrick 2005, 46–7). Cuadro (2018, 110) also provides an insightful discussion of Christian feminism.

5 See Chapter 3 on this 1906 congress.

6 See Ehrick (2005, 34) on the country's early commitment to education. The first director of the Internato Normal para Señoritas (Women's Normal Boarding School) was María Stagnero de Munar who mentored many of the women who later became prominent feminists; she was among the founding members of CNM-U.

7 Paulina was the first female physician, earning her degree in 1908; Clotilde graduated in 1911, both from the Universidad de la República. They attended an all-male secondary school prior to university. In 1910, there were only around 100 women enrolled in men's secondary schools and only 50 at this university, which had around 800 students (Ehrick 2005, 45, 75, 78).

8 *El Día*, April 26, 1911, refers to Batlle's Minister of Public Works issuing such an instruction.

and improved those of widows and expanded the conditions for investigation of paternity to facilitate recognition of those born outside marriage (Cassina 1990, 46, 81).[9]

Heavy immigration from Spain and Italy characterized these decades, and immigrant workers, many of whom brought anarchist ideas with them, made up a large share of the membership of labor organizations. The ranks of anarchists also swelled after Argentina passed its 1902 Residency Law that allowed the government to expel any foreigner involved in strikes and subversive acts, many of whom ended up in Montevideo. Among them were anarchist feminists Virginia Bolten and Juana Rouco Buela, who circulated clandestinely between the two countries. In 1909, Buela founded the periodical *La Nueva Senda, contra toda forma de explotación y tiranía* (New Path: Against all Forms of Exploitation and Tyranny) in Montevideo, which as its name suggests focused on denouncing the multiple forms of women's oppression.[10]

In 1911, Bolten and Uruguayans María Collazo, María Casal y Canda and Delfa Boatti founded the Asociación Feminista Emancipación (Feminist Emancipation Association) as a non-sectarian group that combined anarchist, freethinking and socialist ideas (Rodríguez Díaz 1989, 90–101; Ehrick 2005, 62). Its principal objective was "to emancipate women, the conquest of rights that legitimately correspond to them."[11] Nonetheless, there was no specific mention in its program with respect to women's civil rights. It was committed to fighting the influence of the Catholic Church over women, which it considered a major source of their oppression. It aimed to advance women and children's physical, moral and intellectual education and to combat social conventions prejudicial to women. Its objective was to prepare women to become a man's "real companion, thus being able to realize her mission as a woman and mother" and to join men in the class struggle.[12]

One of the outcomes of the 1910 First International Congress of Women in Buenos Aires was an attempt to organize the first women's regional organization,

9 On intestate inheritance, see "Impuesto de Herencias. Reformas a la Ley," of July 12, 1909, in *Registro Nacional de Leyes y Decretos* (1911, 32, 552–4). Previously, if the deceased had both legitimate and recognized natural children, the latter received only half the share of the former; the share of a natural child now increased to two-thirds of that of a legitimate child. Also, before this reform, the surviving spouse only inherited the deceased's full estate in the absence of legitimate or recognized children, ascendants and siblings. Now the spouse no longer shared the estate with the deceased's siblings. On the recognition of natural children, see the reform of November 25, 1913, in *Registro Nacional de Leyes y Decretos* (1914, 36, 677–8). A reform of September 5, 1914, expanded the conditions for the investigation of paternity; *Registro Nacional de Leyes y Decretos* (1915, 37, 438–9).

10 See Cuadro (2018, 135–59) for a thorough review of anarchist thought on the woman question.

11 "Programa y Reglamento de la Asociación Feminista 'Emancipación," *El Día*, April 25, 1911; and in Rodríguez Díaz (1989, 119–20).

12 Rodríguez Díaz (1989).

the Federación Femenina Panamericana.[13] Uruguayan-born María Abella de Ramírez, a freethinking feminist who resided in Argentina, was among the leaders of this effort, traveling to Montevideo in 1911 to establish a section of the Federation. She recruited members among the 14 Uruguayans who had attended the Buenos Aires congress; those joining included physician Paulina Luisi, who served as the section's first president, lawyer Isabel Pinto de Vidal[14] and Francisca Beretervide (Cuadro 2018, 179).

The Uruguay Section adopted the 15-point program that the Federation had approved at the conclusion of the 1910 Buenos Aires congress.[15] Defining itself as a non-partisan and non-religiously affiliated organization, it was committed to studying the means to advance the position of women, including their intellectual development, economic autonomy and mothering skills. Its demands regarding women's civil and political rights were quite general, for instance, "considering that civil law does not give married women equal rights to men with respect to the free administration of their assets, it is necessary to work to reform those laws and all that diminish women's rights" (point 9). It did not mention women's suffrage directly but alluded to it: "Since women already collaborate in the development of the nation and for the betterment of the race, it follows that they should participate in the business of the State" (point 14). Its platform also called for the expansion of women's secondary education, the opening of all professions and occupations to women, absolute divorce and legal equality between legitimate and illegitimate children. The organization was committed to fighting alcoholism and other social vices, to improving philanthropic approaches to combating indigency and vagrancy, and to promoting national and international peace.

Prior to Abella's trip to constitute the Uruguay Section, the Federation invited the Emancipation group to join this regional association. In a very anti-suffrage speech, Virginia Bolten argued against joining forces since the two groups held different objectives. Emancipation prioritized the organization of working-class women while, in her view, the issues of concern to the Federation were those of elite intellectuals.[16] As a member of Emancipation later explained in an interview in *El Día*,

> we do not aspire to suffrage, we do not want to be deputies; we do not dream of a transformation of the codes. Our principal objective is to educate; [a rational

13 Belén de Sárraga was the official Uruguayan delegate to the 1910 women's congress, representing the Asociación de Damas Liberales; she served as honorary first vice-president and gave a keynote address. Luisi was on its international publicity commission (Asociación de Universitarias Argentinas 1911, 24–9; Ehrick 1998, 410).

14 Pinto, a future senator, was the second woman to graduate with a law degree.

15 "Programa de la Federación Femenina Pan Americano," *El Día*, April 21, 1911, also in Rodríguez Díaz (1989, 117–9). This program differed from the 17-point program presented by María Abella at the 1906 International Congress of Freethinkers, discussed in Chapter 3, contrary to what Cassina (1990, 75–6) suggests.

16 In *El Día*, April 25, 1911; see Rodríguez Díaz (1989, 96–100) on its activities organizing women wage workers.

> education] is the only way to create free men, and women prepared to be their compañeras.
>
> *(Cited in Cuadro 2018, 151)*

Although it is not clear from the Federation's program statement that they advocated pursuing women's suffrage at this time, this quote reflects the classic anarchist position regarding participation in the political system. A few of the socialist-leaning women in Emancipation, such as María Casal y Candas and Delfa Boatti, joined the Federation on an individual basis.

The founding principles of Uruguay's Socialist Party, formally constituted in 1910, included women's equal civil and political rights. It initially collaborated with anarchists, including Emancipation on labor and other issues, for example, the 1911 campaign in favor of separation of church and state; it also allied with the Colorado and Liberal parties on these issues (Rodríguez Díaz 1989, 101). But relations between socialists and anarchists became increasingly strained, including among women militants, and in 1914, the Socialist Party created its own organization for women, the Agrupación Socialista Femenina (Socialist Women's Group) (Ehrick 2005, 64–5). Among its founders was 15-year-old cigarette worker Julia Arévalo Roche who decades later would become one of the first two women deputies in the Congress.

Ehrick (2005, 9, 111–7) shows how another precedent to the emergence of organized liberal feminism were the organizations formed or expanded in conjunction with Batlle's social welfare policies. Between 1910 and 1915, elite women formed several new social assistance organizations targeting poor women and children. She argues that their direct contact with working class communities and their role as "agents of state policy" contributed to politicizing them, catalyzing their feminism. Also, there was often overlapping membership between these and other organizations in which Paulina Luisi was involved, such as the National League of Ladies Against Alcoholism and the Women's Commission of the Uruguayan League Against Tuberculosis, which brought together middle- and upper-class women of different political and ideological tendencies around shared concerns.

Legislative Initiatives and the Founding of Women's Rights Organizations

Paulina Luisi founded the CNM-U shortly after Colorado legislators submitted the first bills to reform women's civil and political rights and just as the government was planning a constitutional convention to consider universal male suffrage and other reforms. She organized a second association, the Alianza Uruguaya para el Sufragio de la Mujer (Uruguayan Alliance for Women's Suffrage), as the Congress began discussion of women's municipal level suffrage. All told, the Congress entertained at least five bills on women's civil rights and two on suffrage between 1914 and 1929; these women's organizations lobbied for most of them.

Colorado Party deputies introduced three relevant bills during 1914. The first, submitted by Horacio Maldonado, was on the property rights of working wives.[17] The 1908 Montevideo census had revealed that women constituted 17% of the economically active population (Rodríguez and Sapriza 1984, 32). Inspired by the recent reforms in Germany and France, the bill gave married women the right to manage and dispose of reserved property – the earnings and assets acquired through their exercise of a profession or occupation – and the ability to participate in relevant lawsuits. Maldonado expected the bill to benefit poor working wives whose irresponsible husbands dissipated their hard-earned wages.

Legal scholar Hector Miranda introduced a complementary bill to enhance all women's civil rights.[18] It removed discriminatory language in the civil, commercial and procedural codes so that women could serve as witnesses, guardians, executors of estates, hold power of attorney and represent others and serve as commercial agents and notary publics. According to Miranda, "the minimum feminist program … is civil equality of the sexes, a prior step to women's political rights."[19] He argued that it was "absurd that to the natural advantages men have on many counts, they add artificial advantages based on privileges and prohibitive laws."[20]

Hector Miranda along with Cesar Miranda and two other Colorado deputies introduced a third bill, on women's political rights, which gave women the same political rights as men.[21] It was supported by a lengthy justification, which argued that it was "unjust, irrational and unconstitutional" to deny women the vote, as well as detrimental to the public welfare and social progress.[22] The only evidence of women's support for this bill at this time was several articles by Julia Arévalo in *El Socialista* (Ehrick 2005, 65).

The commission on codes produced a favorable report on Miranda's civil rights bill but did not further consider the other two.[23] It added an article that required wives to have their husbands' permission for them to exercise any of the civil functions or professions delineated in the bill. It explained that "the rights of women should be explicitly subordinated to the superior interests of the species, of the family and for humanity."[24] In other words, while the commission was ready to expand women's civil rights and public role, it was committed to potestad marital as the foundation of marriage.

17 *Diario de Sesiones de la Honorable Cámara de Representantes* (DSCR) (1915, session 230, 144–6). For the restrictions on wives and the marital regime, see Uruguay (1868, arts. 127–144, 1900–1940); these were unchanged in its next code, Uruguay (1893).
18 DSCR (1915, 231, 382–3).
19 DSCR (1915, 382).
20 DSCR (1915, 383).
21 DSCR (1915, 233, 228–50).
22 DSCR (1915, 228).
23 This June 1915 report is in DSCR (1918, 265, 371–3).
24 DSCR (1918, 371).

The Colorado Party was planning to hold a constitutional convention and in anticipation wanted to expand the size of the electorate in support of a democratic process. The 1915 electoral law instituted universal male suffrage, dropping the literacy requirement (Zeballos 2015, 142). The objectives of the 1917 Constitutional Convention were to formally separate church and state, to institute a rotating presidency among a plural governing council and to enshrine universal male suffrage.[25] Irrespective of his support for women's political rights in principle,[26] Batlle's proposal for constitutional reform did not include women's suffrage since he feared it would be too divisive (Vanger 2010, 50). It was the two Socialist Party delegates, Emilio Frugoni and Celestino Minelli who raised the issue at the Convention,[27] arguing unsuccessfully that the text on citizenship replace "men" with the term "person" to leave the door open for female suffrage.[28]

Women had not mobilized to demand their civil or political rights up to this time, although some women were politically active (Rodríguez and Sapriza 1984, 61). The debate around the electoral law and in the subsequent Constitutional Convention was the impetus behind Paulina Luisi's founding of the CNM-U in 1916, which then became ICW's second Latin American member. It was an umbrella organization of existing women's associations, including some of the recently formed social assistance organizations, and included women of different political tendencies. Between elected and institutional members, some 43 women served on the CNM-U's initial governing council.[29] Among those elected were several who had been part of the earlier Federation section, such as Francisca Beretervide and Isabel Pinto, with Luisi serving as president (Cuadro 2018, 185).

Among the first acts of the CNM-U was to send a petition to the Convention in support of women's civil and political rights, signed by 55 women (*Acción Femenina* 1917, 1, 7). It was in response to a comment made during its deliberations

25 Between presidential terms, Batlle spent four years in Europe and was much impressed by the Swiss form of government that served as the model for his proposed reform of the executive branch. The reform also instituted proportional representation and the secret ballot (Vanger 2010).

26 In a 1912 article in his newspaper, *El Día,* under his pseudonym of "Laura," Batlle viewed women's political rights as a long-term proposition that would result once women had more education and experience in the public realm; Rodríguez and Sapriza (1984, 58) and Ehrick (2005, 74). Giordano (2013) considers that he came to support women's suffrage more actively after his European stay.

27 *Diario de Sesiones de la H. Convención N. Constituyente de la República Oriental del Uruguay, 1916–1917* (DSCC), vol. II, 340–508; and Lavrin (1995, 325–8).

28 Ehrick (2005, 133) says that this constitution did not exclude women from citizenship, but article 7 explicitly defines citizens as men (Uruguay 1918). The Electoral Court recognized women's citizenship in the late 1920s; see comments by Senator Claudio Viera, *Diario de Sesiones de la Cámara del Senado* (DSCS) (1932, 156 (87), December 12, 373–5).

29 At the time of its first assembly in June 1917, the CNM-U had nine institutional members, including two Catholic-affiliated organizations. It invited the Socialist Women's Group and the recently formed Comité de Damas Coloradas (Colorado Party Ladies Committee) to join but they declined (*Acción Femenina* 1917, 1, 1; Ehrick 2005, 130).

that Uruguayan women had not shown interest in suffrage.[30] Over subsequent weeks, more petitions arrived by women demanding suffrage, some the result of a petition drive among women factory workers by the Socialist Women's Group.[31] According to Delegate Frugoni, these petitions showed that suffrage was supported not only by "the most representative and prestigious of feminine intellectual circles of the Republic" but also by women workers.[32] A petition followed from the recently formed Comité de Damas Coloradas Pro Batlle-Viera, with 322 adherents.[33]

Meanwhile, the drafting commission reached a political compromise whereby the legislature could extend the vote to women in the future through a two-thirds vote.[34] While intending to facilitate women's suffrage when appropriate by not requiring a constitutional amendment, it in fact raised the bar. Delegate Minelli argued that under the existing constitution, the legislature could enfranchise women by majority vote; the requirement of a two-thirds majority would only make it that much more difficult.[35]

According to Silvia Rodríguez and Graciela Sapriza (1984, 64), it was not just conservatives who opposed women's political participation that led to postponement of their political rights but also because many Colorado Party members were indifferent, being concerned about women's alleged political conservatism. Nonetheless, the fact that the constitutional convention even discussed women's suffrage and that the new constitution's article 10 explicitly mentioned such raised the expectations of feminists that it was achievable in the not-too-distant future.

In the following years, the CNM-U focused on building broader support for women's suffrage while pursuing other issues through its 15 commissions. These reflected the widespread interests of its members, with some commissions dedicated to furthering a social assistance agenda, while others focused on promoting women's civil and political rights (Ehrick 2005, 132–33). Its initial program did not go into much detail on the reform of women's civil rights, besides calling for equality between the sexes in civil law.[36] The plan of activities of its commission on legislation, chaired by CNM-U's executive secretary, Francisca Beretervide, included studying how the various codes discriminated against women; sponsoring lectures and short courses on the relevancy of the law to women; publishing popular education materials on these topics; and lobbying for legislation.

Another commission, led by Luisa Luisi, focused on women in the liberal professions. It compiled a list of those that either excluded women because they were

30 DSCC (1916–1917, vol. II, 343, 356–7).
31 DSCC (1916–1917, vol. II, 390–1, 408–9, 460–1, 500, 502).
32 DSCC (1916–1917, vol. II, 446).
33 DSCC (1916–1917, vol. II, 508).
34 DSCC (1916–1917, vol. III, 85–9).
35 This requirement ended up being of the total members of each chamber and not just those present at the vote, making its attainment even more difficult; see Uruguay (1918, art. 10).
36 "Programa del Consejo Nacional de Mujeres," reproduced in Luisi (1930, 207–11); *Acción Femenina* (1917, 1, 27–37).

only open to citizens or because of specific prohibitions and lobbied to get these overturned. The CNM-U also launched campaigns against alcoholism, tuberculosis and the White Slave trade, and promoted childcare and child health initiatives. Paulina Luisi edited its periodical, *Acción Femenina*, which kept members informed of the organization's activities. Its pages included critiques of how the civil code discriminated against women and occasional letters by women on the code's detrimental effects.

During 1918, Colorado deputies submitted two more bills that sought to end specific forms of discrimination against women. Cesar Miranda submitted a modest bill to amend the commercial code to end the prohibition on women being commercial agents.[37] He reasoned that if women could be traders and merchants, why should they not engage in related commercial activities. José Salgado presented a broader bill to allow women with the appropriate qualifications to exercise any profession, including government positions and academic posts.[38] He argued that it was incongruous that so many women were now beginning to graduate from secondary and technical schools and university but once they completed their training found that they could not follow their chosen career path because of their sex.

The leadership of the CNM-U followed up with a petition to the Chamber urging its approval of all the bills dealing with women's property and civil rights proposed since 1914. It subsequently sent a delegation to meet with President Feliciano Viera (Batlle's successor, also a Colorado) to urge him to include these bills in the upcoming congressional special session (*Acción Femenina* 1918, 5–6, 88–90). Nonetheless, all of these proposals died in committee (*Acción Femenina* 1919, 265, 370–3).

Paulina Luisi summarized her thinking at the time in a speech she delivered at the Ateneo in Montevideo in late 1918 and early the next year to the Unión Feminista Nacional in Buenos Aires. She argued that women needed the vote now and should not wait to demand it until that day that men considered them "sufficiently prepared to participate in civil life" or they had civil rights (Luisi 1919, 4). She explained that feminists did not plan to abandon the home or their children:[39]

> We are the first to demand the recognition of maternity as the principal mission of women and their primordial duty, and if we ask for intervention in the management of public affairs it is not to preach to women about their duties but to give them a means to meet these in all their nobleness and complexity and with full awareness of their critical influence on the future of the human race.
>
> *(Luisi 1919, 8)*

37 DSCR (1918, 263, 203).

38 DSCR (1918, 320–1).

39 See Osta (2023) on how feminist maternalism shaped the debate on suffrage.

In other words, women needed the vote to meet their responsibilities and to reach their full human potential: "The vote and only the vote gives sufficient power to ask and be heard, to propose and be considered; to demand and have those demands met" (Luisi 1919, 7). Otherwise, she concluded, women would continue to wait for reforms crucial to them.

Encouraging to Luisi was that President Viera proposed a bill allowing women to vote and stand for office in municipal elections (*Acción Femenina* 1919, 22, 132). Although Viera thought the legislature had debated women's suffrage sufficiently that granting it at the local level would not require much further discussion, it proved controversial. The version the Chamber approved excluded mention of women; the Senate then failed to act on it.[40] During Viera's presidency, the only law approved that strengthened women's property rights was one creating the Postal Savings Bank in 1919, which allowed "all persons, irrespective of age or civil status" to open an account in their own name and make deposits and withdrawals.[41] Designed to instill the habit of savings among the working class, it had the inadvertent effect of giving wives greater control over their earnings.[42]

Ostensibly because she felt the need to have a separate organization to focus on women's suffrage, Paulina Luisi founded the Alianza Uruguaya para el Sufragio de la Mujer in 1919, which became IWSA's first Latin American affiliate. In an editorial in *Acción Femenina* (1919, 22, 119–23), Luisi explained how the Alianza grew out of the CNM-U's commission on suffrage; Carmen Cuesta de Nari, the head of that commission, became the Alianza's first president, with Luisi serving as secretary for external relations. One of its first acts was to write Congress in support of including women's suffrage in the municipal elections bill.[43]

According to Lavrin (1995, 334–5), Luisi's international commitments and absence from Montevideo along with personality conflicts led to tensions within the CNM-U, which led her to establish this new organization. There were also ideological and political differences between Luisi and Isabel Pinto in particular. Pinto was an avid Batllista, whereas Luisi was sympathetic to socialist positions although not a party member (Ehrick 2005, 134–6).

When Baltasar Brum, an advocate of women's rights, assumed the presidency in 1919, Luisi lost no time in lobbying him for women's civil and political rights.[44] She asked for the prompt approval of the 1914 bills that had languished in the

40 DSCR (1919, 275, 507–9, 519; 1919, 276, 308).

41 Law 6888, February 27, 1919; www.impo.com.uy/bases/leyes-originales/6888-1919.

42 This law is perhaps why Luisi was able to report to the 1920 IWSA Congress that among Uruguay's accomplishments was that "women disposed freely of their earnings" (*Acción Femenina* 1920, 34–5, 171). In my review of the labor legislation of this period (in which many consider Uruguay a pioneer), I did not find any evidence of married women workers attaining the right to receive and manage their own wages, a measure Chile enacted in 1924.

43 DSCR (1919, 274, 466).

44 Giordano (2012, 89) also stresses how Luisi always advocated in support of both civil and political rights.

legislature, specifically Maldonado's bill on married women's property rights and Hector Miranda's on women's other civil rights. Shortly after, the Chamber began debate on the revised Miranda civil rights bill.[45]

Several National Party deputies were reluctant to expand women's civil rights. Deputy Aureliano Rodríguez Larreta, for example, was willing to vote in favor of the Miranda bill but no other legislation related to women's rights. As he put it:

> ...in what concerns feminism, it is necessary to walk with lead feet. It appears to me that this tendency to try to make women into men, giving them all the rights and obligations of men, will even conspire against population growth...This is a serious matter. If women dedicate themselves to the activities and occupations of men, they will lose their enchantments and marriages are going to decrease.[46]

His main concern was that the expansion of women's civil rights might lead to women considering themselves citizens and begin to press for political rights.

Whether strengthening women's civil rights would lead to political rights generated much debate, since a sizable number of deputies were willing to accept the former but not the latter. As Deputy Ismael Cortinas noted, "The equality of civil rights is a remedy to injustices that are actually quite shocking, while equality of political rights is what will convert women into real *marimachos* ...."[47] He acknowledged that many women wanted civil rights, not just a vocal few, either because of their convictions or because of the limitations that they experienced in daily life.

Even though the deputies approved the first six articles of the revised bill, the discussion on the floor got bogged down over two issues: whether women needed to be citizens to exercise certain professions, such as notary public, and whether wives could exercise the various professions or functions without the approval of their husbands.[48] Some were concerned that being a guardian or a commercial agent might require a married woman to make a contract, and the civil code prevented wives from doing so without their husbands' permission; hence, these provisions were in contradiction. Deputy Salgado noted that the whole point of the Miranda reform was to allow married women to play these roles without requiring their husbands' approval; i.e., that they needed full civil capacity. He tried to assure the deputies that once they considered the revised version of the Maldonado bill on women's property rights, there would be no contradiction between the proposed expansion of their civil rights and the marital regime. Most of the deputies remained unconvinced and after much discussion, the Chamber tabled the bill until the commission presented its report, which did not happen before the end of this session of Congress.

45 DSCR (1919, 270, 311–19; 271, 14–34).
46 DSCR (1919, 23).
47 DSCR (1919, 27).
48 DSCR (1919, 267–73).

To keep the issue of suffrage alive, the Alianza and the CNM-U jointly drafted their own bill on political rights that Deputy César Miranda presented to the Chamber in 1920. It contained two articles that women at age 20 or older could vote and stand for office in local elections and that after two years from the law's promulgation, they could vote in national elections (Onetti 1930, 56). The commission on legislation promptly rejected their proposal. It demonstrates, nonetheless, the thinking of feminists at the time, first, their willingness to accept partial suffrage as an interim measure, and second, their commitment to working for women's civil and political rights simultaneously.

President Brum (1923, 5–6) finally decided to get directly involved in the reform effort, asking the study group of Colorado Party legislators who met weekly to give priority to women's civil and political rights. He himself took on the drafting, presenting his first report to the group in June 1921 along with a draft bill entitled "Women's Civil and Political Rights." It consisted of only four articles: two on women's right to vote and stand for office at the municipal and national level under the same conditions as men; one establishing that "before the law, women are equal to men"; and a final article abrogating any article in the code contrary to these rights (Brum 1923, 19). The lengthy exposition of motives focused primarily on why women should have the vote.[49]

The next year Brum (1923, 65–178) presented his even lengthier treatise on the reform of family law, with a detailed commentary on each article requiring modification or deletion, as well as corresponding changes in the civil procedure, penal and commercial codes. His basic approach was to establish a symmetry of rights and duties between men and women, thus both husband and wife represented the household, managed its affairs and exercised shared patria potestad over their children, all fairly radical ideas at the time.

The way he addressed the administration of the conjugal society was rather unusual. Under the existing code, at marriage, women lost the property rights they exercised as single women, since husbands – without their consent – automatically became their representative and managed their individual property as well as the community property. Brum found this unacceptable and proposed maintaining the default regime of partial community property but making it subject to the presumption that the wife gave the husband an explicit or tacit mandate to administer her assets and the community property and to represent her. The wife could reclaim her right to manage her own assets and co-manage the community property at any time during the marriage. His solution, of presuming the woman's consent to the husband's administration, was a novel way of making the principle of gender equality in marriage compatible with existing practice and sensibilities.

49 The Colorado Party began to discuss women's suffrage at its 1920 party congress and it incorporated the aim of women's equal civil and political rights into its 1922 platform (Rodríguez and Sapriza 1984, 46).

Brum also provided couples with flexibility in managing their economic affairs. In a prenuptial agreement, they could make any arrangement they so wished; thus prior to marriage, they could establish the joint administration of community property with joint representation of the household or the full separation of property; moreover, they could contract for the latter at any point during the marriage. He also wanted to guarantee that working wives be able to control their own earnings and proposed adopting the concept of women's reserved property but with a new twist. Given his commitment to gender equality, he felt compelled to extend this same privilege to husbands. He thus proposed that under any regime, if a person exercised an occupation, they could manage such earnings as if in the regime of separation of property; at its end, the assets acquired by either spouse constituted gananciales, pooled and divided equally. In addition, his proposal established the same conditions for divorce (the adultery of either was sufficient grounds) and allowed all women to be witnesses and guardians. The study group endorsed Brum's proposed reforms, and two Colorado deputies submitted the bill to the Chamber in early 1923.[50] This bill also died in committee.

The relationship between the CNM-U and the Alianza was initially tight,[51] but tensions continued to fester and in 1921, Luisi stepped down from the CNM-U presidency, with Isabel Pinto assuming it.[52] Ehrick (2005, 139–43) shows how the profiles of the members of these two organizations became increasingly distinct. Those in the CNM-U were older, more elite women whereas younger, middle-class and professional women gravitated toward the Alianza. There was also a growing political divide, with those in the Alianza increasingly viewed as anti-Batllista, since most of its membership consisted of either Riveristas or socialists.[53] Nevertheless, the leaders of both organizations were close to President Brum and encouraged his efforts on behalf of women's political and civil rights (*Acción Femenina* 1922, 43–46, 70; 47, 15).

Besides women's suffrage, in its initial years the Alianza focused on women's participation on government advisory councils such as those on education and public assistance as a way for them to assert citizenship and strengthen their claim for

50 DSCR (1923, 305, 124–6). The submitted bill differed only slightly from the January 1923 draft presented in Brum (1923, 15–7).

51 The names of both organizations appeared in the masthead of *Acción Femenina*, but this lasted only from issues 27 through 36 of 1920. Publication of the newsletter then stopped until March–May 1922, when it resumed only under the name of the CNM-U.

52 After her resignation as president, Luisi remained as CNM-U's external secretary (the link to the ICW) but later resigned. There was an apparent rapprochement in 1925; the last issue of *Acción Femenina* focused on Luisi's pioneering role in Uruguayan feminism (Ehrick 2005, 145).

53 Among the noted Riveristas in the Alianza were Fanny Carrió and Sofía Álvarez Vignoli de Demicheli whose husbands were leaders of this Colorado faction. Álvarez Vignoli, who joined after having been a leader in the Catholic youth group at the Women's University, would become one of two women elected senators in 1942. In the 1920s, there were five socialist women in the Alianza (Ehrick 2005, 142).

full political rights. Moreover, growing numbers of women had the expertise to serve in such positions (Onetti 1930, 56; Cuadro 2018, 197–8). In 1923 the Alianza changed its name, dropping the part on suffrage, to become the Alianza Uruguaya de Mujeres, in a move parallel to IWSA's broadening purpose and subsequent name change.[54] Thereafter, it pursued an even broader agenda, addressing labor, educational and moral issues.[55]

Its platform demanding equal civil rights became more specific, for example, regarding the property rights of wives, it demanded that they be able to manage their own earnings and assets and "be emancipated from men's guardianship" (i.e., the end of potestad marital). It asked that married women have the same rights as adult single women to pursue employment without need for anyone's permission. It also called for the equal rights of parents over their legitimate children; the same standard for adultery for both sexes as grounds for divorce; and for women to have similar access as men to all industrial, administrative, judicial and government positions.

The Alianza mounted a successful campaign to rescind the prohibition on women being witnesses and notary publics, which incrementally broadened their civil rights.[56] Also on its agenda was a demand regarding a woman's nationality, that if a woman married someone of a different nationality, she be able to choose whether to maintain or change hers. This point was ambiguous in Uruguay's 1893 Civil Code and the 1918 Constitution, but its 1928 naturalization law cleared it up, perhaps because of pressure from the Alianza.[57]

Paulina Luisi's international activities and stature continued to grow during the 1920s. Her international involvement began through Pan Americanism when she attended the First Pan American Scientific Conference held in Santiago in late 1908 (Swiggett 1916, Appendix A). Following the organization of the International Women's Pan American Committee that resulted from the Ladies Auxiliary Conference of the 1915 Second Pan American Scientific Conference, CNM-U members Luisi, Carmen Cuesta and Anita de Monteverde served as its Uruguayan representatives, with some 20 women participating on the local committee (Cuadro 2018, 238–43).[58]

54 First proposed at its 1920 Geneva congress when its focus broadened beyond suffrage, IWSA's name changed in 1926 to the International Alliance of Women for Suffrage and Equal Citizenship (IAWSEC). Among the priorities announced at its 1923 Rome congress were attaining the right of mothers over their children and women being able to maintain their nationality when they married someone with a different one (IAW 2005, 76; Cuadro 2018, 199–201).

55 "Programa de la Alianza Uruguaya de Mujeres" in Luisi (1930, 199–206). The date the Alianza adopted this platform is not clear; Lavrin (1995, 340) refers to it as a second edition of its platform.

56 Law 8.000, October 14, 1926, that modified the Ley Orgánica Notarial; mentioned by Cassina (1990, 84) and Ehrick (2005, 138).

57 Law 8.196, February 10, 1928; www.impo.com.uy/bases/leyes/8196-1928.

58 This international committee was responsible for organizing the parallel women's auxiliary conference held in conjunction with the Third Pan American Scientific Congress in Lima in 1924. While invited to form part of the organizing committee, Luisi did not attend although some Uruguayan women sent papers.

Invited to the First Pan American Women's Conference organized by National League of Women Voters in Baltimore in 1922, Luisi did not attend. She sent Cecilia Paladino de Vitale as the Alianza's representative along with a proposal to create a Pan American Association of Women (Adams 1922, 12; Marino 2019, 22–5). PAAAW emerged from this conference, with Carrie Chapman Catt and Luisi serving as honorary president and vice president, respectively. When Catt visited Uruguay in January 1923 as part of her South American tour, Luisi was out of the country and the CNM-U hosted Catt's visit, which included an interview with President Baltazar Brum (Cuadro 2018, 243–7).[59]

Luisi became increasingly wary of Pan Americanism, largely because it was a US-led initiative in a period of growing anti-imperialist sentiment as a result of repeated US interventions in Central America and the Caribbean (Cuadro 2018, 247, 254). She thus became involved with the Liga Internacional de Mujeres Ibéricas e Hispanoamericanas (LIMIH), whose primary objective was to promote unity among "la raza" (Hispanic women), to counter the influence of US-based feminism.[60] Luisi served as this association's second vice-president but attended only one of the conferences that it co-sponsored, the 1928 Buenos Aires Women's International Congress hosted by the Club Argentina de Mujeres, where she spoke on behalf of the IAWSEC (Cuadro 2018, 268, 264).

Luisi's most consistent participation was in IWSA/IAWSEC, attending three of its four international congresses during the 1920s and serving a term as second vice president (Cuadro 2018, 230–7). In addition, she participated in multiple League of Nations activities, serving as Uruguay's delegate to the League's commission on the protection of infancy and youth and representing the government at several other international forums (Ehrick 2005, 105–6). The Uruguayan press widely reported her international activities, which assisted in normalizing feminist initiatives on behalf of women's civil and political rights.

The Push for Both Civil and Political Rights

To build momentum for women's suffrage, the Alianza and the CNM-U joined together as the Asociaciones Feministas (Feminist Associations) to host a one-day conference in late 1929. Subsequently, Colorado Party legislators submitted bills on women's civil and political rights and Congress passed the women's suffrage law in 1932. While the Senate approved a civil rights bill, the Chamber did not consider it before the president dismissed the Congress.

In 1929, the IAWSEC launched a global campaign to promote women's suffrage, urging governments to recognize women's political rights. The Feminist

59 According to Catt (1923a), Uruguayan feminists were among the most enthusiastic that she met on her trip. Some 200 met her at the docks when she arrived and 125 showed up to bid her farewell.

60 On LIMIH, see Chapter 6. On Luisi's tensions with feminists in the United States and Europe who looked down on those from elsewhere, see Ehrick (1998).

Associations sent its campaign letter to the Consejo Nacional de Administración (CNA, National Council of Administration)[61] and the Chamber, asking them to follow-up on article 10 of the constitution that allowed the legislature to cede women political rights (Luisi 1930, 181–9). The CNA subsequently urged Congress to do so, saying that "the constitution of the Republic incorporates the principle of the right of women to suffrage at the national or municipal level."[62] Moreover, in a news conference, Luis Alberto de Herrera, the leader of the National Party and a member of the CNA, expressed his support for women's suffrage. The objective of the December 1929 conference was to draw attention to these encouraging developments and demonstrate women's keen interest in securing political rights.

The conference included 11 presentations by well-known women in a variety of professions, chosen to highlight distinct aspects of the importance of giving women the vote and what they might do with it. Paulina Luisi, who chaired the organizing committee, gave the opening address where she highlighted how women now had equal civil rights in 25 and either partial or full political rights in 35 countries. Many of the presentations stressed one of the main themes of her talk, how men and women's priorities often differed, and that optimal legislation required women's input.

Several papers contained critiques of the country's civil code and the many ways that it subordinated women, especially wives. Luisa Machado Bonet de Abella, Uruguay's first female notary public, stressed how unjust it was for a working woman to save her earnings to purchase an asset, only to have her husband sell it without her consent and do as he pleased with the proceeds. Since he was legally the sole administrator of the conjugal society, he was totally within his rights to ignore her wishes (Luisi 1930, 127–130). Law student Olivia de Vasconcellos went into detail on the irrationality behind women's legal incapacity; for example, the rules of the civil code excluded a sister of legal age from being a guardian of her siblings in favor of someone who was not a relative (Luisi 1930, 151–5). Writer Laura Cortinas concluded her presentation on the injustices against women by asking, "how will we get civil rights if men are the only ones who legislate?" (Luisi 1930, 115–6).

The conference organizing committee acknowledged that participants held diverse positions regarding civil and political rights and their timing. Some favored securing women's civil rights prior to aspiring to the vote, while others wanted stronger property rights but were less interested in suffrage (Luisi 1930, 11–23). The committee, nonetheless, maintained the Alianza's earlier position that aimed for both while considering political rights a precondition to obtaining full civil

61 The CNA was the collective executive incorporated into the 1918 Constitution. "Mensaje enviado por la Comisión Directiva de la Alianza Internacional para los Derechos Ciudadanos de las Mujeres," June 1929, in Luisi (1930, 191–4).

62 "Mensaje del Consejo Nacional de Administración con motivo de la nota de la Alianza Internacional," November 6, 1929, in Luisi (1930, 195–7).

rights. If women had the vote, then "showing our weight at the polls, it will be easy to make the necessary modifications in our civil code. Without political rights we will always be dependent on men's will and criteria …" (Luisi 1930, 21).

The Feminist Associations maintained momentum by continuing the suffrage petition campaign begun at this meeting, holding public forums and keeping the issue alive in the press (Cassina 1990, 7–10; Ehrick 2005, 146). This was the context in which in July 1930 Colorado Deputy Alfeo Brum presented a bill on women's political rights in the Chamber,[63] and Colorado Senator Pablo M. Minelli presented one on women's civil rights in the Senate.

The Minelli Bill on Women's Civil Rights

The bill on "Women's Civil Rights," developed by the Senate's commission on legislation under the leadership of Minelli, combined aspects of Brum's earlier proposal with some of the measures in Argentina's 1926 law.[64] The commission's report considered the current legal status of women outdated since it did not reflect the country's level of development, women's growing labor force participation and their role in public life. Moreover, Uruguay was falling behind other countries, specifically Argentina. The Commission found "no reason to maintain any civil inequalities with respect to men" as regards women who were single, divorced or widowed. The bill thus eliminated all restrictions on their activities in the civil code, code of civil procedures and commercial code so that their civil rights were equal to those of men.[65] It also allowed married women to conduct these same civil acts and public functions although for some they still required their husbands' authorization.

The Commission observed how "all the great nations" had reformed married women's property rights, and that England and many US states had gone furthest by giving wives, under the separation of property regime, "absolutely liberty" with respect to their own earnings and assets. Rather than proposing it as the default regime, they wanted to modify the existing conjugal society in two ways, by recognizing the reserved property of working wives and by allowing wives who so wished to manage the assets they brought to marriage. Instituting reserved property meant that wives would no longer require their husband's authorization to pursue a profession or any occupation, to manage the product of their labor or the assets acquired with these earnings, or to join a cooperative or an association; they could appear in suits regarding this property. At the dissolution of the conjugal society, the gananciales from such activities were community property. Their rationale was

63 DSCR (1930, 364, 90).

64 DSCS (1930, 60, 395–439); and in Pinto (1951, 52–108), along with the bill finally approved by the Senate.

65 The only sex-based difference maintained was in the age a person could leave home without parental authorization, which was 21 for men and reduced from 30 to 25 for women.

that "if a married woman was in a position to create wealth with the product of her labor, nothing should constrain her civil capacity with regards to the disposition or administration of such wealth."[66] Minelli expected this measure would prevent abuses by husbands, reduce marital conflict and increase the incentives for women to join the labor force.

With respect to the assets that a woman brought to marriage or inherited (termed *bienes dotales*), the bill proposed that, in principle, these were hers to manage and dispose of freely; however, unless she declared her intention to manage these in a special registry, these assets remained under her husband's management. He could not sell or mortgage them without her consent. This proposal was similar to what Brum had proposed and moreover, like what Argentina had adopted. The gananciales or community property remained under the husband's management.[67] The bill also gave wives the right to declare a total separation of property at any time, without need for justification. The commission rejected Brum's idea that both spouses should have this right, since it considered that equivalent rights assumed equivalent economic and social positions, which was hardly the case, reflecting the thinking of feminism of compensation. Hence, it proposed only women could declare the separation of property as a way of protecting their gananciales from the marriage, just as in this proposal only women had the right to reserved property, not both spouses as in Brum's.

Other advances included eliminating the clause that wives owed their husbands obedience and replacing it with the obligation of mutual protection and support; both spouses determining the couple's domicile; and allowing wives to be executors and receive inheritances or donations without need for a husband's permission. The bill, nonetheless, maintained fathers' patria potestad over children, although in their absence, mothers automatically exercised this right and on the same terms; if either parent widowed and remarried, they maintained their previous rights.

When the bill finally came up for discussion the next year, some conservatives voiced serious misgivings over its scope. National Party senator Juan Bautista Morelli was ready to recognize the equal civil rights of single women but opposed reducing the civil incapacity of wives.[68] He especially objected to wives being able to work without their husbands' permission:

> There are certain obligations that are indispensable…How could it be that a husband not have the right to oppose that she stop nursing a child…or stop caring for the children or their pre-school education? And even more so during pregnancy, the husband has the right to oppose that she engages in a profession

66 DSCS (1930, 60, 407).

67 Unlike Brum's proposal, there was no provision for the joint management of either the wife's property or community property or shared household headship.

68 DDCS (1932, vol. 155, 155–60).

or occupation that could compromise its success, for the superior purpose of matrimony is procreation.[69]

To safeguard the interests of the family, he proposed that a wife need her husband's permission to work although if he denied it, she could appeal to a judge for authorization. The Senate, nonetheless, approved the original wording of the article on reserved property.

Conservatives were successful in modifying the bill's intention to give wives the option of fully and autonomously managing the assets they brought to marriage. Senator Eduardo Rodríguez Larreta was concerned that under the old rules of the dowry if a husband sold his wife's immovable asset without her consent, he had to restitute its value at the end of the marriage; under the proposed new rules, since the wife managed her own property the husband was not accountable. Thus, a husband might persuade his wife to sell an asset to solve his own business problem when it was not in her interest to do so, and he had no obligation to compensate her if he later lost this money. In the interest of protecting them, the senator wanted wives to obtain the approval of a judge to be able to alienate their property.[70]

Other senators agreed that husbands tended to dominate marital decisions and that wives needed protection against their potentially unscrupulous behavior. Senator Minelli opposed this amendment since it undermined the intent of the reform. He argued that one must assume that wives who opted to manage their own assets had sufficient competence to know what was in their interest. The commission eventually recommended adoption of Rodríguez Larreta's amendment as a safeguard on the actions of either spouse regarding women's immovable property. If a husband administered his wife's assets, he could not alienate these without her consent and the approval of a judge; if the wife managed them (or under the separation of property), she also needed a judge's approval. Minelli reluctantly accepted the commission's recommendation since it placed wives in an inferior position to those in Argentina and did not meet international standards.[71] This amendment was the only substantive change to Minelli's original bill, which the Senate approved in June 1932 and sent to the Chamber.[72]

Why Women's Suffrage Came First

While Deputy Alfeo Brum's 1930 bill on women's political rights never made it out of committee, a consensus in favor of women's suffrage was slowly building. The National Party added it to its platform, expecting an expansion in the size of the electorate to favor it, and Catholic groups also began to support it (Lavrin 1995,

69 DDCS (1932, vol. 155, 160).
70 DDCS (1932, vol. 155, 164–7).
71 DDCS (1932, vol. 155, 176–7).
72 DDCS (1932, vol. 155, 314–8), and for the approved version, 350–6.

339–43; Ehrick 2005, 169). Moreover, the economic upheaval of the Great Depression fostered new political alignments. The two major parties each splintered – the Colorados, between Batllistas and supporters of Gabriel Terra (elected president in 1930), and the Nacionales, between those favorable or opposed to long-time leader Luis Alberto de Herrera – foreshadowing the tensions that would lead to the 1933 coup (Sapriza 2011, 384–6).

Having garnered 4,300 signatures, the Alianza found the moment fortuitous to deliver its suffrage petition to Congress (Cuadro 2018, 237). It then formed a new umbrella group, the Comité Pro-Derechos Civiles y Políticos de la Mujer (Committee for Women's Civil and Political Rights or Women's Rights Committee), in 1932 to coordinate the activities of all the organizations backing women's suffrage. Sara Rey Álvarez, secretary-general of the Alianza, assumed coordination of the 23 women's and mixed-sex organizations that joined the campaign. She led a vigorous lobbying effort, meeting with the presidents of the two Chambers and the Chamber's legislation commission as well as with President Terra (Lavrin 1995, 343; Cuadro 2018, 216, 237).[73]

The Senate acted first. Lorenzo Batlle Pacheco (the son of former president José Batlle) and Pablo M. Minelli of the Batllista faction introduced a bill recognizing women's political rights at the national and municipal levels.[74] Minelli referred to how the Senate had just passed the women's civil rights bill and that there was no reason for it not to also approve granting women suffrage. The argument that they were unprepared to vote and hold office no longer was valid. Chastising his Colorado Party colleagues, he argued that women's political rights were not about whether they were more conservative or religious than men, it was "not a matter of convenience but of justice, irrespective of the results …."[75] He stressed how "women have their own interests and rights to defend" and that while the Senate-approved bill on women's civil rights was a major step forward, it did not give wives equal rights in marriage. The code would require further reform, which required women's input.

The commission on legislation then began working on the changes required in the electoral law to accommodate women's suffrage, to include these in the same bill. Minelli and Claudio Viera of the National Party presented the revised bill to the Senate in December 1932 and urged its approval.[76] Viera reported that the Electoral Court had already solved affirmatively the question of whether women were citizens constitutionally, a prerequisite for suffrage. The only opposition was by National Party Senator Luciano Macedo who stated that while a woman "is not

73 In a speech to the American Ladies Club of Montevideo in September 1934, Rey emphasized that women attained suffrage only because of the dedicated lobbying of the Committee on Women's Rights (*Ideas y Acción* 1934, 30, 3).

74 DSCS (1932, 156, 109).

75 DSCS (1932, 156, 109).

76 DSCS (1932, 373–5).

a man's slave, she is born for the home, not politics."[77] Although it went against his personal convictions, in solidarity with his party, he planned to vote in favor of the bill. The Senate approved it that same day, sending it to the Chamber.

Deputies Alfeo Brum and Agustín Minelli immediately introduced a motion to treat the Senate bill as urgent in order to proceed to its discussion without the usual commission report.[78] Since women's suffrage had been under discussion for 20 years and the Senate had managed to approve the bill in one day, Deputy Minelli urged deputies to do likewise. Each of the leaders of the different factions then spoke in favor of the bill, to the applause of the women in the gallery. As Lavrin (1995, 343–4) observes, the most heated debate was over which party could claim credit for advancing women's suffrage. Deputy Eduardo Victor Haedo, a supporter of National leader Herrera, warned that if fellow conservatives did not vote in favor of the bill, the Batllistas would get credit for it rather than Herrera, who had helped turn public opinion in favor of women's suffrage.[79] He also stressed that its attainment represented an achievement of women themselves rather than any political party, recognizing Paulina Luisi's leadership.

Deputies who were hesitant or opposed to the bill focused their objections on not having had sufficient time to study the proposed changes to the electoral law; others viewed this as a delaying tactic and urged a vote. The Chamber ended up approving the bill that same day. Law 8927 on "Women's Civic Rights" gave women equal political rights to men's at the local and national levels; it required both to register to vote at the age of 21 and both could stand for office at that age.[80]

In their analysis of the factors leading to the approval of women's suffrage, Rodríguez and Sapriza (1984) conclude that it had as much to do with the changing political needs and electoral strategies of the political parties as the demands and lobbying of the women's movement. Castillo (2023, 84), nonetheless, emphasizes how by the 1930s it was not clear that any given party would benefit from women's vote, thus strategic considerations were neutral. She, Ehrick (2005) and Cuadro (2018) all note how the 1917 constitutional debate on women's suffrage changed expectations, leading political figures to reckon with the idea that women would eventually gain the vote. With a growing share of women completing secondary schooling, it became difficult to argue that suffrage was unsuitable for women. Moreover, these authors all stress how by the 1920s organized women represented a vocal and visible political force whose demands politicians could no longer ignore.

Why women attained suffrage but not enhanced civil rights at this time is largely because the Chamber ran out of time before the tumultuous economic and political

77 DSCS (1932, 374).
78 DSCR (1932, 381, 124–42).
79 DSCR (1932, 131).
80 Law 8927, *Diario Oficial* 7.909, December 22, 1932, 797. Voting became obligatory with the 1934 Constitution (Uruguay 1934, art. 68).

events of early 1933 led to authoritarian rule. President Terra closed the Congress in March 1933 in an auto-coup. During the discussion of the suffrage bill, however, it was evident that many National Party deputies were ready to approve the civil rights bill.[81] Thus, it was not only intransigent conservative forces who were responsible for the delay in women attaining stronger property rights; the divisions within the Colorado Party that led to the coup played a role as well.

Feminists divided over the coup and formed new alliances. Sofia Álvarez Vignoli, whose husband Alfredo Demicheli was a minister in the Terra government, was among those who signed a manifesto in support of the proposed constitutional reform, the driving issue behind the coup, joining Margarita Uriarte de Herrera, a leader of the Catholic Ladies League and wife of National party leader Luis Alberto de Herrera (Sapriza 2011, 386).

Feminist Initiatives and Incremental Reform

While the events of 1933 divided women politically, momentum toward attainment of equal civil rights continued when Uruguay hosted the 1933 Pan American conference where the CIM presented its Equal Rights Treaty. By then, feminists were developing their own detailed proposals for reform of the marital regime. The enactment of the 1934 Constitution and code of the child met a few of their other demands.

In late 1932, Sara Rey (Figure 8.1), the coordinator of the Women's Rights Committee, founded an autonomous party, the Partido Independiente Democrático Femenino (PIDF, Independent Democratic Women's Party) and in 1933, launched its periodical, *Ideas y Acción*. Attaining women's equal civil rights figured prominently in its ten-point program.[82] Among its demands were for both parents to exercise equal patria potestad over children, the elimination of potestad marital, and that couples be able to choose between the regimes of separation of property or joint administration. What the latter entailed was not very clear, although it seems the PIDF wanted to offer women a choice of regimes and go beyond the Alianza's demand that wives manage their own earnings and assets as they had as single women.[83] Other relevant demands in PIDF's platform were women's access to all professions, occupations and government positions on the same terms as men; equal remuneration for equal work; further expansion in the ability to investigate paternity; and recognition of the equal rights of natural and legitimate children.

81 See the remarks of Amador Sánchez and Anastasio Viera in DSCR (1932, 381, 129, 139).

82 *Ideas y Acción* (1933, 1, 1), which also lays out a 23-point social program and details on its political program. Lavrin (1995, 221, 345–9) says that PIDF's proposals on women's civil rights drew on Brum's original ideas; it did so only in the spirit of equal civil rights, not in terms of the marital regime.

83 The Alianza's general platform is in Luisi (1930, 198–206).

FIGURE 8.1 Uruguayan activist Sara Rey Álvarez (1894–1949), ca. 1930.

Source: Photographer unknown. Courtesy of Schlesinger Library, Harvard Radcliffe Institute.

Sara Rey considered the 1932 Senate-approved Minelli bill an advance but stressed that it fell short of the goal of wives attaining equivalent civil rights to husbands.[84] Foremost in her critique was that it left unchanged a father's right of patria potestad over children during the marriage. She considered the supremacy the code gave fathers unjust because mothers had a stronger biological tie to their children than fathers did and played a critical role in their care. It was also contradictory to social custom, which made wives the pillar of the home. Rey also thought the Minelli bill only minimally strengthened married women's property rights, since it

84 "Los derechos civiles de la mujer. Estudio crítico sobre el proyecto aprobado por el Senado en junio de 1932." *Ideas y Acción* (1933, 10, 1–3).

required them to explicitly declare that they wanted to administer their own property, something they were unlikely to do if it risked producing disharmony in the marriage. In her view, wives should have an automatic right to administer their own assets; if they wished, they could then give their husbands a mandate to manage them but this should be by choice. Moreover, the Minelli bill did not consider the possibility of joint management of community property.[85]

Discussions at the Seventh International Conference of American States held in Montevideo in December 1933 boosted support for strengthening women's civil rights. The CIM had undertaken a detailed study of women's civil and political rights in each country and presented its results along with proposals for an Equal Rights Treaty and a Convention on the Nationality of Women.[86] The wording of the Treaty was as follows: "The contracting states agree that upon the ratification of this treaty men and women shall have equal rights throughout the territory subject to their respective jurisdictions" (Brown 1934, 221).

The Terra government appointed Sofía Álvarez Vignoli as an official delegate and she served on the sub-committee that considered the Equal Rights Treaty. In her impassioned speech in support of a binding treaty, she highlighted how Latin American civil codes were "full of prohibitions on women, which reduce their sphere of action" and that "treat them as retards, idiots and criminals" (Álvarez Vignoli 1934, 21–2). She noted the hypocrisy in the arguments of anti-feminists who defended such restrictions on the grounds of protecting women's femininity. If they wanted to defend women, she asked, why were there not protections for the thousands of working women who labored while pregnant or for those whose husbands appropriated their wages? She argued that an equal rights treaty was the most expeditious means of women achieving four basic rights: recognition of their full rights as mothers (i.e., equal patria potestad); full legal capacity to exercise all civil functions; administration of their own assets; and joint administration of a couple's community property.

The sub-commission rejected the idea of a binding treaty on the grounds that it would impinge on matters of national sovereignty. Nonetheless, it recommended that the conference adopt the following weak resolution, which was subsequently approved:[87]

> ...that [member states] endeavor, so far as the peculiar circumstances of each country will conveniently permit, to establish the maximum of equality between

85 In the above-cited article, Sara Rey mentions that under her direction, the Women's Rights Committee had immediately formed a sub-committee of lawyers to propose an alternative to the Senate-approved bill, one that they were planning to present whenever the Chamber considered the Minelli bill.

86 This 21-volume study (IACW 1933) included an assessment of whether each country's legislation treated men and women equally on over 100 points related to "public" rights, rights in marriage and those of legitimate and illegitimate children.

87 "Informe de la subcomisión," December 12, 1933 (doc. III. No. E), in Doris Stevens Papers, Series V, Sub-Series B. Conferences: Montevideo Conference, Printed Material.

> men and women in all matters pertaining to the possession, enjoyment and exercise of civil and political rights.[88]

Four countries separately endorsed the Equal Rights Treaty – Uruguay, Ecuador, Cuba and Paraguay. In the first three, women already had equal political rights. Ecuador and Cuba had also strengthened married women's property rights although women did not yet have equal civil rights.

To the delight of CIM representatives, the conference approved the Convention on the Nationality of Women. It established that "there will be no distinction based on sex as regards nationality, in their legislation or in their practice."[89] It meant that when women married someone of a different nationality, they had the option of maintaining their own. It represented a major victory for the global women's movement that in international forums had lobbied for this change.[90]

Subsequently, PIDF lobbied the Uruguayan government to ratify the Equal Rights Treaty that it had signed since ratification would require it to remove all inequalities based on sex in the country's codes and other legislation.[91] It also developed a more detailed proposal to attain full legal equality, building on the points mentioned in its founding document.[92] Both marital and familial relations were to be based on equal rights and responsibilities rather than on potestad marital and patria potestad. On the marital regime, husbands would no longer automatically assume the administration of their wives' earnings and assets as well as the gananciales. The new default regime PIDF proposed in 1934 was rather novel, both spouses would jointly manage the individual property of each as well as the community property (termed the *régimen de administración común*), based on equal rights. It also provided couples with alternatives, by mutual consent, each spouse could manage their own earnings and assets (regime of separate administration), or a wife could turn over hers for her husband to manage (regime of marital administration). Irrespective of regime, wives could pursue any profession or form of employment without need for their husbands' authorization.

The PIDF's 1934 proposal also included both parents holding equal rights of patria potestad during the marriage. In the case of separation or divorce,

88 "Derechos civiles y políticos de la mujer [Séptima Conferencia Internacional Americana, Montevideo – 1933], approved December 16, 1933; https://www.dipublico.org/14665/derechos-civiles-y-politicos-de-la-mujer-septima-conferencia-internaciona-americana-montevideo-1933/. Translation from Scott (1934, 222).

89 Translation from Scott (1934, 219).

90 See Bredbenner (1998, chpt. 6) on the background to this treaty, and Marino (2019, 103–13) on the debate at this conference over CIM's future. This conference also strengthened the international ties of Uruguayan feminists. PIDF sponsored a reception for CIM delegates and *Ideas y Acción* interviewed many of them; subsequently, PIDF became a member of the regional organization Unión de Mujeres Americanas.

91 Sara Rey Álvarez, "Los derechos civiles de la mujer" (*Ideas y Acción* 1934, 34, 1).

92 *Ideas y Acción* (1934, 34, 1–2).

guardianship and custody of children under the age of 16 was to remain with the mother irrespective of the child's sex.[93] If a divorced or widowed mother remarried, she was to retain her rights of patria potestad, as fathers currently did if they remarried. If the separation or divorce was due to adultery, the same standard applied to both husbands and wives. The proposal also detailed some of the specific civil functions that women should be able to execute, such as being a guardian, witness and executor of a will, as well the government positions to be open to them on the same terms, such as being a magistrate, a legal advocate or representative.

Not long after the Pan American meeting, President Terra held a referendum to enact a new constitution, a vote in which most eligible women did not participate.[94] Besides getting rid of the collegiate form of the executive in favor of a centralized presidency (the main issue in the 1933 coup), the 1934 Constitution included several points advocated by feminists. It explicitly incorporated women as citizens with the right to vote and hold office (Uruguay 1934, art. 64), conforming to the 1932 law. Since they were now citizens, all forms of government employment were now open to them (art. 69). It also included the principle of both parents holding the same responsibilities irrespective of whether their children were born in or outside marriage (art. 41). This principle permeated the 1934 Code of the Child, drafted by a commission on which Sofia Álvarez Vignoli was also member.[95] Among its measures was repeal of the article in the civil code that restricted most women from being guardians over children.

Feminist organizations hosted the First National Women's Congress in Montevideo in April 1936, which focused on a broad range of topics, from the conditions of working women to the dangers of fascism and the civil war in Spain (Lavrin 1995, 221).[96] Sara Rey presented PIDF's platform for reform of women's

93 In 1929, the Senate had approved a bill that in the case of divorce gave guardianship and custody to mothers of girls under the age of 16 and boys under 12, improving on civil code provisions whereby mothers only automatically had custody of children aged five and under (*Ideas y Acción* 1933, 8, 1–2). This article pointed out how in divorces husbands used the issue of child custody to their material benefit, so that women ended up with fewer assets from the marriage in order to maintain custody.

94 During 1933 and 1934, *Ideas y Acción* published several articles on PIDF's concern that the vote to ratify this constitution would take place before many women were able to register. It complained that the government had not expanded the times or places for registration. Also, those opposed to the Terra regime's coup boycotted the referendum since the constitution was not the product of an elected constitutional assembly.

95 Ley 9342, May 2, 1934; https://www.impo.com.uy/leyes/9342-1934.

96 According to Deutsch (2023, 178), the Unión Femenina Contra la Guerra (Women's Union against the War), an anti-fascist organization, convened this congress. It was a predecessor to Acción Femenina por la Victoria (Feminine Action for Victory), an anti-fascist war relief organization founded in 1942 (with similar objectives to the Victory Board in Argentina) in which most of the leading feminists participated (Deutsch 2023, 179–84).

civil rights, which was endorsed by those attending.[97] PIDF subsequently ran candidates in the 1938 election, the first in which women participated, and had an extremely poor showing. The party never received the backing of some of the main feminist leaders, such as the Luisi sisters, who did not believe in the wisdom of organizing an all-female political party. The publication of *Ideas y Acción* continued until the next year when PIDF disappeared from the public scene (Lavrin 1995, 348–9).

Reaching Consensus on Civil Code Reform

Between 1937 and 1943, legislators introduced five bills on women's civil rights in the Congress before one of the reformulated 1943 bills became law in 1946. Women legislators led the process and their collective efforts resulted in a much better law, one that established men and women's equal civil capacity and equal rights in marriage although not full gender equality.

The Chamber's commission on codes finally agreed to discuss the 1932 Senate-approved Minelli bill in 1937 at the insistence of socialist Deputy Emilio Frugoni. Before it could issue a report, however, the Senate approved a different and less favorable bill (Cámara de Senadores 1939, 92–8). Sponsored by National Party Senator Martín R. Echegoyen, this 1938 bill demonstrates that even conservatives thought that the enhancement of women's civil rights was long overdue.[98] It gave single, divorced and widowed women full civil capacity, for as Echegoyen (Cámara de Senadores 1939, 8) observed, the need for their civil equality with men "does not need to be explained, given the collective consciousness regarding this matter ..." The situation of married women was different although he was willing to meet feminist demands half-way.

Echegoyen's bill expanded what wives could do without their husband's or a judge's authorization. They could be employed and manage their own earnings, including the assets so acquired and its fruits; administer their own assets; accept an inheritance; participate in lawsuits; and exercise patria potestad over minor children from a previous marriage, including managing their assets. It also gave wives greater say in determining a couple's place of residence by requiring mutual consent to mortgage or sell this dwelling. Nonetheless, it maintained certain restrictions on their activities. A husband could oppose his wife being employed or

97 Presentation by Sara Rey on "Derechos civiles de la mujer" summarized in "El Congreso Nacional de Mujeres," *El Día* (April 20, 1936, 8). The only differences that I found between this version of the PIDF proposal and the one adopted in 1934 was the addition of two phrases. One made both spouses equally responsible for the sustenance of the household according to their capabilities, while the other allowed wives to participate in lawsuits without requiring their husbands' authorization.

98 Both he and National Party leader Luis Alberto de Herrera had been official delegates, along with Sofía Álvarez Vignoli, to the 1933 Pan American conference in Montevideo where the Uruguayan government signed the Equal Rights Treaty.

accepting an inheritance, with a judge settling the matter. Moreover, for her to manage her own assets required a wife to declare her intention to do so; otherwise, the default was for the husband to manage these, along with the community property (Cámara de Senadores 1939, 3–7).

Feminist activist Sara Rey found Echegoyen's bill unsatisfactory. Writing in *Ideas y Acción*, she argued that since it maintained the principle of wives owing obedience to their husbands, they could still prevent their wives from earning an income.[99] Moreover, like the 1926 Argentine law, unless a wife went out of her way to declare her intention, her assets remained under her husband's control, thus the right to manage these herself was illusory. The Echegoyen bill also failed to address other issues of concern to feminists such as patria potestad or the unequal treatment of spouses for adultery in the grounds for separation or divorce.

Deputy Frugoni also considered the Echegoyen bill to do only the minimum to strengthen married women's property rights and thus presented a new proposal that drew on the 1932 approved Senate bill, Baltazar Brum's conception of a jointly administered household, and Carlos Vaz Ferreira's feminism of compensation. Frugoni's (1940, 249–79) bill gave women the same civil rights that men held and established that they had full civil capacity irrespective of marital status, ending potestad marital. His innovation was to apply the concept of compensation to the default marital regime, which he termed the "conjugal society of non-reserved gananciales." Each spouse had separate and parallel rights to administer the assets they brought to marriage and what they inherited, as well as the earnings from their separate employment or occupation. The rents and fruits from their separately owned assets brought to marriage or inherited constituted gananciales, managed jointly by both spouses. Treated differently, however, where the earnings and assets each acquired from their employment. Whereas those of the husband were gananciales, the assets a wife acquired with her own earnings constituted her individual property.

Frugoni's reasoning was that a husband was primarily responsible for the household's economic support and his wife for its internal administration, although both had the obligation to contribute to household expenses based on their ability. Wives had a right to half of the gananciales at the dissolution of the conjugal society because they contributed to their generation primarily through their domestic labor and childcare. In his words, "… the work of a good mother and housewife make up a very important contribution to its economy" (Frugoni 1940, 67). If a wife also worked for income, these efforts were in addition to her domestic responsibilities (i.e., the "double day"), and hence she should be able to keep the earnings from such additional labor. He thus found it "logical and just" that a wife's earnings be "reserved for her," although a husband share his earnings with her as gananciales, since she indirectly contributed to their generation. While the concept of feminism of compensation influenced the earlier debate over divorce by demand of the woman, Frugoni's innovative idea to apply it to the marital regime by giving

99 Reproduced in Frugoni (1940, 64).

special treatment to a wife's earnings did not as fare well.[100] Neither his nor Senator Echegoyen's bills made it out of committee.

The Congress did approve one bill relevant to the protection of women and the family, on the creation of family patrimony.[101] Similar to laws adopted in other Latin American countries in the 1930s, if there were children who were minors either or both spouses could request the designation of their family home and/or farm as a *bien de familia* if worth less than 5,000 pesos and not mortgaged. In this case, neither could sell the property nor could creditors seize it for debts. A benefit to wives was that if widowed or divorced, this designation allowed them to remain in the family home until the youngest child reached the age of majority.

As a result of the 1942 elections, the Congress incorporated its first women members, two as senators of the Colorado Party but of different bands – Sofia Álvarez Vignoli of the more conservative Riverista faction and Isabel Pinto, a Batllista and former president of CNM-U – and two as deputies – Magdalena Antonelli Moreno, a Colorada, and Julia Arévalo of the Communist Party. As Lavrin (1995, 223) observes, having women represented in the Congress made the debate over women's civil rights unique in Latin America. In addition, by then most of ideological arguments against women's equal civil rights were exhausted. The primary disagreement among legislators in the early 1940s was over the legal technique to follow, a short bill that laid out the key principles or a longer bill that specified the required revision or abrogation of each relevant civil code article. Nevertheless, there were points of substance enmeshed in these debates, principally, the extent to which the reform should embrace a dual-headed household where husband and wife had fully equal rights.

The next year, Senator Álvarez Vignoli and Deputy Antonelli each led different initiatives to attain women's equal civil rights in their respective Chambers.[102] Álvarez Vignoli (1946), a lawyer, presented a lengthy bill containing detailed revisions of a host of articles in the civil, procedural and commercial codes.[103] This bill was likely the outcome of the effort that began a decade before under the Women's Rights Committee in which she had participated.[104] In her exposition, she

100 Divorce by demand of the woman, however, proved to be popular. Data for 1945–1949 indicate that 50.5% of divorces took place under this condition; 36.7% were for a specific fault and only 12.8% were by mutual consent (Ganón 1964, 180).

101 Law 9.770, April 10, 1938; https://impo.com.uy/bases/leyes-originales/9770-1938.

102 Álvarez Vignoli (1946) contains all the various bills and their discussion (reproducing the congressional record) and the reports of the various commissions. The congressional record does not always include the latter as well as the petitions received.

103 "Proyecto de Ley," May 4, 1946, in Álvarez Vignoli (1946, 9–81).

104 Mentioned by Deputy Magdalena Antonelli; Álvarez Vignoli did not include this antecedent. The group of women lawyers on the Women's Rights Committee had worked on a detailed proposal of needed revisions to Uruguay's civil, procedural, penal and commercial codes. The main difference in its demands from the 1934 PIDF proposal was with respect to the default marital regime. According to Antonelli's summary, the group proposed that either spouse could opt to manage their own earnings and assets, with the gananciales to be jointly managed, and does not mention other alternatives. "Exposición de la Srta. Magdalena Antonelli Moreno," in Álvarez Vignoli (1946, 303–4).

reviewed how her bill differed from the many presented in the Congress over the past 30 years. The Brum, Minelli and Echegoyen bills all required a wife to declare her intention to manage her own assets and those she might acquire via inheritance. She considered this a fatal flaw because it would be difficult for a wife to take such an action without destabilizing the marriage. These bills would thus end up supporting the status quo, with the husband the manager of his wife's assets and the community property.

In Álvarez Vignoli's bill, each spouse automatically managed and disposed of his or her own assets. The wife could opt out of managing these herself, turning over administration to her husband (the regime of "administración marital"). But by changing the default option, she made it easier for women who wanted to manage their own assets to do so. In her view, what was lacking in previous bills was women's input on how to achieve justice and restore their dignity; hers was "the clear and precise expression of a woman's thinking, which speaks her truth in name of her sisters" (Álvarez Vignoli 1946, 14). Other key features were the joint management of the conjugal society by husband and wife and the need for mutual consent for either to alienate immovable assets that formed part of the gananciales or to accept an inheritance. Either spouse could also ask for the separation of property without cause at any point during marriage.[105] Also, the domicile of the couple was to be jointly determined and both parents were to jointly exercise patria potestad.

The Senate's commission on the constitution, which besides Álvarez Vignoli, included Cesar Miranda and Martín Echegoyen, sponsors of earlier bills on women's rights, then revised her lengthy bill. The commission reduced it to three principles, recognition of women's full civil capacity, equal property rights and joint patria potestad, expressed in only 16 articles.[106] The substitute bill established that without need for the wife to declare so, she had the right to administer and freely dispose of her own assets, the fruits of these (the gananciales) and the product of her activities (her earnings), maintaining Álvarez Vignoli's default language. The commission's innovation was to propose full separation of property during the marriage with the pooling of all gananciales at its dissolution. Its intention was to combine the best of two regimes, separation of property and the conjugal society by providing for individual autonomy while maintaining the unity of the marriage bond.[107]

105 According to Lavrin (1995, 346), when the issue of divorce came up in the discussion of PIDF's platform in early 1933, Álvarez Vignoli had argued for a change in the divorce law so that either spouse could demand a divorce without cause. She considered that giving only women the right to unilateral divorce implied their inferiority, thus "a superior understanding of feminism" required its elimination. When she lost this vote, she and a few others left PIDF. Thus, her 1943 proposal on either spouse being able to request the separation of property was consistent with her earlier position.

106 "Informe y proyecto substitutivo de la Comisión de Constitución y Legislación Social," October 26, 1944, in Álvarez Vignoli (1946, 91–107).

107 Álvarez Vignoli (1946, 96–97).

The commission's bill also differed from Álvarez Vignoli's on three other important points: it retained the husband as the administrator of the conjugal society rather than providing for joint administration by the couple; while patria potestad was to be exercised by both parents, only the father was designated as the administrator of the children's assets and their representative; and while in her bill either spouse could opt for the complete separation of property at any point, the substitute bill extended this right only to wives or by mutual consent. The commission reasoned that if a husband had the same right as the wife to demand the separation of property at any time, this would undermine her right to future gananciales, since the equal division of these were a form of compensation to wives for their domestic labor. Moreover, this formulation conformed to Uruguay's divorce legislation whereby only the wife could demand a divorce without cause.[108]

As rapporteur for the commission, Álvarez Vignoli (1946, 108–20) explained how her colleagues had convinced her that it was preferable to opt for a short bill that encompassed the key principles, leaving it to judges to work out the details rather than revising all the articles that required such at this time. She did not mention the specific points mentioned above where the substitute bill departed from her original bill. Since the commission included representatives of all the political parties, she was satisfied that they had reached consensus on core issues; what she wanted most was the Senate's quick approval. Referring to several missives that the commission had received in support of the bill, she stressed how women had been waiting for at least a quarter of a century for recognition of their rights and were not willing to wait any longer.

Nonetheless, aware that the commission was considering a short version of the Álvarez Vignoli bill, Paulina Luisi sent a letter urging it to do a thorough job of revising the code so that it conformed to the constitutional guarantee of equality of all persons before the law.[109] She was not convinced by the argument that a thorough revision would delay the process excessively since so many of the previous bills contained detailed analyses of which articles needed to be rescinded or changed. Feminists were not of a single mind on the issue. Sara Rey sent a letter with a new petition signed by 1,422 women from across the political spectrum urging approval of the commission's revised bill without delay.[110]

Most of the Senate debate focused on the pros and cons of a short bill based on general principles versus a detailed long one. Senator Isabel Pinto was among those most concerned about a short bill that did not repeal specific articles. She

108 Also see Zajtay and Vaz Ferreira's (1950, 839–40) discussion of this bill.

109 Letter from Paulina Luisi and María Inés Villarino of the Alianza Uruguaya de Mujeres, October 2, 1944, in Álvarez Vignoli (1946, 251–2).

110 Letter from Sara Rey and María Inés Navarra of November 6, 1944 (Álvarez Vignoli 1946, 252–3). Another women's organization, the Unión Nacional Femenina, emerged in 1944 under the coordination of the president's wife, Celia Álvarez Mouliá de Amézaga, which also lobbied for married women's property rights and other reforms of concern to women (Deutsch 2023, 236).

feared that if it left to judges to interpret the bill's principles, it could have terrible consequences for women, for example, they would maintain the dual standard for adultery in the grounds for divorce (Álvarez Vignoli 1946, 120–27). Senator Álvarez Vignoli agreed with her that one moral standard should govern marriage but dismissed her concern primarily because she did not want to let the bill's approval get bogged down in intractable issues. Separate future legislation could address the issue of adultery.[111]

Commission member Ledo Arroyo Torres defended the short bill approach as the state of the art in legal circles and suggested that a technical committee could later make the required revisions for the next edition of the code (Álvarez Vignoli 1946, 128–72). In his lengthy exposition, he mentioned how this bill gave wives many more rights than the reforms enacted in other South American countries. Surprisingly, he did not stress how Colombia had previously instituted a mixed regime nor refer to its antecedents in Central America although he mentioned that most jurists who had written treatises on marital regimes considered a mixed regime, such as the commission was proposing, as the most just. The Senate approved the bill with only minor changes that November and sent it to the Chamber.

In the Chamber, a special commission on women's civil rights made up of deputies Magdalena Antonelli, Julia Arévalo and six others had been drafting a bill when they received the Senate's approved bill.[112] Rather than continuing to revise the code article by article, it decided to focus its efforts on the Senate bill. In its November 1945 report, it said it made some changes to the Senate bill but tried to keep these to a minimum to ensure its approval by both Chambers.[113] The commission had also taken the precaution of sending a draft of its reformulated bill to the Supreme Court, the Bar and Notary associations and had incorporated their recommendations. Moreover, it had informally discussed the proposed changes with Senator Álvarez Vignoli and the Senate commission.

The special commissions' substantive changes to the bill included one to the first article. Whereas the Senate version declared that all women had full civil capacity, it proposed that it say, to emphasize the principle of equality, that men and women had equal civil capacity and equal civil rights. To make the bill consistent with these principles, it added new articles specifying that a couple's residency was to be jointly determined by both spouses and that parents shared patria potestad

111 As Giordano (2012, 177) infers, the language that Senator Álvarez Vignoli used to make this point was rather unfortunate, since she made it on moral terms. She said she did not want this law "which gives ample liberties to honest women, becoming mixed up with the problem of adultery … women's debauchery" (Álvarez Vignoli 1946, 182).

112 At Antonelli's insistence, the Chamber set up this special commission in 1944 after its commission on codes failed to act on her proposal that they reconsider the earlier Minelli bill.

113 "Primer Proyecto de Ley de la Comisión Especial sobre Derechos Civiles de la Mujer," September 24, 1945, and "Informe y Proyecto sustitutivo de la Comisión Especial sobre Derechos Civiles de la Mujer," November 22, 1945, in Álvarez Vignoli (1946, 266–91). The Senate's bill and the report of the Special Commission are in DSCR (1946, 485–92).

over their children. However, it left it up to the couple to decide which spouse managed the children's assets and represented them. Whereas the Senate bill specified that only the woman or both could ask for the separation of property at any time, this commission reverted to Álvarez Vignoli's initial proposal that either spouse could request such.

The special commission maintained the same mixed marital regime that the Senate bill proposed. It reported that its members had not fully agreed on what to call this regime, which represented the harmonization of "a regime of separation with gananciales."[114] While it cited debates among legal scholars in France and Argentina over its name and implications, it did not mention if any countries had already adopted such a regime as the default. In its interpretation, the conjugal society continued to exist during the marriage although each spouse administered separately the gananciales each generated.[115] It also maintained the Senate's proposed safeguard on the separate management of gananciales, the requirement of mutual consent for either spouse to sell or mortgage immovable assets. It added a business, farm or factory to the list of assets requiring mutual consent for their alienation.

In her comments before the Chamber, Antonelli emphasized how the commission's consensus around the principle of equal civil rights represented a major step forward and urged its approval of the revised bill.[116] At the same time, she felt compelled to raise its main deficiency, that it did not address the situation of housewives who did not own assets nor earn a wage, salary or steady income, for example, the wife of the white collar worker mentioned in the introduction who wrote *Acción Femenina* about her husband's irresponsible use of his salary. In Antonelli's analysis, the division of labor whereby husbands were the breadwinners and wives cared for the home and children was the result of the social and legal obligations of marriage. This was "the desirable position for married women if she is to be a good mother," and one that benefits the family, society and the state.[117] Moreover, the sharing of gananciales recognized the equivalence of each spouse's position.

The problem in instituting the proposed mixed regime was that in the case of property-less housewives, only the husband's activities generated gananciales directly, and the bill required a wife's consent only if he wished to alienate these. Although she contributed indirectly to their accumulation, the wife did not have a say in their day-to-day management. The bill thus "mutilated the concept of legal equivalency" by not considering the gender division of labor.[118] In her view, it would have been preferable if the bill stipulated that husband and wife jointly managed the gananciales, as proposed in the earlier bills by Brum, Frugoni and Álvarez

114 DSCR (1946, 488).
115 Implicitly, the husband remained the head of the conjugal society, since the bill (art. 3) made the conjugal society subject to the relevant articles of the existing civil code.
116 DSCR (1946, 498–504), and in Álvarez Vignoli (1946, 300–21).
117 DSCR (1946, 502).
118 DSCR (1946, 502).

Vignoli. That would have given a property-less housewife a much stronger voice in the disposition of her husband's wages or salary during the marriage.

Antonelli stressed that her criticism was not based on some "exotic feminism" – a radical egalitarianism – but rather grounded in the recognition of women's fundamental role as mothers. In her view, feminism strove to improve the position of women because by doing so, it improved the position of children and hence, the future of humanity. The most significant aspect of the proposed bill was that it gave mothers and fathers shared patria potestad, and irrespective of her criticism, she supported its approval as a "homage to mothers."[119]

The discussion continued over five days and, as in the Senate debate, a main concern was the pros and cons of a short versus long bill.[120] The 1926 Argentine bill was brought up numerous times, both as a reminder of how that country had acted on women's civil rights almost 20 years earlier and as an example of what could go wrong when a bill did not abrogate specific articles that were offensive to women; i.e., all aspects of potestad marital. The wording of the first article was also a concern, whether granting women equal rights and capacities meant that this would abrogate aspects of the civil code or other legislation that gave preference or protection to women for social, moral or biological reasons. For this reason, the special commission ended up changing its initial wording of this article so that it only established equal civil capacity.[121] After accepting a few other changes, the Chamber approved the revised bill in April 1946.

Since each Chamber had approved a different bill, a special commission of the General Assembly reconciled the two bills, with three of the four women in the Congress (Álvarez Vignoli, Antonelli and Arévalo) participating in this commission. Among the important changes, it made to the final language was that it specified that the bill's provisions overruled those of the civil code relating to the management of the conjugal society; i.e., the husband was no longer its sole administrator.[122] The General Assembly unanimously approved most of the 21 articles of the final bill, and President Amézaga signed it into law on September 18, 1946. Shortly after, at Senator Pinto's insistence, the Congress approved the appointment of a committee of lawyers to reconcile the law with the civil code prior to the publication of its next edition.[123]

119 DSCR (1946, 503). Pinto (1951, 112–25) also later highlighted shared patria potestad over children as the law's greatest "moral conquest," perhaps because this reform had previously faced such strong opposition.

120 In Álvarez Vignoli (1946, 321–436).

121 Álvarez Vignoli (1946, 327–30, 394–7 and 495).

122 "Informe y Proyecto de la Comisión Especial de la Asamblea General," in Álvarez Vignoli (1946, 452–6). Lavrin (1995, 223) considers the final law to resemble Antonelli's bill more closely than Álvarez Vignoli's initial proposal. In my reading, Antonelli's important contribution was to add back into the bill several points that had been in Álvarez Vignoli's original and ignored by the Senate Commission, hence it was a collaborative effort.

123 Álvarez Vignoli (1946, 469–71).

Law 10.783, the Law of Woman's Civil Rights,[124] established men and women's equal civil capacity across the board. It went further than any previous South America reform in eradicating potestad marital and incorporating parallel rights and mutual consent as the governing principles in marriage. Specifically, it was the first reform to establish that the household's residency was to be determined by mutual consent and that parents held shared patria potestad over children, with the couple determining which of them managed the children's assets. Widows or divorced mothers who remarried retained it, including the administration of their children's assets just like fathers.

The reform adopted the marital regime of deferred community property.[125] During the marriage, each spouse had the free administration and disposition of their own assets and their fruits, and of their own earnings and any assets so acquired; at its dissolution, they shared the pooled gananciales equally. Both spouses contributed to the expenses of the household based on their ability. While Uruguay's new marital regime was like that established in Colombia in 1932, it differed in an important way: for either spouse to alienate the immovable assets and businesses they acquired during the marriage, they required the explicit consent of the other. Thus while the law did not incorporate the provision for joint management of the gananciales championed by Senator Álvarez Vignoli and Deputy Antonelli nor address Antonelli's criticism regarding the situation of asset-less housewives, it gave greater protection to women who did not earn income nor own assets compared to Colombia's law.

Uruguay's 1946 civil code reform, nonetheless, left these asset-less housewives vulnerable in another way. In the interest of applying parallel rights consistently, either spouse could demand the separation of property without cause at any point. While this gave couples maximum flexibility, it meant that a wife, against her wishes, could find herself without any future claim on the gananciales generated by her husband.

Feminist scholar Verónica Giordano (2012, 174–8) argues that while the law established the equal civil capacity of all citizens, male and female, it did not establish equality between them nor rid the code of its paternalism. This is because the 1946 law did not rescind or modify all the specific articles of the civil code that violated equal rights, only those referring to women's relative incapacity, as Paulina Luisi and Senator Pinto had warned. The best example is the unequal treatment of adultery as a cause of civil divorce and its unequal consequences, that only wives lost their right to gananciales. Since it was up to the courts to interpret the compatibility of existing articles with the general principle of equal civil capacity, some legal scholars and judges concluded that it was fine to treat adultery differently because this was not a legal incapacity, but rather a moral question (Giordano

124 *Registro Nacional de Leyes y Decretos* (1946, vol. 1, 962).
125 CIM (1948, 157) called it the regime of "participation in the gananciales."

2012, 177). As it turned out, it took another 30 years to establish equal treatment for adultery.[126] The government did not appoint a civil code review commission to update and deal with its inconsistencies until 1986.[127]

Conclusion

Uruguay went against conventional wisdom of feminists and reformists in other countries by granting women political rights before they gained strong property and other civil rights. That the CNM-U emerged in 1916 with both banners in hand had much to do with the political moment in which this organization was born. Colorado deputies had already introduced bills to strengthen women's civil and political rights and shortly thereafter approved universal male suffrage. The arguments in favor of the latter, such as the need to broaden the electorate beyond those who were literate to institutionalize democracy, flew in the face of the exclusion of women who in growing numbers were completing secondary education and joining the professions. Also, the fact that the 1918 Constitution made mention of women attaining the vote by a future vote of the legislature raised expectations regarding its eventual enactment, as did a subsequent electoral court decision to consider women as citizens.

In addition, Paulina Luisi was a uniquely accomplished and determined feminist leader, one committed to the idea that the social change that she envisioned depended crucially on women obtaining political rights. It was she who most clearly made the argument that women needed political rights to meet the responsibilities associated with their primary mission of motherhood and to safeguard the future of humanity. As founder of the CNM-U and later the Alianza, these organizations pursued the dual objective of attaining civil and political rights simultaneously. Feminists in 1932 were almost successful in achieving both before the country's anti-democratic turn abruptly halted the momentum. Luisi surely did not expect that it would take over a decade after the attainment of suffrage for women to gain full civil rights. This delay was partly because of the conservative turn following the 1933 coup, that it was only in 1938 that women had the opportunity to exercise their right to vote and stand for office and not until 1942 that women joined the Congress.

While a CNM-U commission began to study early on the many ways that the civil code discriminated against women, and they and/or the Alianza lobbied heavily to reform specific aspects, such as enabling women to be witnesses and to exercise any profession, they did not tackle reforms to the marital regime beyond advocating for the general principle that wives should be able to manage their own earnings and assets just as single women did. The women's organizations tended

126 Decree Law 14.766, April 18, 1978; https://parlamento.gub.uy/documentosyleyes/leyes/ley/14766.

127 Unofficial publications of the code, for example, Uruguay (1976), appended Law 10.783 of 1946 but maintained the earlier text. The Congress did not approve a new code until 1994.

to follow the lead of allied legislators, whether of the Colorado or Socialist parties, endorsing their proposals to reform the marital regime and advance women's rights.

Even though women began graduating with a law degree in the decade of the teens, it was only after they attained suffrage that feminists undertook systematic work on alternatives to the marital regime, beginning with the lawyers affiliated with the Women's Rights Committee and then as part of the PIDF. Worth noting is that feminists in their proposals did not follow the feminism of compensation, as reflected in the 1930 Minelli or 1939 Frugoni bills that gave wives special privileges. Rather, they focused on attaining parallel and joint rights in marriage.

The final bill on women's civil rights was very much a collaborative effort of the women legislators, all declared feminists. Senator Álvarez Vignoli's bill, with its detailed analysis of the civil code articles that needed elimination or reformulation, provided the initial content. But it was the Senate commission that revised her bill that produced the final formula for the new marital regime, one that combined the separation of property during marriage with community property at its dissolution. In drafting a shorter version of the Álvarez Vignoli bill, the Senate commission also ignored certain proposed changes that were crucial to feminists. Here it was Deputy Antonelli's efforts in the Chamber that resulted in the reincorporation of certain articles of her bill, so that its content more truly reflects equal rights and responsibilities, among them the articles on shared patria potestad and joint determination of a household's residency. Also, the fact that three of the four women legislators served on the final congressional reconciliation commission ensured that these gains remained in the approved law.

The main demand that feminists did not attain was joint management of the gananciales. The trade-off was that wives gained complete autonomy during the marriage to manage their own assets, earnings and individually generated gananciales under the deferred community property regime. Their joint efforts at least safeguarded the interests of housewives who owned no assets nor earned an income by requiring mutual consent for either spouse to alienate gananciales that constituted immovable property or businesses. The next chapter demonstrates how the Uruguayan law of 1946 went further than any other previous legislation in South America in establishing equal civil rights between men and women, and especially in marriage. Nonetheless, Paulina Luisi's and Senator Pinto's warning that it was dangerous not to address and revise each article in the civil code to eliminate all those that were harmful to women proved prescient, for the code did not fully embrace gender equality.

9

THE INFLUENCE OF FEMINISTS' PROPOSALS ON CIVIL CODE REFORM

Reflecting on the achievement of feminism in the region, lawyer and activist Elena Caffarena (1944, 10) observed:

> If women and their organizations have not energetically pushed to obtain the full legal capacity of married women – that is, that they have not launched sustained campaigns and petitioned with the same decisiveness as they have suffrage – it is because of their lack of knowledge of the code that governs them and because of the difficulty of formulating the legal institution that should replace the current one.

As previous chapters have demonstrated, not all women's organizations developed their own ideas on needed reforms to the marital regime, the legal institution to which Caffarena refers. Most of the platforms of secular women's organizations called for "equal civil rights" but did not go into specifics. Among the general concerns frequently voiced in women's publications was that mothers should have a say in the raising of their own children; that with respect to women's civil capacity, they should not be treated the same as minors, the physically or mentally impaired or criminals; that when they held the required qualifications, they should have access to the same professions and government posts as men; and that they should not be made into dependents of their husbands upon marriage.

In the first two university theses written by South American women related to women's civil rights – by Chilean Matilde Brandau (1898) for a doctorate in law and Argentine Elvira López (1901) for a doctorate of philosophy – they both embraced ceding mothers the same rights of patria potestad that fathers held. This was likely because this reform was compatible, even necessary to the accepted mission

DOI: 10.4324/9781003658436-9

of women as wives and mothers and their idealized position of "queen of the home." While both were aware of how more developed countries had strengthened married women's property rights, they did not make specific recommendations as to needed changes in their own country's marital regime. Brandau, nonetheless, went further than López, urging a reform of the Chilean civil code so that wives hold the same legal capacity as single women.

During the subsequent decade, South American women began writing about specific ways to enhance the economic autonomy of wives. Recall that Peruvian writer Zoila Aurora Cáceres (1909) reported favorably on how wives in France had gained stronger property rights through the mechanism of reserved property that, as an exception within the community property regime, gave working wives the right to manage their own earnings. And Ecuadorian journalist Zoila Ugarte de Landívar (1910b) advocated giving couples flexibility to determine how they managed their property. At international congresses in Buenos Aires in 1906 and 1910, a feminist educator and a feminist physician presented the first comprehensive proposals by women for civil code reform that included changes to the marital regime. Note that women entered law schools much later than medical and other professional schools,[1] thus it was not until later decades that female lawyers were among the authors of feminist proposals to reform the marital regime.

This chapter considers the extent to which the ideas and proposals of feminists and their organizations influenced the reforms of family law in South America in the first half of the twentieth century. Whether they could have exerted influence depended partly on the timing of when these organizations emerged, for this differed markedly across the region (see Table 1.1). As Francesca Miller (1991) and Asunción Lavrin (1995) posit, an important precondition for the formation of secular women's organizations was the expansion of women's access to public secondary and higher education. Women in Argentina, Chile, Uruguay and Peru formed organizations demanding rights earlier than in Ecuador, Colombia or Venezuela largely because the expansion of normal schools and women's entry into universities and the professions took place decades earlier.

In the Southern Cone and Peru, the emergence of women's rights groups also coincided with the introduction of the first bills to enhance women's civil rights (Table 1.1). In contrast, in the Andean countries of Ecuador, Venezuela and Colombia legislators presented these, and in Ecuador and Venezuela enacted, important reforms prior to their emergence as well as the notable expansion of public primary education. Once formed, women's rights organizations lobbied in support of many of the bills to reform family law, a process described in previous chapters.

This chapter focuses on the content of feminist proposals for reform of the marital regime. The proposals analyzed in the following section address the issue

1 The first woman lawyer graduated in Chile in 1892; Argentina, 1909; Uruguay, 1911; Peru, 1920; Ecuador, 1927; Venezuela, 1936; and Colombia in 1942; see country chapters for sources.

posed by Caffarena – the "legal institution" that should replace the conjugal society as the default marital regime. In five of the seven countries,[2] feminists wrote at least nine proposals between 1906 and 1944 that went into detail on the management of a couple's individual and community property. While all nine proposals sought greater economic autonomy for married women, they differed on whether the objective was for wives to maintain the same property rights they held as single women or to attain equal rights in marriage. The latter challenged directly the position of the husband as sole manager of the community property and household head. Their proposals on the management of the community property also had different implications for different groups of married women, especially those who owned no assets and did not work for income.

The subsequent section then provides a comparative analysis of what the reforms enacted up through the 1950s achieved, often in a piecemeal fashion. The conclusion summarizes the extent to which feminist demands shaped the content of the respective reforms and where they fell short. As it turned out, it proved more difficult for feminists to modify patria potestad as the sole prerogative of fathers during marriage than to reform the marital regime.

Feminists' Proposals

The range and content of the issues covered in the detailed proposals for reform by feminists and/or their organizations reflected what rights women had already attained as well as what they considered to be the most egregious offenses to their dignity in specific circumstances. All proposed changing the marital regime so that wives – either by choice or automatically – manage their own earnings and/or property without need for a husband's authorization; they differed on whether the husband remained the sole manager of the couple's community property. In three of the four countries where women's rights groups first emerged – Argentina, Chile and Peru – feminists authored detailed civil code reform proposals prior to the 1930s. In Uruguay and Venezuela, it was after previous reform proposals had languished that feminists developed their own proposals in the 1930s and 1940s.[3]

In Argentina, women authored two proposals shortly after its legislature in 1902 entertained the first bill to strengthen married women's property rights. Educator and journalist María Abella de Ramírez presented her 17-point platform for women's rights at the 1906 International Congress of Freethinkers. Abella's ([1908] 1965, 13–5) proposal contained two specific demands regarding the marital regime: that in a prenuptial agreement, women be able to opt to manage all their own

2 In Colombia and Ecuador, where a feminist movement was slow to develop and important civil code reforms preceded it, I did not locate any detailed proposals on the marital regime written by women in the period under study.

3 Several of these proposals were developed in dialogue with various legislative bills. See the respective country chapters for details on these and the appropriate references.

assets (what they brought to marriage and later acquired through inheritance) and earnings; and that they be able to manage directly half of the gananciales during the marriage (what corresponded to their share of the community property at its end). The first demand gave women a choice when they married to avoid being forced to turn over their wealth and earnings to their husbands. Abella reasoned that not all women wanted or were ready to manage their own assets, thus the importance of wives having the option to decide what best served their interests. The second reflected a concern she often expressed in her writings regarding despotic husbands who did not give their wives any money to manage to meet their personal needs, making them especially dependent upon their husbands' goodwill.[4]

Later, in the program of the Liga Feminista Nacional that she founded in 1910, Abella proposed a different mechanism to accomplish this second objective. If a woman did not bring assets to marriage or did not opt to manage her own, a husband was to provide his wife with a monthly allowance for her personal and household needs, with the amount specified in a prenuptial agreement.[5] This suggests her primary concern was in assuring that wives have guaranteed access to income and hence, some economic autonomy rather than establishing equal rights in marriage. Nonetheless, she called for abolishing the need for a husband's authorization for a wife to engage in most transactions and that a household's domicile be determined by mutual consent, demands that indicate she favored ending most aspects of potestad marital.

Abella championed absolute divorce and the right of either spouse to demand it without need to prove fault. In her view, divorce by mutual consent was insufficient because either spouse could be vengeful and refuse to free their partner to marry someone else. Since marriage should be based on love and mutual respect, she saw no need for someone to continue in an intolerable relationship.[6] She also proposed that both parents exercise patria potestad on the same terms, and if a widowed mother remarried, that she maintain the same rights as widowers did when they remarried. In addition, she called for the opening of all professions and government employment to women on the same terms as men, and equal salaries for equal work irrespective of sex.

Elvira Rawson (1911), the physician who led the Centro Feminista, drafted the next feminist proposal for reform of the Argentine civil code likely in dialogue with Abella's proposal and the 1902 legislative bill. She presented it to the 1910 First International Congress of Women in Buenos Aires, which endorsed it. In her proposal, when women married, they automatically retained the same property rights they held as single women; that is, they continued to manage their own

4 See "Una lección de derecho, anecdota" that she wrote prior to this platform and included in her 1908 anthology (Abella [1908] 1965, 122–4).

5 "Liga Feminista Nacional," *La Nueva Mujer*, 2, reprinted in Rey (2021, 157).

6 See "El divorcio por pedido de una sola de las partes" that she presented to the 1908 Congress of Freethinkers in Córdoba (Abella [1908] 1965, 114–20).

earnings and assets with complete autonomy. To leave no doubt what this entailed, she spelled out exactly what wives should be able to do without permission of their husbands: engage in any profession or industry; acquire, rent, sell, mortgage and donate assets; represent themselves in lawsuits regarding this property; and be able to hold their own bank accounts and join cooperatives and mutual associations. She thus proposed eliminating many of the components of potestad marital. At the same time, Rawson assumed that the conjugal society would continue as the default regime, with the husband as manager of the community property. What she wanted was for wives to have a say in the alienation of gananciales; that is, to require mutual consent to sell, mortgage or donate immovable property acquired during the marriage. This demand was not as radical a departure from tradition as Abella's original idea, that wives directly manage half the gananciales but perhaps Rawson thought it more attainable.

Regarding legally separated women, Rawson proposed that they be able to fully control their own assets, so that they no longer require their estranged husbands' or a judge's permission to alienate immoveable assets. Similar to Abella, she demanded that husband and wife exercise patria potestad on the same terms. She also proposed that the civil code allow the investigation of paternity; that unmarried parents hold the same rights over their children as married couples had over legitimate children; and that all female relatives be able to serve as children's guardians and all women as witnesses. Among the points in Abella's proposal that Rawson did not include was the determination of a couple's residency, perhaps because this demand challenged the husband's prerogatives as household head too directly. She also did not include the demand for absolute divorce, surely because it was an issue that divided Catholic and secular women.

Over a decade later in Chile, the Consejo Nacional de Mujeres under the leadership of educator Amanda Labarca developed its first proposal, written in 1922 in dialogue with the first two legislative bills on married women's property rights. This proposal centered on three principles: women attaining full civil capacity, wives managing their own earnings and mothers assuming patria potestad over children in the father's absence. The CNM-C proposal did not demand equal patria potestad because Chile's 1855 code did not automatically convey it to the mother in a father's absence; rather, if the father had not specified a guardian in his will, a judge appointed one. Thus, this demand was a first step toward recognition of a mother's rights. While the proposal asked for widows to exercise patria potestad under the same terms as widowers, if a widow remarried, it accepted her losing such rights, likely because these were the terms of the 1915 bill submitted by liberal Senator Luis Claro Solar.

The CNM-C proposed that married women be free to pursue any form of employment and that their wages or salaries as well as any savings and investments resulting from such earnings be theirs to manage. It differed from Claro Solar's bill to adopt married women's reserved property, which followed the French rules, in its emphasis on wives determining whether they wished to be employed and on its provision for their earnings (including any assets acquired with such) becoming the wife's *exclusive* property rather than community property. Recognizing that many wives collaborated with their husbands in family enterprises, it also proposed that half of the net profits constitute women's exclusive property.[7] The CNM-C proposal, nonetheless, accepted the traditional conjugal society as the default regime, with the husband controlling both the assets that women brought to marriage or later inherited as well as the community property.

The CNM-C proposal was then reformulated by two liberal deputies who dropped the special treatment of the gananciales from women's earnings in favor of instituting separation of property as the default regime, the key feature of Senator Eliodoro Yañez's 1922 bill. The CNM-C adopted this Maza-Sánchez bill as its own, and Amanda Labarca (1924) explained that she came to favor the separation of property regime largely because it was the most straightforward way of assuring that wives maintain the same property rights they held as single women. According to her, there were too many deficiencies to the conjugal society to consider partially reforming this regime. Also, since a Liberal senator had proposed adopting the separation of property regime, this may have seemed more politically acceptable than giving wives special privileges that husbands did not have, as in the original CNM-C proposal.

Labarca (1924) was aware that under the regime of separation of property, wives did not have access to the gananciales generated by their husbands. A way to compensate women for this loss was to give widows control of their children's assets, which the Maza-Sánchez bill did, and improve spousal inheritance rights. The bill also gave wives the option of giving their husbands a mandate to manage their earnings and assets in which case they would share the gananciales. She praised the bill for allowing women to choose what was in their best interests rather than forcing them into becoming their husbands' dependents.

During these same years, Peruvian feminists developed two original proposals, both prior to the legislature entertaining any relevant bills. Miguelina Acosta Cárdenas (1920) wrote a comprehensive proposal for civil code reform for her doctoral thesis in law. She proposed that wives who brought assets to the marriage or later inherited them be able to freely manage these and moreover, that husbands and wives *jointly* manage the gananciales generated by either of them. Her idea to substitute the concept of potestad marital with a dual-headed household where both spouses managed its affairs was quite novel. Cognizant that not all women brought assets to marriage, she also proposed that working wives have access to reserved property, that is, full control over their earnings and the assets so acquired. She also demanded equal rights of patria potestad during the marriage, in widowhood and if a widowed parent remarried. To achieve equal civil rights, Acosta proposed a

7 These two ideas were features of Enrique del Valle's (1918) bill in Argentina, a proposal that Labarca may have known about through her correspondence with feminists in Argentina and Uruguay.

rewriting of the code so that the neutral word "persons" replaces "men" wherever it referred to rights, giving women the same capacity to exercise civil functions such as being a witness or guardian. Absolute divorce was under discussion in Peru, and Acosta did not hesitate to endorse it.

María Jesús Alvarado ([1923] 2019) developed Evolución Femenina's 1922 proposal that it presented to the Civil Code Review Commission, likely in dialogue with Acosta's thesis. It differed from Acosta's thesis by advocating parallel rights in marriage. It proposed something like the separation of property regime during the marriage (although not called that), whereby each spouse managed their own earnings, assets and the gananciales so generated. It required mutual consent, nonetheless, for either spouse to alienate gananciales, which suggests it assumed their pooling and division at the marriage's dissolution. This proposal foreshadowed the regime of deferred community property, although this option was not part of discussions in Peruvian legal circles. It also demanded equal rights of patria potestad, the investigation of paternity, and making all women eligible to be guardians and witnesses.[8]

In Venezuela in the twenties, married women's property rights were already as strong as what Chile had achieved in its reforms of 1925 and 1934. Already in the last quarter of the nineteenth century couples had the option of choosing separation of property in a prenuptial agreement; moreover, its 1916 civil code reform allowed wives to manage their earnings as reserved property, reforms enacted under the banner of liberalism. When women's rights groups emerged in the transition to democracy, these joined together rather quickly to develop their own proposal for reform, which with further refinements became the 1940 platform of the Frente de Asociaciones Unidas Pro-Reforma del Código Civil (AUPR1942).

The Frente's demands centered on ending the obligation of wives to obey their husbands and that wives manage their own assets with full legal capacity to contract and appear in suits, going beyond the 1916 law that focused only on women's earnings. It assumed that provisions for married women's reserved property continued, and similarly, the conjugal society under the direction of the husband. The change it proposed in the latter was requiring mutual consent for husbands to donate any gananciales.[9] With respect to civil divorce (instituted in 1904), it asked that the grounds go beyond fault to include mutual consent as well as equal treatment of spouses in the case of adultery. Other demands were that mothers

8 After Alvarado went into exile, journalist Zoila Aurora Cáceres and her group, Feminismo Peruano, assumed the banner of civil code reform. Its proposal was more modest, calling for wives to have full legal capacity so that they could manage their own assets and have a say in the management of the gananciales; that parents share patria potestad over children; and for the code to allow the investigation of paternity (Pachas 2019, 42).

9 The earlier 1937 petition had called for mutual consent for alienation of gananciales, not just donations, but the Frente later accepted the consensus of jurists that it was more important for wives to have a veto over donations that reduced the gross value of gananciales than their sale, which did not.

exercise equal patria potestad; that irrespective of marital status, women be eligible to serve as guardians and family judges; and for the code to allow the investigation of paternity. Its most innovative proposal was to give women in consensual unions the same property rights as married women with respect to community property generated during the union.

In Uruguay, where strong women's organizations developed in the late teens, it was not until after many unsuccessful legislative efforts dating from 1914 that feminists began to develop their own proposals for civil code reform. Soon after women attained suffrage in 1932, the newly formed Partido Independiente Democrático Femenino (PIDF) developed its platform drawing on the work of the group of women lawyers affiliated with the earlier Women's Civil and Political Rights Committee, a group that included Sofía Álvarez Vignoli de Demicheli, a future senator. It presented its full civil code reform proposal in 1934, which the 1936 First National Women's Congress endorsed.

PIDF's proposal called for women's equal civil rights across the board, including ending all aspects of potestad marital.[10] It proposed a unique default marital regime whereby all assets, irrespective of who acquired them and when, and including all gananciales, be jointly managed by husband and wife.[11] By mutual consent, however, a couple could opt for the separation of property regime or for the husband to administer his wife's property, thus providing couples with maximum flexibility. The platform also called for equal patria potestad over children, with widows and divorcees to maintain their rights if they remarried, and for the code to allow the investigation of paternity.

Once elected senator, Álvarez Vignoli (1946, 9–67) presented a lengthy bill in 1943 that contained detailed revisions to many civil code articles drawing on the earlier work of the Women's Rights Committee. Its content was similar to the PIDF platform. It rid the code of the need for the wife's obedience and a husband's permission for her to conduct any act, contract or lawsuit. The main difference in the default regime was that each spouse managed their own earnings and assets and jointly administered the gananciales. A feature of her bill was its parallelism, with husband and wife having the same rights and responsibilities. Either spouse could designate the other to manage the gananciales, but to alienate them required mutual consent. In other words, a wife could also renounce her right to manage her own property and give her husband a mandate to do so in which case he required her authorization to sell them. Either spouse could opt for the separation of property regime either prior to or at any time during the marriage. Both spouses

10 Recall that Uruguay's 1868 Civil Code, like those of Argentina and Venezuela, did not include the Chilean definition of potestad marital but its content was similar, and included the phrase requiring the wife's obedience to the husband.

11 This idea had similarities to the regime of full community property, which was Brazil's default marital regime in this period, although it was fully under control of husbands. PIDF's proposal did not include pooling ownership of all property, only its management.

exercised patria potestad including jointly administering children's assets. In the case of separation and divorce, the same grounds of adultery applied to either spouse.

In this same period in Chile, lawyer Elena Caffarena (1944) developed a proposal for what she considered to be the ideal marital regime, deferred community property. Previously, the program of Movimiento Pro-Emancipación de Mujeres de Chile (MEMCH), the broad-based women's organization that she co-founded in 1935, had only sought an improvement in the country's 1925 and 1934 reforms so that separation of property were an option at any point during the marriage, not limited to a prenuptial agreement. As a result of MEMCH's lobbying, a 1943 partial reform of the civil code met this demand. Caffarena was aware that even with greater flexibility, few couples pursued this option (see Table 4.1). If wives were ever to gain greater economic autonomy, the default regime had to change so that they manage the assets that they brought to marriage or later inherited. Thus in her 1944 book, Caffarena proposed the adoption of deferred community property as the default regime since it combined the best aspects of separation of property with the benefits of the conjugal society. It gave wives full legal capacity and autonomy to manage and dispose of their own assets, earnings and gananciales, while the equal division of the gananciales at its end recognized women's contribution to the accumulation of community property through their domestic and caring labor.

Earlier, other feminists, such as Ecuadorian journalist Zoila Ugarte, had raised the point of how women's domestic and caring labor contributed to the generation of gananciales. Moreover, at various points, legislators in Ecuador, Argentina, Peru and Uruguay justified the maintenance of the conjugal society because the sharing of gananciales was a just compensation for women's domestic labor. Advocates of Colombia's 1932 law were likely the first to apply this argument to justify the adoption of deferred community property as the default regime, how it provided the ideal manner of giving wives full economic autonomy while recognizing their contribution to the formation of gananciales. Caffarena's distinction was being the first South American feminist to write explicitly about its benefits in these terms.

A Continuum toward Equal Rights in Marriage

To facilitate comparative analysis, Table 9.1 summarizes the content of these nine proposals for reform of the marital regime. First, the very heterogeneity of these proposals suggests how difficult it was for feminists to decide on an ideal regime. They were cognizant that no one arrangement perfectly suited the situation of all married women. Not all brought assets to marriage or stood to inherit later. This was not simply a class divide, for any woman who worked while single might accumulate assets prior to marriage, whether a business, real estate or household

TABLE 9.1 Feminist Proposals to Reform the Marital Regime

Year and country/ author	*Marital contracts*	*Default: MW same property rights as single women*	*Default: MW equal or parallel rights as husbands*	*Default: Management of gananciales*
1906 Argentina María Abella	Prenuptial: Women opt to manage own property			Husband; wife given half to manage
1910 Argentina Elvira Rawson		She manages own earnings and assets		Husband; wife's consent to alienate
1920 Peru Miguelina Acosta		Reserved property over earnings; manages own assets		Joint
1922 Chile CNM-C/Amanda Labarca		She manages own earnings and its fruits (excluded from CP)		Husband
1922 Peru Evolución Femenina/María Jesús Alvarado			Each manages assets, earnings and gananciales; consent to alienate	Implicit: pooled and divided at end
1934 Uruguay PIDF/Sara Rey	Prenuptial: Couple opt for full separation of property or the conjugal society		Jointly manage assets and earnings of each	Joint
1940 Venezuela Frente de Asoc. Unidas Pro-Reforma		(Reserved property over earnings, 1916); she manages own assets		Husband; wife's consent to donate
1943 Uruguay Sofía Álvarez	Either could opt for full separation of property any time		Each manages own assets, earnings	Joint
1944 Chile Elena Caffarena			Each manages assets, earning and gananciales	Gananciales pooled and divided at end

Note: MW, married women; CP, community property.

goods and savings.[12] At the same time, many were undoubtedly asset-less housewives who did not earn income and were in a different position from those who earned a wage or salary or who collaborated with their husbands in a family enterprise.

Second, none of these initial reform proposals recommended adopting the marital regime of separation of property as the default, as in the Anglo-Saxon reforms, likely for the above reason. Feminists recognized that the great benefit of the partial community property regime was the sharing of gananciales at its end since it occurred irrespective of each spouse's monetary contribution. They were acutely aware of how wives were likely to generate fewer labor earnings than husbands due to social conventions against their working outside the home, unequal labor market opportunities and wage discrimination. Thus, the nine proposals maintained this basic feature of the conjugal society, the sharing and equal division of community property at its dissolution. The main points of divergence were over management of this community property and how much flexibility to offer couples.

As Table 9.1 shows, only three proposals offered a choice of regimes. María Abella in Argentina wanted women to have the option of choosing to manage their property and earnings in a prenuptial agreement.[13] Feminists in Uruguay, probably more realistically, framed this demand in terms of couples being able to opt for the separation of property regime by mutual consent. Where the 1934 PIDF proposal and Senator Álvarez Vignoli's 1943 bill differed was that in the latter, either spouse could also demand the separation of property at any time, not just adopt it by mutual consent prior to marriage. This reflected her commitment to seeking fully parallel and equal rights in marriage.[14]

A frequent concern in feminist writings and the central focus in four of these proposals was that women when they marry not lose the rights they had as single women to manage their own earnings and assets. Only the initial 1922 CNM-C proposal in Chile focused exclusively on wives' control over their earnings and on terms particularly favorable to them. This focus on earnings may have been because there was broader consensus among elite Chilean women that working-class women needed control over their wages than over the idea that they themselves needed to manage their own property.[15] The other three – Rawson's 1910, Acosta's 1920 and the 1940 Frente proposals – all wanted wives to manage their own

12 Recall from Table 2.1 the broad range of movable and immovable property that when given the opportunity, Ecuadorian women excluded from the conjugal society to manage themselves.

13 Amanda Labarca voiced a similar concern, that women have a choice, when she backed the bill making separation of property the default, feeling assuaged that it allowed couples to maintain the conjugal society if they so wished. The Uruguayan PIDF proposal also provided for this choice.

14 As critics pointed out during the congressional debate, parallel rights to demand separation of property could have negative consequences since it left wives vulnerable because a husband could unilaterally leave his wife without access to his future gananciales.

15 Recall from Chapter 4 that the Chilean League of Catholic Ladies at their 1918 congress had endorsed Claro Solar's bill, which only featured wives' control over their own wages.

earnings as well as the assets they brought to marriage or later inherited. The proposals noted in the fourth column of Table 9.1, which demanded that married women have equal or parallel rights as husbands, also assumed that wives not lose rights they previously held as single women when they married; however, these set their sights on a different goal, changing the authority structure within marriage.

Where these nine proposals differed most profoundly was with respect to management of gananciales. They spanned a continuum ranging from maintaining the status quo–where husbands remained the sole managers of the community property–to equal rights in marriage. Four proposals maintained the husband as the principal manager and head of the conjugal society (last column). The 1922 CNM-C proposal accepted the status quo, with husbands managing both the assets wives brought to marriage and the gananciales. The proposals of Elvira Rawson in Argentina and the Frente in Venezuela moved further along the continuum by demanding that wives at least have a say in the decision to alienate or donate, respectively, the community property. María Abello's formulation was unique, for although she maintained husbands as heads of the conjugal society, she wanted them to turn over half of the gananciales (which would include a husband's earnings) for wives to manage to meet daily expenses and their own needs, an implicit form of parallel management.

The other five proposals explicitly asked for the joint or parallel management of the gananciales by husband and wife, in effect, eliminating the husband as the sole decision-maker. Peruvian lawyer Miguelina Acosta, in 1920, was the first to propose their joint management. In the mid-1930s, the PIDF proposal in Uruguay included joint management of gananciales as well as of each spouse's individual earnings and assets. In her senate bill, Sofia Álvarez Vignoli modified this idea so that each spouse manages their own assets and earnings but jointly manage the gananciales.

The 1922 proposal of Peruvian María Jesús Alvarado envisioned a marital regime where husbands and wives each had parallel and independent rights over their property during the marriage, subject to a parallel constraint (neither could alienate such assets without the other's consent), although they would pool and divide the gananciales at the end. This combination of regimes – separation of property during the marriage but community property at its end – is what Chilean Elena Caffarena came to advocate decades later as best establishing the conditions for equal property rights in marriage.

Not all feminists agreed, however, that this was the ideal marital regime, even in Uruguay that adopted this mixed regime, because not all wives could benefit directly from separation of property during the marriage. During the legislative debates in Uruguay, Deputy Magdalena Antonelli was concerned about the situation of housewives who neither brought nor inherited property nor earned income and thus would not have gananciales to manage during marriage (Álvarez 1946, 300–21). The main way to give them access to income was if the gananciales were jointly managed. Thus, she and Senator Álvarez agreed that the ideal arrangement was parallel management by each spouse of individual earnings and assets with joint management of the gananciales.

Equal civil rights in marriage, nonetheless, required not only establishing equal property rights but also abolishing all the elements of potestad marital that underpinned male household headship, for instance, determination of the couple's domicile and patria potestad over children. While almost all these proposals called for mothers and fathers to have equal patria potestad, only those of María Abella and Sofía Álvarez included the joint determination of where a couple resided although this was implicit in Miguelina Acosta's demand for a dual-headed household. Senator Álvarez's proposal as amended was the basis for Uruguay's 1946 law, the one that came closest to achieving equal rights in marriage.

Reforms Enacted by Mid-Century

By the mid-twentieth century, all seven South American countries had strengthened married women's property rights and women had attained many of the other civil rights that men had. These countries differed not only in terms of the process through which women acquired these but also in the scope of their reforms. This section summarizes the reforms enacted in the marital regime and potestad marital, spousal inheritance rights, patria potestad over children, divorce and legal separation and women's other civil rights.

The Marital Regime and Potestad Marital

A defining feature of the reforms of the marital regime adopted by the seven countries through the 1950s was that they maintained the centrality of community property: at the dissolution of the marriage, the couple (and/or their estates) pooled and divided the gananciales in equal shares. Whereas these reforms weakened potestad marital with respect to a husband's control over a wife's property, most maintained key elements of his control over her person. Only one country came close to fully eliminating it.

To facilitate cross-country comparison of these legal changes, Table 9.2 summarizes how these reforms changed the main components of the marital regime and three other dimensions of potestad marital. Five countries – Argentina Chile, Ecuador, Peru and Venezuela – maintained the conjugal society or partial community property as the default regime with the husband as its head and manager of the gananciales, with wives gaining varying degrees of autonomy over their earnings and assets as well as voice over the disposition of the gananciales. Two, Colombia and Uruguay, adopted the regime of deferred community property that combined separation of property during the marriage with community property at its dissolution.

The reform that garnered the earliest consensus in the region was regarding the right of working wives to manage their own earnings, a measure that

TABLE 9.2 Reforms to the Marital Regime and Potestad Marital Enacted through the Early 1950s

Country/year of reform[a]	*Default marital regime*	*If wife manages own earnings*	*If wife manages own assets*	*Who manages community property*	*If option of separation of property is available*	*If wife owes husband obedience*	*If wife has right to be employed*	*Who decides on domicile*
Argentina (1926)	Conjugal society	Yes, as reserved property	Option	Husband, but wife's consent to donate	No	No	Yes	Husband
Chile (1925/1934)	Conjugal society	Yes, as reserved property	No	Husband; 1952 – wife's consent to alienate	In prenuptial; 1943 – by mutual consent after marriage	Yes	Yes, husband can appeal	Husband
Colombia (1932)	Deferred community property	Yes	Yes	Parallel control over own gananciales	No	Yes	Yes	Husband
Ecuador (1911)	Conjugal society	Option; 1939 – if wage worker; 1950 – if professional	Option	Husband, but if wife excludes her assets, the gananciales hers; 1936 – wife's consent to alienate	No	Yes	Assumed, he could revoke	Husband
Peru (1936)	Conjugal society	Yes, as reserved property	Yes	Husband	No	No	Assumed, if he revokes, wife can appeal	Husband, she has redress
Uruguay (1946)	Deferred community property	Yes	Yes	Parallel control over own gananciales, mutual consent to alienate	Yes, at any point by demand of either	No	Yes	By mutual consent
Venezuela (1942)	Conjugal society	1916 – yes, as reserved property	Yes	Husband, mutual consent to donate	1873 – yes, in prenuptial	No	Yes	Husband, she has redress

Note:
[a] *Year of major reform; if a year appears in another column, it is of a previous or subsequent partial reform of the civil code.*

responded to the notable increase women's wage labor force participation. Prior to the enactment of broader civil code reform, specific legislation often gave certain groups of women the right to manage their own savings accounts – such as Chile in 1907, Argentina in 1914, Uruguay in 1919 and Colombia in 1928 – and/or enacted labor codes that gave wives control over their own wages – such as Chile in 1924 and Colombia in 1931. Such legislation provided momentum to the recognition of the right of all working wives, including professionals and own-account workers, to control their own earnings in subsequent code reform efforts.

By 1946, wives who earned income derived from their independent labor had the right to manage their earnings in all seven countries (Table 9.2), meeting the minimum demand of most feminists. In two, Colombia and Uruguay, this was because the separation of property regime prevailed during the marriage. In four – Argentina, Chile, Peru and Venezuela – their earnings constituted reserved property, following variations of the German and French models. This meant that wives had the automatic right to collect their own wages and salaries and decide how to use these earnings. They could save their earnings in their own bank accounts, purchase movable or immovable assets without need for their husbands' approval, and manage these assets, including deciding on their disposition. At the end of the marriage, the assets so acquired constituted gananciales, pooled and divided between the spouses.

Only in Ecuador was a wife's control over her own earnings not automatic, but rather still just an option. Under its 1911 law, via a notarized document, wives could exclude their earnings from the conjugal society to manage them, with the gananciales these generated belonging to them alone. This option was thus more favorable to them than the mechanism of reserved property. However, it was not until the 1938 reform of its labor code that all wives who were wage workers acquired the right to directly receive and manage their own wages automatically without needing to declare such before a notary public.

When married women gained the right to control their own earnings, this did not necessarily mean that they automatically had the right to work outside the home. Under potestad marital, they were subject to their husbands' authority and often explicitly required by law to obey their husbands. The nineteenth-century civil codes of all these countries had similar provisions regarding wives working for an income: they required their husband's permission to do so, whether tacit or explicit (via a general or specific license), and the husband could revoke this permission at any time. Table 9.2 (second-to-last column) shows where and when the reforms lifted such restrictions.

Argentina in its 1926 reform was the first to give wives the right to decide on their own employment without need for their husbands' permission. Wives also acquired this right under the main reforms undertaken in Venezuela, Colombia and Uruguay, in the latter two via the adoption of separation of property in the deferred community property regime. Chile in its 1925 decree and 1934 law took a different approach, granting married women the right to work in principle, but giving husbands the right to appeal this action before a judge to prohibit such for reasonable cause. In its 1936 reform, Peru's civil code still assumed that if a wife was employed, she had her husband's tacit or explicit permission; if he revoked it, however, she gained the right to appeal this action before a judge. Ecuador's civil code maintained its traditional restrictions under potestad marital.

Turning to the management of the assets married women brought to marriage or subsequently acquired through inheritance, except in Chile, the reforms of the default marital regime gave women either the option or absolute right to manage these themselves (Table 9.2, fourth column). In Ecuador, and initially in Argentina, wives had to register their intent to manage such assets in the property registry. If they did not opt to do so, the husband continued to manage these assets. Judicial interpretations in Argentina dismissed this requirement over time, as the courts began to consider contracts executed by wives with their own property as legally valid irrespective of whether they had declared their right to manage such property. In four of the six countries where married women could manage their own property – Ecuador (if they had excluded this property), Argentina, Peru and Colombia – they could rent, mortgage, donate and sell this property and participate in lawsuits regarding it without need for their husband's authorization. Two countries placed some restrictions on what women could do that also applied to men's own individual property, requiring mutual consent either to donate such property (Venezuela) or to alienate it (Uruguay).

Regarding the management of the community property (the next column in Table 9.2), in five countries – Argentina, Chile, Ecuador, Peru and Venezuela – the husband remained the head of the conjugal society and thus, by right, managed the gananciales of the marriage. Since men remained the household heads, the CIM (1948, 125) report to the Ninth Inter-American Conference in Bogota concluded that married women in these countries remained legally, relatively incapable. In contrast, in Colombia and Uruguay, since each spouse managed their own gananciales during the marriage, there was no sole head.

In those countries where women's labor earnings formed reserved property – Chile, Argentina, Peru and Venezuela – the treatment of the assets they acquired with their earnings (that technically constituted gananciales) was an exception to the rules of the conjugal society since wives could manage these and any subsequent gains. At the end of the marriage, however, these gananciales formed part of the community property. In Argentina, Peru and Venezuela, where wives could now manage the assets they brought to marriage or later inherited, the gananciales generated by this individual property (such as rent and interest) were legally under the control of the husband, as was any property acquired jointly.

Some countries instituted restrictions on the husband's ability to freely dispose of community property. These were important safeguards for housewives who did not work for an income or who did not own individual assets, since their half of the community property represented the only assets upon which they could rely when the marriage dissolved. From its inception, Argentina's 1869 Civil Code constrained the husband's management of the community property since he could not donate immovables without the wife's consent or the approval of a judge; its 1926 reform did not alter this restriction. Venezuela instituted a similar restriction in its 1942 reform, requiring a wife's consent for the donation of any community property. Recall that the legal thinking behind this restriction was that while the sale of community property did not diminish the gross value of the assets of the conjugal society (since the cash generated belonged to it), a donation reduced it; thus it was more important to subject donations and not sales or mortgages to mutual consent. This interpretation, nonetheless, was not standard across the region.

When Ecuador, Uruguay and Chile constrained the husband's traditional right to freely dispose of community property they focused on its alienation, perhaps fearful of the fungibility of cash generated from such sales. Under Colombia's and Uruguay's deferred community property regime, each spouse managed all the gananciales generated by their own earnings and assets. In Uruguay, nonetheless, each spouse needed the consent of the other to sell or mortgage immovable assets or a business. According to legal scholars Imre Zajtay and Eduardo Vaz Ferreira (1950), the reason that Uruguay mutually conditioned the sale of these assets was related to a criticism raised of the Colombian version of deferred community property: that an irresponsible husband could dissipate his property and gananciales but at the end of the marriage, benefit unjustly from the gananciales generated by his wife. Thus, Uruguay's reform gave each spouse protection against actions that might be prejudicial to their interests at the cost of the economic autonomy of each.

As mentioned, no South American country adopted full separation of property as the default marital regime. Recall that the only nineteenth-century South American code to explicitly allow the option of full separation of property in a prenuptial agreement was Venezuela's 1873 Civil Code.[16] Bello's 1855 Chilean code and those codes based on it stipulated that in a prenuptial agreement, a woman could choose to manage some but not all the assets she brought to marriage. Hence, the significance of Chile's 1925 decree and 1934 law that allowed couples to opt for the separation of property regime in these. Later, this country adopted even greater flexibility through its 1943 law that allowed couples by mutual consent to opt for it at any point during the marriage. This was also a feature of Uruguay's 1946 law, although it could be by demand of either spouse. In their reforms, Ecuador and Argentina did not change the rules governing prenuptials; these could only cover some of a woman's property.[17] By the 1950s, Venezuela, Chile and Uruguay

16 The language of Uruguay's 1868 Civil Code did not prohibit such (arts. 1909–1920), but neither did it mention the possibility of couples freely deciding on the administration of the property which they brought to marriage, as did Venezuela's codes from 1873 on. Peru's 1852 Civil Code did not include the possibility of prenuptial agreements at all.

17 Colombia maintained its traditional language on prenuptial agreements, but according to CIM (1948, 127), in these a couple could opt to give the husband a mandate to administer his wife's property and gananciales (i.e., choose the conjugal society as an alternative to the deferred community property regime).

were the countries that offered couples the greatest flexibility with respect to marital regimes, where they could choose separation of property prior to, or in the latter two, at any point during the marriage.

Otherwise, separation of property could only result from a judicial action due to fault, or because of a permanent legal separation. The codes of Argentina, Ecuador and Peru maintained the nineteenth-century provision regarding the right of wives to demand the separation of property because of their husband's mismanagement of the gananciales, if they committed fraud or went into bankruptcy. Ecuador expanded the conditions for a separation of property when in 1938, it gave husbands the right to demand it if a women excluded her property from the conjugal society; in 1956, both husbands and wives acquired this right but such an action only originated from a wife's exclusion of property, thus restricting its applicability. Other countries made this action more gender-neutral. In Colombia, where the civil code in 1950 still contained the traditional language in which requesting a separation of property was only a privilege of the wife due to a husband's mismanagement, after its 1932 reform, the courts began considering this action as available to either spouse (Ortega Torres 1950, 93). In its 1942 reform, Venezuela allowed either spouse to demand the separation of property due to the other's poor administration of the gananciales if these were at risk.

The most innovative solution to the dilemma of how to attain the benefits of the separation of property regime while preserving the right of wives to half of the gananciales of the marriage was by instituting the regime of deferred community property, as Colombia and Uruguay did. Argentina's legislature discussed and rejected this approach in the late teens. Peruvian María Jesús Alvarado proposed a sketch of such a regime in the early twenties, while Elena Caffarena proposed it for Chile several decades later; neither Peru nor Chile seriously considered this alternative.

In its report to the Pan American Union, CIM (1948, 125–6) concluded that the deferred community regime, "was the regime that offers women the most advantages and which best suits the cultural and economic conditions of women in Latin America." But it also warned that no one regime perfectly suited all wives. The CIM thus recommended that civil codes should offer couples a choice of regimes as well as the option of being able to change the regime during the marriage, this freedom being a feature of the most "modern and progressive legislation."

While all seven countries reformed their marital regime to enhance married women's control over their earnings and property to some degree, they did not fully eliminate all aspects of potestad marital, especially the husband's control over the person of his wife. In their nineteenth-century civil codes, both Colombia and Ecuador had incorporated jurist Andrés Bello's 1855 definition of potestad marital in the Chilean civil code. Irrespective of their subsequent reform of married women's property rights, all three countries maintained this article in their civil codes.[18]

18 For Colombia, see Ortega Torres (1950, art. 177) and on how as of 1952 Chile maintained it, Lira (1961, art. 132). Ecuador (1970) shows its removal.

Particularly, aggravating to feminists was the requirement that wives obey their husbands. All the South American nineteenth-century codes except for Argentina copied or paraphrased the French civil code article that defined marriage as based on a husband's protection and the wife's obedience. The phrase on the wife's obedience disappeared in the 1936 Peruvian, 1942 Venezuelan and 1946 Uruguayan reforms. It remained in the codes of Chile, Ecuador and Colombia until the second wave of feminism.

Another aspect of potestad marital that feminists considered unjust and was a source of family discord was the husband's exclusive right to determine a couple's place of residence and its correlate, that the wife must follow him wherever he determined unless it threatened her life. By mid-century, the only reform that had made the determination of the couple's domicile subject to mutual consent was the 1946 Uruguayan reform (Table 9.2, last column). Peru in its 1936 reform moved in this direction by modifying the original language to oblige a couple to live together unless "it endangers the health, honor or business interests" of either spouse; nonetheless, the husband continued to determine the place of residence although the wife could seek redress (Peru 1939, arts. 160–163). Venezuela's 1942 Civil Code maintained the requirement that a wife live with and follow her husband wherever he determined with the proviso (introduced in its 1896 code) that a judge could exempt her from doing so for a grave proven cause. Chile, Ecuador, Argentina and Colombia maintained the nineteenth-century language of this provision.[19] In sum, by the mid-1950s, married women were in a much stronger position than they had been at the beginning of this century with respect to their property rights although, except for Uruguay, they did not have close to equal rights in marriage.

Since the share of women in consensual unions was not small, it is noteworthy that only one country, Venezuela, gave attention to their property status. Such men and women were technically single and implicitly operated under separation of property, whereby neither partner had any claim on the other's assets. In its 1942 reform, Venezuela gave women who had been in such a union for at least two years a right to the gananciales generated although only if they had brought assets or earned an income. In contrast to marriages, having contributed domestic labor alone was insufficient to entitle such women to half of the gananciales. In other countries, it was only during second-wave feminism that the property and inheritance rights of women in consensual unions became an issue.

19 For Chile, see Lira (1961, art. 133); Colombia, Ortega Torres (1950, art. 178), and for the status of this article in Argentina in the 1960s, Rébora and Gnecco (1965, 74–75). Ecuador (1970, art. 135) modified the language when it allowed a wife to appeal her husband's decision on residency for a compelling reason.

Spousal Inheritance Rights

Historically wives have been more likely than husbands to widow; thus, the provisions of the inheritance regime were as important to their long-run well-being as those in the marital regime. South American women's higher probability of widowhood in the nineteenth century was primarily because of the large age difference at marriage; in the twentieth, it was because of the gender gap in life expectancy.[20] Feminists, nonetheless, gave little attention to spousal inheritance rights during the first half century since their priority was securing reform of the marital regime.[21]

The lack of attention to inheritance was also because under the partial or deferred community property regimes each spouse received half of the gananciales at the dissolution of the marriage. Women sometimes thought of their half as an inheritance from their husbands although the sharing of the gananciales was a property right, not an inheritance. This sharing principle protected a wife if she widowed although there were not always gananciales at the end, either because of the inability to accumulate assets or debt. Moreover, the estate of a deceased spouse consisted of two components, his/her half of the gananciales plus his/her individual property. Whether and how much spouses inherited from each other was crucially important in whether a wife retained the controlling share of the family home, farm or business.[22]

In the nineteenth-century codes, if a person died without leaving a will, intestate rules privileged the deceased's legitimate children who were always in the 1st order of succession. Surviving spouses had the strongest inheritance rights in Venezuela and Argentina (Deere 2023). In both countries, in the 1st order, the spouse had an unconditional right to an inheritance share equal to that of a child, in Venezuela of the deceased's full estate, and in Argentina only of the individual property of the deceased. Spouses were in the weakest position in those countries where their relative wealth determined whether they inherited, such as in Chile and those countries that followed the 1855 Bello code. In these codes, the surviving spouse could request a *porción conyugal*, which was determined by a judge based on relative need and whether they owned assets and received gananciales from the marriage; it could not exceed one-fourth of the estate.

20 See Szuchman (1988), for example, on the large but declining gender age gap at marriage in nineteenth-century Buenos Aires. Arriaga and Davis (1969, Table A-1) show the increasing gender gap in life expectancy at birth, which in most South American countries began in the early twentieth century.

21 Amanda Labarca (1924) was the exception for she recognized that instituting separation of property as the default would require a reform of inheritance rules to ensure adequate protections for widows.

22 For example, if acquired during the marriage, the family home constituted part of the gananciales, and if a wife had no inheritance rights, the widow received half of it as a property right and the children the other half as an inheritance. If the wife also inherited from the husband, she would have the controlling share and greater bargaining power over its disposition.

In the first half of the century, the inheritance rights of surviving spouses improved in those countries where their rights had been weakest, often as part of reforms focused on improving the inheritance rights of recognized natural children. Both Peru and Chile strengthened the position of the surviving spouse in the 1st order of intestate. In Peru's 1936 code, which for the first time gave widows and widowers parallel rights, the spouse became automatically entitled to a share equal to a child up to a maximum of one-quarter of the estate. This share no longer depended on their pleading poverty although the final amount received was determined by whether they received gananciales, with this sum deducted. Chile in 1952 also gave the surviving spouse an automatic right to inherit alongside children, and up to twice the share of a child; the final amount, however, continued to depend on whether they owned assets and received gananciales, with these values deducted from the final amount.

Uruguay in 1914 and Ecuador in 1935 maintained the traditional *porción conyugal* but improved the position of spouses at the expense of the siblings of the deceased. In the third order, in the absence of legitimate descendants, natural children and ascendants, the surviving spouse now inherited the full estate. Colombia in 1936 only bettered the position of the spouse in the 2nd and 3rd orders by giving them a slightly larger portion of the estate than previously.

No South American country in this period recognized inheritance rights between partners in a consensual union, nor was this raised as a demand by feminists. The main concern of feminists and legislators was in making the conditions for recognition of paternity easier so that children born outside of marriage could inherit from their fathers. Between 1913 (in Uruguay) and 1952 (in Chile), every country except Argentina broadened the ability to investigate paternity and improved the inheritance rights of recognized natural children. Nonetheless, if a parent had legitimate children, the share of such a child was always less than that of a legitimate one although the tendency was toward an improvement in the size of their share.

Mothers' Exercise of Patria Potestad

Patria potestad, a father's control over the person and assets of his minor children, was a moral, practical and economic issue for mothers, which is why most feminist proposals included the demand for equal rights over their children. Given the importance of its moral and practical aspects, the economic dimension has received less attention although it was crucially important to the property rights of widows. On the death of a father, the largest share of his patrimony automatically went to his legitimate children. The administration of the inheritance of children who were minors was relevant to the well-being of mothers because the gains generated by such property accrued to the children's guardian as compensation for services rendered. If widowed mothers did not automatically assume patria potestad, this compensation would go to someone else rather than to them.

Of the nineteenth-century civil codes, Argentina's 1869 code was the most favorable to mothers. In principle, both parents exercised patria potestad together although the father alone administered the children's assets. Upon his death, the widow automatically assumed it, including the administration of the children's assets. All the other South American nineteenth-century civil codes defined it as the exclusive right of fathers, while only three – Venezuela, Ecuador and Uruguay – automatically gave this right to the mother if the father died or was otherwise incapacitated. Nonetheless, in Ecuador and Venezuela, a husband in his will could name an advisor to manage the children's assets with his wife, diminishing her autonomy.

Even in Argentina's favorable 1869 code, if a widowed mother subsequently remarried, she lost the right to exercise patria potestad over her own children. She had to inform a judge of her impending marriage, who then appointed a guardian; at his discretion, the judge could appoint her or someone else. If a widow failed to inform the court of her remarriage, she and her new husband were jointly liable for her children's assets and the gains from their management accrued to the new conjugal society. In Ecuador, if a widow remarried, she lost the right to administer the children's assets although she retained other aspects of patria potestad, such as the right to determine their education. Venezuela's initial code provided a bit more flexibility, for if she remarried, a tribunal made up of family members determined if the mother continued to manage the children's assets; if so, she and her new husband assumed joint responsibility for these assets and shared the benefits. In Uruguay, a widow also lost this right and it was the prerogative of a judge to determine the guardian; as in Argentina, if she failed to report that she was remarrying, she and her new husband assumed joint responsibility.

In the twentieth century, mothers automatically assuming patria potestad if they widowed became standardized when the reforms in Chile, Colombia and Peru finally incorporated this measure. Whether widows should retain the right to manage their children's assets if they remarried remained controversial. In Colombia's 1936 and Chile's 1925 reforms, they lost this right, although in the 1934 Chilean updating of these provisions, the language changed to resemble that of Uruguay's 1893 code, with the default being that the widow shared joint responsibility with her new husband. Mothers were in the most favorable position as a result of the 1926 Argentine, 1942 Venezuelan and 1946 Uruguayan reforms, for if widows remarried, they automatically continued to exercise patria potestad on the same terms as widowers, with the gains from children's assets accruing to the surviving parent.

The most controversial issue was whether parents should exercise equal patria potestad *during* the marriage. Only two other countries went as far as Argentina's 1869 code in principle. Peru's 1936 code recognized both spouses although it still gave fathers the final word in any dispute and stipulated that only they were to manage children's assets. Venezuela's 1942 code adopted similar rules to Peru's, considering both parents to share it although the father managed the children's assets. Uruguay's 1946 reform was the first to place parents on equal footing, including in managing children's assets; however, it assumed that only one of them would manage these assets, leaving it to the couple to decide which parent would do so. This likely favored the continuation of fathers as sole managers of these assets.

Divorce and Legal Separation

Among the most enduring restrictions on the civil rights of both husbands and wives in three countries, Argentina, Chile and Colombia, was not being able to divorce and remarry.[23] Ecuador in 1902 and Venezuela in 1904 instituted absolute divorce in the context of their early twentieth-century liberal revolutions, as did Uruguay in 1907 under a progressive social-democratic regime. Peru approved civil divorce in 1930 in the context of regime change and it became more accessible in its 1936 civil code.

Civil divorce in Ecuador and Peru was initially possible only on the grounds of fault of one spouse but mutual consent was subsequently added, in 1910 and 1934, respectively. In contrast, Uruguay's initial civil divorce law included mutual consent. It later added divorce by sole demand of the wife, the only country to adopt this feature.[24] In Venezuela, divorce by mutual consent was controversial for decades. The compromise reached in its 1942 reform went only as far as allowing mutual consent for a permanent legal separation although after two years either spouse could request a no-fault divorce.

Following their colonial heritage, the grounds for a legal separation (termed "divorce," but without the right to remarry) in the nineteenth-century codes differed for husbands and wives when it came to adultery. Any form of adultery by a wife was grounds, whereas for a husband it required scandalous public behavior or concubinage.[25] Feminists found this double moral standard reprehensible which is why many of their proposals addressed it. Of those that instituted absolute divorce, Ecuador and Peru adopted the same standard for husbands and wives in their respective 1935 and 1936 reforms. The reformed codes of Venezuela and Uruguay continued to treat adultery differently irrespective of their having strengthened women's civil rights.[26]

Most countries strengthened women's property rights in the case of a legal separation. Recall that in the nineteenth-century codes, this judicial action dissolved the

23 Argentina instituted a lasting civil divorce law in 1987; Colombia, divorce for all in 1991; and Chile not until 2004. On why it was so controversial, see Lavrin (1985), Rojas (1997) and Htun (2003).

24 See Chapter 8.

25 Only Argentina in its original 1869 Civil Code treated the adultery of wives or husbands similarly as grounds for a permanent separation (Argentina 1870, Book I, Section 2, Chapter IX, art. 46).

26 Venezuela (1942, art. 185); Uruguay (1976, arts. 148, 187). In Uruguay, Law 14.766 of 1976 finally made the conditions of adultery equal as grounds for divorce.

conjugal society, with women gaining control over their earnings, assets and half of the gananciales. They could not, however, alienate their immovable property without their husband's or a judge's authorization. Venezuela removed this restriction in 1904 when it instituted full divorce, Colombia in 1930 legislation, and Chile and Peru in their civil code reforms. It remained in the codes of Ecuador, Argentina and Uruguay through mid-century even after they strengthened married women's property rights.

Women's Civil Capacity

By the 1950s, women who were single (never married, divorced or widowed) attained equal civil rights to men in most countries. Some of the civil code reforms that strengthened married women's property rights simultaneously lifted the restrictions on women being witnesses such as those of Argentina in 1926, Chile in 1925, Peru in 1936 and Venezuela in 1942. Colombia and Uruguay enacted such legislation a decade or more prior to reform of the marital regime, in 1922 and 1926, respectively. Ecuador was an outlier with respect to women being legal witnesses in two respects. Most of the nineteenth-century codes prohibited women from being witnesses except to a marriage; Ecuador's 1860 code allowed them to be a witness to both marriages and a will but not for other public acts, a restriction that continued through mid-century.[27]

Most of the nineteenth-century civil codes prohibited women from being a guardian over minor children unless they were a child's mother or grandmother. Venezuela's 1896 reform included sisters and aunts as potential guardians as long as they remained single or were widows; the restriction on wives being guardians remained until its 1942 reform. Chile, beginning with its 1925 decree, allowed all women to be guardians, although wives required the permission of their husbands, a limitation that remained past mid-century.[28] Ecuador was the only one not to broaden eligibility to include other women relatives.[29]

Finally, except for Chile, by mid-century, countries had abrogated previous restrictions on women's appointment to public posts, such as becoming public advocates, notaries and judges and the in the civil service more generally. These processes were quite heterogeneous: in Argentina, it came about through judicial interpretation of its 1926 reform law; in Ecuador and Uruguay, due to women acquiring full political rights in their respective 1929 and 1934 constitutions; in Colombia and Venezuela, through constitutional recognition, in 1936 and 1944,

27 Ecuador's prohibition on women being a witness to public instruments was in its code of civil procedures (Ecuador 1938, 178).

28 See Lira (1961, art. 137) where this requirement remained.

29 Uruguay's 1934 Code of the Child repealed the restriction on most women being guardians although this discriminatory article remained in its civil code (Uruguay 1976, art. 329).

respectively, prior to women attaining suffrage; and in Peru, through special 1946 legislation, also prior to suffrage.

Conclusion

The proposals by feminists and their organizations for civil code reform had an impact on the content of the final legislation enacted in all five countries where women made these in that the revised codes incorporated at least some of their ideas. The demands most easily incorporated were, of course, those on which the legal community and politicians were already reaching consensus, such as removing restrictions on women exercising certain civil functions like being a witness or a guardian of children, mothers exercising patria potestad in the fathers' absence or married women workers controlling their own income.

The most modest feminist demand across countries (including where women did not develop their own full proposals) was for wives to at least maintain the same property rights they held as single women. They acquired such in all seven, at least as an option. In the two that adopted deferred community property, Colombia and Uruguay, wives automatically retained the right to manage their own earnings and assets. An important difference in the reforms of the other five was whether a wife's management of her earnings and property became the default position – applicable to all wives – or a choice. A further difference is whether a wife's earnings and the property they brought to marriage or later inherited received similar treatment. The dominant tendency was to treat the independent earnings of all wives as reserved property (Argentina, Chile, Peru and Venezuela); how they treated the assets wives brought to marriage or later inherited was more heterogeneous.

The default in Peru and Venezuela was that wives managed these assets. In contrast, in the 1911 Ecuadorian, 1926 Argentine and 1925 and 1934 Chilean legislation, wives had to explicitly opt to manage their own property, in Ecuador and Argentina (initially) by registering it and in Chile by choosing the separation of property regime in a prenuptial. In Argentina, the legislation was consistent with María Abella's thinking that what was important was to give women a choice, so that the law not forcibly convert them into dependents. However, it met Elvira Rawson's demand only part way since she wanted wives' management of their property to be the automatic default, applicable to all. If wives had to act to exercise this right, the concern was that the status quo would prevail.

Feminists and allied legislators raised similar concerns in other countries regarding the option of offering the separation of property regime as an option in prenuptial agreements. Couples rarely made these since any departure from the rules of the conjugal society signaled that a wife did not have confidence in her husband; also prior to marriage, she would rarely be aware that he might not be a good manager nor act in their joint interests. In Chile, where feminists and legislators seriously debated adopting separation of property as the default regime, and enacted it as an option, Elena Caffarena and MEMCH lobbied to improve upon it, by making this option available at any point during the marriage, a reform later adopted. Nonetheless, couples still rarely took advantage of this flexibility, meaning that few wives ended up managing their own property through this means. Thus in practice, Chile enacted the most modest of these reforms, centering principally on wives' control over their wages and salaries.

All the initial feminist proposals maintained the concept of community property in their proposed default regime. Most feminists were hesitant to abandon the known advantages of spouses sharing the gananciales, given gender inequalities in employment opportunities and earnings. As shown, their proposals differed on the extent of wives' participation in the management of gananciales, from none to the wife having a say on their disposition, to spouses having either parallel or joint rights. Just allowing wives to have a say in the sale or mortgaging of community property was sufficiently controversial that Argentine legislators ignored Rawson's modest proposal to give women a voice in its 1926 law, this in a country that already recognized the need for mutual consent to donate gananciales. Two decades later, the latter was a demand of feminists in Venezuela and they did attain mutual consent for donations from either the individual or community property under the control of each spouse. In Ecuador and Chile, after their initial reforms, when women's organizations lobbied for mutual consent for the sale or mortgage of gananciales they achieved such in subsequent legislation.

The most radical feminist demand was for either parallel or joint management of the gananciales since it ended a husband's sole control that underpinned male household headship. It was part of feminist proposals of the early 1920s in Peru and the 1930s in Uruguay but attained only in Uruguay and Colombia, the two countries that adopted deferred community property as the default. No country adopted the joint management of gananciales. An achievement of first-wave feminism, nonetheless, was that in most countries wives gained at least a voice in their management.

Feminists in only one country, Venezuela, raised the demand for recognition of the property rights of couples in consensual unions, a reform that had not been previously in discussion in legal circles. They successfully attained recognition of the community property generated in such unions, although on terms less favorable for wives than they envisioned. Feminists in most countries lobbied for other measures to improve the status of unmarried mothers whether or not they were in a union – for their civil codes to allow the investigation of paternity of children born outside of marriage and the strengthening of the inheritance rights of such children, reforms widely enacted in this period.

The most persistent feminist demand across countries and decades, and one that turned out to be especially controversial, was that spouses share patria potestad during the marriage. By mid-century, all countries had at least recognized a mother's right to assume such in the father's absence and in most widows and widowers exercised the same rights if they remarried, with Colombia and Ecuador being the laggards. Equal rights over children during marriage were another matter. While

Argentina, Peru and Venezuela recognized a mother's right of patria potestad, the father either had the last word or retained control over children's assets. Uruguay's reform went furthest in instituting the principle of equal rights but at the same time left it to the couple to decide who exercised such in practice, which may have discouraged any change from traditional practice. It is consistent that it was the three countries whose initial codes explicitly barred mothers from ever exercising patria potestad –Chile, Colombia and Ecuador –that registered the least progress in this regard.

As the country chapters showed, first-wave feminists tended to make their demands for equal civil rights on maternalist grounds, so that women better exercise the roles of wives and mothers, not in a repudiation of these roles. This chapter has argued that the main differentiating factor in their demands was where they stood on a continuum relative to a husband's role as household head and sole manager of the community property. In most countries, the idea of equal rights in marriage was ahead of its time; it was not yet among the aspirations of most women nor acceptable to most politicians. It is thus not surprising that it was in the last reform before mid-century in the only country where women were in the legislature that went furthest in attaining it. Uruguay's 1946 reform then served as the bridge, becoming the model for the demands of second-wave feminists in the other countries.

10

CONCLUSION

After her 1923 trip to South America, IWSA president Carrie Chapman Catt (1923b) disparaged the state of feminism in the region, calling it a "backward movement," being some 40 years behind the United States. While South American women were aware of the oppressive nature of their civil codes, she considered their demands to be timid. Moreover, she reported that they were not yet interested in political rights. Catt was also aware that they faced more stubborn barriers to acquiring rights than women in North America, among them a high rate of illiteracy, a tight relation between the Catholic Church and the state, and broad acceptance of the traditional gender division of labor that venerated women as mothers and wives. She also understood that participating in the political system might not seem like a pressing need to many women, given the region's history of civil wars and dictators. Thus, she recognized that "the road to emancipation in these countries may be a very different one," that is, women's organizations might not follow the same historic progression in their demands as had those in the more advanced countries (Catt 1923a, 26).

Catt, nonetheless, thought South American women held an advantage that women in the United States had not had, which might influence the timing of reforms – the power of example, the fact that women elsewhere had already achieved strong civil and political rights. They were thus aware "that their countries have fallen behind in the procession" (Catt 1923b, 1030). Her visit, coming shortly after the ratification of US women's suffrage, coincided with the moment when growing numbers of South American feminists began to embrace and organize around the demand for political rights.

The preceding chapters show that many South American intellectuals did, indeed, consider what the more advanced countries had achieved with respect to

DOI: 10.4324/9781003658436-10

women's civil and political rights as a measure of a country's progress toward "civilization."[1] These chapters trace in detail the complex process that in distinct socioeconomic and political contexts led to the strengthening of women's civil and political rights in seven countries, each in their own unique way. This concluding chapter summarizes the main paths to reform of the marital regime, the ideas that its protagonists – feminists, jurists and politicians – adopted or discarded, and how the struggles for women's civil and political rights interacted. It then discusses the potential impacts of these reforms on women's economic autonomy, which requires considering the scope and uptake of these laws and the social change to which they contributed, as well as the challenges of documenting these changes.

Forging Different Pathways to Reform

Overall, two paths led to reforms of married women's property rights in South America distinguished by the political context and whether organized women were part of the process. In the Northern Andes, liberal jurists and politicians led these initiatives prior to the expansion of women's education and wage employment and the emergence of women's rights groups. Ecuador and Venezuela enacted their initial reforms during periods of liberal hegemony with minimal conservative opposition. In contrast, in the Southern Cone where women's education and labor force participation were far more advanced, feminist groups demanding rights emerged at about the same time that liberal and socialist legislators began to propose such reforms. While economic analysis predicts that these reforms advance in countries with higher levels of wealth, urbanization and education, they began in the lesser developed Andean countries rather than in the more developed Southern Cone. Because of differing political contexts, these reforms were more contentious in the latter, requiring compromise between progressive and conservative political forces and often limiting their scope.

In Ecuador and Venezuela, the initial reforms of married women's property rights were part of a radical liberal political package, conducted in the name of expanding individual freedom, which included separation of church and state and enactment of civil marriage and absolute divorce, similar to the earlier processes in Central America.[2] This study reveals how liberal revolutionary ideals circulated in the circum-Caribbean/Northern Andes; moreover, that these liberal reforms reflected legal change taking place in advance of socioeconomic change with the objective of promoting economic and social progress.

1 See Towns' (2019) discussion on how suffragists in Europe and the United States were able to invert the initial conception of "civilization," which excluded women from politics, to one that required their incorporation.

2 In Central America, the reform of family law also included the enactment of testamentary freedom to facilitate the transmission of wealth and promote the free circulation of capital and development of markets (Deere and León 2005). Testamentary freedom was on the agenda in Ecuador although not enacted; I found no evidence of its discussion in Venezuela.

Many of the same ideas and antecedents that drove the revolutions in Central America and Ecuador as well as Venezuela's liberal "Regeneration" influenced liberal jurists and the politicians of the Liberal, Socialist and Radical parties in the Southern Cone, but these never came to hold similar political hegemony. Except for Uruguay, which under a social-democratic regime enacted the separation of church and state and civil divorce in the same period as Ecuador and Venezuela, reformers elsewhere faced a more powerful Catholic Church and often vehement conservative opposition. This made the enaction of both civil divorce and the reform of women's property rights contentious issues. Nonetheless, the factors favorable to women's organizing in the Southern Cone also produced changes in social norms and in the views of some sectors of the Church, conditions that eventually proved favorable to reform of married women's property rights, if not always regarding other rights, such as divorce or shared patria potestad over children.

While the conditions that prompted reform efforts differed across South America, discussions over how to go about strengthening married women's property rights shared similar features. The reforms proposed to change the same inherited marital regime, partial community property with potestad marital, and participants were part of the same broader circuit of ideas, which included awareness of the reforms enacted earlier in the United States and Europe.

In discussions, jurists and politicians everywhere discussed the costs and benefits of the separation of property regime. Its main appeal to liberals was its grounding in the principle of economic freedom. It fully recognized the legal personality of wives so that they managed their earnings and the assets they brought to marriage or later acquired with full autonomy. Moreover, advocates stressed how well this regime worked in the United States and England, promoting individual initiative and economic growth, while being compatible with the stability of the family. But it was one thing to transition from Common Law and equity courts to the separation of property regime as in the Anglo-Saxon countries, and quite another to abandon the community property tradition.

Defenders of this tradition argued that community property best captured the unity of spouses that marriage required. There was a fair amount of consensus across the political spectrum that the collective interests of the family took precedence over the individual interests of its members. While some feminists found the separation of property regime appealing, most agreed with this assessment. Moreover, they generally accepted that the unity of the family depended upon the traditional gender division of labor, even glorifying women's responsibility for home and childrearing. But they did not want these roles to limit their activities and contributions. When feminists demanded rights such as greater economic autonomy or later the vote, it was to better fulfill their responsibilities as wives and mothers. In addition, privileging the family above individual needs was a way of contrasting South American feminism from that of North America and England, which many considered too individualistic and extreme, given the infamous example of the British suffragettes in the teens.

The partial community property regime also offered wives concrete economic benefits, principally the sharing and equal division of the gananciales at the dissolution of the marriage irrespective of each spouse's relative contribution to their generation. Reflecting the Hispanic colonial heritage, traditionalists justified this sharing principle as based in the obligation of husbands to provide wives with protection, either because women were the weaker sex and/or because they viewed them as intellectually inferior. As women's education began to improve in the early decades of the century, the rationale behind the sharing principle of community property also changed.

Some jurists and politicians began to argue that the sharing principle recognized women's domestic and caring labor within the separate spheres and was a just compensation for the services provided by wives. Moreover, this argument was more compatible with the supposed elevated status of wives as "queen of the home" than earlier rationalizations based on women's inferiority as illustrated in the 1911 debate in Ecuador's Senate. Others who advocated maintaining the conjugal society as the only regime or adopting the deferred community property regime made similar equity arguments later on. Another equity argument employed by advocates of the sharing principle was that husbands were in a better position to generate gananciales than wives, given men's much higher economic activity rates as well as the gender gap in earnings.[3] Not raised very frequently, even by feminists, was how these inequalities were related to the ideological construct of separate spheres that maintained wives as queens of the home and discouraged their labor force participation.

Worth stressing is how no South American country adopted separation of property as the default regime as most US states and England had. The legislatures of only two countries, Ecuador and Chile, seriously considered replacing the conjugal society with the regime of separation of property but ultimately rejected doing so. Many reformers were open to the idea of offering it as an option, principally in prenuptial agreements. A choice of regimes was in keeping with the principle of individual freedom and conformed to the international trend.[4] Nonetheless, by mid-century, only the codes of three countries, Chile, Uruguay and Venezuela, offered couples such flexibility.

The challenge before reform-oriented jurists, politicians and feminists was how to maintain the benefits of the conjugal society while giving wives greater

3 Although I found no evidence of the use of this argument, another factor that generated potential gender inequality in wealth was inheritance. Legitimate children irrespective of sex inherited equally in intestate but as mentioned in Chapter 1, inequality among siblings could be produced by a will through a parent's use of the mejora and/or the designation of the share that they were free to will to only one child. In addition, even when the value of inheritance shares was equal, men and women tended to inherit different assets, with men oftentimes favored with land or businesses (Deere and León 2001, Chapter 7).

4 Recall that France's 1804 and Germany's 1896 civil codes and the reforms in Mexico and Central America all offered at least two or more regimes.

economic autonomy. In this regard, the adoption of the mechanism of reserved property for wives from the 1896 German and 1907 French reforms was appealing because it was an exception within the community property regime and it addressed what many considered to be the most pressing need – to ensure the welfare of working-class families by giving the growing number of working wives the right to manage their own earnings. Moreover, the adoption of such a partial reform did not impinge on a husband's control of the assets that women of means brought to marriage or later inherited, what was likely of most concern to middle- and upper-class legislators personally. This largely explains why wives' control over their earnings was the reform that garnered the most consensus and one that all South American countries adopted.

Women's control over the assets they brought to marriage or inherited was more contentious, seen in how in Ecuador and Argentina's early legislation this became an option rather than an automatic right, and how Chile limited this possibility to those who chose separation of property in a prenuptial. Moreover, except in those countries that adopted deferred community property, where wives gained the right to manage all of their own property as the default, husbands still managed their gananciales.

The most novel and far-reaching way of combining wives' greater economic autonomy with the benefits of community property was instituting the regime of deferred community property since it allowed separation of property during the marriage with the pooling and equal division of the gananciales at its end. While this is what in effect four Central American countries adopted between 1887 and 1906, it was rare for jurists or legislators to refer to this antecedent. The exception was Argentine Senator Enrique del Valle (1918), who in the justification for adopting this regime in his 1918 bill referenced the reforms in Costa Rica, El Salvador and Nicaragua. In contrast, in Colombia, which adopted deferred community property in 1932, jurist Luis Felipe Latorre referred only to the reforms in Hungary and Scandinavia as models. In Uruguay, where this mixed regime emerged as a compromise among reformers, legislators mentioned debates around this regime in Europe but not its adoption in Colombia or Central America. Nonetheless, given the degree of interaction between intellectuals in Argentina and Uruguay, it is likely that jurists and politicians in Uruguay were aware of the debate over the del Valle bill in the neighboring country.[5] It clearly was more acceptable for legislators to ground their proposals in the debates and experience of the more advanced countries of Europe, which embodied the notion of progress, than in the lesser developed countries of Central America.

Also worth noting is how in several countries, legislators presented bills that were particularly favorable to wives, giving them special privileges within the partial

5 After Uruguay adopted the deferred community property, French legal scholar Imre Zajtay and Uruguayan Eduardo Vaz Ferreira (1950) summarized its origin being in customary law in Hungary, the 1887 Costa Rican Civil Code, the reforms in Scandinavia of the 1920s, the Colombian reform of 1932 and debates in France in the 1930s.

community property marital regime that went beyond the German or French formulation of married women's reserved property. In Argentina, Deputy Drago's 1902 and Senator del Valle's 1918 bills, as well as Uruguayan Senator Frugoni's 1939 bill, all excluded from the gananciales women's earnings and the assets acquired with such. Similarly, Peruvian Deputy Paz Varela's 1925 bill excluded from the community property the gananciales that wives generated from the management of the non-dowry property they brought to marriage. In addition, in both Uruguayan Senator Minelli's 1930 bill and the original Colombia 1930 capitulaciones bill, only wives could declare a separation of property at any time during the marriage, without need to give cause. The justification for such measures was either because wives needed special protection, being the weaker sex, or because they were at a disadvantage with respect to their socioeconomic roles and required compensation. Only the Uruguayan legislators directly referenced Vaz Ferreira's feminism of compensation as justification for their proposals although his work was likely known in Argentina in the teens, given the circulation of people and ideas between Buenos Aires and Montevideo.

Since none of these bills giving wives special privileges were successful, it is noteworthy that the very first law to strengthen married women's property rights in South America did so. Recall that Ecuador's 1911 law allowed wives if they opted to manage their own assets and/or earnings to exclude their gananciales from the community property while still benefiting from sharing in those generated by their husbands. Interestingly, of the feminist proposals analyzed in Chapter 9, only one gave wives favored treatment, Amanda Labarca's 1922 CNM-C proposal regarding the gananciales generated from women's reserved property. Feminists whose sights were set on equal rights in marriage focused on attaining either parallel or joint rights in the management of gananciales, as in other aspects of marriage.

Of the seven countries, only in Uruguay was the possibility of joint management of the gananciales, a feature of several legislative proposals, including those of President Brum in the 1920s and senators Frugoni and Alvarez in the 1940s. This helps place the proposals by Peruvian feminists in perspective, especially how radical an idea it was in 1920 for Miguelina Acosta to propose the joint management of gananciales as part of the default regime. María Jesús Alvarado's 1922 proposal, on the other hand, focused on parallel rights in all aspects of marriage, including in the management of individual property and the gananciales, with the pooling of the latter at the end, similar to Senator del Valle's proposal in Argentina. It is unknown whether Alvarado was aware of his proposal. It was only in Uruguay and not until the 1930s and 1940s that feminists explicitly addressed the relative benefits of parallel versus joint management of the gananciales, with the main concern being what best served the interests of housewives who owned no assets nor worked for income.

Turning to the approved reforms, what most stands out is their heterogeneity. While jurists, legislators and feminists were often aware of the discussions and reforms adopted in neighboring countries, it was their own interaction within specific national circumstances and the politics of the process that tended to determine their content. In most cases where feminists made detailed proposals, these tended to be further reaching than the compromises reached in the legislative process.

The minimum demand of feminists was that when they marry, women maintain the same rights over their earnings and assets as they had as single women. They achieved this in all cases with respect to their earnings and, except in Chile, regarding the assets they brought to marriage or inherited. Notably, the first feminist proposal in Chile did not demand the latter; wives attained the capacity to manage their inherited assets only if they opted for separation of property.

Regarding the management of community property, worth highlighting is how even a modest proposal for wives to have a say in its alienation was unacceptable in Argentina in the 1920s, this in a country where husbands' donation of community property already required mutual consent. Giving wives a say over the disposition of gananciales only slowly became more acceptable, seen in how Venezuela adopted mutual consent for their donation and Ecuador and Chile eventually did so for their alienation.

Only one country, Uruguay, seriously considered the more radical feminist demand in the continuum of wives having joint or parallel rights over the gananciales, which also enacted the most profound reform. While attaining deferred community property as the default regime guaranteed wives parallel property rights in marriage, not all feminists in this country were convinced that this was the ideal regime. Leading feminists preferred that the couple jointly manage the gananciales because of the protection and access to income it offered housewives who owned no individual assets nor earned income directly. Second-wave feminists across the region would resume this discussion of the benefits of joint versus parallel rights over gananciales.

A recurrent problem in these debates was that it was difficult for legislators to disentangle management of community property from the concept of potestad marital. Both traditionalists and most liberal reformers could not imagine the family having more than one person at its head, and this was always the husband. Thus, most of the Latin American countries that adopted the mixed regime of deferred community property, such as those in Central America and Colombia, maintained potestad marital, Uruguay being the exception. The steadfast commitment to maintaining the husband as head, that is, the patriarchal family, explains the difficulty that most legislatures had of even considering proposals for the joint or parallel management of the community property, shared patria potestad, or the undoing of the other ways that husbands legally controlled the persons of their wives.

Thus in no country did first-wave feminists achieve all for which they had hoped. Except in Uruguay, their demands for equal patria potestad and an end to all vestiges of potestad marital went unheeded, although several other countries dropped the odious requirement of wives needing to obey their husbands. Once organized women achieved some reform of the civil code, they tended to move on to other pressing issues, which by the 1930s was women's suffrage. In Argentina, during that decade, they also had to defend the civil rights already attained; in Ecuador, they had to defend the vote.

Interactions in the Struggles for Civil and Political Rights

At the beginning of the century, there was broad consensus among South American intellectuals, both men and women, that the expansion of women's access to education and their civil rights must come prior to recognizing their political rights. This consensus was because the exercise of citizenship required women to have full civil capacity, and wives to have greater individual autonomy. This view also reflected the trajectory toward women's equal rights in North America and Europe where property rights preceded political rights. It was after women gained the vote in a growing number of more developed countries that South American feminists began to think that political rights might be necessary if they were ever to attain stronger property and other civil rights. While freethinking women's groups in Argentina had called for both civil and political rights early on, Paulina Luisi in Uruguay formed the first national organization, the CNM-U, in 1916 dedicated to actively pursuing both simultaneously.

By the beginning of the 1920s, a growing number of women's rights groups were also incorporating suffrage into their immediate demands, resulting in the resolution approved at the 1926 Inter-American Congress of Women in Panama that for the first time called for women's equal civil and political rights (Marino 2019, 40–51). Nonetheless, there continued to be relatively well-educated women who opposed women's suffrage, at least for national elections up through the 1930s and 1940s because they either considered it inappropriate for their sex and/or found politics distasteful.

In several countries, it was once feminists began demanding both enhanced civil rights and the vote that reformist and conservative politicians reached compromises to reform the marital regime, most notably in Argentina although there is evidence of such a process in Chile and Peru as well. The first country to recognize women's full political rights, nonetheless, was Ecuador in 1929 after women had already attained stronger property rights and in a period of economic and political upheaval. It was during the tumultuous years of the Great Depression that women's organizations everywhere expanded and formed broad-based coalitions, which included working-class women, in pursuit of both civil and political rights.

Argentina and Uruguay came close to recognizing both. Following the approval of its 1926 civil code reform, Argentina's Chamber of Deputies approved a women's suffrage bill in 1932 although its Senate refused to consider it. Also in 1932, Uruguay's Senate approved both a women's suffrage bill and a reform of the marital regime; its Chamber only passed the one on suffrage before the president dismissed the Congress in an auto-coup. Women's suffrage was also on the agenda in this decade in Peru and Chile, but women gained political rights only at the municipal level, coincident with approval of their civil code reforms.[6]

The jurists and politicians who first championed reform of the marital regime were always liberals, radical or socialists or combinations of these currents (as in Colorado party adherents in Uruguay). In contrast, in two countries, Chile and Colombia, conservative legislators made the first proposals to give women the vote. In both, liberals supported women's eventual political rights while blocking suffrage initiatives over several decades because of strategic considerations. They were afraid that given women's greater religiosity, if they had the vote women would favor conservatives.

While the civil code reforms attained usually fell short of feminists' demands, the priority women's organizations placed on suffrage from the 1930s on meant that there was subsequently little progress in deepening these reforms, particularly in Argentina and Peru. Sometimes this task fell to jurists or the courts, motivated by the need to make their codes more internally consistent. Beginning in the 1930s, some governments relied on specialized bodies, such the Institute for the Study Legislation in Chile or the Academy of Legal Scholars in Ecuador to recommend updates to their civil codes. In both cases, women's rights organizations advocated specific code reforms that were subsequently proposed by these bodies and enacted by their legislatures. In contrast, in Colombia, after attaining stronger property rights in 1932, organized women did not pay much attention to further civil code reforms for at least another generation.

One of the longest struggles for married women's property rights was in Uruguay, where the enactment of suffrage preceded women securing strong civil rights. Suffrage is, of course, what led to women's representation in congress and their leading the comprehensive reform effort of the mid-1940s, an achievement that coincided with the approval of the Pan American conventions on women's civil and political rights. This came in the wake of the signing of the United Nations Charter, which embraced these rights, and which provided momentum in the post-World War II period to women's demands for suffrage in countries that had not yet enacted it.

By 1955, women had attained full political rights in all seven countries, the ability to vote and stand for office at the same age and literacy level and other conditions as men. The only difference based on sex was Ecuador's 1946 reversal that made women's vote optional, while men's was obligatory. The main differences

6 Towns (2010, 785) draws attention to how women got the vote in Latin America either during a first wave of "turbulence" around the Great Depression or after World War II "in another wave of regime change." While she is not always right on specifics, in five of the seven South American cases studied women attained full political rights in moments of disruption of the political system, after a revolution or military coup, when conditions required a reconstitution of political alignments. In only two cases (Uruguay and Chile) did women obtain suffrage during periods of relatively stable democratic rule, although it was soon disrupted in Uruguay and under threat in Chile.

between countries were related to whether they had instituted universal suffrage and at what age, 18 or 21. Three countries, Argentina, Uruguay and Colombia, had already adopted universal male suffrage prior to women gaining political rights; when women eventually obtained the vote, it served to enshrine universal suffrage. Having earlier given the vote to illiterate men to broaden democratic participation does not appear to have hastened women's suffrage. In Argentina, it took an additional 35 years and in Uruguay and Colombia, 17 and 18 years, respectively, before women attained it. Only in Venezuela in 1947 did illiterate men and women achieve suffrage at the same time.

Most countries debated whether women should have the same qualifications as men to vote, although it was primarily in Argentina where this was a contentious issue. Debates over whether women should be older or required to have more education than men served to delay the process of women attaining political rights much like the issue of whether it should be in phases. Only three countries, Peru, Chile and Venezuela (if only briefly), ended up following a phased process, with women first attaining suffrage at the municipal level and then in national elections. Uruguay and Colombia also entertained this approach.

Of the country differences in suffrage requirements, that of literacy was the most consequential for women because their literacy rates lagged behind men's for much of the twentieth century. Comparable census data show that at mid-century, the share of women (15 years or older) who were illiterate was over 50% in Venezuela, Ecuador and Peru, countries that also had large gender gaps (UNESCO 1988, Table 5). Literacy continued as a requirement for citizenship in Ecuador, Peru and Chile. In the former two, countries with relatively large indigenous populations, this requirement served to exclude large numbers of indigenous women from political rights. In contrast, in Chile, a relatively small share of women (21%) were illiterate and the gender gap was small, so here exclusion was class-based rather than primarily related to gender or ethnicity.

The most exclusionary aspect of the process of civil code reform was lack of attention to the property rights of women in consensual unions, a group where lower income and, in the Andean countries, indigenous rural women were also over-represented. A number of countries addressed the rights of children born outside marriage, such as by facilitating recognition of paternity and improving their inheritance rights. Nonetheless, except for Venezuela, countries did not address the rights of women in these unions until the second half of this century when their share began to grow as more middle-class women also began to opt for this status.

Impact of the Reforms

The potential impact of marital regime reform on women depends on at least three factors, its scope, use and how the process of attaining it affects gender norms and expectations. Chapter 9 showed how the scope of legislation reforming married women's property rights varied across countries, which at the outset determines its potential to transform marital relations and the lives of women. In addition, subsequent judicial interpretation of these laws influenced their scope – whether the courts solved disputes narrowly or broadly and in women's favor. Their impact also depended critically on whether wives availed themselves of their new rights, especially when these were options rather than automatically applicable to all. Ultimately, the impact of these legal changes depended on how these factors and the very struggle for women's rights changed gender norms and practices. This section highlights the challenges of documenting these potential impacts and this again requires examining specific features.

A frequent observation of contemporaries was how few couples ever utilized traditional prenuptial agreements whereby a wife could specify that she retained some but not all of the assets that she brought to marriage to manage these herself. This was largely because it went against social norms that privileged marital unity and the expectation that couples married for love, not material considerations. The information for the two countries, Venezuela and Chile, whose reforms allowed couples to declare a full rather than just a partial separation of property in premarital agreements suggest that this alternative did not prove much more attractive.

This was lawyer Panchita Soublette's (1941) conclusion after this reform had been in effect in Venezuela for at least four decades. National administrative data for Chile also showed how few couples made capitulaciones prior to marriage either before or after its 1925 decree that allowed these to include the full separation of property (Table 4.1). This was likely because it was difficult for couples to know prior to marriage if this arrangement suited them. Moreover, the consequences of choosing separation of property were risky for women; for under this regime, a wife did not have access to the gananciales generated directly by her husband. Thus, whether this option was in a woman's interest depended on her circumstances, among other factors, on her relative current and potential future wealth compared to her husband's.

Chilean lawyer Elena Caffarena (1928; 1944) argued that it was only after marriage that wives really knew if their husbands were good managers of their assets and whether separation of property served their interests. This was the reasoning behind the 1946 reform that she supported, which allowed couples to choose separation of property at any point during the marriage. While this reform led to an immediate increase in the number of couples choosing this regime, these continued to represent a minuscule share of Chilean married couples.

Contemporaries also observed how few wives ever utilized the only traditional legal redress available to them if their husband mismanaged the community property – to file suit for separation of property. Judicial records for Quito and administrative data for Chile confirmed this. In Argentina, jurist Bibiloni (1939) concluded that few women availed themselves of the traditional or new legal options available to them, including its 1926 law, at least in the immediate post-reform period. Here, the courts began to interpret this law broadly, recognizing married women's right to manage the property they brought to marriage or later inherited irrespective of whether they registered this intent (Spota 1953). It is thus difficult to ascertain how common it subsequently became for wives to manage their own property.

The only other law that had a similar feature to Argentina's, requiring wives to register their intent to avail themselves of its benefits, was the 1911 Ecuadorian law. Hence, the importance of the availability of Property Registry data for Quito which revealed that by 1950, 4.3% of married women had opted to manage their property. Given that relatively few people owned immovable property, particularly urban real estate, this share is a credible uptake rate.[7] Moreover, it likely constitutes a minimum estimate of potential beneficiaries since wives only had to register immovable property; their management of movable property (such as a business or financial assets) required only a notarized document. In addition, women had to pay a tax to inscribe such a document in the registry, which may have discouraged some from fully completing the procedure. Still, the fact that so many willingly paid a tax indicates that a good number of wives were eager to manage their assets and earnings themselves.

Recall that Ecuador's 1911 law was unusually favorable law to women since those who opted to manage their own property or earnings kept the gananciales these generated while they shared in those generated by their husbands. It was thus a much less risky alternative than choosing the separation of property regime, which required wives to give up the right to share in their husbands' future gananciales. Ecuador's law was also more favorable to women than the Argentine, Peruvian and Venezuelan reforms that now allowed wives to manage their own property but where husbands remained the administrators of the gananciales they generated.

Little is known about the implementation of this aspect of the reform in these three countries although its limitations are evident. For example, if a wife inherited a dwelling, it meant that she alone could decide whether to sell or rent it and to whom and on what terms. Rental income, nonetheless, constituted gananciales and these legally accrued to the husband as the manager of community property. Thus the question if this advance provided anything more than an illusional gain in women's property rights. In contrast, under the mechanism of reserved property if a wife purchased such a dwelling with her wages and leased the property, the rental income was hers alone to manage, at least for the duration of the marriage; hence, its greater potential for it to impact women's daily lives and their sense of being autonomous and capable actors. This also explains why some feminist proposals demanded either the parallel or joint management of gananciales; only in this way would women effectively manage their property.

7 An examination of population censuses and surveys for the seven countries showed that data on the share of adults who owned immovable property is only available in one source, the 1931 Lima provincial census, a predominantly urban province. Recall from Chapter 5 that only 8.5% of adult men and 7.7% of adult women reported owning either individual or joint community property.

It is challenging to document the use of either of these mechanisms of strengthening married women's property rights. Notarial records are the most likely source of information on rental, mortgage and sales transactions, but these are not always catalogued for this period. Moreover, while such documents usually include a person's marital status, they do not always contain information on the initial form of acquisition of the property or if it was related to a specific legal provision for wives. Nonetheless, it would be useful to know if subsequent to these reforms, there was at least an increase in women's presence in the archives, a task awaiting future researchers.

The implementation of the deferred community property regime in Colombia and Uruguay should have also left a trace in notarial archives since these reforms required married couples to delineate the property that was under a husband's management so that henceforth, each spouse manage half the community property accrued to that point along with their individual assets and future gains. These reforms also allowed new marriages to formally renounce this option. Future research in Colombia might shed light on the difficulties of implementing this novel regime and perhaps explain why this country later discarded deferred community property as the default in favor of partial community property but under new rules that provided for joint management of gananciales.[8]

Since many wives in this period did not work for an income nor bring assets to marriage or later inherit them, the reform that may have touched the lives of the largest share directly was where they gained a voice in the disposition of gananciales. Moreover, the requirement of mutual consent to alienate these (as in Ecuador and Chile) probably had a larger impact than where this held only for donations (as in Argentina and Venezuela) because the sale, rental or mortgaging of community property was surely more common than its gifting. Also, this measure was relatively straightforward to implement since if a married person purchased or sold an immovable asset, both spouses needed to sign the bill of sale.

Qualitative research in Ecuador in 2009 revealed that women across social classes were aware of the double signature requirement and that it had become standard practice (Deere, Contreras and Twyman 2014, 149–50). Husbands sometimes circumvented it by falsifying their wife's signature or by asking a trusting wife to sign a piece of paper without revealing its content. Nonetheless, these authors found that wives considered this measure as empowering, since it gave them a say in consequential household decisions and provided them with greater economic security. Moreover, working-class women considered it a factor that made marriage preferable to living in a consensual union. It would be useful to replicate this type of qualitative research in the other countries that adopted this mechanism.

Turning to broader socioeconomic impacts, one would expect that the strengthening of the property rights of wives proved an incentive for women stay in or

8 Decree 2820 of 1974, see Deere and León (2021, 230).

join the labor force. Both the mechanism of reserved property and the deferred community property regime allowed wives to manage their earnings and its gains with autonomy. The incentive effect was likely larger in the countries that adopted deferred community property (Colombia and Uruguay) than in those where the husband remained the sole administrator of the gananciales generated by the assets women brought to marriage or later inherited (Argentina, Peru and Venezuela). Only in the former could single women be confident that the assets they acquired with their savings would continue under their management if they married.

A challenge in researching whether these reforms contributed to an increase in women's labor force participation is the inconsistency in the measurement of women's economic activity in most censuses prior to the 1980s, which stymies a rigorous analysis of trends across time and countries. Moreover, published census data prior to 1960 rarely provide information on women's labor force participation by marital status, needed to at least suggest whether the adoption of a specific reform feature was subsequently associated with changes in the labor participation of wives. A rigorous analysis, of course, requires disentangling the independent effect of married women's property law reform from the steady increase in urbanization and women's education and lower fertility that also contributed to the rising rates of female labor force participation from the Great Depression on in most countries.

With regard to the impact of these reforms on marriage rates, the strengthening of the property rights of wives undoubtedly made marriage more attractive to women since they stood to lose less personal autonomy. At the same time, these reforms may have made marriage less appealing to men notwithstanding the fact that husbands maintained many of their traditional prerogatives. The lack of comparable census data across countries on the share of adult women living in consensual unions also makes it difficult to estimate how these reforms impacted the trade-off between these alternatives prior to the 1970s.[9]

One might expect the impact on marital relations to have been most profound in Uruguay, the country that enacted the most comprehensive reform, since its 1946 law granted husbands and wives equal property rights under deferred community property, eradicated potestad marital and recognized equal rights of patria potestad. This reform was also unusual because it allowed either spouse to demand the separation of property during the marriage without cause. Future archival research might shed light on whether husbands pursued this latter alternative more frequently than wives as a way of protesting their loss of rights over the management of their wives' property and earnings, and the impact of such actions on divorce rates. Also, since it was up to couples to determine which of them managed the

9 The available data show that by the 1970s, the share of women in consensual unions was substantially higher in the Andean region than in the Southern Cone (Deere and León 2022, Table 1). The surge in this share across South America, and as a cross-class phenomenon, took place largely in the 1990s.

assets of their minor children and to register such, archival records might indicate if this reform changed the traditional gender division of responsibilities.

Overall, stronger property rights undoubtedly increased the dignity of wives by their recognition as autonomous persons with the right to make decisions affecting their and their families' well-being. This effect was surely largest among the women who were part of the organizations that led the struggle for civil code reform. One might expect that its emancipatory effect was broadest where these organizations formed successful coalitions to mobilize women across class and religious divides. Such coalitions, however, were more of a characteristic of the struggle for suffrage rather than for women's civil rights.

Both struggles drew women into the public arena, a position only made secure through the combined recognition and exercise of their civil and political rights. Once women had the vote, political parties generally began to court them, both directly and indirectly. One of the unexpected outcomes was that many women joined these at the expense of women's organizations, which began to decline. The greatest continuity between the first and second waves of feminism was in Colombia, which was among the last to attain suffrage in the mid-1950s. Once they gained the vote, organized women turned almost immediately to deepening the reform of its civil code; in most countries, there was a generational gap.

These trends occurred within an overall context of rapid urbanization and industrialization that in the post-World War II period came to privilege the male breadwinner model of the family. The contradictions it sowed generated the conditions for a new generation of women to assume many of the unfulfilled aspirations of first-wave feminists, taking up the banner of attaining the dual-headed household and ending potestad marital in all its dimensions.

SOURCES AND REFERENCES

Primary Sources

Archives

AGFJ, Archivo General de la Función Judicial, Quito, Ecuador; archives of the First and Second Civil Court, 1936–1954.
RPCQ, Registro de la Propiedad del Cantón Quito, Quito, Ecuador; subseries "Exclusión de Bienes," 1911–1970.

Electronic Archives

BDF, Biblioteca Digital Feminista Ofelia Uribe de Acosta, Universidad Nacional de Colombia, https://repositorio.unal.edu.co/handle/unal/161.
CCCP, Carrie Chapman Catt Papers, Library of Congress, https://www.loc.gov/item/mss154040024/
DSP, Doris Stevens Papers, Schlesinger Library on the History of Women in the Americas, Harvard University, https://hollisarchives.lib.harvard.edu/repositories/8/archival_objects/1490356
LLMC Digital Collection, https://llmc.com
HathiTrust Collection, https://hathitrust.org

Congressional and Governmental Records[1]

Argentina:
Boletín Oficial
Diario de Sesiones de la Cámara de Diputados
Diario de Sesiones de la Cámara del Senado

1 If no year is noted, the series runs for the whole period of study and multiple volumes were consulted.

Chile:
Diario de Sesiones de la Cámara de Diputados
Diario de Sesiones de la Cámara del Senado
Diario Oficial

Colombia:
Anales de la Cámara de Representantes
Anales del Congreso
Anales del Senado
Diario Oficial

Ecuador:
Actas de la Asamblea Nacional Constituyente, 1928–1929
Actas de la Cámara de Diputados, 1909–1911
Actas de la Cámara del Senado, 1909–1911
Diario de Debates de la Asamblea Constituyente de 1944
Diario de Debates de la Cámara de Diputados
Diario de Debates de la Cámara del Senado
Registro Oficial

Peru:
Diario de los Debates de la Asamblea Nacional de 1919
Diario de los Debates de la Cámara de Diputados
Diario de los Debates de la Cámara Nacional de Diputados
Diario de los Debates de la Cámara del Senado
Diario de los Debates del Congreso Constituyente de 1931
Diario de los Debates del Senado de la República

Uruguay:
Diario Oficial
Diario de Sesiones de la H. Convención N. Constituyente de la República Oriental del Uruguay, 1916–1917
Diario de Sesiones de la Honorable Cámara del Senado
Diario de Sesiones de la Honorable Cámara de Representantes
Registro Nacional de Leyes y Decretos

Venezuela:
Boletín de la Comisión Codificadora Nacional, 1937–1942
Gaceta Jurídica, 1913–1915
Gaceta Oficial

Periodicals[2]

Acción Femenina (Montevideo), 1919–1925
Acción Femenina (Santiago), 1922–1923
Agitación Femenina (Tunja, Colombia), 1944–1946
Boletín Mensual del Museo Social Argentino (Buenos Aires), 1918
El Día (Montevideo), 1910–1911, 1936
El Eco de la Liga de Damas Chilenas (Santiago), 1912
El Mercurio (Santiago), 1923
Ideas y Acción (Montevideo), 1933–1934

2 Years given correspond to those of issues consulted.

La Crítica (Lima), 1917–1919
La Mujer (Quito), 1905
La Mujer Nueva (Santiago), 1936–1941
La Mujer Ecuatoriana (Guayaquil), 1918–1921
La Prensa (Buenos Aires), 1906
La Union Patriótica de Mujeres de Chile (Santiago), 1925–1926
La Voz Femenina (Santiago), 1916–1917
La Voz Femenina, Revista para la Mujer y el Hogar (Santiago), 1925
Letras y Encajes (Medellín), 1926–1952
Mireya, Revista Femenina (Bogotá), 1943–1945
Mujeres de América (Buenos Aires), 1933
Nuevos Horizontes (Guayaquil), 1933–1937
Nosotras (Valparaíso), 1932–1933
Revista Argentina de Ciencias Políticas (Buenos Aires), 1913–1922
Revista de Derecho y Legislación (Caracas), 1914–1915, 1934–1935
Revista del Consejo Nacional de Mujeres (Buenos Aires), 1901–1906
Revista Forense (Quito), 1913–1940
Revista de la Sociedad Jurídica (Quito), 1908–1915
Unión Femenina de Chile (Valparaíso), 1934–1935
Vida Femenina (Buenos Aires), 1935–1938
Vida Femenina, Revista del Hogar y la Mujer (Montevideo), 1918–1931

Other Primary Sources and References

AASF, Asociación Argentina del Sufragio Femenino. 1932. *Fines y propósitos de los estatutos*. Buenos Aires: AASF. DSP.

Abella de Ramírez, María. (1908) 1965. *En pos de la Justicia*. Reprinted as *Ensayos Feministas*. Montevideo: Ed. El Siglo Ilustrado.

Abella de Ramírez, María. (1919) 2004. "La mujer moderna o feminista." *Nuestra Causa* 1 (5), reproduced in *Nuestra Causa, revista mensual feminista, 1919–1921. Estudio e índice general*, edited by Rosalía Gallo, 77–78. Buenos Aires: Instituto de Investigaciones Históricas Cruz del Sur.

Acosta Cárdenas, Miguelina A. (1920) 2020. *Reformas necesarias del Código Civil común peruano tendientes a hacer efectiva la igualdad civil y jurídica del hombre y la mujer*. Thesis for a doctorate in law, Universidad Mayor de San Marcos. In *Miguelina Acosta Cárdenas. Escritos selectos*, edited by Joel Rojas Huaynates. Lima: Heraldos Eds., 33–53.

Acosta Prieto, Héctor S. 1989. "El establecimiento del divorcio en Venezuela y la iglesia católica." *Ensayos Históricos. Anuario del Instituto de Estudios Hispanoamericanos* 1: 71–94.

Adams, Mildred. 1922. "All the Americas meet at Baltimore." *The Woman Citizen*, May 6: 10–12. CCCP.

Aguilar Gil, Roisida. 2002. "El sufragio de la mujer: debate en el Congreso Constituyente de 1931–1932." *Elecciones* 1: 123–64. https://doi.org/10.53557/Elecciones.2002.v1n1.05.

Aguilar Gil, Roisida. 2006. "La 'aurora' del sufragio femenino en el Perú: Zoila A. Cáceres, 1924–1933." In *Mujeres, familia y sociedad en la Historia de América Latina, siglos XVIII-XXI*, edited by Scarlett O'Phelan Godoy and Margarita Zegarra Flórez, 517–35. Lima: CENDOC-Mujer, Pontificia Universidad Católica del Perú, Instituto Riva Agüero and Instituto Francés de Estudios Andinos.

Aguilar Gil, Roisida. 2019. "Acción colectiva transnacional por los derechos femeninos en la Octava Conferencia Internacional Americana, Perú, 1938." In *Género y mujeres en la historia del Perú. Del hogar al espacio público*, edited by Scarlett O'Phelan Godoy and Margarita Zegarra Flórez, 441–61. Lima: Fondo Ed. Pontificia Universidad Católica.

Aguilar Gil, Roisida. 2024. "Collective Action for Women's Suffrage in Peru: Political Contexts, Women's Organizations, and Public Actors." In *Women's Suffrage in the Americas*, edited by Stephanie Mitchell, 273–301. University of New Mexico Press.

Aguilera, Alberto. 1997. "Referencias en publicaciones periódicas sobre el voto de la mujer en Colombia." In *40 años del voto de la mujer en Colombia*, edited by María Victoria Londoño, German Patiño, and Garcés Mariana, 65–175. Cali: Feriva S.A.

Alcibíades, Mirla. 2004. *La heroica aventura de construir una república. Familia-nación en el ochocientos venezolano (1830–1865)*. Caracas: Monte Ávila.

Alessandri Rodríguez, Arturo. 1935. *Tratado práctico de las capitulaciones matrimoniales, de la sociedad conyugal y de los bienes reservados de la mujer casada*. Santiago: Imprenta Universitaria.

Alessandri Rodríguez, Arturo. 1943. "Reformas introducidas al Código Civil por la ley 7.612." Revista de Derecho y Jurisprudencia 40 (1): 105–22. October 23. https://app.vlex.com/#vid230993333.

Alfaro, Eloy. (1897) 1907. "Mensaje del presidente de la República solicitando la protección especial a la mujer y participación a los empleos públicos." In *Recopilación de Mensajes Dirigidos por los Presidentes…*, edited by Alejandro Noboa, 334–36. Vol. IV. Guayaquil: Imp. de El Tiempo.

Alvarado Rivera, María Jesús. 1911. "Femenismo." In *Primer Congreso Femenino Internacional de la República Argentina. Historia, actas y trabajos*, edited by Asociación Universitarias Argentinas, 265–74. Buenos Aires: Imprenta A. Ceppi.

Alvarado Rivera, María Jesús. (1912) 2012. *El Feminismo. Conferencia leída en la Sociedad Geográfica de Lima el 28 de octubre de 1911*. Reproduced. Lima: Centro de la Mujer Peruana Flora Tristán.

Alvarado Rivera, María Jesús. 1914. *Institución "Evolución Femenina." Exposición de Principios y Estatutos*. Lima: Imprenta Peruana.

Alvarado Rivera, María Jesús. 1922. *Amor, matrimonio y divorcio*. Lima: Tip. Evolución Femenina.

Alvarado Rivera, María Jesús. (1923) 2019. "Los derechos civiles de la mujer i del niño." In *María Alvarado Rivera: documentos*, edited by Leonardo Ysla, 44–48. Lima: Editor's edition.

Álvarez, María del Mar. 2010. *Historia de lucha de la mujer venezolana*. Caracas: Fundación Editorial El Perro y La Rama. http://www.elperroylarana.gob.ve/wp-content/uploads/2017/07/historia_de_lucha_de_la_mujer_venezolana.pdf.

Álvarez Giménez, María Elvira. 2019. "The Transnational Feminist Movement in the Americas in the 1930s." *Ciencia Nueva. Revista de Historia y Política* 3 (1): 113–33. https://doi.org/10.22517/25392662.22661.

Álvarez Vignoli de Demicheli, Sofía. 1934. *Derechos civiles y políticos de la mujer*. Montevideo: Comité Ejecutivo del Homenaje a Sofia Alvarez V.

Álvarez Vignoli de Demicheli, Sofía. 1946. *Derechos civiles de la mujer. Antecedentes Parlamentarios*. Montevideo: Ed. Alfa y Omega.

Amézquita de Almeida, Josefina, with Magdalena León de Leal and Lilian Motta de Correa. 1977. "Condiciones de la mujer en el derecho de familia." In *La mujer y el desarrollo en Colombia*, edited by Magdalena León de Leal, 273–315. Bogotá: ACEP.

Angelo J., Enriqueta. 1931. "Nuestro feminismo." *Letras y Encajes* 61: 953–54.

Antezana-Pernet, Corinne A. 1996. *Mobilizing Women in the Popular Front Era: Feminism, Class and Politics in the Movimiento Pro-Emancipación de la Mujer Chilena (MEMCh), 1935–1950*. Ph.D. Dissertation. Irvine, CA: University of California Irvine.

Anzola, Nicasio. 1918. *Lecciones elementales de derecho civil colombiano*. Bogotá: Librería Colombiana.

Araujo, Kathya. 2009. *Dignos de su arte: sujeto y lazo social en el Perú de las primeras décadas del siglo XX*. Ed. Iberoamericana/Vervuert. ProQuest.

Archila, José Antonio. 1942. *Código civil colombiano y disposiciones sustantivas que la adicionan y reforman*. 3rd ed. Bogotá: Ed. Librería Siglo XX.
Argentina, República de. 1874. *Código civil de la República Argentina redactado por Dalmacio Vélez Sársfield y sancionado como ley por el honorable congreso de la república*. Buenos Aires: P. E. Coni. HathiTrust.
Argentina, República de. 1936. *Reforma del Código Civil. Antecedentes, informe, proyecto*. Buenos Aires: Gmo. Kraft Ltda. LLMC Digital.
Arriaga, Eduardo E., and Kingsley Davis. 1969. "The Pattern of Mortality Change in Latin America." *Demography* 6 (3): 223–42. https://doi.org/10.2307/2060393.
Arismendi, José Loreto. 1916. "Sobre los derechos de la mujer soltera, casada, viuda y divorciada." *Revista de Ciencias Políticas* 7: 135–47. HathiTrust.
Aristizábal, Miguel, ed. 1896. *Somaten. Artículos escogidos de El Pichincha, primer diario Radical publicado en Quito en 1895–1896*. Quito: Imprenta el Pichincha. HathiTrust.
Arrom, Silvia M. 1985. "Changes in Mexican Family Law in the Nineteenth Century: The Civil Codes of 1870 and 1884." *Journal of Family History* 10 (3): 305–17. https://doi.org/10.1177/036319908501000308.
Arteaga Infante, Claudio. 1922. *La mujer chilena, esclava de la ley*. Santiago: Ed. Minerva. HathiTrust.
Asociación Universitarias Argentinas, ed. 1911. *Primer Congreso Femenino Internacional de la República Argentina. Historia, actas y trabajos*. Buenos Aires: Imprenta A. Ceppi. HathiTrust.
AUPR, Asociaciones Unidas Pro-Reformas del Código Civil. 1942. *La mujer ante la Ley*. Caracas: Cooperativa de Artes Gráficas.
Avellán Férres, Enrique. 1940. *Comentarios a la Ley de Emancipación Económica de la Mujer Casada*. Doctoral thesis, Faculty of Law and Social Sciences, Universidad Central del Ecuador. Quito: Imp. de la Universidad.
Ayala Mora, Enrique. 1988. "De la revolución Alfarista al régimen oligárquico liberal (1895–1925). In *Nueva historia del Ecuador*, edited by Enrique Ayala Mora, 161–66. Vol. 9. Quito: Corporación Editora Nacional. ProQuest.
Ayala Mora, Enrique. 1994. *Historia de la Revolución Liberal Ecuatoriana*. Quito: Corporación Editora Nacional.
Backhouse, Constance B. 1988. "Married Women's Property Law in Nineteenth-Century Canada." *Law and History Review* 6 (2): 211–57. https://doi:10.2307/743684.
Balarezo, Manuel R. 1937. "Informe presentado por el Sr. Presidente de la Academia de Abogados, Dr. Manuel R. Balarezo, a la Junta General del Colegio de Abogados, diciembre 19 de 1936." *Revista Forense* 24 (122): 91–95.
Bando Femenino. 1928. *Declaración de Principios, Estatutos y Reglamentos del Bando Femenino Social y Cultural de Chile*. Santiago: Imp. Excelsior. DSP.
Barrancos, Dora. 2002. *Inclusión//Exclusión. Historia con mujeres*. Buenos Aires: Fondo de Cultura Económica.
Barrancos, Dora. 2007. *Mujeres en la sociedad argentina. Una historia de cinco siglos*. Buenos Aires: Ed. Sudamericana.
Barriga Alarcón, Enrique. 1907. *Capitulaciones matrimoniales*. Lima: Librería Escolar e Imp. de E. Moreno.
Barrister of the Inner Temple, trans. (1904) 1999. *Code Napoleon or the French Civil Code*. Washington, DC: Beard Books.
Barros, Martina, with Alejandra Castillo. 2009. *Prólogo a La Esclavitud de la Mujer (estudio crítico por Stuart Mill)*. Santiago: Palinodia. http://bibliotecadigital.indh.cl/handle/123456789/451.
Barry, Carolina. 2011. "Una cruzada de Evita? El peronismo y la Ley de Sufragio Femenino." In *Sufragio Femenino. Prácticas y debates políticos, religiosos y culturales en la Argentina y América Latina*, edited by Carolina Barry, 113–44. Caseros, Argentina: Ed. de la Universidad Nacional de Tres de Febrero.

Basch, Norma. 1986. "The Emerging Legal History of Women in the United States: Property, Divorce and the Constitution." *Signs: Journal of Women in Culture and Society* 12 (1): 97–117. https://doi.org/10.1086/494299.

Bedoya Bonelli, Carlos Alonso. 2020. "Sufragio femenino en el Perú en las Juntas Municipales Transitorias de 1945." *Elecciones* 19 (20): 231–62. https://doi.org/10.53557/Elecciones.2020.v19n20.09.

Bellotta, Araceli. 2001. *Julieta Lanteri. La pasión de una mujer*. Buenos Aires: Ed. Planeta.

Beltrán y Puga Murai, Alma Luz. 2020. *Movilización feminista y derecho de familia: la regulación del divorcio civil en Colombia (1930–1991)*. Doctoral thesis, Faculty of Law. Bogotá: Universidad de los Andes.

Benería, Lourdes. 1981. "Conceptualizing the Labor Force: The Underestimation of Women's Economic Activities." *Journal of Development Studies* 17 (3): 10–28. https://doi.org/10.1080/00220388108421795.

Bertola, Luis. 2011. "Institutions and the Historical Roots of Latin American Divergence." In *The Oxford Handbook of Latin American Economics*, edited by Jose Antonio Ocampo and Jaime Ros, 26–49. Oxford University Press.

Bibiloni, Juan Antonio. 1939. *Reforma del Código Civil. Anteproyecto*. Buenos Aires: Gmo. Kraft Ltda. HathiTrust.

Boletín Mensual. 1918. "Derechos civiles de la mujer. Informe de los doctores Esteban Lamadrid, Hector Lafaille, Enrique del Valle Iberlucea, Raimundo M. Salvat, Juan A. Figueroa y Enrique Jorge." *Boletín Mensual del Museo Social Argentino* 7: 530–73. Google Books.

Bordagaray, María Eugenia. 2014. "Anarquistas, comunistas y los debates en torno al divorcio. Argentina, 1932–1954." *La manzana de la discordia* 9 (2): 19–30. https://dialnet.unirioja.es/ejemplar/628265

Boring, Nicolas. 2014. "France." In *Inheritance Laws in the Nineteenth and Twentieth Centuries*, edited by Law Library of Congress, 1–5. Washington, DC: The Law Library of Congress. https://tile.loc.gov/storage-services/service/ll/llglrd/2014504249/2014504249.pdf.

Brandau G., Matilde. 1898. *Derechos civiles de la mujer*. Santiago: Imprenta Cervantes. https://www.memoriachilena.gob.cl/602/w3-propertyvalue-145664.html

Bravo, Mario. 1927. *Derechos civiles de la mujer. El código, los proyectos, la ley*. Buenos Aires: El Ateneo. HathiTrust.

Bredbenner, Candace Lewis. 1998. *A Nationality of their Own: Women, Marriage and the Law of Citizenship*. University of California Press.

Brum, Baltasar. 1923. *Los derechos de la mujer: reforma a la legislación civil y política del Uruguay*. Montevideo: José María Serrano, Ed. HathiTrust.

Bulmer-Thomas, Victor. 1994. *The Economic History of Latin America since Independence*. Cambridge University Press.

Búrgos B., Guillermo. 1917. *De la emancipación de la mujer i especialmente de los derechos de la mujer casada sobre los productos de su trabajo*. Thesis, Faculty of Law and Political Science, Universidad de Concepción. Concepción, Chile: Imp. i Enc. Universitaria. HathiTrust.

Burns, Kathryn. 1983. "Mas allá del 'esencial femenino': Los comienzos del feminismo peruano." *Socialismo y participación* 22: 117–30. https://cedoc.sisbib.unmsm.edu.pe/biblioteca-digital/revistas/socialismo-y-participacion/22

Cáceres, Zoila Aurora. 1909. *Mujeres de ayer y de hoy*. Paris: Ganier. HathiTrust.

Cáceres, Zoila Aurora (n.d. a) 2019. "Discurso pronunciado por la publicista Aurora Cáceres, en la actuación de Unión Americana de Mujeres ofrecida a la Comisión del Mandato Popular Pro-Paz de Mujeres Americanas." In *Zoila Aurora Cáceres y la ciudadanía femenina. La correspondencia de Feminismo Peruano*, edited by Sofia Pachas Maceda, 375–79. Lima: Fondo Editorial UNMSM.

Cáceres, Zoila Aurora. (n.d. b) 2019. "Temario B Asuntos Internacionales. V. Derechos especiales de la Mujer." Draft manuscript. In *Zoila Aurora Cáceres y la ciudadanía femenina. La correspondencia de Feminismo Peruano*, edited by Sofia Pachas Maceda, 381–91. Lima: Fondo Editorial UNMSM.

Cáceres, Zoila Aurora. (1938) 2019. "Los derechos de la mujer." Draft manuscript. In *Zoila Aurora Cáceres y la ciudadanía femenina. La correspondencia de Feminismo Peruano*, edited by Sofia Pachas Maceda, 367–74. Lima: Fondo Editorial UNMSM.

Caffarena Morice, Elena. 1928. "Situación jurídica de la mujer chilena." In *Actividades femeninas en Chile*, edited by Sara Guérin de Elgueta, 75–84. Santiago: La Ilustración. https://www.memoriachilena.gob.cl/602/w3-article-126684.html.

Caffarena de Jiles, Elena. 1944. *Capacidad de la mujer casada con relación a sus bienes*. Santiago: Imp. Universitaria. https://www.memoriachilena.gob.cl/602/w3-article-61859.html.

Caffarena de Jiles, Elena. 1952. *Un capítulo en la historia del feminismo. Las sufragistas inglesas*. Santiago: Ed. del Memch. https://www.memoriachilena.gob.cl/602/w3-article-61865.html.

Camacho, Nemesio, Antonio Samper Uribe, and Fabio Lozano. 1919. "Informe del Directorio Liberal." In *Convención Nacional del Partido Liberal*, 11–48. Bogotá: Casa Ed. de Arboleda & Valencia.

Cámara de Senadores. 1939. *Derechos civiles de la mujer*. Montevideo: Imprenta Nacional.

Cannon, Mary M. 1943. "Women's Organizations in Ecuador, Paraguay and Peru." *Bulletin of the Pan American Union* 77 (11): 601–607. Hein Online.

Cárdenas de Bustamante, Hipatia. 1943. *Oro, Rojo y Azul*. Quito: Ed. Artes Gráficas.

Carlson, Marifran. 1988. *¡Feminismo! The Woman's Movement in Argentina from its Beginnings to Eva Perón*. University of Chicago Press.

Cassina de Nogara, Alba G. 1990. *Hacia una democracia integral. Apuntes para una historia del feminismo en Uruguay*. Montevideo: CONAMU.

Castillo, Isabel. 2023. "Motivation, Alignment, Historical Cleavages, and Women's Suffrage in Latin America." *Perspectives on Politics* 21 (1): 78–93.

Castorino de, María Sara L. 1969. "Una mujer extraordinaria, María J. Alvarado Rivera. Síntesis de su Cruzada Social…" In *Una mujer extraordinaria*, edited by Dora T. Cordova, 7–64. Lima: Evolución Femenina.

Catt, Carrie Chapman. 1923a. "Summing up South America." *The Woman Citizen*. June: 7–8, 26. CCCP.

Catt, Carrie Chapman. 1923b. "Anti-feminism in South America." *Current History* 18 (6): 1028–36. HathiTrust.

CECIM, Comité Ecuatoriano de Cooperación con la CIM. 2006. *CECIM. 30 años construyendo equidad de género*. Quito: Ed. Ecuador.

Chaney, Elsa. 1979. *Supermadre. Women in Politics in Latin America*. University of Texas Press.

Chatfield, Sara. 2018. "Married Women's Economic Rights Reform in State Legislatures and Courts, 1839–1920." *Studies in American Political Development* 32: 236–56.

Chavarriaga Meyer, José Luis. 1940. *Derechos y reivindicaciones de la mujer colombiana*. Thesis for a Doctorate in Political Science and Law, Universidad Nacional. Bogotá: Ed. ABC.

Chile, República de. 1856. *Código Civil de la República de Chile, aprobada diciembre 14, 1855*. Santiago: Imprenta Nacional. HathiTrust.

Chile, República de. 1925. *Constitución Política de Chile de 1925*. https://www.bcn.cl/Books/Constitucion_politica_de_Chile_1925/index.html#p=39.

Chile, República de. 1952/n.d. *XII Censo General de Población y I de Vivienda levantado el 24 de abril de* 1952. Vol. 1. Santiago: Servicio Nacional de Estadística y Censos.

Chile-INE, Instituto Nacional de Estadística. 1958. *Demografía Año 1955*. Santiago: Dirección de Estadística.

Chile-INE, Instituto Nacional de Estadística. 1963. *Demografía Año 1960*. Santiago: Dirección de Estadística.
Chiossone, Tulio. 1942. "Comunicación del Ministro de Relaciones Interiores al Presidente de la Cámara de Diputados." *Revista de Derecho y Legislación* 31: 125–35. HathiTrust.
CIM, Comisión Interamericana de Mujeres. 1933. *Derechos Civiles y Políticos de la Mujer. Chile*. Draft report, October. DSP.
CIM, Comisión Interamericana de Mujeres. 1948. *Informe de la Comisión Interamericana de Mujeres a la Novena Conferencia Internacional Americana sobre Derechos Civiles y Políticos de la Mujer*. Washington, DC: OAS and CIM.
Clagett, Helen. 1947. *A Guide to the Law and Legal Literature of Venezuela*. Washington, DC: Library of Congress.
Clark, A. Kim. 2005. "Feminismos estéticos y antiestéticos en el Ecuador de principios del siglo XX: Un análisis de género y generaciones." *Procesos. Revista Ecuatoriana de Historia* 22: 85–105. https://doi.org/10.29078/rp.v1i22.
Clark, A. Kim. 2012. *Gender, State and Medicine in Highland Ecuador. Modernizing Women, Modernizing the State, 1895–1950*. University of Pittsburgh Press.
Claro Solar, Luis. 1902. *Explicaciones de derecho civil chileno y comparado. De las personas*, Vol. 2. Santiago: Imp. Cervantes. HathiTrust.
Claro Solar, Luis. 1915a. "Proyecto de reforma del código civil." *Revista de Derecho, Jurisprudencia y Ciencias Sociales* 12 (1): 1–25. HathiTrust.
Claro Solar, Luis. 1915b. "Condición civil de la mujer, necesidad de la reforma del código civil." *Revista de Derecho, Jurisprudencia y Ciencias Sociales* 12 (10): 217–25. HathiTrust.
Cocca, Aldo Armando. 1948. *Ley de sufragio femenino*. Buenos Aires: El Ateneo.
Cocker González, Charity. 2000. "Agitating for their Rights: The Colombia Women's Movement, 1930–1947." *Pacific Historical Review* 69 (4): 689–706.
Cohen, Lucy M. 2001. *Colombianas en la vanguardia*. Medellín: Universidad de Antioquia.
Colombia, República de. 1895. *Código civil colombiano expedido por el congreso de 1873 y adoptado por la ley 57 de 1887*. Ed. oficial. Bogotá: Imprenta Nacional. LLMC Digital.
Colombia, República de. 1932. *Historia de las leyes. Legislativa de 1930*, Vol. XVI. Bogotá: Imprenta Nacional.
Colombia, República de. 1939. *Historia de las leyes. Legislativa de 1932*, Vol. 1-B. Bogotá: Imprenta Nacional.
Comisión Codificadora Nacional. (1942) 1968. "Exposición de motivos del proyecto de Código Civil." In *Código Civil, anotado y concordado*, edited by Mariano Arcaya, 9–107. Vol. I. Caracas: Empresa el Cojo.
Coontz, Stephanie. 2006. *Marriage, a History. How Love Conquered Marriage*. New York: Penguin.
Congreso de la República. 1987. *Gobierno y época del presidente Isaías Medina Angarita. El debate parlamentario 1941–1945*. Tome 9, vols. 19 and 21. Caracas: Congreso de la República.
Congreso Mariano Femenino. 1918. *Relaciones y documentos del Congreso Mariano Femenino*. Santiago: Escuela Tip. La Gratitud Nacional. https://www.memoriachilena.gob.cl/602/w3-article-298253.html.
Cordova, Dora T., ed. 1969. *Una mujer extraordinaria. María J. Alvarado Rivera*. Lima: Evolución Femenina.
Cornejo, A. Gustavo. 1921. *Comentarios al Código Civil de 1852*. Vol. 1. 3rd ed. Chiclayo: Librería y Casa Editora Dionisio Mendoza. HathiTrust.
Coronel, Valeria. 2022. *La última Guerra del Siglo de las Luces. Revolución Liberal y republicanismo popular en Ecuador*. Quito: Ed. FLACSO.
Corte Suprema de Justicia. 1927. *Anales Judiciales de la Corte Suprema de Justicia. Año Judicial de 1926*. Vol. 22. Lima: Imp. Americana.

Corva, María Angélica, and Rosario Gómez Molla. 2021. "La matriculación de abogada de María Angélica Barreda ante la Suprema Corte de la provincia de Buenos Aires, Argentina (1910)." *Revista Historia y Justicia*, 16. http://journals.openedition.org/rhj/8215.

Costa Rica, República de. 1887. *Código Civil de la República de Costa Rica*. San José: Imp. Nacional. https://ecollections.law.fiu.edu/civil_codes/11.

CRCC, Comisión Reformadora del Código Civil. 1923. *Actas de las Sesiones de la Comisión Reformadora del Código Civil Peruano creado por Supremo Decreto de 26 de agosto de 1922. Primer Fascículo*. Lima: Imprenta el Progreso Editorial. In *The Making of Modern Law: Foreign Primary Sources, 1600–1970*.

CRCC, Comisión Reformadora del Código Civil. 1924. *Actas...Segundo Fascículo*. Lima: Imprenta el Progreso Editorial. In *The Making of Modern Law: Foreign Primary Sources, 1600–1970*.

CRCC, Comisión Reformadora del Código Civil.1925. *Actas...Cuarto Fascículo*. Lima: Imprenta el Progreso Editorial. In *The Making of Modern Law: Foreign Primary Sources, 1600–1970*.

CRCC, Comisión Reformadora del Código Civil.1926a. *Actas...Sexto Fascículo*. Lima: Imprenta la Tradición. In *The Making of Modern Law: Foreign Primary Sources, 1600–1970*.

CRCC, Comisión Reformadora del Código Civil.1926b. *Segundo Anteproyecto, Libro I, III*. Lima: Imprenta Minerva.

CRCC, Comisión Reformadora del Código Civil. 1929a. *Actas...Séptimo Fascículo*. Lima: Imprenta La Editorial. In *The Making of Modern Law: Foreign Primary Sources, 1600–1970*.

CRCC, Comisión Reformadora del Código Civil.1929b. *Segundo Anteproyecto del Libro Segundo del Código Civil del Perú*. Lima: Imprenta Minerva.

CRCC, Comisión Reformadora del Código Civil.1930. *Actas...Octavo Fascículo*. Lima: Imprenta El Progreso. In *The Making of Modern Law*: Foreign Primary Sources, 1600–1970.

CRCC, Comisión Reformadora del Código Civil.1936. *Proyecto de Código Civil elaborado por la Comisión creada según resolución suprema de 11 de agosto de 1922*. Lima: Librería e Imprenta Gil. LLMC Digital.

Cuadro Cawen, Inés. 2018. *Feminismos y Política en el Uruguay del novecientos*. Montevideo: Ed. de la Banda Oriental y Asociación Uruguaya de Historiadores.

Cueva, Agustín. 1983. "El Ecuador de 1925 a 1960." In *Nueva historia del Ecuador*, edited by E. Ayala Mora, 87–121. Vol. 10. Quito: Corporación Editora Nacional.

C.V.M., Conferencia Venezolana de Mujeres. 1941. *Conferencia preparatoria del Primer Congreso Venezolano de Mujeres, efectuada en Caracas en los días 13 al 16 de junio de 1940*. Caracas: Ed. Bolivar.

Dagnino, Maruja. 2019. *Mujeres del siglo XX: Venezolanas que cambiaron nuestra historia*. Caracas: Transparencia Venezuela and Asamblea Nacional.

De Paula Soria, Francisco. (1909) 1912. "Feminismo. La redención doméstica, civil y política de la mujer ecuatoriana." In F. de Paula Soria, *Ideales. Retazos de mi labor periodística*, 1–6. Quito: Casa Ed. de J. I. Gálvez. HathiTrust.

De Sárraga, Belén, and Federico R. Tonda. 1913. *Conferencias sociológicas y de crítica religiosa dadas en Santiago de Chile en enero y febrero de 1913*. Santiago: La Razón. HathiTrust.

Deere, Carmen Diana. 2023. "Beyond 'Death Do Us Part': Spousal Intestate Inheritance in Nineteenth Century Latin America." *Law and History Review* 41 (4): 619–51. https://doi.org/10.1017/S0738248023000354.

Deere, Carmen Diana. 2025. "Hacia la autonomía económica de la mujer casada: la ley de 1911 y las reformas de los años treinta en el Ecuador." In *De la sublevación a la participacion: las mujeres en la historia del Ecuador* (siglo XIII–XX), edited by Ana Maria Goetschel. Quito: FLACSO ed., forthcoming.

Deere, Carmen Diana, Jacqueline Contreras, and Jennifer Twyman. 2014. "Patrimonial Violence. A Study of Women's Property Rights in Ecuador." *Latin American Perspectives* 41 (1): 143–65. https://doi.org/10.1177/0094582X13492133.
Deere, Carmen Diana, and Cheryl Doss. 2006. "The Gender Asset Gap: What Do We Know and Why Does it Matter?" *Feminist Economics* 12 (1&2): 1–50. https://doi.org/10.1080/13545700500508056.
Deere, Carmen Diana, and Magdalena León. 1982. *Women in Andean Agriculture: Peasant Production and Rural Wage Employment in Colombia and Peru.* Geneva: International Labour Office.
Deere, Carmen Diana, and Magdalena León. 2001. *Empowering Women. Land and Property Rights in Latin America.* University of Pittsburgh Press. https://doi.org/10.2307/j.ctt5hjpf6.
Deere, Carmen Diana, and Magdalena León. 2005. "Liberalism and Married Women's Property Rights in Nineteenth-Century Latin America." *Hispanic American Historical Review* 85 (4): 627–78. https://doi.org/10.1215/00182168-85-4-627.
Deere, Carmen Diana, and Magdalena León. 2021. "De la potestad marital a la violencia económica y patrimonial en Colombia." *Revista de Estudios Socio-Jurídicos* 23 (1): 1–33. https://doi.org/10.12804/revistas.urosario.edu.co/sociojuridicos/a.9900.
Deere, Carmen Diana, and Magdalena León. 2022. "Consensual Unions, Property Rights and Patrimonial Violence against Women in Latin America." *Social Politics: International Studies in Gender, State & Society* 29 (2): 608–33. https://doi.org/10.1093/sp/jxab001.
Deere, Carmen Diana, and Magdalena León. 2023. "Identidad de las mujeres casadas: el uso del 'de' en sus apellidos en Colombia." *Revista de Estudios Sociales* 84: 19–39. https://doi.org/10.7440/res84.2023.02.
Delgado, Pedro Genaro. 1922. *La mujer ante la ley o el abogado de la mujer peruana.* Lima: San Martín y Cía.
Del Valle Iberlucea, Enrique. 1918. "Derechos civiles de la mujer." *Boletín Mensual del Museo Social Argentino* 7: 418–78. HathiTrust.
Deutsch, Sandra McGee. 2012. "Argentine Women Against Fascism: The Junta de la Victoria, 1941–1947." *Politics, Religion & Ideology* 13 (2): 221–36. https://doi.org/10.1080/21567689.2012.675707.
Deutsch, Sandra McGee. 2023. *Gendering Antifascism. Women's Activism in Argentina and the World, 1918–1947.* University of Pittsburgh Press.
Díaz de Guíjarro, Enrique. 1942. *La compra de bienes raíces por la mujer casada.* Buenos Aires: Antología Jurídica.
Doepke, Matthias, and Michèle Tertilt. 2009. "Women's Liberation: What's in it for Men." *Quarterly Journal of Economics* 124 (4): 1541–91. https://doi.org/10.1162/qjec.2009.124.4.1541.
Dominici, Anibal. 1897. *Comentarios al Código Civil Venezolano (reformado en 1896)*, Vol. 1. Caracas: Imprenta Bolivar.
Dreier, Katherine S. 1920. *Five Months in the Argentine from a Woman's Point of View, 1918 to 1919.* New York: F. Fairchild Sherman.
Dueñas Vargas, Guiomar. 2024. "Women's Suffrage in Colombia." In *Women's Suffrage in the Americas*, edited by Stephanie Mitchell, 141–64. University of New Mexico Press.
Duve, Thomas, and Tamar Herzog, eds. 2024. *The Cambridge History of Latin American Law in Global Perspective*. Cambridge University Press.
Ecuador, República de. 1860. *Código Civil de la República del Ecuador*. Quito: Imprenta de los Huérfanos de Valencia. HathiTrust.
Ecuador, República de. 1889. *Código Civil de la República del Ecuador*. 3rd ed. New York: Imprenta de Las Novedades. HathiTrust.
Ecuador, República de. 1897. *Constitución de 1897*. https://constitutionnet.org/sites/default/files/1897.pdf.

Ecuador, República de. 1906. *Constitución Política de la República del Ecuador decretada por la Asamblea Nacional de 1906–1907*. https://derechoecuador.com/constituciones
Ecuador, República de. 1912. *Anuario de Legislación Ecuatoriana 1911*, Vol. 10. Quito: Imprenta y Encarnación Nacional. HathiTrust.
Ecuador, República de. 1913. *Anuario de Legislación Ecuatoriana 1912*, Vol. 11. Quito: Imprenta y Encarnación Nacional. HathiTrust.
Ecuador, República de. 1929. *Constitución de 1929*. https:///www.cancilleria.gob.ec
Ecuador, República de. 1930. *Código Civil de la República del Ecuador*. 4th ed. Quito: Talleres Gráficos Nacionales. LLMCDigital.
Ecuador, República de. 1938a. *Código de Procedimientos Civiles*. Quito: Imprenta del Ministerio de Gobierno. LLMCDigital.
Ecuador, República de. 1938b. *Constitución Política de la República del Ecuador expedida por la Asamblea Nacional de 1938*. Proyecto en curso. http://archivobiblioteca.asambleanacionalgob.ec/constituciondelecuador/constitucion1938.pdf
Ecuador, República de. 1945. *Constitución Política de la República del Ecuador dictada por la Asamblea Nacional Constituyente de 1944–1945*. Quito: Talleres Gráficos Nacionales.
Ecuador, República de. 1946. *Constitución de 1946*. https:///www.cancilleria.gob.ec
Ecuador, República de. 1950. *Código Civil de la República del Ecuador*. 5th ed. Quito: Talleres Gráficos Nacionales.
Ecuador, República de. 1952. *Información Censal. Resumen de los Resultados Definitivos del Censo Nacional de Población de 1950*. Quito: Dirección General de Estadística y Censos, Talleres Gráficos del Censo.
Ecuador, República de. 1960. *Código Civil*. In Comisión Legislativa, *Constitución y Leyes de la República*, 614–1040. Quito: Talleres Gráficos Nacionales.
Ecuador, República de. 1970. *Código Civil de la República del Ecuador*. 7th ed. *Registro Oficial*. LLMC Digital.
Ehrick, Christine. 1998. "*Madrinas* and Missionaries: Uruguay and the Pan-American Women's Movement." *Gender & History* 10 (3): 406–24. https://doi.org/10.1111/1468-0424.00111.
Ehrick, Christine. 2005. *The Shield of the Weak. Feminism and the State in Uruguay, 1903–1933*. University of New Mexico Press.
Eltit, Diamela. 1994. "Elena Caffarena, una mujer de todos los tiempos." In *Crónica del Sufragio Femenino en Chile*, edited by Diamela Eltit, 97–108. Santiago: SERNAM. https://www.memoriachilena.gob.cl/archivos2/pdfs/MC0031311.pdf.
Errázariz Tagle, Javiera. 2005. "Discursos en torno al sufragio femenino en Chile 1865–1949." *Historia* 38 (vol. II): 257–86. https://dx.doi.org/10.4067/S0717-71942005000200002.
Espina, Gioconda. 1994. "Entre sacudones, golpes y amenazas. Las venezolanas organizadas y las otras." In *Mujeres y participación política. Avances y desafíos en América Latina*, edited by Magdalena León, 167–80. Bogotá: T M Editores.
Estrada, Jenny. 1980. *Una Mujer total. Matilde Hidalgo de Procel (Biografía)*. Imprenta de la Universidad de Guayaquil.
Estrada Ayala de Ramírez Pérez, Aurora. (1934) 2006. "La mujer trabajadora en la vida social." *La Pólvora* (Quito), 78. Reproduced in *Orígenes del feminismo en el Ecuador*, edited by Ana María Goetschel, 343–52. Quito: CONAMU and FLACSO. https://biblio.flacsoandes.edu.ec/libros/digital/52830.pdf.
Evans, Richard J. 1976. *The Feminist Movement in Germany*. Sage.
Evans, Richard J. 1977. *The Feminists. Women's Emancipation Movements in Europe, America and Australasia 1840–1920*. Croom Helm.
Ewell, Judith. 1984. *Venezuela. A Century of Change*. Stanford University Press.
Ezama Gil, Angeles. 2014. "Una historia de asociación de mujeres más allá de las fronteras. La Liga Internacional de Mujeres Ibéricas e Hispanoamericanas y la Cruzada de la Mujer Española." In *Mujeres en la Frontera*, edited by Almeda Margarita,

Lorenzo María García, and Guzman Helena, 53–82. Madrid: Universidad Nacional de Educación a Distancia.
Fernández, Raquel. 2014. "Women's Rights and Development." *Journal of Economic Growth* 19: 37–80.
Font, Miguel J., ed. 1921. *La Mujer. Encuesta feminista Argentina.* Buenos Aires: Imp. Costa Hnos. HathiTrust.
Freire López, Ana María. 2021. "La Biblioteca de la Mujer de Emilia Pardo Bazán. Historia y cronología de un proyecto editorial." In *Et amicitia et magisterio. Estudios en honor de José Manuel González Herrán*, 262–74. Madrid: Biblioteca Virtual Miguel de Cervantes.
Friedman, Elisabeth J. 2000. *Unfinished Transitions. Women and the Gendered Development of Democracy in Venezuela, 1936–1996*. Pennsylvania State University Press.
Friedman, Lawrence M. 1984. "Rights of Passage: Divorce Law in Historical Perspective." *Oregon Law Review* 63 (4): 649–70. Hein Online.
Frugoni, Emilio. 1940. *La mujer ante el derecho*. Montevideo: Ed. Indoamérica.
Fuentes, Manuel Atanasio, and Miguel Antonio de la Lama. 1870. *Código Civil de 1852*. Lima: Imprenta del Estado.
Gago, Verónica. 2009. "El programa político de una vanguardista prudente." Prologue. In Elvira López, *El movimiento feminista: primeros trazos del feminismo en Argentina*, 7–19. Buenos Aires: Biblioteca Nacional.
Gallo, Rosalía. 2004. *Nuestra Causa, revista mensual feminista, 1919–1921. Estudio e índice general*. Buenos Aires: Instituto de Investigaciones Históricas Cruz del Sur.
Gallo Chinchilla, Margarita. 1945. *La mujer ante la legislación chilena. Derechos político y social*. Universidad de Chile.
Galván. 1831. Novísima Recopilación de las Leyes de España. Vol. 3. Mexico City: Galván, Librero.
Ganón, Isaac. 1964. "Sobre la familia Uruguaya." *Revista Mexicana de Sociología* 26 (1): 173–90. https://doi.org/10.2307/3538495.
García de Astorga, Amarilis. 1983. "La mujer en la administración de la comunidad conyugal." In *Venezuela: Biografía inacabada, evolución social 1936–1983*, edited by Ministro de Estado para la Participación de la Mujer en el Desarrollo, 239–67. Banco Central de Venezuela.
García y García, Elvira. 1925. *La mujer peruana a través de los siglos. Serie historiada de estudios y observaciones*. Vol. 2. Lima: Imprenta Americana. HathiTrust.
García Moreno, Alejo. 1897. *Texto y comentarios al Código Civil del Imperio Alemán promulgado el 18 agosto 1896*. Madrid: Centro Ed de Góngora. https://ecollections.law.fiu.edu/civil_codes/18.
García Naranjo Morales, Aída. 2009. *Peruanas notables. Presencia de las mujeres en los movimientos sociales de los siglos XX y XXI*. Lima: Centro de Derechos y Desarrollo.
Gargarella, Roberto. 2004. "Towards a Typology of Latin American Constitutionalism, 1810–60." *Latin American Research Review* 39 (2): 141–53. https://www.jstor.org/stable/1555404.
Gaviola A., Edda, Ximena Jiles M., Lorella Lopresti M. and Claudia Rojas M. 1986. *Queremos votar en las próximas elecciones. Historia del movimiento sufragista chileno 1913–1952*. Santiago: Centro de Análisis y Difusión de la Condición de la Mujer 'La Morada' and others.
Geddes, Rick, and Dean Lueck. 2002. "The Gains from Self-ownership and the Expansion of Women's Rights." *American Economic Review* 92 (4): 1079–92. https://www.jstor.org/stable/3083297.
Geddes, Rick, and Sharon Tennyson. 2013. "Passage of the Married Women's Property Acts and the Earnings Acts in the United States: 1850 to 1920." *Research in Economic History* 29: 145–89.
Giddens, Anthony. 1992. *The Transformation of Intimacy*. Cambridge, UK: Polity Press.

Giordano, Veronica. 2012. *Ciudadanas incapaces. La construcción de los derechos civiles de las mujeres en Argentina, Brazil, Chile y Uruguay en el siglo XX*. Buenos Aires: Teseo.

Giordano, Veronica 2013. "Modernidad, modernización y sufragio universal: La experiencia de Argentina, Brasil, Chile y Uruguay." In *Formas de ciudadanía en América Latina*, edited by Mirta Zaida Lobato, 41–63. Madrid and Frankfurt: Ed. Iberoamericana and Vervuert.

Glendon, Mary Ann. 1989. *The Transformation of Family Law. State, Law, and Family in the United States and Western Europe*. University of Chicago Press.

Goetschel, Ana María, 2006. "Estudio Introductorio." In *Orígenes del feminismo en el Ecuador*, edited by A.M. Goetschel, 13–56. Quito: CONAMU and FLACSO. https://biblio.flacsoandes.edu.ec/libros/digital/52772.pdf

Goetschel, Ana María. 2007. *Educación de la mujeres, maestras y esferas públicas*. Quito: FLACSO and Abya Yala. https://biblio.flacsoandes.edu.ec/libros/digital/59706.pdf

Goetschel, Ana María. 2010. "Las paradojas del liberalismo y las mujeres: coyuntura 1907–1909." In *Celebraciones centenarias y negociaciones por la nación ecuatoriana*, edited by Valeria Coronel and Mercedes Prieto, 209–40. Quito: Ed. FLACSO. https://biblio.flacsoandes.edu.ec/libros/digital/52523.pdf

Gómez Camargo, Lisa Cristina. 2019. *Construcción de la ciudadanía de las mujeres en Colombia. Cuatro acontecimientos históricos*. Doctoral thesis. Bogotá: Universidad Externado. https://doi.org/10.2307/j.ctv1k03pb6.

Gómez Molina, Paola Marcela. 2015. "Régimen patrimonial del matrimonio: contexto histórico que rodeo la promulgación de la Ley 28 de 1932." *Revista de Estudios Socio-Jurídicos* 17 (1): 41–76. https://dx.doi.org/10.12804/esj17.01.2014.02

Gómez R., José J. 1961. *Régimen de bienes en el matrimonio*. 3rd ed. Bogotá: Ed. Temis.

Gómez de Monroy, Hilda Emma. 2002. *La mujer colombiana y el proceso histórico de sus derechos*. Tunja: Ed. Artes Gráficas.

González, Cesar. 1942. "Circular del Ministro de Relaciones Interiores Relativa al nuevo Código Civil." *Boletín de la Academia de Ciencias Políticas y Sociales,* 41–62.

González Fanning, Teresa. 1911. "Educación doméstica y social de la mujer." In *Primer Congreso Femenino Internacional de la República Argentina. Historia, actas y trabajos*, edited by Asociación Universitarias Argentinas, 275–80. Buenos Aires: Imprenta A. Ceppi.

González del Riego, Delfina. 2005. *50 años del voto femenino en el Perú: Historia y realidad actual*. Lima: Ministerio de la Mujer y el Desarrollo Social. https://bvs.minsa.gob.pe/local/minsa/1316_gob526-1.pdf,

Grierson, Cecilia. 1902. "Marcha progresiva de la ideal del Consejo Nacional de Mujeres." *Revista del Consejo Nacional de Mujeres* 2 (8): 24–34.

Guardia, Sara Beatriz. 1985. *Mujeres peruanas. El otro lado de la historia*. Lima: Imp. Ed. Humboldt.

Guatemala, República de. 1877. *Código Civil de la República de Guatemala, 1877*. Guatemala City: Imp. El Progreso. https://ecollections.law.fiu.edu/civil_codes/3.

Guérin de Elgueta, Sara, ed. 1928. *Actividades femeninas en Chile*. Santiago: La Ilustración. https://www.memoriachilena.gob.cl/602/w3-article-126684.html.

Guy, Donna J. 2009. *Women Building the Welfare State. Reforming Charity and Creating Rights in Argentina, 1880–1955*. Duke University Press.

Guzmán Brito, Alejandro. 2000. *La codificación civil en Iberoamérica. Siglos XIX y XX*. Santiago: Ed. Jurídica.

Hammond, Gregory. 2011. *The Women's Suffrage Movement and Feminism in Argentina from Roca to Perón*. University of New Mexico Press.

Handelsman, Michael M. 1976. *Amazons and Artists: A Study of Ecuadorian Women's Prose*. Ph.D. dissertation. Gainesville, FL: University of Florida. https://ufdc.ufl.edu/UF00097505/00001/images.

Henault, Mirta. 2002. *Alicia Moreau de Justo. 'Dad paso a la honradez, al trabajo, a la justicia*. Buenos Aires: CUATA Eds.
Herchenroder, M. F. P. 1938. "The Capacity of Married Women in French Law." *Journal of Comparative Legislation and International Law* 20 (4): 196–203. https://www.jstor.org/stable/755031.
Herrarte, Alberto, ed. 1956. *Documentos de la Unión Centroamericana*. Guatemala City: Secretaría General de la Organización de Estados Centroamericanos (ODECA). http://www.sice.oas.org/sica/Studies/DocUnionCentroamericana.pdf.
Herrera, Gioconda. 2010. "El congreso católico de mujeres de 1909 y la regeneración de la nación." In *Celebraciones centenarias y negociaciones por la nación ecuatoriana*, edited by Valeria Coronel and Mercedes Prieto, 241–63. Quito: Ed. FLACSO. https://biblio.flacsoandes.edu.ec/libros/digital/52524.pdf
Herrera García, Mercedes. 1956. "Situación legal, política y social de la mujer en el Ecuador." Paper presented to the 9th Conference of the International Federation of Lawyers. *Revista Forense*, Época II, 5: 100–109.
Holcombe, Lee. 1983. *Wives and Property: Reform of the Married Women's Property Law in Nineteenth-Century England*. University of Toronto Press.
Honduras, República de. 1906. *Código Civil 1906*. Tegucigalpa: Tip. Nacional.
Htun, Mala. 2003. *Sex and the State. Abortion, Divorce, and the Family under Latin American Dictatorships and Democracies*. Cambridge University Press.
Huggins Castañeda, Magally. 2010. "Re-escribiendo la historia. Las venezolanas y sus luchas por los derechos políticos." *Revista Venezolana de Estudios de la Mujer* 15 (34): 163–90. http://saber.ucv.ve/ojs/index.php/rev_vem/issue/view/322.
Hünefeldt, Christine. 2000. *Liberalism in the Bedroom: Quarreling Spouses in Nineteenth Century Lima*. Pennsylvania State University Press.
IAC, International American Conference. 1940. "Eighth International Conference of American States. Lima, December 9-27, 1938." *International Conferences of American States, First Supplement 1933–1940*. Washington, DC: Carnegie Endowment for International Peace. Hein Online.
IACW, Inter-American Commission on Women. 1933. *Report of the IACW on the Political and Civil Rights of Women* (21 volumes). DSP.
IACW, Inter-American Commission on Women 1935. *Documents concerning its creation and Organization*. Washington, DC: Pan American Union. DSP.
IACW, Inter-American Commission on Women 1938. *Report of the Inter- American Commission of Women to the Eighth International Conference of American States on the Political and Civil Rights of Women*. Lima. Hein Online.
IAW, International Alliance of Women. 2005. *Centenary Edition. International Alliance of Women (1904–2004)*. https://womenalliance.org/wp-content/uploads/2018/10/IAW-Centenary-Edition-1904-2004-webversion.pdf
ICW, International Council of Women. 1966. *Women in a Changing World. The Dynamic Story of the International Council of Women since 1888*. Routledge & Kegan Paul.
Idrobo, María Angélica. (1928) 2006. "Discurso en la velada del Centro Cultura y Renovación," *La Nación* (Guayaquil). Reproduced in *Orígenes del feminismo en el Ecuador*, edited by Ana María Goetschel, 111–14. Quito: CONAMU and FLACSO.
Irarrázaval de Pereira, Isabel. 1918. "Sobre algunos derechos que la mujer debe aspirar." In *Relaciones y Documentos del Congreso Mariano Femenino*. Santiago: Escuela Tip. La Gratitud Nacional.
Iregui-Bohórquez, Ana María, Ligia Alba Melo-Becerra, María Teresa Ramírez-Giraldo and Ana María Tribin-Uribe. 2021. *El camino hacia la igualdad de género en Colombia. Todavía hay mucho por hacer*. Bogotá: Banco de la República.
Jaramillo Sierra, Isabel C. 2013. *Derecho y familia en Colombia. Historias de raza, género y propiedad (1540–1980)*. Bogotá: Universidad de los Andes.

Jiménez Pacheco, Julio. 1913. *La mujer ante el derecho*. Doctoral thesis, Faculty of Law, Universidad Nacional de San Antonio Abad. Cuzco: Tip. Lib. H.G. Rozas. HathiTrust.

Karl, Terry L. 1997. *The Paradox of Plenty. Oil Booms and Petro States*. University of California Press.

Kirkwood, Julieta. 1986. *Ser política en Chile. Las feministas y los partidos*. Santiago: FLACSO-Chile.

Klarén, Peter. 2004. *Nación y sociedad en la historia del Perú*. Lima: IEP. ProQuest.

Klimpel, Felícitas. 1962. *La mujer chilena (El aporte femenino al progreso de Chile) 1910–1960*. Santiago: Ed. Andrés Bello. https://www.memoriachilena.gob.cl/602/w3-article-126686.html.

Labarca H., Amanda. 1914. *Actividades femeninas en los Estados Unidos*. Santiago: Imprenta Universitaria. HathiTrust.

Labarca H., Amanda. 1924. "Un estudio sobre el feminismo en Chile." *Atenea* 1 (5): 376–86. https://doi.org/10.29393/At5-74ALES10074.

Labarca H., Amanda. 1934. *¿A dónde va la mujer?* Santiago: Talleres Empresa Letras.

Labarca H., Amanda. 1947. *Feminismo Contemporáneo*. Santiago: Zig-Zag. http://bibliotecadigital.indh.cl/handle/123456789/447.

Labarca H., Amanda. 1952. "Evolución femenina." In *Desarrollo de Chile en la primera mitad del siglo XX*, 107–30. Santiago: Universidad de Chile.

LaGreca, Nancy. 2009. *Rewriting Womanhood: Feminism, Subjectivity, and the Angel of the House in the Latin American Novel*. Penn State University Press.

Landívar de Arteaga, Myriam, ed. 2015. *Zoila Ugarte de Landívar, la escritora, pensamiento y obra. Semblanzas y necrologías, 1892–1948*. Quito: Casa de la Cultura Ecuatoriana Benjamín Carrión.

Lanteri Renshaw, Julieta. (1919) 2004. "La mujer en la política," *Nuestra Causa*, 2. In *Nuestra Causa, revista mensual feminista*, edited by R. Gallo, 74–76. Buenos Aires: Instituto de Investigaciones Históricas Cruz del Sur.

Latorre U., Luis F. 1934. "Proyecto de Ley sobre reformas civiles. Régimen patrimonial en el matrimonio." In *Trabajos jurídicos de Luis F. Latorre U. como abogado consultor de la presidencia*, edited by L.F. Latorre U., 26–32. Bogotá: Imprenta Nacional.

Lavrin, Asunción. 1995. *Women, Feminism and Social Change in Argentina, Chile and Uruguay 1890–1940*. University of Nebraska Press.

Leonardi de, María Teresa R. 1983. "El movimiento femenino 1932–1983." In *Venezuela: Biografía inacabada, evolución social 1936–1983*, edited by Ministro de Estado para la Participación de la Mujer en el Desarrollo, 381–482. Banco Central de Venezuela.

Lira Urquieta, Pedro. 1961. *Código Civil de Chile. Estudio Preliminar del Dr. Pedro Lira Urquieta*. Madrid: Instituto de Cultura Hispánica.

Londoño, Patricia. 1995. "Publicaciones periódicas dirigidas a la mujer en Colombia, 1858–1930." In *Las mujeres en la historia de Colombia*, edited by Magdala Velásquez Toro, 355–81. Vol. 3. Bogotá: Consejería Presidencial y Grupo Ed. Norma.

Lodoño López, Jenny. 2011. "El liberalismo y las mujeres." In *El crimen de El Ejido*, edited by Enrique Ayala, 73–80. Quito: Corporación Editorial Nacional.

López, Elvira V. 1901. *El movimiento feminista*. Ph.D. Thesis, Universidad de Buenos Aires. Buenos Aires: Imp. Mariano Moreno. HathiTrust.

López Oseira, Ruth. 2013. "El declive de la potestad marital. Norma y costumbre en torno a la reforma del Código Civil Colombiano de 1932." In *Género, prácticas y representaciones en la historia colombiana siglo XIX y XX*, edited by Ruth López Oseira, 244–78. Medellín: Universidad Nacional de Colombia. ProQuest.

Lorenzo Modía, María Jesús. 2003. "La vindicación de los derechos de la mujer antes de Mary Wollstonecraft." *Philologia Hispalensis* 17 (2): 105–14. https://doi.org/10.12795/PH.2003.v17.i02.09.

Luisi, Paulina. 1919. *Movimiento sufragista*. Montevideo: Imp. El Siglo Ilustrado. HathiTrust.

Luisi, Paulina, ed. 1930. *La mujer uruguaya reclama sus derechos*. Montevideo: Alianza Uruguaya and Consejo de Mujeres.
Luna, Lola G. 1985. "Los movimientos de mujeres: feminismo y feminidades en Colombia (1930–1943)." *Boletín Americanista* 35: 169–90. https://hdl.handle.net/2445/166140
Luna, Lola G. 2001a. "La feminidad y el sufragismo colombiano durante el periodo 1944–48." *Otras Miradas* 1 (1): 108–25. https://www.redalyc.org
Luna, Lola G. 2001b. "El logro del voto femenino en Colombia: la violencia y el maternalismo populista, 1949–1957." *Boletín Americanista* 51: 81–94. https://dialnet.unirioja.es/servlet/articulo?codigo=2936874
Luna, Lola G. 2004. *El sujeto sufragista, feminismo y feminidad en Colombia, 1930–1945*. Cali: Ed. La Manzana.
Machado, José Enrique. 1940. "Historia del código civil venezolano." *Revista de Derecho y Legislación* 29 (344): 3–39. HathiTrust.
Machado, José Olegario. (1898) 1922. *Exposición y comentario del código civil argentino*. Vol. 1. Buenos Aires: Ed. Científica y Literaria Argentina. HathiTrust.
Mannarelli, María Emma. 1999. *Limpias y modernas. Género, higiene y cultura en la Lima de novecientos*. Lima: Ed. Flora Tristán.
Marino, Katherine M. 2014. "Marta Vergara, Popular-Front Pan-American Feminism and the Transnational Struggle for Working Women's Rights in the 1930s." *Gender & History* 26 (3): 642–60. https://doi.org/10.1111/1468-0424.12093.
Marino, Katherine M. 2019. *Feminism for the Americas. The Making of an International Human Rights Movement*. University of North Carolina Press.
Marino, Katherine M., and Susan Ware. 2022. "Rethinking 'First Wave' Feminisms: An Introduction." *Signs: Journal of Women in Culture and Society* 47 (4): 811–16. https://doi.org/10.1086/718868.
Márquez Macías, Rosario. 2022. "El Hogar Americano en Madrid. Una institución de corta vida con trayectoria internacional." *Temas Americanistas* 48: 143–66. https://doi.org/10.12795/Temas-Americanistas.2022.i48.08.
Martínez, Luisa. 1937. *Reformas del Código Civil Venezolano para la Mujer*. (Pamphlet of October 21, 1937, radio speech on La Voz de la Espera). Caracas: Ed. Bolivar. DSP.
Martínez Macias, María Esther. 1933. "El problema feminista en el Ecuador." *Nuevos Horizontes* 1 (2): 7, 27.
Martínez Macias, María Esther. 1934. "La mujer y el sufragio." *Nuevos Horizontes* 1 (5): 7, 27.
Martínez Paz, E. 1917. "El código civil venezolano de 1916."*Revista de Derecho y Legislación* 6: 148–51. HathiTrust.
Martínez V., Emma D. 2008. "La educación de las mujeres en Venezuela, 1870–1940 o reconstruir la historia Venezolana incluyendo a las mujeres." *Revista Venezolana de Estudios de la Mujer* 13 (31): 127–50. https://ve.scielo.org/scielo.php?script=sci_isoref&pid=S1316-37012008000200009&lng=es&tlng=es.
Mateos Alarcón, Manuel. 1904. *Código Civil del Distrito Federal, concordado y anotado por M. Mateo Alarcón*. México, D.F: Librería de la vda de Ch. Bouret. HathiTrust.
Mayer, Dora. 1911. "La moral femenina." In *Primer Congreso Femenino Internacional de la República Argentina. Historia, actas y trabajos*, edited by Asociación Universitarias Argentinas, 241–58. Buenos Aires: Imprenta A. Ceppi.
Maza Valenzuela, Erika. 1995. "Catolicismo, anticlericalismo y la extensión del sufragio a la mujer en Chile." *Estudios Públicos* No. 58: 137-97. https://www.estudiospublicos.cl/index.php/cep/article/view/1218.
Maza Valenzuela, Erika. 1998. "Liberales, Radicales y la ciudadanía de la mujer en Chile (1872–1930)," *Estudios Públicos* No. 69: 319–56. https://www.estudiospublicos.cl/index.php/cep/article/view/1044.
McCammon, Holly J., Karen E. Campbell, Ellen M. Granberg, and Christine Mowery. 2001. "How Movements Win: Gendered Opportunity Structures and U.S. Women's Suffrage

Movements, 1866 to 1919." *American Sociological Review* 66 (1): 49–70. https://doi.org/10.1177/000312240106600104.

McCammon, Holly J., Sandra C. Arch, and Erin M. Bergner. 2014. "A Radical Demand Effect: Early US Feminists and the Married Women's Property Acts." *Social Science History* 38: 221–50. https://doi.org/10.1017/ssh.2015.17.

MEMCH, Movimiento Pro-Emancipación de las Mujeres de Chile. 1936. "Programa del MEMCH, 1936." Fondo Elena Caffarena. https://www.archivonacional.gob.cl/archivos-mujeres-y-generos/galerias/memch-movimiento-pro-emancipacion-de-las-mujeres-de-chile.

MEMCH, Movimiento Pro-Emancipación de las Mujeres de Chile 1983. *MEMCH. Antología para una historia del movimiento feminista en Chile*. Santiago: MEMCH.

Méndez, Luis. (1873) 1897. "La verdad histórica sobre la formación del Código Civil." In *Revisión del proyecto de código civil mexicano del Dr. Justo Sierra por la Comisión formade de... durante los años de 1861 a 1866*, edited by Agustín Verdugo, 9–29. Vol. 1. México, D.F.: Talleres de la Librería Religiosa.

Mendoza Mora, Lucía. 2018. *En busca del reconocimiento. Las primeras feministas colombianas, 1926-1944*. Thesis, Department of History. Bogotá: Universidad de los Andes. https://repositorio.uniandes.edu.co.

Metz, Annie. 2007. "Jeanne Schmahl et la loi sur le libre salaire de la femme." *Bulletin de Archives du Feminisme* 13. https://www.archivesdufeminisme.fr/metz-jeanne-schmahl-loi-libre-salaire-femme/.

México, República de. 1870. *Código Civil del Distrito Federal y Territorio de la Baja California*. México, D.F.: Tip. de J. M. Aguilar.

Milanich, Nara B. 2009. *Children of Fate. Childhood, Class and the State in Chile, 1850–1930*. Duke University Press.

Miller, Francesca. 1991. *Latin American Women and the Search for Social Justice*. Hanover, NH: University Press of New England.

Miller, Francesca. 2010. "Latin American Feminism and the Transnational Arena." In *Globalizing Feminisms 1789–1945*, edited by Karen Offen, 193–203. Routledge.

Miloslavich Túpac, Diana. 2015. "Feminismo y sufragio 1931–1955." *Elecciones* 14 (15): 109–43. https://doi.org/10.53557/Elecciones.2015.v14n15.05.

Miranda Salcedo, Dalín. 2011. "La dinámica de la construcción legal y eclesiástica de la familia en Colombia 1850–1930." *Advocatus* (Barranquilla) 16: 133–58.

Mirow, Michael C. 2004. *Latin American Law: A History of Private Law and Institutions in Spanish America*. University of Texas Press.

Moehling, Carolyn M., and Melissa A. Thomasson. 2020. "Votes for Women: An Economic Perspective on Women's Enfranchisement." *Journal of Economic Perspectives* 34 (2): 3–23. https://doi.org/10.1257/jep.34.2.3.

Molyneux, Maxine. 2001. "'No God, No Boss, No Husband!' Anarchist Feminism in Nineteenth Century Argentina." In *Women's Movements in International Perspective*, edited by Maxine Molyneux, 13–37. Palgrave.

Moreau, Alicia. 1919a. *La emancipación civil de la mujer*. Buenos Aires: Biblioteca Feminista, Unión Feminista Nacional. https://www.scribd.com/document/512618874/Alicia-Moreau-de-Justo-La-emancipacion-civil-de-la-mujer.

Moreau, Alicia. (1919b) 2004. "El movimiento feminista en la República Argentina." *Nuestra Causa*, 1. In R. Gallo, *Nuestra Causa, revista mensual feminista*, 71–73. Buenos Aires: Instituto de Investigaciones Históricas Cruz del Sur.

Morel, Isabel (Delia Ducoing de Arrate). n.d. *Charlas Femeninas. Unión Femenina de Chile: sus finalidades, su organización*. Valparaíso: Unión Femenina de Chile. https://www.memoriachilena.gob.cl/archivos2/pdfs/MC0023601.pdf.

Mori y Chávez, Lorenzo. 1906. *Condición civil de la mujer*. Thesis presented for the doctorate in Law, Universidad Mayor de San Marcos. Lima: Imprenta San Pedro. HathiTrust.

Moscoso, Martha. 1996a. "Imagen de la mujer y la familia a inicios del siglo XX." *Procesos. Revista Ecuatoriana de Historia* 6: 67–82. https://repositorio.uasb.edu.ec/handle/10644/1249.

Moscoso, Martha. 1996b. "Discurso religioso y discurso liberal: mujeres sumisas." In *Y el amor no era todo... Mujeres, imágenes y conflictos*, edited by M. Moscoso, 22–57. Quito: Abya Yala, DGIS/Holanda.

Nari, Marcela M.A. 2000. "Maternidad, política y feminismo." In *Historia de las mujeres en Argentina*, edited by Fernanda Gil Lozano, Valeria Silvina and María Gabriela Ini, 192–216. Vol. 2. Buenos Aires: Taurus.

Nari, Marcela M.A. 2004. *Políticas de maternidad y maternalismo político. Buenos Aires, 1890–1940*. Buenos Aires: Ed. Biblos.

Newland, Carlos. 1994. "El Estado Docente and its Expansion: Spanish America Elementary Education, 1900–1950." *Journal of Latin American Studies* 26 (2): 449–67. https://doi.org/10.1017/S0022216X00016291.

O'Connor, Erin. 2007. *Gender, Indian, Nation. The Contradictions of Making Ecuador, 1830–1925*. University of Arizona Press.

O'Connor, Erin. 2024. "Without Consideration of Their Sex? The Uneven Path to Female Suffrage in Ecuador, ca. 1883–1940." In *Women's Suffrage in the Americas*, edited by Stephanie Mitchell, 245–72. University of New Mexico Press.

Offen, Karen. 1988. "Defining Feminism: A Comparative Historical Perspective." *Signs: Journal of Women in Culture and Society* 14 (1): 119–57. https://doi.org/10.1086/494494.

Offen, Karen. 2018. *Debating the Woman Question in the French Third Republic, 1870–1920*. Cambridge University Press.

Oliver, María Rosa. 1969. *La vida cotidiana*. Buenos Aires: Ed. Sudamericana.

Onetti, Carmen. 1930. "Gestiones de las asociaciones feministas por los derechos de la mujer," in *La mujer uruguaya reclama sus derechos políticos*, edited by Paulina Luisi, 50–65. Montevideo: Alianza Uruguaya and Consejo de Mujeres.

Ortega Torres, Jorge. 1950. *Código civil con notas, concordancias, jurisprudencia de la corte suprema y normas legales complementarias*. Bogotá: Ed. Temis.

Osta Vázquez, María Laura. 2023. "El argumento maternalista en el proceso de aprobación de los derechos políticos de las mujeres durante las primeras discusiones de Brasil y Uruguay a 90 años de su legislación." *Historia Regional* 36 (49): 1–17. http://historiaregional.org/ojs/index.php

Ots y Capdequi, José María. 1969. *Historia del Derecho Español en América y del Derecho Indiano*. Madrid: Ed. Aguilar.

Pachas Maceda, Sofía. 2019. "Estudio preliminar. Esclavas ayer, ciudadanas hoy." In *Zoila Aurora Cáceres y la ciudadanía femenina. La correspondencia de Feminismo Peruano*, edited by Sofia Pachas Maceda, 27–92. Lima: Fondo Editorial UNMSM, Jurado Nacional de Elecciones and Centro de la Mujer Peruana Flora Tristán.

Páez, Federico. 1939. *Explico*. Quito: Ed. El Comercio. http://repositorio.casadelacultura.gob.ec/bitstream/34000/521/1/FR1-F-000375.02-Paez-Explico.pdf.

Palacios, Lucila. 1985. *Espejo Rodante (páginas autobiográficas, 1902 a 1949)*. Caracas: Venediciones.

Palermo, Silvana A. 1998. "El sufragio femenino en el Congreso Nacional: Ideologías de género y ciudadanía en la Argentina (1916–1955)." *Boletín del Instituto de Historia Argentina y Americana Dr. Emilio Ravignani*. Series 3, (16 and 17): 151–78. https://repositoriouba.sisbi.uba.ar/gsdl/cgi-bin/library.cgi?a=d&c=bolravi&d=16-17-6_htm

Parra-Aranguren, Gonzalo. 1974. *La codificación de Páez (Código Civil de 1862)*. Caracas: Biblioteca de la Academia Nacional de Historia.

Paul, Catharine Manny. 1968. *Amanda Labarca H.: Educator to the Women in Chile*. CIDOC Cuaderno No. 1. Cuernavaca, Mex: CIDOC. ProQuest.

Peláez Echeverri, Gabriela. 1944. *La condición social de la mujer en Colombia*. Caracas: Ed. Cromos.

Peñaherrera, Victor M. 1922. *La mujer casada ante el derecho civil ecuatoriana*. Quito: Imprenta Nacional. https://hdl.handle.net/10469/12512.

Pereira, Teresa. 1978. "La mujer en el siglo XIX." In *Tres ensayos sobre la mujer chilena*, edited by Lucía Santa Cruz, Teresa Pereira, Isabel Zegers and Valeria Maino, 72–182. Santiago: Ed. Universitaria. https://www.memoriachilena.gob.cl/archivos2/pdfs/MC0023907.pdf.

Pérez Borja, Francisco. 1913. "Estudio de la Ley de Emancipación Económica de la Mujer Casada." *Revista de la Sociedad Jurídico-Literaria* 1 (3-4): 123–132, 235-242. HathiTrust.

Pérez E., José M., and Viteri L. Homero. 1924. "Cuestionario sobre el estado legal de las mujeres (solicitado por la Unión Panamericana)." *Revista Forense* 13 (31): 209–20.

Pérez Echanique, José María. (1946) 1954. "La igualdad de derecho entre los conyugues." *El Comercio*, reproduced in *Revista Forense*, Época II (1): 188–91.

Pérez Guerrero, Alfredo. (1946) 1954. "La igualdad de derecho de los conyugues." *El Comercio*, reproduced in *Revista Forense*, Época II (1): 180–88.

Pérez Guevara, Ada. 1944. *Sufragio femenino. Aspectos venezolanos*. Caracas: Impresores Unidos.

Pérez Perdomo, Rogelio. 1983. "Ensayo de periodización de la historia social del derecho en Venezuela." In *Libro Homenaje a José Melich Orsini*, edited by Instituto de Derecho Privado, 704–33. Universidad Central de Venezuela.

Pérez Perdomo, Rogelio. 2013. *Los juristas académicos de Venezuela: Historia institucional y biografía colectiva*. Faculty Books. 1. https://ecollections.law.fiu.edu/faculty_books/1.

Pernet, Corinne A. 2000. "Chilean Feminists, the International Women's Movement, and Suffrage, 1915–1950." *Pacific Historical Review* 69 (4): 663–88. https://www.jstor.org/stable/3641229.

Perú, República de. 1852. *Código Civil del Perú*. Lima: Imprenta del Gobierno, por Eusebio Aranda. HathiTrust.

Perú, República de. 1927. *Resumen del Censo de las provincias de Lima y Callao levantado el 17 de diciembre de 1920*. Lima: Min. de Hacienda e Imp. Americana. Google Books.

Perú, República de. 1932. *Censo de las provincias de Lima y Callao levantado el 13 de noviembre de 1931*. Lima: Junta Departamental de Lima Pro-Desocupados and Imp. Torres Aguirre. Google Books.

Perú, República de.1933. *Constitución Política del Peru (29 de marzo de 1933)*. https://www.leyes.congreso.gob.pe.

Perú, República de. 1939. *Código Civil promulgado por Decreto Supremo de 30 de agosto de 1936 en uso de la autorización contenida en la Ley No. 8305*. 2nd Oficial Edition. Lima: Imprenta Americana. LLMC Digital.

Pinto de Vidal, Isabel. 1951. *El batllismo precursor de los derechos de la mujer*. Montevideo: n.p.

Pinzón de Lewin, Patricia. 2014. *Esmeralda Arboleda. La mujer y la política*. Bogotá: Taller de Ed. Rocca.

Plaza, Leonidas. (1905) 1908. "Mensaje del Presidente de la República al Congreso Nacional." In Alejandro Noboa, ed., *Recopilación de Mensajes Dirigidos por los Presidentes…*, 264–351. Vol. V. Guayaquil: Imp. de El Tiempo. HathiTrust.

Poblete Poblete, Olga. 1993. *Una mujer, Elena Caffarena*. Santiago: Ed. Cuarto Propio. https://www.memoriachilena.gob.cl/602/w3-article-61875.html.

Portal, Magda. 1978. "Yo soy Magda Portal." In *Ser Mujer en el Perú*, edited by Esther Andradi and Ana María Portugal, 209–32. Lima: Ed. Mujer y Autonomía.

Portillo, José María. 2024. "Constitutions." In *The Cambridge History of Latin American Law in Global Perspective* edited by Thomas Duve and Tamar Herzog, 283–321. Cambridge University Press.

Posada y Díaz, Carlos G. 1915. "La institución de bienes reservados de la mujer casada." *Revista General de Legislación y Jurisprudencia* 63 (126): 280–95.

Posso, Rodolfo, and Reinaldo L. Cortés. 1946. "La mujer casada ante la nueva Constitución Política de la República." *Revista Forense* 29 (139): 9–30.

Poulsen, Karen. 2016. "Mujer y ciudadanía: La consecución del sufragio femenino en el Perú (1933–1955)." *Revista del Instituto Riva-Agüero* (RIRA) 1 (2): 141–97. https://doi.org/10.18800/revistaira.201602.005.

Prieto, Mercedes, and Ana María Goetschel. 2007. "El sufragio femenino en Ecuador 1884–1940." In *Mujeres y escenarios ciudadanos*, edited by Mercedes Prieto. Quito: FLACSO, 299–330. https://biblio.flacsoandes.edu.ec/libros/109583-opac.

Quintero, Inés. 2000. "Itinerarios de la mujer o el 50 por ciento que se hace mitad." In *Venezuela siglo XX. Visiones y testimonios*, edited by Azdrúbal Baptista, 245–72. Caracas: Fundación Polar.

Quintero, Inés. 2001. "Madres y ciudadanas (la lucha por el sufragio femenino en Venezuela)." *Cuadernos del CENDES* 46: 53–71.

Quintero, Rafael. 1980. *El mito del populismo en el Ecuador*. Quito: FLACSO. https://biblio.flacsoandes.edu.ec/libros/6052-opac.

Ramón Vaello, Yolanda. 1985. *La mujer en la vida nacional y en la prensa*. Caracas: Ed. Arte.

Ramos, Angela. 1990. *Una vida sin tregua*. Lima: Ed. Minerva.

Ramos Nuñez, Carlos. 2011. *Historia del derecho civil peruano. Siglos XIX y XX*. Tome VI, vols. 1–3. Lima: Fondo Editorial PUCP. Digitalia.

Rangel Lamus, Amenodoro. 1936. "Régimen patrimonial de la mujer casada." *Revista de Derecho y Legislación* 25: 79–85. HathiTrust.

Rawson de Dellepiane, Elvira. 1911. "Modificaciones al código civil argentino." In *Primer Congreso Femenino Internacional de la República Argentina*, edited by Asociación Universitarias Argentinas, 428–29. Buenos Aires: Imprenta A. Ceppi.

Rawson de Dellepiane, Elvira. (1919) 2004. "La importancia social de la mujer." Conference presented to the Ateneo Hispano-Americano summarized under "Asociación Pro-Derechos de la Mujer," *Nuestra Causa*, 6. In *Nuestra Causa, revista mensual feminista*, edited by R. Gallo, 79–84. Buenos Aires: Instituto de Investigaciones Históricas Cruz del Sur.

Rawson de Dellepiane, Elvira. 1921. "La campaña feminista en la Argentina." In *La Mujer. Encuesta feminista Argentina*, edited by Miguel J. Font, 73–87. Buenos Aires: Imp. Costa Hnos.

Reaño García, José. 1928. *Historia del Leguíismo, sus hombres y sus obras*. Lima: E. E. Balarezo.

Rébora, Juan Carlos. 1926. *La Familia (Boceto sociológico y jurídico)*. Parte General. Buenos Aires: Libreros-Editores Juan Roldán & Cía. HathiTrust.

Rébora, Juan Carlos. 1927. *El estatuto de la mujer y las relaciones emergentes del matrimonio*. Buenos Aires: Lib.-Eds. Juan Roldán y Cia. HathiTrust.

Rébora, Juan Carlos. 1929. *La emancipación de la mujer (el aporte de la Jurisprudencia)*. Buenos Aires: Lib. y Ed. La Facultad.

Rébora, Juan Carlos and Emilio Pedro Gnecco. 1965. *El Código civil de la República Argentina*. Buenos Aires: Tip. Ed. Argentina.

Rendón, Zoila C. 1923. *La mujer en el hogar y en la sociedad*. Quito: Talleres Tipográficos Nacionales. HathiTrust.

Rendón de Mosquera, Zoila. (1928) 2006. "Come se juzga el feminismo verdadero." *La Aurora* (Guayaquil). Reproduced in *Orígenes del feminismo en el Ecuador*, edited by Ana María Goetschel, 93–95. Quito: CONAMU and FLACSO. https://biblio.flacsoandes.edu.ec/libros/digital/52780.pdf.

Rendón de Mosquera, Zoila. (1948) 2006. *La mujer en los diversos organismos humanos*. Quito: Imprenta Nacional. Excerpt. Reproduced *Orígenes del feminismo en el Ecuador*, edited by Ana María Goetschel, 103–109. Quito: CONAMU and FLACSO. https://biblio.flacsoandes.edu.ec/libros/digital/52782.pdf.

Rey, Ana Lía. 2021. "María Abella de Ramírez: librepensadora, maestra, periodista y feminista en *Nosotras* y *La Nueva Mujer*." *Mora* 27 (2): 139–57. https://doi.org/10.34096/mora.n27.11099.

Reyes, Oscar Efrén. 1938. n.d. *Breve historia general del Ecuador*. 14th ed. Quito: Publisher unknown.

Reyes Cárdenas, Catalina and Magdala Velásquez Toro. 1995. "Proceso histórico y derechos de las mujeres, años 50 y 60." In *Las mujeres en la historia de Colombia*, edited by Magdala Velásquez Toro, 229–257, Vol. 1. Bogotá: Consejería Presidencial and Grupo Ed. Norma.

Rheinstein, Max, and Mary Ann Glendon. 2004. "Interspousal Relations." In *International Encyclopedia of Comparative Law*, edited by Aleck Chloros, 4.01–4.170. Vol. 4. Leiden: Mohr Siebeck et al.

Rioseco Enriquez, Emilio. 1948. "Explicaciones sobre el Proyecto de Ley del Instituto Chileno de Estudios Legislativos que modifican el Codigo Civil." *Revista de Derecho* 16 (66): 489–537.

Risolia, Marco Aurelio. 1940. "El espíritu de la legislación civil y su reforma." In *La Reforma del Código Civil Argentino. Extractos del "Boletín Mensual" del Seminario de Ciencias Jurídicas y Sociales Nos. 93/94*, edited by Facultad de Derecho de la Universidad de Buenos Aires, 7–63. Universidad de Buenos Aires.

Rivarola, Rodolfo. 1901. *Instituciones del Derecho Civil Argentino*. Buenos Aires: Imp, Lit. y Encuadernación de J. Peuser. HathiTrust.

Rivas Sarache, María Teresa. 2006. "Mujeres y reivindicaciones civiles en Venezuela: La reforma del código civil en 1942." *Boletín de la Academia Nacional de la Historia* 89 (356): 179–207.

Rocchi, Fernando. 2000. "Concentración de capital, concentración de mujeres. Industria y trabajo femenino en Buenos Aires, 1890–1930." In *Historia de las mujeres en Argentina*, edited by Fernanda Gil Lozano, Valeria Silvina and María Gabriela Ini, 223–43. Vol. 2. Buenos Aires: Taurus.

Rodas Morales, Raquel. 2009. "De los inicios de la República a la Revolución Juliana." In *Historia del voto femenino en el Ecuador*, edited by Raquel Rodas Morales, 18–134. Quito: Consejo Nacional de Mujeres.

Rodas Morales, Raquel. 2011. *Zoila Ugarte de Landívar. Patriota y repúblicana, heroína ejemplar del feminismo*. 2nd ed. Quito: Co misión de Transición.

Rodríguez, Gustavo Humberto. 1979. *Olaya Herrera. Político, estadista y caudillo*. Bogotá: Imprenta Nacional.

Rodríguez Díaz, Universindo. 1989. *Los sectores populares en el Uruguay del novecientos. Primera Parte (1907–1911)*. Montevideo: Ed. Compañero.

Rodríguez Fonnegra, Jaime. 1965. *De la sociedad conyugal o régimen de los bienes determinado por el matrimonio*. Vol. 2. Bogotá: Ed. Lerner.

Rodríguez Piñeres, Eduardo. 1899. "Condición civil de la mujer en Colombia (Estudio de legislación y derecho positivo)." Conferencia dictada en la Sociedad Colombiana de Jurisprudencia el 19 de noviembre de 1898. *Anales de Jurisprudencia* 4 (41 & 42): 129–72. HathiTrust.

Rodríguez Piñeres, Eduardo. 1923. *Código Civil Colombiano y Leyes Vigentes que lo Adicionan y Reforman*. 5th ed. Bogotá: Librería Americana. https://ecollection.law.fiu.edu/civil_codes/19.

Rodríguez Villamil, Silvia, and Graciela Sapriza. 1984. *Mujer, Estado y política en el Uruguay del siglo XX*. Montevideo: Ed. de la Banda Oriental.

Rojas, Joel. 2020. "Estudio preliminar, Miguelina Acosta Cardenas: Pensamiento y acción." In *Miguelina Acosta Cárdenas. Escritos selectos*, edited by Joel Rojas, 9–15. Lima: Heraldos Eds.

Rojas Mira, Claudia F. 1997. "Contradicciones de la modernidad. El no divorcio en Chile." *Debate Feminista* 16: 341–356. http://www.jstor.org/stable/42624452.

Rojas Mira, Claudia F. 2011. "'Rumbo a La Moneda' historia del movimiento sufragista en Chile, 1913–1952." In *Sufragio Femenino. Prácticas y debates políticos, religiosos y culturales en la Argentina y América Latina*, edited by Carolina Barry, 391–412. Caseros, Argentina: Ed. de la Universidad Nacional de Tres de Febrero.

Rojas Mira, Claudia F., and Ximena Jiles Moreno. 2017. *Epistolario emancipador del MEMCH. Catálogo Histórico Comentado (1935-1949)*. Santiago: Ed. del Archivo Nacional de Chile. https://www.archivonacional.gob.cl/sites/www.archivonacional.gob.cl/files/images/articles-83326_recurso_1.pdf.

Rojas Mira, Claudia F., and Ximena Jiles Moreno. 2020. "La extraordinaria política protagonizada por el Movimiento de Emancipación de la Mujer Chilena (MEMCH): 1935–1949." *Revista Izquierdas* 49: 3252–72. https://dx.doi.org/10.4067/S0718-50492022000100209.

RomoLeroux de Morales, Ketty. 1975. *Situación jurídica y social de la mujer en el Ecuador*. Universidad de Guayaquil.

Rosemblatt, Karin Alejandra. 2000. *Gendered Compromises. Political Cultures & the State in Chile, 1920–1950*. University of North Carolina Press. ProQuest.

Rubio de Laverde, Lucila. 1965. *Perfiles de Colombia*. Bogotá: Ed. Guadalupe.

Rupp, Leila. 2010. "Constructing Internationalism: The Case of Transnational Women's Organizations, 1888–1945." In *Globalizing Feminisms, 1789–1945, Rewriting Histories*, edited by Karen Offen, 139–52. Routledge.

Salazar Cortez, Tatiana Alejandra. 2018. "Una lectura a la versátil militancia de la Alianza Femenina Ecuatoriana, 1938–1950." *Trashumante. Revista Americana de Historia Social* 11: 164–186. https://doi.org/10.17533/udea.trahs.n11a08.

Salazar Herrera, Catalina. 2001. *Actuación política de mujeres peruanas durante el siglo XX. Tentando una cronología*. Lima: Manuela Ramos.

Salmon, Marylynn. 1986. *Women and the Law of Property in Early America*. University of North Carolina Press.

Salvat, Raymundo J. 1922. *Tratado de derecho civil argentino (parte general)*. 2nd ed. Bueno Aires: Lib. y Casa Editora de Jesús Menéndez. HathiTrust.

Sánchez Manríquez, Karin. 2006. "La costumbre y la ley en tensión: Las primeras mujeres universitarias en Chile, 1877–1893." *Boletín de la Academia Chilena de Historia* 72 (115): 291–328. https://www.institutodechile.cl/wp-content/uploads/2019/02/boletin_115.pdf

Sanojo, Luis. 1873. *Instituciones de Derechos Civil Venezolano*. Vol. 3. Caracas: Imprenta Nacional. Google Books.

Santos Zelaya, J., and Fernando Abaunza. 1903. *Código Civil de la República de Nicaragua*. Managua: Tip. Nacional.

Sapriza, Gabriela. 2011. "El voto femenino en Uruguay, 1900–1932." In *Sufragio Femenino. Prácticas y debates políticos, religiosos y culturales en la Argentina y América Latina*, edited by Carolina Barry, 357–89. Caseros, Argentina: Ed. de la Universidad Nacional de Tres de Febrero.

Scott, James Brown. 1934. "The Seventh International Conference of American States." *American Journal of International Law* 28 (2): 219–30. https://www.doi:10.2307/2190923.

Sebree, J. Emmett. 1928. "Outlines of Community Property." *New York University Law Review* 6: 32–52. Hein Online.

Segovia, Lisandro. 1881. *El Código Civil de la República Argentina (copia de la edición oficial integra) con su explicación y crítica bajo la forma de notas*. Vols. 1 and 2. Buenos Aires: Imprenta de Pablo E. Coni. HathiTrust.

Shammas, Carole, Marylynn Salmon, and Michel Dahlin. 1987. *Inheritance in America: From Colonial Times to the Present*. Rutgers University Press.

Shanley, Mary Lyndon. 1989. *Feminism, Marriage, and the Law in Victorian England, 1850–1895*. University of Princeton Press.

Shumway, Jeffrey. 2005. *The Case of the Ugly Suitor and other Histories of Love, Gender and Nation in Buenos Aires, 1776–1870*. University of Nebraska Press.

Sieben, Graciela N. 2012. *El proceso legislativo de la Ley 11.357 de los derechos civiles de la mujer: los debates en el Congreso Nacional*. Master's thesis. Quilmes, Argentina: Universidad Nacional de Quilmes. http://ridaa.unq.edu.ar/handle/20.500.11807/112.

Siegel, Reva B. 1994. "Home as Work: The First Woman's Rights Claims Concerning Wives' Household Labor, 1850–1880." *Yale Law Journal* 103 (95): 1073–1217. https://openyls.law.yale.edu/bitstream/20.500.13051/290/2/Home_As_Work___The_First_Woman_s_Rights_Claims_Concerning_Wives__Household_Labor__1850_1880.pdf.

Sinardet, Emmanuelle. 1998. "La mujer en el proyecto nacional de la revolución liberal ecuatoriana (1895–1925)." In *Coloquio de Historia Canaria Americana*, edited by Casa de Colón, 1441–57. Vol. 13. Las Palmas: Cabildo de Gran Canaria. https://hdl.handle.net/20.500.12285/coloquios/1113.

Sosa, Ximena. 2020. *Hombres y mujeres velasquistas, 1934–1972*. Quito: FLACSO. https://doi.org/10.46546/20202atrio.

Soublette S., Panchita. 1941. "Ponencia de la Asociación Venezolana de Mujeres relativa a derechos civiles de la mujer." In *Conferencia preparatoria del Primer Congreso Venezolano de Mujeres, efectuada en Caracas en los días 13 al 16 de junio de 1940*, edited by C.V.M., 95–109. Caracas: Ed. Bolivar.

Speth, Linda E. 1982. "The Married Women's Property Acts, 1839–1865." In *Women and the Law: The Social Historical Perspective*, edited by D. Kelly Weisberg, 69–91. Vol. 2. Cambridge: Schenkman.

Spota, Alberto G. 1953. "Ley 11.347 de Derechos Civiles de la Mujer." *Anales de Legislación Argentina*, 199–202. Vol. 1920–1940. Buenos Aires: Ed. Ley.

Staves, Susan. 1990. *Married Women's Separate Property in England, 1660–1883*. Harvard University Press.

Stetson, Dorothy McBride. 1987. *Women's Rights in France*. Westport, CT: Greenwood.

Stuven, Ana María, and Claudia Araya. 2004. "Liberalismo y divorcio en la historia de Chile: una encrucijada ideológica y valórica." *Bicentenario* 3 (2): 99–124. ProQuest.

Suárez, Belarmino. 1911. *El Código Civil del año de 1860 con sus modificaciones hasta el año 1911 por el Dr. Belarmino Suárez*. San Salvador: Tip. La Unión.

Suárez, Paula S. 2012. "Las mujeres abogadas en la historia y en la Facultad de Derecho de la Universidad de Buenos Aires." *Academia. Revista sobre Enseñanza del Derecho* 10 (20): 143–83. http://revistas.derecho.uba.ar/index.php/academia/article/view/633.

Suárez M., José María. 1913. "Algo acerca de la condición jurídica de la mujer casada." *Revista de la Sociedad Jurídica-Literaria* 8: 65–102. HathiTrust.

Subercaseaux, Bernardo. 2011. *Historia de las ideas y de la cultura en Chile: desde la Independencia hasta el Bicentenario*. Vol. 2. Ed. Universitaria de Chile.

Swiggett, Glen Levin. 1916. *Report on the Women's Auxiliary Conference Held in the City of Washington in Conjunction with the Second Pan American Scientific Congress December 28, 1915-January 7, 1916*. Washington, DC: Government Printing Office.

Szuchman, Mark D. 1988. *Order, Family and Community in Buenos Aires, 1810–1860*. Stanford University Press.

Terán C., Luciano. 1906. *Censo de la Población de Quito, 1 de Mayo de 1906*. Informe del Director General de Estadística al Ministerio del Rango. Quito: Imp. El Comercio. http://hdl.handle.net/10469/12568

Throup S., Matilde. 1911. "Libertades y derechos civiles de la mujer." In *Primer Congreso Femenino Internacional de la República Argentina*, edited by Asociación Universitarias Argentinas, 388–99. Buenos Aires: Imprenta A. Ceppi.

Toledo Más, César. 1938. *Legislación matrimonial en el Perú*. Lima: Ed. Lumen.

Torres, Anabel. 1986. "Una voz insurgente. Entrevista con Ofelia Uribe de Acosta." In *Voces insurgentes*, edited by María Cristina Laverde Toscano and Luz Helena Sánchez Gómez, 23–45. Bogotá: Fund. Universidad Central Servicio Colombiano de Comunicación Social.

Torres, Julio T., ed. 1942. *Compilación de reformas al código civil, leyes y reglamentos conexos*. Quito: Talleres Gráficos del Ministerio de Gobierno. LLMCDigital.

Towns, Ann. 2010. "The Inter-American Commission of Women and Women's Suffrage, 1920–1945." *Journal of Latin American Studies* 42 (4): 779–807. https://doi.org/10.1017/S0022216X10001367.

Towns, Ann. 2019. "Global Patterns and Debates in the Granting of Women's Suffrage." In *The Palgrave Handbook of Women's Political Rights*, edited by Susan Franceschet, Mona Lena Krook, and Netina Tan, 3–19. Palgrave Macmillan.

Travieso, Carmen Clemente. (1944) 1977. "La evolución social de la mujer." In *Las mujeres en el pasado y en el presente* edited by Carmen Clemente Travieso, 91–166. Caracas: Agrupación Cultural Femenina.

Travieso, Carmen Clemente. 1961. *Las luchas de la mujer venezolana*. Caracas: Agrupación Cultural Femenina.

Troya, Pilar, Valeria Coronel, Daniela Schreeder, and Iván Orosa. 2022. *Nela Martínez Espinosa (1912–2004)*. Estudios Feministas No. 3. Instituto Tricontinental de Investigación Social and Archivo Martínez-Meriguet. https://thetricontinental.org/es/estudios-feminismos-3-nela-martinez/.

Ugarte de Landívar, Zoila. 1905a. "Notas Editoriales." *La Mujer* 1 (1): 31–32.

Ugarte de Landívar, Zoila. 1905b. "Aspiraciones." *La Mujer* 1 (4): 97–102.

Ugarte de Landívar, Zoila. 1910a. "La Emancipación de la Mujer." *La Prensa*, September 9, 10, 12, 13, 14, 15, and 22. Quito.

Ugarte de Landívar, Zoila. 1910b. "La Sociedad Conyugal." *La Prensa*, no. 330, September 15. Quito.

UMA, Unión de Mujeres Americanas. 1936/n.d. *Objetivo y bases de organización de los consejos nacionales y reglamento interior del Consejo Internacional en Nueva York*. DSP.

UMA Peruana. 1936/n.d. *Estatuto de la UMA Peruana*. DSP.

UNESCO, United Nations Educational, Scientific and Cultural Organization. 1988. *Compendium of Statistics on Illiteracy*, 30. Paris: Division of Statistics on Education, Office of Statistics.

Uribe de Acosta, Ofelia. 1931. "Contribución al estudio de la reforma Olaya-Restrepo sobre el régimen de las capitulaciones matrimoniales," paper presented to the Fourth International Conference of Women, reproduced as "El proyecto de capitulaciones matrimoniales en el Congreso Femenino," *El Tiempo*, January 1, 23 and 25.

Uribe de Acosta, Ofelia. 1963. *Una voz insurgente*. Bogotá: Ed. Guadalupe. https://repositorio.unal.edu.co/handle/unal/49522.

Uribe Escobar, Ricardo. 1914. *Notas feministas*. Doctoral thesis, Faculty of Law and Political Science. Medellín: Universidad de Antioquia. https://www.scribd.com/doc/236912108/Escobar-Notas-Feministas-1914

Uribe-Uran, Victor M. 2023. "Filiation, Marriage, Family and Domestic Conflicts." In *A Companion to Latin American Legal History*, edited by M.C. Mirow and Victor Uribe-Uran, 452–76. Brill Legal History Library Vol. 64. Leiden: Koninklijke Brill NV.

Urrutia, Francisco José. 1902. *Estudios de legislación y de derecho civil. La autoridad marital*. Vol. I. Quito: Librería Americana. HathiTrust.

Uruguay, República Oriental del. 1868. *Código Civil para el Estado Oriental del Uruguay promulgado por el Gobierno Provisorio*. Ed. Oficial. Montevideo: Imprenta de La Tribuna. HathiTrust.

Uruguay, República Oriental del. 1893. *Código Civil de la República Oriental del Uruguay*. Ed. Oficial. Montevideo: Imprenta de la Nación. HathiTrust.

Uruguay, República Oriental del. 1914. *Código Civil de la República Oriental del Uruguay, nueva edición con todas las reformas promulgadas al día*. Montevideo: Talleres Gráficos Barreiro y Ramos. https://ecollections.law.fiu.edu/civil_codes/25.

Uruguay, República Oriental del. 1918. *Constitución de La República. Constitución 1918 Plebiscitada el 25 de Noviembre de 1917*. http://parlamento.gub.uy/documentosyleyes/constitucion.

Uruguay, República Oriental del. 1934. *Constitución de La República. Constitución 1918 Plebiscitada el 19 de abril de 1934.* https://parlamento.gub.uy/documentosyleyes/documentos/8/HTML.

Uruguay, República Oriental del. 1976. *Código Civil de la República Oriental del Uruguay, con las leyes y decretos que reforman y complementan su texto primitivo.* Montevideo: Talleres Gráficos Barreiro y Ramos.

Valdés Riesco, Alejandro. 1922. *La mujer ante las leyes chilenas.* Santiago: Imp. y Lic. La Ilustración.

Valdivia, María Inés. 2019. "El feminismo maternalista de la obra de Zoila A. Cáceres (1877–1958). In *Género y mujeres en la historia del Perú. Del hogar al espacio público*, edited by Claudia Rosas Lauro, 419–40. Lima: Fondo Ed. Pontifica Universidad Católica.

Valencia Zea, Arturo y Álvaro Ortíz Monsalve. 1995. *Derecho Civil. Derecho de familia.* Vol. 5. 7th ed. Bogotá: Temis.

Valladares Chamorro, Odalis. 2012. "La incursión de las mujeres a los estudios universitarios en el Perú: 1875–1908." *Cuadernos del Instituto Antonio de Nebrija (CIAN)* 15 (1): 105–23. https://e-revistas.uc3m.es/index.php/CIAN/article/view/1544/758

Valobra, Adriana María. 2005. "Partidos, tradiciones y estrategias de movilización social: De la Junta de la Victoria a la Unión de Mujeres de la Argentina." *Prohistoria* 9 (9): 67–82. https://www.memoria.fahce.unlp.edu.ar/art_revistas/pr.7389/pr.7389.pdf.

Valobra, Adriana María. 2012. "Recorridos, tensiones y desplazamientos en el ideario de Alicia Moreau." *Revista Nomadías* 15: 139–69. https://www.memoria.fahce.unlp.edu.ar/art_revistas/pr.7390/pr.7390.pdf

Valobra, Adriana María. 2024. "History and Interpretations of Women's Suffrage in Argentina." In *Women's Suffrage in the Americas*, edited by Stephanie Mitchell, 125–44. University of New Mexico Press.

Valverde, Emilio F. 1942. *El derecho de familia en el Código Civil Peruano.* Vol. 1. Lima: Imp. Ministerio de la Guerra.

Vanger, Milton I. 2010. *Uruguay's José Batlle y Ordoñez. The Determined Visionary, 1915–1917.* Lynne Rienner Pubs.

Vargas Arenas, Iraida. 2007. *Resistencia y participación. La saga del pueblo venezolano.* Caracas: Monte Ávila. https://monteavilaeditores.com/libros/resistencia-y-participacion/.

Vasallo, Alejandra. 2000. "Entre el conflicto y la negociación. Los feminismos argentinos en los inicios del Consejo Nacional de Mujeres, 1900–1910." In *Historia de las mujeres en Argentina*, edited by Fernanda Gil Lozano, Valeria Silvina y María Gabriela Ini, 172–90. Vol. 2. Buenos Aires: Taurus. ProQuest.

Vassalis, Idalia. 1934. "Triunfos Femeninos." *Nuevos Horizontes* 1 (7): 9.

Vásconez Cuvi, Victoria. 1922a. "Por la mujer," in *Ensayos literarios.* Quito: n.p.

Vásconez Cuvi, Victoria. 1922b. *Honor al feminismo.* Quito: Talleres Tipográficos Nacionales. HathiTrust.

Vásconez Cuvi, Victoria. 1925. *Actividades domésticas y sociales de la mujer.* Quito: Talleres Tipográficos Nacionales. HathiTrust.

Vásquez Rencoret, Humberto. 1922. *Los derechos civiles de la mujer.* Santiago: Imprenta Echeverría. HathiTrust.

Vaz Ferreira, Carlos. (1933) 1945. *Sobre feminismo.* Buenos Aires: Ed. Losada. Vega Ugalde, Silvia. 1987. *La Gloriosa. De la revolución del 28 de mayo de 1944 a la contrarevolución Velasquista.* Quito: El Cornejo.

Velasco Galdós, Adelaida. (1914) 2006. "¿Feminismo?," *El Hogar Cristiano.* In *Orígenes del feminismo en el Ecuador*, edited by A.M. Goetschel, 81–82. Quito: CONAMU and FLACSO.

Velásquez Ocampo, Olga Patricia. 2015. "'Compañera y no sierva.' Los avatares hacia el sufragio femenino en Colombia." *Ambiente Jurídico* 18: 11–34. https://revistasum.umanizales.edu.co/ojs/index.php/Ambientejuridico/article/view/1739/1825

Velásquez Toro, Magdala. 1986. "Aspectos históricos de la condición sexual de la mujer en Colombia." In *Voces insurgentes*, edited by María Cristina Laverde Toscano and Luz Helena Sánchez Gómez, 181–201. Bogotá: Fund. Universidad Central and Servicio Colombiano de Comunicación Social.

Velásquez Toro, Magdala. 1989. "Condición jurídica y social de la mujer." In *Nueva historia de Colombia*, edited by Álvaro Tirado Mejía, 9–60. Vol. 4. Bogotá: Planetas.

Velásquez Toro, Magdala. 1995. "La República Liberal y la lucha por los derechos civiles y políticos de las mujeres." In *Las mujeres en la historia de Colombia*, edited by Magdala Velásquez Toro, 183–228. Vol. 1. Bogotá: Consejería Presidencial and Grupo Ed. Norma.

Velásquez Toro, Magdala. 1997. "Reflexiones históricas en torno a los derechos políticos de las mujeres en los cuarenta años del voto femenino." In *40 años del voto de la mujer en Colombia*, edited by María Victoria Londoño, German Patiño, and Garcés Mariana, 9–37. Cali: Feriva S.A.

Venezuela, Estados Unidos de. (1862) 1974. In *La codificación de Páez (Código Civil de 1862)*, edited by Gonzalo Parra-Aranguren. Vol. 1. Caracas: Biblioteca de la Academia Nacional de Historia.

Venezuela, Estados Unidos de. 1867. *Código civil sancionado por el Congreso de los Estados Unidos de Venezuela en 1867*. Caracas: Imprenta de José R. Henríquez. HathiTrust.

Venezuela, Estados Unidos de. (1873) 1973. *Código civil sancionado por el General Guzmán Blanco*. Caracas: Imprenta Nacional. Reproduced in *Código civil sancionado por el General Guzmán Blanco*. Caracas: Congreso de la República.

Venezuela, Estados Unidos de. 1896. *Código civil sancionado por el Congreso de los Estados Unidos de Venezuela en sus sesiones ordinarias de 1896*. Caracas: Tip. del Comercio. HathiTrust.

Venezuela, Estados Unidos de. 1904. *Código civil sancionado por el Congreso de los Estados Unidos de Venezuela*. Caracas: Imprenta Bolivar. HathiTrust.

Venezuela, Estados Unidos de. 1915. *Anuario Estadístico de Venezuela 1912*. Caracas: Dirección General de Estadísticas, Imprenta Nacional. HathiTrust.

Venezuela, Estados Unidos de. 1916. *Código Civil de los Estados Unidos de Venezuela, 1916*. Caracas: Lit. y Tip. del Comercio. HathiTrust.

Venezuela, Estados Unidos de. (1922) 1928. *Código Civil de los Estados Unidos de Venezuela, 1922*. Caracas: Lit. y Tip. del Comercio. https://ecollections.law.fiu.edu/civil_code/21.

Venezuela, Estados Unidos de. 1929. *Constitución de 1929 (29 de mayo de 1929)*. https://derechodelacultura.org.

Venezuela, Estados Unidos de. 1936. *Constitución de 1936 (20 de julio de 1936)*. https://derechodelacultura.org.

Venezuela, Estados Unidos de. 1942. *Código Civil de los Estados Unidos de Venezuela, 1942*. Caracas: Imprenta Nacional.

Venezuela, Estados Unidos de. 1945a. *Constitución política de los Estados Unidos de Venezuela*. https://derechodelacultura.org.

Venezuela, Estados Unidos de. 1945b. *Código de Comercio*. Caracas: *Gaceta Oficial de los Estados Unidos de Venezuela*, No. 148 Extraordinario, September 19.

Venezuela, Estados Unidos de. 1947. *Constitución política de los Estados Unidos de Venezuela*. https://derechodelacultura.org.

Venezuela, Estados Unidos de. 1955. *Código de Comercio*. Caracas: *Gaceta Oficial de los Estados Unidos de Venezuela*, No. 475 Extraordinario, December 21.

Venezuela, Estados Unidos de. 1957. *Octavo Censo General de Población (26 de noviembre de 1950)*. Vol. XII, Resumen General. Caracas: Dirección General de Estadística y Censos Nacionales.

Verba, Ericka Kim. 1995. "The *Círculo de Lectura de Señoras* [Ladies' Reading Circle] and the *Club de Señoras* [Ladies' Club] of Santiago, Chile: Middle- and Upper-class

Feminist Conversations (1915-1920).” *Journal of Women's History* 7 (3): 6–33. https://doi.org/10.1353/jowh.2010.0453.
Vigil, Mercedes. 2003. *Matilde, la mujer de Batlle*. Montevideo: Planeta.
Vignoli, Marcela. 2018. “El Consejo Nacional de la Mujer en Argentina y su dimensión internacional, 1900–1910.” *Travesía* 20 (2): 121–47. https://www.scielo.org.ar/scielo.php?script=sci_isoref&pid=S2314-27072018000200006&lng=es&tlng=es.
Vignoli, Marcela. 2021. “Cecilia Grierson y las damas de la Beneficencia oficial en los orígenes del Consejo Nacional de Mujeres de Argentina (1887–1906).” *Boletín del Instituto de Historia Argentina y Americana* 55: 1–26. https://doi.org.10.34096/bol.rav.n55.10348
Villarreal Méndez, Norma. 1994. “Movimientos de mujeres y participación política en Colombia, 1930–1991.” In *Historia, género y política. Movimientos de mujeres y participación política en Colombia 1930–1991*, by Lola G. Luna and Normal Villarreal, 59–203. University of Barcelona.
Villavicencio, Maritza (with Margarita Zegarra, ed.). 1992. *Del silencio a la palabra. Mujeres peruanas en los siglos XIX–XX*. Lima: Flora Tristán.
Warbasse, Elizabeth Bowles. 1987. *The Changing Legal Rights of Married Women, 1800–1861*. New York: Garland.
Wills Obregón, María Emma. 2007. *Inclusión sin representación. La irrupción política de las mujeres en Colombia, 1970–2000*. Bogotá: Grupo Ed. Norma.
Wisnoski, Alex. 2023. “Women.” In *A Companion to Latin American Legal History*, edited by M.C. Mirow and Victor Uribe-Uran, 287–309. Brill Legal History Library Vol. 64. Leiden: Koninklijke Brill NV.
Women's Auxiliary Committee. 1921. *Bulletin of the Women's Auxiliary Committee of the United States of the Second Pan American Scientific Congress in Cooperation with the International Committee*. Washington, DC: Pan American Union.
Yarrington, Doug. 2014. “Political Transition in an Age of Extremes: Venezuela in the 1930s.” In *The Great Depression in Latin America*, edited by Paulo Doinot and Alan Knight, 160–87. Duke University Press.
Ysla Heredia, Leonardo. 2022. *María Jesús Alvarado. Retrato de una intelectual y activista peruana*. Lima: Editorial UPC. http://dx.doi.org/10.19083/978-612-318-425-4.
Zahler, Reuben. 2013. *Ambitious Rebels. Remaking Honor, Law and Liberalism in Venezuela, 1780–1850*. University of Arizona Press.
Zajtay, Imre, and Eduardo Vaz Ferreira. 1950. “Contribución al estudio de los regímenes matrimoniales de participación.” *Revista de la Facultad de Derecho y Ciencias Sociales* (Montevideo) 1 (3): 813–65.
Zeballos, Camila. 2015. “La extensión del sufragio en el Uruguay de 1915: Una coyuntura pactada.” *Revista Uruguaya de Ciencias Políticas* 24 (1): 133–51. https://rucp.cienciassociales.edu.uy/index.php/rucp/article/view/83/60.
Zeberio, Blanca. 2005. “Un código para la nación. Familia, mujeres, derechos de propiedad y herencia en Argentina durante el siglo XIX.” In *¿Ruptura de la inequidad? Propiedad y género en la América Latina del siglo XIX*, edited by Magdalena León and Eugenia Rodríguez Sáenz, 131–181. Bogotá: Siglo del Hombre.
Zegarra Flórez, Margarita Delfina. 2006. “María Jesús Alvarado y el rol de las mujeres peruanas en la construcción de la patria.” In *Mujeres, familia y sociedad en la historia de América Latina, siglos XVIII–XXI*, edited by Scarlett O'Phelan Godoy and Margarita Zegarra Flórez, 489–515. Lima: CENDOC-Mujer, Pontificia Universidad Católica del Perú, Instituto Riva Agüero and Instituto Francés de Estudios Andinos.
Zegers, Julio. 1918. “Los derechos civiles de la mujer en la legislación chilena.” *Revista Chilena* 2 (10): 449–56. HathiTrust.

GLOSSARY

Capitulaciones contracts between spouses over the ownership and administration of property; in the nineteenth century, prenuptial agreements.

Deferred community property regime the marital regime whereby each spouse manages the assets each brings to marriage or acquires thereafter via any means (including from wages, salaries and other independent earnings) autonomously, while at the end of the marriage the gains each generated are pooled and divided equally.

Gananciales the community property of the marriage; acquest and gains during the marriage.

Patria potestad rights of the father over the person and property of his legitimate children.

Potestad marital rights of the husband over the person and property of his wife.

Reserved property the right of wives under the partial community property regime to manage and dispose of their own wages, salaries and other independent earnings, and any assets acquired with such; at the end of the marriage the gains form part of the community property to be divided.

Separation of property regime the marital regime whereby each spouse owns and manages the assets each brings to marriage or acquires thereafter via any means (including from wages, salaries and other independent earnings) autonomously. There is no community property at the end of the marriage.

Sociedad conyugal conjugal society; the marital regime of partial community property. It recognizes three types of property in marriage, his, hers and community property. The individual property consists of the assets each brings to marriage or later inherits. The gains on such property and the wages, salaries and other earnings of each and any assets purchased with such constitute community property to be divided equally at its dissolution. In the nineteenth-century civil codes, the husband administered all three forms of property.

INDEX

Note: Page numbers in **bold** refer to tables and page numbers followed by "n" refer to notes.

For Product Safety Concerns and Information please contact our EU
representative GPSR@taylorandfrancis.com
Taylor & Francis Verlag GmbH, Kaufingerstraße 24, 80331 München, Germany

www.ingramcontent.com/pod-product-compliance
Ingram Content Group UK Ltd.
Pitfield, Milton Keynes, MK11 3LW, UK
UKHW020155200926
475702UK00016B/2723
* 9 7 8 1 0 4 1 1 1 1 3 0 6 *